EVERYTHING

YOU NEED TO KNOW ABOUT

EVERYTHING

YOU NEED TO KNOW ABOUT...

Baby
Names

LISA SHAW

D&C

David and Charles

A DAVID & CHARLES BOOK

David & Charles is a subsidiary of F+W (UK) Ltd.,
an F+W Publications Inc. company

First UK edition published in 2005
First published in the USA by Adams Media, an F+W Publications Inc. company,
as The Everything® Baby Names Book in 1997

Cover Design Ali Myer

A catalogue record for this book is available from the British Library.

ISBN 0 7153 2224 9

Printed in Great Britain by CPI Bath
for David & Charles
Brunel House   Newton Abbot   Devon

Visit our website at www.davidandcharles.co.uk

David & Charles books are available from all good bookshops;
alternatively you can contact our Orderline on (0)1626 334555 or
write to us at FREEPOST EX2110, David & Charles Direct,
Newton Abbot, TQ12 4ZZ (no stamp required UK mainland).

Introduction

Once upon a time, parents-to-be didn't think much about what they were going to name their babies. They figured they would either name their child after a favourite relative, or perhaps give him or her one of the names that were currently popular and that, more often than not, had religious origins.

Today, times have changed. Though there are still some parents who tend to pick a name out of a hat—or use the same name selection methods their parents and grand-parents used—the majority of new parents today carefully consider a large variety of names before settling on one.

Why has this happened? Because *we've* changed. Even though a name is just a label we've put on a child in order to distinguish him or her from other children, a name is something to which people attach a lot of expectations and stereotypes, as much as we don't like to admit it.

Today, there are a wealth of names to choose from: the multicultural movement has exposed names from hundreds of ethnic groups, so you can select one that will be a first in your family; or you can choose a name that reflects on a well-loved relative; or you can even learn how to invent a name. Besides the fact that there have been many studies that indicate that the name a child bears—indeed, even an adult—has some influence on how he or she will be regarded by peers, the names you choose for your baby-to-be are the first links that you have to it. Once you choose a name for your girl or boy, you can begin to think of your baby in concrete ways, instead of just as an amor-phous being that you'll get to meet a number of months down the road.

There are more than 25,000 names to choose from in this book. Some of them are variations of a tried-and-true name, while others are so unique that a child who is given one of them might forever have to explain what it means or what his or her parents had in mind. But a lot of what's involved in bearing an unusual name revolves around attitude: many parents who bestow an uncommon name on a child are proud of the fact that their child stands out, and will convey that attitude to their child.

Should You Choose A Popular Name?

Throughout this book, you'll read about names that were popular for girls and boys during certain periods of time. Sometimes it's impossible to determine why a particular name was popular; frequently, it starts out as a snowball and gradually—or rapidly, in some cases—turns into an avalanche. For instance, Jennifer and Justin were around when I was growing up in the '60s, but they didn't make the top ten name lists until the '80s, when they virtually exploded in popularity. But now, while they're still around, they appear less frequently, replaced by Chelsea and Sophie for girls and Jordan and Dylan for boys. Sometimes, what makes a name become suddenly popular is that a public figure with the name becomes especially prominent. In fact, Jennifer may indeed enjoy a renaissance in the '90s now that an actress with the last name of Aniston has been cast into the spotlight.

The problem with giving your child a currently popular name is the chance that he or she will be in a class with four other children who all have the same name. When I was growing up, I always thought it was a little bit sneaky when children with the same names always ended up in different classes. But back then, the choices were David, Robert, Laura, and Nancy, solid, untrendy names. Today, the more exotic names are, the more popular they are. But then again, David, Robert, Laura, and Nancy didn't appear on any Most Popular Name lists prior to the '60s, so who knows, maybe the parents who chose these names were bucking tradition even back then.

But when a name is popular today, it means they are *really* popular. How much? Here's a breakdown: today, one out of every five girls has a name that falls into the top ten, while for boys, the figure jumps to one in three; one out of every two girls has a name that is in that year's list of top fifty names, while for boys, the frequency jumps to three in five.

Names and Stereotypes

One thing that you have absolutely no control over when choosing a name for your baby is the associations that other people will have with it. Think about that bratty kid in your third-grade class named Henry who teased you relentlessly. Be honest: today, whenever you

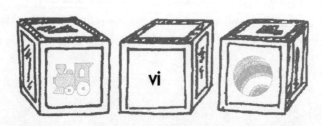

meet someone with the same name as a former tormentor, isn't there even the tiniest assumption that this new person has the same characteristics of the boy or girl who bugged you back then?

Similarly, some of the associations that we have with celebrity names can be just as damning—or complimentary, depending upon the name. In the late '70s, many parents rushed to name their daughters Farrah. When you meet one of these young women today named Farrah, what's the first thing you think of?

And the nature-oriented names that hippie parents christened their kids with back in the '60s through the mid-'70s today stand out. In the last year, I've met twenty-somethings named Cinnamon and Charity. Of course, I didn't want to make a big deal out of their names, since they probably got this treatment all the time, but it was the name itself that initially cornered my thoughts, and not the person behind the name tag. Of course, after you get to know the person a bit, the initial surprise about the person's name tends to fade into the background. But keep in mind that some people are never able to get past *that name*, and therefore make instant assumptions about a person.

But then again, a name doesn't have to belong to a celebrity or serve as a barometer of the social times to provide people with a stereotyped image of the person behind the name. Some names just have a certain sound to them that helps paint a picture in our minds. Just try to imagine the different physical characteristics you would expect the following names to embody: Bertha, Blythe, Chloe, Gladys.

People frequently say they eschew labels, but in the end, slapping a label—or in this case, a name—on things or people before you get a chance to become familiar with them is the brain's natural way to make sense of something new. Unfairly, certain names also help us to decide whether to spend the time to know more about that person.

In quieter, more personable times, a name was an expression of virtue. During the 1800s, names such as Patience, Prudence, and yes, Chastity and Charity embodied traits to strive for. And yet, these and other names specific to a particular decade or century are in themselves labels. Think about it: what did a rebellious teenager in Victorian times do with a name like Prudence if she clearly wasn't prudent? The fact that she was christened with this very name might have encouraged the adults around her to become more impatient with her if it was clear that she wasn't anything like her name.

Today, those big blue *"hi-my-name-is"* tags tell a whole lot more about you to the

world than you really want. So take some time to think about what you'd like your child's name tag to convey to the world.

How to Use This Book

Today, we all hear stories about the parents who put their children on waiting lists for the top private kindergartens—when these children haven't even been born yet. As we are a nation of people who ponder every move for how it will affect us in the future, our concerns for our soon-to-be-born children fall along the same lines. You can read about the kind of music to listen to, the foods you should eat during pregnancy to ensure a larger-than-normal brain in your baby, and even the type of work and leisure activities you should undertake in order to keep your baby calm both before and after it is born.

As you thumb through the listings, circle the names that seem like possibilities to you, and try to imagine your child outside playing while you call him or her in to dinner. How will it sound? One person I know applied this rule to the future pets she planned to get, after one of her cats was lost temporarily and she found herself running down the street yelling, "Euripides! It's time for dinner, Euripides!"

Then, imagine your child as an adolescent, with all the joys and terrors that this implies. No matter what name you give your baby, whether common or unusual, you should know now that your teenager will probably hold it against you in some way because the coolest kid in her grade has a name that is either more traditional or more unusual. You can't win.

But then, picture your baby as an adult with children of his own. What does his wife call him? And does your grown child fit the name you gave him so many years ago?

As I've said, a name is such a personal thing that it makes sense to spend some time making the all-important decision of what to call your new baby. This book will help you to make this momentous choice.

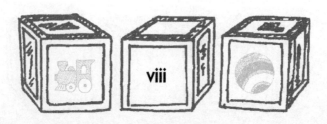

IT'S A BOY!

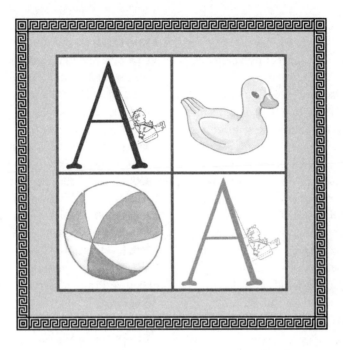

AADI (Hindu) Beginning.

AAKAV (Hindu) Shape.

AAKESH (Hindu) Lord of the sky.

AAKIL (Hindu) Intelligent.

AALOK (Hindu) Light of God.

AAMIN (Hindu) Grace of God.

AANAN (Hindu) Face.

AANDALEEB (Hindu) Bluebird.

AARON (Hebrew) Lofty or exalted. It appears in the bible as the older brother of Moses, appointed by God to be his brother's keeper, and is traditionally regarded as the founder of the Jewish priesthood. Also taken up by English Puritans in the 17th century, it reached a peak of popularity in the 1970s and 1980s. Famous people from the past with the name include the US vice-president Aaron Burr, the American composer Aaron Copland, and English poet Aaron Hill. Variations: *Aarao, Aharon, Arek, Aron, Aronek, Aronne, Aronos, Arran, Arren, Arrin, Arron.*

AATMADEVA (Hindu) God of the soul.

AATMIK (Hindu) Soul.

ABAYOMI (African: Nigerian) Brings happiness.

ABBA (Hebrew) Father.

ABBAS (Arabic) Stern. Also an informal name for a lion, it was borne by Muhammad's uncle Abbas ibn Abd-al-Muttalib in the sixth century.

ABDAL ATI (Arabic) One who serves Allah. Variation: *Abdel Ati.*

ABDAL AZIZ (Arabic) One who serves the Mighty One. Variations: *Abdel Aziz, Abdul Aziz.*

ABDAL FATTAH (Arabic) One who serves the one who provides nourishment. Variation: *Abdel Fattah.*

ABDAL HADI (Arabic) One who serves a leader. Variation: *Abdel Hadi.*

ABDAL HAKIM (Arabic) One who serves a wise one. Variation: *Abdel Hakim.*

ABDAL HALIM (Arabic) One who serves the patient one. Variation: *Abdel Halim.*

ABDAL HAMID (Arabic) One who serves a praiseworthy one. Variations: *Abdel Hamid, Abdul Hamid.*

ABDAL JABIR (Arabic) One who serves the comforter. Variations: *Abdal Jabbar, Abdul Jabir.*

ABDAL JAWWAD (Arabic) One who serves the noble one. Variation: *Abdel Gawwad.*

ABDAL KARIM (Arabic) One who serves the generous one. Variations: *Abdel Kerim, Abdel Krim.*

ABDAL LAFIF (Arabic) One who serves the kind one. Variations: *Abdel Lafif, Abdul Lafif.*

ABDAL MAJID (Arabic) One who serves the glorious one. Variations: *Abdul Magid, Abdul Majid, Abdul Medjid, Abdul Mejid.*

ABDAL MALIK (Arabic) One who serves the king. Variation: *Abdel Malik.*

ABDAL MUFI (Arabic) One who serves the donor. Variation: *Abdel Mufi.*

ABDAL MUHSIN (Arabic) One who serves a charitable one. Variation: *Abdul Muhsen.*

ABDAL QADIR (Arabic) One who serves the capable. Variations: *Abdal Kadir, Abdel Adir, Abdel Kadir, Abdel Qadir, Abdul Qader.*

ABDAL RAHIM (Arabic) One who serves the compassionate. Variations: *Abder Rahim, Abdul Rahim.*

ABDAL RAHMAN (Arabic) One who serves the merciful. Variations: *Abdar Rahman, Abder Rahman, Abdul Rahman, Abdur Rahman.*

ABDAL RAUF (Arabic) One who serves the compassionate.

ABDAL RAZIQ (Arabic) One who serves the provider. Variations: *Abdal Razzaq, Abder Razi, Abder Razza, Abdur Razzaq.*

ABDAL SALAM (Arabic) One who serves peace. Variations: *Abdel Salam, Abdul Salam, Abdus Salam.*

ABDAL WAHAB (Arabic) One who serves the giving.

ABDALLAH (Arabic) One who serves Allah. Variations: *Abdalla, Abdulla, Abdullah.*

ABDUL (Arabic) Servant.

ABDUL HAFEEZ (Arabic) Servant of the master. Variation: *Abdul Hafiz.*

ABDUL HAKIM (Arabic) Servant of a wise man. Variations: *Abdul Hakeem, Abdul Hakeen.*

ABDUL HAMID (Arabic) Servant of the worthy one.

ABDUL JABBAR (Arabic) Servant of the comforter.

ABDUL KARIM (Arabic) Servant of a generous man. Variation: *Abdul Kareem.*

ABDUL LATIF (Arabic) Servant of a kind man. Variation: *Abdul Lateef.*

ABDUL MAJID (Arabic) Servant of a glorious man. Variation: *Abdul Majeed.*

ABDUL QADIR (Arabic) Servant of a capable man. Variation: *Abdul Kadir.*

ABDUL RAHMAN (Arabic) Servant of a merciful man. Variations: *Abdul Rehman, Abdur Rahman, Abdur Rehman.*

ABDULLAH (Arabic) Servant of God. Variation: *Abdulla.*

ABDUR RAHIM (Arabic) Servant of a compassionate man.

ABDUR RASHID (Arabic) Servant of a righteous man.

ABEEKU (African: Ghanian) Born on Wednesday.

ABEJIDE (African: Nigerian) Born in winter.

ABEL (Hebrew) Breathing spirit or breath. In the Bible, Abel was the second son of Adam.

ABHIRAJA (Hindu) Great king.

Choosing a Name Is Fun!

During the process of pregnancy and getting everything ready for the baby, deciding what you're going to name your baby can sometimes seem like just another chore to fit into your overpacked schedule.

How can you make choosing a name for your baby less like work and more like the joy it should be? Here are some ideas you can try:

🦆 Leaf through all the entries in the book. Try to work out what names your friends and family would pick if *they* were allowed to name your baby.

🦆 Hold a lottery. Tell all your friends and relatives that you're looking for suggestions, and that you'd like their input. Of course, you don't have to commit to any of the names that are provided to you, and indeed, some of the entries will be good for a laugh or two. Put all of the entries into a box, and pick the winning entry out of the hat a week before your due date. Make the prize relevant to the birth of your baby. The winner gets to serve as the baby's first sitter when you and your partner find the time and energy to go out for your first dinner in a restaurant after the baby arrives.

🦆 Pick five names that just sound good when you say them. Write them down on a card, and every day for a month, pull the card out and read them aloud to see how they sound. At the end of the month, one will probably become your favourite.

5

ABID (Arabic) One who worships Allah. Variation: *Abbud.*

ABIEL (Hebrew) God is my father. Variation: *Aviel.*

ABIODUN (African: Nigerian) Born during war.

ABIOLA (African: Nigerian) Born during the New Year.

ABNER (Hebrew) Father of light. Biblical. Variations: *Aviner, Avner.*

ABORNAZINE (Native American: Abnaki) Keeper of the flame. Variation: *Bornbazine.*

ABRAHAM (Hebrew) Father of many. If the name Abraham conjures up an image of a wise old man to you, you may scoff at the idea of making an infant put up with the name until it fits, say, oh, in sixty years or so. But as more and more parents decide to give their children names with a historical basis, Abraham will continue to have a growing place in baby names. Variations: *Abe, Abrahamo, Abrahan, Abram, Abramo, Abran, Abrao, Avraham, Avram, Avrum.*

ABSALOM (Hebrew) Father of peace. The handsome son of the King. Variation: *Absalon.*

ACE (English) Unity. Nickname given to one who excels. It's also the name of a member of the rock group Kiss.

ACESTES (Greek) Mythological Trojan king.

ACHAIUS (Irish) Horseman.

ACHARON (Hebrew) Last.

ACHATES (Greek) Ancient mythological figure.

ACHAV (Hebrew) Uncle. Variation: *Ahab.*

ACHAZYA (Hebrew) God has taken. Variations: *Achazia, Achaziah, Achazyahu, Ahaziah, Ahaziahu.*

ACHBAN (Hebrew) Brother of a smart man.

ACHELOUS (Greek) God of the river.

ACHER (Hebrew) Other.

ACHERON (Greek) River of woe.

ACHIDA (Hebrew) Smart brother.

ACHILLES (Greek) The mythological hero who appears in Homer's *Iliad*, where he successfully fights the Trojans. His mother helped to make him unbeatable when she held him by the ankle and submerged him in the River Styx. His ankle was the only part of him that could be injured, which is why today we refer to that part of the anatomy as an *Achilles' heel.*

ACHIMELECH (Hebrew) The king is my brother. Variation: *Ahimelech.*

ACHISAR (Hebrew) The prince is my brother.

ACHISHAR (Hebrew) My brother is a song. Variation: *Ahishar.*

ACHIYA (Hebrew) God is my brother. Variations: *Achiyahu, Ahia, Ahiah.*

ACTAEON (Greek) Ancient mythological figure.

ACTON (English) Town in Great Britain.

ADAD (Greek) God of storms and floods.

ADAEL (Hebrew) God's ornament. Variation: *Adiel.*

ADAIAH (Hebrew) Witness of God. Variations: *Adaia, Adaya.*

ADAM (Hebrew) Man of the red earth. According to the Judaeo-Christian tradition, Adam was the first man in the world, and his name has always been popular in many countries and in many religions. A very common name in 13th-century England, its popularity increased again during the 1960s with a slew of positive, almost macho, associations in the entertainment world. Adam West, who played Batman in the television series, and British pop singer Adam Faith undoubtedly served as the inspiration for many men named Adam today. Many parents pick the name for their first son. Variations: *Adamec, Adamek, Adamh, Adamik, Adamka, Adamko, Adams, Adamson, Adamsson, Adan, Adao, Addam,*

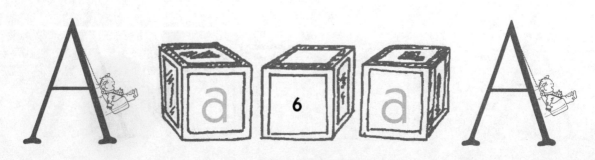

Addams, Addamson, Addie, Addis, Addy, Adhamh, Adnet, Adnot.

ADAMNAN (Irish) Little Adam. Variation: *Adhamhnan.*

ADAMYA (Hindu) Difficult.

ADAPA (Greek) Ancient mythological figure.

ADAR (Syrian) Ruler or prince.

ADDAE (African: Ghanian) Morning sun.

ADDISON (English) Son of Adam.

ADE (African: Nigerian) Royal.

ADEBAYO (African: Nigerian) He was happy.

ADEBEN (African: Ghanian) Twelfth-born son.

ADEJOLA (African: Nigerian) The crown needs honour.

ADESOLA (African: Nigerian)The crown honoured us.

ADHEESHA (Hindu) King.

ADHIDEVA (Hindu) Supreme god.

ADIKA (African: Ghanian) First child from second husband.

ADIL (Arabic) Fair.

ADIN (Hebrew) Attractive. Variation: *Aden.*

ADIO (African: Nigerian) Righteous.

ADIR (Hebrew) Noble.

ADISA (African: Nigerian) One who is clear.

ADITSAN (Native American: Navajo) Listener.

ADITYA (Hindu) The sun. Variation: *Aaditva.*

ADIV (Hebrew) Gentle.

ADLAI (Hebrew) God's justice.

ADLER (English) An eagle.

ADMON (Hebrew) Red peony.

ADNAN (Arabic) Settled.

ADOEETE (Native American: Kiowa) Tree. Variations: *Adoerte, Adooeette.*

ADOFO (African: Ghanian) Warrior.

ADOLPH (German) Noble wolf. Variations: *Adolf, Adolfo, Adolphe.*

ADOM (African: Ghanian) God's blessing.

ADON (Hebrew) Lord.

ADONIAH (Hebrew) The Lord is my God. Variations: *Adonia, Adonijah, Adoniya, Adoniyah.*

ADONIS (Greek) Handsome.

ADRI (Hindu) Fortress; rock. Adri is a minor god in the Hindu religion.

ADRIAN (Latin) Black; dark. Variations: *Adrean, Adren.*

ADRIEL (Hebrew) God's flock.

ADUNBI (African: Nigerian) Pleasant.

ADUSA (African: Ghanian) Thirteenth-born.

AEACUS (Greek) Son of Zeus.

AEDUS (Irish) Fire.

AEGEUS (Greek) Goatskin shield of Zeus. Variation: *Aegis.*

AEGYPTUS (Greek) King of Egypt.

AENEAS (Irish) To praise. Variation: *Eneas.*

AEOLUS (Greek) The changeable one.

AESON (Greek) Ancient mythological figure.

AETIOS (Greek) Eagle.

AFA (Polynesian) Hurricane.

AFI (Polynesian) Fire.

AFU (Polynesian) Hot.

AGANJU (African: Yoruban) The son and husband of the earth-goddess Odudua.

AGAPIOS (Greek) Love.

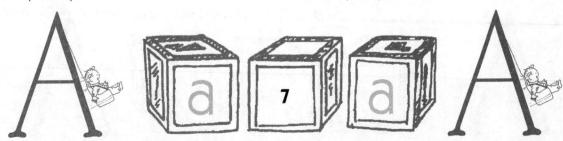

AGASTYA (Hindu) Patron saint of southern India.

AGATHIAS (Greek) Good.

AGNI (Hindu) Fire deity in the Hindu religion.

AHANU (Native American) One who laughs.

AHARNISH (Hindu) Day and night.

AHIMELEKA (Hawaiian) Biblical priest.

AHIO (Polynesian) Whirlwind.

AHMAD (Arabic) More deserving. Variation: *Ahmed.*

AHMED (Arabic) Praise. Variation: *Ahmad*

AHOHAKO (Polynesian) Storm.

AHOMANA (Polynesian) Thunder.

AHSAN (Hindu) Gratitude.

AHUSAKA (Native American: Winnebago) Wings.

AIAKOS (Greek) The son of Zeus.

AIDAN (Irish, Gaelic) Warm. Aidan has become popular in recent years due to the success of the ice-blue-eyed actor Aidan Quinn. It is also the name of an Irish saint from 600 CE.

AILBHE (Irish) Bright.

AILESH (Hindu) King of all.

AILILL (Irish) Sprite.

AILPEAN (Scottish) Unknown definition. Variations: *Ailpein, Alpine.*

AINEAS (Greek) To praise. Variation: *Aeneas.*

AINMIRE (Irish) Great lord.

AIOLOS (Greek) Change.

AISAKE (Polynesian) He laughs.

AISEA (Polynesian) God saves.

AIYETORO (African: Nigerian) Peace on earth.

AJANABH (Hindu) A mountain.

AJANI (African: Nigerian) He fights for possession.

AJAX (Greek) Ancient mythological figure.

AKALANKA (Hindu) Pale.

AKAMU (Hawaiian) Red earth. Variation: *Adamu.*

AKANDO (Native American) Ambush.

AKANNI (African: Nigerian) Our encounter brings wealth.

AKBAR (Hindu) Muslim King in sixteenth century.

AKE (Scandinavian) Ancestor. Variation: *Age.*

AKECHETA (Native American: Sioux) Warrior.

AKELA (Hawaiian) Lucky. Variation: *Asera.*

AKELIELA (Hawaiian) The majesty of God. Variation: *Aderiela.*

AKEMI (Japanese) Beautiful dawn. Variation: *Akeno.*

AKHILENDRA (Hindu) Lord of the universe.

AKIHIKO (Japanese) Bright boy. Variations: *Akio, Akira.*

AKIHITO (Japanese) Bright.

AKIIKI (African: Ugandan) Friend.

AKILESH (Hindu) King of all.

AKILIANO (Hawaiian) One from the city of Adrian. Variation: *Adiriano.*

AKIM (Russian) God.

AKINLABI (African: Nigerian) We have a boy.

AKINLANA (African: Nigerian) Brave. Variation: *Akins.*

AKIVA (Hebrew) Heel. Variations: *Akavia, Akaviah, Akavya, Akiba, Kiba, Kiva.*

AKOLO (Polynesian) Fence.

AKONIIA (Hawaiian) The Lord is my God. Variation: *Adoniia.*

AKONO (African: Nigerian) My turn.

AKSHAN (Hindu) Eye.

AKSHAY (Hindu) Forever.

AKUA (African: Ghanian) Born on Thursday.

AKWETEE (African: Ghanian) Second of twins.

ALA (Arabic) Superior.

ALADDIN (Arabic) Very faithful.

ALAHMOOT (Native American: Nez Perce) Elm branch.

ALAKA'I (Hawaiian) Leader.

ALAN (English, Celtic) Fair; handsome. I think of Alan as somewhat of a name of the 1950s and 1960s, since

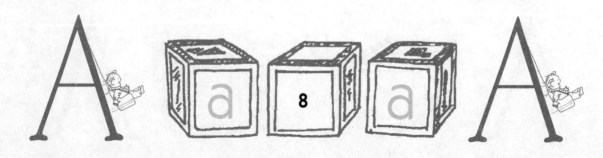

so many of the children I knew then were named Alan, as well as popular film and TV stars, like Alan Ladd and Alain Delon. For this reason, some parents might shy away from the name, and never even consider it, but if you want a steadfast name that will stand out, Alan is a good choice. Today, famous Alans include Alan Jay Lerner, Alan Alda and Allen Ginsberg. Variations: *Ailean, Ailin, Al, Alain, Aland, Alano, Alanson, Alao, Alen, Alin, Allan, Allayne, Allen, Alleyn, Alleyne, Allin, Allon, Allyn, Alon, Alun.*

ALARIK (Scandinavian) Leader of all. Variation: *Alaric.*

ALASTAIR (Greek) One who rules.

ALBANY (English) The city.

ALBERT (Old English) Bright; brilliant. Variations: *Alberto, Albie, Albin, Albrecht.*

ALBION (Latin) White mountain.

ALCYONEUS (Greek) Kingfisher.

ALDEN (English) Wise; old.

ALDRICH (English) An old and wise leader.

ALEEKCHEAAHOOSH (Native American: Crow) Accomplished.

ALEKANEKELO (Hawaiian) Protector. Variations: *Aleka, Alekanedero, Alika.*

ALEKONA (Hawaiian) Old town. Variation: *Aletona.*

ALEMANA (Hawaiian) Warrior. Variations: *Amana, Aremana.*

ALEPANA (Hawaiian) From Alba. Variation: *Alebana.*

ALEPELEKE (Hawaiian) Counsellor. Variations: *Alapai, Aleferede.*

ALEWINA (Hawaiian) Friend to elves. Variation: *Alevina.*

ALEXANDER (Greek) Protector; helper and defender of mankind. Alexander is one of those great, strong names that stands well on its own as well as in one of its many versions. So if you like the name as it is, fine. If your boy later decides that he'd rather be called Alex, Alek, or chooses the wonderfully sensual Spanish name Alessandro, it's all possible. Famous Alexanders include Alexander the Great, Alexander Hamilton, actor Alec Baldwin, Alexander Haig, and Aleksandr Solzhenitsyn. Variations: *Alasdair, Alastair, Alaster, Alec, Alejandro, Alejo, Alek, Alekos, Aleksander, Aleksandr, Alesandro, Alessandre, Alessandri, Alessandro, Alex, Alexandre, Alexandro, Alexandros, Alexei, Alexi, Alexio, Alik, Alisander, Alissander, Alissandre, Alistair, Alister, Alistir, Allistair, Allister, Allistir, Alsandair, Alsandare, Sacha, Sande, Sander, Sanders, Sanderson, Sandey, Sandie, Sandor, Sandy, Sascha, Sasha, Sashenka, Sashka (Russian), Saunders, Saunderson.*

ALFRED (English) Elf; wise listener. Variation: *Alfredo.*

ALGOT (Scandinavian) Last name.

ALI (Arabic) Elevated.

ALIIMALU (Hawaiian) Peaceful leader.

ALIKKEES (Native American: Nez Perce) Haircut.

ALIPATE (Polynesian) Bright.

ALITZ (Hebrew) Happy. Variation: *Aliz.*

ALLAHKOLIKEN (Native American: Nez Perce) Antlers.

ALLARD (English, French) Brave; noble one.

ALLON (Hebrew) Oak tree. Variation: *Alon.*

ALOHALANI (Hawaiian) Compassionate. Variation: *Alohilani.*

ALOIKI (Hawaiian) Famous war. Variation: *Aloisi.*

ALPHEUS (Greek) God of the rivers.

ALPHONSE (German) One who is ready to fight. Most adults today who have the name are commonly known as Al, but when it comes to naming their own children, it's Alphonse, probably after a grandfather. Variations: *Alfonse, Alfonso, Alfonze, Alfonzo, Alonzo, Alphonso.*

ALTAIR (Greek) Bird.

ALTON (English) One who lives in an old town.

ALVIN (German) Friend. A couple of generations ago, chiefly in America, Alvin was a common choice

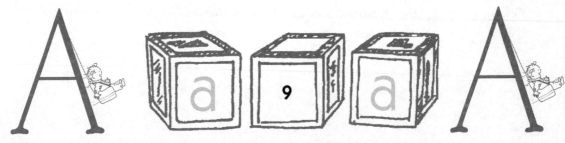

among new parents. One famous Alvin is US ballet dancer and choreographer Alvin Ailey. Variations: *Ailwyn, Alion, Aluin, Aluino, Alva, Alvan, Alven, Alvie, Alvino, Alvy, Alvyn, Alwin, Alwyn, Alwynn, Aylwin.*

ALVIS (Scandinavian) Unknown definition.

AMADEUS (Latin) One who loves God. Of course this name was popularized in the mid-1980s film *Amadeus*, about the composer Wolfgang Amadeus Mozart. Will your child turn out to be a prodigy if you give him this name? Variations: *Amadeo, Amado.*

AMADI (African: Nigerian) Fated to die at birth.

AMAL (Hindu) Pure.

AMALESH (Hindu) Clean.

AMANAKI (Polynesian) Hope.

AMARIAH (Hebrew) God has spoken. Variations: *Amaria, Amariahu, Amarya, Amaryahu.*

AMASA (Hebrew) Hardship. Variations: *Amasai, Amasia, Amasiah, Amasya.*

AMBONISYE (African: Tanzanian) God rewards me.

AMBROSE (English) Immortal being.

AMIEL (Hebrew) Lord of the people.

AMIL (Hindu) Unattainable.

AMIN (Arabic) Trustworthy.

AMIR (Hebrew) Powerful.

AMIRAM (Hebrew) Powerful country.

AMJAD (Arabic) More gratifying.

Some Popular Names from the 1940s

Perhaps it is telling that I could not locate a list of popular baby names from the 1940s that contained more than ten names apiece. And you don't have to look closely at these names to see that they seem almost utilitarian, as though there was an air of 'Let's just choose a name and get it over with.'

The 1940s was a decade that was quite different from the ones that have passed since. Today, we receive news of countless regional wars occurring all over the world; back then, there was one war, a *world* war, and in the first half of the 1940s, the number one thing that concerned most people was when that war was going to be over. Of course,

similar concerns have continued to plague us in the decades that have followed, but we were not as unified in our cause as we were in the 1940s.

For parents-to-be in the 1940s, choosing simple names for their children was a clear indication of the atmosphere and tenor of the times. During the second half of the decade and into the 1950s, after the war ended, the baby boom was beginning, and people gradually started to feel that they could lavish attention on their children. In time, the most popular names would clearly reflect this sense of newfound personal freedom. The following names are listed in order of popularity:

Boys' Names

- James
- John
- Robert
- William
- Charles
- David
- Jerry
- Thomas
- Richard
- Jose

Girls' Names

- Mary
- Maria
- Linda
- Barbara
- Patricia
- Betty
- Sandra
- Carolyn
- Gloria
- Martha

ANNAR (Scandinavian) The second.

ANNAWON (Native American: Algonquin) Chief. Variation: *Annawan*.

ANOKI (Native American) Actor.

ANSEL (French) One who follows; someone with a nobleman. Variations: *Ancel, Anselm*.

ANSHU (Hindu) Sunbeam. Variation: *Anshul*.

ANSON (English) Son of Anne. Anson can also mean Son of God. Variations: *Annson, Ansson*.

ANTAEUS (Greek) Enemy. Variation: *Antaios*.

ANTHONY (Latin) Praiseworthy; valuable. Descended from the Roman Antonius. Saint Anthony was a hermit who lived in the third century in what is today Italy; he is the patron saint for poor people. You don't have to be Italian to be named Anthony; my father,  who was 100 per cent Polish, was christened with Anthony as his middle name. A list of famous people who have Anthony or Tony as their first names is a veritable *Who's Who* of class: Anthony Quinn, Anthony Hopkins, Anton Chekhov, Anthony Eden, Anthony Burgess, Tony Curtis, Tony Bennett, Tony Blair and Anthony Perkins. Variations: *Andonios, Andonis, Anntoin, Antin, Antoine, Anton, Antone, Antonello, Antoney, Antoni, Antonin, Antonino, Antonio, Antonius, Antons, Antony, Antos*.

ANUENUE AKUA (Hawaiian) Spirit of the rainbow.

ANUM (African: Ghanian) Fifth-born.

ANWAR (Arabic) Shafts of light.

AODH (Irish) Fire. Variations: *Aodha, Aodhaigh, Aodhan, Aodhfin, Aodhgan, Aoidh*.

APARA (African: Nigerian) A child that comes and goes.

APASH WYAKAIKT (Native American: Nez Perce) Necklace of flint.

APEKALOMA (Hawaiian) Peaceful father. Variation: *Abesaloma*.

APELA (Hawaiian) Breathing spirit or breath. Hawaiian version of Abel. Variation: *Abela*.

APELAHAMA (Hawaiian) Father of many. Hawaiian version of Abraham. Variation: *Aberahama*.

APELAMA (Hawaiian) Many children. Variations: *Aberama, Abiram, Apilama*.

APIA (Hawaiian) God is my father. Variation: *Abia*.

APIATAN (Native American: Kiowa) Lance. Variations: *Ahpeatone, Ahpiatom, Apiaton*.

APIKAI (Hawaiian) Gift from God. Variation: *Abisai*.

APOLLO (Greek) Manly destroyer. Apollo, the god of medicine and healing, is known as one of the more powerful Greek gods. He is best known for flying through the sky in a chariot and giving a famous oratory at Delphi. Variations: *Apollon, Apollos, Apolo*.

APOSTOLOS (Greek) An apostle.

APPANOOSE (Native American: Sauk) Child.

AQUILO (Greek) The north wind.

ARACH (Hebrew) Prepared.

ARAPOOSH (Native American: Crow) Upset stomach. Variation: *Arrapooish*.

ARCAS (Greek) The son of Jupiter and Callisto.

ARCHER (English) Named after a man who's good with a bow and arrow. Variations: *Archibald, Archie, Archy*.

ARCHIMEDES (Greek) To first think about.

ARDAL (Irish) Valour. Variations: *Ardghal, Artegal, Arthgallo*.

ARDEN (Celtic) Eager.

ARDON (Hebrew) Bronzed. From the Bible.

ARE (Scandinavian) Eagle.

ARES (Greek) The god of war.

ARGUS (Greek) Bright.

ARI (Hebrew) Lion. Variation: *Arie.*

ARIEL (Hebrew) Lion of God; sprite. Ariel can also be a girls' name. Variations: *Arel, Ari.*

ARIES (Greek) The ram.

ARIOCH (Hebrew) Royal. Variation: *Aryoch.*

ARION (Greek) Mythological talking horse.

ARISTAEUS (Greek) Noble.

ARISTIDES (Greek) The best.

ARISTOKLES (Greek) The most famous.

ARISTOTLE (Greek) Superior. The Greek philosopher who was known only by his first name was the most famous example of Aristotle until Jacqueline Kennedy married the Greek shipping tycoon Aristotle Onassis. Variations: *Ari, Arie, Arri, Ary.*

ARJUN (Hindu) White.

AR-KE-KEE-TAH (Native American: Oto) Stay.

ARKHIPPOS (Greek) Ruler of the horse.

ARLEN (Irish, Gaelic) Pledge; oath. Variations: *Arlan, Arlin, Arlyn.*

ARLES (Hebrew) Promise. Variations: *Arlee, Arleigh, Arley, Arlie, Arlis, Arliss, Arly.*

ARLO (Spanish) Bayberry tree. Even though the only Arlo you may have heard of is Arlo Guthrie, the name is actually a common Italian version of Charles.

ARMAND (French) Man of the army. French variant of Herman. Variations: *Arman, Armande, Armando, Armin, Armon, Armond, Armonde, Armondo.*

ARMON (Hebrew) High place.

ARMSTRONG (English) One who has a strong arm.

ARNBJORN (Scandinavian) Eagle bear.

ARNOLD (German) Strong as an eagle could certainly describe one of this century's most famous Arnolds, the one with the last name of Palmer. Undoubtedly, Arnold Schwarzenegger has also helped to rejuvenate the reputation of this name and its popularity in American culture and among its boys. Variations: *Arnaud, Arne, Arnie, Arno, Arnolde, Arnoldo.*

ARNON (Hebrew) Rushing stream.

ARNOST (Czech) Determined.

ARRE-CATTE WAHO (Native American: Omaha) Big elk.

ARRIO (Spanish) Fierce; warlike. Variations: *Ario, Arryo, Aryo.*

ARSENIO (Greek) Virile; masculine. The first time you probably ever heard this name was when you got your first glimpse of Arsenio Hall.

ARSHAD (Hindu) Devoted.

ARTEMUS (Greek) One who follows Artemis, the Greek goddess of the hunt. Variations: *Artemas, Artemis, Artimas, Artimis, Artimus.*

ARTHUR (Celtic) Bear; rock. Famous in the English-speaking world and beyond as the semi-legendary English King Arthur. Though Arthur is not a common name today, it was used in the early part of the 20th century with some frequency. Famous Arthurs include British comedian Arthur Askey, US tennis player Arthur Ashe, playwright Arthur Miller and singer Art Garfunkel. Variations: *Art, Artair, Arte, Artek, Artie, Artis, Arto, Artur, Arturo, Arty, Atur.*

ARUN (Cambodian) Sun.

ARUNDEL (English) Valley of the eagle.

ARVAD (Hebrew) Exile.

ARVE (Scandinavian: Norwegian) Heir.

ARVID (Scandinavian: Norwegian) Eagle in a tree.

ARVIN (German) Friend of the people. Variations: *Arv, Arvid, Arvie, Arvy, Arwin, Arwyn.*

ARVIND (Hindu) Red lotus. Variations: *Arvinda, Aurobindo.*

ARWYSTLI (Welsh) Good counsel.

ARYABHATA (Hindu) Astronomer.

ARYEH (Hebrew) Lion.

ASA (Hebrew) Doctor. Variation: *Ase.*

AMMAR (Arabic) Long life.

AMMIEL (Hebrew) People of God. Variation: *Amiel*.

AMNON (Hebrew) Loyal. Variation: *Aminon*.

AMOKA (Hawaiian) Strong one. Hawaiian version of Amos. Variation: *Amosa*.

AMON (Hebrew) Secret. Variation: *Ammon*.

AMORY (German) Leader.

AMOS (Hebrew) Strong one. Famous Amoses in the past have been named after the book of Amos in the Old Testament, who was a prophet. Variations: *Amotz, Amoz*.

AMPHION (Greek) Ancient mythological figure.

AMUL (Hindu) Valuable.

AMYCUS (Greek) Friendly.

AN (Vietnamese) Peace.

AN TOAN (Vietnamese) Safe.

ANAD (Hindu) God. Variation: *Anaadi*.

ANAEL (Greek) Guardian for Librans.

ANAIAH (Hebrew) God answers. Variations: *Anaia, Anaya*.

ANAKALE (Hawaiian) Crown. Variation: *Anadar*.

ANAKLETOS (Greek) To call forth. Variations: *Anacletus, Cletus, Kletos*.

ANAKONI (Hawaiian) Valuable.

ANAND (Hindu) Happiness.

ANANE (African: Ghanian) Fourth son.

ANANTA (Hindu) Eternal.

ANANYA (Hindu) Unique.

ANASTASIO (Italian) Resurrection. Variation: *Anastasius*.

ANCHISES (Greek) Ancient mythological figure.

ANDAL (Hindu) Unknown definition.

ANDOR (Scandinavian) Eagle and Thor.

ANDRE (French) Manly. French version of Andrew. Variations: *Ahndray, Andrae, Andray, Aundray*.

ANDREW (English) Manly; brave. The apostle Andrew became the patron saint of Scotland, Russia and Greece, which may be the reason why Andrew has always been a popular name for boys, not only in English but in many languages since medieval times. It has remained current ever since reaching a recent peak in the 1960s and 1970s. The name Andrew conjures up both dignity and informality, traits that served United States Presidents Andrew Johnson and Andrew Jackson. Other famous Andrews include Andy Warhol, Prince Andrew and Andy Williams. Variations: *Aindrea, Aindreas, Anders, Andi, Andonis, Andor, Andre, Andreas, Andrei, Andres, Andrey, Andy*.

ANDWELE (African: Tanzanian) God brings me.

ANEKELEA (Hawaiian) Manly. Variation: *Anederea*.

ANGELO (Italian, Portuguese, Spanish) Messenger; angel. Though the name Angel used to be the most popular form of this name, Angelo has come into favour because Angel has been used more often as a girls' name. Variation: *Angel*.

ANGUS (Scottish, Gaelic) Only choice. I think of a steakhouse or a man in a kilt playing the bagpipes whenever I hear this name, but Angus Og is a Celtic god who benefits his people with his wisdom and intelligence. Variation: *Aengus*.

ANGVARIATIONU TOKECHA (Native American: Sioux) Another day.

ANIKETOS (Greek) Unconquered.

ANIL (Hindu) Air.

ANITELU (Polynesian) Manly.

ANIWETA (African: Nigerian) A spirit brings it.

ANJAY (Hindu) Unconquerable.

ANKER (Scandinavian) Harvester.

ANKUR (Hindu) Blossom.

ANLUAN (Irish) Great champion. Variation: *Anlon*.

ASAD (Arabic) More fortunate. Variation: *Assad*.

ASADEL (Arabic) Successful.

ASAPH (Hebrew) Gather. Variations: *Asaf, Asif, Asiph*.

ASARIEL (Greek) Guardian of Pisceans.

ASCANIUS (Greek) Ancient mythological figure.

ASCOT (English) Eastern cottage. Variation: *Ascott*.

ASEEM (Hindu) Eternal.

ASHBY (English) Ash tree farm. Variations: *Ash, Ashbey, Ashbie, Ashburn*.

ASHER (Hebrew) Happy. Asher was one of Jacob's sons in the Bible. One of the most common nicknames for Asher – along with the other names listed here that start with 'A-s-h' – is Ash, which has an interesting superstition connected with it. The ash tree commonly brings good luck; the belief is that if you give a bit of sap from an ash tree to an infant, he will be lucky for the rest of his life. Variations: *Anschel, Anshel, Anshil, Ashu*.

ASHFORD (English) Place to cross a river near ash trees. Variations: *Ash, Ashenford*.

ASHISHISHE (Native American: Crow) Crow. Variation: *Shishiesh*.

ASHKII DIGHIN (Native American: Navajo) Sacred child.

ASHLEY (English) Meadow of ash trees. Variations: *Ashlea, Ashlee, Ashlee, Ashleigh*.

ASHLIN (English) Ash trees that encircle a pond. Variation: *Ashlen*.

ASHRAF (Arabic) More noble.

ASHTON (English) Town with ash trees.

ASHUR (Assyrian) The god of war; (Arabic) Islamic month of Ashur.

ASHVAGHOSHA (Hindu) Neigh of a horse.

ASIM (Arabic) Guardian.

ASMUND (Scandinavian) God is protector.

ASRIEL (Hebrew) Prince of God.

ASTON (English) Eastern town.

ASTRAEUS (Greek) The starry one.

ASTYANAX (Greek) King of the city.

ASWAD (Arabic) Black.

ASWIN (English) Friend with a spear. Variations: *Aswinn, Aswyn, Aswynn*.

ATA (African: Ghanian) Twin.

ATAGULKALU (Native American: Cherokee) Pitched trees. Variation: *Attakullakulla*.

ATAIAH (Hebrew) God helps. Variation: *Ataya*.

ATHELSTAN (English) Highborn rock.

ATHERTON (English) Town by the spring.

ATIAH (Arabic) Ready.

ATID (Thai) Sun.

ATIF (Arabic) To sympathize.

ATLEY (English) Meadow. Variations: *Atlea, Atlee, Atleigh, Attlee, Attleigh, Attley*.

ATMAN (Hindu) Soul.

ATREUS (Greek) Ancient mythological figure.

ATSIDI (Native American: Navajo) Blacksmith.

ATSU (African: Ghanian) Second of twins.

ATU (African: Ghanian) Born on Saturday.

ATUANYA (African: Nigerian) Unexpected.

ATWATER (English) Water.

ATWELL (English) The well.

ATWOOD (English) The wood.

ATWORTH (English) The farm.

ATYAANANDA (Hindu) Joyful.

ATZEL (Hebrew) Noble. Variation: *Azel*.

AUBREY (English) Ruler of the elves.

AUDLEY (English) Unknown definition.

AUDRIC (German) Noble ruler.

AUGUST (Latin) Worthy of respect. Roman name derived from Augustus in use since the 18th century. It was most popular in the19th century, but has since become rare. A famous Augustus is British painter Augustus John. Variations: *Agostino, Agosto, Aguistin,*

Agustin, Agustino, Augie, Augustin, Augustine, Augustino, Augusto, Augustus, Augy.

AUKAI (Hawaiian) Sailor.

AUKAKE (Hawaiian) Wise. Variations: *Augate, Auguseto, Augutino, Aukukeko, Aukukino.*

AULAY (Scottish) Forefather.

AULELIO (Hawaiian) Golden. Variation: *Aurelio.*

AUREK (Polish) Fair-haired. Variations: *Aurel, Aurele, Aureli, Aurelian, Aurelio, Aurelius.*

AURIEL (Hebrew) Lion of God.

AUSTIN (English) Majestic. Derived from Augustine. Has been in use since medieval times. Austin, along with its variants, is currently one of the more popular names, especially with the recent newfound popularity of the books of the writer Jane Austen. Apart from Dr Austin Sloper in Henry James' novel *Washington Square*, famous Austins are still few and far between, until those in the current crop hit their stride. Variations: *Austen, Austyn.*

AVANINDRA (Hindu) Lord of the earth.

Creating a Name from Scratch

What are you saying? That out of the more than 25,000 names in this entire book, you can't find one name that you like?

Well, not exactly...*maybe.* But perhaps you're looking for a name that's unusual but that also just hits you in a different way than a name that's considered to fall within the realm of conventionality.

Just what does this mean? Well, you could make up a name by creating a word that doesn't mean anything, or you could use a word that is a name for something else, but not usually a person.

That's how the current trend in naming babies after places came about. Somebody named their son or daughter Montana, someone else heard it and thought it was a good idea, and now, while Montana isn't exactly commonplace, people don't look at you strangely when you tell them this is the name you've chosen for your little girl.

If you want to give your baby a name that you create from scratch, the first bit of advice that I have is to look around you. What do you have that really means a lot to you? Or what in your life represents Nirvana? You must be a bit careful not to allow this name to serve as a projection of all your wishes and hopes for your child, because it's possible you could run into trouble down the road with

expectations for your baby that are too high. However, choosing a name that represents something close to your heart is a great way to transfer that love to your new baby.

Another way you can create a name from scratch is to pick an existing name and then change the spelling of it. However, it's easy for people to think that your version of a more common name is just a misspelling; this could result in people tending to use the more common name whenever they spell it out, and lots of energy on your part spent correcting them.

African-American parents have been at the forefront of creating unusual names for the last couple of decades. When you see a name in this book that is of African-American origin and the definition reads 'newly created', the chances are that the name was formed by taking an existing name and then changing a couple of letters in it. After its changeover, it still rhymes with the original name, but is just a bit different.

A good example is how Leticia becomes Lakisha. One plus is that it's usually easy to pronounce based on the way it's spelled. Other names have been created by adding 'La' or 'De' in front of a common name, like LaTonya or LaDonna for girls, and Deshawn for boys.

AVENALL (French) Oat pasture. Variations: *Aveneil, Aveneill, Avenel, Avenell, Avenil, Avenill.*

AVERILL (English) Fighting boar. Borne by a seventh-century English saint and has enjoyed a modest revival since the early years of the 20th century. Variations: *Ave, Averel, Averell, Averil, Averyl, Averyll, Avrel, Avrell, Avrill, Avryll.*

AVERY (English) Counsellor. Derived from Alfred in medieval times, it has been in occasional use since the end of the 19th century. This name fits tidily into the trend of naming a baby after a town or place, and also as an androgynous name that suits both boys and girls equally well.

AVI (Hebrew) My God.

AVIAH (Hebrew) My father is Lord. Variations: *Abia, Abiah, Abijah, Avia, Aviya.*

AVIDAN (Hebrew) God is fair.

AVIDOR (Hebrew) Father of a people.

AVIKAR (Hebrew) My father is priceless; (Hindu) Flawlessness.

AVINOAM (Hebrew) Pleasant father.

AVIRAM (Hebrew) My father is strong. Variation: *Abiram.*

AVISHAI (Hebrew) Gift from God. Variations: *Abishai, Avisha, Avshai.*

AVITAL (Hebrew) Father of dew. Variations: *Abital, Avitul.*

AVIUR (Hebrew) Father of fire.

AVIV (Hebrew) Spring.

AVNIEL (Hebrew) My God is my strength.

AWAN (Native American) Somebody.

AWST (Welsh) Great.

AXEL (Scandinavian) Father of peace; reward from God. Axel is a common name in both Norway and Sweden. In occasional use chiefly in the US where it was introduced by Scandinavian immigrants. The first time many people got wind of the name was from the lead singer of the rock group Guns 'N Roses, Axl Rose. Another famous Axel is Swedish physician and writer Axel Munthe. Variations: *Aksel, Ax, Axe, Axell, Axil, Axill, Axl.*

AYIZE (African: Zulu) Let it come.

AYLWARD (English) Noble guardian.

AYMAN (Arabic) Lucky.

AYO (African: Nigerian) Happiness.

AZ (Hebrew) Powerful.

AZAD (Turkish) Free.

AZAI (Hebrew) Strength. Variation: *Azzai.*

AZANIAH (Hebrew) God listens. Variations: *Azania, Azaniya, Azanyahu.*

AZARAEL (Hebrew) God helps. Variations: *Azareel, Azarel, Azaria, Azariah, Azariahu, Azarya, Azaryahu.*

AZI (African: Nigerian) Youth.

AZIEL (Hebrew) God is my power.

AZIM (Arabic) Defender. Variations: *Aseem, Asim, Azeem.*

AZIZ (Arabic) Powerful.

AZIZI (Arabic) Precious.

AZRAEL (Hebrew, Greek) Help from God. Variation: *Azriel.*

AZRIEL (Hebrew) God is my help. Variations: *Azuria, Azuriah.*

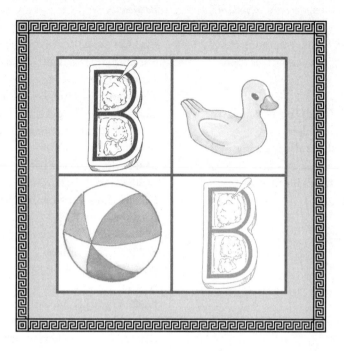

BAASU (Hindu) Prosperous.

BABAFEMI (African: Nigerian) My father loves me.

BABAR (Hindu) Lion. Variation: *Baber*.

BACCHUS (Latin) God of wine.

BACHIR (Hebrew) Oldest son.

BACHUR (Hebrew) Young man.

BADAR (Arabic) Full moon.

BADEN (English) Last name.

BADR (Arabic) Full moon.

BADR ALDIN (Arabic) Led by Allah.

BADRU (Arabic) Full moon.

BAHA (Arabic) Brilliance, magnificent.

BAHIR (Arabic) Luminous.

BAHJAT (Arabic) Happiness. Variation: *Bahgat*.

BAILEY (English) This name has become popular for girls in the last decade; it originally meant a steward or bailiff. Variations: *Bailee, Bailie, Baillie, Baily, Baylee, Bayley, Bayly*.

BAINBRIDGE (English) Bridge. Variations: *Bain, Baynbridge, Bayne, Baynebridge*.

BAIRD (Irish) A travelling singer. Variations: *Bard, Barde, Barr, Bayerd, Bayrd*.

BAKARI (African: Swahili) Promising.

BAKER (English) One whose job is to bake. Last name. Variations: *Bax, Baxter*.

BAKR (Arabic) Camel. Variation: *Bakor*.

BAL (Hindu) An infant with a full head of hair.

BALA (Hindu) Child. Variations: *Balen, Balu, Balun*.

BALABHADRA (Hindu) Lucky. Variation: *Balu*.

BALAKRISHNA (Hindu) Young Krishna.

BALDER (English) Brave warrior; (Scandinavian) Prince. Variations: *Baldur, Baudier*.

BALDEV (Hindu) Strong god.

BALDRIC (German) Brave ruler. Variations: *Baldrick, Baudric.*

BALDWIN (German) Brave friend. Variations: *Bald, Baldovino, Balduin, Baldwinn, Baldwyn, Baldwynn, Balldwin, Baudoin.*

BALENDIN (Latin) Fierce.

BALFOUR (Gaelic) Grazing land. Town in northern Scotland. Variations: *Balfor, Balfore.*

BALIN (Hindu) Soldier. Balin is also the name of the monkey king in Hindu mythology, who is said to be able to instantly weaken any of his enemies by just wishing it. Variation: *Bali.*

BALLARD (German) Mighty.

BALRAJ (Hindu) Strong king.

BALTHASAR (Greek) One of the Three Kings of Christmas. Variation: *Balta.*

BANAN (Irish) White.

BANBHAN (Irish) Piglet.

BANCROFT (English) Field; pasture. Variations: *Bancrofft, Bankroft.*

BANNING (Gaelic) Small boy.

BAO (Chinese) Treasure.

BAOTHGHALACH (Irish) Foolish pride. Variations: *Behellagh, Beolagh, Boetius.*

BARAK (Hebrew) Lightning. Variation: *Barrak.*

BARAM (Hebrew) Son of the people.

BARCLAY (English) Valley of the birches. Variations: *Barcley, Barklay, Barkley, Barklie, Barrclay.*

BARDOLF (English) Wolf that wields an axe. Variations: *Bardolph, Bardou, Bardoul, Bardulf, Bardulph.*

BARDRICK (German) Soldier with an axe. Variation: *Bardric.*

BAREND (Scandinavian) Firm bear.

BARKER (English) Shepherd.

BARLOW (English) Hillside. Variations: *Barlowe, Barrlow.*

BARNABAS (Hebrew) Comfort. This name appears in the bible as one of the companions of Saint Paul and was taken up by English speakers during the medieval period. It has now been eclipsed by Barnaby which was famously featured as the title character in Charles Dickens' novel Barnaby Rudge. Variations: *Barnabie, Barnabus, Barnaby, Barnebas, Barney, Barnie, Burnaby.*

BARNES (English) The barns.

BARNETT (English) Baronet.

BARNUM (English) A baron's home. Variation: *Barnham.*

BARON (English) Warrior. Variation: *Barron.*

BARRA (Irish) Fair head.

BARRINGTON (English) Last name. Place name in Britain.

BARRY (Gaelic) Pointed object. Barry is also increasingly being used as a girls' name with the spelling of Barrie. The name, however, is not as popular as it was a couple of decades ago. Variation: *Barrymore.*

BARTHOLOMEW (English) Farmer's son. The basic version of this English surname may be given as a first name, usually after a family member. There are countless derivatives that come from Bartholomew, which was the name of one of the twelve apostles. Today, the most famous celebrity who goes by a shortened version of Bartholomew is none other than Bart Simpson. Variations: *Bart, Bartel, Barth, Barthel, Barthelemy, Barthelmy, Barthlomeo, Bartholome, Bartholomieu, Bartlett, Bartoli, Bartolo, Bartolomeo, Bartram.*

BARTON (English) Field of barley.

BARTRAM (English) Fame.

BARUCH (Hebrew) Blessed.

BARUTI (African: Botswana) Teacher.

BASANT (Hindu) Spring.

BASIL (English) Royal. The great British actor Basil Rathbone is the most famous person to have come along with this name, but the Catholic Church also has its own Saint Basil. Other well known Basils include television puppet Basil Brush and John Cleese's character Basil Fawlty Variations: *Basile, Basilio, Basilios, Basilius, Bazil, Bazyl.*

BASIM (Arabic) Smile. Variation: *Bassam.*

BASIR (Turkish) Smart.

BASSETT (English) Short person. Because the most popular usage of Bassett, excepting its service as a last name, is as the name of a hound, the name hasn't become as popular as it could be. Variation: *Basset.*

BAUL (English) Snail.

BAURICE (African-American) Variation of Maurice.

BAVOL (English) The wind.

BAY (Vietnamese) Born on Saturday.

BAYARD (English) Brown hair. Variations: *Baiardo, Bay, Bayarde.*

BEACAN (Irish) Small. Variations: *Beag, Bec, Becan.*

BEACHER (English) Near beech trees. Variations: *Beach, Beachy, Beecher, Beechy.*

BEAGAN (Gaelic) Small child. Variations: *Beagen, Beagin.*

BEAL (French) Handsome. Variations: *Beale, Beall, Beals.*

BEAMAN (English) Beekeeper. Variations: *Beamann, Beamen, Beeman.*

BEANON (Irish) Good. Variations: *Beinean, Beineon, Binean.*

BEARACH (Irish) Spearlike. Variations: *Bearchan, Bercnan, Bergin.*

BEATTIE (Gaelic.) One who brings joy. Masculine version of Beatrice.

BEAU (French) Beautiful. Variation: *Bo.*

BEAUFORT (French) A beautiful fort.

BEAUMONT (French) Beautiful mountain.

BEAUREGARD (French) Beautiful gaze. Variations: *Beau, Bo.*

BECHER (Hebrew) First-born. Variation: *Bechor.*

BECK (English) Brook.

BEDE (English) Prayer. Also the name of a saint from the seventh century.

BEDFORD (English) Last name. Place name.

BEDRICH (Czech) Ruler of peace.

BEINISH (Hebrew) Son of the right hand.

BEIRCHEART (Irish) Shining army.

BELA (Czech) White.

BELDON (English) Beautiful valley. Variations: *Belden, Beldin, Bellden, Belldon.*

BELEN (Greek) Arrow.

BELLAMY (English) Handsome companion. Variations: *Belamy, Bell, Bellamey, Bellamie.*

BELLO (African) Assistant.

BEM (African: Nigerian) Peace.

BEMIDII (Native American: Ojibwa) River by a lake.

BENAIAH (Hebrew) God builds. Variations: *Benaya, Benayahu.*

19

What Celebrities Are Naming Their Babies

It's obvious that we have all become more celebrity-conscious in the last couple of decades. And this fact can't help but be mirrored in the names we give our children. Not only do we name our kids after celebrities, we also name them after the children that the stars are having. Many Hollywood types lean towards the unusual, which, to some people, gives a green light to their own choices of uncommon names. Of course, unusual should be taken into perspective. It could be a name like Jett, which Kelly Preston and John Travolta chose for their son, or a name that was previously an ordinary one in years gone by – like Harry – that is turning into a trendy name because it now appears so rarely – or is it because it happened to be Prince Charles and Diana's choice for their second son?

Here are some of the names that celebrities have picked for their own children:

- Sasha, Sawyer, Theo, Mikaela
  Steven Spielberg and Kate Capshaw

- Annie, Tommy
  Christopher Guest and Jamie Lee Curtis

- Isabella, Connor
  Tom Cruise and Nicole Kidman

- Claudia Rose, John Henry
  David Kelley and Michelle Pfeiffer

- Dexter (daughter)
  Diane Keaton

- Taylor (daughter)
  Kate Jackson

- William, Lillie
  Parker Stevenson and Kirstie Alley

- Roberto
  Isabella Rossellini

- P.J. (son)
  Rosie O'Donnell

- Molly
  Teri Garr

- Jake, Skylar
  Sheena Easton

- Mary Clementine
  Linda Ronstadt

- Joseph Marlon
  Robert Lieberman and Marilu Henner

- Tara
  Oliver Stone and Chong Son Chong

- Jack Henry, Miles, Eva
  Tim Robbins and Susan Sarandon

- Danielle
  Jerry and SanDee Lewis

- Michael Garrett
  Bruce Boxleitner and Melissa Gilbert

- Nicolas
  Jean-Claude Van Damme and Darcy LaPier

- Taylor Mayne Pearl
  Garth and Sandy Brooks

- Jett
  John Travolta and Kelly Preston

- Renee
  Rod Stewart and Rachel Hunter

- Cody
  Robin and Marsha Williams

- Hayley
  David Hasselhoff and Pamela Bach

- Chianna, Chesare
  Sonny and Mary Bono

- Alexander James
  Andy Mill and Chris Evert

- Jack Henry
  Dennis Quaid and Meg Ryan

- Christina Aurelia
  Arnold Schwarzenegger and Maria Shriver

- Brooklyn, Romeo
  David and Victoria Beckham

- Apple
  Gwyneth Paltrow and Chris Martin

BEN-AMI (Hebrew) Son of the people.

BENEDICT (English) Blessed. Borne by 6th-century saint Benedict, who founded the Benedictine order of monks. The name was given to no less than fifteen different popes. In his play *Much Ado About Nothing*, Shakespeare used the name for a bachelor who married with great hesitation. The name had a resurgence in popularity in the 1980s and 1990s. Some parents have been choosing Benedict as an alternative to the prospect of their child's facing nurseries filled with Benjamins – the names are similar, but Benedict may be more distinctive. Variations: *Bence, Benci, Bendek, Bendict, Bendix, Benedek, Benedetto, Benedick, Benedicto, Benedictus, Benedik, Benedikt, Benito.*

BENES (Czech) Blessed.

BENJAMIN (English) In the Bible, Benjamin was the youngest son of Jacob. The name translates to son of my right hand. The name Benjamin has become extremely popular in recent years. Famous Benjamins include US President Benjamin Franklin, British Prime Minister Benjamin Disraeli and British composer Benjamin Britten. For me, Benjamin is a great name not only for a toddler running around in tiny overalls but also for a sensitive teenage poet. Variations: *Benejamen, Beniamino, Benjaman, Benjamen, Benjamino, Benjamon, Benji, Benjie, Benjiman, Benjimen, Benjy, Bennie, Benny, Minyamin, Minyomei, Minyomi.*

BENJIRO (Japanese) Peaceful.

BENNETT (English) Formal version of Benjamin. Variations: *Benet, Benett, Bennet.*

BENONI (Hebrew) Son of a sorrowful mother.

BENSON (English) Son of Ben. Last name. Variations: *Bensen, Benssen, Bensson.*

BENTLEY (English) Meadow. Though Bentley had its origins as a name for boys, it is starting to catch on among girls as well. Parents who dream of great things for their children – including fancy cars – may opt for the name Bentley. Variations: *Bentlea, Bentlee, Bentlie.*

BENTON (English) Town in Britain.

BENZI (Hebrew) Good son.

BER (Hebrew) Bear.

BERDY (Russian) Very smart.

BERESFORD (English) Field of barley. Variation: *Berresford.*

BERG (German) Mountain. Variations: *Bergh, Burg, Burgh.*

BERGEN (Scandinavian) Hillside dweller. Variations: *Bergin, Birgin.*

BERGER (French) Shepherd.

BERK (Turkish) Stable.

BERKELEY (English) Last name. Town in Britain meaning birch wood. Berkeley is also sometimes used as a girls' name. It is pronounced 'barklee' in Britain and 'burklee' in the USA. Variations: *Barcley, Barklay, Barkley, Barklie, Berkley.*

BERNAL (German) A strong bear. Variations: *Bernald, Bernhald, Bernhold, Bernold.*

BERNARD (German) Brave. Bernard has a long and illustrious history, even though it is not frequently on the top fifty lists. Two saints from medieval days went by the name of Bernard, as does the heroic type of dog that is considered to be the patron saint for hikers. Variations: *Barnard, Barnardo, Barney, Barnhard, Barnhardo, Barnie, Barny, Bernardas, Bernardel, Bernardin, Bernardino, Bernardo, Bernardyn, Bernhard, Bernhardo, Bernie, Berny, Burnard.*

BERRY (English) Flower. This name was quite popular towards the end of the 19th century. Unlike some flower and fruit names that were common at the time, Berry fell from favour early in the 20th century and is now very rare.

BERT (English) Bright light. Bert is more common as a shortened version of Robert, Gilbert, and other names that end in '-bert'. Famous Berts include Bert Lahr, who played the lion in *The Wizard of Oz*, Burt Reynolds, Burt Lancaster, Burt Bacharach, and the best friend of Ernie in *Sesame Street*. Variations: *Berthold, Bertie, Bertold, Bertolde, Berty, Burt, Burtt, Burty*.

BERTHOLD (German) Bright strength. Variations: *Berthoud, Bertold, Bertolde*.

BERTIL (Scandinavian) Bright. Variation: *Bertel*.

BERTIN (Spanish) Good friend. Variation: *Berton*.

BERTRAM (German) Brightly coloured raven. Variations: *Bert, Bertrand*.

BERWIN (English) Friend at harvest time. Variations: *Berwyn, Berwynn, Berwynne*.

BERWYN (Welsh) White hair.

BESHILTHEENI (Native American: Navajo) Metalworker.

BETHEL (Hebrew) House of God. Variation: *Bethell*.

BETSERAI (African: Zimbabwean) Help.

BETZALEL (Hebrew) In God's shadow.

BEVAL (English) Like the wind.

BEVAN (Welsh) A son of a man named Evan. Its usage today is becoming popular among parents who like the name Evan, but are looking for something a little different. Variations: *Beavan, Beaven, Beven, Bevin, Bevon*.

BEVERLY (English) A stream of beavers. Variations: *Beverlee, Beverleigh, Beverley*.

BEVIS (French) A town in France, though a recent popular variation of the spelling – from *Beavis and Butthead* – will probably make you think twice about giving your baby boy this name. Variations: *Beauvais, Beavis*.

BHAKATI (Hindu) Devotion.

BHANU (Hindu) The sun.

BHARAT (Hindu) Maintenance.

BHASKARA (Hindu) Provides light. Variation: *Bhaskar*.

BHASVAN (Hindu) Light. Variation: *Bhaswar*.

BHAVNISH (Hindu) King.

BHOJA (Hindu) Eleventh-century king.

BIALAS (Polish) White. Variation: *Bialy*.

BICKFORD (English) Town in Britain.

BILAL (Arabic) The chosen one.

BILL (English) Bill is rarely a given first name. It is a variation of the more formal name William, which most parents of 'Bills' choose to name their boys. Variations: *Billy, Byll*.

BING (German) This literally means a hollow in the earth that's shaped like a pot; also, a type of cherry. Although the most famous person known by this name had the last name of Crosby, his birth name was actually Harry.

BINH (Vietnamese) Section.

BIRCH (English) A tree. If nature names ever catch on again the way they did in the 1970s, an arbour-loving family might decide to name all their children after trees. Variations: *Birk, Burch*.

BIRGER (Scandinavian) To help. Variations: *Birghir, Borge, Borje, Borre, Byrghir, Byrgir*.

BIRGER (Scandinavian: Norwegian) Rescue.

BIRKETT (English) Area with birch trees. Variations: *Birket, Birkit, Birkitt, Burket, Burkett, Burkitt*.

BIRKEY (English) Island of birch. Variations: *Birkee, Birkie, Birky*.

BIRLEY (English) Cow pasture. Variations: *Birlie, Birly*.

BIRNEY (English) Brook with an island. Variations: *Birnie, Birny, Burney, Burnie*.

BIRTLE (English) Hill with birds.

BISAHALANI (Native American: Navajo) Speaker.

BISHAMON (Japanese) God of war.

BISHOP (English) Bishop.

BISHVAJIT (Hindu) Victor of the world.

BIX (English) Nickname for Bixby, a last name.

BJORN (Scandinavian) Bear.

BLACKBURN (English) A black brook.

BLAGDEN (English) Dark valley

BLAINE (Gaelic) Thin. Blaine is also used as a girls' name. Variations: *Blain, Blane, Blayne.*

BLAIR (English) Flat piece of land. Like Blaine, Blair is also commonly given to girls. Variations: *Blaire, Blayr, Blayre.*

BLAISE (Latin) Stutterer. Variations: *Blaize, Blase, Blayse, Blayze, Blaze.*

BLAKE (English) This name could be given to both boys and girls, and strangely enough, could mean either light or dark. Blake is a name that became synonymous with a famous TV character of the 1980s, *Dynasty's* Blake Carrington, who was played by John Forsythe. The husband of actress Julie Andrews, Blake Edwards, has long been known for his offbeat movies. Variations: *Blaike, Blayke.*

BLAKELY (English) Dark or light meadow. Variations: *Blakelee, Blakeley, Blakelie.*

BLANCO (Spanish) White.

BLANFORD (English) Ford of the grey man. Variation: *Blandford.*

BLAZEJ (Czech) Stutterer.

BLEDDYN (Welsh) Wolf hero.

BLISS (English) Joy.

BLYTHE (English) Happy. Variation: *Blithe.*

BOAZ (Hebrew) Quick. Boaz is an obscure name from the Old Testament, and although the last time it appeared with any regularity was during the 17th century, it does seem to be making tiny inroads among parents who are looking for something that's completely different, but can be shortened to a familiar nickname: Bo. Variations: *Boas, Boase.*

BOB (English) Bright; famous. Like its common counterpart Bill, Bob is rarely given as the name that will appear on the birth certificate; Robert is typically the given name of choice. Variations: *Bobbey, Bobbie, Bobby.*

BOBO (African: Ghanian) Born on Tuesday.

BODAWAY (Native American) Fire maker.

BODEN (French) One who delivers the news. Variations: *Bodin, Bowden, Bowdoin.*

BODIL (Scandinavian: Norwegian) Dominant.

BODUA (African: Ghanian) Animal tail.

BOGART (French) Strength of a bow. Of course, the most famous Bogart went by the name of Humphrey, and even though it appears most often as a last name in this country, Bogart is gaining in popularity as a first name. Variations: *Bogey, Bogie, Bogy.*

BOGUCHWAL (Polish) God's glory. Variations: *Bogufal, Boguslaw, Bogusz, Bohusz.*

BOGUMIERZ (Polish) God is great.

BOGUMIL (Polish) God's love.

BOHDAN (Czech) Gift from God. Variations: *Bogdan, Bogdashka.*

BOHUMIL (Czech) God's love.

BOHUMIR (Czech) God is great.

BOHUSLAV (Czech) God's glory.

BOJAN (Czech) War. Variations: *Bojanek, Bojek, Bojik.*

BOLESLAV (Czech) Great glory. Variation: *Bolek.*

BOLESLAW (Polish) Great glory.

BOLTON (English) Town in Britain.

BOMANI (African: Malawian) Strong soldier.

BONAR (French) Gentle. Variations: *Bonnar, Bonner.*

BOND (English) Man of the land. Variations: *Bonde, Bondon, Bonds.*

BON-HWA (Korean) Glorious.

BONIFACE (Latin) Fortunate. Variations: *Bonifacio, Bonifacius.*

BOOKER (English) Slang for the Bible. Booker T. Washington was a famous American musician

BOONE (French) Good.

BOOTH (English) House. Variations: *Boot, Boote, Boothe.*

BORDEN (English) Boar's house. Variations: *Bordin, Bordon.*

BORG (Scandinavian) Castle dweller.

BORIS (Slavic) Warrior. Boris is one of those names that brings up memories of Saturday morning cartoons or monster movies. Famous Borises include Boris Karloff, Boris Pasternak, Boris Yeltsin and Boris Becker. Variations: *Boriss, Borris, Borys.*

BORIVOJ (Czech) Great soldier. Variations: *Bovra, Bovrek, Bovrik.*

BORNANI (African: Malawian) Warrior.

BORR (Scandinavian: Swedish) Youth.

BORYSLAW (Polish) Glory in battle.

BOSEDA (African: Nigerian) Born on Sunday.

BOSTON (English) Named for the city.

BOTAN (Japanese) Long life.

BOTOLF (English) Wolf. Variations: *Botolph, Botulf.*

BOUR (African) Rock.

BOUREY (Cambodian) County.

BOWEN (Gaelic) Small son. Variation: *Bow.*

BOWIE (Gaelic) Blond. Famous Bowies include David Bowie and Colonel James Bowie, who invented the Bowie knife.

BOY (English) Boy.

BOYCE (French) Forest. Variations: *Boice, Boise.*

BOYD (Gaelic) Blond. Variation: *Boid.*

BOYNE (Irish) White cow. Variations: *Boine, Boyn.*

BOZIDAR (Czech) Gift from God. Variations: *Bovza, Bovzek.*

BOZYDAR (Polish) A gift of God.

BRADEN (English) Broad meadow. Variations: *Bradon, Braeden, Brayden, Braydon.*

BRADFORD (English) A wide stream. Northern English place name. Variations: *Brad, Bradburn, Braddford, Bradfurd.*

BRADLEY (English) A wide meadow. Bradley is one of those names that seems to always skirt the edge between extreme popularity and obsolescence. When I was at school in the 1970s, it seemed like a slightly nerdy name, but was saved by the virile sound of its nickname: *Brad.* Undoubtedly, its growing popularity today is due to the fame of film star Brad Pitt. Variations: *Brad, Bradlea, Bradlee, Bradleigh, Bradlie, Bradly.*

BRADSHAW (English) Wide forest.

BRADY (English) Wide island.

BRAHMA (Hindu) Prayer.

BRAINARD (English) Brave raven. Variation: *Brainerd.*

BRAM (Gaelic) Raven. Variations: *Bramm, Bran, Brann.*

BRAMWELL (English) Town in Britain. A famous Bramwell was William Bramwell Booth, leader of the Salvation Army . Variations: *Brammell, Bramwel, Branwell.*

BRAN (Welsh) Raven.

BRAND (English) Firebrand.

BRANDEIS (German) One who dwells in a land burned by fire.

BRANDON (English) Sword; hill afire. Brandon is one of those names that appears to be suddenly cool, especially in the USA, where its popularity peaked in the 1980s. Variations: *Bran, Brandan, Branden, Brandin, Brandyn.*

BRANT (English) Proud. Variation: *Brannt.*

BRASIL (Irish) War. Variations: *Brazil, Breasal, Bresal, Bressal.*

BRATISLAV (Czech) Glorious brother.

BRATUMIL (Polish) Brotherly love.

BRAWLEY (English) Meadow.

BRAXTON. (English) Literally, Brock's town.

BREDE (Scandinavian) Glacier.

BRENCIS (Czech) Crown of laurel.

BRENDAN (Irish) Foul-smelling hair. I'd venture a guess that most parents who give their sons this name haven't a clue what it really means – including me; my son's middle name is Brendan. Famous Brendans include American actor Brendan Frasier, Irish playwright Brendan Behan and British athlete Brendan Foster. Brendan was also an Irish saint nicknamed the Voyager who, rumour has it, was the first Irishman to sail to America. It was among the top fifty names in Australia in the 1970s. Variations: *Brenden, Brendin, Brendon.*

BRENNAN (Irish) Raven. Variation: *Brennen.*

BRENT (English) Mountaintop. Though Brent is very popular today, it has been used as a first name only since the 1930s. It enjoyed a peak of popularity on both sides of the Atlantic in the 1970s and 1980s. A famous Brent includes the fictional character Brent Tarleton in *Gone With the Wind*. Variations: *Breneon, Brentan, Brentin, Brenton, Brentyn.*

BRETISLAV (Czech) Glorious noise.

BRETT (English) British man. Brett is a name that is very popular in Australia. Brett is also frequently used as a girls' name today, which, unlike many popular androgynous names, hasn't diminished its popularity among boys. The US writer Bret Harte is a famous Brett, as is Bret Easton Ellis. Variations: *Bret, Brette, Bretton, Brit, Britt.*

BREWSTER (English) Brewer. Variation: *Brewer.*

BRIAN (Celtic) Brave; virtuous. Irish names are currently popular among parents-to-be and Brian may be ready for a comeback. It's a solid name with lots of possibilities for variety, yet it has a bit of a lilt to it, and it doesn't seem overexposed – *yet*. There are many famous Brians, including musicians Brian Adams, Brian Wilson and Bryan Ferry, actors Brian Blessed and Brian Dennehy, directors Bryan Forbes and Brian De Palma and cricketer Brian Close. Variations: *Briano, Brien, Brion, Bryan, Bryon.*

BRIAREUS (Greek) Mythological hundred-armed giant.

BRIDGELY (English) Meadow near a bridge. Variation: *Bridgeley.*

BRIDGER (English) One who lives near a bridge. Variation: *Bridge.*

BRIDON (African-American) Unknown definition.

BRIGHAM (English) Village near a bridge. Variations: *Brigg, Briggs.*

BRIGHTON (English) Town in Britain.

BRINLEY (English) Burnt wood. Variations: *Brindley, Brinly, Brynley, Brynly.*

BRISHEN (Gypsy) Born during a rainstorm.

BROCK (English) Badger. Variations: *Broc, Brockley.*

BRODER (Scandinavian) Brother. Variations: *Brolle, Bror.*

BRODERICK (Scottish) Brother of Roderick. Variations: *Brod, Broddy, Broderic, Brodric, Brodrick.*

BRODNY (Slavic) Person dwelling near a stream.

BRODY (Scottish) Second son. Variations: *Brodee, Brodey, Brodi, Brodie.*

BROMLEY (English) Town in Britain.

BRON (African) Origin.

BRONE (Irish) Sadness.

BRONISLAV (Czech) Glorious armour. Variations: *Branek, Branik, Branislav, Bronislaw.*

BRONSON (English) Dark man's son. With the popularity of other boys' names that start with 'B-r-' and have two syllables, Bronson certainly seems like a candidate for an increase in usage. Variations: *Bron, Bronnson, Bronsen, Bronsin, Bronsonn, Bronsson.*

BROOK (English) Brook; stream. Variations: *Brooke, Brookes, Brooks.*

BROUGHTON (English) Town in Britain.

BROWN (English) Colour.

BRUCE (English) Thick brush. Variations: *Brucey, Brucie.*

BRUNO (English) Dark-skinned. Variation: *Bruns.*

BRUNON (Polish) Brown.

BRYCE (Celtic) Unknown definition. Variation: *Brice.*

BRYCHAN (Welsh) Speckled.

BRYDEN (English) Town in Britain.

BRYNMOR (Welsh) Great hill. Variation: *Bryn.*

BRYSON (English) Nobleman's son.

BU (Vietnamese) Leader.

BUADHACH (Irish) Victory. Variations: *Buach, Buagh.*

BUCK (English) Male deer. Made popular by by the space adventures of the cartoon strip character Buck Rogers, which were first published in the 1920s. Its Greek definition is 'weaver', but because of its stag-like association, some parents will shy away. Variations: *Buckey, Buckie, Bucky.*

BUCKLEY (English) Meadow where deer graze. Variations: *Bucklie, Buckly.*

BUDDY (English) Friend. Buddy, along with its derivatives, has rarely been the name that appears on a baby's birth certificate; its common usage is as a nick-name, with such notables as actor Bud Abbott, bandleader Buddy Rich, and rock and roll singer Buddy Holly. Variations: *Bud, Budd, Buddey, Buddie.*

BUDINGTON (English) Area in Britain.

BUDISLAV (Czech) Glorious awakening. Variation: *Budek.*

BUDZISLAW (Polish) Awakening glory. Variations: *Budzisz, Budzyk.*

BUGONEGUIG (Native American: Chippewa) Hole in the sky. Variation: *Bagwunagijik.*

BURCHARD (English) Strong castle. Variations: *Burckhardt, Burgard, Burgaud, Burkhart.*

BURFORD (English) Town in Britain.

BURGESS (English) Citizen. Variations: *Burges, Burgiss.*

BURKE (French) Fortress dweller. Variations: *Berk, Berke, Birk, Birke, Bourke, Burk.*

BURL (English) Forest. Most familiar as the first name of US actor and singer Burl Ives.

BURLEIGH (English) Town in Britain. Variations: *Burley, Burlie, Byrleigh, Byrley.*

BURNABY (Norse) Warrior's land.

BURNE (English) Brook. Town in Britain. Variations: *Bourn, Bourne, Bourne, Burn, Byrn, Byrne, Byrnes.*

BURNELL (French) Small brown child. Variation: *Burnel.*

BURNETT (English) Unknown definition. Variations: *Burnet, Burnitt.*

BURNEY (English) Town in Britain.

BURR (Scandinavian) Youth.

BURTON (English) Fort. Variations: *Bert, Burt.*

BUSBY (Scottish) Village in the forest.

BUSTER (English) Unknown definition. Nickname.

BUTCHER (English) Butcher. Variation: *Butch.*

BYFORD (English) Town in Britain.

BYRAM (English) Town in Britain.

BYRD (English) Like a bird. Variation: *Bird.*

BYRON (English) Cow barn. Variation: *Biron.*

Names from Locations

One of the most popular trends in names for boys and girls today is the practice of naming a baby after a place: a town, a county, a region of the country, or even an alma mater.

While I wouldn't go so far as to name a baby Newark, or some other less-than-appealing venue, the names that are getting the most attention at the moment are American place names with far-flung Western connotations: Montana, Cheyenne, Dakota and Sierra are a few of the more popular choices.

Names of certain cities are also becoming more commonplace: Phoenix, Boston and Philadelphia are a few names that have cropped up recently.

In the recent past, place names that have been popular in America have been from the southern part of the country and have been names for girls, such as Carolina, Florida and Georgia.

Names can be drawn from countries like India and counties like Devon. Since many place names like Devon don't have any connotations attached to them as to whether they're clearly a boys' or girls' name, today's parents are choosing them in equal numbers for their sons and their daughters. Although names that end with the letter 'a' are more likely to be used for girls since a name that ends in 'a' has a traditionally female association, this is not a hard and fast rule.

- Acton: Town in Britain.
- Clyde: A river in Scotland.
- Carinthis: A region in Germany.
- Daryl: Area in France.
- Elba: Area in Italy.
- Fraser: Town in France.
- Jordan: Country in the Middle East.
- Kailash: A Himalayan mountain.

- Kerry: County in Ireland.
- Louvain: A city in Belgium.
- Moneka: Sioux for the Earth.
- Nevada: Western US state (Spanish origin).
- Paazani: Hindu for the Ganges river.
- Sidney: City in Australia.
- Vail: Colorado city.

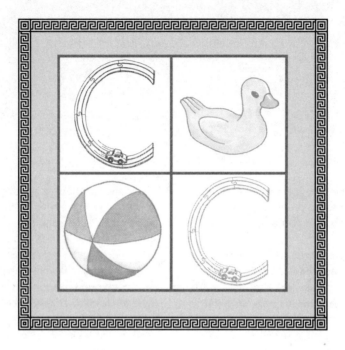

CABLE (English) Rope marker. Variation: *Cabe.*

CACHI (Spanish) He brings peace.

CADAO (Vietnamese) Song.

CADBY (English) Soldier's estate.

CADDOCK (Welsh) Ready for war.

CADELL (Welsh) Small battle. Variations: *Caddell, Cade, Cadel.*

CADHLA (Irish) Handsome.

CADI (Arabic) Luck.

CADMAN (Welsh) Soldier.

CADMUS (Greek) One who excels.

CADWALADR (Welsh) Battle leader. Variations: *Cadwalader, Cadwaladyr.*

CADWALLON (Welsh) Battle arranger. Variation: *Cadwallen.*

CAELAN (Irish) Powerful warrior. Variations: *Caelin, Calin, Caulan.*

CAERWYN (Welsh) White fortress. Variation: *Carwyn.*

CAESAR (Latin) Hairy. Has appeared since the 18th century in tribute to the celebrated Roman emperor. Variations: *Caezar, Cesar, Cesare, Cesareo, Cesario, Cesaro, Cezar, Cezary, Cezek.*

CAFFAR (Irish) Helmet.

CAHIR (Irish) Warrior. Variation: *Cathaoir.*

CAI (Welsh) Joy. Variations: *Caio, Caius.*

CAILEAN (Scottish) Triumphant in war.

CAIN (Hebrew) Spear.

CAIRBRE (Irish) One who rides a chariot.

CALBHACH (Irish) Bald. Variation: *Callough.*

CALDER (English) Brook.

CALDWELL (English) Stream; cold well. Variation: *Cal.*

CALEB (Hebrew) Brave; dog. Caleb was a popular name among Puritans, since the Biblical Caleb was one of the people who spent time wandering with Moses on his excursion in the wilderness. Starting in the 19th century, common usage of the name began to fall off. However, in the current trend to look for baby names that are traditional yet different, the prevalence of Caleb among boys has grown. Variations: *Cale, Kalb, Kaleb.*

CALEY (Irish) Slender.

CALHOUN (Irish) Small forest. Variations: *Colhoun, Colquhoun.*

CALLAGHAN (Irish) An Irish saint.

CALLUM (Irish) Dove. Variation: *Calum.*

CALVERT (English) Calf herder. Variation: *Calbert.*

CALVIN (English) Bald. Name taken up in the 16th century in tribute to French Protestant theologian Jean Calvin. Other famous Calvins include US President Calvin Coolidge and fashion designer Calvin Klein. Variations: *Cal, Calvino, Kalvin.*

CAMDEN (English) Twisting valley.

CAMERON (Gaelic) Crooked nose or river. Though the name is very popular today, it was rare until the 1950s. Notable bearers of the name include theatrical producer Cameron Mackintosh. Variation: *Camron.*

CAMEY (Irish) Champion. Variation: *Camy.*

CAMILLUS (Latin) One who assists a priest. Variation: *Camillo.*

CAMLINE (Latin) Song.

CAMLO (Gypsy) Beautiful.

CAMPBELL (Gaelic) Crooked mouth. Best known as the surname of one of the most famous Scottish clans, historically the sworn enemies of the MacDonalds. No matter what name you give your child, he's still going to get teased about it. There was a boy at school named Campbell, and of course, the other kids called him a soup can. But the ribbing would probably have escalated had they known the real meaning of Campbell. Variations: *Cam, Camp.*

CAN (Vietnamese) Advice.

CANICE (Irish) Handsome. Variation: *Coinneach.*

CANNON (French) Official of a church. Variations: *Cannan, Canning, Canon.*

CANOWICAKTE (Native American: Sioux) Forest hunter.

CANUTE (Scandinavian) Knot. Variation: *Knute.*

CAOIMHIN (Irish) Noble. Variation: *Caoimhghin.*

CAOLAN (Irish) Thin.

CAPPI (Italian) Luck.

CAPTAIN (English) In charge.

CARADOC (Welsh) Affection. Variation: *Caradog, Carthage.*

CAREY (Welsh) Near a castle. Variation: *Cary.*

CARL (English) Man. Nickname for Charles. Carl is one of those names that rolls off the tongue and sounds like it has more than one syllable. Famous Carls include US astronomer Carl Sagan and composer Carl Davis. Variation: *Karl.*

CARLETON (English) Farmer's land. Variations: *Carlton, Charleton.*

CARLIN (Gaelic) Little champion. Variations: *Carling, Carly, Carolan, Carollan.*

CARLISLE (English) Protected tower. Town in Britain. Variation: *Carlyle.*

CARLOS (Spanish) Man. Spanish version of Charles. Variations: *Carlino, Carlo, Carolo.*

CARMEL (Hebrew) Garden.

CARMICHAEL (Gaelic) One who follows Michael.

CARMINE (English) Garden. Variations: *Carmel, Carmelo.*

CARNEY (Irish) Champion. Variations: *Carny, Karney, Karny.*

CARR (English) Swamp. Variations: *Karr, Kerr.*

CARROLL (English) Man. Version of Charles. Though Carol is more popular as a girls' name, it does seem to be making inroads into the male side of the chart,

which is where it originally started out. It's often been reserved for children born at Christmas. Famous Carrolls include British film director Carol Reed Variations: *Caroll, Carolus, Carrol, Caryl*.

CARSON (English) Son who lives in a swamp. Variation: *Karsen*.

CARSWELL (English) Watercress.

CARTER (English) Driver of the cart. President Carter may be responsible for this surname catching on as a first name among both boys and girls.

CARTHACH (Irish) Loving. Variations: *Cartagh, Carthage*.

CARTWRIGHT (English) One who builds carts.

CARVEL (French) One who lives in a swamp. Variation: *Carvell*.

CARVER (English) Woodcarver.

CARY (English) Stream.

CASE (English) He who brings peace.

CASEY (Irish) Observant. Popular among both girls and boys, Casey is being chosen by many parents today because it sounds like a name that suits both a child and an adult. Some names are great for children but falter when you try them out on an adult, and vice versa. Casey works well for all ages, and both sexes, which will only continue to contribute to its popularity. Famous Caseys include American engineer Casey Jones, who lost his life saving his passengers on the *Cannonball Express*. Variations: *Cacey, Cayce, Caycey, Kasey*.

CASHESEGRA (Native American: Osage) Large animal tracks. Variation: *Koshisigre*.

CASIMIR (Polish) He brings peace. Variations: *Casimire, Casimiro, Castimer, Kazimir*.

CASPAR (English) Wealthy man. Variations: *Cash, Casper, Cass*.

CASSIDY (Irish) Smart. It literally translates from O'Caiside, which means one who dwells in an area of Ireland called Caiside. Caiside itself means bent love, which somehow turned into smart. Cassidy is another wildly popular name for both boys and girls that may have begun to bloom at the peak of the 1970s TV show *The Partridge Family*, featuring David Cassidy. Variation: *Cassady*.

CASSIEL (Greek) Guardian of Capricornians.

CASSIUS (Latin) Narcissistic.

CASTLE (English) Castle. Variation: *Castel*.

CASTOR (Greek) Beaver.

CATER (English) Caterer.

CATHAL (Irish) Ready for war. Variation: *Cahal*.

CATO (Latin) Smart. Variation: *Caton*.

CAVAN (Irish) Good-looking.

CAW (Welsh) Joyous.

CEALLACH (Irish) War. Variations: *Ceallachan, Cillan, Cillian, Keallach*.

CEARBHALL (Irish) Man.

CECIL (English) Blind. Has a reputation as an aristocratic name. Famous Cecils include US film director Cecil B. de Mille, Cecil Rhodes, after whom Rhodesia was named, and Irish poet Cecil Day-Lewis. Variations: *Cecilio, Cecillo, Cecillus, Celio*.

CEDRIC (Welsh) Leader of war. Variations: *Cedrick, Cedrych*.

CELESTIN (Czech) Heaven.

CEMAL (Arabic) Beauty.

CENON (Spanish) To receive life from Zeus. Variations: *Xenon, Zenon*.

CEPHAS (Hebrew) Rock.

CEPHEUS (Greek) Ancient mythological figure.

CERDIC (Welsh) Cherished. Variations: *Ceredig, Ceretic*.

CEREK (Slavic) Unknown definition.

CESLAV (Czech) Glorious honour. Variation: *Ctislav*.

CETANWAKUWA (Native American: Sioux) Attacking hawk.

CHAD (English) Protector. Strong, one-syllable names became popular for a while in the late 1960s and early 1970s. Variations: *Chadd, Chadwick.*

CHADLAI (Hebrew) Stop. Variation: *Hadlai.*

CHAGIAH (Hebrew) Festival. Variations: *Chagia, Chagiya, Haggiah, Hagia.*

CHAGO (Spanish) Heel. Variation: *Chango.*

CHAI (Hebrew) Life. Variation: *Hail.*

CHAITANYA (Hindu) Cognizance.

CHAL (Gypsy) Boy.

CHALFON (Hebrew) Change. Variations: *Chalfan, Halfon, Halphon.*

CHALIL (Hebrew) Flute. Variations: *Halil, Hallil.*

CHALMERS (Scottish) Head of the household. Variation: *Chalmer.*

CHAM (Hebrew) Hot. Variation: *Ham*; (Vietnamese) Hard-working.

CHAN (Vietnamese) Right.

CHANANIAH (Hebrew) God's sympathy.

CHANCE (English) Good fortune.

CHANCELLOR (English) Secretary.

CHAND (Hindu) Shining moon. Variations: *Chanda, Chandak, Chander, Chandra, Chandrabha, Chandrak, Chandrakant.*

CHANDAN (Hindu) Sandalwood.

CHANDLER (English) Candle maker. This name has become popular in the last few years, due perhaps to its appearance as first and last names among both male and female TV characters. The most famous Chandler in the last decade must be Matthew Perry's character in the long-running hit US television series *Friends.*

CHANDRARAJ (Hindu) Moon king.

CHANDRESH (Hindu) Moon leader.

CHANEY (French) Oak tree. Variation: *Cheney.*

CHANG (Chinese) Smooth.

CHANIEL (Hebrew) God's grace. Variations: *Channiel, Haniel, Hanniel.*

CHANKRISNA (Cambodian) Tree.

CHANNING (English) Wise; church official.

CHANOCH (Hebrew) Devoted. Variations: *Enoch, Hanoch.*

CHANTI (Hispanic) Supplanter.

CHAPMAN (English) Peddler. Variations: *Chap, Chappy.*

CHARAKA (Hindu) One who roams.

CHARLES (English) Man. Charles has spawned a number of variations in all cultures throughout the centuries. The name has a rich and varied history, as the name of the patron saint of Catholic bishops and boasts many links to royalty – two kings of England, ten kings of France, the Scottish pretender Bonnie Prince Charlie and the current heir to the British throne Prince Charles. Then there are cartoon characters like Charlie Brown, and a slew of actors, from Charles Bronson to Charlie Chan. Other famous Charleses include Chick Corea, Charles Darwin, Charles de Gaulle, Charles Dickens and Charlie

Chaplin. Variations: *Charley, Charlie, Chas, Chaz, Chick, Chip, Chuck.*

CHARLTON (English) House where Charles lives. The most famous Charlton is US film actor Charlton Heston. Variations: *Carleton, Carlton.*

CHARUDATA (Hindu) Beautiful. Variation: *Charvaka.*

CHASE (English) Hunter. Variations: *Chace, Chaise.*

CHASID (Hebrew) Devout. Variation: *Chasud.*

CHASIEL (Hebrew) God's refuge. Variation: *Hasiel.*

CHASIN (Hebrew) Strong. Variations: *Chason, Hasin, Hassin.*

CHASKA (Native American: Sioux) First son.

CHAU (Vietnamese) Pearl.

CHAUNCEY
(English)

Chancellor. Variations: *Chance, Chancey, Chaunce, Chauncy.*

CHAVIV (Hebrew) Dear. Variations: *Habib, Haviv.*

CHAYIM (Hebrew) Life. Variations: *Chaim, Chaimek, Chayyim, Chayym, Haim, Hayyim, Hayym.*

CHAZAIAH (Hebrew) God sees. Variations: *Chazaya, Chaziel, Hazaia, Hazaiah, Haziel.*

CHE (Spanish) God will add. Hispanic nickname for Joseph.

CHEASEQUAH (Native American: Cherokee) Red bird.

CHEAUKA (Native American: Hopi) Clay.

CHEBONA BULA (Native American: Creek) Boy who laughs.

Names of Famous Historical References

Perhaps you live near a famous historical site. Or one of your ancestors participated in one of the events that helped to shape your region or the entire country. Or you've always just liked the name of a famous person who played a pivotal role in a historical event. So now you're thinking about turning the event or the person into your baby's name.

It's a good possibility that any name that reflects pride in history will be different from the names of your child's classmates, so you should consider this before you decide on a name. But some of these names also follow the current trend of naming babies after counties, cities, and countries, so your baby may not stand out so much.

Here are some of the first names I've seen that are directly influenced by historical events:

- Arlington (Massachusetts)
- Cape (Cod)
- Concord
- Lexington
- Machias (Maine)
- Montpelier (Vermont)
- Parker (House)
- Patriot
- Salem
- Sturbridge
- Thoreau
- Walden

Of course, there are more recent historical events that could serve as candidates, but I don't know many people who want to name their babies after Watergate, Whitewater, or any other political controversy!

CHECHE (Spanish) God will add.

CHEILEM (Hebrew) Power. Variation: *Chelem.*

CHEN (Chinese) Great.

CHENCHE (Spanish) To conquer.

CHENCHO (Spanish) Crowned with laurel.

CHENG-GONG (Chinese) Success.

CHENZIRA (African: Zimbabwean) Born while travelling.

CHEPE (Spanish) God will increase. Variation: *Chepito.*

CHESLAV (Russian) Camp.

CHESMU (Native American) Abrasive.

CHESTER (English) Campsite. Chester seems to be a fussy name that conjures up Victorian tea in the afternoons and bow ties. What's more popular, however, is one of Chester's nicknames: Chet. US country and western musician Chet Atkins is an example of a celebrity with the name. Variations: *Cheston, Chet.*

CHETWIN (English) House on a winding road.

CHETZRON (Hebrew) Walled town. Variation: *Hezron.*

CHEVALIER (French) Knight. Variations: *Chev, Chevi, Chevy.*

CHEYENNE (English) A city in Wyoming.

CHI (African: Nigerian) God.

CHICO (Spanish) Boy. Variation: *Chicho.*

CHIK (Gypsy) Earth.

CHIKAE (African-American) Power of God.

CHILO (Spanish) Frenchman.

CHILTON (English) Farm near a well.

CHIM (Vietnamese) Bird.

CHINESE (African: Nigerian) God protects. Variation: *Cinese.*

CHIN-HWA (Korean) Wealthiest.

CHIN-MAE (Korean) Truth.

CHINTAK (Hindu) To think.

CHINUA (African: Nigerian) Blessings of God.

CHIOKE (African: Nigerian) Gift from God.

CHIONESU (African: Zimbabwean) Protector.

CHIP (English) Nickname for Charles that is sometimes given as the full name.

CHIRAM (Hebrew) Exalted brother. Variation: *Hiram.*

CHIRANJIV (Hindu) One who lives long. Variation: *Chirayu.*

CHISULO (African: Malawian) Steel.

CHITTO (Native American: Creek) Brave.

CHIUMBO (African: Kenyan) Small child.

CHIZKIAH (Hebrew) God enriches. Variations: *Chizkia, Chizkiya, Chizkiyahu, Hezekiah.*

CHOKICHI (Japanese) Good luck.

CHONEN (Hebrew) Gracious.

CHONG DUY (Vietnamese) Eat like a bird.

CHOZAI (Hebrew) Prophet. Variation: *Hozai.*

CHRISTIAN (English) Anointed one; Christ. Variations: *Chresta, Chris, Christiaan, Christianos, Chrystian, Cris, Kris, Kriss, Kristian.*

CHRISTMAS (English) The holiday. Christmas used to be a somewhat popular name through the 1800s. Perhaps parents who loved the holiday – and who were fondly remembering their own holiday celebrations before the children arrived – hoped that with a boy with this name, every day would be Christmas. Of course, after the annual rites of the children waking up at 4 a.m., anxious to see what Father Christmas brought, any sane parent would have second thoughts about the wisdom of being reminded of this day the other 364 days of the year.

CHRISTOPHER (English) One who holds Christ in his heart. Famous Christophers include St. Christopher, the patron saint of people who travel, the actor Christopher Plummer, Winnie-the-Pooh's friend Christopher Robin, and explorer Christopher Columbus. Christopher just started to become popular among new parents in the 1980s; now class-

rooms are filled with Christophers and its variations. Variations: *Chris, Christof, Christofer, Christoff, Christoffer, Christoforus, Christoph, Christophe, Christophoros, Christos, Christos, Cris, Cristobal, Cristoforo, Kit, Kitt, Kristofer, Kristofor.*

CHUIOKE (African: Nigerian) Talented. Variations: *Chike, Chinelo.*

CHUL (Korean) Firm.

CHUL-MOO (Korean) Iron weapon.

CHUMA (African: Zimbabwean) Bead.

CHUMIN (Spanish) Lord. Variation: *Chuminga.*

CHUMO (Spanish) Twin.

CHUNG-HEE (Korean) Righteous. Variation: *Chung-Ho.*

CHURCHILL (English) Church on a hill.

CHUSLUM MOXMOX (Native American: Nez Perce) Yellow bull.

CHWALIBOG (Polish) Praise God.

CIAN (Irish) Ancient; old. Variation: *Cianan.*

CIARAN (Irish) Black; black hair. Variations: *Ciardha, Ciarrai.*

CIBOR (Hebrew) Strong.

CICERO (Latin) Chickpea. Variation: *Ciceron.*

CID (Spanish) Rooster; God.

CILOMBO (African) Camp near the road.

CINNEIDID (Irish) Helmet head. The Anglicized version of this name is Kennedy. Variations: *Cinneide, Cinneidigh.*

CIRO (Spanish) Throne.

CISCO (Spanish) Frenchman.

CLANCY (Irish) Son of a red-headed soldier. Variation: *Clancey.*

CLARENCE (English) Clear. Variations: *Clair, Clarance, Clare, Clarey.*

CLARK (English) Scholar. Variations: *Clarke, Clerc, Clerk.*

CLAUDE (Latin) With a limp. Claude was quite a prolific name in the arts in the late 19th century, with luminaries such as Debussy, Monteverdi and Monet. Variations: *Claud, Claudio, Claudius, Klaudio.*

CLAY (English) Maker of clay. Clay can stand on its own, but it's also short for some of the following names that have Clay as their first syllable.

CLAYBORNE (English) Stream near a bed of clay. Variations: *Claiborn, Claiborne, Claybourne, Clayburn.*

CLAYTON (English) House or town near a clay bed. Clayton is a name that has always been popular to some extent; today, however, when it is given to a newborn baby, parents are more likely to use its nickname, Clay, and not the full version. Variations: *Clayten, Claytin.*

CLEARY (Irish) Educated man.

CLEAVON (African-American) Cliff. Variations: *Clevon, Kleavon, Klevon.*

CLEDWYN (Welsh) Rough and blessed. River in Wales.

CLEMENT (English) Gentle. The name of several saints and no fewer than fourteen popes, it has been in use since medieval times. Famous Clements include British Prime Minister Clement Atlee and British politician, food critic and media personality Clement Freud. The most common nickname for Clement is Clem. Variations: *Clem, Cleme, Clemen, Clemens, Clemente, Clementius, Clemento, Clemmie, Clemmons, Clemmy.*

CLEON (Greek) Famous. It is also a popular African-American variation of Cleo or Leon.

CLEVELAND (English) High cliff.

CLIAMAIN (Scottish) Gentle.

CLIFFORD (English) Place to cross a river near a cliff. Cliff has been a good name for celebrities: think of Cliff Richard, US playwright Clifford Odets

and Cliff Claven from *Cheers*. Variations: *Cliff, Clyff, Clyfford.*

CLIFTON (English) Town near a cliff. Variations: *Clift, Clyfton.*

CLINTON (English) Town near a hill. Before President Clinton came into international prominence, the name Clinton had appeared now and then as a first name: Clint Eastwood and Clint Black are two examples. Variations: *Clint, Clynt.*

CLIVE (English) Cliff. Variation: *Clyve.*

CLOVIS (German) Famous fighter.

CLUNY (Irish) Meadow.

CLYDE (Scottish) River in Scotland.

COB (English) Heel. Variation: *Cobb.*

COCHISE (Native American: Apache) Wood.

CODY (English) Cushion. Cody used to be known as a town in Wyoming and the name of various Western outlaws from the second part of the 19th century. Maybe it is the association with the Wild West hero Buffalo Bill Cody that makes it such a favourite. Cody is not only popular for boys but also for girls. When I was growing up, Cody – actually, Coty, one of its variations – got most of its recognition as a brand of nail varnish, which just goes to show you how much things change in a short period of time. Variations: *Codey, Codie, Coty, Kodey, Kodie, Kody.*

COILEAN (Irish) Puppy. Variation: *Cuilean.*

COINNEACH (Irish) Handsome.

COISEAM (Scottish) Stable, steady.

COLBERT (English) Famous sailor. Variations: *Colvert, Culbert.*

COLBY (English) Dark farm. Variation: *Collby.*

COLEMAN (English) Dove; one who follows Nicholas; (Irish) Little dove. Cole Porter helped to make this name popular in the 20th century. Variations: *Cole, Colman.*

COLIN (English) Triumphant people; also, young boy. Colin and its various spellings have become popular for boys, and to a lesser extent, girls, in the last ten years or so. The name sounds dignified and worthy of respect. Famous Colins include cricketer Sir Colin Cowdry and British actors Colin Welland and Colin Firth. Variations: *Colan, Cole, Collin, Colyn.*

COLLEY (English) Black hair. Variation: *Collis.*

COLLIER (English) Coal miner. Like Colin, the name Collier evokes a lot of professional respect.

COLLINGWOOD (English) Forest.

COLLINS (Irish) Holly.

COLM (Irish) Dove. Variations: *Colum, Columba.*

COLONEL (English) Military designation.

COLSTON (English) Unknown property owner. Variations: *Colson, Colt.*

COLTER (English) A herd of colts.

COLTON (English) One from a dark town. Variations: *Collton, Colt.*

COLVILLE (French) Town in France. Variations: *Colvile, Colvill.*

COLVIN (English) Last name of unknown origin.

COLWYN (Welsh) River in Wales. Variations: *Colwin, Colwynn.*

COMAN (Arabic) Noble.

COMHGHALL (Irish) Hostage.

COMHGHAN (Irish) Twin. Variation: *Comdhan.*

CONAIRE (Irish) Unknown definition. Variations: *Conary, Connery, Conrey, Conroy, Conry.*

CONALL (Irish) High and mighty. Variation: *Connell.*

CONAN (Irish) Elevated. Conan the Barbarian aside, Conan is beginning to appear with a little more regularity. The creator of Sherlock Holmes, Sir Arthur Conan Doyle, also bears the name. Variation: *Conant*.

CONARY (Irish) Last name.

CONCETTO (Italian) Refers to the Immaculate Conception.

CONCHOBHAR (Irish) Strong dog. Variations: *Concobhar, Conquhare*.

CONG (Chinese) Smart.

CONLAN (Irish) Hero. Variations: *Con, Conlen, Conley, Conlin, Conlon, Connlyn*.

CONN (Irish) Wisdom.

CONNLAODH (Irish) Pure fire. Variations: *Connlaoi, Connlaoth*.

CONNOR (Irish) Much desire. Connor appears in mythology as a legendary Irish king. Another popular name that could serve as last name or first, male or female; it is starting to appear in both sexes more frequently. Irish writer Conor Cruise O'Brien bears the name. Variations: *Conner, Conor*.

CONRAD (German) Courageous adviser. Four German kings and the US writer Conrad Aitken are famous Conrads. Variations: *Conn, Connie, Conny, Conrade, Conrado, Konrad, Kurt, Kurtis*.

CONROY (Irish) Wise man.

CONSTANTINE (English) Stable, steady. Variations: *Constant, Constantin, Constantino, Constantinos, Costa, Konstantin, Konstanz*.

CONWAY (Welsh) Holy river. Variation: *Conwy*.

COOK (English) Cook. Variation: *Cooke*.

COOPER (English) Barrel maker.

COOWESCOOWE (Native American: Cherokee) Egret.

CORBET (English) Black hair. Variations: *Corbett, Corbin, Corbit, Corbitt*.

CORCORAN (Irish) Cork.

CORDELL (English) Rope maker.

CORDERO (Spanish) Lamb.

COREY (Irish) The hollow. This name is very popular and it's not difficult to see why. It fits one of the main criteria for why certain names are popular today: it's unisex – both girls and boys are comfortable with the name. However, it does show signs of being overtaken by other popular names. Variations: *Corin, Correy, Cory, Korey*.

CORLISS (English) Generous. Variation: *Corley*.

CORMAG (Scottish) Raven.

CORMICK (Gaelic) Chariot driver. Variations: *Cormac, Cormack*.

CORNELIUS (Latin) Horn. Variations: *Cornelious, Cornelus, Cornilius*.

CORNELL (English) Town name; college. Variations: *Cornal, Cornall, Cornel*.

CORNWALLIS (English) Man from Cornwall, England.

CORT (German) Courageous. Variation: *Kort*.

CORTEZ (Spanish) South American explorer.

CORWIN (English) Friend of the heart. Variations: *Corwyn, Corwynn*.

CORYDON (English) Ready for war.

CORYELL (English) One who wears a helmet.

COSGROVE (Irish) Triumphant one. Variation: *Cosgrave*.

COSMO (Greek) Order. Cosmo is the patron saint of Milan and of doctors. Variations: *Cos, Cosimo, Cosme*.

COSTA (Greek) Stable, steady. Variation: *Kostas*.

COTY (French) Small hill. Variation: *Koty*.

COULSON (English) Triumphant people. Variation: *Colson.*

COURTLAND (English) Farm land. Variations: *Cortland, Cortlandt, Courtlandt.*

COURTNEY (English) One who lives in the court. Variations: *Cortney, Courtenay, Courtnay.*

COVELL (English) Hill with a cave.

COWAN (Irish) Valley in a hill. Variation: *Coe.*

COY (English) Forest.

COYLE (Irish) Soldier.

CRADDOCK (Welsh) Affection.

CRAIG (Scottish) Rock. Craig was once uniquely Scottish but now is fairly widespread in English-speaking countries. Variation: *Kraig.*

CRANDALL (English) Valley of cranes. Variations: *Crandal, Crandell.*

CRANLEY (English) Meadow with the cranes. Variations: *Cranleigh, Cranly.*

CRANSTON (English) Community of cranes.

CRAVEN (English) Unknown definition.

CRAWFORD (English) Ford of crows.

CREIGHTON (English) Rocky area. Variations: *Crayton, Crichton.*

CREON (Greek) Prince.

CRESSWELL (English) River of watercress. Variation: *Creswell.*

CRISDEAN (Scottish) Christ.

CRISPIN (Latin) Curly hair. Variations: *Crepin, Crispen, Crispian, Crispino, Crispo, Crispus.*

CROFTON (English) Colony of cottages.

CROMWELL (English) Twisting stream.

CROSBY (English) By the cross. Variations: *Crosbey, Crosbie.*

CROSLAND (English) Land of the cross. Variation: *Crossland.*

CROSLEY (English) Meadow with a cross. Variations: *Croslea, Crosleigh, Crossley.*

CROWTHER (English) Fiddler.

CTIBOR (Czech) Honourable fight. Variation: *Ctik.*

CUINN (Irish) Wisdom.

CULLEN (Gaelic) Handsome. Variations: *Cullan, Cullin.*

CULLENT (Irish) Holly. Variations: *Cullan, Cullin, Cully.*

CULVER (English) Dove. Variations: *Colver, Culley, Cully.*

CUMHAIGE (Scottish) Hound of the plain.

CUNNINGHAM (Gaelic) Village with a milk pail.

CURCIO (Spanish) Friendly.

CURRAN (Irish) Hero.

CURRO (Spanish) Frenchman.

CURTIS (English) Polite. Variations: *Curt, Kurt, Kurtis.*

CUTHBERT (English) Famous. Variations: *Cuithbeart, Cuithbrig.*

CUTLER (English) Maker of knives.

CWRIG (Welsh) Master.

CYNAN (Welsh) Chief. Variation: *Kynan.*

CYNDDELW (Welsh) Chief statue.

CYNDEYRN (Welsh) Head chief.

CYPRIAN (Greek) Man from Cyprus.

CYRANO (Greek) From Cyrene, a Greek Island.

CYRIL (Greek) Lord. Variations: *Cirilio, Cirillo, Cirilo, Cyrill, Cyrille, Cyrillus.*

CYRUS (Latin) Sun. Variation: *Cy.*

CYSTENIAN (Welsh) Stable, steady.

CZCIBOR (Polish) Fight with honour. Variations: *Cibor, Gcibor.*

CZESLAW (Polish) Honour and glory. Variations: *Czech, Czesiek.*

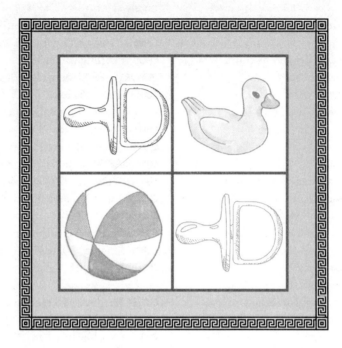

DABIR (African) Teacher.

DACEY (Gaelic) A man from the south. Variations: *Dace, Dacia, Dacian, Dacy.*

DACIAN (Latin) One from Dacia in Rome.

DACSO (Hungarian) God judges.

DADA (African: Nigerian) Child with curly hair.

DADGAYADOH (Native American: Seneca) Gambling men.

DAFYDD (Welsh) Beloved.

DAG (Scandinavian) Day. Variations: *Daeg, Dagen, Dagny.*

DAGAN (Hebrew) Earth. Variation: *Dagon.*

DAGWOOD (English) Bright forest.

DAHY (Irish) Capable. Variation: *Daithi.*

DAI (Japanese) Large; (Welsh) To shine.

DAIBHIDH (Irish) Beloved. Variations: *Daibhid, Daith, Daithi, Daithm.*

DAIRE (Irish) Last name.

DAIVAT (Hindu) Powerful.

DAIVIK (Hindu) Divine.

DAKARAI (African: Zimbabwean) Happiness.

DAK-HO (Korean) Deep lake.

DAKOTA (Dakota) Friend. Dakota is also used as a name for girls, as are many of the other currently popular names that describe locations.

DAKSH (Hindu) Competent.

DALAL (Hindu) Salesman.

DALBERT (English) Bright one. Variation: *Delbert.*

DALE (English) One who lives in a dale or valley. Variations: *Dal, Daley, Daly, Dayle.*

DALFON (Hebrew) Raindrop. Variation: *Dalphon.*

DALIBOR (Czech) To fight far away. Variations: *Dal, Dalek.*

DALLAS (Scottish) Town in Scotland. Dallas can also be used as a name for girls. Dallas Green and Dallas Townsend are two big reasons for the popularity of the name.

DALLIN (English) Proud. Variations: *Dalan, Dallan, Dallen, Dallon, Dalon.*

DALTON (English) A town in a valley. Variations: *Dallton, Dalten.*

DALY (Irish) To gather together. Variations: *Dailey, Daley.*

DALZIEL (Scottish) A small field.

DAMASKENOS (Greek) The city of Damascus. Variations: *Damaskinos, Damasko.*

DAMEK (Czech) Red earth.

DAMIAN (Greek) Tame. Damian was a popular name in the 1970s, until its appearance in several horror movies. The name isn't used much for boys for fear that the child might actually live up to the potential of his name. However, now Liz Hurley has called her son Damian, it may become more popular again. Damian is also the name of the patron saint of hairdressers. Variations: *Dameon, Damiano, Damien, Damion, Damyan, Damyen, Damyon.*

DAMODAR (Hindu) Rope around the abdomen.

DAMON (Greek) Gentle one. Variations: *Daemon, Daimen, Daimon, Daman, Damen, Damone, Daymon.*

DAN (Vietnamese) Positive.

DANA (English) A resident of Denmark. Dana can be either a girls' or boys' name.

DANAUS (Greek) Ancient mythological king.

DANE (English) Brook. Variations: *Dain, Dayne.*

DANFORTH (English) Town in Britain.

DANG (Vietnamese) Valuable.

DANIEL (Hebrew) God is my judge. Daniel has always been one of my favourite names. Every time you use the full, formal version, it sounds somewhat distin-guished and knowing, yet a bit mischievous. The name is Biblical in origin – as in the tale of Daniel being thrown to the lions – but it is an approachable name, not stuffy at all. There are a slew of famous Daniels to help cement your choice: Danny DeVito, Danny Kaye, Daniel Defoe, Daniel Boone, Daniel Barenboim, and Daniel Day-Lewis. Variations: *Dan, Danakas, Danek, Dani, Daniele, Daniels, Danil, Danila, Danilkar, Danilo, Danko, Dannie, Danniel, Danny, Dano, Danya, Danylets, Danylo, Dasco, Donois, Dusan.*

DANIOR (Gypsy) Born with teeth.

DANLADI (African) Born on Sunday.

DANNO (Japanese) Meeting in a pasture.

DANTE (Latin) Everlasting. Some parents might shy away from this name for their newborn boys because of its association with hell from Dante's *Inferno*, but this name is actually a sound choice for those who like the name Damien but are looking for something a bit less threatening. Variations: *Dontae, Donte.*

DANVEER (Hindu) Benevolent.

DAR (Hebrew) Pearl.

DARA (Cambodian) Stars.

DARBY (English) Area where deer graze. Darby is also commonly used as a girls' name. Variations: *Dar, Darb, Derby.*

DARCY (Irish) Dark one. Like Darby, Darcy is also occasionally used to name girls. Variations: *Darce, Darcey, Darsey, Darsy.*

DAREIOS (Greek) Persian king.

DAREN (Nigeria) Born at night.

DARIN (Greek) Gift. Variations: *Dare, Daron, Darren, Darrin, Darron.*

DARIUS (Greek) Wealthy. Variations: *Dario, Darrius.*

DARNELL (English) Hidden area. Variations: *Darnal, Darnall, Darnel.*

DARRAGH (Irish) Black oak. Variation: *Darrah.*

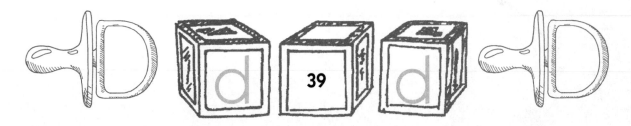

US Politicians

If you are expecting great things from your child, perhaps naming them after a politician or even a president may stand them in good stead. If you look at a list of past U.S. presidents, you'll see that as far as their names go, plain works. These name show that if you have any aspirations for your child's political future, you might not want to name him Sebastian or her Dianna.

James, John and William are the names that have appeared more than once on the list of presidential names. Some vice-presidents who never made it to the top spot – maybe because of their names? – include Garret, Spiro, Levi and Schuyler.

Among recent politicians, Robert – shortened to Bob to make it more palatable, perhaps – Newt, George, Al, Pete, Dan, William (there it is again), and John have all made it to top political office.

Of course, local and regional politicians can also serve as an inspiration for your child's name. In my neck of the woods, I've noticed a small increase in the number of little girls named Madeline, probably in deference to the former Vermont governor of the same name – Madeline Albright.

So if you're looking towards politics to help narrow down your choices, you don't necessarily have to look around on a national basis – the best possibilities may be closer to home.

Names of the Presidents

- George Washington
- John Adams
- Thomas Jefferson
- James Madison
- James Monroe
- John Quincy Adams
- Andrew Jackson
- Martin Van Buren
- William Henry Harrison
- John Tyler

- James K. Polk
- Zachary Taylor
- Millard Fillmore
- Franklin Pierce
- James Buchanan
- Abraham Lincoln
- Andrew Johnson
- Ulysses S. Grant
- Rutherford B. Hayes
- James Garfield
- Chester A. Arthur

- Grover Cleveland
- Benjamin Harrison
- William McKinley
- Theodore Roosevelt
- William H. Taft
- Woodrow Wilson
- Warren G. Harding
- Calvin Coolidge
- Herbert Hoover
- Franklin D. Roosevelt
- Harry S. Truman

- Dwight Eisenhower
- John F. Kennedy
- Lyndon B. Johnson
- Richard M. Nixon
- Gerald Ford
- Jimmy Carter
- Ronald Reagan
- George Bush
- Bill Clinton
- George W. Bush

DARREN (Gaelic) Great. Variations: *Daran, Daren, Darin, Darran, Darrin, Darron, Darryn, Daryn.*

DARRICK (English) Ruler of the land. Variations: *Darik, Darrik.*

DARRIE (Irish) Red hair. Variation: *Darry.*

DARRYL (English) An English last name. Darryl was a popular name in the 1980s. Famous Darryls include singer Darryl Hall and US film producer Darryl F. Zanuch. Variations: *Darrel, Darrell, Darrill, Darrol, Darryll, Daryl, Daryll.*

DARSHAN (Hindu) To see.

DARTON (English) Place where deer graze.

DARWESHI (African: Swahili) Devout.

DARWIN (English) Friend. Variations: *Danvin, Derwin, Derwynn.*

DASAN (Native American) Chief.

DASHIELL (English) Unknown definition.

DATIEL (Hebrew) What God knows.

DAUD (Hindu) Beloved.

DAUDI (African: Swahili) Beloved. Variation: *Dawud.*

DAVID (Hebrew) Cherished. Even though the name David has been around since medieval times, it has never really gone out of style. The fact that David is a Biblical name – David opposed mighty Goliath – and that so many famous people have lived with the name may combine to account for its continued popularity: David Bowie, David Mamet, David Cassidy, Dave Brubeck, David Niven and David Beckham. The name has significance in both the Christian and Jewish religions: David is the patron saint of Wales, while the Star of David is the cornerstone symbol of Judaism. Variations: *Dave, Daveed, Davi, Davidek, Davie, Davy, Dewey, Dodya.*

DAVIN (Scandinavian) Shining.

DAVIS (English) Son of David. Variations: *Davison, Dawson.*

DAWSON (English) Last name.

DAWUD (Arabic) Beloved.

DAX (English) Water.

DAYANAND (Hindu) Compassionate joy.

DAYARAM (Hindu) One who is pleased by being compassionate.

DAYLON (African-American) Unknown definition.

DAYTON (English) Illuminated town.

DE (Chinese) Virtue.

DE OLE (African-American) Unknown definition. Variation: *Deole.*

DEACON (Greek) Servant. Variations: *Deke, Dekel, Dekle.*

DEAN (English) Valley. Dean was wildly popular back in the 1950s and 1960s, probably because of actor Dean Martin, but today no such actor carries the torch for the name. Variations: *Deane, Dene.*

DEANDRE (African-American) Newly created. Variations: *D'Andre, Deondre, Diondre.*

DEANGELO (Italian) From the angel. Variations: *D'Angelo, DiAngelo.*

DEARBORN (English) River of deer. Variations: *Dearbourn, Deerborn.*

DECHA (Thai) Powerful.

DECIMUS (Latin) The tenth.

DECLAN (Irish) Irish saint. Declan is slowly but surely becoming more popular among parents with Irish roots who want to give their boys a name that reflects their family background and has a somewhat romantic sound to it. Variation: *Deaclan.*

DECO (Hungarian) Lord.

DEEMS (English) Child of a judge.

DEGATAGA (Native American: Cherokee) Gathering.

DEJUAN (African-American) Newly created name, though it technically means 'of John'. Variations:

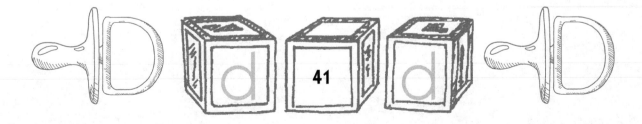

D'Juan, D'Won, DaJuan, Dawon, Dewaun, Dewon, Dujuan.

DEKANAWIDA (Native American: Iroquois) Two rivers running. Variation: *Deganawidah.*

DEKEL (Arabic) Palm tree.

DEKER (Hebrew) To pierce.

DELANEY (Irish) Child of a competitor. Variations: *Delaine, Delainey, Delainy, Delane, Delany.*

DELANO (Irish) Black man; also could mean of the night.

DELBERT (English) Sunny day. This name appears to have been introduced relatively recently in the early part of the 20th century on both sides of the Atlantic mainly within Black communities.

DELEWIS (African-American) De + Lewis. Variation: *DLewis.*

DELL (English) Valley. Dell has been used both as a boys' and girls' name, though in the US it has appeared more as a female name, sometimes spelled with only one 'l'. Variation: *Del.*

DELLINGER (Scandinavian) Dayspring.

DELMAR (Spanish) Oceanside. Variations: *Delmer, Delmor, Delmore.*

DELON (African-American) Unknown definition. Variations: *Deelon, DeLon, DeLonn, Delonn, Dlon, DLonn.*

DELROY (English) The king.

DELSIN (Native American) He is so. Variation: *Delsy.*

DELVIN (English) Good friend. Variations: *Dalwin, Dalwyn, Delavan, Delevan, Delwyn, Delwynn.*

DEMA (Russian) Calm.

DEMARCO (African-American) Demarco is a newly created name that literally means of Mark. Variations: *D'Marcus, Damarcus, Demarcus, Demario, Demarkis, Demarkus.*

DERNAS (Hebrew) A colleague of Paul.

DEMETRIUS (Greek) Lover of the earth. Variations: *Demeter, Demetre, Demetri, Demetrio, Demetris, Demetrois, Dimetre, Dimitri, Dimitry, Dmitri, Dmitrios, Dmitry.*

DEMOND (African-American) Of man. Newly created.

DEMOS (Greek) People.

DEMOTHI (Native American) Talks while walking.

DEMPSEY (Irish) Proud.

DEMPSTER (English) Judge.

DENBY (Scandinavian) Denmark village. Variations: *Danby, Denbey.*

DENELL (African-American) Unknown definition.

DENHAM (English) Town in a dell.

DENHOLM (Scottish) Village in Scotland.

DENIZ (Turkish) Ocean that flows.

DENLEY (English) Meadow near a valley. Variations: *Denlie, Denly.*

DENMAN (English) Dweller of a valley.

DENNIS (Greek) One who follows Dionysius, the Greek god of wine. Denis is also the patron saint of France. Dennis the Menace is undoubtedly the most famous Dennis around, but a number of other Dennises have made their mark on the world: Dennis Potter, Denis Healey, Denis Compton and Denis Quilley, among others. Variations: *Denies, Denis, Denka, Dennes, Denney, Denny, Dennys, Denys.*

DENNISON (English) Son of Dennis. Variations: *Denison, Dennyson, Dyson.*

DENTON (English) Valley town. Variations: *Dent, Denten, Dentin.*

DENVER (English) Green valley. Capital of Colorado. Denver is also popularly used as a girls' name.

DENZELL (African-American) Unknown definition. Actor Denzel Washington bears this name. Variations: *Denzel, Denziel, Denzil, Denzill, Denzyl.*

DENZIL (English) Town in Britain.

DEONTAE (African-American) Newly created. Variations: *D'Ante, Deante, Deonte, Diante, Diontay, Dionte, Donte.*

DEORSA (Scottish) Farmer.

DERBY (English) Village with deer.

DEREK (English) Leader. Eric Clapton and his group Derek and the Dominoes probably gave us our first exposure to this name. It is also distinguished by the many British actors who share it: Derek Nimmo, Derek Jacobi, as well as film director Derek Jarman are just a few. Variations: *Dereck, Derick, Derik, Derreck, Derrek, Derrick, Derrik, Deryck, Deryk.*

DERMOT (Irish) Free of jealousy. Variations: *Dermod, Dermott.*

DERON (African-American) Newly created. Variations: *Daron, Daronn, Deronne.*

DEROR (Hebrew) Independence. Variation: *Derori.*

DERRY (Irish) Red-haired. City in Ireland. Variation: *Derrie.*

DERWARD (English) Deer herder.

DERWIN (English) Good friend. Variations: *Darwin, Darwyn, Derwynn, Durwin.*

DESHAD (Hindu) Nation. Variations: *Deshal, Deshan.*

DESHAWN (African-American) Newly created. Variations: *D'chaun, DaShaun, Dashawn, DeSean, DeShaun, Deshaun.*

DESHI (Chinese) Moral.

DESMOND (Irish) From South Munster, an old civilization in Ireland. South African Archbishop Desmond Tutu and author Desmond Morris have helped to make this name more visible recently. Variations: *Desmund, Dezmond.*

DESTIN (French) Fate. Variation: *Deston.*

DEVAK (Hindu) God.

DEVAL (Hindu) Divine.

DEVANAND (Hindu) Joy from the gods.

DEVDAS (Hindu) God's servant.

DEVEN (Hindu) God.

DEVENDRA (Hindu) God of the sky.

DEVERELL (English) Riverbank.

DEVIN (Irish) Poet. Variations: *Dev, Devan, Deven, Devon, Devonn, Devyn.*

DEVINE (Irish) Ox.

DEVLIN (Irish) Courageous. Variations: *Devland, Devlen, Devlyn.*

DEVMANI (Hindu) Gem from God.

DEVRAJ (Hindu) Ruler of the gods.

DEWAYNE (African-American) Newly created. Dewayne is one of many popular African-American names that are created by adding the prefix 'De-' to another name, most often with one syllable. No-one knows exactly how this custom started, but it certainly helps to set these names apart, and the practice creates hundreds of new names to play with. Variations: *D'Wayne, DeWayne.*

DEWEI (Chinese) Highly noble.

DEWEY (English) Last name.

DEWI (Welsh) Darling.

DEXTER (Latin) Right-handed. Variation: *Dex.*

DEZYDERY (Polish) To desire.

DHAVAL (Hindu) White. Variations: *Dhavlen, Dhavlesh.*

DHIMANI (Hindu) Smart. Variations: *Dheemant, Dhimant.*

DIAMOND (English) Jewel.

DIARMAD (Scottish) Freeman.

DIARMAID (Irish) Free. Variations: *Dermod, Dermot, Dermott.*

DIARMUID (Irish) Free of jealousy.

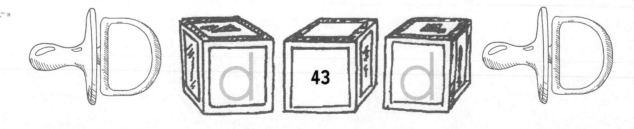

DICHALI (Native American) Speaks later.

DICKENS (English) Last name. Variations: *Dickon, Dickons.*

DIDIER (French) Desire.

DIEDERIK (Scandinavian) Ruler of the people. Variations: *Diderik, Didrik, Dierk.*

DIEGO (Spanish) Hispanic form of James. Diego is starting to become popular because it is a place name – San Diego. It was also the first name of Frida Kahlo's husband, the famous Mexican artist Diego Rivera.

DIETER (German) People's army.

DIETRICH (German) Leader of the people.

DIEU HIEN (Vietnamese) Amaryllis flower.

DIGBY (English) Village by a ditch.

DILIP (Hindu) Protector.

DILLON (Irish) Loyal. Variations: *Dillan, Dilon, Dilyn.*

DILWYN (Welsh) Blessed truth. Variation: *Dillwyn.*

DIMA (Russian) Powerful warrior.

DIMITRI (Russian) Lover of the earth. Variations: *Dimitr, Dimitre, Dimitrios, Dimitry, Dmitri.*

DIN (Vietnamese) Calm.

DINESH (Hindu) God of the day.

DINGBANG (Chinese) Protect the country.

DINH (Vietnamese) Stable.

DINH HOA (Vietnamese) Flower at the apex.

DINO (Italian) Small sword. Nickname for Dean.

DINSMORE (Irish) Fort on the hill.

DION (African-American) God. Variations: *Deion, DeOn, Deon.*

DIONYSUS (Latin) God of wine. Variations: *Dionis, Dionusios, Dionysius.*

DIPAK (Hindu) Lamp. Variation: *Deepak.*

DIRK (German) Dagger.

DISHI (Chinese) Virtuous man.

DISHON (Hebrew) Walk upon.

DIVEROUS (Greek) Unknown definition. Variations: *Divarus, Diveros, Diverus, Divorus.*

DIVES (English) Rich man. Variation: *Divers.*

DIVON (Hebrew) To walk gently.

DIVYENDU (Hindu) The moon.

DIWALI (Native American: Cherokee) Bowl.

DIXON (English) Son of Dick.

DIYA (Arabic) To shine.

DIYA ALDIN (Arabic) Shining religion.

DLNENDRA (Hindu) God of the sky.

DOANE (English) Hilly area.

DOB (English) Brilliant.

DOBIESLAW (Polish) Striving for glory.

DOBROMIERZ (Polish) Good and famous.

DOBROMIL (Czech, Polish) Good grace.

DOBROMIR (Czech) Good fame.

DOBROSLAV (Czech) Good glory.

DOBROSLAW (Polish) Good glory.

DOBRY (Polish) Good.

DOCTOR (English) Physician; teacher.

DODEK (Polish) Gift.

DOHASAN (Native American: Kiowa) Cliff. Variations: *Dohate, Dohosan.*

DOHERTY (Irish) Wicked. Variation: *Dougherty.*

DOLAIDH (Scottish) Ruler of the world. Variation: *Domhnall.*

DOLAN (Irish) Black hair.

DOMINICK (English) Lord. Variations: *Dom, Dome, Domek, Domenic, Domenico, Domicio, Domingo, Domingos, Dominic, Dominik, Dominique, Domo, Domokos, Nic, Nick, Nik.*

DONAGH (Irish) Brown warrior. Variations: *Donaghy, Donnchadh, Donogh, Donough.*

DONAHUE (Irish) Dark. Variations: *Donahoe, Donohue.*

DONALD (Scottish) Mighty. Donald was a very popular name fifty or so years ago, with Donald Trump,

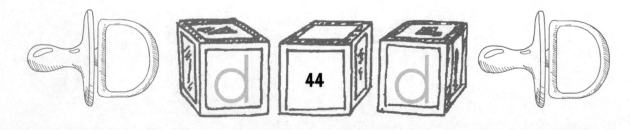

Donald Sutherland and Donald O'Connor all succeeding with the name. Variations: *Don, Donal, Donaldo, Donalt, Donnie, Donny.*

DONAT (Polish) Given by God.

DONATO (Italian) Present. Variations: *Don, Donat, Donatello, Donati, Donatien, Donatus.*

DONG (Korean) East.

DONG-SUN (Korean) Integrity from the East.

DONG-YUL (Korean) Passion from the East.

DONNAN (Irish) Brown. Variation: *Donn.*

DONNCHADH (Irish) Brown warrior.

DONNELLY (Irish) Dark-skinned man. Variations: *Don, Donnell.*

DONOVAN (Irish) Dark. Variations: *Don, Donavan, Donavon, Donoven, Donovon.*

DONYELL (African-American) Unknown definition.

DOOLEY (Irish) Dark-skinned hero.

DOR (Hebrew) Home.

DORAN (Irish) Stranger. Variations: *Doron, Dorran, Dorren.*

DORIAN (Greek) A region in Greece. Variations: *Dorean, Dorien, Dorion, Dorrian, Dorryen.*

DORON (Hebrew) Gift from God.

DOTAN (Hebrew) Law. Variation: *Dothan.*

DOUGAL (Scottish) Dark-skinned stranger. Variations: *Dougald, Dougall, Dugal, Dugald, Dugall.*

DOUGLAS (English) Dark water. River in Ireland. Common Scottish last name. It was used as frequently for girls as for boys when it first began to catch on back in the 17th century. Famous Douglases include General Douglas MacArthur, actors Douglas Fairbanks and British war hero Sir Douglas Bader. Variations: *Doug, Douglass.*

DOV (Hebrew) Bear.

DOVEV (Hebrew) Whisper.

DOVIDAS (Lithuanian) Friend.

DOW (Irish) Dark hair.

DOWAN (Irish) Black.

DOYLE (Irish) Black stranger.

DRAKE (English) Dragon.

DRENG (Scandinavian: Norwegian) Farmhand.

DREW (English) Wise. Diminutive of Andrew. Drew also became a popular girls' name in the 1980s. Variations: *Drewe, Dru.*

DRUMMOND (Scottish) Common Scottish last name.

Keeping Your Last Name in Mind

When you finally settle on the first name that you're going to give your baby, you may be dismayed to discover that you're not really done. You need to see how it fits with your last name.

This may not be as easy as it seems; also, people frequently have different ideas about what works and what doesn't. The combination that seems to run most smoothly off the tongue is when both the first and last names have multiple syllables and the pronunciation emphasis is on the first syllable of both. However, when the number of syllables in each name differs, primarily when one of the names has only one syllable, it's a good idea that the other name has more than one.

Pay attention to how the names sound together: watch for rhymes, alliterations and onomatopoeia. I remember reading an interview with Billy Joel once about his name. His given name is William Joel, and he picked Billy Joel because he thought that Bill Joel sounded like a doorbell.

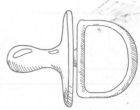

DRURY (French) Cherished.

DRYDEN (English) Dry land.

DRYSTAN (Welsh) Sad.

DU (Vietnamese) Play.

DUANE (Irish) Dark-skinned. Variations: *Duwayne, Dwain, Dwaine, Dwane, Dwayne.*

DUARTE (Portuguese) One who watches over the land.

DUBH (Irish) Black hair. Variation: *Dubhan.*

DUBHGHALL (Scottish) Dark-haired stranger.

DUBHGLAS (Irish) Black and grey. Variation: *Dughlas.*

DUC (Vietnamese) Virtuous.

DUCK-HWAN (Korean) Integrity returns.

DUCK-YOUNG (Korean) Integrity lasts.

DUDLEY (English) Field where people gather. Variation: *Dudly.*

DUFF (Celtic) Dark-skinned. Variations: *Duffey, Duffy.*

DUGAN (Irish) Swarthy. Variations: *Doogan, Dougan, Douggan, Duggan.*

DUKE (English) Leader. Shortened version of Marmaduke.

DUKKER (Gypsy) Fortune teller.

DULANI (African: Malawian) Cutting.

DUMAKA (African: Nigerian) Help out.

DUMAN (Turkish) Smoky.

DUMICHEL (African-American) Of Michael. Newly created.

DUMIN (Czech) Lord.

DUNCAN (Scottish) Brown-skinned soldier. Duncan has a long history as a Scottish name, being borne by a seventh-century saint and three 11th-century kings. Duncan is a great name that I don't think is chosen enough. Just the sound of the name, the heft of it, along with its roots, makes it a great candidate to become more popular. Variations: *Dun, Dune, Dunn.*

DUNHAM (Celtic) Dark-skinned man.

DUNLEY (Celtic) Meadow on a hill.

DUNLOP (Scottish) Muddy hill.

DUNMORE (Scottish) Fort on a hill.

DUNN (Scottish) Brown. Variation: *Dunne.*

DUNSTAN (English) Rocky hill.

DUNTON (English) Town on a hill.

DUOC (Vietnamese) Ethical.

DUR (Hebrew) To accumulate.

DURAND (Latin) Lasting. Variation: *Durant.*

DURELL (Scottish) Doorman for the King. Variation: *Durrell.*

DURIEL (Hebrew) God is my home.

DURKO (Czech) Farmer.

DURRIKEN (Gypsy) Forecaster.

DURRIL (Gypsy) Gooseberry.

DUSAN (Czech) Spirit. Variations: *Dusa, Dusanek, Duysek.*

DUSTIN (English) Dusty place or courageous soldier. When Dustin Hoffman's career first began to take off back in the 1960s and 1970s, parents didn't respond to the possibility of using this name for their own babies. Maybe today's parents are, and there are little Dustins walking around everywhere. You may decide to go the same route, or to choose one of the variations. Variations: *Dust, Dustan, Duston, Dusty, Dustyn.*

DWIGHT (Flemish) Blond.

DWYER (Irish) Dark wisdom.

DYAMI (Native American) Eagle.

DYER (English) One who dyes clothing for a living.

DYLAN (Welsh) Son of the ocean. Variations: *Dillan, Dillon.*

DYMOKE (Unknown) Unknown definition.

DYNAWD (Welsh) Donation.

DYRE (Scandinavian: Norwegian) Valuable.

DYSON (English) Last name. Shortened version of Dennison.

DYZEK (Polish) He who loves the earth.

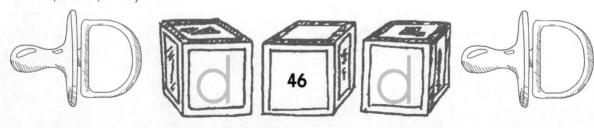

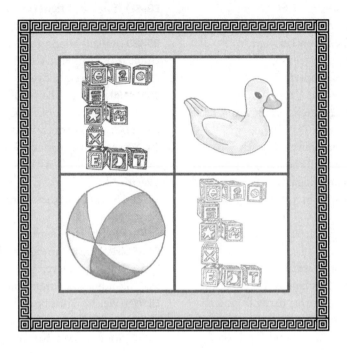

EA (Irish) Fire. Variation: *Eth.*

EACHANN (Irish) Horse lover.

EADBHARD (Irish) Wealthy protector. Variation: *Eadbard.*

EAIRRDSIDH (Scottish) Genuinely brave. Variation: *Eairrsidh.*

EALAHWEEMAH (Native American: Nez Perce) Sleep.

EALAOT WADASS (Native American: Nez Perce) Earth.

EALAOTHEK KAUNIS (Native American: Nez Perce) Birds in flight coming to earth.

EALLAIR (Scottish) Steward in a monastery. Variation: *Ellar.*

EAMON (Irish) Rich protector. Variation: *Eamonn.*

EANRAIG (Scottish) Home ruler.

EAPALEKTHILOOM (Native American: Nez Perce) Pile of clouds.

EARDLEY (English) Region in England. Last name. Variation: *Eardly.*

EARL (English) Leader; nobleman. Famous Earls include US crime fiction writer Erle Stanley Gardner and famous US jurist Earl Warren. Rarely used as a first name these days; Earl is often chosen as a good middle name. Variations: *Earle, Earlie, Early, Erl, Erle, Errol, Erryl.*

EATON (English) Town on a river. Variations: *Eatton, Eton, Eyton.*

EBEN (Hebrew) Stone. Variations: *Eban, Even.*

EBENEZER (Hebrew) Ebenezer literally means rock that helps, but who could hear this name without thinking of Charles Dickens' story *A Christmas Carol*? Whenever I go wandering around old cemeteries, I invariably come across a whole slew of Ebenezers among the Johns and Davids. Surprisingly enough, Ebenezer was once one of the top ten names to give boys. Variations: *Ebbaneza, Eben, Ebeneezer, Ebeneser, Ebenezar, Ebenezeer.*

EBERHARD (German) The bravery of a boar. Variations: *Eberhardt, Everard, Everhardt, Everhart.*

EBISU (Japanese) The god of labour and luck.

EBO (African: Ghanian) Born on Tuesday.

EDAN (Celtic) Fire.

EDEK (Polish) Guardian of property.

EDEL (German) Noble.

EDEN (Hebrew) Delight. Variations: *Eaden, Eadin, Edan, Edin.*

EDENSAW (Native American: Tlingit) Glacier.

EDGAR (English) Wealthy man who holds a spear. US writers Edgar Allan Poe and Edgar Rice Burroughs are notable men with this name. Variations: *Edgard, Edgardo.*

EDISON (English) Edward's son. Variations: *Ed, Eddison, Edson.*

EDMUND (English) Wealthy guardian. As a given name, Edward is more popular than Edmund, even though the variations and nicknames that derive from each are basically the same. Variations: *Ed, Eddie, Eddy.*

EDRIC (English) Powerful man who holds property. Variation: *Edrick.*

EDSEL (English) Home of a rich man.

EDWARD (English) Guardian of property. Edward has a touch of nobility to it, along with a number of famous, distinguished men who go by the name: Edward G. Robinson, Prime Minister Edward Heath and Edouard Manet, as well as the Queen's youngest son Prince Edward. Of course, some of the more exotic spellings can only help to enhance the image of Edward. Variations: *Ed, Eddie, Edouard, Eduardo, Edvard.*

EDWIN (English) Rich friend. Variation: *Edwyn.*

EDWY (English) War.

EDZARD (Scandinavian) Strong edge.

EFRON (Hebrew) Bird. Variation: *Ephron.*

EGAN (Gaelic) Fire. Variations: *Egann, Egon.*

EGBERT (English) Bright sword.

EGERTON (English) Last name. Region in Britain.

EGIDIO (Italian) Young goat.

EGIDIUSZ (Polish) Protective shield.

EGIL (Scandinavian) Edge.

EGINHARD (German) Power of the sword. Variations: *Eginhardt, Egon, Einhard, Einhardt.*

EGOR (Russian) Farmer. Variation: *Igor.*

EHIOZE (African: Nigerian) Not jealous.

EIDEARD (Scottish) Wealthy protector. Variation: *Eudard.*

EIFAH (Hebrew) Darkness. Variations: *Efa, Efah, Eifa, Epha, Ephah.*

EIFION (Welsh) Last name.

EIGNEACHAN (Irish) Strong man. Variation: *Ighneachan.*

EILAM (Hebrew) Forever. Variation: *Elam.*

EILIF (Scandinavian) Immortal. Variation: *Eiliv.*

EILWYN (Welsh) White brow. Variation: *Eilwen.*

EIMHIN (Irish) Quick.

EINAR (Scandinavian: Norwegian) Leader. Variation: *Ejnar.*

EINION (Welsh) Anvil. Variation: *Einwys.*

EINRI (Irish) Ruler at home. Variations: *Anrai, Hannraoi, Hanraoi.*

EKAANTA (Hindu) Solitude.

EKANA (Hawaiian) Strength. Variation: *Etana.*

EKEKA (Hawaiian) Wealth. Variation: *Edega.*

EKEKIELA (Hawaiian) Powerful god. Variation: *Ezekiela.*

EKELA (Hawaiian) Help. Variation: *Ezera.*

EKEMONA (Hawaiian) Rich protector. Variations: *Edemona, Edumona, Edwada, Ekewaka, Ekualo, Ekumena.*

EKER (Hebrew) Root.

ELAM (English) Area in Britain.

ELAN (Hebrew) Tree. Variation: *Ilan.*

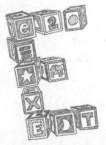
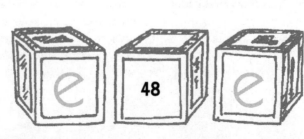

ELASKOLATAT (Native American: Nez Perce) Animal running into the ground.

ELAZAR (Hebrew) God helps.

ELBA (Italian) Area in Italy.

ELBERT (English) Noble; shining.

ELCHANAN (Hebrew) God is good. Variations: *Elhanan, Elhannan.*

ELDER (English) Older person. A kind of tree.

ELDON (English) Consecrated hill. Area in England.

ELDRED (English) Elderly counsellor.

ELDRIDGE (German) Wise leader.

ELEDON (English) Leader's hill.

ELENEK (Hawaiian) Eager. Variations: *Eneki, Eneti, Ereneti.*

ELEUTHERIOS (Greek) Liberty. Variation: *Eleftherios.*

ELI (Hebrew) God is great. Variations: *Elie, Ely.*

ELIAKIM (Hebrew) God will develop. Variations: *Elika, Elyakim, Elyakum.*

ELIAZ (Hebrew) My God is powerful.

ELIHU (Hebrew) God.

ELIJAH (Hebrew) The Lord is my God. Variations: *Elek, Elias, Eliasz, Elie, Eliya, Eliyahu, Ellis, Elya.*

ELIKAI (Hawaiian) God is my salvation. Variation: *Elisai.*

ELIRAN (Hebrew) My God is song. Variation: *Eliron.*

ELISHUA (Hebrew) God saves. Variation: *Elisha.*

ELJASZ (Polish) God is Lord.

ELKANAH (Hebrew) God creates. Variations: *Elkan, Elkin.*

ELKI (Native American) To drape over.

ELLARD (German) Noble; brave.

ELLERY (English) Island with elder trees. Last name. Variation: *Ellary.*

ELLIOT (English) God on high. Variations: *Eliot, Eliott, Elliott.*

ELLISON (English) Son of Ellis. Variations: *Elison, Ellyson, Elson.*

ELLMELECH (Hebrew) God is King.

ELLSWORTH (English) Home of a great man. Variations: *Ellswerth, Elsworth.*

ELMAN (German) Elm tree.

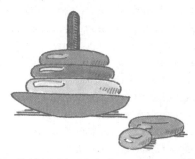

ELMER (English) Noble. Variations: *Aylmar, Aylmer, Aymer, Ellmer, Elmir, Elmo.*

ELMO (Latin) Helmet from God.

ELMORE (English) Valley with elm trees.

ELOF (Scandinavian) Sole descendant. Variations: *Elov, Eluf.*

ELON (African-American) Spirit.

ELONI (Polynesian) Lofty.

ELOY (Spanish) Famous warrior.

ELPIDIOS (Greek) Hope.

ELRAD (Hebrew) God is the king. Variation: *Elrod.*

ELRIC (English) Wise ruler.

ELROY (African-American) The king. Variations: *El Roy, Elroi.*

ELSTON (English) From a farm. Variation: *Ellston.*

ELSU (Native American) Falcon in flight.

ELTA (Hawaiian) The Lord is my God.

ELTON (English) Ella's town; old town.

ELVET (English) Stream of swans.

ELVIN (English) Old friend.

ELVIO (Spanish) Fair.

ELVIS (Scandinavian) Wise.

ELWELL (English) Old well.

ELWIN (Welsh) Old friend.

ELWOOD (English) Old wood. Variation: *Ellwood*.

ELWYN (Welsh) Fair.

EMANUEL (Hebrew) God is among us. The name given to the Messiah. Biblical names are popular, and Emanuel, which appears in Isaiah 7:14, signifies prophecy and promise and is given by parents to a son who they believe is capable of accomplishing great things. Though the shortened versions of Manny and Manuel are directly derived from Emanuel, today's parents are tending toward the full, more formal version. Variations: *Emmanuel, Emmanuil; Immanuel, Manny, Manuel*.

EMBER (English) Ashes.

EMEK (Hebrew) Valley.

EMERSON (German) Emery's son.

EMERY (German) Leader of the house. Variations: *Emmery, Emory*.

EMILE (French) Eager. The French novelist Emile Zola is perhaps the most famous Emile around, although actor Emilio Estevez has helped to make the name more visible in recent years. England footballer Emile Heskey may help build its profile. Variations: Emil, Emilek, Emilio, Emilo, Emils.

EMLYN (Welsh) Area in Wales.

EMMETT (German) Powerful. This name is beginning to catch on for girls as well. Variations: *Emmet, Emmot, Emmott*.

EMOBI (Polynesian) Birth.

EMRYS (Welsh) Immortal.

EMYR (Welsh) Ruler.

ENAM (African: Ghanian) Gift from God.

ENAPAY (Native American: Sioux) Proceeds with courage.

Names of Angels

Why all this interest in angels? Some people point to the dearth of spirituality in the world, as well as an overall disdain for organized religion. And so this trend has naturally spilled over into the choices available to name your baby. However, while author Sophy Burnham tells of many different named angels, the Bible lists only two: Michael and Gabriel. You might also be inspired, though, by the names of the books in the Bible where angels have appeared: Judah, Gideon, Ezekiel and Daniel. (I don't think you'd be interested in naming your baby *Numbers*.)

Of course, the number of recognizable angels heads into the stratosphere when people give a name to the spirit that they feel has served them well as their own personal guardian angel. I've heard these angels referred by name as everything from 'Snickers' to 'Deborah'.

The word *angel* means messenger in the Bible, and angels appear in both the Old and New Testament. Of course, instead of naming your baby after a specific angel – whatever its name – you could always take a different route and name him or her, well, *Angel*.

Some Angel Names

- Attarib: Guardian angel of winter.
- Gabriel: Guardian angel of fire.
- Michael: Guardian angel of the threshold.
- Torquaret: Guardian angel of autumn.
- Tubiel: Guardian angel of summer.
- Zadkiel: Guardian angel of benevolence, mercy and memory.

ENDERBY (English) Last name.

ENGELBERT (German) Bright like an angel. Variations: *Englebert, Ingelbert, Inglebert.*

ENLAI (Chinese) Appreciation.

ENLI (Native American) I saw a dog.

ENNIS (Gaelic) Only choice.

ENOCH (Hebrew) Educated. Variation: *Enock.*

ENOKA (Hawaiian) Learned.

ENOS (Hebrew) Man. Variations: *Enosa, Enosh.*

ENRICO (Italian) Leader of the house. Variations: *Enric, Enrikos, Enrique.*

ENZIO (Italian) Ruler at home.

ENZO (Italian) To win.

EOCHAIDH (Irish) Horseman.

EOGHAN (Scottish) Youth. Variation: *Eoghann.*

EOIN (Irish) God is good.

EPELAIMA (Hawaiian) Fertile. Variation: *Eperaima.*

EPENA (Hawaiian) Stone. Variation: *Ebena.*

EPHRAYIM (Hebrew) Fertile. Another Bible name for boys that starts with an 'E' that is beginning to appear among children again. It was the name of Joseph's second son. A character with this name also appears in Dickens' *Little Dorrit*. Variations: *Efraim, Efrain, Efrayim, Efrem, Efren, Ephraim, Ephrain.*

ERAN (Hebrew) Observant. Variation: *Er.*

ERASMUS (Greek) Loved. A famous school in New York, Erasmus High, produced several of today's celebrities, including Barbra Streisand. Variations: *Erasme, Erasmo, Erastus.*

ERCOLE (Italian) Gift.

EREL (Hebrew) I see God.

ERHARD (German) Determination. Variations: *Erhardt, Erhart.*

ERIC (Scandinavian) Ruler of the people. The name was taken up on a regular basis in the 19th century as a response to the F. W. Farrar's school story *Eric; or Little by Little*. Eric was very popular in the first half of the 20th century and appears to have reached its peak in the mid-1970s, helped along, no doubt, by the fame of Eric Clapton. Other famous Erics include British comedians Eric Sykes and Eric Morecombe. Variations: *Erek, Erich, Erick, Erico, Erik.*

ERLAND (English) Land of a nobleman.

ERLEND (Scandinavian) Stranger.

ERLING (English) Son of a nobleman.

ERNAN (Irish) One who is experienced or wise. Variation: *Earnan.*

ERNEST (English) Earnest. Variations: *Earnest, Ernestino, Ernesto, Ernie, Ernst.*

ERROL (Scottish) Area in Scotland. Variations: *Erroll, Erryl.*

ERSKINE (Scottish) Green cliff.

ERVIN (Scottish) Beautiful. Also a form of Irvin. Variations: *Erving, Ervyn.*

ERWIN (English) A boar and a friend. A number of men with the name Erwin have been involved behind the scenes in films, including producer Erwin Allen. Author Erwin Shaw wrote the book *Rich Man, Poor Man* and Erwin was German Field Marshall Rommel's first name. Variations: *Erwinek, Erwyn, Erwynn, Irwin.*

ERYX (Greek) The son of Aphrodite and Poseidon.

ESAIAS (Greek) God saves.

ESAU (Hebrew) Hairy. One of Isaac and Rebecca's twin sons in the bible Variation: *Esaw.*

ESDRAS (French) Help.

ESBJORN (Scandinavian) Divine bear. Variations: *Asbjorn, Ebbe, Esben, Esbern.*

ESKAMINZIM (Native American: Apache) Big mouth.

ESKET (Scandinavian) Divine cauldron. Variation: *Eskil.*

ESME (French) Esteemed.

ESMOND (English) Rich protector.

ESPOWYES (Native American: Nez Perce) Mountain light.

ESSIEN (African) Sixth-born.

ESTEBAN (Spanish) Crown. Variation of Stephen.

ETHAN (Hebrew) Steady. The novel *Ethan Frome* and the Revolutionary War hero Ethan Allen are the best-known examples of this name. It should be among the top contenders for parents who are looking for a dignified name that fits a child as well as it does an adult. Variations: *Eitan, Etan.*

ETHELBERT (English) Noble and bright.

ETIENNE (French) Crown. Variation of Stephen.

ETTORE (Italian) Loyal.

ETU (Native American) The sun.

EUCLID (Greek) Last name. Greek developer of geometry theories.

EUFEMIUSZ (Polish) Pleasant voice.

EUGENE (Greek) Well born. Eugene O'Neill and conductor Eugene Ormandy were christened with this name, as well as four popes, but today its nickname – Gene – is more popular as a given name than its original source. Variations: *Eugen, Eugeni, Eugenio, Eugenius, Gene.*

EUKAKIO (Hawaiian) Steady. Variation: *Eutakio.*

EUKEPIO (Hawaiian) To worship well. Variation: *Eusebio.*

EUMANN (Scottish) Wealthy protector.

EUNAN (Scottish) Unknown definition.

EUSEBIOS (Greek) To worship well. Variation: *Eusebius.*

EUSTACE (Greek) Fertile. Variations: *Eustache, Eustachius, Eustasius, Eustazio, Eustis.*

EUSTACHY (Polish) Stable, steady.

EUSTON (Irish) Heart. Variation: *Uistean.*

EVAK (Hindu) Equal.

EVAN (Welsh) God is good. Evan is a version of John that is picking up speed as a common name for boys today. However much they like the name, we wouldn't suggest that parents with the last name of Evans go so far as the parents of Evan Evans, a Welsh poet from the 18th century. Variations: *Ev, Evann, Evans, Evin, Ewan.*

EVANDER (Scottish) Good man.

EVERETT (English) Literally, boar plus hard. Everett is most commonly known as a last name. Variations: *Everard, Everet, Everhard, Everitt.*

EVERILD (English) Boar battle.

EVERLEY (English) Boar meadow.

EVERTON (English) Boar town.

EVZEN (Czech) Well born. Variations: *Evza, Evzek, Evzenek.*

EWALD (English) Powerful in the law. Variation: *Evald.*

EWAN (Scottish) Youth. Variations: *Euan, Euen, Ewen.*

EWART (Scottish) Shepherd. Variation: *Ewert.*

EWIND (Scandinavian) Island of the Wends, an ancient Scandinavian tribe.

EWING (English) Friend of the law.

EYANOSA (Native American: Sioux) Big both ways.

EYOTA (Native American) Great.

EYULF (Scandinavian) Lucky wolf. Variation: *Eyolf.*

EZEKIEL (Hebrew) The strength of God. Variation: *Zeke.*

EZER (Hebrew) Help.

EZIO (Italian) Unknown definition.

EZRA (Hebrew) Helper. It seems that names with an unusual letter like 'z' or 'x' are becoming very popular; this may be one explanation for why Ezra is starting to appear more often on boys' birth certificates. The poet Ezra Pound is the most famous holder of this name. Variations: *Esra, Ezera, Ezri.*

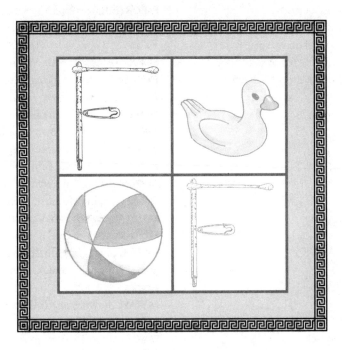

FA (Chinese) Beginning.

FAAS (Scandinavian) Firm counsel.

FABIAN (Latin) One who grows beans. The US pop singer Fabian from the 1950s – whose full name was Fabian Forte – may make this name a good choice for parents who fondly remember that decade. Variations: *Faba, Fabek, Faber, Fabert, Fabiano, Fabien, Fabio, Fabius, Fabiyan, Fabyan, Fabyen.*

FABRICE (French) He who works with his hands. Variations: *Fabrizio, Fabrizius.*

FABRON (French) Blacksmith. Variations: *Fabre, Fabroni.*

FACHNAN (Irish) Unknown definition. Variations: *Fachtna, Faughnan.*

FADEY (Russian) Bold. Variations: *Faddei, Fadeaushka, Fadeuka.*

FADI (Arabic) To save.

FADIL (Arabic) Generous.

FADL (Arabic) Grace. Variation: *Fadhl.*

FAGAN (Irish) Eager child. Variation: *Fagin.*

FAHD (Arabic) Panther. Variations: *Fahad, Fahid.*

FAHIM (Hindu) Intelligent.

FAINGA (Polynesian) Confront.

FAIPA (Polynesian) Bait the hook.

FAIRFAX (English) Blond.

FAIRLEIGH (English) Meadow with bulls. Variations: *Fairlay, Fairlee, Fairlie, Farleigh, Farley.*

FAISAL (Arabic) Stubborn. Variation: *Faysal.*

FAKHR (Arabic) Glory. Variations: *Fakhir, Fakhri.*

FAKHR ALDIN (Arabic) Glorious religion. Variations: *Fakhir Aldin, Fakhrid Adin.*

FAKIH (Arabic) Intelligent.

FALAK (Hindu) Heaven.

FALAN (Hindu) Fertile. Variations: *Faleen, Falit.*

FALE (Polynesian) House.

FALEAKA (Polynesian) House of plants.

FALKNER (English) Falcon trainer. Falkner is a first name/last name that is ripe for an increase in use among parents who are looking for something distinctive and distinguished. Variations: *Falconer, Falconner, Faulkner, Fowler.*

FANE (English) Happy.

FANG (Chinese) Wind.

FANGALOKA (Polynesian) Beach.

FANGATUA (Polynesian) Wrestle.

FAOLAN (Irish) Little wolf. Variations: *Felan, Phelan.*

FARAJ (Arabic) Cure. Variation: *Farag.*

FARDORAGH (Irish) Dark-skinned man. Variation: *Feardorcha.*

FAREED (Hindu) Unique.

FAREWELL (English) The greeting; also, beautiful spring.

FARID (Arabic) Unrivalled.

FARIS (Arabic) Knight.

FARNELL (English) Hill of ferns.

FARNHAM (English) Meadow of the ferns. Variations: *Farnam, Farnum, Fernham.*

FARNLEY (English) Field with ferns. Variations: *Farnlea, Farnleigh, Fernleigh, Fernley.*

FAROLD (English) Voyager.

FARON (English) Unknown definition. Last name. Variations: *Faran, Farin, Farran, Farrin, Farron, Farrun, Farun.*

FAROUK (Arabic) Truth. Variations: *Faraq, Faroqh.*

FARQUHAR (Scottish) Dear one. Variations: *Farquar, Farquarson, Farquharson, Fearchar.*

FARR (English) Wayfarer.

FARRAR (Irish) Unknown definition. Last name.

FARRELL (Irish) Courageous man. Variations: *Farall, Farrel, Farrill, Farryll, Ferrel, Ferrell, Ferrill, Ferryl.*

FARROW (Irish) Unknown definition. Last name.

FARUQ (Hindu) Moralist. Variations: *Farook, Farooq.*

FATHI (Arabic) To win. Variation: *Fath.*

FAU (Polynesian) Tree.

FAUIKI (Polynesian) Small trees.

FAUST (Latin) Good luck. Variations: *Faustino, Fausto, Faustus.*

FAUTAVE (Polynesian) Tall trees.

FAVIAN (Latin) Brave man.

FAWZ (Arabic) To accomplish.

FAXON (German) Long hair.

FAYIZ (Arabic) Winner.

FEAGH (Irish) Raven.

FEARADHACH (Irish) Masculine.

FEARGHALL (Irish) Brave man. Variation: *Fearghus.*

FEARGHAS (Scottish) Strong man. Variations: *Feargus, Fergus.*

FEATHERSTONE (English) Region in Britain.

FEHIN (Irish) Little raven. Variations: *Fechin, Feichin.*

FEIDHLIM (Irish) Forever good. Variations: *Feidhlimidh, Felim, Phelim.*

FEILO (Polynesian) Familiar.

FEIVEL (Hebrew) Bright one. Variation: *Feiwel.*

FEKITOA (Polynesian) Two men gather.

FELETI (Polynesian) Peace.

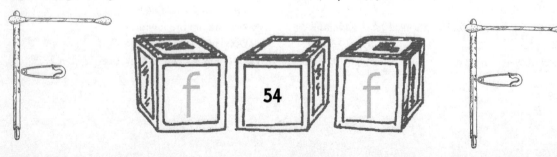

FELIPE (Spanish) Lover of horses. Derivative of Philip.

FELIX (Latin) Happy; lucky.

FELTON (English) Town in a field. Variations: *Felten, Feltin.*

FENRIS (Scandinavian) Scandinavian mythological figure.

FENTON (English) Town by a swamp.

FENWICK (English) Farm by a swamp.

FENYANG (African: Botswana) Conqueror.

FEORAS (Irish) Rock.

FERDINAND (German) Brave traveller. Ferdinand is a very old name. It enjoyed a brief period of favour among English speakers during the 1550s when Mary I married Philip II of Spain, which created a short-lived fashion for everything Spanish. It was used by Shakespeare in *Love's Labour's Lost* as well as *The Tempest*. The name is currently enjoying a renaissance in some of its variations. Variations: *Ferdinando, Ferdynand, Fernand, Fernando.*

FERGAL (Irish) Brave. Variation: *Forgael.*

FERGUS (Scottish) Best choice. Variation: *Ferris.*

FERGUSON (Scottish) Son of Fergus.

FERMIN (Spanish) Powerful.

FERNLEY (English) Meadow of ferns. Variation: *Fernleigh.*

FEROZ (Persian) Lucky.

FERRAND (French) Grey hair. Variations: *Farand, Farrand, Farrant, Ferrant.*

FIACHRA (Irish) Saint.

FIANCE (French) Engaged.

FIDEL (Latin) Faith. The major connection that people have with this name is with the ruler of Cuba, Fidel Castro, who by chance is the literal embodiment of the definition of the name – faithful. The variations for the name are highly lyrical and lack the connota-

tions. For a baby born during the month of December, Fidel may be a good choice because of the Christmas carol 'Adeste Fidelis'. Variations: *Fidal, Fidele, Fidelio, Fidelis, Fidello.*

FIELDING (English) In the field. Variation: *Field.*

FIFE (Scottish) County in Scotland. Variation: *Fyffe.*

FIKRI (Arabic) Smart person.

FILBERT (English) Smart. Hazelnut.

FILIMOEIKA (Polynesian) Shark's enemy.

FILMORE (English) Famous. Variations: *Fillmore, Filmer, Fylmer.*

FINAN (Irish) Blonde child. Variation: *Fionan.*

FINBAR (Irish) Blond hair. Borne by several early Irish saints, including a sixth-century bishop of Cork. Variation: *Fionnbharr.*

FINEEN (Irish) Fair birth. Variations: *Finghin, Finin, Finneen, Finnin.*

FINGALL (Scottish) Fair-haired stranger. Variation: *Fingal.*

FINIAN (Irish) Fair. Although borne by two sixth-century Irish bishops, the musical *Finian's Rainbow* is probably how most people were first exposed to this name. Its wonderful lilt and Irish connotations may cause Finian to become more popular than it has been. Variations: *Finnian, Fionan, Fionn.*

FINLAY (Scottish) Fair hero. The name of the father of Macbeth, King of Scotland. Variations: *Findlay, Findley, Finleigh, Finley.*

FINN (Irish) From Finland.

FINNEGAN (Irish) Fair. Like Finian, Finnegan seems to be poised for an increase in popularity among boys' names because it meets the popularity criteria of last name, unisex usage, and the association with Ireland. Variation: *Finegan.*

FIONNLAGH (Scottish) Fair-haired soldier. Variation: *Fionnla.*

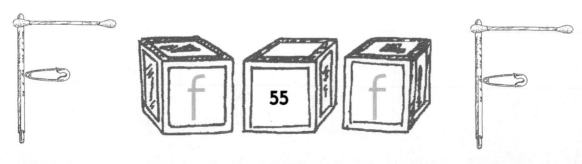

FIORELLO (Italian) Little flower.

FIRDOS (Hindu) Paradise. Variations: *Firdaus, Firdose, Firdoze.*

FIROZ (Hindu) Winner. Variations: *Feroz, Feroze, Firuz.*

FIRTH (English) Forest.

FISK (English) Fish. Variation: *Fiske.*

FISKE (Scandinavian) Fish. Variation: *Fisk.*

FITCH (English) Name of a mammal similar to a ferret.

FITZ (English) Son.

FITZGERALD (English) Son of the mighty spearholder.

FITZHUGH (German) Son of an intelligent man.

FITZPATRICK (Irish) Son of a statesman.

FITZWILLIAM (Irish) Son of the soldier.

FITZROY (English) Son of a king. It was used initially as a nickname of illegitimate sons of English monarchs.

FLAMINIO (Spanish) Priest.

FLANNERY (Irish) Red hair. Though Flannery is more popularly known as a girls' name, the choice seems appropriate for a red-haired boy. Variations: *Flaine, Flann, Flannan.*

FLAVIAN (Latin) Yellow hair. Variations: *Flavia, Flavien, Flavio.*

FLAWIUSZ (Polish) Blond.

FLEMING (English) Man from the valley. Variation: *Flemming.*

FLETCHER (English) One who makes arrows. It is perhaps best known as the name of Fletcher Christian, the English naval officer who led the infamous mutiny on the Bounty. It's an attractive choice for a boy today. Variation: *Fletch.*

FLINT (English) Stream. Flint rhymes with Clint, another macho name, but Flint is even tougher-sounding.

FLORENT (French) Flower. Variation: *Florenz.*

FLORIAN (Latin) In bloom. Variations: *Florien, Florino, Floryan.*

FLORIS (Scandinavian) Blossoming.

FLOYD (Welsh) Grey hair. US heavyweight Boxer Floyd Patterson was the antithesis of this almost-feminine name, but his reputation hasn't increased the popularity of the name very much.

FLURRY (Irish) In bloom.

FLYNN (Irish) Red-haired man's son. Variations: *Flin, Flinn, Flyn.*

FOLANT (Welsh) Strong.

FOLAU (Polynesian) Travel.

FOLKE (Scandinavian) People. Variation: *Folki.*

FOLUKE (African: Nigerian) Placed in God's hands.

FORBES (Scottish) Field.

FORD (English) River crossing.

FOREST (French) Woods. Popular again today following Tom Hanks' role in the film *Forrest Gump.* However, back in the 19th century it was favoured after the US Confederate commander Nathan Bedford Forrest. Variations: *Forester, Forrest, Forrester, Forster, Foster.*

FORTUNE (French) Lucky. Variations: *Fortunato, Fortunatus, Fortunio.*

FRANCIS (Latin) Frenchman. Descended from the Roman Franciscus, the name is supposed to have its origin in St Francis of Assisi. Notable bearers include Sir Francis Drake, Francis Bacon and Sir Francis Chichester. Its derivatives were very popular in the 20th century; top names include Frank Sinatra, Franco Zeffirelli, Frank Lloyd Wright, Frankie Valli, Frank Capra, and Frank Loesser, among many others. Though Francis was frequently in the top ten list of names from the late 19th century through the 1940s, it doesn't even crack the top fifty names today. All that may change, however, as more parents opt for traditional names from their own family trees.

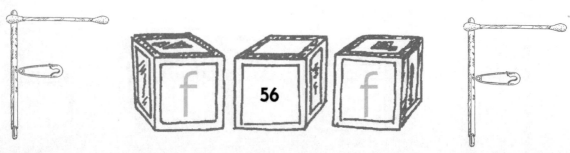

New Age Names

Since the beginning of time, parents have always been on the lookout for a name that best expresses the essence of their baby as well as what the child will become. Current traditions also play a big role in the naming game. This explains the renaissance in what could be described as New Age names. Often, this translates to a name that relates to the environment or people's growing interest in multiculturalism – sometimes, both.

In the case of an environmentally based name, parents of girls have much more to choose from than parents of boys, since many of the things that appear in nature – crystal, rose, heather – are traditionally associated with the feminine. Traditional masculine-sounding names from the natural world include Clay, Rock and Forrest.

Multiculturalism, however, throws the door wide open for both sexes. Today, New Age parents can look to a large variety of sources to name their children, including Japanese, Turkish, Greek, African, and – as is becoming increasingly common – Native American. And since many of these names in other languages describe nature, parents who want their baby's name to fulfill a variety of roles can easily be satisfied. For example, the girl's name Azami describes a thistle flower in Japanese, while Misu for boys means rippling water in the Miwok Indian language.

Then again, some New Age parents throw all caution to the wind to invent an entirely new name, which can be accomplished by changing the spelling of a more traditional name: Michelle can become Nichelle; Travis can turn into Trevis. Or, they choose a name that is known as a label for something other than a human: Boston, Mountain and Castle are some that I've come across. If this appeals to you, flip through the pages of this book to find a name that comes close to what you want for your baby, and then play around with it. Today, more than ever, the rule about baby names is to do what is true for you and your child.

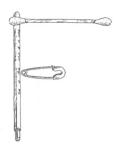

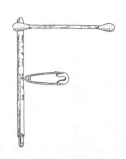

Variations: *Fran, Franc, Franchot, Francisco, Franco, Francois, Frank, Frankie, Franky.*

FRANG (Scottish) Frenchman. Variation: *Frangag.*

FRANKLIN (English) A free property owner. Variations: *Frank, Franki, Frankie, Franklyn, Franklynn, Franky.*

FRANZ (German) Frenchman. Franz Kafka and composers Franz Liszt and Schubert are the men who come to mind with this name. Variations: *Frans, Franzen, Franzl.*

FRANTISEK (Czech) French man. Variations: *Fanousek, Frana, Franek, Franta, Frantik.*

FRASER (English) Town in France. Undoubtedly, Fraser will become a popular name in the next decade, due to the success of the TV character played by Kelsey Grammer. Variations: *Frasier, Fraze, Frazer, Frazier.*

FRAYNE (English) Foreign. Variations: *Fraine, Frayn, Freyne.*

FREDERICK (German) Merciful leader. Fred Astaire, Freddie Mercury, actors Fred MacMurray and Freddie Bartholomew, and film director Fred Zinnemann serve as some well-known men with this name. Variations: *Fred, Freddie, Freddy, Fredek, Frederich, Frederico, Frederik, Fredric, Fredrick, Friedrich, Fritz.*

FREEBORN (English) Born into freedom.

FREEDOM (English) Liberty.

FREEMAN (English) Free man. Variation: *Freemon.*

FREMONT (German) Protector of liberty.

FREWIN (English) Free friend. Variation: *Frewen.*

FREY (Scandinavian) Supreme Lord.

FRICK (English) Brave.

FRIDOLF (English) Calm wolf.

FRIEND (English) Friend.

FRITJOF (Scandinavian) Peace thief. Variations: *Fridtjof, Fridtjov, Fritjov.*

FRITZ (German) Peaceful ruler. Fritz started out as a nickname for Frederick, but started to appear as an independent name among babies born in the late 19th century. Variations: *Fritzchen, Fritzroy.*

FRODE (Scandinavian) Wise.

FRODI (Scandinavian) Ancient Danish king.

FUAD (Arabic) Heart. Variation: *Fouad.*

FUANILEVU (Polynesian) Great.

FULBRIGHT (German) Bright.

FULEHEU (Polynesian) A bird.

FULLER (English) One who shrinks cloth.

FULTON (English) Town of the people.

FULUMIRANI (African: Malawian) A trip.

FUNSAN (African: Malawian) Request.

FUTKEFU (Polynesian) Grass skirt.

FYNN (African: Ghanian) River in Ghana.

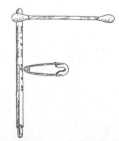

GABRIEL (Hebrew) Man of God. The name of the Archangel who informed Mary of the forthcoming birth of Jesus. Gabriel is a wonderfully diverse name with plenty of choices for the parent – and later, the son – who wants a variant of the name, yet wishes to remain true to the root. Famous Gabriels include Gabriel Garcia Marquez and Gabriel Byrne. Variations: *Gab, Gabby, Gabe, Gabi, Gabko, Gabo, Gabor, Gabriele, Gabrielli, Gabriello, Gabris, Gabys, Gavi, Gavriel.*

GADDIEL (Hebrew) Fortune from God. Variation: *Gadiel.*

GADI (Arabic) My fortune.

GAETAN (Italian) An area in Italy.

GAGE (French) Pledge.

GAHUJ (African: Rwandan) The hunter.

GAIR (Irish) Small one. Variations: *Gaer, Geir.*

GAIUS (Welsh) Rejoice.

GALBRAITH (Irish) Variations: *Galbrait, Galbreath.*

GALE (Irish) Foreigner. Variations: *Gael, Gail.*

GALEGINA (Native American: Cherokee) Stag. Variation: *Galagenoh.*

GALEN (Greek) Healer. Variation: *Galeno.*

GALLAGHER (Irish) Foreign partner.

GALLOWAY (Irish) Foreigner. Variations: *Gallway, Galway.*

GALT (Scandinavian: Norwegian) One from a region in Norway called Galt. The fashion designer Jean Paul Gaultier has given this name some panache. Variations: *Galtero, Gaultier, Gautier.*

GALTON (English) Landlord. Variation: *Gallton.*

GALVIN (Irish) Sparrow. Variations: *Gallven, Gallvin, Galvan, Galven.*

GAMAL (Arabic) Camel.

GAMBA (African: Zimbabwean) Warrior.

GAMBLE (Norse) Old.

GAMLIEL (Hebrew) God is my reward. Variation: *Gamaliel.*

GAN (Chinese) Adventure.

GANDY (English) A railroad worker who helps to lay tracks.

GANEODIYO (Native American: Iroquois) Pristine lake. Variations: *Ganyodaiyo, Kaniatario.*

GANESH (Hindu) Lord of them all.

GANNON (Irish) Light-skinned.

GANUNDALEGI (Native American: Cherokee) Walking on a mountain ridge.

GARAI (African: Zimbabwean) Settled.

GARAKONTHIE (Native American: Iroquois) The sun moves across the sky.

GARBHAN (Irish) Small, tough child. Variation: *Garvan.*

GARDNER (English) Gardener.

GAREK (Polish) Wealth with a spear. Variation of Edgar. Variations: *Garreck, Garrik.*

GARETH (Welsh) Gentle. Variations: *Garith, Garreth, Garyth.*

GARFIELD (English) Field of spears. Both a cartoon cat and a president have had this name, but it is a relatively rare choice today.

GARIANA (Hindu) Shout.

GARLAND (French) Wreath. Variations: *Garlan, Garlen, Garlyn.*

GARNER (English) To harvest grain. Variation: *Gar.*

GARNET (English) Shelter; jewel; red. Variation: *Garnett.*

GARNOCK (Welsh) River of alder trees.

GARRETT (Irish) Brave with a spear. Variations: *Garett, Garrat.*

GARRICK (English) He who rules with a spear. Variations: *Garreck, Garryck, Garyk.*

GARRIDAN (Gypsy) He who hides.

GARRISON (English) Fort.

GARROWAY (English) He who fights with a spear. Variation: *Garraway.*

GARSON (English) Son of Gar.

GARTH (English) Gardener. Garth is most popular today because of the country singer Garth Brooks, but it was even more popular in the 19th century, when a number of writers, from George Eliot to Charlotte Yonge, chose the name for main characters in their novels.

GARTON (English) Town shaped like a triangle.

GARVEY (Irish) Peace. Variations: *Garvie, Garvy.*

GARVIN (English) Friend with a spear. Variations: *Garvan, Garven, Garvyn.*

GARWOOD (English) Forest with pine trees.

GARY (English) Spear. Gary Cooper is singlehandedly credited with creating this name as a possibility for modern use in the 1940s and 1950s. Before he began using it as his first name – his real name was Frank – its only use was as a last name and as a town in Indiana immortalized in the musical *The Music Man.* Today, while Gary isn't as popular as it was in the middle part of the 20th century, two sporting celebrities bearing the name include golfer Gary Player and footballer Gary Lineker. Variations: *Garey, Garrey, Garry.*

GASPARD (French) Wealthy man. French variation of Jasper. Variations: *Gaspar, Gasper.*

GASTON (French) Man from Gascon. An area in France. Many children – and parents – today are familiar with Gaston only as the name of a villain in a Disney movie. Variation: *Gascon.*

GAURAV (Hindu) Pride.

GAUTIER (French) Powerful leader. Variations: *Gauther, Gauthier.*

GAVIN (Welsh) White falcon. Variations: *Gavan, Gaven, Gavyn, Gawain, Gawaine, Gawayn, Gawayne, Gawen.*

GAWASOWANEH (Native American: Iroquois) Snow snake.

GAWATN (Welsh) Battle hawk.

GAYLORD (French) Lively.

GAYNOR (Irish) Son of a pale man.

GAYNWAWPIAHSIKA (Native American: Shawnee) Leader. Variation: *Gaynwah.*

GAYTAHKIPIAHSIKAH (Native American: Shawnee) Feral cat.

GEARY (English) Changeable. Variation: *Gearey.*

GEDALIAH (Hebrew) God is great. Variations: *Gedalia, Gedaliahu, Gedalya, Gedalyahu.*

GEFANIAH (Hebrew) God's orchard. Variations: *Gefania, Gefanya, Gephania, Gephaniah.*

GELELEMEND (Native American: Delaware) The leader.

GEMINI (Latin) Twins.

GENE (English) Well born. Derived from Eugene. Gene is a friendly, approachable name, probably made so by actors Gene Kelly, Gene Wilder and Gene Hackman. Variations: *Genek, Genio, Genka, Genya.*

GENOS (Phoenician) Sun worshippers.

GENT (English) Gentleman. Variation: *Gentle.*

GENTY (English) Snow.

GEOFFREY (German) Peace. Alternative spelling for Jeffrey.

GEORGE (Greek) Farmer. Became a popular choice after the succession to the throne of George I in 1714. Its royal status was strengthened with another five English monarchs bearingthe name. While George as a given name has not been the most popular choice in the last couple of decades, it seems to be making a mini-comeback, particularly among parents who wish to honour an older relative with the name. Famous Georges include George Washington, George Patton, Giorgio Armani, and US Presidents George Bush and George W. Bush. Well-known Georges are musicians George Harrison and George Michael and actor George Clooney. Although a woman novelist in the 19th century became famous under the pseudonym George Sand, the name George is overwhelmingly more popular for boys than for girls. Variations: *Georg, Georges, Georgi, Georgios, Georgy, Giorgio, Giorgos.*

GERAINT (Latin) Old.

GERALD (German) Ruler with a spear. The name had something of an aristocratic reputation in the 19th century and but fell out of favour and is used infrequently nowadays. Variations: *Geralde, Geraldo, Geraud, Gerrald, Gerrold, Gerry, Jerald, Jeralde, Jeraud, Jerold, Jerrald, Jerrold, Jerry.*

GERARD (German) Brave with a spear. Variations: *Garrard, Gerhard, Gerrard, Gerrit, Gerry.*

GERLACH (Scandinavian) Javelin.

GERMAIN (French) One from Germany. Variations: *Germaine, German, Germane, Germayn, Germayne, Jermain, Jermaine, Jermane, Jermayn, Jermayne.*

GERONIMO (Native American: Apache) A famous Apache Indian chief.

GERSHOM (Hebrew) Exile. Variations: *Gersham, Gershon, Gerson.*

GERVASE (German) Honour. Variation: *Gervais.*

GERWYN (Welsh) Fair love. Variation: *Gerwen.*

GESHEM (Hebrew) Rain.

GETHIN (Welsh) Murky. Variations: *Geth, Gethen.*

GEVARIAH (Hebrew) God's might. Variations: *Gevaria, Gevarya, Gevaryah, Gevaryahu.*

GHALIB (Arabic) Defeat.

GHASSAN (Arabic) Young. Variation: *Ghassam.*

GHAYTH (Arabic) Rain. Variation: *Ghaith.*

GHOSHAL (Hindu) Commentator. Variation: *Ghoshil.*

GI (Korean) Brave.

GIANCARLO (Italian) Combination of John and Charles.

GIANNIS (Greek) God is good; variation of John. Variations: *Giannes, Gianni, Giannos.*

GIBIDH (Scottish) Famous pledge.

GIBOR (Hebrew) Hero.

GIBSON (English) Son of Gilbert. Variations: *Gibb, Gibbons, Gibbs.*

GIDEON (Hebrew) One who cuts down trees. Variations: *Gideone, Gidon, Gidoni.*

GIFFORD (English) Brave provider; also, puffy-faced. Variations: *Gifferd, Giffyrd.*

GIG (English) Horse cart.

GIL (Hebrew) Joy.

GILAD (Arabic) Camel's hump. Variations: *Giladi, Gilead.*

GILAM (Hebrew) Joy of a people.

GILBERT (German) Bright pledge. In the past, Gilbert hasn't been a name to choose if you're looking for your son to grow into a suave, debonair adult, but Johnny Depp's role in the film *What's Eating Gilbert*

Grape? might have helped to change that. Variations: *Gib, Gil, Gilberto.*

GILBY (Norse) Hostage's home. Variations: *Gilbey, Gillbey, Gillby.*

GILCHRIST (Irish) Servant of Christ. Variation: *Giolla Chriost.*

GILDEA (Irish) Servant of God. Variation: *Giolla Dhe.*

GILES (English) Young goat. Variations: *Gil, Gilles, Gyles.*

GILLANDERS (Scottish) Servant of St. Andrew. Variations: *Gille Ainndreis, Gille Anndrai.*

GILLEAN (Scottish) Servant of St. John. Variations: *Gillan, Gillen, Gillian.*

GILLEONAN (Scottish) Servant of St. Adomnan. Variation: *Gille Adhamhnain.*

GILLESPIE (Irish) Servant of the bishop. Variations: *Gilleasbuig, Gillis, Giolla Easpaig.*

GILLETT (French) Young. Variations: *Gelett, Gelette, Gillette.*

GILLIE (Gypsy) Song.

GILMER (English) Famous hostage.

GILMORE (Irish) Servant of the Virgin Mary. Variations: *Gillmore, Gillmour, Gilmour, Giolle Maire.*

GILON (Hebrew) Joy.

GILROY (Irish) Servant of the redhead. Variations: *Gilderoy, Gildray, Gildrey, Gildroy, Gillroy.*

GILSON (English) Unknown definition. Last name.

GILUS (Scandinavian) Shield.

GINO (Italian) Living forever.

GINTON (Hebrew) Garden.

GIONA (Italian) Dove.

GIOVANNI (Italian) God is good. Italian version of John.

GIPSY (English) Wanderer. Variation: *Gypsy.*

GIRIOEL (Welsh) Lordly.

GIRVIN (Irish) Small, tough child. Variations: *Girvan, Girven, Girvon.*

GIUSEPPE (Italian) God will increase. Italian version of Joseph.

GIVON (Hebrew) Hill.

GLADSTONE (Scottish) Scottish last name.

GLADUS (Welsh) Lame.

GLADWIN (English) Happy friend. Variations: *Gladwinn, Gladwyn, Gladwynne.*

GLAISNE (Irish) Unknown definition. Variation: *Glasny.*

GLANVILE (French) Town with oak trees. Variation: *Glanville.*

GLASGOW (Scottish) Capital of Scotland.

GLEN (Irish) Narrow valley. In the past, parents have chosen Glen for their children – boys and, to a lesser extent, girls – because the name is a smooth one, non-threatening, and already claimed by such equally unflappable celebrities as Glenn Miller and Glen Ford. Today, it may seem to be a bit plain for some parents, but others are choosing it just for that reason alone. Variation: *Glenn.*

GLENDON (Scottish) Town in a glen. Variations: *Glenden, Glendin, Glenton, Glentworth.*

GLENDOWER (Welsh) Last name.

GLENVILLE (English) Town in a valley. Variation: *Glenvil.*

GLYN (Welsh) Small valley.

GLYNDWR (Welsh) Valley of water. Variations: *Glyn, Glynn, Glynne.*

GOBIND (Hindu) Cowherder.

GODDARD (German) A hard God. Variations: *Godard, Godart, Goddart, Godhardt, Godhart, Gothart, Gotthard, Gotthardt, Gotthart.*

GODFREY (German) God is peace. Variation of Geoffrey. Variations: *Goddfrey, Godfried, Gotfrid, Gottfrid, Gottfried.*

GODWIN (English) Good friend. Variations: *Godwinn, Godwyn, Godwynn.*

GOEL (Hebrew) The saviour.

GOFRAIDH (Irish) Peaceful God. Variations: *Gothfraidh, Gothraidh.*

GOHACHIRO (Japanese) Thirteenth child.

GOLDING (English) Little gold one.

GOLDWIN (English) Golden friend. Variations: *Goldewin, Goldewyn, Goldwinn, Goldwyn, Goldwynn.*

GOLIATH (Hebrew) Exile. Variation: *Golliath.*

GOMDA (Native American: Kiowa) Wind.

GOMER (English) Good fight.

GONZALO (Spanish) Wolf. Variation: *Gonzales.*

GORDON (Scottish) Round hill. A name with strong Scottish connotations being a famous clan name. A relative of Gordon – Jordan – is currently popular and making the rounds among new parents. Those who want to be a bit different might choose Gordon, the original. Famous Gordons include actor Gordon Jackson and footballer Gordon Banks. Variations: *Gordan, Gorden, Gordie, Gordy.*

GORE (English) Spear.

GORMAN (Irish) Child with blue eyes.

GORO (Japanese) Fifth son.

GOSHEVEN (Native American) Jumper.

GOTAM (Hindu) Best cow. Variations: *Gautam, Gautama.*

GOWER (Welsh) Pure.

GOWON (African: Nigerian) Rain maker.

GOYATHLAY (Native American: Apache) Yawning.

GOZAL (Hebrew) Bird.

GRADY (Irish) Famous. Variations: *Gradey, Graidey, Graidy.*

GRAHAM (Scottish) Grey house. Scottish surname from the 12th century that was taken on as a first name in the English-speaking world. Its popularity peaked in the 1950s. Famous bearers of the name are a varied bunch – writer Graham Greene, racing driver

Sports Heroes

Whatever your passion for sports, many parents-to-be are naming their babies after a top figure in the sport that they follow.

Golf? Jack, Tom, Ben, Gary, and now Phil, Colin, Lee, Tiger and Ernie are your top choices.

When it comes to football, of course, it depends upon which team you follow, and if you're known around the neighbourhood as an Arsenal fan, better not inadvertently name your son or daughter after a player for Manchester United, or else you and your child will never hear the end of it.

Tennis is always a fertile ground for names that are somewhat exotic, especially since most of the winners of the top competitions in the last few decades have been from many different countries. Tennis can inspire names like Martina, Serena, Venus and Steffi for girls and Andre, Stefan, Bjorn and Pete for boys.

If your baby is born during the two weeks that an Olympics is being held somewhere in the world, the odds are more than likely that you may lean toward a name that belongs to one of the more prominent medal winners.

Giving your child a name that belongs to one of the top athletes in his or her field also runs the risk of sounding dated in ten or twenty years, especially if that athlete has left active competition. But overall, prominent sports figures provide a wealth of great names for your budding athlete.

Graham Hill and Irish TV presenter Graham Norton. Variations: *Graeham, Graeme, Grahame, Gram.*

GRANGER (French) Farmer. Variations: *Grainger, Grange.*

GRANT (Scottish) Great.

GRANTLAND (English) Sizeable fields.

GRANTLY (English) Grey meadow. Variations: *Grantlea, Grantleigh, Grantley.*

GRANVILLE (French) Big town. Variations: *Granvil, Granvile, Granvill, Grenville.*

GRAY (English) Grey. Last name. Variations: *Graydon, Grey.*

GRAYSON (English) Son of a man with grey hair. Variation: *Greyson.*

GREELEY (English) Grey meadow. Variations: *Greelea, Greeleigh, Greely.*

GREENWOOD (English) Green wood. Last name. Variations: *Green, Greener, Greenshaw.*

GREGORY (Greek) Observant. Gregory and its off-shoots have been popular since Gregory Peck

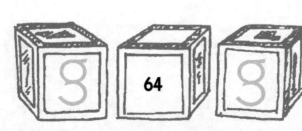

appeared in the film of *To Kill a Mockingbird*. Before that watershed event, it was more frequently chosen by popes – sixteen of them, to be precise, including Gregory the Great in the sixth century. Variations: *Greg, Gregg, Gregoire, Gregor, Gregorio, Gregorios, Gregos, Greig, Gries, Grigor.*

GRESHAM (English) Last name. Variation: *Grisham.*

GREVILLE (English) Last name.

GRIFFIN (Latin) One with a hooked nose. Variations: *Griff, Griffon, Gryphon.*

GRIFFITH (Welsh) Powerful leader. Variations: *Griff, Griffyth, Gryffyth.*

GRIMSHAW (English) Dark forest.

GRISWOLD (English) Grey forest.

GROSVENOR (French) Great hunter.

GROVER (English) Grove of trees. Grover is a name that both sounds cute for a baby and appropriately grown-up for an adult. Chiefly used in the USA, Grovers who have been famous include the *Sesame Street* Muppet and President Stephen Grover Cleveland.

GUADALUPE (Spanish) Valley of the wolf. Variations: *Guadaloup, Guadaloupe.*

GUATON-BIAN (Native American: Kiowa) Large ribs.

GUILFORD (English) Ford with yellow flowers. Variations: *Gilford, Guildford.*

GULSHAN (Hindu) Garden.

GULZAR (Arabic) Blooming.

GUNADHYA (Hindu) Virtuous. Variation: *Gunaadhya.*

GUNNAR (Scandinavian) Battle. Variations: *Gun, Gunder.*

GUNTHER (Scandinavian) Warrior. Variations: *Guenther, Gun, Gunnar, Guntar, Gunter, Guntero, Gunthar.*

GUR (Hebrew) Lion cub.

GURPREET (Pakistani) Religious guru.

GURUDATTA (Hindu) Guru's gift.

GURYON (Hebrew) Lion. Variations: *Garon, Gorion, Gurion.*

GUS (English) Majestic. Gus was originally a shortened form of Augustus, but came into its own as an independent name over the course of the 19th century.

GUSTAF (Scandinavian: Swedish) Staff of the gods. Variations: *Gus, Gustaff, Gustav, Gustave, Gustavo, Gustavs, Gusti, Gustik, Gustus, Gusty.*

GUTHRE (Irish) Windy area. Variations: *Guthrie, Guthry.*

GUTIERRE (Spanish) Ruler of the people.

GUTPAGHO (Native American: Kiowa) Wolf.

GUY (French) Guide; forest; man. Variations: *Gui, Guion, Guyon.*

GUYAPI (Native American) Frank.

GWALCHMAI (Welsh) Battle with a hawk.

GWANDOYA (African: Ugandan) Miserable.

GWATCYN (Welsh) Surname. Variation: *Gwatkin.*

GWYNEDD (Welsh) Blessed. Variations: *Gwyn, Gwynfor, Gwynn, Gwynne.*

GWYTHYR (Welsh) Winner. Variation: *Gwydyr.*

GYAN (Hindu) Knowledge. Variation: *Gyani.*

GYANDEV (Hindu) God of knowledge.

GYANTWAKA (Native American: Iroquois) He who plants.

GYASI (African: Ghanian) Wonderful.

GYLFI (Scandinavian) Ancient mythological king.

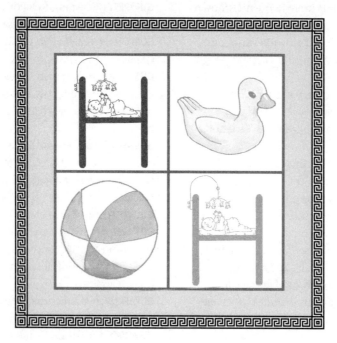

HAAKON (Scandinavian) Chosen son. Variations: *Hagen, Hakan, Hakon.*

HABIB (Arabic) Dear.

HABIMANA (African: Rwandan) God exists. Variation: *Habimama.*

HACHEHI (Native American: Arapaho) Wolf.

HACHIUMA (Japanese) Eight horses.

HADAD (Arabic) The Syrian god of virility.

HADAWAKO (Native American: Iroquois) Falling snow.

HADI (Arabic) Guide.

HADLEY (English) Meadow of heather. Variations: *Hadlea, Hadlee, Hadleigh, Hadly, Headley, Hedley, Hedly.*

HADRIAN (Scandinavian: Swedish) Black earth.

HADRIEL (Hebrew) God's glory.

HADWIN (English) Friend in war. Variations: *Hadwinn, Hadwyn, Hadwynne.*

HAFIZ (Arabic) Protector.

HAFOKA (Polynesian) Big.

HAGAN (Irish) Home ruler. Variations: *Hagen, Haggan.*

HAGLEY (English) Surrounded by hedges. Variations: *Haglea, Haglee, Hagleigh, Haig.*

HAHNEE (Native American) Beggar.

HAHTALEKIN (Native American: Nez Perce) Echo.

HAI (Vietnamese) Sea.

HAIDAR (Arabic) Lion.

HAILAMA (Hawaiian) Famous brother. Variations: *Hairama, Hilama, Hirama.*

HAJJ (African: Swahili) Born during the pilgrimage to Mecca.

HAKADAH (Native American: Sioux) Last.

HAKAN (Native American) Fiery.

HAKEEM (Arabic) Wise. Hakeem is common in Muslim countries, as it is one of the ninety-nine qualities of Allah that are detailed in the Koran, but it is becoming more popular, particularly among African-American and Muslim families. Variations: *Hakem, Hakim.*

HAKIZIANA (African: Rwandan) God saves.

HAK-KUN (Korean) Foundation.

HAKON (Scandinavian) Of the highest race. Variation: *Hako.*

HALA (Hindu) Unknown definition.

HALAPOLO (Polynesian) Place where chili peppers grow.

HALATOA (Polynesian) The grove of trees.

HALBERT (English) Bright hero. Variation: *Halburt.*

HALDAN (Scandinavian) Half Danish. Variations: *Haldane, Halden.*

HALDOR (Scandinavian) Thor's rock. Variations: *Halldor, Halle.*

HALE (English) Healthy. Variation: *Haley.*

HALEN (Scandinavian: Swedish) Hall.

HALFDAN (Scandinavian) Half Danish.

HALFORD (English) Ford in a valley. Variation: *Hallford.*

HALI (Greek) Sea.

HALIAN (Native American) Downy.

HALIL (Turkish) Good friend.

HALIM (Arabic) Gentle.

HALL (English) Worker at the manor.

HALLALHOTSOOT (Native American: Salish) To talk.

HALLAM (English) Valley.

HALLEWELL (English) Holy well. Variations: *Hallwell, Hellewell.*

HALLEY (English) Meadow near the manor.

HALLUTEEN (Native American: Nez Perce) Large stomach.

HALLWARD (English) Protector of the manor. Variation: *Halward.*

HALOLA (Hawaiian) Powerful army. Variation: *Harola.*

HALPUTTA HADJO (Native American) Crazy crocodile.

HALSEY (English) The island that belongs to Hal. Variations: *Hallsey, Hallsy, Halsy.*

HALSTEAD (English) Lands of the manor. Variation: *Halsted.*

HALSTEN (Scandinavian) Rock and stone. Halston is perhaps best known as the last name of a designer who was famous in the 1970s. Though some image-conscious parents may have chosen the name for their sons born then, it is an unusual choice today. Variations: *Hallstein, Hallsten, Hallston, Halston.*

HALTON (English) Manor on the hill.

HALYARD (Scandinavian) Defender of the rock. Variations: *Hallvard, Hallvor, Halvor, Halvar.*

HAM (Hebrew) Hot.

HAMADI (Arabic) Praised. Variation: *Hamidi.*

HAMAL (Arabic) Lamb.

HAMAR (Norse) Hammer.

HAMID (Arabic) Greatly praised. Derivative of Mohammed. Variations: *Hammad, Hammed.*

HAMIDI (African: Kenyan) Admirable.

HAMILL (English) Scarred. Variations: *Hamel, Hamell, Hamil, Hammill.*

HAMILTON (English) Fortified castle. Variation: *Hamelton.*

HAMISH (Scottish) He who removes. Hamish is appearing more frequently among parents who want their son's name to convey an Arabic feel – even though it originates in Scotland. The name also has its roots in Yiddish, where it means comfortable.

HAMISI (African: Swahili) Born on Thursday. Variation: *Hanisi.*

HAMLET (English) Village.

HAMLIN (German) One who loves to stay at home. Variations: *Hamelin, Hamlen, Hamlyn.*

HAMMET (English) Village. Variations: *Hammett, Hammond.*

HAMUND (Scandinavian) Mythological figure.

HAMZA (Arabic) Powerful.

HANAN (Hebrew) God is good.

HANANIAH (Unknown) Unknown definition.

HANDEL (German) God is good.

HANAUHOU (Hawaiian) Renewal.

HANAUHOULANI (Hawaiian) Heavenly rebirth.

HANDLEY (English) Clearing in the woods. Variations: *Handlea, Handleigh, Hanley.*

HANEK (Czech) God is good. Variation of John. Variations: *Hanus, Hanusek, Johan, Nusek.*

HANFORD (English) High ford.

HANI (Arabic) Happy.

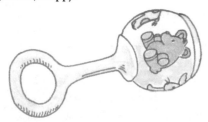

HANIF (Arabic) Follower of Islam. Variation: *Hanef.*

HANK (English) Ruler of the estate. Diminutive of Henry. Hank is a homely, unpretentious name that, because of the famous men who have lived with the name – Hank Marvin and Hank Williams – is a good choice for parents who are also home bodies and unpretentious. However, most people use Hank as the nickname and instead give Henry as the full name.

HANNES (Scandinavian) God is good. Variation of John. Variations: *Haensel, Hannu, Hans, Hansel, Hansl.*

HANNIBAL (English) Unknown definition.

HANRAOI (Irish) Ruler of the home. Variation of Henry.

HANSON (Scandinavian) Son of Hans. Variations: *Hansen, Hanssen, Hansson.*

HANSRAT (Hindu) Swan king.

HANUMAN (Hindu) Chief of the monkeys.

HAO (Chinese) Good.

HAO NGOC (Vietnamese) Jade.

HAOA (Hawaiian) Observer. Hawaiian version of Howard.

HARAL (Scottish) Leader of the army. Variation: *Arailt.*

HARATH (Arabic) To provide. Variation: *Harith.*

HARB (Arabic) War.

HARBERT (Scandinavian) Bright army.

HARBIN (French) Little bright warrior.

HARCOURT (French) Fortified house. Variation: *Harcort.*

HARDEEP (Punjabi) Loves God. Variation: *Harpreet.*

HARDEN (English) Valley of rabbits. Variation: *Hardin.*

HARDING (English) Son of a brave man.

HARDWIN (English) Brave friend. Variations: *Hardwyn, Hardwynn.*

HARDY (English) Brave.

HAREL (Hebrew) Mountain of God.

HARFORD (English) Ford of the hares.

HARGROVE (English) Grove with hares. Variations: *Hargrave, Hargreaves.*

HARI (Hindu) Tawny. Some people may think this is another way to spell Harry, but it is the name for the Hindu sun god; a Sikh guru from the 17th century also claimed this name.

HARISH (Hindu) Lord. Variation: *Haresh.*

HARITH (Arabic) Capable. Variation: *Harithah.*

HARJEET (Hindu) Victorious.

HARKIN (Irish) Dark red. Variation: *Harkan, Harken.*

HARLAN (English) Army land. Variations: *Harland, Harlen, Harlenn, Harlin, Harlyn, Harlynn.*

HARLEY (English) Rabbit pasture. Variations: *Arlea, Arleigh, Arley, Harlea, Harlee, Harleiah, Harly.*

HARLOW (English) Army hill.

HARMON (German) Army man. Variation: *Harman*.

HARO (Japanese) First son of a boar.

HAROLD (English) Army ruler. The name of the Saxon King killed in 1066 at the Battle of Hastings. The name Harold conjures up a feel of the good life as it was experienced about a hundred years ago, in smoking jackets and libraries. It is rare today but famous Harolds include Harold Pinter, Harold Lloyd and Prime Ministers Harold Macmillan and Harold Wilson. Variations: *Hal, Harailt, Harald, Haraldo, Haralds, Haroldas, Haroldo*.

HAROUN (Arabic) High-class. Variation: *Harun*.

HARPER (English) Harp player. Harper is a great name for parents who are looking for an androgynous last name as first name that hasn't been around much yet and possesses no negative connotations. Harper is also used as a girls' name.

HARRINGTON (English) Last name.

HARRIS (English) Last name.

HARRISON (English) Harry's son. Popular in the States, possibly influenced by the presidents William H. Harrison and Benjamin Harrison. In recent decades, actor Harrison Ford may have something to do with its reappearance. Variation: *Harrisen*.

HARRY (English) Ruler at home. Variation of Henry. Today Harry seems to be one of those previously nerdy names that is on its way back in style. Britain's young Prince Harry and the success of J. K. Rowling's *Harry Potter* books may have something to do with the revival. Variations: *Harrey, Harri, Harrie*.

HARSHAD (Hindu) One who gives joy.

HARSHAL (Hindu) Happy. Variations: *Harshil, Harshul*.

HART (English) Stag. Variation: *Harte*.

HARTFORD (English) Ford where stags graze.

HARTLEY (English) Meadow where stags graze. Variations: *Hartlea, Hartlee, Hartleigh, Hartly*.

HARTMAN (German) Hard man. Variation: *Hartmann*.

HARTWELL (English) Well where stags drink. Variations: *Harwell, Harwill*.

HARUE (Japanese) Born in the spring.

HARVEY (French) Eager for battle. It came to England with the Normans and makes several appearances in the Domesday Book. I remember when I was at school, a boy in my class named Harvey was the cutest and sweetest boy there. Did he feel he had to compensate for his unpopular name with his behaviour? Children today with the name probably won't have half the problems that my friend Harvey had when he was relentlessly teased about his name throughout his childhood and teenage years. Harvey is back with a vengeance, and growing in popularity. US playwright Harvey Fierstein and actor Harvey Keitel may have helped the reputation of the name. Variations: *Herve, Hervey*.

HARWOOD (English) Wood of hares.

HASAD (Turkish) Harvest.

HASANT (African: Swahili) Handsome. Variations: *Hasan, Hasin, Hassan, Hassani, Husani*.

HASHIM (Arabic) Destroyer of evil. Variation: *Hasheem*.

HASHKEH NAABAH (Native American: Navajo) Mad fighter.

HASIM (Arabic) To determine.

HASIN (Hindu) Laughing.

HASKEL (Hebrew) Wisdom. Variations: *Chaskel, Haskell, Heskel*.

HASLETT (English) Land of hazel trees. Variation: *Hazlitt*.

HASSEL (English) From Hassall, the witches' corner. Variations: *Hassal, Hassall, Hassell*.

HASTIN (Hindu) Elephant.

HASTINGS (English) Son of a miserly man.

HATCHOOTUCKNEE (Native American: Choctaw) Snapping turtle.

HATDAR (Hindu) Lion. Variations: *Haider, Haydar, Hayder, Hyder.*

HATFEZ (Hindu) Protector.

HATIM (Arabic) To decide.

HAU (Vietnamese) Desire.

HAVEA (Polynesian) In charge.

HAVEL (Czech) Small. Variations: *Hava, Havelek, Havlik.*

HAVELOCK (Scandinavian) Seaport.

HAVEN (English) Sanctuary. Variation: *Havin.*

HAWARD (Scandinavian) High defender.

HAWLEY (English) Meadow with hedges. Variations: *Hawleigh, Hawly.*

HAWTHORN (English) Where hawthorns grow. Variation: *Hawthorne.*

HAYDEN (English) Hill of heather; (Welsh) Valley with hedges. Hayden and its variants are quite popular in Great Britain and Wales and the name is beginning to catch on in the USA. Parents-to-be whose childhoods were filled with piano lessons are familiar with another spelling of the name, Haydn, as in Franz Joseph, but children today are more likely to know it through actor Aidan Quinn. Variations: *Aidan, Haddan, Haddon, Haden, Hadon, Hadyn, Haydn, Haydon.*

HAYES (English) Hedges. Variation: *Hays.*

HAYTHAM (Arabic) Proud.

HAYWARD (English) Protector of hedged area.

HAYWOOD (English) Forest with hedges. Variation: *Heywood.*

HEATHCLIFF (English) Cliff near an open field. Heathcliff is indelibly linked with the character in Emily Bronte's classic romance *Wuthering Heights*. The given name of Heath is more common than the full name these days, with the actor Heath Ledger no doubt making it popular. Variation: *Heath.*

HEATON (English) High town.

HEBER (Hebrew) Gathering. Variation: *Hebor.*

HECTOR (Greek) Holding fast. Actor Hector Elizondo and composer Hector Berlioz are the most famous Hectors in the last one hundred years, and the families who choose the name for their sons today are most often of Hispanic descent. Variation: *Hektor.*

HEDDWYN (Welsh) Blessed peace.

HEDEON (Russian) Logger.

HEDRICK (English) Unknown definition.

HEIMDALL (Scandinavian) White god.

HEINMOT ILPPILP (Native American: Nez Perce) Red thunder.

HEINMOT TOOYALAKEKT (Native American: Nez Perce) Moving thunder.

HEINMOT TOSINLIKT (Native American: Nez Perce) Crowded lightning.

HEINRICH (German) Ruler of the estate. Variation of Henry. Variations: *Heinrick, Heinrik, Henrik, Henrique, Henryk.*

HEKEKA (Hawaiian) To hold fast. Variation: *Heketa.*

HELAKU (Native American) Sunny.

HELEMANO (Hawaiian) Army man. Variation: *Heremano.*

HELEUMA (Hawaiian) Mooring.

HELGI (Scandinavian) Happy. Variations: *Helge, Helje.*

HELMUT (French) Helmet. Helmut Kohl and Helmut Newton have made this name visible, but it tends not to be very popular..

HEMACHANDRA (Hindu) Golden moon.

HEMAN (Hebrew) Faithful.

HEMATUTE HIKAITH (Native American: Nez Perce) Eyes of thunder.

HEMENE (Native American: Nez Perce) Wolf.

Names from the New Testament

Frequently, parents who consider themselves to be Christians will turn to the Bible – specifically, the New Testament – for inspiration in naming their children. For boys, they might choose a book of the Bible – Matthew, Mark, Luke, John, Timothy, James or Peter – or one of the twelve apostles: Thomas, Andrew or Philip for example.

For girls, parents can select one of the female characters from the New Testament – Mary, of course – or turn to the patron saints of Catholicism for inspiration. Of course, you can pick the patron saint first instead

of choosing the name, especially if it is appropriate to your life. For instance, if you or your spouse are involved in music and you'd like to give your baby a name that relates to your profession, you might look to the patron saints for musicians: Cecilia or Gregory. Interestingly, there is a patron saint of television – Clare of Assissi. Other professional saints include Barbara for architects, Sebastian for athletes, and Matthew for tax collectors. And you don't necessarily have to be Catholic to enjoy picking the name of a patron saint – you just need a good sense of humour.

Boys' Names

- Alexander: Son of the man who carried Jesus' cross.
- Andrew: Disciple of Jesus.
- Demas: A colleague of Paul.
- Elias: Variation of the Old Testament's Elijah.
- Galio: Older brother of Seneca.
- Jairus: Leader of the synagogue at Capernaum.
- James: Brother of Jesus.
- Jason: A colleague of Paul.
- John: Apostle.
- Joseph: Father of Jesus.
- Luke: Apostle.
- Nathaniel: Disciple of Jesus.
- Paul: Apostle.
- Stephen: Martyr.
- Timothy: Disciple of Paul.

Girls' Names

- Anna: Prophetess who called Jesus the messiah.
- Bethany: Village in the book of Luke.
- Candace: Eunuch in the book of Acts.
- Eunice: Mother of Timothy.
- Julia: Woman greeted by Paul in the book of Romans.
- Magdala: Town of Mary Magdalene.
- Mary: Mother of Jesus.
- Phoebe: Woman in book of Romans.
- Salome: Mother of John the apostle.
- Tabitha: Woman in the book of Acts.

HEMENE ILPPILP (Native American: Nez Perce) Red wolf.

HEMENE ISTOOPTOOPNIN (Native American: Nez Perce) Bald wolf.

HEMENE MOXMOX (Native American: Nez Perce) Yellow wolf.

HEMOLELEKEAKUA (Hawaiian) Perfect God.

HENDERSON (English) Son of Henry. Last name.

HENELI (Hawaiian) Ruler at home. Variations: *Hanale, Henele, Heneri.*

HENLEY (English) High meadow. Last name.

HENNING (Scandinavian) Home ruler.

HENRY (German) Ruler of the house. Like Harry, another previously unpopular name in recent decades, Henry is one of the more popular choices around. Famous Henrys include Henry Fonda, Henry James and Henry Longfellow. But perhaps an unconscious influence for the name's increasing popularity is Henry David Thoreau. He seems to be in the environmental news on a regular basis, which is pretty good considering that he's been dead for more than a hundred years. Variations: *Henery, Henri, Henrik, Henrique, Henryk.*

HE-PING (Chinese) Peace.

HERALD (English) Bearer of news.

HERBERT (German) Shining army. Variations: *Heibert, Herb, Herbie.*

HERCULES (Greek) Zeus's son. Variations: *Herakles, Hercule.*

HEREWARD (English) Military.

HERLEIF (Scandinavian) Beloved army. Variations: *Harlief, Herlof, Herluf.*

HERMAN (German) Army man. Herman Munster and Herman Melville, the author of *Moby Dick*, are among the most famous recipients of the name. Variations: *Hermann, Hermon.*

HERMES (Greek) Mythological messenger of the Greek gods.

HERMOD (Scandinavian) Ancient mythological figure.

HERNANDO (Spanish) Brave traveller.

HEROMIN (Polish) Estate head.

HERRICK (German) Leader in war.

HESPEROS (Greek) Evening star. Variation: *Hespero.*

HESUTU (Native American) Taking a wasps' nest from the earth.

HETNMOT (Native American: Nez Perce) Thunder.

HEVEL (Hebrew) Breath.

HEWITT (English) Last name.

HEWLETT (English) Last name. Variation: *Hewlitt.*

HEWNEY (Irish) Green. Variations: *Aney, Oney, Owney, Oynie, Uaithne.*

HEWSON (English) Hugh's son.

HIALMAR (Scandinavian) Warrior's helmet. Variation: *Hialmar.*

HIAWATHA (Native American: Iroquois) Maker of rivers.

HIBAH (Arabic) Gift.

HIDEAKI (Japanese) Wise.

HIDEO (Japanese) Superb.

HIEN (Vietnamese) Sweet.

HIEREMIAS (Greek) The Lord will uplift.

HIERONYMUS (Greek) Sacred name. Variation: *Hieronimos.*

HIEU (Vietnamese) Respect.

HIFO (Polynesian) Atonement.

HIKILA (Polynesian) To raise the sail.

HIKMAT (Arabic) Knowledge.

HILARION (Greek) Cheerful. Variation: *Ilarion.*

HILARY (Greek) Happy. Before it became popular as a girls' name, Hilary was used for boys. Variations: *Hilaire, Hilarie, Hillary, Hillery.*

HILDEBRAND (German) Sword used in battle.

HILEL (Arabic) The new moon.

HILLARD (German) Tough soldier. Variations: *Hilliard, Hillier, Hillyer.*

HILLEL (Hebrew) Highly praised. Jewish families are choosing this name more frequently for their sons. Hillel was the name of one of the first great Talmudic scholars.

HILMAR (Scandinavian) Renowned nobleman.

HILTON (English) Town on a hill. Variation: *Hylton.*

HIMERONIM (Polish) Strong army.

HIMESH (Hindu) Snow king.

HIMSLEHKIN (Native American: Nez Perce) Raw.

HINMATON YALATKIT (Native American: Nez Perce) Rolling thunder.

HINUN (Native American) God of rain.

HIPPOCRATES (Greek) The father of medicine.

HIPPOLYTE (Greek) Horse.

HIPPOLYTOS (Greek) One who frees horses.

HIRAM (Hebrew) Most noble man. Variations: *Hirom, Hyrum.*

HIROHITO (Japanese) Emperor.

HIROMASA (Japanese) Direct.

HIROSHI (Japanese) Generous.

HIRSH (Hebrew) Deer. Variations: *Hersch, Herschel, Hersh, Hershel, Hersz, Hertz, Hertzel, Herz, Herzl, Heschel, Hesh, Hirsch, Hirschel.*

HISHAM (Arabic) To break. Variation: *Hishim.*

HISOKA (Japanese) Restrained.

HITOSHI (Japanese) First.

HIUWE (Hawaiian) Heart. Variations: *Hiu, Huko.*

HIYATOMMON (Native American: Nez Perce) One who shouts.

HO (Chinese) Good.

HOA (Vietnamese) Flower.

HOAALOHAKUPAA (Hawaiian) Faithful friend. Variation: *Kahoaalohakopaa.*

HOANG (Vietnamese) Completed.

HOBSON (English) Son of Robert. Hobson is a very refined name – the sort that might be good to select if you want your son to be a butler when he grows up.

HOC (Vietnamese) Learn.

HOD (Hebrew) Wonderful.

HODDING (Dutch) Bricklayer.

HODER (Scandinavian) Ancient mythological figure. Variation: *Hodur.*

HODGSON (English) Son of Roger.

HODIAH (Hebrew) God is great. Variations: *Hodia, Hodiya.*

HOENIR (Scandinavian) Ancient mythological figure. Variation: *Honir.*

HOGAN (Irish) Youth.

HOHANONIVAH (Native American: Cheyenne) Armour.

HOHOTS (Native American: Nez Perce) Bear.

HOHOTS ILPPILP (Native American: Nez Perce) Red bear.

HOHOTS TAMALWEYAT (Native American: Nez Perce) Leader of the grizzly bears.

HOKEA (Hawaiian) Salvation. Hawaiian version of Hosea.

HOKU (Hawaiian) Star.

HOLA (Polynesian) Run away.

HOLAKIO (Hawaiian) Hawaiian version of Horatio. Variations: *Holeka, Horesa.*

HOLATA (Native American: Seminole) Alligator.

HOLBROOK (English) Brook near the hollow. Variation: *Holbrooke.*

HOLCOMB (English) Deep valley.

HOLDEN (English) Hollow valley.

HOLIC (Czech) Barber.

HOLISI (Polynesian) House built of reeds.

HOLLAND (English) Country.

HOLLEB (Polish) Dovelike. Variations: *Hollub, Holub.*

HOLLIS (English) Near the holly trees.

HOLMES (English) Islands in a stream.

HOLT (English) Forest.

HOMER (Greek) Hostage. Homer is a noble name, now perhaps more associated with the hapless father on *The Simpsons* and not the great Greek epic poet who wrote *The Odyssey*. Variations: *Homere, Homeros, Homerus, Omer.*

HONDO (African: Zimbabwean) War.

HONOK (Polish) One who leads at home.

HONON (Native American) Bear.

HONORE (Latin) Honoured one.

HONOVI (Native American) Strong.

HONZA (Czech) God is good.

HOPKIN (English) Bright renown. Last name. Variation of Robert.

HORACE (Latin) Old Roman clan name. Neither Horace nor its variant, Horatio, has ever been a wildly popular name. But Horatio actually has a bit of potential these days, as its illustrious past shows: Navy hero (Nelson), composer (Palmer), and aircraft pioneer (Phillips). Variations: *Horacio, Horatio.*

HORST (German) Undergrowth.

HORTON (English) Grey town. Variation: *Horten.*

HOSA (Native American: Arapaho) Crow.

HOSEA (Hebrew) Deliverance. Variations: *Hoseia, Hosheia.*

HOSHAMA (Hebrew) God hears you.

HOSYU (Japanese) Reserved.

HOTAIA (Polynesian) Mine.

HOTHLEPOYA (Native American: Creek) Crazy warrior.

HOTOTO (Native American) Whistler.

HOUGHTON (English) Town on the cliff.

HOUSTON (English) Town on the hill.

HOWARD (English) Observer. Last name. Howard isn't widely used today, but earlier in the century it was chosen with great frequency because people felt that it had a decidedly aristocratic feel. Howard is a saint's name, too. The name's most famous association is perhaps with eccentric billionaire Howard Hughes. Other stars with the name include film director Howard Hawks and actor Howard Keel. It's not clear why this name went out of fashion after being one of the top twenty names for boys from the late 19th century through to the 1950s. Variation: *Howie.*

HOWE (English) Hill.

HOWELL (Welsh) Exceptional.

HOWI (Native American: Miwok) Turtledove.

HOWIN (Chinese) A swallow.

HOWLAND (English) Land with hills. Variations: *Howlan, Howlen.*

HOYOUWERLIKT (Native American: Nez Perce) Good necklace.

HOYT (Irish) Spirit.

HU (Chinese) Tiger.

HUAKAVA (Polynesian) Drink made from kava root.

HUANG (Chinese) Wealthy.

HUANG-FU (Chinese) Wealthy future.

HUAN-TOA (Native American: Kiowa) Sword.

HUANU (Hawaiian) God is good.

HUBERT (German) Bright mind. Variations: *Hubbard, Hube, Huber, Huberto, Huey, Hugh, Hughes, Hugo, Uberto.*

HUDSON (English) Son of Hugh.

HUGH (English) Intelligent. It came to England with the Normans and has remained in use ever since, enjoying a resurgence in recent years, possibly fol-

lowing the success of the films of British actor Hugh Grant, who may give it an air of sophistication. Other famous Hughs include architect Sir Hugh Casson, British novelist Sir Hugh Walpole and TV presenter Sir Huw Wheldon. Variations: *Hew, Huey, Hughes, Hughie, Huw.*

HUHUEWAHEHLE (Native American: Creek) Good boy.

HULA (Native American: Osage) Eagle.

HULAMA (Hawaiian) Brilliant.

HULBERT (German) Shining grace.

HULWEMA (Native American) Dead grizzly bear.

HUMAYD (Arabic) To praise.

HUMBERT (German) Famous giant. Most notable as the character Humbert Humbert in Vladimir Nabokov's novel *Lolita*. Variations: *Humberto, Umberto.*

HUMPHREY (English) Peaceful. Humphrey has long been popular as a last name. As a first name, it was considered quite aristocratic but gradually became more widely used. It is personified by the legendary American actor Humphrey Bogart. Another famous bearer of the name is jazz musician and radio presenter Humphrey Lyttleton. Commonly shortened to Humph. Variations: *Humfredo, Humfrey, Humfrid, Humfried, Humphery, Humphry.*

HUNG (Vietnamese) Courageous.

HUNT (English) The hunt.

HUNTER (English) Hunter. Although by definition the name Hunter sounds refined and mannered, parents may consider that writer Hunter S. Thompson has earned a reputation as a maverick.

HUNTINGTON (English) Hunter's estate. Variation: *Huntingdon.*

HUNTLEY (English) Meadow of the hunter. Variations: *Huntlea, Huntlee, Huntleigh, Huntly.*

HURLBERT (English) Bright army.

HURLEY (Irish) Ocean tide. Variations: *Hurlee, Hurleigh, Hurly.*

HURST (English) Grove of trees. Variation *Hearst.*

HUSAYN (Arabic) Beautiful. Variations: *Hisein, Husain, Hussain, Hussein.*

HUSIS MOXMOX (Native American: Nez Perce) Yellow head.

HUSISHUSIS KUTE (Native American: Nez Perce) Bald.

HUSLU (Native American) Shaggy bear.

HUSNI (Arabic) Perfection.

HUSSEIN (Arabic) Little beauty. Variations: *Husain, Husein.*

HUTCHINSON (English) Thought. Variation: *Hutcheson.*

HUTTON (English) Town on the bluff. Variation: *Hutten.*

HUXFORD (English) Hugh's ford.

HUXLEY (English) Hugh's meadow. Variations: *Hux, Huxlea, Huxlee, Huxleigh, Huxly.*

HUY (Vietnamese) Light.

HUYA-NA (Native American: Sioux) Young eagle.

HUYU (Japanese) Winter.

HY (Vietnamese) Hope.

HYATT (English) High gate.

HYDE (English) Measure of land in England in the Middle Ages.

HYMAN (English) Life. Variation: *Hyam.*

HYO (Korean) Childhood devotion.

HYUN-KI (Korean) Foundation of wisdom. Variation: *Hyun-Shik.*

HYWEL (Welsh) Famous. Borne by several early Welsh rulers, it is quite rare outside Wales despite a resurgence in the 20th century. British actor Hywel Bennett is a famous example. Variation: *Hywell.*

IAGO (Italian) He who grabs by the heel. Iago was an evil character in Shakespeare's play *Othello*, but the name is perhaps best known today as the name of the parrot in the Walt Disney film *Aladdin*.

IAKEPA (Hawaiian) Hawaiian version of Jasper. Variations: *Iasepa, Kakapa, Kasapa*.

IAKONA (Hawaiian) To heal. Variation: *Iasona*.

IALEKA (Hawaiian) Descendant. Variation: *Iareda*.

IAN (Scottish) God is good. British novelist Ian Fleming penned all of the *James Bond* stories, and the name hit its peak in both Britain and the United States in the mid-1960s, which some would say was the time when the best Bond films were made. Other notable bearers of the name include British actors Ian Carmichael and Sir Ian McKellen. The variant Iain is largely confined to Scotland and includes the novelist Iain Banks. Variations: *Ean, Iain, Iancu, Ianos*.

IARFHLAITH (Irish) Tributary lord. Variation: *Jarlath*.

IBN-MUSTAPHA (Arabic) Son of the Mustapha.

IBRAHIM (Arabic) Father of many. Variation of Abraham.

ICARUS (Greek) Greek mythological figure who flew too close to the sun; his wings, attached to his body with wax, fell off and he plummeted to earth.

ICHABOD (Hebrew) The glory is no more. Most associate this name with the character from Washington Irving's story *The Legend of Sleepy Hollow*, played by Johnny Depp in the film. Variations: *Ikabod, Ikavod*.

ICHIRO (Japanese) First son.

IDI (African: Swahili) Born during the Idd festival.

IDRIS (Welsh) Impulsive.

IDWAL (Welsh) Lord + wall.

IEKE (Hawaiian) Wealth. Variation: *Iese*.

IELEMIA (Hawaiian) God will lift up. Variation: *Ieremia*.

IESTYN (Welsh) Moral.

IFOR (Welsh) Archer.

IGASHO (Native American) Traveller.

IGNAAS (Scandinavian) Fire.

IGNATIUS (English) Fervent; on fire. The only famous personality I know with this name is Iggy Pop. Historically, Ignatius was a martyr in the Catholic church as well as the name of several saints. Variations: *Iggy, Ignac, Ignace, Ignacek, Ignacio, Ignatious, Ignatz, Ignaz, Ignazio, Inigo, Nacek, Nacicek.*

IGOR (Russian) Russian version of the Norwegian name Ingeborg, the guardian of the Norse god of peace. It has never been very popular in recent years, perhaps because of its association with Doctor Frankenstein's assistant.

IHAB (Arabic) Present.

IHSAN (Arabic) Benevolence.

IISHIM (Hindu) Spring.

IKAAKA (Hawaiian) Laughter. Variations: *Aikake, Isaaka.*

IKAIA (Hawaiian) God is my saviour. Variation: *Isaia.*

IKAIKALANI (Hawaiian) Spiritual power.

IKALE (Polynesian) Eagle.

IKAMALOHI (Polynesian) Fish.

IKANI (Polynesian) Small, hot-headed child.

IKE (English) Short for Isaac, it has sometimes stood alone as an independent name. Variations: *Ikey, Ikie.*

IKENAKI (Hawaiian) Fire.

ILIAS (Greek) The Lord is my God. Greek version of Elijah. Variation: *Ilia.*

ILLINGWORTH (English) Town in Britain.

ILLTUD (Welsh) Land of many people. Variation: *Illtyd.*

ILOM (African: Nigerian) I have enemies.

IL-SUNG (Korean) Superior.

ILYA (Russian) Nickname for Elias, which has become its own name. Variation: *Ilja.*

IMAD (Arabic) Support, pillar.

IMAROGBE (African: Nigerian) Child born to a good family.

IMRAN (Arabic) Host.

IMRICH (Czech) Strength at home. Variation: *Imrus.*

INAR (English) Individual.

INCE (Hungarian) Innocent.

INCENCIO (Spanish) White one.

INEK (Polish) Boar friend.

INEN TOXXOUKE (Native American: Nez Perce) Echo.

INGEMAR (Scandinavian) Son of Ing, Norwegian god of peace. Variations: *Ingamar, Inge, Ingmar.*

INGER (Scandinavian) Ing's army. Variation: *Ingar.*

INGHAM (English) Area in Britain.

INGRAM (English) Raven. Variations: *Ingraham, Ingrim.*

INGVAR (Scandinavian) Protector of Ing, the Norwegian god of peace.

INIGO (Spanish) Variant of Ignatius. Records of its use in England go back at least to the 16th century, when it was borne by the famous English architect Inigo Jones. It enjoyed another brief period of popularity in the 19th century.

INIKO (African: Nigerian) Hard times.

INKPADUTA (Native American: Sioux) Red point.

INNES (Scottish) Island. Variations: *Inness, Innis, Inniss.*

INNOCENZIO (Italian) Innocent. Variations: *Inocencio, Inocente.*

INOKE (Polynesian) Devoted.

INOKENE (Hawaiian) Innocent.

INTEUS (Native American) Unashamed.

IOAKIM (Russian) God will build.

IOELA (Hawaiian) God is Lord.

IOKEPA (Hawaiian) God will increase. Variations: *Iokewe, Iosepa.*

IOKIA (Hawaiian) God heals.

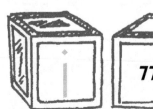
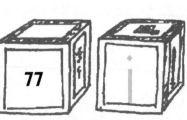

77

IOKINA (Hawaiian) God will develop. Variation: *Wakina.*

IOKUA (Hawaiian) God helps.

ION (Irish) God is good.

IONA (Hawaiian) Dove.

IONAKANA (Hawaiian) God will give. Variation: *Ionatana.*

IONGI (Polynesian) Young.

IORWERTH (Welsh) Handsome lord. Variation: *Yorath.*

IPPAKNESS WAYHAYKEN (Native American: Nez Perce) Mirror necklace.

IPYANA (African: Tanzanian) Grace.

IRA (Hebrew) Observant. Famous Iras include US lyricist Ira Gershwin, brother of George, and US writer Ira Levin.

IRAM (English) Shining.

IRATEBA (Native American: Mojave) Pretty bird. Variations: *Arateva, Yaratev.*

IROMAGAJA (Native American: Sioux) Crying. Variation: *Iromagaju.*

IRVIN (Scottish) Beautiful. Variation: *Irvine.*

IRVING (English) Sea friend. Though Irving is not as popular as the other previously nerdy names that seem to be making a comeback these days, there is no

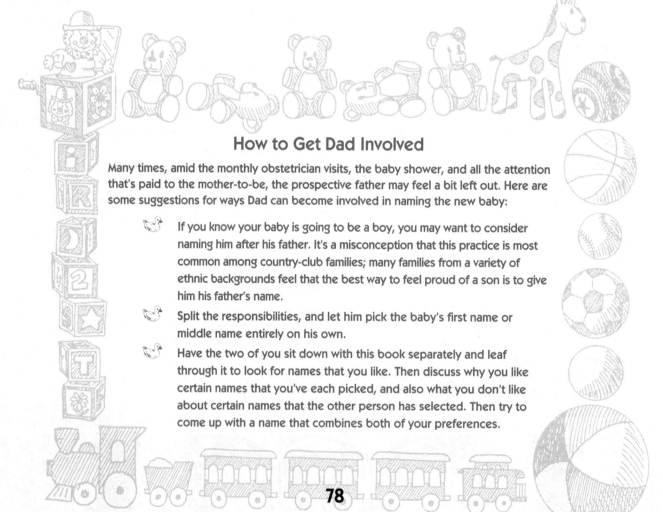

How to Get Dad Involved

Many times, amid the monthly obstetrician visits, the baby shower, and all the attention that's paid to the mother-to-be, the prospective father may feel a bit left out. Here are some suggestions for ways Dad can become involved in naming the new baby:

- If you know your baby is going to be a boy, you may want to consider naming him after his father. It's a misconception that this practice is most common among country-club families; many families from a variety of ethnic backgrounds feel that the best way to feel proud of a son is to give him his father's name.

- Split the responsibilities, and let him pick the baby's first name or middle name entirely on his own.

- Have the two of you sit down with this book separately and leaf through it to look for names that you like. Then discuss why you like certain names that you've each picked, and also what you don't like about certain names that the other person has selected. Then try to come up with a name that combines both of your preferences.

doubt that it is being selected more now than it was ten or twenty years ago. Famous Irvings include Russian born US song writer Irving Berlin. Variation: *Irv.*

ISAAC (Hebrew) Laughter. The name appears in the Bible as the son of Abraham and Sarah whose birth brought delight to his elderly parents. It's obvious that people have become more aware and proud of their ethnic heritage as they are choosing names that have clear connections to their backgrounds. Isaac is a great example of this trend, as it is beginning to appear with greater frequency. Isaacs who have made a name for themselves include US violinist Isaac Stern, US science fiction author Isaac Asimov, English writer and angler Izaak Walton and scientist Sir Isaac Newton . Variations: *Isaak, Isak, Itzak, Ixaka, Izaak.*

ISAIAH (Hebrew) God helps me. Variations: *Isa, Isaia, Isia, Isiah, Issiah.*

ISAM (Arabic) To pledge.

ISAS (Japanese) Valuable.

ISHA (Hindu) Lord.

ISHAAN (Hindu) Sun. Variation: *Ishan.*

ISHAM (English) Area in Britain.

ISHAQ (Arabic) Laughter.

ISHARA (Hindu) Sign.

ISHIEYO NISSI (Native American: Cheyenne) Two moons. Variation: *Ishaynishus.*

ISHMAEL (Hebrew) God will hear. Variations: *Ismael, Ismail, Yishmael.*

ISHNA WITCA (Native American: Sioux) Single man.

ISI (Japanese) Rock.

ISIDORE (Greek) Gift from Isis. Variations: *Isador, Isadore, Izzy.*

ISIKELI (Polynesian) God is strong.

ISKANDAR (Arabic) Protector. Variation: *Iskander.*

ISKEMU (Native American) Stream.

ISLWYN (Welsh) Grove.

ISMAH (Arabic) God listens. Variation: *Ismatl.*

ISMAT (Arabic) Protector.

ISOROKU (Japanese) Fifty-six.

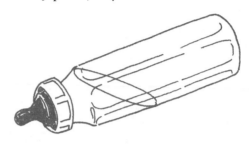

ISRAEL (Hebrew) Struggle with God. The country. Israel has been given to both Jewish boys and African-Americans in the last few decades. Variation: *Yisrael.*

ISSA (African: Swahili) Protection.

ISTU (Native American) Pine sap.

ISTVAN (Hungarian) Crown. Variation: *Isti.*

ITHEL (Welsh) Charitable lord.

ITZA-CHO (Native American: Apache) Eagle.

IUKEKINI (Hawaiian) Righteous.

IUKINI (Hawaiian) Well born. Variation: *Iuaini.*

IVAN (Czech) God is good. Variations: *Ivanchik, Ivanek, Ivano, Ivas.*

IVES (English) Yew wood. Variations: *Ivo, Ivon, Yves.*

IVOR (Scandinavian: Norwegian) Norwegian god. Variations: *Ivar, Iver.*

IVORY (African-American) Ivory.

IYAPO (African: Nigerian) Tribulation.

IYE (Native American) Smoke.

IZZ ALDIN (Arabic) Power of faith. Variations: *Izz Alden, Izz Eddin.*

JA (Korean) Attraction.

JAAN (Estonian) Anointed.

JABARI (Arabic) To comfort.

JABBAR (Hindu) One who comforts.

JABEZ (Hebrew) Born in pain. Because this name ends in a 'z' I always thought it was Spanish. However, it shows up on the gravestones in many old cemeteries, a testament to its Puritan roots. Variations: *Jabes, Jabesh, Jabus.*

JABIN (Hebrew) God has created.

JABIR (Arabic) Healer. Variations: *Gabir, Gabr, Jabbar, Jabr.*

JABULANI (African: Zimbabwean) Happy.

JACHYM (Czech) God will develop. Variation: *Jach.*

JACINTO (Spanish) Hyacinth. Variations: *Ciacintho, Clacinto, Jacindo.*

JACKSON (English) Son of Jack. Variation: *Jakson.*

JACOB (Hebrew) Supplanter or heel. Jacob first appears in the book of Genesis in the Bible; Jacob was the youngest son of Isaac and Rebecca. It is very popular among parents these days, possibly because it displays a sense of forthrightness and openness. No upper-crust pretentions here. Perhaps the most famous literary Jacob was created by Charles Dickens in *A Christmas Carol.* Variations: *Jaco, Jacobus, Jacoby, Jacquet, Jakab, Jake, Jakie, Jakiv, Jakob, Jakov, Jakub, Jakubek, Kiva, Kivi.*

JACY (Native American) Moon. Variation: *Jace.*

JADON (Hebrew) God has heard. Variations: *Jacdon, Jaden, Jaydon.*

JADRIEN (African-American) Combination of Jay and Adrien.

JAEGAR (German) Hunger.

JAE-HWA (Korean) Wealthy.

JAEL (Hebrew) Goat.

JAFAR (Arabic) River. Variations: *Gafar, Jafari.*

JAGANNATH (Hindu) God of all.

JAGGER (English) To haul something.

JAGJIT (Hindu) Victor of the world.

JAHAN (Hindu) World.

JAHI (African: Swahili) Dignity.

JAIDEV (Hindu) God of victory.

JAIMINI (Hindu) Victorious one.

JAINENDRA (Hindu) Victorious lord of the sky. Variation: *Jinendra.*

JAIRAJ (Hindu) Victorious lord.

JAIRUS (Hebrew) God clarifies.

JAJA (African: Nigerian) Honour.

JAJUAN (African-American) Newly created.

JAKEEM (Arabic) Noble.

JAKUB (Czech) Supplanter. Variations: *Jakoubek, Kuba, Kubes, Kubicek.*

JAL (Gypsy) Wanderer.

JALADHI (Hindu) Ocean.

JALAL (Arabic) Great. Variations: *Galal, Jaleel.*

JALEN (African-American) Calm.

JAMAL (Arabic) Handsome. Variations: *Gamal, Gamil, Jamaal, Jamahl, Jamall, Jameel, Jamel, Jamell, Jamil, Jamill, Jammal.*

JAMAINE (Arabic) German.

JAMAR (African-American) Newly created. Variations: *Jamarr, Jemar, Jimar.*

JAMES (English) He who replaces. Variation of Jacob. James – by itself and in its many incarnations – has never really gone out of style. It can be formal or casual, and a boy with the name of James will either love it or prefer one of the more informal versions. Later on, however, having the option to be called James as an adult adds to the respect the name possesses. Famous Jameses include James Taylor, James

Stewart, James Cagney, James Mason, and Jimi Hendrix. Variations: *Jacques, Jaime, Jaimey, Jaimie, Jaimito, Jamey, Jamie, Jayme, Jaymes, Jaymie, Jim, Jimi, Jimmey, Jimmie, Jimmy.*

JAMESON (English) Son of James. Variations: *Jamieson, Jamison.*

JAN (Czech) God is good. Variations: *Janco, Jancsi, Jando, Janecek, Janek, Janik, Janika, Jankiel, Janne, Jano, Janos, Jenda.*

JANESH (Hindu) Lord of the people.

JANSON (Scandinavian) Son of Jan. Variations: *Jansen, Jantzen, Janzen.*

JANUARIUS (Polish) The first month of the year. Variations: *Janiusz, Janiuszek, Jarek.*

JANUS (English) Born in January. Roman god.

JAPHETH (Hebrew) He increases. Japheth was the oldest son of Noah. Variation: *Japhet.*

JARAH (Hebrew) Sweet.

JAREB (Hebrew) He struggles. Variations: *Jarib, Yarev, Yariv.*

JARED (Hebrew) Descend. Jared, with its many variants, has been very popular since the mid-1960s, when it first began to appear with some regularity. Jared, however, was around as a common name in the 17th century with the Puritans, after which it fell out of favour for a while. Variations: *Jarad, Jarid, Jarod, Jarrad, Jarred, Jerad, Jered, Jerod, Jerrad, Jerrod, Jerryd, Yarden, Yared.*

JAREK (Czech) Spring. Variations: *Jariusz, Jariuszek, Jarousek.*

JARELL (African-American) Newly created. Variations: *Jarel, Jarrel, Jarrell, Jarul.*

JARETH (African-American) Newly created. Variations: *Jarreth, Jerth.*

JARMAN (German) German. Variation: *Jerman.*

JAROGNIEW (Polish) Spring anger.

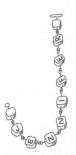

JAROMIERZ (Polish) Famous spring.

JAROMIL (Czech) One who loves spring. Variation: *Jarmil.*

JAROMIR (Czech) Great spring.

JARON (Hebrew) To shout. Variations: *Gerron, Jaran, Jaren, Jarin, Jarran, Jarren, Jarron, Jeran, Jeren, Jeron, Jerrin, Jerron.*

JAROPELK (Polish) Spring people.

JAROSLAV (Czech) Glorious spring. Variations: *Jarda, Jaroslaw.*

JARRETT (English) Brave with a spear. Variations: *Jarret, Jarrete.*

JARVIS (German). Honourable. Variation: *Jervis.*

JASHA (Russian) He who replaces. Variation of Jacob.

JASHON (African-American) Unknown definition. Variations: *JaShaun, JaShonn.*

JASON (Hebrew) God is my salvation. Jason Priestley, Jason Robards, Jason Donovan and a variety of other TV and Hollywood stars combined to turn Jason into one of the hottest names of the 1970s and 1980s Sean Connery has probably helped by calling his son Jason. Names that start with the letter 'J' constitute a sizable percentage of names today, and when Jason first began to catch on, it represented a fresh new approach to 'J' names. Today, Jason is still popular, but it can border on overuse in some places; selecting a form of Jason with a different spelling will help your son to stand apart. Variations: *Jace, Jacen, Jaison, Jase, Jasen, Jayce, Jaycen, Jaysen, Jayson.*

JASPAL (Pakistani) Virtuous.

JASPER (English) Wealthy one. Variation: *Jaspar.*

JAVAN (English) Son of the Biblical Japheth. Variations: *Javin, Javon.*

JAVARIS (Latin) Unknown definition.

JAVAS (Hindu) Fast.

JAVIER (Spanish) Homeowner. Variation of Xavier.

JAVON (African-American) Newly created. Variations: *Javonne, Jevon.*

JAWAHARLAL (Hindu) Victory.

JAWDAT (Arabic) Good. Variation: *Gawdat.*

JAWHAR (Arabic) Jewel.

JAY (Latin) Blue jay. US writer Jay McInerney and the wealthy Jay Gatsby from F. Scott Fitzgerald's novel *The Great Gatsby* are a couple of the famous men with this name who have pierced the public consciousness. Parents like Jay as a choice for their sons because it's a simple name, yet still conveys a bit of a sophisticated image, probably from the Gatsby connection. Variations: *Jae, Jai, Jave, Jaye, Jeays, Jeyes.*

JAYAKRISHNA (Hindu) Victorious Krishna.

JAYANT (Hindu) Victorious.

JAZEPS (Latvian) God will increase.

JAZON (Polish) Healer.

JEAN (French) He replaces. French version of John. Variations: *Jean-Francois, Jean-Michel, Jean-Phillipe, Jeannot.*

JEDEDISH (African-American) Unknown definition.

JEDIDIAH (Hebrew) Beloved of God. Variations: *Jed, Jedd, Jedediah, Jedidia, Yedidia, Yedidiah, Yedidya.*

JEDREK (Polish) Powerful man. Variations: *Jedrick, Jedrus.*

JEFFERSON (English) Son of Jeffrey.

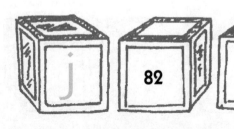

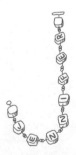

JEFFREY (German) Peace. Jeffrey was one of the most popular names in the 1970s, but like many names that are strongly tied with a particular point in time, Jeffrey is declining in popularity today. When parents do choose it, they tend to select one of its more unusual spellings. Jeffrey and its variations beginning with 'G' have been extremely popular throughout Europe for many centuries. Notable Geoffreys include Geoffry Chaucer, British politician Sir Geoffrey Howe and cricketer Geoffrey Boycott. Variations: *Geoff, Geoffrey, Geoffry, Gioffredo, Jeff, Jefferies, Jeffery, Jeffries, Jeffry, Jefry.*

JEHAN (French) God is good.

JEHU (Hebrew) The Lord is King.

JELA (African: Swahili) The father is in jail during birth.

JELANI (African: Nigerian) Strong. Variations: *Jalani, Jehlani.*

JENDA (Czech) God is good.

JENKIN (Flemish) Little John. Variations: *Jenkins, Jenkyn, Jenkyns.*

JENSI (Hungarian) Well born. Variations: *Jenci, Jens.*

JEPHTHA (Hebrew) God sets free.

JEREMY (Hebrew) The Lord exalts. Jeremy has been a popular name among parents in the last couple of decades. Famous Jeremys include actor Jeremy Irons and a frog in one of Beatrix Potter's books named Jeremy Fisher. However, like its counterpart Jason, Jeremy has become a bit too popular for some, who decide to opt for one of the many variants available. Variations: *Jem, Jemmie, Jemmy, Jeramee, Jeramey, Jeramie, Jere, Jereme, Jeremey, Jeremi, Jeremia, Jeremias, Jeremie, Jerimiah, Jeromy, Jerr, Jerrie, Jerry.*

JERIAH (Hebrew) God sees.

JERICHO (Arabic) City of the moon. Variation: *Jerico.*

JERMAINE (German) German. Variations: *Jermain, Jermane, Jermayne.*

JERNEY (Slavic) Unknown definition.

JEROME (Greek) Sacred name. Name of a saint. Other notable bearers are Jerome K. Jerome, Jerome Kern and Jerome Robbins. Variations: *Jeron, Jerone, Jerrome.*

JERRELL (African-American) Newly created. Variations: *Gerrell, Jarell, Jarrel, Jarrell, Jeriel, Jerriel, Jerul.*

JERRICK (African-American) Newly created. Variations: *Jerick, Jerrie.*

JERVIS (English) Unknown definition. Variation: *Gervase.*

JERZY (Polish) Farmer. Variation: *Jersey.*

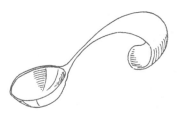

JESSE (Hebrew) God exists. Jesse Jackson, Jesse James and Jesse Owens are the most popular people with this name. Even though it has been thought of more as a girls' name in recent years, at its peak in the 1970s, it was extremely popular for boys. I've always liked Jesse more as a boys' name than for girls. Like a lot of other names that begin with the letter 'J', Jesse is great for all ages: little kids, teenagers, young fathers, and then even grandfathers. Jesse has staying power, and is hip to boot. Variations: *Jesiah, Jess, Jessey, Jessie, Jessy.*

JESUS (Hebrew) The Lord is my salvation.

JETHRO (Hebrew) Fame. Variation: *Jeth.*

JETT (English) Airplane.

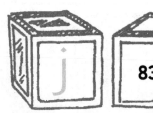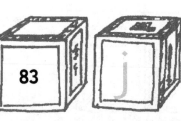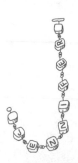

JEVIN (African-American) Unknown definition. Variation: *Jevon.*

JEX (English) Unknown definition.

JI (Chinese) Order.

JIAO-LONG (Chinese) Dragon.

JIBBEN (Gypsy) Life.

JIBRI (Arabic) Powerful.

JIE (Chinese) Wonderful person.

JIMOH (African: Swahili) Born on Friday.

JIN (Chinese) Gold.

JINAN (Arabic) Garden.

JINDRICH (Czech) Home ruler. Variations: *Jindra, Jindrik, Jindrisek, Jindrousek.*

JING (Chinese) Capital.

JING-QUO (Chinese) Ruler of a nation.

JING-SHENG (Chinese) Born in the capital.

JIRI (Czech) Farmer. Variations: *Jira, Jiran, Jiranek, Jiricek, Jirik, Jirka, Jirousek.*

JIRO (Japanese) Second son.

JITENDRA (Hindu) One who wins over the lord of the sky. Variations: *Jeetendra, Jitender.*

JIVAN (Hindu) Life. Variation: *Jivin.*

JOAB (Hebrew) Praise the Lord. Variation: *Jobe.*

JOACHIM (Hebrew) God will determine. Variations: *Joaquim, Joaquin.*

JOAH (Hebrew) God is his brother.

JOB (Hebrew) Oppressed. Variations: *Joab, Jobe, Joby.*

JOEL (Hebrew) God is Lord.

JOERGEN (Scandinavian) Farmer.

JOFFRE (French) Last name.

JOHAR (Hindu) Jewel.

JOHN (Hebrew) God is good. If you count all of the variations, spellings, and the language usages around the world, it's possible that more boys are named John than any other name. John cuts across all categories: in religion, there's John the Baptist and St. John the Divine; in movies, it seemed for a while in the 1950s, there was no other name to give to the lead male character (Johnny Angel, Johnny Guitar, Johnny Cool); and in entertainment, there's John Wayne, John Lennon, Sir John Gielgud, John Osborne, Sir John Betjeman, Johnny Depp, Johnny Cash, and Johnny Weissmuller, the actor who played Tarzan. With this prestige and a wide variety of Johns to choose from, it's a good bet that John in one or more of its forms will never be out of style. Variations: *Jack, Jackie, Jacky, Joao, Jock, Jockel, Jocko, Johan, Johann, Johannes, Johnie, Johnnie, Johnny, Jon, Jonam, Jone, Jonelis, Jonnie, Jonny, Jonukas, Jonutis, Jovan, Jovanus, Jovi, Jovin, Jovito, Jovon, Juan, Juanito.*

JOHNSON (English) Son of John. Variations: *Johnston, Jonson.*

JOJI (Japanese) Farmer.

JOJO (African: Ghanian) Born on Monday.

JOLON (Native American) Valley of the oak trees.

JO-LONG (Chinese) Large dragon.

JOMEI (Japanese) Light.

JONAH (Hebrew) Dove. Biblical book. Variations: *Jonas, Yonah, Yonas, Yunus.*

JONATHAN (Hebrew) Gift from God. In the Bible, Jonathan was King Saul's oldest son and was best known as King David's best friend. Parents have liked Jonathan because it is based on a classic name – John – but is more distinctive. Other Jonathans include British theatre director Jonathan Miller, Irish clergyman and writer Jonathan Swift, British actor Jonathan Pryce and broadcasters Jonathan Dimbleby and Jonathan Ross. Variations: *Johnathan, Johnathen, Johnathon, Jon, Jonathen, Jonathon, Jonnie, Jonny, Jonothon.*

JONIGAN (African-American) Newly created.

JONTE (African-American) Newly created. Variations: *Johatay, Johate, Jontae.*

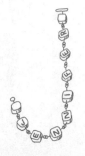
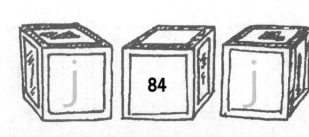

Some Popular Names from the 1950s

People in the 1950s were ripe with postwar optimism about the future of the world and their own kids.

Perhaps more so in the 1950s than in any other decade, parents travelled the tried-and-true route when it came to selecting names for their babies:

safe, almost corporate, names that also provided for some degree of variation as a baby grew into an adult.

Of course, who could predict that the decade that followed would bring such changes in the way we lived and in the choice of names?

Boys' Names

Robert	Gerald
Michael	Douglas
James	George
John	Frank
David	Patrick
William	Anthony
Thomas	Philip
Richard	Raymond
Gary	Bruce
Charles	Jeffrey
Ronald	Brian
Dennis	Peter
Steven	Frederick
Kenneth	Roger
Joseph	Carl
Mark	Dale
Daniel	Walter
Paul	Christopher
Donald	Martin
Gregory	Craig
Larry	Arthur
Lawrence	Andrew
Timothy	Jerome
Alan	Leonard
Edward	Henry

Girls' Names

Linda	Marilyn
Mary	Brenda
Patricia	Beverly
Susan	Carolyn
Deborah	Ann
Kathleen	Shirley
Barbara	Jacqueline
Nancy	Joanne
Sharon	Lynn
Karen	Marcia
Carol	Denise
Sandra	Gloria
Diane	Joyce
Catherine	Kathy
Christine	Elizabeth
Cynthia	Laura
Donna	Darlene
Judith	Theresa
Margaret	Joan
Janice	Elaine
Janet	Michelle
Pamela	Judy
Gail	Diana
Cheryl	Frances
Suzanne	Maureen

JORDAN (Hebrew) To descend. Jordan is a unisex name as well as an occasional last name, which has helped to make it as popular as it is. During the Crusades, the name caught on when soldiers brought water from the River Jordan back home with them to baptize their children. Variations: *Jorden, Jordy, Jori, Jorrin.*

JORGE (Spanish) Farmer. Variation: *Jorgen.*

JOSEPH (Hebrew) God will increase. Joseph is perhaps best known as Mary's husband in the Bible. This fact, and its many varieties around the world, may be the reason why the name has never fallen out of style. Famous Josephs have included Franz Joseph Haydn, novelist Joseph Conrad and US actor Joseph Cotten. Variations: *Jodi, Jodie, Jody, Jose, Josecito, Josef, Joselito, Josephe, Josephus, Josip.*

JOSHA (Hindu) Satisfaction.

JOSHUA (Hebrew) God is my salvation. Joshua was the leader of the Jews after Moses, and a book in the Bible is named for him. However, Joshua has only started to become popular since the 1960s, although other Biblical names have been used for centuries. Variations: *Josh, Joshuah.*

JOSIAH (Hebrew) God supports.Variations: *Josia, Josias, Josua.*

JOTHAM (Hebrew) God is perfect.

JOZA (Czech) God will increase. Variations: *Jozanek, Jozka.*

JUBAL (Hebrew) Ram's horn.

JUDE (Hebrew) Praise God. Once best known as the title character in Thomas Hardy's book *Jude the Obscure*, the Beatles song 'Hey Jude' brought it to prominence again, and the success of British actor Jude Law may make it fashionable once again. Variations: *Juda, Judah, Judas, Judd, Judson.*

JULIAN (Latin) Version of Julius. Saint. Variations: *Julien, Julion, Julyan.*

JULIUS (Latin) Young. Roman clan name. Variations: *Giulio, Julio.*

JUMAANE (African: Swahili) Born on Tuesday.

JUMAH (African: Swahili) Born on Friday. Variation: *Juma.*

JUMOKE (African: Nigerian) Child is beloved.

JUN (Chinese) Truth.

JUN LITZOQUE (Native American: Apache) Yellow horse.

JUNG-HWA (Korean) Virtuous.

JUNIOR (English) Young.

JURGEN (German) Farmer. Variation of George.

JURI (Slavic) Farmer. Variation of George.

JUSTIN (Latin) Just. Variations: *Justen, Justino, Justo, Juston, Justus, Justyn.*

JUWAN (African-American) Newly created.

JVALANT (Hindu) Bright. Variation: *Jwalant.*

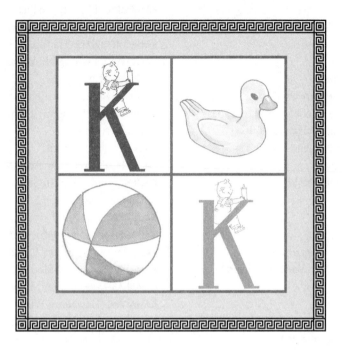

KABIL (Turkish) Last name.

KABIR (Hindu) Spiritual leader.

KABR (Hindu) Grass.

KACEY (English) He announces peace. Nickname for Casimir. Variation: *Kasey*.

KADAR (Arabic) Powerful. Variations: *Kade, Kedar*.

KADE (Gaelic) Swamp.

KADEEM (African-American) Newly created.

KADIN (Arabic) Friend. Variation: *Kadeen*.

KADIR (Arabic) Green. Variation: *Kadeer*.

KADMIEL (Hebrew) God is first.

KADO (Japanese) Entrance.

KAELAN (Gaelic) Powerful soldier. Variations: *Kalan, Kalen, Kalin*.

KAEMON (Japanese) Right-handed.

KAFELE (African: Malawian) Worth dying for.

KAGA (Native American) Writer.

KAHAAHEO (Hawaiian) We are proud of this one.

KAHAIAOKAPONIA (Hawaiian) One who sacrifices.

KAHAKUOKAHALE (Hawaiian) Ruler at home.

KAHANA (Hebrew) Priest.

KAHANU (Hawaiian) He breathes.

KAHATUNKA (Native American: Osage) Raven. Variation: *Caxe Tonkah*.

KAHAWAI (Hawaiian) River. Variation: *Kaheka*.

KAHEKAALOHI (Hawaiian) Pool that shines.

KAHELEMEAKUA (Hawaiian) He who walks with God.

KAHGEGWAGEBOW (Native American: Ojibwa) Eternal.

KAHIL (Turkish) Young. Kahil is a name that is popular in many different countries, not just Turkey. In Hebrew, it means perfect; in Greece, it means beautiful. Up until the 1970s, the form of the name most often seen was Cahil, the English version of this name. However, African-American families have made this name more popular. Variations: *Cahil, Kahlil, Kaleel, Khaleel, Khalil.*

KAHO (Polynesian) Arrow.

KAHUA (Hawaiian) Fort.

KAI (Hawaiian) Sea.

KAIHAU (Polynesian) Leader.

KAIHE (Hawaiian) One who throws a spear.

KAIHEKOA (Hawaiian) One who is brave with a spear.

KAIKALA (Hawaiian) Caesar. Variation: *Kaisara.*

KAIKEAPONA (Hawaiian) One who learns.

KAILAHI (Polynesian) To gorge.

KAILINEMO (Hawaiian) Smooth skin.

KAIPO (Hawaiian) Lover.

KAISER (Bulgarian) Hairy.

KAJ (Greek) Earth.

KAJETAN (Polish) Unknown definition.

KAKAIO (Hawaiian) God remembers. Variations: *Kakalia, Zakaria.*

KAKANA (Hawaiian) Powerful.

KAKAU (Polynesian) Swim.

KAKELAKA (Hawaiian) Biblical name.

KAKUMULANI (Hawaiian) Bottom of the sky.

KALA (Hindu) Black.

KALAILA (Hawaiian) Unknown definition. Variation: *Kalaida.*

KALANI (Polynesian) Gallon.

KALAUKA (Hawaiian) Hawaiian version of Claude. Roman clan name. Variation: *Kalauda.*

KALAWINA (Hawaiian) Hairless. Variation: *Kalavina.*

KALE (Hawaiian) Man. Variations: *Kalolo, Karolo.*

KALEA (Hawaiian) Joy.

KALECHI (African: Nigerian) Praise God.

KALEO (Hawaiian) One voice.

KALEOLANI (Hawaiian) Heavenly sounds.

KALEPA (Hawaiian) Faithful. Variation: *Kaleba.*

KALHANA (Hindu) Name of twelfth-century poet.

KALIDASA (Hindu) Black servant. Variation: *Kalidas.*

KALIKAU (Polynesian) Athletic.

KALIKIANO (Hawaiian) One who follows God.

KALIKOHEMOLELE (Hawaiian) Perfect son.

KALIL (Hebrew) Wreath. Variation: *Kailil.*

KALINGA (Hindu) Bird.

KALINO (Hawaiian) Brilliant.

KALIPEKONA (Hawaiian) Town on a cliff. Variation: *Kalifetona.*

KALIQ (Arabic) Artistic.

KALIU (Hawaiian) Unknown definition. Variation: *Dariu.*

KALKIN (Hindu) Hindu god.

KALMIN (Scandinavian) Man. Variation: *Kalle.*

KALOGEROS (Greek) Fair old ace.

KALOOSH (Armenian) Blessed event.

KALU (Hindu) Name of founder of the Sikh religion.

KAMAHA (Hawaiian) Sleeping one.

KAMAKAKOA (Hawaiian) Brave eye.

KAMAKANI (Hawaiian) Wind.

KAMAL (Arabic) Perfect. Like many of the other Arabic and Turkish names for boys that begin with 'K' Kamal is becoming more popular, especially among African-American families. Variations: *Kameel, Kamil.*

KAMALIELA (Hawaiian) God is my reward.

KAMALUHIAKAPU (Hawaiian) Serenity.

KAMANGENI (African: Malawian) Relative.

KAMAU (African: Kenyan) Warrior.

KAMBAN (Hindu) Twelfth-century poet.

KAMEKONA (Hawaiian) Strong man. Variation: *Samesona.*

KAMENOSUKE (Japanese) Turtle's helper.

KAMOKU (Hawaiian) Island.

KAMUELA (Hawaiian) Biblical prophet. Variation: *Samuela.*

KAMUZU (African: Nguni) Medicine.

KANA (Hawaiian) God is my judge. Variations: *Dana, Daniela, Dano, Kaniela.*

KANAI (Hawaiian) Winner.

KANAKANUI (Hawaiian) Big man.

KANALE (Hawaiian) Hawaiian version of Stanley. Variation: *Sanale.*

KANALOA (Hawaiian) A major Hawaiian god.

KANE (Welsh) Beautiful; (Japanese) Golden. First taken up by English speakers in the 1950s, it is chiefly used in Australia and the USA, where it is becoming more popular for both boys and girls. One popular variation has been introduced by superstar actor Keanu Reeves. Variations: *Kain, Kaine, Kayne, Keanu.*

KANEHOOMALU (Hawaiian) Peaceful man.

KANG (Chinese) Healthy.

KANG-DAE (Korean) Powerful.

KANGI (Native American: Sioux) Raven. Variation: *Kangee.*

KANGI SUNKA (Native American: Sioux) Crow dog.

KANIEL (Hebrew) Reed. Variations: *Kan, Kani, Kanny.*

KANJI (Japanese) Tin.

KANTU (Hindu) Happy.

KANU (Hindu) Beautiful.

KANZAN (African-American) Unknown definition.

KAPA (Polynesian) Attack.

KAPALAOA (Hawaiian) Ivory.

KAPALEKANAKA (Hawaiian) Protector of man.

KAPALI (Hawaiian) Cliff.

KAPELIELA (Hawaiian) God is my strength. Variation: *Gaberiela.*

KAPENI (African: Malawian) Knife.

KAPILA (Hindu) Monkey.

KAPILDEV (Hindu) Hindu god.

KARAM (Arabic) Charitable. Variations: *Kareem, Karim.*

KARDAL (Arabic) Mustard seed.

KARDAMA (Hindu) Kapila's father.

KARE (Scandinavian: Norwegian) Large.

KAREEM (Arabic) Its definition, generous, is one of the ninety-nine qualities ascribed to God in the Koran. Variations: *Karim, Karime.*

KAREL (Czech) Man. Variations: *Karlicek, Karlik, Karlousek, Karol, Karoly.*

KARIF (Arabic) Born in the autumn. Variation: *Kareef.*

KARIM (Hindu) Valuable. Variation: *Kareem.*

KARIO (African-American) Variation of Mario.

KARL (German) Man. Variations: *Karlen, Karlens, Karlin.*

KARNAK (Hindu) Heart.

KARNEY (Irish) The winner. Variations: *Carney, Carny, Karny.*

KARNIK (Hindu) Control.

KARR (Scandinavian) Swamp.

KASEKO (African: Zimbabwean) To tease.

KASI (Hindu) Bright.

KASIB (Arabic) Fertile. Variation: *Kaseeb.*

KASIM (Arabic) Divided. Variation: *Kaseem.*

KASIMIR (Slavic) He announces peace.

KASIYA (African: Malawian) Trip.

KASPAR (Persian) Protector of wealth. Variation: *Kasper.*

KASS (German) Blackbird. Variations: *Kasch, Kase.*

KATEB (Arabic) Writer.

KATOA (Polynesian) Complete.

KATSUTOSHI (Japanese) Outsmart.

KAUFANA (Polynesian) Bow.

KAUL (Arabic) Trustworthy. Variations: *Kahlil, Kalee, Khaleel, Khalil.*

KAULANA (Hawaiian) Famous.

KAULO (Hawaiian) To borrow. Variation: *Saulo*.

KAUMAVAE (Polynesian) Split up.

KAVANAGH (Irish) One who follows Kevin.

KAVI (Hindu) Poet.

KAVINDRA (Hindu) God of the poets.

KAWA (Native American: Apache) Great.

KAWIKA (Hawaiian) Beloved. Variations: *Davida, Kewiki*.

KAWIKANI (Hawaiian) Strong man.

KAY (Welsh) Joy.

KAYAM (Hebrew) Stable.

KAYIN (African: Nigerian) Famous.

KAYODE (African: Nigerian) Brings joy.

KAZUO (Japanese) First son.

KEAHI (Hawaiian) Fire.

KEAHILANI (Hawaiian) Heavenly fire.

KEAKA (Hawaiian) God is good.

KEALA (Hawaiian) Pleasant odour.

KEALAALOHI (Hawaiian) Brilliant path.

KEALAMAULOA (Hawaiian) Everlasting road.

KEANE (English) Sharp. Once common in Ireland, where it was particularly associated with the O'Hara family. Variations: *Kean, Keen, Keene*.

KEARN (Irish) Dark. Variation: *Kern*.

KEARNEY (Irish) The winner. Variations: *Karney, Karny, Kearny*.

KEATON (English) Hawk nest. Variations: *Keeton, Keiton, Keyton*.

KEAZIAH (African-American) Cassia.

KEB (Egyptian) Egyptian god.

KEDAR (Hindu) God of mountains.

KEDEM (Hebrew) Old.

KEEFE (Irish) Beloved. Variations: *Keefer, Keifer*.

KEEGAN (Irish) Small and passionate. Besides being a perfect name for a little boy who's always getting into trouble, Keegan is also considered to be the astrolog-

ical sign of fire, which includes Sagittarius, Leo and Aries. Variations: *Kagen, Keagan, Keegen, Kegan*.

KEELAN (Irish) Small and skinny.

KEELEY (Irish) Handsome. Variations: *Kealey, Kealy, Keelie, Keely*.

KEENAN (Irish) Small and old. Variations: *Keenen, Keenon, Kenan, Kienan, Kienen*.

KEFENTSE (African: Botswana) Conqueror.

KEFIR (Hebrew) Lion cub.

KEFU (Polynesian) Blond hair.

KEHINDE (African: Nigerian) Second-born of twins.

KEIJI (Japanese) Careful.

KEIKEMAMAKE (Hawaiian) Desired.

KEINTIKEAD (Native American: Kiowa) White armour.

KEIR (Irish) Dark-skinned; swarthy. Variations: *Keiron, Kerr, Kieran, Kieron*.

KEITARO (Japanese) Blessed.

KEITH (Scottish) Forest. Keith was cool in the 1970s when a Rolling Stone had the name.

KEKA (Hawaiian) Appointed. Variation: *Seta*.

KEKILA (Hawaiian) Hawaiian version of Roman clan name. Variation: *Kikila*.

KEKOA (Hawaiian) Tree.

KEKOANU (Hawaiian) Powerful fighter.

KELALA (Hawaiian) Leader with a spear.

KELAYA (Hebrew) Dry grain.

KELBY (German) A farm by a spring. Variations: *Kelbey, Kelbie, Kellby*.

KELE (Native American: Hopi) Sparrow. Variation: *Kelle*.

KELEKOUO (Hawaiian) Observer. Variation: *Keli*.

KELEMENETE (Hawaiian) Gentle. Variation: *Kelemeneke*.

KELEPT (Polynesian) Faithful.

KELII (Hawaiian) Wealthy.

KELL (English) Spring.

KELLAGH (Irish) War.

KELLEN (English) Soldier. Variations: *Keelan, Keilan, Kelden, Kellan, Kelle.*

KELLI (Hawaiian) Chief.

KELLY (Irish) Warrior. Not too long ago, Kelly was a name given in equal measure to both boys and girls. But today, a boy with the name of Kelly is a rare thing indeed. Variations: *Kelley, Kellie.*

KELSEY (English) Island. Variations: *Kelsie, Kelsy.*

KELTON (English) Town of ships.

KELVIN (African-American) Unknown definition. Variations: *Keloun, Kelvan, Kelven, Kelvyn.*

KEMAL (Turkish) Honour.

KEMIKIUO (Hawaiian) Fertile.

KEMP (English) Fighter.

KEMPTON (English) Town of fighters.

KEMUEL (Hebrew) To help God.

KENAKUK (Native American: Kickapoo) Stubborn.

KENAN (Hebrew) To attain. Variation: *Cainan.*

KENDALL (English) Last name. Valley of the river Kent. Variations: *Kendal, Kendell.*

KENDRICK (English) Royal hero. Variations: *Kendricks, Kendrik, Kendryck.*

KENEKE (Hawaiian) Handsome. Variations: *Keneki, Kenete, Keneti.*

KENELM (English) Brave helmet.

KENIDS (African-American) Unknown definition.

KENIKA (Hawaiian) Hawaiian version of Dennis.

KENJI (Japanese) Second son.

KENLEY (English) Meadow of the king. Variations: *Kenlea, Kenlee, Kenleigh, Kenlie, Kenly.*

KENN (Welsh) Brilliant water.

KENNARD (English) Brave; powerful. Variations: *Kennaird, Kennerd.*

KENNEDY (Irish) Helmet head; ugly head. In the 1960s, Kennedy was a name given to boys to honour the esteemed family from Massachusetts and in tribute to the assassinated President John F. Kennedy. Variations: *Canaday, Canady, Kenneday.*

KENNETH (Irish) Handsome; sprung from fire. Helped along by the macho image of Barbie's boyfriend Ken, this name was the epitome of masculinity through the 1950s and 1960s. Today, however, it conjures up images of medieval England and the Knights of the Round Table, due to its appearance in a novel by Sir Walter Scott. Variations: *Ken, Kendall, Kenney, Kennie, Kennith, Kenny, Kenyon.*

KENT (English) County in England. This name seems to have first appeared in the mid-20th century.

KENTON (English) Town of kings.

KENTRELL (English) Unknown definition.

KENWARD (English) Brave protector.

KENWAY (English) Brave fighter.

KENYA (African-American) African country.

KENYON (Irish) Blond.

KEO (Hawaiian) God will increase.

KEOIA (Hawaiian) Life.

KEOKI (Hawaiian) Farmer.

KEOKUK (Native American: Sauk) Alert moves.

KEOLA (Hawaiian) Alive.

KEOLAMAULOA (Hawaiian) Redemption.

KEON (Irish) Well born. Variations: *Keyon, Kion.*

KEONI (Hawaiian) God is good.

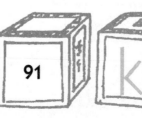

Some Popular Names from the 1960s

Even though the 1960s have a reputation as a free-wheeling, anything-goes decade, as the following lists show, the names parents were choosing for their babies were actually quite conventional. Most of the radical activity in politics, social outlook, and baby names took place in the second half of the decade, and of course, these choices are averaged with the more sedate first half; but the more unusual names didn't surface until the 1970s.

Boys' Names	Girls' Names
Michael	Mary
David	Susan
James	Lisa
John	Karen
Robert	Linda
William	Deborah
Mark	Kimberly
Richard	Donna
Jeffrey	Patricia
Charles	Cynthia

KEPAKIANO (Hawaiian) Hawaiian version of Sebastian. Variation: *Pakiana*.

KEPANO (Hawaiian) Crown. Variations: *Kekepana, Setepana, Tepano*.

KEREENYAGA (African: Kenyan) Mysterious mountain.

KEREL (African) Young man.

KEREM (Hebrew) Orchard.

KERILL (Irish) Unknown definition. Variation: *Coireall*.

KERMIT (Irish) Free of jealousy. This name will undoubtedly be associated with a frog for the next hundred years. However, there are some brave parents who are forging ahead and naming their baby boys after the *Sesame Street* muppet.

KERR (Scandinavian) Swamp.

KERRY (Irish) County in Ireland. Variations: *Kerrey, Kerrie*.

KERS (Hindu) A plant.

KERSEN (Indonesian) Cherry.

KERWIN (Irish) Dark. Variations: *Kerwen, Kerwinn, Kerwyn, Kirwin*.

KES (English) Falcon.

KESAVA (Hindu) Hairy.

KESHA (African-American) Newly created.

KESHON (African-American) Version of Sean. Variations: *Ke Sean, Ke Shon, Kesean*.

KESIN (Hindu) Panhandler with long hair.

KESSE (African: Ghanian) Fat.

KESTER (English) One who carries Christ in his heart. Variation of Christopher.

KETTIL (Scandinavian) Sacrificial cauldron. Variations: *Keld, Kjeld, Kjell, Kjetil*.

KEVIN (Irish) Handsome. This name was confined to Ireland until the early 20th century, when it was taken up by English speakers more widely. It reached its peak in the 1960s but it became a subject of ridicule in the 1980s – being a Kevin was the same as

being a nerd. However this does not seem to have hurt the fame of actors Kevin Kline, Kevin Bacon and Kevin Spacey. The name originated with a saint in the seventh century CE who headed a monastery in Dublin. Even today, St. Kevin is the patron saint of Dublin. Variations: *Kavan, Kev, Kevan, Keven, Kevon, Kevyn.*

KEWINI (Hawaiian) Beautiful birth.

KHALDUN (Arabic) Eternal.

KHALFANI (African: Swahili) Born to lead.

KHALID (Arabic) Eternal. Variations: *Khaled, Khaleed.*

KHAMISI (African: Swahili) Born on Thursday. Variation: *Khamidi.*

KHAN (Hindu) Expected.

KHANG (Vietnamese) Strong.

KHARAVELA (Hindu) Name of a king from the area of Kalinga.

KHAYRAT (Arabic) Beneficial act. Variation: *Khayri.*

KHUONG (Vietnamese) Help.

KHWAIA (Hindu) Master.

KIJANA (African-American) Unknown definition.

KIBBE (Native American) Bird of the night.

KIDD (English) Young goat.

KIEFER (German) Barrel maker. Variation: *Keefer.*

KIERAN (Irish) Dark. Variations: *Keiran, Keiren, Keiron, Kieron, Kyran.*

KIFIMBO (African: Swahili) A twig.

KIHO (African: Ugandan) Fog.

KIJIH (Native American) Walks quietly.

KIKEONA (Hawaiian) Man who hews. Variation: *Kileona.*

KIKIKWAWASON (Native American: Creek) Flash in the sky.

KIKINE (Hawaiian) Hawaiian version of Sidney. Variation: *Kikane.*

KILAB (Arabic) Dog.

KILCHD (Native American: Navajo) Red boy.

KILEY (English) Narrow land.

KILIAHOTE (Native American: Choctaw) Firebuilding.

KILILA (Hawaiian) Lord. Variation: *Kirila.*

KILIPEKA (Hawaiian) Famous oath. Variation: *Kilipaki.*

KILLIAN (Irish) Conflict. Killian is a noble name and was borne by several early Irish saints. Variations: *Kilian, Killie, Killy.*

KILOHANA (Hawaiian) Supreme.

KIM (Vietnamese) Gold.

KIM HU (Vietnamese) Golden jar.

KIMBALL (English) Leader in war. Variations: *Kim, Kimbal, Kimbell, Kimble.*

KIMEONA (Hawaiian) He has heard. Variation: *Kimona.*

KIMO (Hawaiian) To seize.

KIMOKEO (Hawaiian) Respect God. Variation: *Timoteo.*

KIN (Japanese) Golden.

KINCAID (Celtic) Leader in war.

KING (English) King. Famous Kings are film director King Vidor and jazz musician King Oliver.

KINGMAN (English) King's man. Variation: *Kinsman.*

KINGSLEY (English) Meadow of the King. If it weren't for the actor Ben Kingsley, the writer Charles Kingsley and the novelist Kingsley Amis, most parents-to-be would not be aware of the possibility of using Kingsley for their sons. Variations: *Kingslea, Kingslie, Kingsly.*

KINGSTON (English) Town of the king. Variation: *Kinston.*

KINGSWELL (English) Well of the king.

KINNARD (Irish) Top of the hill. Variation: *Kinnaird.*

KIONIKIO (Hawaiian) Hawaiian version of Dionysius. Variation: *Dionisio.*

KIPILIANO (Hawaiian) One from Cyprus. Variation: *Kipiriano.*

KIPP (English) Hill with a sharp peak. Variations: *Kip, Kipper, Kippie, Kippy.*

KIRAL (Turkish) King.

KIRAN (Hindu) Ray of light.

KIRBY (English) Village of the church. Variations: *Kerbey, Kerbi, Kerbie, Kirbey, Kirbie.*

KIRI (Cambodian) Mountain.

KIRIL (Greek) The Lord. Variations: *Kirillos, Kyril.*

KIRK (Scandinavian: Norwegian) Church. Kirk was once an extremely appealing name, owing to the success of Michael's father, Kirk Douglas. Variations: *Kerk, Kirke.*

KIRKLEY (English) Church meadow. Variations: *Kirklea, Kirklee, Kirklie, Kirkly.*

KIRKWELL (English) Church spring.

KIRKWOOD (English) Church forest.

KIRTON (English) Church town.

KISTNA (Hindu) Delightful. Variation: *Kistnah.*

KITO (African: Swahili) Jewel.

KITSTSUI SHAMKIN (Native American: Nez Perce) Metal shirt.

KITWANA (African: Swahili) Pledged to live.

KIUKIKOPA (Hawaiian) Christlike. Variation: *Kirisitopa.*

KIVI (African-American) One who lives by a stone.

KIYIYAH (Native American: Nez Perce) Wailing wolf.

KIYOKAYA (Native American: Sauk) Alert.

KIYOSHI (Japanese) Silent.

KIZZA (African: Ugandan) Born after twins.

KLAH (Native American: Navajo) Left-handed.

KLAUS (German) Victorious people. Short for Nicholas. I don't think this name is going to be on the top ten list anytime soon, what with such personalities as Klaus Barbie, Claus von Bulow, and the ubiquitous Santa all boasting this name. Variations: *Claes, Claus, Clause, Klaas, Klaes.*

KLEMENS (Polish) Mild; compassionate. Variation: *Klement.*

KLIMENT (Czech) Gentle.

KNIGHT (English) Unknown definition. Last name.

KNOTON (Native American) The wind.

KNOWLES (English) Grassy hill. Variations: *Knolls, Nowles.*

KNOX (English) Hills.

KNUD (Scandinavian: Danish) Kind.

KNUTE (Scandinavian: Danish) Knot.

KOAMALU (Hawaiian) Brave peace.

KODWO (African: Ghanian) Born on Monday.

KOFI (African: Ghanian) Born on Friday.

KOHANA (Native American: Sioux) Fast.

KOI (Native American: Choctaw) Panther.

KOICE (African-American) Variation of Royce.

KOJI (Japanese) Child.

KOJO (African: Ghanian) Born on Monday.

KOKAYI (African: Zimbabwean) Call the people.

KOKUDZA (African) Short-lived.

KOLAIAH (Hebrew) Voice of God. Variations: *Kolaia, Kolaya, Kolia, Koliya, Kolya.*

KOLOMALU (Polynesian) Shelter.

KOMAKI (Hawaiian) Hawaiian version of Tom. Variations: *Kamaki, Koma, Toma.*

KOMINIKO (Hawaiian) Belonging to God. Variation: *Dominigo.*

KOMOKU (Japanese) God of the south.

KONA (Hawaiian) Leader of the world. Variation: *Dona.*

KONANE (Hawaiian) Bright moonlight.

KONANIAH (Hebrew) God is settled. Variations: *Konania, Konanya.*

KONDO (African: Swahili) War.

KONDWANI (African: Malawian) Happy.

KONG (Chinese) Empty.

KONIESCHGUANOKEE (Native American: Delaware) God of daylight.

KONISH AUTASSIN (Native American: Nez Perce) Injured bird.

KONO (Native American: Miwok) Squirrel with a pine nut.

KONTAR (African: Ghanian) Only child.

KONUR (Scandinavian) Ancient mythological figure.

KOOLKOOL SNEHEE (Native American: Nez Perce) Red owl.

KOOPNEE (Native American: Nez Perce) Broken.

KOPANO (African: Botswana) Union.

KORB (German) Basket.

KOREN (Hebrew) Shining.

KORESH (Hebrew) To dig. Variations: *Choreish, Choresh.*

KORNEL (Czech) Horn. Variations: *Kornek, Nelek.*

KORT (Scandinavian) Wise counsellor.

KORUDON (Greek) Man with a helmet.

KOSMY (Polish) Universe.

KOSOKO (African: Nigerian) Without hoe.

KOSTI (Scandinavian: Finnish) Staff of God.

KOUKAKALA (Hawaiian) Black. Variation: *Dougalasa.*

KOVAR (Czech) Smith.

KPODO (African: Ghanian) First-born of twins.

KRISHNA (Hindu) Pleasing. Variations: *Krisha, Krishnah.*

KRUIN (African) Mountaintop.

KSAWERY (Polish) Polish version of Xavier.

KUAIKA (Hawaiian) White. Variation: *Duaita.*

KUBA (Czech) One who replaces. Variation of Jacob. Variation: *Kubo.*

KUDYAUKU (African: Malawian) Feast.

KUFUO (African: Ghanian) Father feels the pains of birth.

KUKANE (Hawaiian) Masculine.

KULAKINAH (Native American: Cherokee) Stag. Variations: *Kilakina, Kullageenah.*

KULAMAUU (Hawaiian) Pasture.

KULIKEFU (Polynesian) Yellow dog.

KULTANO (Hawaiian) Light beard.

KUMAKICHI (Japanese) Lucky.

KUMAR (Hindu) Son.

KUN (Chinese) Universe.

KUNEI (Polynesian) He is present.

KUPAALANI (Hawaiian) Loyal in spirit.

KUPER (Hebrew) Red hair.

KUZIH (Native American) Fast talker.

KWABENA (African: Ghanian) Born on Tuesday.

KWACHA (African: Malawian) Morning.

KWAKOU (African: Ghanian) Born on Wednesday. Variations: *Kwako, Kwaku.*

KWAMIN (African) Born on Saturday.

KWAN (Korean) Powerful.

KWANG-SUN (Korean) Benevolence.

KWAS (African: Ghanian) Born on Sunday.

KWAYERA (African: Malawian) Sunrise.

KWENDE (African: Malawian) Let's go.

KWESI (African) Born on Sunday.

KWIATOSLAW (Polish) Glorious flower.

KWINTYN (Polish) Fifth.

KYAN (African-American) Variation of Ryan.

KYLE (Scottish) Narrow land. When I was at the beach last summer, there must have been at least four little boys under the age of five with the name of Kyle running around. Though Kyle is also a popular choice for girls these days, the name for boys made it into the top twenty most popular names of the 1990s. In Hebrew, it means crowned with laurel. Since the name is so newly popular, expect it to be prominent for the next five to ten years. Variations: *Kiel, Kile, Ky, Kyele, Kyler.*

KYROS (Greek) Master.

KYUBOK (Korean) Blessed.

KYUBONG (Korean) Distinguished.

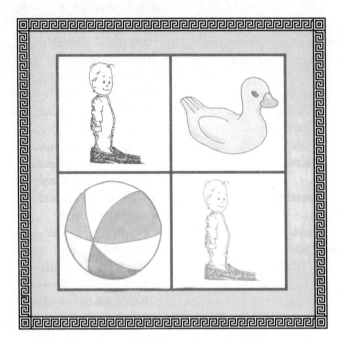

LA ROY (African-American) The king.

LA VONN (African-American) The small one. Variations: *La Vaun, La Voun*.

LAAKEA (Hawaiian) Holy light.

LABAN (Hebrew) White. Variation: *Lavan*.

LABHRAS (Irish) One from Laurentum. Variation: *Lubhras*.

LACHLAN (Scottish) Hostile. Variation: *Lachlann*.

LACHTNA (Irish) Grey.

LACY (French) Unknown definition. Variation: *Lacey*.

LADAN (Hebrew) Witness.

LADD (English) Young man. Variations: *Lad, Laddey, Laddie, Laddy*.

LADO (African) Second-born son.

LAEL (Hebrew) Belongs to God.

LAFAYETTE (French) Last name.

LAFI (Polynesian) Concealed.

LAHAHANA (Hawaiian) Sun's warmth.

LAHPATUPT (Native American: Nez Perce) Broken bone.

LAHPEEALOOT (Native American: Nez Perce) Geese landing in water.

LAIONELA (Hawaiian) Lion.

LAIRD (Scottish) Leader of the land.

LAIS (East Indian) Lion.

LAKE (English) Body of water.

LAKISTA (African-American) Unknown definition.

LAKOCHETS KUNNIN (Native American: Nez Perce) Blanket.

LAKSHMAN (Hindu) Wealthy.

LAKSHMIDAS (Hindu) Servant of the goddess of beauty.

LAL (Hindu) Lovely.

LALLO (Native American: Kiowa) Little boy.

LAMAR (Latin) The sea. In German, the name Lamar also means having lots of land. Variations: *Lamarr, Lemar, Lemarr.*

LAMBERT (German) Bright land. Variations: *Lambard, Lampard;* (Scandinavian) Famous land. Variation: *Lammert.*

LAMOND (African-American) Lawyer. Variations: *La Mond, La Monde, Lammond.*

LAMONTE (African-American) Mountain. Variation: *Lamont.*

LANCELOT (French) Servant. Variations: *Lance, Lancelott, Launcelot.*

LANDER (English) Landlord. Variations: *Landers, Landor.*

LANDON (English) Grassy meadow. The name Landon is a great name for a boy with literary aspirations. Variations: *Landan, Landen, Landin.*

LANDRY (English) Leader.

LANE (English) One who lives near the lane. Variations: *Laine, Layne.*

LANG (Norse) Tall. Variation: *Lange.*

LANGDON (English) Long hill. Variation: *Langden.*

LANGFORD (English) Long ford.

LANGILEA (Polynesian) Thunder.

LANGILOA (Polynesian) Storm.

LANGLEY (English) Long meadow. Variations: *Langlea, Langlee, Langleigh, Langly.*

LANGSTON (English) Long town. Variations: *Langsden, Langsdon.*

LANGUNDO (Native American) Serene.

LANGWARD (English) Tall protector.

LANGWORTH (English) Long paddock.

LANI (Hawaiian) Sky.

LANTY (Irish) Servant of St. Secundus. Variations: *Laughun, Leachlainn, Lochlainn, Lochlann.*

LANU (Native American: Miwok) Circle around a pole.

LAOGHAIRE (Irish) One who herds calves.

LAOISEACH (Irish) One from Leix, a county in Ireland. Variation: *Laoiahseach.*

LAP (Vietnamese) Independent.

LAPAELA (Hawaiian) God heals. Variation: *Lapaele.*

LAPHONSO (African-American) Noble. Variations: *Lafonso, LaPhonso.*

LAPIDOS (Hebrew) Torches. Variation: *Lapidoth.*

LARKIN (Irish) Cruel. Larkin is another one of those androgynous last-name names that is, as of this point, pretty underutilized. This makes it a great choice for parents who want to give their little boys a name that's different but not that different.

LARON (French) Thief.

LARRIMORE (French) One who provides arms. Variations: *Larimore, Larmer, Larmor.*

LARRY (English) Originally a nickname for Lawrence, but it's recently been considered a stand-alone name. Variations: *Larrie, Lary.*

LARS (Scandinavian) Crowned with laurel. It was one of the most popular boys names in Scandinavia in the 1960s and 1970s. Variation: *Larse.*

LASAIRIAN (Irish) Flame. Variations: *Laisrian, Laserian.*

LASZLO (Hungarian) Famous leader. Variations: *Laslo, Lazuli.*

LATAVAO (Polynesian) Homebody.

LATEEF (Arabic) Gentle. Variation: *Latif.*

LATHIUM (Scandinavian) Barn.

LATHROP (English) Farm with barns. Variations: *Lathe, Lay.*

LATIMER (English) Interpreter. Variation: *Latymer.*

LATUHILANG (Polynesian) Leader in the sky.

LAUAKI (Polynesian) Best.

LAULIWASIKAU (Native American: Shawnee) Rattle.

LAVAN (Hebrew) White.

LAVANAA (Hindu) Shining.

LAVESH (Hindu) Crumb.

97

LAVI (Hebrew) Lion.

LAWFORD (English) Ford on a hill.

LAWLER (Irish) One who mutters. Variations: *Lawlor, Lollar, Loller*.

LAWRENCE (English) Crowned with laurel. The name Lawrence has been popular with great regularity since it first emerged in the third century CE; St. Lawrence was a martyr. Throughout the ages, this name has made regular appearances in the work of Shakespeare and in other literature and films, including *Lawrence of Arabia*. Lawrence was a very popular name in the 1940s and 1950s, but even back then parents were actively considering variations of the name, which is how we ended up with Lorne Green, of *Bonanza* fame. Today, parents are once again choosing the name Lawrence for their sons. Other notable Larrys are Sir Laurence Olivier, Larry Hagman, Lawrence Durrell and Larry Adler. Variations: *Larry, Laurance, Laurence, Laurencio, Laurens, Laurent, Laurenz, Laurie, Lauris, Laurus, Lawrance, Lawrey, Lawrie, Lawry, Loren, Lorence, Lorencz, Lorens, Lorenzo, Lorin, Lorry, Lowrance*.

LAWSON (English) Son of Lawrence.

LAWTON (English) Town on a hill. Variation: *Laughton*.

LAZARUS (Hebrew) God's help. Variations: *Eleazer, Laza, Lazare, Lazaro, Lazzro*.

LE SONN (African-American) Newly created.

LEANDER (Greek) Lion man. Variations: *Leandre, Leandro, Leandros*.

LEBEN (Hebrew) Life.

LEBNA (Ethiopian) Spirit.

LECHOSLAW (Polish) Glory of the Poles. Variations: *Lech, Leslaw, Leszek*.

LEE (English) Meadow. Since the time of Confederate general Robert E. Lee, it seems that this name has always been hugely popular, both as a first and last name and as a good name for both boys and girls. Today, parents who see the simple spelling of Lee as a bit too run-of-the-mill are frequently choosing the variant Leigh. Or, more frequently, they are tacking it on to the end of another boys' name, creating names like Lynnlee and Huntleigh. Actors Lee J. Cobb and Lee Marvin and golfers Lee Trevino and Lee Westward have contributed to the visibility of this name. Variation: *Leigh*.

LEE RON (African-American) Newly created.

LEGGETT (French) Messenger. Variations: *Legate, Leggitt, Liggett*.

LEI (Chinese) Thunder.

LEIBEL (Hebrew) My lion. Variation: *Leib*.

LEIF (Scandinavian: Norwegian) Beloved. Leif is a great choice for parents who like the name Lee but who need something a little bit more exciting. Famous Leifs have included Leif Garrett and Leaf Phoenix, brother of the late River. Variations: *Leaf, Lief*.

LEIGHTON (English) Town by the meadow. Variations: *Layton, Leyton*.

LEITH (Scottish) Broad river.

LEKEKE (Hawaiian) Powerful leader.

LEL (Gypsy) He takes.

LELAND (English) Meadow land.

LEMUEL (Hebrew) Devoted to God. Variations: *Lem, Lemmie, Lemmy, Lemy*.

LEN (Native American: Hopi) Flute.

LENI (Polynesian) Now.

LENNO (Native American) Man.

LENNON (Irish) Cape.

LENNOR (Gypsy) Summer.

LENNOX (Scottish) Many elm trees. Scottish and English surname occasionally used as a first name. Notable bearers include British composer Sir Lennox Berkely and British boxer Lennox Lewis. Variation: *Lenox*.

LENSAR (Gypsy) With his parents. Variation: *Lendar.*
LEO (Polynesian) Protect. Several early saints, various emperors of Constantinople, thirteen popes and, more recently, actors Leo G. Carroll and Leo McKern all shared the name. It was given a boost when Prime Minister Tony Blair and Cherie Booth named their fourth child Leo. Variations: *Leokau, Leontios, Leopold.*
LEON (Greek) Lion. Variations: *Leo, Leonas, Leone, Leonek, Leonidas, Leosko.*

LEONARD (German) Bold as a lion. Leonard owes most of its present visibility to popular culture. Hollywood actor Leonardo di Caprio, who has appeared in some very successful films including *Titanic, Romeo and Juliet*, and *Catch Me If You Can*, may be popularizing the name. In fact, given the name's positive and some-what exotic connotations, Leonard might be making a comeback. Nevertheless, several men who were named Leonard promptly gave up the name once they got into the entertainment field, including Tony Randall and Roy Rogers. Variations: *Len, Lenard, Lennard, Lenny, Leonardo, Leonek, Leonhard, Leonhards, Leonid, Leontes, Lienard, Linek, Lon, Lonnie, Lonny.*
LEONDRA (African-American) Lion.

LEOPOLD (German) Brave people. Variations: *Leo, Leupold.*
LEOR (Hebrew) I have light.
LEPEET HESSEMDOOKS (Native American: Nez Perce) Two moons.
LEPOLO (Polynesian) Attractive.
LERON (Hebrew) My song. Variations: *Lerone, Liron, Lirone, Lyron.*
LEROY (French) The king. Variations: *Le Roy, LeeRoy, Leeroy, LeRoi, Leroi, LeRoy.*
LESLIE (Scottish) Low meadow. One famous Leslie who held onto his name is the actor Leslie Howard; one who let go of it was Bob Hope. He had to or else he would have been known as Less Hope! Variations: *Les, Leslea, Lesley, Lesly, Lezly.*
LESTER (English) Last name. Area in Britain, Leicester. Like its cousin Leslie, Lester has gone way out of fashion. The most famous Lesters in recent years include US jazz musician Lester Cole and British jockey Lester Piggott. Variation: *Les.*
LETALESHA (Native American: Pawnee) Old knife.
LEVERETT (French) Baby rabbit. Variations: *Lev, Leveret, Leverit, Leveritt.*
LEVERTON (English) Farm town.
LEVI (Hebrew) Attached. Variations: *Levey, Levin, Levon, Levy.*
LEWIN (English) Beloved friend.
LEWY (Irish) Unknown definition. Variation: *Lughaidh.*
LEX (English) Lex, a shortened version of Alexander, has turned into an independent name.
LEYLAND (English) Uncultivated land.
LI (Chinese) Strength.
LIANG (Chinese) Good.
LIBERIO (Portuguese) Freedom.
LIBOR (Czech) Freedom. Variations: *Libek, Liborek.*

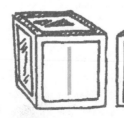

99

LIDIO (Portuguese) Masculine version of Lydia, area in Asia.

LIEM (Vietnamese) Honest.

LIF (Scandinavian) Life.

LIHAU (Hawaiian) Light rain.

LIKE (Chinese) Buddha is my guardian.

LIKO (Chinese) Buddhist nun.

LI-LIANG (Chinese) Powerful.

LIMU (Polynesian) Seaweed.

LINCOLN (English) Town by a pool. Variations: *Linc, Link*.

LINDBERG (German) Mountain of linden trees.

LINDELL (English) Valley of the linden trees. Variations: *Lindall, Lindel, Lyndall, Lyndell*.

LINDSAY (English) Island of linden trees. From the 19th century, Lindsay was used as a boys name, but since the 1930s it has been increasingly used for girls. A prominent male Lindsay is UK film director Lindsay Anderson. Variations: *Lindsee, Lindsey, Lindsy, Linsay, Linsey, Lyndsay, Lyndsey*.

LINFORD (English) Ford of linden trees. Variation: *Lynford*.

LINFRED (German) Gentle peace.

LINLEY (English) Meadow of linden trees. Variations: *Linlea, Linlee, Linleigh, Linly*.

LINTON (English) Town of linden trees. Variations: *Lintonn, Lynton, Lyntonn*.

LINUS (Greek) Flax. Probably most notable as Charlie Brown's companion in the Charles Schulz comic strip *Peanuts*.

LIONEL (Latin) Little lion. Variations: *Leonel, Lionell, Lionello, Lonell, Lonnell*.

LIRON (Hebrew) My song. Variation: *Lyron*.

LISIATE (Polynesian) Brave king.

LISIMBA (African: Malawian) Harmed by a lion.

Scandinavian Names – Cultural Traditions

Many of the names that we choose for our children are derived from names that are similar in other cultures, and, in some cases, identical.

Scandinavian names are certainly distinctive, but not that different, in many cases.

Here are some of the top names for boys and girls from Scandinavia in alphabetical order:

Boys' Names

Anders	Jens
Bjorn	Karl
Dag	Lars
Erik	Nils
Gunnar	Olaf
Gustaf	Oskar
Hans	Per
Ingvar	Rolf

Girls' Names

Anna	Heide
Astrid	Inga
Berta	Ingrid
Britta	Kari
Christina	Karin
Dagmar	Margareta
Elisabeth	Merete
Erna	Siane
Eva	Ulla
Grete	Ulrika

LISTER (English) A dyer.

LITTON (English) Town on the hill. Variation: *Lytton.*

LIU (African) Voice.

LIVINGSTON (English) Leif's settlement. Singer Livingston Taylor is perhaps the best-known Livingston around. The name itself is rarely used, but presents a good choice for parents who are looking for a name that is distinctive and just a bit different, but still commands respect. Variation: *Livingstone.*

LIWANU (Native American: Miwok) Growling bear.

LLEWELLYN (Welsh) Lionlike. Variations: *Lewellen, Lewellin, Llewelin, Llewelleyn.*

LLOYD (Welsh) Grey or sacred. Variation: *Loyd.*

LOCHAN (Hindu) Eyes.

LOCKE (English) Fort. Variations: *Lock, Lockwood.*

LODEWUK (Scandinavian) Famous in war. Variations: *Lodewijk, Ludovic.*

LODUR (Scandinavian) Ancient mythological figure.

LOGAN (Irish) Hollow in a meadow. Logan is one of those names that manages to convey a wealth of different connotations, all of them positive. What comes to mind? Swift, smart, sexy, and just a bit intriguing.

LOKELA (Hawaiian) Famous spear.

LOKENE (Hawaiian) Hawaiian version of Rodney.

LOKNI (Native American) Raining through the roof.

LOMAN (Irish) Little bare one; (Serbian) Delicate.

LOMAS (English) Unknown definition. Last name.

LOMBARD (Latin) Long beard.

LON (Irish) Brutal. Variations: *Lonnie, Lonny.*

LONATO (Native American) Flint.

LONG (Vietnamese) Dragon.

LONO (Hawaiian) God of farming.

LOPAKA (Hawaiian) Bright and famous.

LOPATI (Polynesian) Bright fame.

LORCAN (Irish) Little fierce one.

LORD (English) Lord.

LORIMER (Latin) Harness maker. Variation: *Lorrimer.*

LORING (German) Son of a famous soldier. Variation: *Lorring.*

LORNE (Scottish) Area in Scotland. Variation: *Lorn.*

LOT (Hebrew) Concealed.

LOU (Polynesian) Leaf. Variation: *Lu.*

LOUDON (German) A low valley. Variations: *Louden, Lowden, Lowdon.*

LOUIS (French) Famous warrior. Louis is an old and highly esteemed French name. Dating from the sixth century CE, Louis has been the name of no fewer than eighteen kings in France, a great jazz trumpeter, and my own father. Today, Louis is on the verge of making a comeback. It is that kind of traditional yet non-boring name that might just appeal to parents today. Variations: *Lew, Lewe, Lotario, Lothair, Lothar, Lothario, Lou, Luigi, Luis.*

LOUKANOS (Greek) Man from Lucania, an area in southern Italy. Variation: *Lukianos.*

LOUVAIN (French) City in Belgium.

LOVELL (English) Last name. Variation: *Lovel.*

LOWELL (English) Young wolf. Variation: *Lowel.*

LUBOMIERZ (Polish) Great love. Variation: *Lubomir.*

LUBOMIL (Polish) Lover of grace.

LUBORNIR (Czech) Great love. Variations: *Luba, Lubek, Lubor, Luborek, Lubornirek, Lubos, Lubosek, Lumir.*

LUBOSLAW (Polish) Lover of glory.

LUCAN (Irish) Light.

LUCAS (English) An area in southern Italy. Lucas is cool. It is a very popular name today, partially because it makes a great name for a little boy toddling around and a teenager who grows six inches a year as well as for a sensitive, handsome adult who you'd be proud to call your son. Lucas conveys a sense of intrigue, and I'd venture a guess that it's on the verge of becoming more frequently chosen, even for girls.

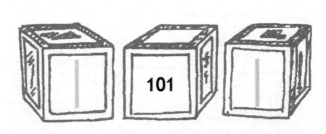

Luke, another version of the name, is also very popular, though it seems to be on the downswing while Lucas has not yet peaked. Variations: *Loukas, Luc, Lukas, Luke.*

LUCIUS (Latin) Light. Variations: *Luca, Lucan, Lucca, Luce, Lucian, Luciano, Lucias, Lucien, Lucio.*

LUDGER (Scandinavian) People with spear.

LUDLOW (English) Hill of the leader. Variation: *Ludlowe.*

LUDOMIERZ (Polish) Famous people.

LUDOMIR (Czech) Famous people. Variation: *Ludek.*

LUDOSLAV (Czech) Great people.

LUDOSLAW (Polish) Glorious people. Variation: *Lutoslaw.*

LUDVIK (Czech) Famous at war.

LUDWIG (German) Famous soldier.

LUGHAIDH (Irish) Unknown definition.

LUGONO (African: Malawian) Sleep.

LUISTER (African) One who listens.

LUKMAN (North African) Forecaster.

LULANI (Hawaiian) Pinnacle of heaven.

LUMHE CHATI (Native American: Creek) Red eagle.

LUNDY (Scottish) Child born on Monday.

LUNN (Irish) Strong; warlike. Variations: *Lon, Lonn.*

LUNT (Scandinavian) Grove of trees.

LUONG (Vietnamese) Bamboo.

LUTALO (African: Ugandan) Warrior.

LUTHER (German) Army people. Luther has been popular in the past as a middle name, probably owing to Martin Luther King. The visibility of singer Luther Vandross, however, has helped to make the name more popular as a first name.

LEA (Native American) Head shaker.

LYLE (French) The island. Lyle is one those wonderful, lazy names that conjures up long summer afternoons in the garden when it's too hot to do anything but drink a glass of lemonade. Singer Lyle Lovett only encourages this image and probably also the name's usage in coming years. Variations: *Lisle, Ly, Lyall, Lyell, Lysle.*

LYMAN (English) One who lives in the meadow. Variations: *Leaman, Leyman.*

LYNCH (Irish) Mariner.

LYNDAL (English) Valley with lime trees. Variations: *Lindal, Lineal.*

LYNDEN (English) Hill with lime trees. Variations: *Linden, Lyndon, Lynne.*

LYNFORD (English) Ford with lime trees. Variation: *Linford.*

LYNTON (English) Town with lime trees. Variation: *Linton.*

LYSANDER (Greek) Liberator. Variation: *Lisandro.*

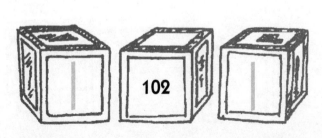

102

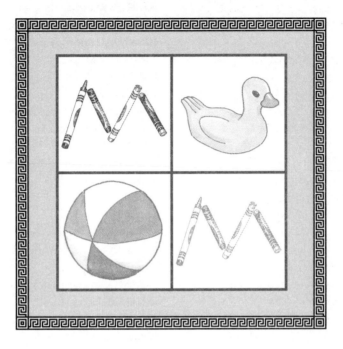

MAAKE (Polynesian) Warrior.

MAALIN (Hindu) Wreath.

MAANA (Polynesian) His.

MAASEIYA (Hebrew) God's work. Variations: *Maaseiah, Masai.*

MAASI (Polynesian) March.

MAC (Scottish) Son of. Variation: *Mack.*

MACADAM (Scottish) Son of Adam. Variations: *MacAdam, McAdam.*

MACALLISTER (Irish) Son of Alistair. Variations: *MacAlister, McAlister, McAllister.*

MACARDLE (Irish) Son of bravery. Variations: *MacArdell, McCardell.*

MACAULAY (Scottish) Son of the moral one.

MACBRIDE (Irish) Son of St. Brigid. Variations: *Macbryde, McBride.*

MACCABEE (Hebrew) Hammer. Variations: *Macabee, Makabi.*

MACCOY (Irish) Son of Hugh. Variations: *MacCoy, McCoy.*

MACCREA (Irish) Son of grace. Variations: *MacCrae, MacCray, MacCrea, McCrea.*

MACDONALD (Scottish) Son of Donald. The Macdonalds were a powerful Scottish clan. Variations: *MacDonald, McDonald.*

MACDOUGAL (Scottish) Son of the dark stranger. Variations: *MacDougal, McDougal.*

MACGOWAN (Irish) Son of the blacksmith. Variations: *MacGowan, Magowan, McGowan.*

MACHIR (Hebrew) Commerce.

MACHUPA (African: Swahili) One who likes to drink.

MACKENZIE (Irish) Son of a wise leader. Variations: *Mack, MacKenzie, Mackey, Mackie, McKenzie.*

MACKINLEY (Irish) Learned ruler. Variations: *MacKinley, McKinley.*

MACMAHON (Irish) Son of the bear. Variation: *McMahon.*

MACMURRAY (Irish) Son of the mariner. Variation: *McMurray.*

MACON (English) City in Georgia.

MACY (French) Matthew's estate. Variation: *Macey.*

MADDOX (Welsh) Generous. Variations: *Maddock, Madock, Madox.*

MADHAV (Hindu) Young.

MADISON (English) Son of the mighty warrior. Whether it's an avenue, a president, or a baby name, Madison is an up-and-comer, for both girls and boys. Variations: *Maddie, Maddison, Maddy, Madisson.*

MADU (African: Nigerian) People.

MADZIMOYO (African: Malawian) Water of life.

MAELEACHLAINN (Irish) Servant of St. Secundinus. Variations: *Maelsheachlainn.*

MAFI (Polynesian) Winner.

MAFILEOKAVEKA (Polynesian) Attractive winner.

MAFITEA (Polynesian) White-skinned winner.

MAFIULIULI (Polynesian) Dark-skinned winner.

MAGEE (Irish) Son of Hugh. Variations: *MacGee, McGee.*

MAGHNUS (Irish) Great. Variations: *Magnus, Manus.*

MAGUIRE (Irish) Son of the beige man. Variations: *MacGuire, McGuire, McGwire.*

MAHADEV (Hindu) Great god.

MAHARAJ (Hindu) Great king.

MAHASKA (Native American: Sioux) White cloud. Variations: *Mahushkah, Mohaska, Mohoska.*

MAHAVIRA (Hindu) Great hero. Variation: *Mahavir.*

MAHENDRA (Hindu) Great god of the sky.

MAHESA (Hindu) Great lord. Variation: *Mahisa.*

MAHESH (Hindu) Great ruler.

MAHIN (Hindu) Great.

MAHIR (Arabic) Capable.

MAHKAH (Native American: Sioux) Earth.

MAHMOUD (Hindu) Worthy. Variations: *Mahmood, Mahmud, Mehmood, Mehmoud, Mehmud.*

MAHON (Irish) Bear.

MAHPEE (Native American: Sioux) Sky.

MAIKALKEAKUA (Hawaiian) God is great.

MAIMUN (Arabic) Lucky.

MAINCHIN (Irish) Little monk. Variation: *Mannix.*

MAITLAND (English) Town in Britain.

MAJID (Hindu) Magnificent. Variations: *Magid, Majeed.*

MAJOR (Latin) Greater. Variations: *Majar, Majer, Mayer, Mayor.*

MAKALOHI (Polynesian) Slate.

MAKANAAKUA (Hawaiian) Gift from God. Variation: *Makanaokeakua.*

MAKANI (Hawaiian) The wind.

MAKARIOS (Greek) Blessed. Variations: *Macario, Macarios, Maccario, Maccarios, Makar.*

MAKARY (Polish) Blessed.

MAKATAIMESHEKIAKIAK (Native American: Sauk) Black sparrow.

MAKHPIA-LUTA (Native American: Sioux) Red cloud. Variations: *Makhpia-Sha, Makhpiya-Luta.*

MAKIMO (Hawaiian) Great.

MAKOTO (Japanese) Honesty.

MAKRAM (Arabic) Noble.

MAKYA (Native American: Hopi) One who hunts for eagles.

MALACHI (Hebrew) Messenger. Malachi was both a book in the Bible and the name of an Irish saint. As such, you wouldn't expect it to appear with any great frequency today, but this very old-fashioned name is suddenly becoming very popular. Variations: *Malachai, Malachie, Malachy, Malechy.*

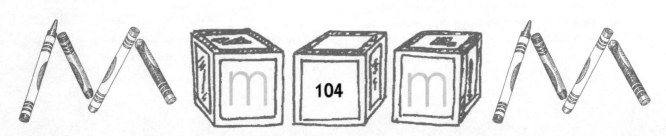

MALAKI (Hawaiian) Servant. Variation: *Malakoma*.

MALAWA (African: Malawian) Flowers.

MALCOLM (English) A servant. Popular in Scotland, four Scottish kings bore this name, one of whom succeeded Macbeth. It was taken up in England on a significant scale in the 1920s and 1930s and reached a peak in the 1950s before going into decline. Famous Malcolms include British land speed record holder Sir Malcolm Campbell, British conductor Sir Malcolm Sargent, novelist Malcolm Bradbury and US Black activist Malcolm X. Variations: *Malcolum, Malcom, Malkolm*.

MALEKO (Hawaiian) Warlike.

MALIK (Hindu) King. Variations: *Maliq, Mallik*.

MALIN (English) Little strong warrior. Variations: *Mallin, Mallon*.

MALKAM (Hebrew) God is their king. Variations: *Malcam, Malcham*.

MALKI (Hebrew) My king.

MALKIAH (Hebrew) God is my king. Variations: *Malkia, Malkiya, Malkiyahu*.

MALLORY (French) Sad. Variations: *Mallery, Mallorie, Malory*.

MALO (Polynesian) Winner.

MALONEY (Irish) Regular churchgoer. Variations: *Malone, Malony*.

MALU (Polynesian) Breeze.

MALUCH (Hebrew) Leader.

MALUHIA (Hawaiian) Peaceful.

MALUHIALAN (Hawaiian) Spiritual peace. Variation: *Malulani*.

MALUOKEAKUA (Hawaiian) Peace of God.

MALVERN (Welsh) Bare hill.

MAMDUH (Arabic) To approve.

MAMMEDATY (Native American: Kiowa) Walking.

MAMO (Hawaiian) Yellow bird.

MAMUN (Arabic) Faithful.

MAN (Vietnamese) Sharp mind.

MAN YOUNG (Korean) Long life and wealth.

MANAL (Arabic) To achieve.

MANAR (Arabic) Role model.

MANASE (Polynesian) Forgetful.

MANCHU (Chinese) Pure.

MANCO (Native American) King.

MANDALA (African: Malawian) Flowers.

MANDEL (German) Almond. Variation: *Mandell*.

MANDELA (African-American) Name of the former South African president.

MANDER (Gypsy) From me.

MANDONDO (African: Malawian) Drops.

MANFRED (English) Man of peace. Well known South African-born British pop singer Manfred Mann is probably best known with this name. Variations: *Manafred, Manafryd, Manfrid, Manfried, Mannfred, Mannfryd*.

MANIPI (Native American) Walking wonder.

MANISHEE (Native American: Sioux) Lame.

MANKATO (Native American: Sioux) Blue earth. Variations: *Mah-e-ca-te, Mahecate, Mon-eca-to, Monecato*.

MANLEY (English) Man's meadow. Variations: *Manlea, Manleigh, Manly*.

MANNING (English) Son of a man.

MANOACH (Hebrew) To rest. Variations: *Manoa, Manoah*.

MANSA (African) King.

MANSEL (English) In a clergyman's house. Variation: *Mansell*.

MANSFIELD (English) Field by a river.

MAN-SHIK (Korean) Foundation.

MANSOOR (Hindu) Victor.

MANSUR (Arabic) Divine assistance. Variation: *Mansour*.

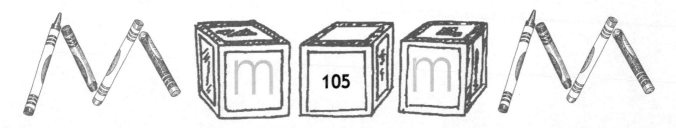

MANTON (English) Man's town. Variations: *Mannton, Manten.*

MANU (African: Ghanian) Second son; (Hawaiian) Bird. Variation: *Manuku;* (Hindu) God who gives laws.

MANUETOAFA (Polynesian) A bird in the desert.

MANUMAKALII (Hawaiian) Small bird.

MANUTAPU (Polynesian) Sacred bird.

MANVILLE (French) Good town. Variations: *Mandeville, Manvill.*

MAOLBHEANNACHTA (Irish) One looking for or who hopes for blessings.

MAOLCHOLM (Irish) Servant of St. Columba. Variations: *Maolcholuim, Maolcolm.*

MAOLMORDHA (Irish) Majestic chief.

MAON (Hebrew) House.

MAOZ (Hebrew) Strength.

MAQUI-BANASHA (Native American: Mesquakie) Bear cub.

MARAR (African: Zimbabwean) Earth.

MARCELLUS (Latin) Young warrior. Variations: *Marceau, Marcel, Marcelin, Marcello.*

MARCH (English) One who lives by a border.

African-American Names – Cultural Traditions

Back in my primary school, the white children had names like Larry, Henry, Danny, Michael; the typical white names of the 1960s and 1970s.

But there was one particular boy named Marquez, who was African-American, and I thought he had the most unusual name around.

Of course, since those days, African-American parents have basically cornered the market on coining names that are so pretty and/or distinctive that they virtually roll off the tongue: Ayeesha, LaRonda, Deshawn.

Technically, these are not specifically African names, but instead they combine African heritage with an African-American style that results in a name that is unique and attractive but not altogether unfamiliar.

Some critics eschew the trend because they view this as one example of how African-Americans are still considered to be far from the mainstream – 'A name shouldn't be a person's primary way she says, "Look at me, I'm here!"' is how one critic put it – but others view the names as wonderful examples of creativity as well as individuality.

Basically, many African-American names are created by taking a prefix – such as 'La-' for girls, and 'De-' for boys – and then adding another, frequently used, common name as the suffix.

Following is a list of these names:

Boys' Names

- Deandre
- Dejuan
- Delewis
- Delon
- Demarco
- Demond
- Denell
- Deole
- Deontae
- Deron
- Deshawn

Girls' Names

- Lapaula
- Larita
- Lashannon
- Lasharon
- Lashaun
- Lasheba
- Lashell
- Lasherri
- Lashona
- Latania
- Latasha
- Latesha
- Latrecia
- Latrice

MARCUS (Latin) Warlike. Common in ancient Rome, it was taken up in the middle of the 19th century by English speakers and is one of the more popular names that parents have been giving their sons these days. Variations: *Marco, Marcos.*

MARDEN (English) Valley with a pool.

MAREK (Czech) Warlike. Variations: *Marecek, Mares, Marik, Marousek.*

MARESHA (Hebrew) Peak.

MARID (Arabic) Defiant.

MARIO (Italian) Roman clan name. Considered to be the male version of Maria. Notable bearers of the name include singer Mario Lanza and racing driving Mario Andretti.

MARION (French) Bitter; defiant. The most famous bearer of the name was John Wayne, whose real name was Marion Michael Morrison.

MARK (English) Warlike. It seemed as if there were a million Marks in my school when I was growing up in the 1970s, and no one could really put their finger on why the name became so suddenly popular in the early 1960s when these kids were being named. In 1976, of course, Olympic swimmer Mark Spitz and his victories set off a whole new wave of babies named Mark, but it didn't seem to last as long as the first wave. Before these two recent waves, the most famous Marks were Mark Antony, St. Mark, and the writer Samuel Clemens, who is known by his pen name, Mark Twain. Today, parents who are partial to the name tend to choose one of the variations listed here and not its original incarnation. Variations: *Marc, Marco, Marko, Markos.*

MARKHAM (English) Homestead on the border.

MARLAND (English) Land near a lake.

MARLEY (English) Meadow near a lake. Variations: *Marlea, Marleigh, Marly.*

MARLON (French) Little hawk. Variation: *Marlin.*

MARLOW (English) Hill near a lake. Variation: *Marlowe.*

MARMION (French) Small one.

MARO (Japanese) Myself.

MARQUIS (African-American) Nobleman. Variations: *Markeece, Markeese, Markese, Marques, Marqui, Marquise.*

MARSDEN (English) Swampy valley. Variation: *Marsdon.*

MARSH (English) Swamp.

MARSHALL (French) One who cares for horses. It seems to me that the name Marshall conveys a sense of authority. Because it conveys such an in-charge tone, perhaps people in the military will prefer it for their kids, but for the rest of us, expect it to be quite an unusual choice. Variations: *Marschal, Marsh, Marshal.*

MARSTON (English) Town by a marsh.

MART (Turkish) Born during the month of March.

MARTIN (Latin) Warlike. Martin was always much more popular as a last name than a first name, except of course in the case of the reverend Martin Luther King, Jr., who was first christened with the name Michael. The feminine forms of Martin – Martina and Martine – seem to be more popular today than the male version. Most parents who use the name for their sons today tend to use it as a middle name. Notable celebrities with the name include Marty Wilde, Marty Feldman, Martin Amis and the central character in Charles Dickens' novel *Martin Chuzzlewit.* Variations: *Mart, Martan, Martel, Marten, Martey, Martie, Martinas, Martiniano, Martinka, Martino, Martinos, Martins, Marto, Marton, Marty, Martyn, Mertin.*

MARVIN (English) Mariner. Marvin Gaye and Marvin Hamlisch share the name. Variations: *Marv, Marvyn.*

MARWAN (Arabic) Unknown definition.

MARWOOD (English) Lake in a forest.

MASAHIRO (Japanese) Sage.

MASAMBA (African: Malawian) Leaves.

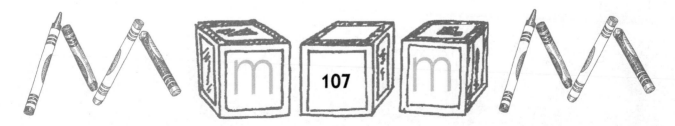

MASAO (Japanese) Sacred.

MASATO (Japanese) Fairness.

MASHAMA (African: Zimbabwean) Surprise.

MASHEMA (Native American: Kickapoo) Elk antlers. Variation: *Mashumah*.

MASIO (African-American) Twin. Nickname of Tomasio. Variation: *Macio*.

MASKA (Native American) Powerful.

MASLIN (French) Little twin. Variations: *Maslen, Masling*.

MASON (French) Stone carver or worker. Variations: *Mace, Masson*.

MASPERA MOHE (Native American: Sioux) Moose.

MASSE OLA (Native American: Creek) Sunrise.

MASUD (Arabic) Lucky. Variation: *Masiud*.

MASUN (French) Young

MATAFEO (Polynesian) Coral.

MATAIO (Hawaiian) Gift from God. Variation: *Makaio*.

MATANIAH (Hebrew) Gift from God. Variations: *Matania, Matanya, Matitia, Matitiah, Matityah, Matityahu, Mattaniah, Mattathias, Matya*.

MATEJ (Czech) Gift from God. Variations: *Mata, Matejek, Matejicek, Matejik, Matousek, Matyas, Matys, Matysek*.

MATENI (Polynesian) Warrior.

MATHER (English) Mighty army.

MATHGHAMHAIN (Irish) Bear.

MATO (Native American: Mandan) Bear.

MATO TOPE (Native American: Mandan) Four bears.

MATO WATAKPE (Native American: Sioux) Attacking bear.

MATOHINSDA (Native American: Sioux) Bear with no hair.

MATOK (Hebrew) Sweet.

MATOLO (Polynesian) Scour.

MATOPE (African: Zimbabwean) Last child.

MATOSKAH (Native American: Sioux) White bear.

MATSLMELA (Lesotho) Roots.

MATTAN (Hebrew) Gift. Variations: *Matan, Matena, Maton, Mattun*.

MATTHEW (Hebrew) Gift of the Lord. This name features in the Bible as one of the four evangelists and the author of the first gopsel. Matthew has been a very popular name, both 2,000 years ago and today. Matthew is a more interesting name than many of the other traditional Biblical names, for instance, John and James, but it is also immensely helped by the multitudes of attractive Hollywood men with the name. There's Matthew Broderick, Matthew Modine and Matt Dillon. And if Matthew doesn't strike your fancy, there are many variations for you to choose from to inject a little spice into your son's name. Variations: *Mateo, Mateus, Mathe, Mathew, Mathia, Mathias, Mathieu, Matias, Matt, Matteo, Matthaus, Matthia, Matthias, Mattias, Matty*.

MAUI (Hawaiian) God who discovered fire.

MAULI (Hawaiian) Dark-skinned.

MAURICE (Latin) Dark-skinned. The name came to England with the Normans and was relatively popular in medieval times, when it was usually given as Morris. It became fashionable again in the mid-19th century, by which time the modern spelling had evolved. Variations: *Maurey, Mauricio, Maurie, Mauris, Maurise, Maurizio, Maury, Morey, Morice, Morie, Moris, Moriss, Morrice, Morrie, Morris, Morriss, Morry*.

MAVERICK (American) Non-conformist.

MAWULI (African: Ghanian) God exists.

MAXFIELD (English) Mack's field.

MAXIMILIAN (Latin) Greatest. Variations: *Maksim, Maksimka, Maksum, Massimiliano, Massimo, Max, Maxi, Maxie, Maxim, Maxime, Maximilano, Maximiliano, Maximillian, Maximino, Maximo, Maximos, Maxy*.

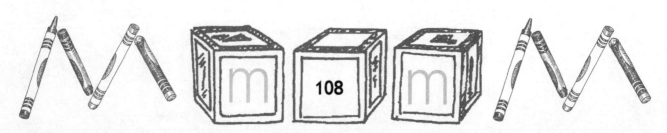

MAXWELL (Scottish) Marcus's well. Twenty years ago who could have ever foreseen the vast popularity of the name Max today? Parents who are choosing this name for their sons invariably give them the full name of Maxwell but refer to them as Max. Max is probably cool because it has an 'x' in it. In this case, and in the case of the name Max, the 'x' does not refer to a movie that you need to be eighteen or over to see, but a trend that is very hot that shows no signs of burning out anytime soon. Famous bearers include Canadian-born newspaper proprietor Max Aitkin, US playwright Maxwell Anderson and British comedian Max Wall. Variation: *Max*.

MAYER (Latin) Larger. Variations: *Mayor, Meier, Meir, Meirer, Meuer, Myer*.

MAYFIELD (English) Strong man's field.

MAYHEW (French) Gift from the Lord. Variation of Matthew.

MAYNARD (English) Hard strength. Variations: *Maynhard, Meinhard, Menard*.

MAYO (Irish) County in Ireland.

MAZI (African: Nigerian) Sir.

MAZIN (Arabic) Cloud.

MBWANA (African: Swahili) Master.

MEAD (English) Meadow. Variations: *Meade, Meed*.

MEALLAN (Irish) Little pleasant one. Variations: *Meldan, Mellan*.

MECISLAV (Czech) Glorious father. Variations: *Mecek, Mecik, Mecislavek*.

MEDWIN (German) Powerful friend.

MEHITABEL (Hebrew) God benefits. Mehitabel, another Biblical name, is perhaps best known as one of the characters in the book *Archy and Mehitabel* by the author Don Marquis; Archy was a cockroach and Mehitabel was a cat.

MEHTAR (East Indian) Prince.

MEIR (Hebrew) Bright one. Variations: *Mayer, Meyer, Myer*.

MELBOURNE (English) City in Australia. Variations: *Melborn, Melburn, Milbourne, Milburn, Millburn, Millburne*.

MELCHIOR (Polish) King.

MELDON (English) Mill on a hill. Variation: *Melden*.

MELDRICK (English) Boss at the mill.

MELECH (Hebrew) Ruler.

MELVILLE (English) Mill town.

MELVIN (Irish) Great chief. Although other clearly nerdy names have become popular today, even an actor with Mel Gibson's appeal doesn't seem to be popularizing this name – notice that he goes by the short form. Variations: *Malvin, Malvinn, Malvon, Malvonn, Mel, Melvern, Melvyn, Melwin, Melwinn*.

MENACHEM (Hebrew) Comforting. Variations: *Menahem, Mendel*.

MENASHE (Hebrew) Forgetful. Variations: *Mana, Manasseh, Mani, Menashi, Menashya*.

MENDEL (Hebrew) Wisdom. Variations: *Mendeley, Mendell*.

MENEWA (Native American: Creek) Great warrior. Variation: *Menawa*.

MENSAH (African: Ghanian) Third-born son.

MERCER (English) Shopkeeper. Variation: *Merce*.

MERED (Hebrew) Rebellion.

MEREDITH (Welsh) Great leader. Variations: *Meredyth, Merideth, Meridith*.

MERFIN (Welsh) Welsh king in the ninth century. Variation: *Merfyn*.

MERLIN (English) Falcon. Merlin actually originated as a name for girls, but the name gradually gravitated to common use for males. While actress Merle Oberon is the most famous female of this name, the name and its variations are mostly claimed by male celebrities:

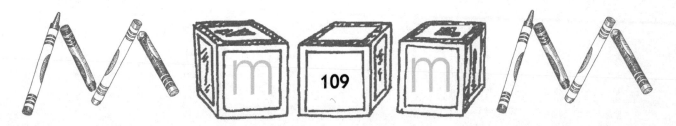

US country singer Merle Haggard and Merlyn Rees. Variations: *Marlin, Marlon, Merle, Merlen, Merlinn, Merlyn, Merlynn.*

MERRICK (English) Dark-skinned. Variation: *Merryck.*

MERRILL (English) Bright as the sea. Masculine version of Murie. Variations: *Meril, Merill, Merrel, Merrell, Merril, Meryl.*

MERRIPEN (Gypsy) Life.

MERRITT (English) Small and famous. Variations: *Merit, Meritt, Merrett.*

MERTON (English) Town by a lake. Variations: *Mertin, Mirtin, Murton, Myrton.*

MERVILLE (French) Small village.

MERVIN (Welsh) Sea hill. Variations: *Mervyn, Murvin, Murvyn.*

MESHACH (Hebrew) Unknown definition.

MESTIPEN (Gypsy) Fortune.

METHODIOS (Greek) Fellow traveller.

METHUSHELACH (Hebrew) Messenger. Variations: *Methuselah, Metushelach.*

METODEJ (Czech) Fellow traveller. Variations: *Metodek, Metousek.*

MEYER (German) Farmer. Variation: *Mayer.*

MHINA (African: Swahili) Delightful.

MICANOPY (Native American: Seminole) Chief. Variation: *Micco.*

MICHAEL (Hebrew) Who is like God? Along with Mohammed and John, Michael could be one of the most popular boys' names in the world in any language. The reasons? Famous Michaels get lots of press, both good and bad, and as a result, the name is always out there. In addition, the name is liberally scattered through both the Old and New Testaments as well as throughout the Koran. Today's famous Michaels include Michael Owen, Michael J. Fox, Michael Jackson, Michael Jordan, Michael Caine and Michael Douglas, plus others with variations of the name: Mickey Rourke, Mickey Rooney, Mickey Spillane, Mike Tyson, Mike Hucknall and Mick Jagger. Michael has been one of the names at the top of the list for over four decades. Variations: *Makis, Micah, Micha, Michail, Michak, Michal, Michalek, Michau, Micheal, Michel, Michele, Mick, Mickel, Mickey, Mickie, Micky, Miguel, Mihail, Mihailo, Mihkel, Mikaek, Mikael, Mikala, Mike, Mikelis, Mikey, Mikhail, Mikhalis, Mikhos, Mikkel, Mikko, Mischa, Misha, Mitch, Mitchel, Mitchell.*

MIDDLETON (English) Town in the middle.

MIECZYSLAW (Polish) Glorious sword. Variations: *Maslaw, Mieszko, Mietek.*

MIKASI (Native American: Omaha) Coyote.

MIKOLAS (Czech) Victorious people. Variation: *Mikuls.*

MILAN (Hindu) Meeting.

MILBOROUGH (English) Middle borough. Variation: *Milbrough.*

MILES (English) Soldier. Variations: *Milo, Myles.*

MILFORD (English) Ford at the mill.

MILLARD (English) Guard of the mill.

MILLER (English) One who mills grain.

MILLS (English) The mills.

MILO (German) Generous.

MILOSLAV (Czech) Glorious love. Variations: *Milda, Milon, Milos.*

MILOSLAW (Polish) Lover of glory. Variations: *Milek, Milosz.*

MILSON (English) Son of Miles.

MILTAIYE (Native American) Ocean waves.

MILTON (English) Mill town.

MINCO (Native American: Choctaw) Chief.

MINGAN (Native American) Grey wolf.

MING-HOA (Chinese) Prestigious.

MINH (Vietnamese) Brilliant.

MINOR (Latin) Younger. Variation: *Mynor.*

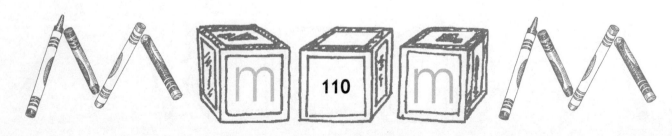

MIROSLAV (Czech) Famous glory. Variation: *Mirek.*

MIROSLAW (Polish) Great glory. Variations: *Mirek, Miroslawy.*

MISU (Native American: Miwok) Flowing water.

MITSU (Native American: Osage) Grizzly bear.

MLENGALENGA (African: Malawian) Heaven.

MOC VAN (Vietnamese) The sun and moon both rise.

MODRED (English) Brave adviser. Variation: *Mordred.*

MOHAJIT (Hindu) Handsome. Variations: *Mohan, Mohandas, Mohanshu.*

MOHAMMED (Arabic) Greatly praised. If Michael is the most popular name in the western world, then Mohammed and its numerous variations is probably the most popular name in Muslim countries, if not actually the world. Mohammed is the name of the prophet of Islam, and the popularity of the name could possibly be explained by an old Muslim proverb: if you have a hundred sons, give them all the name of Mohammed. The name is also becoming hugely popular among African-Americans. The most famous recent bearer of this name is the great fighter Mohammed Ali (Cassius Marcellus Clay). Variations: *Ahmad, Amad, Amed, Hamdrem, Hamdum, Hamid, Hammad, Hammed, Humayd, Mahmed, Mahmoud, Mahmud, Mehemet, Mehmet, Mohamad, Mohamed, Mohamet, Mohammad, Muhammad.*

MOHAN (Hindu) Enchanting.

MOHE (Native American: Cheyenne) Elk.

MOIAG (Native American) Noisy. Variation: *Mojag.*

MOJIESZ (Polish) Drawn from the water.

MOKO (Polynesian) Crooked.

MOMUSO (Native American) Yellowjacket nest.

MONAHAN (Irish) Monk. Variations: *Monaghan, Monohan.*

MONGO (African: Nigerian) Famous.

MONROE (Irish) Red marsh. Variations: *Monro, Munro, Munroe.*

MONTAGUE (French) Sharp mountain peak. Variations: *Montagu, Montaqu, Montaque.*

MONTEL (English) Unknown definition.

MONTGOMERY (English) Rich man's mountain. Variations: *Monte, Montgomerie, Monty.*

MONTSHO (African: Botswana) Black.

MOOTSKA (Native American: Hopi) Yucca plant. Variation: *Mootzka.*

MORAN (Hebrew) Guide.

MORDECAI (Hebrew) Name commonly given to boys born during Purim. Variations: *Mordche, Mordechai, Mordi, Motche.*

MORAY (Scottish) Last name.

MORELAND (English) Uncultivated land. Variations: *Moorland, Morland.*

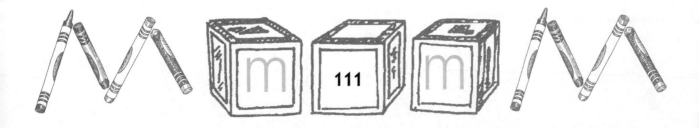

MORGAN (Welsh) Great and bright. This name has a long history among the Welsh and was famous as the seventh-century Welsh prince commemorated today in the name of Glamorgan. Also a girls' name. Famous male Morgans include British writer Edward Morgan Foster and US actor Morgan Freeman. Variations: *Morgen, Morrgan.*

MORI (Hebrew) My guide. Variations: *Morie, Moriel.*

MORLEY (English) Meadow on a moor. Variations: *Moorley, Moorly, Morlee, Morleigh, Morly, Morrley.*

MORRISON (English) Son of Morris. Variation: *Morrisson.*

MORSE (English) Son of Maurice.

MORTIMER (French) Still water. If Walt Disney had gone along with his first choice and named his mouse Mortimer instead of Mickey, there would be many more Mortimers around today. Variations: *Mort, Mortmer, Mortym.*

MORTON (English) Town by a moor. Variation: *Morten.*

MORVEN (Scottish) Big mountain peak.

MOSES (Hebrew) Arrived by water. Variations: *Moise, Moises, Moisey, Mose, Mosese, Mosha, Moshe, Moss, Moyse, Moze, Mozes.*

MOSI (African: Swahili) First-born.

MOSTYN (Welsh) Fort in a field.

MOSWEN (African) Light-coloured.

MOTEGA (Native American) New arrow.

MOTSQUEH (Native American: Nez Perce) Chipmunk.

MOUNGA (Polynesian) Mountain.

MOUSA (Arabic) From water.

MTIMA (African: Malawian) Heart.

MUA (Polynesian) Supreme.

MUAMOHOLEVA (Polynesian) Attractive chief.

MUATA (Native American) Yellowjackets.

MUBARAK (Arabic) Blessed.

MUDADA (African: Zimbabwean) The provider.

MUHANNAD (Arabic) Sword.

MUHSIN (Arabic) Generous.

MUIR (Scottish) Moor.

MUIREADHACH (Irish) Sailor. Variations: *Murchadh, Murrough.*

MUIRGHEAS (Irish) Sea choice.

MUKHTAR (Arabic) To choose.

MUNCHIN (Irish) Little monk.

MUNDAN (African) Garden.

MUNGO (Scottish) Friendly. Variation: *Mongo.*

MUN-HEE (Korean) Learned.

MUNIM (Arabic) Charitable.

MUNIR (Arabic) Bright light.

MUNNY (Cambodian) Smart.

MUNYIGA (African: Ugandan) Nest.

MURACO (Native American) White moon.

MURDOCH (Scottish) Sailor. Variations: *Murdo, Murdock, Murtagh.*

MURIEL (Irish) Bright as the sea.

MURPHY (Irish) Sea fighter.

MURRAY (Scottish) Mariner. Murray is another one of those great last-names-as-first-names that is perfectly posed for rejuvenation. Somewhat popular during the 1940s and 1950s, Murray has fallen out of favour and has since been used mostly as a middle name. I like the name, so be the first down your street to use it. Variations: *Murrey, Murry.*

MUSA (African: Swahili) Child.

MUSAD (Arabic) Lucky. Variations: *Misid, Musaed.*

MUSENDA (African) Nightmare.

MUSTAPHA (Arabic) Chosen. Variation: *Mustafa.*

MUTASIM (Arabic) Shelter.

MUTAZZ (Arabic) Strong.

MWAI (African: Malawian) Prosperity.

MWAMBA (African: Tanzanian) Strong.

MWLA (African: Malawian) Rain.

MYERS (English) One who lives in a swamp. Variation: *Myer.*

MYRON (Greek) Aromatic oil. Variations: *Miron, Myreon.*

MYUNG DAK (Korean) Virtuous.

MYUNG-KI (Korean) To rise up shining.

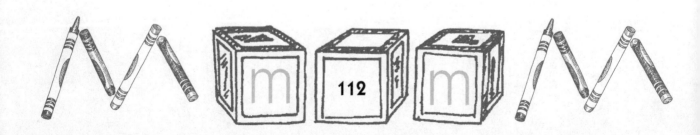

Names from the Old Testament

The names of the books of the Old Testament have provided a wealth of names for parents to ponder over for their babies.

Joshua, Samuel, Joel, Malachi, Ruth and Daniel are just a few of the names that represent centuries of history and respect for the past.

These days, the names that Jewish families select for their children are often determined by the form of Judaism that they follow. Orthodox Jews tend to select exact Biblical names for their sons and daughters. Reformed and non-practising Jews often pick names that seem a bit more anglicized, although occasionally they will do what is referred to as double-naming their babies. In this case, the first name won't be a traditional Jewish name, but the middle name will.

One thing that both Orthodox and reformed Jews have in common, however, is that they consider the naming of a new baby to be the perfect way to honour a deceased relative. Orthodox Jews tend to recycle the same names; reformed Jews often choose a more modern name that starts with the same letter as the relative's name. For instance, instead of choosing Sidney or Stanley for a new baby, they'll use Sam.

Sephardic Jews from western Europe and the Middle East tend to use a naming practice that is prevalent in Egypt: they name their newborn babies after older relatives who are still alive. They believe that this will add years to the adult's life while enhancing the baby's.

Boys' Names

- Abel: Adam's son.
- Adam: First man.
- Asher: Son of Jacob and Zilpah.
- Daniel: Prophet.
- Eleazar: Aaron's son.
- Elijah: Prophet; travelled to heaven in a chariot of fire.
- Gideon: Hero of the Israelites.
- Isaac: Son of Abraham; Rebecca's husband.
- Japheth: Son of Noah.
- Jonah: Prophet; swallowed by large fish.
- Joseph: Son of Jacob and Rachel.
- Levi: Son of Jacob and Leah.
- Mordecai: The uncle of Esther.
- Nathan: Prophet.
- Noah: Builder of ark.
- Samuel: Prophet.
- Seth: Adam's son.
- Uriah: Husband of Bathsheba.

Girls' Names

- Abigail: Wife of David.
- Asenath: Wife of Joseph.
- Bathsheba: Wife of Uriah and then David.
- Delilah: Mistress of Samson.
- Eve: Wife of Adam.
- Hagar: Mother of Ishmael.
- Leah: First wife of Jacob.
- Naomi: Mother-in-law of Ruth.
- Orpah: Wife of Clioin.
- Rachel: Wife of Jacob; mother of Joseph and Benjamin.
- Rebecca: Wife of Isaac.
- Ruth: Wife of Mahlon.
- Sarah: Wife of Abraham.
- Tamar: Daughter of David.
- Zilpah: Mistress of Jacob.

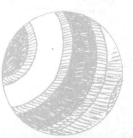

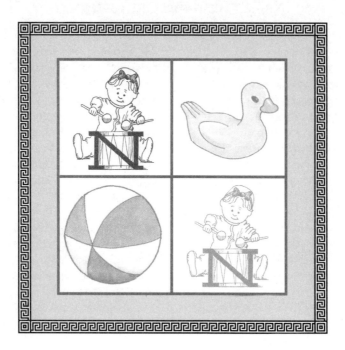

NABIL (Arabic) Noble.

NACHUM (Hebrew) Comfort. Variations: *Nabum, Nachman, Nechum, Nehum.*

NADIM (Hindu) Friend. Variation: *Nadeem.*

NADIR (Hebrew) Pledge.

NAGARJUNA (Hindu) Second-century philosopher.

NAGATAKA (Japanese) Childhood obligation.

NAGID (Hebrew) Leader. Variation: *Nageed.*

NAHELE (Hawaiian) Forest.

NAHMA (Native American) Trout.

NAHOR (Hebrew) Light. Variations: *Nahir, Nahur, Nehor.*

NAIJA (African: Ugandan) Next-born.

NAIM (Arabic) Happy. Variation: *Naeem.*

NAIRNE (Scottish) River. Variation: *Nairn.*

NAJ (Arabic) To save. Variations: *Nagi, Naji.*

NAJIB (Arabic) Smart. Variations: *Nagib, Najeeb.*

NAKAI (Native American: Navajo) Mexican.

NAKISISA (African: Ugandan) Child of the shadows.

NALDO (Spanish) Good advice.

NALIN (Hindu) Lotus.

NALREN (Native American) To thaw.

NALUNANI (Hawaiian) Beautiful ocean.

NAM (Vietnamese) South.

NAMID (Native American) Star dancer.

NAMIL (Arabic) To achieve.

NAMIR (Hebrew) Leopard.

NAM-KYU (Korean) Southern.

NANAK (Hindu) Name of the founder of the Sikh religion.

NANDAN (Hindu) Happiness.

NANDIN (Hindu) Destroyer.

NAOKO (Japanese) Direct.

NAOMHAN (Irish) Little holy one. Variation: *Nevan.*

NAPANA (Hawaiian) Gift. Variation: *Natana.*

NAPEZI (Native American: Cheyenne) Yellow hand.

NAPOLEON (African-American) Lion in a new city.

NAPTHALI (Hebrew) Conflict.

NARAIN (Hindu) The Hindu god Vishnu.

NARAYANA (Hindu) Man.

NARCISSUS (Greek) Daffodil. Variation: *Narcisse.*

NARD (Persian) Chess game.

NAREN (Hindu) Superior man.

NARESH (Hindu) Ruler of men.

NASHASHUK (Native American: Sauk) Thunder.

NASHEAKUSH (Native American: Sauk) Son of Chief Black Hawk and Asshewequa. Variation: *Nasomsee.*

NASHOBA (Native American: Choctaw) Wolf. Variation: *Neshoba.*

NASR (Arabic) Victory. Variations: *Nasser, Nassor.*

NATAL (Spanish) Birthday. Variations: *Natale, Natalio.*

NATANE (Polynesian) Gift.

NATHAN (Hebrew) Gift from God. The real name of the late, great comedian George Burns was Nathan, and though the name might seem really stodgy or old-fashioned, it is actually very popular today. Not only is it in the top hundred boys' names of the 1990s, but it was also on the top hundred list back in George Burns's day. Nathan was the name of a prophet who appeared in the Old Testament book of II Samuel, and it's been around ever since. Nathan is a pretty common name in many English-speaking countries and popular in Great Britain, Australia and the United States. Famous Nathans who kept their names include Nathanial Hawthorne and Nat King Cole. Variations: *Nat, Natan, Nataniele, Nate, Nathanial, Nathaniel, Nathen, Nathon, Natt, Natty.*

NAULEO (Polynesian) Observant.

NAV (Hungarian) Name.

NAVARRO (Spanish) Land. Variation: *Navarre.*

NAVEED (Hindu) Good thoughts.

NAVIN (Hindu) New.

NAWAT (Native American) Left hand.

NAYATI (Native American) Wrestler.

NAYLAND (English) Island resident.

NDALE (African: Malawian) A trick.

NDULU (African: Nigerian) Dove.

NECHEMYA (Hebrew) God's comfort. Who would have ever thought that Jeremiah would become popular? Nechemya could be headed in the same direction if there are enough parents out there who take the first step. Variations: *Nechemia, Nechemiah, Nehemiah.*

NEDAVIAH (Hebrew) Charity of the Lord. Variations: *Nedabiah, Nedavia, Nedavya.*

NEEL (Hindu) Blue. Variations: *Neelendra, Neelmani.*

NEGASI (Ethiopian) He will become royalty.

NEHRU (East Indian) Canal.

NEIL (Irish) Champion. This name predates the Norman Conquest and can be found in the Domesday Book. It reached a peak in popularity in the 1960s, with the first man on the moon bearing the name – Neil Armstrong. Neil is an easygoing name that has always been independent; its original spelling is Niall. Famous Neils include Neil Simon, Neil Sedaka and Neil Young. Variations: *Neal, Neale, Neall, Nealle, Nealon, Neile, Neill, Neille, Neils, Nels, Niadh, Nial, Niall, Nialle, Niel, Niels, Nigel, Niles, Nilo.*

NEKTARIOS (Greek) Nectar. The drink of the gods. Variation: *Nectarios.*

NELEK (Polish) Like a horn.

NELSON (English) Son of Neil. Adopted as a first name in tribute to Admiral Horatio Nelson after his death in the Battle of Trafalgar. It has remained in occasional use, becoming more common in the USA than elsewhere. Other Nelsons include Nelson Rockefeller,

Nelson Mandela and singer Nelson Eddey. Variations: *Nealson, Neilson, Nilson, Nilsson.*

NEMESIO (Spanish) Justice.

NEMO (Hawaiian) Smooth.

NEN (Egyptian) Spirit.

NENNEN CHEKOOSTIN (Native American: Nez Perce) Raven.

NEPER (Spanish) New city.

NEPTUNE (Latin) Roman god of the sea.

NERO (Latin) Strong. Variations: *Neron, Nerone.*

NESBIT (English) Curve in the road. Variations: *Naisbit, Naisbitt, Nesbitt, Nisbet, Nisbett.*

NESTOR (Greek) Traveller.

NETO (Spanish) Earnest one.

NETANIAH (Hebrew) Gift of Jehovah. Variations: *Netania, Netanya, Nethaniah.*

NETOTWEPTUS (Native American: Nez Perce) Three feathers.

NEVADA (Spanish) Snow-covered. Like the names of other American western states and cities, Nevada is catching on among parents who are looking for something different for their sons.

NEVILLE (French) New town. Variations: *Nevil, Nevile, Nevill, Nevyle.*

NEVIN (Irish) Holy. Variations: *Nev, Nevan, Nevins, Niven.*

NEWELL (English) New hall. Variations: *Newall, Newel, Newhall.*

NEWLAND (English) New land.

NEWLIN (Welsh) New pond. Variations: *Newlun, Newlyn.*

NEWMAN (English) Newcomer.

NEWTON (English) New town.

NGAI (Vietnamese) Herb.

NGHI (Vietnamese) Suspicious.

NGHIA (Vietnamese) Forever.

The Trend Toward Ethnic Names

If you want to give your baby a name that sounds a bit exotic, but is really just a variation of a more common name, you might want to think about giving him or her a particular nationality's version of that name.

For instance, the Spanish variation of William is Guillermo, while Paul becomes Pavel in Polish. Jane is Juana in Spanish; Jana in Hungarian.

Of course, you could also pick a name from your own ethnic background that doesn't necessarily correspond with any equivalent – Welsh and Irish names are currently popular, as well as a wealth of names from many African countries. Or you could select a name from an ethnic group that you share no roots with, just because you like the name.

The good news about giving your baby an ethnic name is that there are no rules: if you like the name, then go ahead. In the last couple of decades, people have begun to travel more frequently to all corners of the globe, and it has become possible to meet people from many different places. We will continue to be exposed to an increasingly wide community of people, and this will continue to be reflected in the names we choose for our children.

In addition, once these previously exotic names are used more and start to become part of the mainstream, they won't stand out as much in the coming years – which means that parents thirty years from now who want something new and different for their own kids will continue to push the envelope toward increasingly exotic baby names.

NGOC ANH (Vietnamese) Flower.

NGOLINGA (African: Malawian) Whiner.

NGOZI (African: Nigerian) Good luck.

NGUNDA (African: Malawian) Dove.

NHEAN (Cambodian) All-seeing.

NIAZ (Hindu) Gift.

NIBAW (Native American) To stand up.

NICABAR (Spanish) To steal.

NICHOLAS (Greek) People of victory. Nicholas has been popular for about the last two decades. Nicholas was first mentioned in the Book of Acts, and the Biblical figure was followed by St. Nicholas, who is considered to be the patron saint of children. Why is Nicholas so popular? It just sounds like a folksy, friendly name that will serve a boy well from toddlerhood all the way through to grandfatherhood. Whether it's little Nicky or Grandad Nick, Nicholas fits no matter what the age. Famous Nicholases, besides Santa Claus, include the protagonist of *Nicholas Nickleby* by Dickens, Nick Nolte and Nick Faldo. Though some feel the name is too popular, most parents who choose the name for their sons won't agree.
Variations: *Nic, Niccolo, Nichol, Nick, Nickolas, Nickolaus, Nicky, Nicol, Nicolaas, Nicolai, Nicolas, Nikita, Nikki, Nikky, Niklas, Niklos, Niko, Nikolai, Nikolais, Nikolas, Nikolaus, Nikolo, Nikolos, Nikos, Nikula.*

NICODEMUS (Greek) Jewish leader.

NIEN (Vietnamese) Year.

NIGAN (Native American) In the lead.

NIGEL (Irish) Champion. Variation of Neil. Variations: *Nigal, Nigiel, Nigil.*

NIHOPALAOA (Hawaiian) Whale tooth.

NIKODEM (Polish) Victorious people.

NIKODEMOS (Greek) Victory of the people. Variation: *Nicodemus.*

NIKOLAO (Hawaiian) Winning people. Variation: *Nikolo.*

NIKOMEDES (Greek) To ponder victory. Variation: *Nicomedes.*

NIKOSTRATOS (Greek) Victorious army. Variation: *Nicostratos.*

NILI (Hebrew) Israel's glory.

NIMROD (Hebrew) Rebel.

NINASTOKO (Native American: Blackfoot) Chief.

NINIAN (Scottish) Unknown definition.

NIPTON (English) Another name for the Isle of Wight.

NIRAM (Hebrew) Fertile meadow.

NIRVAN (Hindu) Bliss.

NISAN (Hebrew) Miracle. Variation: *Nissan.*

NISHAD (Hindu) Seventh note of a scale.

NITIS (Native American) Good friend. Variation: *Netis.*

NITOH MAHKWI (Native American: Blackfoot) Lone wolf.

NIUTEI (Polynesian) Coconut tree.

NIXON (English) Son of Nicholas.

NIZAR (Arabic) Unknown definition.

NJAU (African: Kenyan) Young bull.

NNAMDI (African: Nigerian) My father is alive.

NOADIAH (Hebrew) Meeting with God. Variations: *Noadia, Noadya.*

NOAH (Hebrew) Rest. Ever child knows who Noah is, and so do an increasing number of parents who are choosing this name for their baby boys. Of course, any child with this name should expect the requisite ribbing: where's your Ark? Variations: *Noach, Noak, Noe, Noi, Noy.*

NOAM (Hebrew) Delight.

NOBLE (Latin) Well-bred.

NOCONA (Native American: Comanche) Wanderer. Variation: *Nokoni.*

NODIN (Native American) The wind. Variation: *Noton.*

NOE (Polish) Quiet.

NOEL (French) Christmas. Variations: *Natal, Natale, Nowel, Nowell.*

NOELANI (Hawaiian) Heavenly rain.

NOHEA (Hawaiian) Handsome.

NOHOKA (Hawaiian) One who lives by the ocean.

NOKONYU (Native American) The nose of a katydid.

NOKOSI (Native American: Seminole) Bear.

NOLAN (Irish) Little proud one. Variations: *Noland, Nolen, Nolin, Nollan, Nuallan.*

NOOR (Hindu) Light.

NO-PAWALLA (Native American: Osage) Fear of thunder. Variations: *Napawalla, Nepawalla, Nopawalla.*

NORBERT (German) Famous northerner. Variation: *Norberto.*

NORMAN (English) Northerner. The name Norman originated from the French tribe in Normandy, which is most famous for invading England in the year 1066. It was among many medieval names in vogue in Victorian times. It was very popular in the first half of the 20th century, but fell into decline in the 1950s. Famous Normans include British film comedian Norman Wisdom, novelist Norman Mailer, and British politicians Norman Tebbitt and Norman Lamont. Variations: *Norm, Normand, Normando, Normen, Normie.*

NORRIS (English) Northerner. Variations: *Noris, Norreys, Norrie, Norriss, Norry.*

NORTHCLIFF (English) Northern cliff. Variations: *Northcliffe, Northclyff, Northclyffe.*

NORTHROP (English) Northern farm. Variation: *Northrup.*

NORTON (English) Northern town.

NORVAL (Scottish) Northern village. Variations: *Norvil, Norvill, Norville, Norvylle.*

NORVELL (English) North well. Variation: *Norvel.*

NORVIN (English) Northern friend. Variations: *Norvyn, Norwin, Norwinn, Norwyn, Norwynn.*

NORWARD (English) Guardian of the north.

NORWOOD (English) Northern woods. What is it about names that begin with the prefix 'Nor'? Other names with nerdier histories are currently making a comeback, but no such bright future holds for boys' names beginning with 'Nor', Norwood included.

NOY (Hebrew) Beauty.

NUMA (Arabic) Kindness. Masculine form of Naomi.

NUMAIR (Arabic) Panther.

NUNCIO (Italian) Messenger. Variation: *Nunzio.*

NUNNA HIDIHI (Native American: Cherokee) Mountain man.

NUR (Arabic) Light.

NUR ALDIN (Arabic) Light of faith.

NUREN (Hindu) Brilliance.

NURI (Arabic) Light. Variations: *Noori, Nur, Nuria, Nuriel, Nury.*

NURU (African: Swahili) Light.

NUSAIR (Arabic) Vulture.

NWA (African: Nigerian) Son.

NWABUDIKE (African: Nigerian) The son is powerful.

NWAKE (African: Nigerian) Son born on market day.

NYE (Welsh) Honour.

OAKES (English) Near oak trees. Variations: *Oak, Ochs.*

OAKLEY (English) Meadow of oak trees. Variations: *Oaklee, Oakleigh, Oakly.*

OBA (African: Nigerian) King.

OBADIAH (Hebrew) Servant of God. There is a Book of Obadiah in the Old Testament and the name is borne by a dozen biblical characters. Obadiah has the potential to catch on among parents who would like to give their baby boys a name from the Bible that is just a bit different. One of its nicknames, Obie, is close to Opie. Variations: *Obadias, Obe, Obed, Obediah, Obie, Ovadiach, Ovadiah.*

OBASI (African: Nigerian) Honouring God.

OBATAIYE (African: Nigerian) King of the world.

OBAYANA (African: Nigerian) The king warms himself at the fire.

OBERON (German) Noble and bearlike. Variations: *Auberon, Auberron.*

OBERT (German) Wealthy and brilliant.

OBI (African: Nigerian) Heart.

OBIKE (African: Nigerian) A strong family.

OCEAN (English) Ocean. Variation: *Oceanus.*

OCTAVIUS (Latin) Eighth child. Variations: *Octave, Octavian, Octavien, Octavio, Octavo, Ottavio.*

ODAKOTA (Native American: Sioux) Friends.

ODELL (English) Forested hill. Variations: *Ode, Odey, Odi, Odie.*

ODHRAN (Irish) Pale green. Variations: *Odran, Oran.*

ODIN (Scandinavian) One-eyed Norse god.

ODINAN (African) Fifteenth child.

ODION (African: Nigerian) First-born of twins.

ODISSAN (African) Thirteenth son.

ODOLF (German) Wealthy wolf. Variation: *Odolff.*

ODYSSEUS (Greek) One of the leaders of the Trojan War.

OGALEESHA (Native American: Sioux) Red shirt.

OGANO (Japanese) Deer pasture.

OGDEN (English) Valley of oak trees. Variations: *Ogdan, Ogdon.*

OGHE (Irish) Horseman. Variations: *Oghie, Oho.*

OGUN (African: Nigerian) War god. Variations: *Ogunkeye, Ogunsawo, Ogunsheye.*

OHANKO (Native American) Careless.

OHANZEE (Native American: Sioux) Shadow.

OHIN (African) Chief.

OHITEKAH (Native American: Sioux) Courageous.

OHIYESA (Native American: Sioux) Victor.

OH-OH-E-SO-TO-WHO (Native American: Osage) Seven bulls.

OISIN (Irish) Young deer. Variations: *Ossian, Ossin.*

OISTIN (Irish) Respected.

OJORE (African: Ugandan) Soldier.

OKECHUKU (African: Nigerian) Gift from God.

OKELLO (African: Ugandan) Born after twins.

OKEMOS (Native American) Small chief.

OKO (African: Nigerian) The god Ogun.

OKON (African) Born at night.

OKOTH (African: Ugandan) Born during a rainstorm.

OKPARA (African: Nigerian) First-born son.

OKTAWIAN (Polish) Eighth.

OLA (African: Nigerian) Money.

OLADELE (African: Nigerian) We are honoured at home.

OLAF (Scandinavian) Forefather. Olaf is a very common name in Norway. There have been many other ethnic names that have become part of modern culture, but Olaf doesn't seem as if it will ever totally fit in. What comes to my mind is that the name is just too close to the word oaf. And so despite its esteemed background – Olaf served as the name of no fewer than five Norwegian kings – I don't see it as an up

and comer. Variations: *Olaff, Olav, Olave, Olen, Olin, Olof, Olov, Olyn.*

OLAFEMI (African: Nigerian) Fortunate.

OLAKEAKUA (Hawaiian) God lives.

OLANIYAN (African: Nigerian) Surrounded by honour.

OLDRICH (Czech) Noble king. Variations: *Olda, Oldra, Oldrisek, Olecek, Olik, Olin, Olouvsek.*

OLEG (Russian) Holy. The chance of Oleg's reaching the top hundred names list in this country is just a little less remote than the chances for Olaf, primarily because of Oleg's association with the designer Oleg Cassini. Variation: *Olezka.*

OLERY (French) Leader.

OLIVER (Latin) Olive tree. Variations: *Oliverio, Olivero, Olivier, Olivor, Olley, Ollie, Olliver, Ollivor.*

OLIWA (Hawaiian) Olive.

OLNEY (English) Town in Britain.

OLORUN (African: Nigerian) Nigerian god.

OLUBAYO (African: Nigerian) Joy.

OLUFEMI (African: Nigerian) God loves me. Variation: *Olviemi.*

OLUGBALA (African: Nigerian) God of the people.

OLUHYODE (African: Nigerian) God makes me happy.

OLUJIMI (African: Nigerian) Given by God.

OLUMIDE (African: Nigerian) God arrives.

OLUMOI (African: Nigerian) God awakens.

OLUSHEGUN (African: Nigerian) God is champion.

OLUSHOLA (African: Nigerian) Blessed by God.

OLUWA (African: Nigerian) Our God.

OLUYEMI (African: Nigerian) Satisfied.

OMANAND (Hindu) Joy from a meditation chant.

OMAR (Hebrew) Eloquent. A biblical name occasionally surfacing in English-speaking countries since the 19th century, although it is the Arabic form that is more common now. Omar Sharif and poet Omar

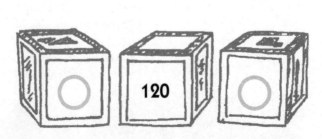

Khayyam have all lent exposure to this name. Despite the lack of a public figure with this name today, some parents are beginning to consider this name for their own sons. Variations: *Omarr, Omer.*

OMRI (Hebrew) Servant of God.

ONACONA (Native American: Cherokee) White owl. Variation: *Oukounaka.*

ONAN (Turkish) Wealthy.

ONANI (African) A glance.

ONAONA (Hawaiian) Sweet-smelling.

ONDREJ (Czech) Manly. Variations: *Ondra, Ondravsek, Ondrejek, Ondrousek.*

ONGWATEROHIATHE (Native American: Iroquois) White sky.

ONSLOW (English) Fan's hill. Variation: *Ounslow.*

ONUR (Turkish) Dignity.

ONWARENHIIAKI (Native American: Mohawk) One who cuts trees.

ONWOACHI (African: Nigerian) God's world.

OQWAPI (Native American: Tewa) Red cloud.

ORAN (Irish) Green. Variations: *Orin, Orran, Orren, Orrin.*

ORBAN (Hungarian) Urbanite.

OREN (Hebrew) Ash tree. Variations: *Orin, Orrin.*

ORESTES (Greek) Mountain. Variations: *Aresty, Oreste.*

OREV (Hebrew) Raven.

ORFORD (English) Ford of cattle.

ORION (Greek) Son of fire or light; sunrise. Mythological son of Poseidon.

ORJI (African: Nigerian) Sturdy tree.

ORLANDO (Italian) Famous land. Variations: *Ordando, Orland, Orlande, Orlo.*

ORMAN (German) Sailor. Variations: *Ormand, Ormond, Ormonde.*

ORO (Spanish) Gold.

ORON (Hebrew) Light.

ORRICK (English) Old oak tree. Variation: *Orric.*

ORSON (Latin) Bearlike. Orson Welles – whose real first name was George – put this name on the map. Today the name seems to be making a comeback, probably in deference to the late great actor from *Citizen Kane*. Variations: *Orsen, Orsin, Orsini, Orsino.*

ORTON (English) Shore town.

ORUNJAN (African: Nigerian) God of the noontime sun.

Bizarre Meanings When Combining First, Middle and Last Names

Some people collect things like stamps, shells and antiques. Then there are those who just have to be different.

One of these guys goes by the name of Dick Crouser and he collects names. Not just any names; he looks for names that may seem innocent by themselves, but that are quite strange when taken in the context of a middle and last name.

Here are some of the highlights from his collection:

- Hazel Mae Call
- Seldom Wright
- Harley Worthit
- Daily Goforth
- Hazel B. Good

I'm sure if you try, you can come up with some examples that Dick can add to his collection.

ORVILLE (French) Golden town. Variations: *Orv, Orval, Orvell, Orvelle, Orvil.*

ORVIN (English) Friend with a spear. Variations: *Orwin, Orwynn.*

OSAKWE (African: Nigerian) God agrees.

OSANMWESR (African: Nigerian) God made me complete.

OSAYABA (African: Nigerian) God forgives.

OSBERT (English) Divine and bright.

OSBORN (English) Divine bear. Variations: *Osborne, Osbourn, Osbourne, Osburn, Osburne.*

OSCAR (English) Divine spear. Back when Oscar the Grouch first arrived on the scene, Jack Klugman was starring as Oscar Madison in *The Odd Couple*. The reputations that both of these Oscars had back then tended to discourage parents from choosing the name for their own kids. Today, however, Oscar is considered to be cool, and actually a way to poke fun at our earlier associations with the name. The great success of Steven Spielberg's movie *Schindler's List*, about Oskar Schindler, probably helped to enhance the name. Other famous Oscars have included Oscar Wilde, Oscar Hammerstein and Oscar de la Renta. Variations: *Oskar, Osker, Ossie.*

OSCEOLA (Native American: Creek) Black drink.

OSEI (African: Ghanian) Noble.

OSGOOD (English) Divine and good. Variations: *Oz, Ozzi, Ozzie, Ozzy.*

OSHEA (Hebrew) Helped by God. Variation: *Oshaya.*

OSILEANI (Polynesian) Speaks up.

OSMAN (Polish) God protects.

OSMAR (English) Divine and marvellous.

OSMOND (English) Divine protector. Variations: *Osman, Osmand, Osmonde, Osmund, Osmunde.*

OSRED (English) Divine adviser.

OSRIC (English) Divine ruler. Variation: *Osrick.*

OSSIOLACHIH (Native American: Creek) Screaming eagle.

OSTEN (Latin) Esteemed. Variations: *Ostin, Ostyn.*

OSWALD (English) Divine power. Variations: *Ossie, Osvald, Oswaldo, Oswall, Oswell.*

OSWIN (English) Divine friend. Variations: *Osvin, Oswinn, Oswyn, Oswynn.*

OTA (Czech) Wealthy. Variation: *Otik.*

OTADAN (Native American) Abundance.

OTEE EMATHLA (Native American: Seminole) Sensible.

OTETIANI (Native American: Iroquois) Prepared.

OTHMAN (German) Rich man.

OTHNIEL (Hebrew) Lion of God. Variation: *Otniel.*

OTIS (English) Son of Otto.

OTOKAR (Czech) One who watches his wealth.

OTSKAI (Native American: Nez Perce) Leaving.

OTSTOTPOO (Native American: Nez Perce) Fire.

OTTAH (African: Nigerian) Skinny boy.

OTTO (German) Wealthy. Otto is so out on a limb that there are some people who consider it to be a cutting-edge name to give their sons. Otto is popular all over the world, including in Hungary, Germany, Sweden and Russia. Variations: *Odo, Otello, Othello, Otho, Othon, Oto, Ottomar.*

OURAY (Native American: Ute) Arrow.

OVED (Hebrew) Worshiper. Variation: *Obed.*

OWEN (Welsh) Well born. Owen could easily be considered a second cousin to the name Evan. Some parents consider Owen to be a better name than Evan these days, since the latter is a bit overused. Variations: *Owain, Owin.*

OXFORD (English) Oxen crossing a river.

OZ (Hebrew) Power.

OZNI (Hebrew) To listen.

OZURU (Japanese) Stork.

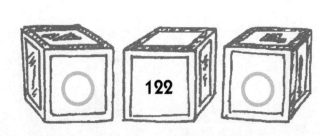

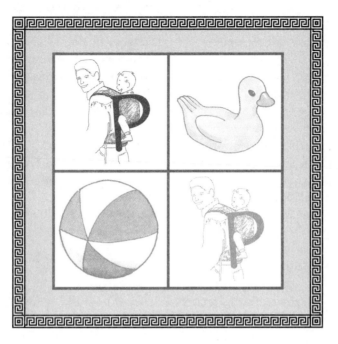

PAAHANA (Hawaiian) Busy.

PACO (Spanish) Diminutive of Francisco. Variations: *Pacorro, Paquito.*

PADDY (Irish) Nickname for Patrick. Variations: *Paddey, Paddie.*

PADGET (English) Young assistant. Variations: *Padgett, Paget, Pagett.*

PAGE (French) Intern. Variation: *Paige.*

PAGIEL (Hebrew) Worships God.

PAHKATOS (Native American: Nez Perce) Five cuts.

PAHKATOS QOHQOH. (Native American: Nez Perce) Five ravens.

PAHKOWYALKELAKED (Native American: Nez Perce) Five turns.

PAINTER (English) Painter.

PAKELIKA (Hawaiian) Nobleman.

PAKI (South African) Witness.

PAKILE (Hawaiian) Royal. Variation: *Bakile.*

PAL (Gypsy) Brother.

PALAKI (Polynesian) Black. Variations: *Palefu, Peleki.*

PALAKIKO (Hawaiian) Free man. Variation: *Farakiko.*

PALANI (Hawaiian) Frenchman. Variation: *Farani.*

PALAUNI (Polynesian) Brown.

PALEKOLOMAIO (Hawaiian) Hill. Variation: *Baretolomaio.*

PALENAPA (Hawaiian) Hawaiian version of Barnabas. Variation: *Barenaba.*

PALLATON (Native American) Fighter. Variations: *Palladin, Pallaten.*

PALMER (English) Carrying palm branches. Palmer is one of those mild-mannered last names that is quickly catching on as a popular first name for both boys and girls. Look for Palmer to make gentle inroads into the top hundred names for boys. Variations: *Pallmer, Palmar.*

PANAS (Greek) Immortal.

PANCHO (Spanish) Frenchman. Variation: *Panchito.*

PANOS (Greek) Rock.

PANTNI (Hindu) Name of the developer of Sanskrit.

PAPIANO (Hawaiian) Hawaiian version of Fabian. Variation: *Fabiano.*

PARIS (English) The city. Variation: *Parris.*

PARKER (English) Park keeper. Parker started out as a popular boys' name during the 1800s in America and has always been more common there than in other countries. There is a Dr Parker Peps in Charles Dickens' novel *Dombey and Son.* Variations: *Park, Parke, Parkes, Parks.*

PARLAN (Scottish) Farmer.

PARNELL (French) Little Peter. Variations: *Parkin, Parnel, Parrnell.*

PARR (English) Castle park. Variations: *Parrey, Parrie.*

PARRISH (English) County; church area. Variation: *Parish.*

PARRY (Welsh) Son of Harry.

PARVAIZ (Hindu) Happy. Variations: *Parvez, Parviz, Parwiz.*

PASCAL (French) Easter child. Variations: *Pascale, Pascalle, Paschal, Pascoe, Pascow, Pasqual, Pasquale.*

PASSACONAWAY (Native American: Pennacook) Bear cub.

PATABSU (Native American) Fire ant.

PATAMON (Native American) Raging man.

PATANJAU (Hindu) Fallen palm tree.

PATRICK (Irish) Noble man. Today, parents who have absolutely no ethnic connection to Ireland are choosing the name Patrick for their sons. St. Patrick, the patron saint of Ireland, has been popular all over the world for the last two centuries. However, in

Ireland before the 17th century, the name was considered too holy for general use and it was left to the Scots and English to take it up. There are a slew of famous Patricks, including Patrick Macnee, Patrick Moore and Patrick Swayze. Parents who like the name but who want something just a little bit different for their own sons are choosing one of the many variations of the name. Some well-known examples are Pat Cash, Pat Boone, Paddy Ashdown and Irish playwright Padraic Colum. Variations: *Paddey, Paddie, Paddy, Padraic, Padraig, Padruig, Pat, Patek, Patric, Patrice, Patricio, Patricius, Patrik, Patrizio, Patrizius, Patryk.*

PATTIN (Gypsy) A leaf.

PATTON (English) Soldier's town. Variations: *Paten, Patin, Paton, Patten, Pattin.*

PATWIN (Native American) Man.

PAUL (Latin) Small. All the children I've seen running around lately with the name Paul have actually been given one of the name's more exotic varieties, of which there are many to choose from. One little boy I know down the road is named Pavel, and it so fits him – his father's ethnic background is Polish – that I could not imagine his parents calling him in for dinner by screaming 'Paul!' Paul itself was big in the 1960s, which could be solely due to the fame of Paul McCartney. Variations: *Pablo, Pal, Pali, Palika, Pall, Paolo, Pasha, Pashenka, Pashka, Paska, Paulin, Paulino,*

Paulis, Paulo, Pauls, Paulus, Pauly, Pavel, Pavils, Pavlicek, Pavlik, Pavlo, Pavlousek, Pawel, Pawl, Pol, Poul.

PAWHUSKA (Native American: Osage) White hair. Variations: *Pabhuska, Pahuska, Paubuska.*

PAWISHIK (Native American: Fox) To flick something off the body. Variation: *Poweshiek.*

PAXTON (English) Peaceful town. Variations: *Packston, Pax, Paxon, Paxten.*

PAYAT (Native American) He is coming. Variations: *Pay, Payatt.*

PAYNE (Latin) Countryman. Variation: *Paine.*

PAZ (Spanish) Peace.

PEADAR (Irish) Rock. Variation: *Peadair.*

PEARSON (English) Son of Piers. Variation: *Pierson.*

PEDAHEL (Hebrew) God redeems. Variation: *Pedael.*

PEDAT (Hebrew) Atonement.

PEKELO (Hawaiian) Stone. Variation: *Peka.*

PELAGIOS (Greek) From the sea.

PELANEKELINA (Hawaiian) Hawaiian version of Franklin. Variations: *Farani, Feranekelina, Palani.*

PELEKE (Hawaiian) Wise counsellor. Variation: *Ferede.*

PELEKI (Hawaiian) Hawaiian version of Percy.

PELEKINAKO (Hawaiian) Hawaiian version of Ferdinand. Variation: *Feredinado.*

PELHAM (English) Region in Britain.

PELL (English) Parchment paper.

PEMBROKE (Irish) Cliff. Variation: *Pembrook.*

PENEKIKO (Hawaiian) Blessed. Variations: *Benedito, Beni, Peni.*

PENLEY (English) Fenced meadow. Variations: *Penlea, Penleigh, Penly, Pennlea, Pennleigh, Pennley.*

PENMINA (Hawaiian) Hawaiian version of Benjamin. Variation: *Beniamina.*

PENN (English) Enclosure. Variation: *Pen.*

PEOPEO (Native American: Nez Perce) Bird.

PEOPEO HIHHIH (Native American: Nez Perce) White bird.

PEOPEO IPSEWAHK (Native American: Nez Perce) Lone bird.

PEOPEO MOXMOX (Native American: Nez Perce) Yellow bird.

PEOPEO THOLEKT (Native American: Nez Perce) Bird alighting.

PEPIN (German) One who perseveres. Variations: *Pepi, Peppi, Peppie, Peppy.*

PERACH (Hebrew) Flower. Variation: *Perah.*

PERACHIAH (Hebrew) God's flower. Variations: *Perachia, Perachya.*

PERCIVAL (English) Pierce the valley. Variation: *Perceval.*

PERCY (English) Valley prisoner. Variations: *Pearce, Pearcey, Pearcy, Percey.*

PEREGRINE (Latin) Falcon. Variations: *Peregrin, Peregryn.*

PERETZ (Hebrew) Spring forward. Variations: *Perez, Pharez.*

PERICLES (Greek) Famous Greek orator.

PERKIN (English) Little Peter. Variations: *Perkins, Perkyn.*

PERRY (English) Traveller.

PESACH (Hebrew) Spared. The name for Passover. Variation: *Pessach.*

PESEKAVA (Polynesian) Song about kava.

PETER (Greek) Rock. Peter is a common, friendly name that seems to be one of the oldest names around. It appears in the Bible as a saint's name, in a much-loved children's book, and in nursery rhymes – Peter Rabbit, Peter Piper – as well as on stage and in films: consider Peter O'Toole, Peter Sellers and Peter Ustinov. Though it was popular as a Biblical name up until the 16th century, Peter fell out of favour

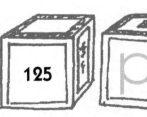
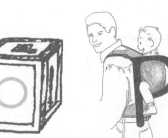

until almost the early part of the 20th century in both the United States and Europe. Peter has never been a trendy name; it's rock-solid, just like its definition. Variations: *Pearce, Pears, Pearson, Pearsson, Peat, Peder, Pedro, Peers, Peet, Peeter, Peirce, Petey, Petie, Petras, Petro, Petronio, Petros, Petter, Pierce, Piero, Pierre, Pierrot, Pierrson, Piers, Pierson, Piet, Pieter, Pietro, Piotr, Pyotr*.

PEUKE (Hawaiian) Happy. Variation: *Felike*.

PEVERELL (French) Piper. Variations: *Peverall, Peverel, Peveril*.

PEWLIN (Welsh) Small. Variation: *Peulan*.

PEYTON (English) Soldier's estate. Variation: *Payton*.

PEZI (Native American: Sioux) Grass.

PHARAOH (Egyptian) King. Variation: *Pharoah*.

PHELAN (Irish) Wolf.

PHELPS (English) Son of Philip.

PHILANDER (Greek) Loves men.

PHILEMON (Greek) Kiss.

PHILIP (Greek) Lover of horses. In recent times, Philip has had a bit of a regal feel to it, possibly owing to Britain's Prince Philip. Philip was also one of the original twelve apostles in the Bible and Philip II of Macedonia was Alexander the Great's father. Though the name was pretty popular in the 1960s, it seems that Philip is more common as a last name these days. The name Philip strikes many people as an exclusively French name; however, it is found in the languages of most European countries. Some well known Philips are US television comedian Phil Silvers, British rock musican Phil Collins, and British poet Philip Larkin. Variations: *Felipe, Felipino, Fil, Filib, Filip, Filipo, Filippo, Fillipek, Fillipp, Fillips, Phil, Philippel, Phill, Phillip, Phillipe, Phillipos, Phillipp, Phillippe, Phillips, Pilib, Pippy*.

PHILO (Greek) Loving.

PHINEAS (Hebrew) Oracle. The first name of US showman P.T. Barnum Variation: *Pinchas*.

PHIRUN (Cambodian) Rain.

PHOENIX (Greek) Immortal. Variation: *Phenix*.

PHTHISIS (Greek) Wasting.

PHUOC (Vietnamese) Good.

PIAO (Chinese) Handsome.

PICH (Cambodian) Diamond.

PIAS (Gypsy) Fun.

PICKFORD (English) Ford at a peak.

PIERCY (English) Pierced hedge. Variation: *Piercey*.

PILA (Hawaiian) Hawaiian version of Bill.

PILAR (Spanish) Pillar.

PILI (African: Swahili) Second-born.

PILLAN (Native American) Highest essence. Variation: *Pilan*.

PILTPO (Hawaiian) Hawaiian version of Philip.

PIN (Vietnamese) Faithful.

PINCHAS (Hebrew) Snake's mouth. Variations: *Phineas, Phinehas, Pinchos, Pinhas*.

PINO (Italian) God will add.

PINON (Native American) Constellation.

PIO (Latin) Pious. Variation: *Pius*.

PIRAN (English) Cornish place name. It is the name of the Celtic abbot St. Piran, the patron saint of Cornish miners. Variations: *Peran, Pieran*.

PIRRO (Greek) Red hair.

PITALESHARU (Native American: Pawnee) Chief. Variation: *Pitaresharu*.

PITNEY (English) Island of a headstrong man. Variation: *Pittney*.

PITT (English) Ditch.

PIZI (Native American: Sioux) Man in the middle.

PLACIDO (Spanish) Peaceful. Singer Placido Domingo has added some degree of visibility to this name, and

it might make the short list for parents who are looking for specifically Italian names for their sons. Variations: *Placid, Placidus, Placyd, Placydo.*

PLATO (Greek) Broad-shouldered. Variation: *Platon.*

PLATT (French) Flat land. Variation: *Platte.*

POCANO (Native American: Pueblo) Spirits coming.

PODALADALTE (Native American: Kiowa) Snake head.

POHDLOHK (Native American: Kiowa) Old wolf.

POLLARD (English) Bald. Variations: *Poll, Pollerd, Pollurd.*

POLLUX (Greek) Crown. Variations: *Pol, Pollack, Polloch, Pollock.*

POLOIKA (Hawaiian) Hawaiian version of Floyd. Variation: *Foloida.*

POLYNICES (Greek) Ancient mythological figure.

POMEROY (French) Apple orchard. Variations: *Pommeray, Pommeroy.*

PO-NA-KAH-KO-WAH (Native American: Delaware) Falling leaf.

PONCE (Spanish) Fifth.

PONIFAKE (Hawaiian) Good fortune. Variation: *Bonifake.*

PONTUS (Greek) God of the sea.

PORFIRIO (Greek) Purple stone. Variations: *Porphirios, Prophyrios.*

Androgynous Names

Another popular trend is for parents to provide their daughters with a name that's clearly male. Certainly, some of the place-as-name monikers accomplish this feat, but many parents are going one step further by giving their daughters a name that won't cause potential employers to rule out these young women once they hit the workforce. Most parents who want their daughters to go as far as they can certainly feel that a male name couldn't hurt their chances in the workplace.

Again, pointing to the studies that exist regarding the right baby name as an indication of future success, in a college course with 400 students, professors have been shown to give higher grades to students whom they think are male. In other instances, when judging a batch of CVs that were blindly submitted to prospective employers, some human resource managers have tended to favour candidates for certain jobs who they think are male. This explains the popularity for girls' names such as Glenn, Shannon and Michael.

Note, however, that androgynous in this case means a male name for a girl, not a female name for a boy. Though some may argue that men don't need a leg up, so to speak, giving a girls' name to a boy does not happen as frequently, and is often thought of as being problematic.

Boys' Names

Brice	Lindsay
Dana	Marion
Haley	Robin
Kelly	Stacy
Leslie	Terry

Girls' Names

Blair	Michael
Blake	Sam
Brett	Taylor
Casey	Tyler
Drew	Whitney

PORTER (Latin) Gatekeeper.

POSOA (Polynesian) Flirting.

POV (Gypsy) Ground or mud.

POVYESHIEK (Native American: Fox) One who shakes. Variation: *Pawishik*.

POWA (Native American) Rich.

POWELL (English) Last name. General Colin Powell has brought this name to the forefront. There's no telling what the future for Powell as a first name will be now the general has left politics, but I'd venture a guess to say that more parents have considered it as a first name for their sons recently. Variation: *Powel*.

POWHATAN (Native American: Algonquin) Location of the powwow.

PRABHAT (Hindu) Light at dawn.

PRADEEP (Hindu) Light. Variation: *Prakash*.

PRADOSH (Hindu) Light at night.

PRAMOD (Hindu) Joy.

PRASAD (Hindu) Brilliant.

PRATAP (Hindu) Great.

PRAVAT (Thai) History.

PRAVIN (Hindu) Capable.

PREM (Hindu) Love.

PREMYSL (Czech) First. Variations: *Myslik, Premek, Premousek*.

PRENTICE (English) Apprentice. Variations: *Pren, Prent, Prentis, Prentiss*.

PRESCOTT (English) Priest's cottage. Variations: *Prescot, Prestcot, Prestcott*.

PRESLEY (English) Priest's meadow. Variations: *Presleigh, Presly, Pressley, Prestley, Priestley, Priestly*.

PRESTON (English) Priest's town. Preston seems to be one of those names that has great potential, but it still retains a bit of prissiness that keeps many parents from considering it for their sons.

PREWITT (French) Brave little one. Variations: *Prewett, Prewit, Pruitt*.

PRIBISLAV (Czech) To help glorify. Variations: *Priba, Pribik, Pribisek*.

PRICE (Welsh) The son of an ardent man. Variation: *Pryce*.

PRIMO (Italian) First son. Variations: *Preemo, Premo*.

PRINCE (Latin) Prince. Variations: *Prinz, Prinze*.

PROCTOR (Latin) Official. Variations: *Prockter, Procter*.

PROKOP (Czech) Very progressive.

PROSPER (Latin) Fortunate. Variation: *Prospero*.

PRYDERI (Welsh) Concern.

PRYOR (Latin) Leader of the monastery. Variation: *Prior*.

PRZBYSLAW (Polish) Helper of glory.

PUAKAEAFE (Polynesian) One thousand pigs.

PUAKATAU (Polynesian) Boar.

PULIKEKA (Polynesian) Attractive.

PULUKE (Hawaiian) Hawaiian version of Bruce. Variation: *Buruse*.

PULUNO (Hawaiian) Brown. Variation: *Buruno*.

PUNAWAI (Hawaiian) Water.

PURVIS (English) Purveyor. Variations: *Purves, Purviss*.

PUTNAM (English) One who lives near a pond.

QABIL (Arabic) Able.

QADIM (Arabic) Ancient.

QADIR (Arabic) Talented. Variation: *Qadar*.

QAMAR (Arabic) Moon.

QASIM (Arabic) Provider.

QING-NAN (Chinese) The younger generation.

QOHQOH ILPPILP (Native American: Nez Perce) Red raven.

QUADREES (African-American) Four. Variations: *Kwadrees, Quadrhys*.

QUAN VAN (Vietnamese) Authorized.

QUANAH (Native American: Comanche) Aromatic.

QUANG THIEU (Vietnamese) Smart.

QUED (Native American: Kiowa) Decorated robe.

QUELATIKAN (Native American: Salish) Blue horn.

QUENNELL (French) Oak tree. Variation: *Quennel*.

QUENTIN (Latin) Fifth. Names with 'x's and 'z's in them seem to be pretty popular right now and you would expect the same thing to be true of names with 'q's in them. Quentin is probably the leading candidate for the most common name that begins with a 'Q', especially since actor and director Quentin Tarantino hit the big time with his film *Pulp Fiction*. Variations: *Quent, Quenten, Quenton, Quint, Quinten, Quintin, Quinton, Quito*.

QUIGLEY (Irish) One with messy hair.

QUILLAN (Irish) Cub. Variation: *Quillen*.

QUIMBY (Norse) A woman's house. Variations: *Quenby, Quim, Quin, Quinby*.

QUINCY (French) The estate of the fifth son. Famous Quincys in recent years include the composer and singer Quincy Jones as well as the TV medical examiner Quincy played by actor Jack Klugman. Variation: *Quincey*.

QUINLAN (Irish) Strong man. Variations: *Quindlen, Quinley, Quinlin, Quinly*.

QUINN (Irish) Wise. Variation: *Quin*.

QUINTO (Spanish) Home ruler. Variation: *Quiqui*.

QUIRIN (English) A magic spell.

QUIRINUS (Latin) Roman god of war.

QUNNOUNE (Native American: Narragansett) Tall.

QUON (Chinese) Bright.

QUSAY (Arabic) Distant. Variation: *Qussay*.

Eastern European Names – Cultural Traditions

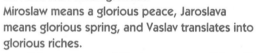

The names that parents from Russia, Poland, the Czech Republic, and other countries in eastern Europe give their children conjure up wonderful images of young girls and boys with exotic, guttural accents running around in a field, the girls with scarves on their heads and the boys with tiny braces holding their trousers up.

At least that's my vision. The names Irina and Igor also bring to mind wizened old men and women, sitting around a dented oaken table, too many talking at once and gesturing with their hands while the aforementioned children are still running around, trying to get their grandparents' attention.

Russia, Poland and the Czech Republic have produced many names that have a rich, earthy sound to them. Of course, if you grew up in the 1960s and 1970s like me, names like Natasha and Boris conjure up an image of Saturday morning cartoons; for our parents, these same names may have brought images of fallout shelters into their consciousness.

Today, Slavic names still have an otherworldly feel to them, but this time it is tinged with romance and allure. Many names that originate in eastern

Europe contain '-slav' or '-slava' as a suffix; in Polish, it turns to '-slaw' and '-slawa'. Slav and slaw mean glorious. Miroslaw means a glorious peace, Jaroslava means glorious spring, and Vaslav translates into glorious riches.

Of course, not all Slavic names use this suffix; other popular names include Ludmilla, Pavel, Bela, and Karel, as well as Slavic versions of English names we're familiar with: Tomas, Filip, and Zofie.

I have a Polish background, and though none of my grandparents had traditionally Polish first names – or maybe they did and changed them early in life when they arrived in this country – I can appreciate the heritage that is evident whenever I think of my grandmother telling me as a child to go take my chumchoo, which is Polish for bath.

My parents' names were strictly Americanized. After all, my grandparents wanted their children to be Americans more than anything else: my maternal grandparents – Lottie, short for Ludmilla, and Myron – chose Jean for their daughter, my mother.

These are the current top ten eastern European names for boys and girls:

Boys' Names

Alexi	Konstantin		
Dmitri	Nicolai		
Feodor	Oleg		
Igor	Vladimir		
Ivan	Yuri		

Girls' Names

Galina	Natalya		
Irina	Olga		
Larisa	Sofia		
Lyudmila	Tatiana		
Marina	Yelena		

RAAMAH (Hebrew) Thunder. Variations: *Raam, Raamia, Raamiah, Raamya.*

RAANAN (Hebrew) Fresh. Variation: *Ranan.*

RABBI (Hebrew) My master.

RABI (Arabic) Breeze.

RABY (Scottish) Famous and bright. Variations: *Rab, Rabbie, Rabi.*

RACHIM (Hebrew) Compassion. Variations: *Racham, Rachmiel, Raham, Rahim.*

RAD (Arabic) Thunder.

RADBORNE (English) Red stream. Variations: *Rad, Radborn, Radbourn, Radbourne, Radburn, Radburne, Radd.*

RADCLIFF (English) Red cliff. The name Radcliff has a tweedy, uppercrust sound to it. Name of the British writer Radclyffe Hall, author of the novel *The Well of Loneliness.* Variations: *Radcliffe, Radclyffe.*

RADEK (Czech) Famous ruler. Variations: *Radacek, Radan, Radik, Radko, Radouvsek, Radovs.*

RADFORD (English) Red ford or ford with reeds. Variations: *Rad, Radd, Radferd, Radfurd, Redford.*

RADHI (East African) Goodwill.

RADHULBH (Irish) Wolf counsellor.

RADIMIR (Czech) Happy and famous. Variations: *Radim, Radomir.*

RADLEY (English) Red meadow. Variations: *Radlea, Radlee, Radleigh, Radly.*

RADMAN (Slavic) Joy.

RADNOR (English) Red shore.

RADOMIL (Slavic) Lover of peace.

RADOSLAV (Czech) Happy and glorious.

RADOSLAW (Polish) Glad for glory. Variations: *Raclaw, Slawek.*

RADWAN (Arabic) Delight.

RAFA (Hebrew) Cure. Variation: *Rapha*.

RAFAT (Arabic) Merciful.

RAFFERTY (Irish) Prosperous. Variations: *Rafe, Rafer, Raferty, Raff, Raffarty, Raffer, Raffi, Raffy*.

RAFI (Arabic) Exalted.

RAFIQ (Hindu) Friend. Variations: *Rafee, Rafi, Rafiki*.

RAGHID (Arabic) Cheerful.

RAGHNALL (Irish) Powerful judgment. Variation: *Rognvaldr*.

RAGNAR (Scandinavian) Warrior of judgment. Variations: *Ragnor, Regner*.

RAGNER (Norse) Power. Variations: *Rainer, Rainier, Rayner, Raynor*.

RAGNVALD (Scandinavian) Powerful judgment.

RAHIM (Hindu) Compassionate.

RAHMAN (Arabic) Compassionate. Variation: *Rahmet*.

RAIDEN (Japanese) God of thunder.

RAINART (German) Great judgment. Variations: *Rainhard, Rainhardt, Reinart, Reinhard, Reinhardt, Reinhart*.

RAINI (Native American) A god.

RAJAB (Arabic) Seventh month. Variation: *Ragab*.

RAJENDRA (Hindu) King of the sky. Variations: *Rajender, Rajinder*.

RAJESH (Hindu) King of kings.

RAJIV (Hindu) Striped.

RAJNISH (Hindu) Ruler of the night. Variation: *Rajneesh*.

RALEIGH (English) Deer meadow. Variations: *Rawleigh, Rawley, Rawly*.

RALPH (English) Wolf-counsellor. Notable Ralphs include actors Sir Ralph Richardson and Ralph Fiennes, US philosopher Ralph Waldo Emerson, the British composer Ralph Vaughn Williams and the British cartoonist Ralph Steadman. Variations: *Ralphie, Raoul, Raul, Raulas, Raulo, Rolf, Rolph*.

RALSTON (English) Ralph's town.

RAM (Hindu) One who pleases others. Variations: *Rama, Ramananda*.

RAMADAN (Arabic) Ninth month of the Muslim year.

RAMAKRISHNA (Hindu) Pleasing god.

RAMIRO (Portuguese) Great judge. Variation: *Ramirez*.

RAMNATH (Hindu) Lord Rama is lord.

RAMSAY (English) Island of rams. Variations: *Ramsey, Ramsy*.

RAMSDEN (English) Valley of rams.

RANCE (African) Borrower. Variations: *Rancel, Rancell, Ransel, Ransell*.

RAND (English) Fighter.

RANDOLPH (English) Wolf with a shield. One of the variations for Randolph, Randy, has become more popular as a given name than the original. Variations: *Randal, Randall, Randel, Randell, Randey, Randie, Randil, Randle, Randol, Randolf, Randy*.

RANEN (Hebrew) Joyful song. Variation: *Ranon*.

RANGER (French) Protector of the forest. Variations: *Rainger, Range*.

RANIER (English) Mighty army.

RANIT (Hebrew) Song. Variation: *Ronit*.

RANJIT (Hindu) Delightful.

RANKIN (English) Shield.

RANSFORD (English) Raven ford.

RANSLEY (English) Raven meadow. Variations: *Ransleigh, Ransly*.

RANSOM (English) Son of the protector. Variations: *Ransome, Ranson*.

RAOUL (French) Variation of Ralph. Variation: *Raul*.

RAPHAEL (Hebrew) God has healed. Contrary to popular opinion, Raphael is not a variation of Ralph, but a name that has stood on its own ever since Biblical times, where it was the name of an archangel. It is much more common in South European countries.

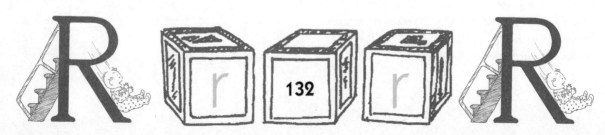

One famous Raphael was the great Italian Renaissance painter.Variations: *Rafael, Rafel, Rafello, Raffaello*.

RAPIER (French) As strong as a sword.

RASHAD (Arabic) Moral work. Variation: *Rashid*.

RASHARD (African-American) Variation of Richard.

RASHAUN (African-American) Newly created. Variations: *Rayshaun, Rayshawn*.

RASHID (Turkish) Righteous. Variations: *Rasheed, Rasheid, Rasheyd*.

RASHIDI (African: Swahili) Good advice.

RASHON (African-American) Newly created. Variations: *Rachan, Rashaan, Rasham, Rashan, Rashawn, Reshaun, Reshawn*.

RASMUS (Greek) Beloved.

RATAN (Hindu) Gem.

RAUF (Arabic) Sympathy.

RAV (Hindu) Sun god.

RAVI (Hindu) Sun. Variation: *Ravee*.

RAVINDRA (Hindu) Sun power.

RAVIV (Hebrew) Rain.

RAVIYA (Hebrew) Fourth. Variation: *Ravia*.

RAWDON (English) Craggy hill.

RAWLINS (French) Last name. Variations: *Rawlinson, Rawson*.

RAY (English) Royal. Variations: *Rayce, Raydell, Rayder, Raydon, Rayford, Raylen, Raynell*.

RAYBURN (English) Brook for deer. Variations: *Rayborn, Raybourne, Rayburne*.

RAYHAN (Arabic) Favoured by God.

RAYMOND (German) Counsellor and protector. Raymond began to catch on only in the mid-19th century, before becoming one of the most popular names for boys in 1900. Famous Rays include Raymond Burr, the character that Dustin Hoffman played in the movie *Rainman*, Raymond Chandler and Raymond Carver. St. Raymond is considered to be the patron saint of lawyers, so if you don't particularly care for lawyers, better not choose that name for your son. Variations: *Raimondo, Raimund, Raimunde, Raimundo, Rajmund, Ramon, Ramond, Ramone, Ray, Rayment, Raymonde, Raymondo, Raymund, Raymunde, Raymundo, Reimond*.

RAZA (Hindu) Content.

RAZI (Hebrew) My secret. Variations: *Raz, Raziel*.

READ (English) Red-haired. Variations: *Reade, Reed, Reid, Reide, Reyd*.

READING (English) Son of the red-haired one. Variations: *Redding, Reeding, Reiding*.

REDLEY (English) Red meadow. Variations: *Radley, Redlea, Redleigh, Redly*.

REDMAN (English) Rider.

REDMOND (Irish) Counsellor. Variation of Raymond. Variations: *Radmond, Radmund, Redmund*.

REECE (Welsh) Fiery, zealous. Rhys was the name of an 11th-century Welsh king, but is not commonly in use outside the Welsh community around the world. Variations: *Rees, Reese, Rhys*.

REEVE (English) Bailiff. Variations: *Reave, Reeves*.

REGAN (Irish) Little king. Variations: *Reagan, Reagen, Regen*.

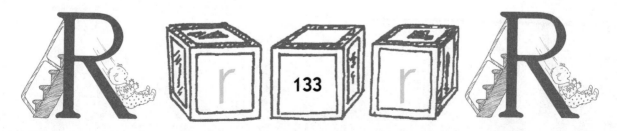

REGIN (Scandinavian) Judgment.

REGINALD (English) Strong counsellor. Reginald is almost never used as a proper name except when it stands in as the formal version of the much more popular Reggie. Famous Reggies include British television news reader Reginald Bosanquet and the fictional character in the TV series *The Rise and Fall of Reginald Perrin*. More often than not, famous men who were born with the name Reggie or Reginald have changed their names for ones they consider to be more suitable – like Rex Harrison and Elton John. Variations: *Reg, Reggie, Reginalt*.

REHOR (Czech) To awaken. Variations: *Horek, Horik, Rehak, Rehorek, Rehurek*.

REI (Japanese) Law.

REMIGIUSZ (Polish) Oarsman.

REMINGTON (English) Family of ravens. Variations: *Rem, Remee, Remi, Remie, Remmy*.

REMUS (Latin) Swift.

REMY (French) From Rheims, a town in central France. Variations: *Remee, Remi, Remie, Remmy*.

RENAUD (French) Powerful.

RENDOR (Hungarian) Policeman.

RENE (French) Reborn. Variations: *Renat, Renato, Renatus, Renne, Rennie, Renny*.

RENFRED (English) Strong peace.

RENFREW (Welsh) Calm river.

RENJIRO (Japanese) Pure.

RENNY (Irish) Small and mighty.

RENSHAW (English) Forest of ravens. Variation: *Renishaw*.

RENTON (English) Deer habitat.

RENZO (Italian) Laurel. Diminutive form of Lorenzo.

RESHEPH (Hebrew) Flame. Variation: *Reshef*.

REUBEN (Hebrew) Behold a son. Reuben is showing signs of bubbling up, especially among parents who are looking for a name with tradition and spirit; the Biblical Reuben was Jacob's eldest son and founded one of the tribes of Israel. Who knows if this name will catch on? Think of the singer Ruben Blades. Variations: *Reuban, Reubin, Reuven, Reuvin, Rube, Ruben, Rubin, Rubu*.

REUEL (Hebrew) Friend of God. Variation: *Ruel*.

REX (Latin) King.

REXFORD (English) King's ford.

REY (Spanish) King. Variation: *Reyes*.

REYHAM (Arabic) God's choice.

REYNARD (French) Fox. Variation: *Renard*.

REYNOLD (English) Powerful adviser. Variations: *Ranald, Renald, Renaldo, Renauld, Renault, Reynaldo, Reynaldos, Reynolds, Rinaldo*.

REZ (Hungarian) Red hair.

RHAMADHANI (African: Swahili) Born during the month of Ramadan.

RHETT (Welsh) Fiery. Variation: *Rhys*.

RHODES (Greek) Island of roses. Variations: *Rhoades, Rhodas, Rodas*.

RHODRI (Welsh) Ruler of the wheel.

RHYDDERCH (Welsh) Reddish brown.

RICHARD (German) Strong ruler. The Normans introduced the modern form of this name and established one of the most enduring of all English names. There have been many famous bearers of the name including three English kings as well as celebrities such as Richard Burton, Richard Chamberlain, Richard Attenborough, Richard Branson, Richard Gere and Richard Todd, among others. Others with the common diminutive Rick or Ricky include US country singer Rick Nelson, UK pop musician Rick Wakeman and British TV comedian Rik Mayall. In America its popularity took a nose dive in the mid-1970s at the same time as

Richard Nixon left office. Variations: *Dic, Dick, Dickie, Dicky, Ricard, Ricardo, Riccardo, Ricciardo, Rich, Richardo, Richards, Richart, Richerd, Richi, Richie, Rick, Rickard, Rickert, Rickey, Rickie, Ricky, Rico, Rihards, Riki, Riks, Riocard, Riqui, Risa, Ritch, Ritchard, Ritcherd, Ritchie, Ritchy, Rostik, Rostislav, Rostya, Ryszard.*

RICHMOND (French) Lush mountain.

RICKWARD (English) Mighty guardian. Variations: *Rickwerd, Rickwood.*

RIDA (Arabic) Satisfied. Variations: *Reda, Rida, Ridha.*

RIDER (English) Horseman. Variations: *Ridder, Ryder.*

RIDGE (English) Ridge. Variation: *Rigg.*

RIDGEWAY (English) Road on a ridge.

RIDGLEY (English) Meadow on a ridge. Variations: *Ridgeleigh, Ridgeley, Ridglea, Ridglee, Ridgleigh.*

RIDLEY (English) Red meadow. Variations: *Riddley, Ridlea, Ridleigh, Ridly.*

RIGEL (Arabic) Foot.

RILEY (Irish) Brave. Riley seems to be a good candidate for becoming more popular as a name for boys since it is Irish and is traditionally thought of as a last name. Variations: *Reilly, Ryley.*

RIMON (Hebrew) Pomegranate.

RING (English) Ring.

RINGO (Japanese) Apple.

RIO (Spanish) River. Variation: *Reo.*

RIORDAN (Irish) Minstrel. Variations: *Rearden, Reardon.*

RIP (Dutch) Ripe.

RIPLEY (English) Shouting man's meadow. Variations: *Ripleigh, Riply, Ripp.*

RISHON (Hebrew) First.

RISLEY (English) Meadow with shrubs. Variations: *Rislea, Rislee, Risleigh, Risly.*

RISTON (English) Town near shrubs.

RITHISAK (Cambodian) Strong.

RITTER (German) Knight.

RIVAI (Hebrew) Conflict.

RIVE (French) River.

RIYAD (Arabic) Garden. Variation: *Riyadh.*

ROALD (German) Famous leader.

ROARK (Irish) Mighty. Variations: *Roarke, Rorke, Rourke.*

ROBERT (English) Bright fame. Its modern form came from France and was the name of William the Conqueror's father. There are many appearances of it in the Domesday Book. The Scottish king Robert the Bruce also made it very popular in Scotland. Robert is one of the most popular names in the world. It has endless variations in every language, and one theory holds that so many men were named Robert from the time of the Middle Ages up until today that many variants were necessary so that people could distinguish one Robert from another. Famous Roberts include US politician Robert Kennedy, Scottish writer Robert Louis Stevenson, British Prime Minister Robert Peel, Scottish poet Robert Burns, US General Robert E. Lee and actors Robert Wagner, Robert Redford, and Robert de Niro. Variations: *Bob, Bobbey, Bobbie, Bobby, Riobard, Rob, Robb, Robbi, Robbie, Robbin, Robby, Robbyn, Rober, Robers, Roberto, Roberts, Robi, Robin, Robinet, Robyn, Rubert, Ruberto, Rudbert, Ruperto, Ruprecht.*

ROBERTSON (English) Son of Robert.

ROBINSON (English) Son of Robert. Variations: *Robbinson, Robeson, Robson, Robynson.*

ROCCO (Italian) Rest. Variations: *Rock, Rockie, Rocky.*

ROCHESTER (English) Stone fortress.

ROCK (English) Rock. Variations: *Rockford, Rockie, Rocky.*

ROCKLEY (English) Rock meadow. Variations: *Rocklee, Rockleigh, Rockly.*

ROCKWELL (English) Well by the rocks.

Some Popular Names from the 1970s

During the 1970s, parents-to-be chose names for their children that were solid and traditional, probably as a reaction to the wild, anything-goes atmosphere that was rampant in the previous decade.

Safe but common Biblical names – like David and

John – were big for boys, while names for girls tended toward something a touch more exotic – like Angela and Theresa. These lists include fifty of the most popular boys and girls names chosen by parents in the 1970s.

Boys' Names

Michael	Sean
Robert	Gregory
David	Ronald
James	Todd
John	Edward
Jeffrey	Derrick
Steven	Keith
Christopher	Patrick
Brian	Darryl
Mark	Dennis
William	Andrew
Eric	Donald
Kevin	Gary
Scott	Allen
Joseph	Douglas
Daniel	George
Thomas	Marcus
Anthony	Raymond
Richard	Peter
Charles	Gerald
Kenneth	Frank
Matthew	Jonathan
Jason	Lawrence
Paul	Aaron
Timothy	Phillip

Girls' Names

Michelle	Heather
Jennifer	Susan
Kimberly	Sandra
Lisa	Denise
Tracy	Theresa
Kelly	Christina
Nicole	Tina
Angela	Cynthia
Pamela	Melissa
Christine	Patricia
Dawn	Renee
Amy	Cheryl
Deborah	Sherry
Karen	Donna
Julie	Erica
Mary	Rachel
Laura	Sharon
Stacey	Linda
Catherine	Barbara
Lori	Jacqueline
Tammy	Rhonda
Elizabeth	Andrea
Shannon	Rebecca
Stephanie	Wendy
Kristin	Maria

RODERICK (German) Famous ruler. Actor Roddy McDowell and singer Rod Stewart have brought attention to this name. Rod and Roderick have always been fairly popular choices for names in Britain. Variations: *Rod, Rodd, Roddie, Roddy, Roderic, Roderich, Roderigo, Rodique, Rodrich, Rodrick, Rodrigo, Rodrique, Rurich, Rurik.*

RODMAN (English) Famous man.

RODNEY (English) Island clearing. Variations: *Rodnee, Rodnie, Rodny.*

ROE (English) Roe deer.

ROGAN (Irish) Redhead.

ROGER (German) Renowned spearman. There have been plenty of famous Rogers throughout the last couple of decades, including Roger Moore, Roger Daltrey, and even Roger Rabbit. Variations: *Rodger, Rogelio, Rogerio, Rogerios, Rogers, Ruggerio, Ruggero, Rutger, Ruttger.*

ROHAN (Irish) Red.

ROHIN (East Indian) Striving.

ROKA (Japanese) Wave.

ROLAND (German) Famous land. Introduced by the Normans in the 11th century, in medieval history Roland was the most gallant of all knights. Shakespeare used the name Roland in his play *As You Like It*, and in three others. Variations: *Rolle, Rolli, Rollie, Rollin, Rollins, Rollo, Rollon, Rolly, Rolo, Rolon, Row, Rowe, Rowland, Rowlands, Rowlandson.*

ROMAN (Latin) One from Rome. Variations: *Romain, Romano, Romanos, Romulo, Romulos, Romulus.*

ROMANY (Gypsy) Gypsy.

ROMEO (Italian) Pilgrim visiting Rome.

ROMNEY (Welsh) Curving river.

RONALD (English) Powerful adviser. The name reached a peak in the UK in the 1920s and in the USA in the 1940s. Famous Ronalds include British film actor Ronald Coleman and actor and US President Ronald Reagan. Variations: *Ranald, Ron, Ronn, Ronney, Ronni, Ronnie, Ronny.*

RONAN (Irish) Little seal.

RONDRE (African-American) Newly created. Variation: *Ron Dre.*

RONEL (Hebrew) Song of God.

RONI (Hebrew) Joyful.

RONSON (English) Son of Ronald.

ROONEY (Irish) Red-haired. Variations: *Roonie, Roony.*

ROOSEVELT (Dutch) Field of roses.

ROPER (English) Maker of rope.

RORY (Irish) Red. Rory is very popular now. To me, it brings images of a small child galloping down the street. Rory is such a spirited name that many parents are choosing it for their sons. Variations: *Ruaidri, Ruairi, Ruaraidh.*

ROSARIO (Portuguese) The rosary.

ROSCOE (Scandinavian) Deer forest.

ROSH (Hebrew) Chief.

ROSHAN (Hindu) Light at dawn.

ROSHAUN (African-American) Newly created. Variations: *RoShawn, Roshon.*

ROSLIN (Scottish) Small redheaded child. Variations: *Roslyn, Rosselin, Rosslyn.*

ROSS (Scottish) Cape. Variations: *Rosse, Rossie, Rossy.*

ROSTISLAV (Czech) Grabs glory. Variations: *Rosta, Rostecek, Rostek.*

ROSWELL (English) Rose spring.

ROTH (German) Red.

ROTHWELL (Norse) Red spring.

ROUSSE (French) Red-haired.

ROVER (English) Wanderer.

ROWAN (Irish) Red. Variation: *Rowen.*

ROWELL (English) Deer spring.

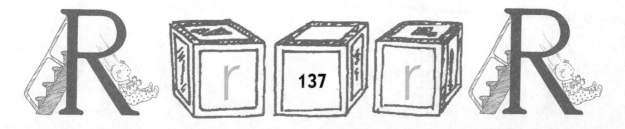

ROWLEY (English) Unevenly cleared meadow. Variations: *Rowlea, Rowlee, Rowleigh, Rowlie, Rowly.*

ROXBURY (English) Town of the rook.

ROY (Irish) Red. Roy was a very popular boys' name in the 1950s because of the cowboy singer Roy Rogers. In these days when parents prefer a baby name with lots of possibilities, Roy presents only one: Roy. Variation: *Roi.*

ROYAL (French) Royal. Variation: *Royall.*

ROYCE (American) Roy's son. Variations: *Roice, Royse.*

ROYD (Scandinavian) Forest clearing.

ROYDEN (English) Hill of rye. Variations: *Roydan, Roydon.*

ROYSTON (English) Last name. Variation: *Roystan.*

ROZEN (Hebrew) Leader.

RUADHAN (Irish) Little red-haired one. Variation: *Rowan.*

RUDD (English) Ruddy skin.

RUDO (African: Zimbabwean) Love.

RUDOLPH (German) Famous wolf. If you want your son to spend the first ten Decembers of his life with his peers asking him where his red nose is, then name your son Rudolph. The great Russian dancer, Rudolph Nureyev, unfortunately has done little to help redeem this name. Variations: *Rodolfo, Rodolph, Rodolphe, Rolf, Rolfe, Rolle, Rollo, Rolph, Rolphe, Rudey, Rudi, Rudie, Rudolf, Rudolfo, Rudolpho, Rudolphus, Rudy.*

RUDYARD (English) Red paddock.

RUFORD (English) Red ford. Variation: *Rufford.*

RUFUS (Latin) Red-haired. Variations: *Ruffus, Rufo, Rufous.*

RUGBY (English) Rook fortress.

RUMFORD (English) To cross a wide river.

RUNAKO (African: Zimbabwean) Handsome.

RUNE (Scandinavian) Secret lore.

RUPERT (German) Bright fame. Variation of Robert. Variations: *Ruperto, Ruprecht.*

RURIK (Scandinavian) Famous king. Variations: *Roar, Rorek, Roth, Rothrekr.*

RUSH (English) Red-haired.

RUSHFORD (English) Ford with rushes.

RUSKIN (French) Child with red hair.

RUSSELL (French) Red-haired. Variations: *Rus, Russ, Russel.*

RUSTY (French) Red-haired. Variation: *Rustie.*

RUTHERFORD (English) Cattle crossing. Variation: *Rutherfurd.*

RUTLAND (Norse) Red land.

RUTLEY (English) Red meadow.

RUUD (Scandinavian) Famous wolf.

RYAN (Irish) Last name. The growth in popularity of Ryan seemed to coincide with both the celebrity of Ryan O'Neal and modern women's desire for the sensitive man. Ryan is not a name you'd think of for a bully. But again, a big reason for its popularity is that it is an Irish name and a last name all rolled into one, and most names today that fit this description can count on some degree of popularity. Variations: *Ryne, Ryon, Ryun.*

RYCROFT (English) Field of rye. Variation: *Ryecroft.*

RYE (Polish) Strong ruler.

RYLAND (English) Land of rye. Variation: *Ryeland.*

RYSZARD (Polish) Brave ruler. Variant of Richard.

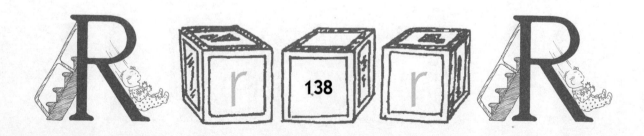

SAAD (Hebrew) Assistance. Variations: *Saadia, Saadiah, Saadya, Saadyah.*

SAARIK (Hindu) Bird.

SABER (French) Sword. Variation: *Sabre.*

SABIN (Latin) The name of an ancient Roman clan. Variations: *Sabine, Sabino.*

SABIR (Arabic) Patient. Variation: *Sabri.*

SABOLA (African: Malawian) Pepper.

SABURO (Japanese) Third son.

SACHDEV (Hindu) Truth of god.

SACHIEL (Greek) Guardian of Sagittarians.

SADDAM (Arabic) Unknown definition. In the wake of the Iraq War, the name Saddam has to be among the rarest names to appear on birth certificates in the world.

SADIKI (African: Swahili) Faithful.

SADLER (English) Saddle maker. Variation: *Saddler.*

SAEBHREATHACH (Irish) Noble judge.

SAEED (African: Swahili) Happy.

SAFA (Arabic) Pure child.

SAFFORD (English) River crossing at the willows.

SAFWAT (Arabic) Select.

SAGAR (English) Champions.

SAGOYEWATHA (Native American: Iroquois) He wakes them up.

SAHAJ (Hindu) Natural.

SAHALE (Native American) Overhead.

SAHEN (Hindu) Falcon.

SAHIL (Hindu) Leader.

SAHKONTEIC (Native American: Nez Perce) White eagle.

SAHN (Vietnamese) Comparable.

SAID (Arabic) Happy. Variations: *Saeed, Saied, Saiyid, Sayeed, Sayid, Syed.*

SAJAN (Hindu) Beloved.

SAJJAN (Hindu) Gentle.
SAKARIA (Scandinavian) God remembers. Variation of Zachariah. Variations: *Sakari, Sakarias.*
SAKARISSA (Native American: Tuscarora) Spear. Variations: *Sagarissa, Sequareesa.*
SAKHR (Arabic) Rock.
SAKIMA (Native American) King.
SAKNGEA (Cambodian) Ambassador.
SAKURUTA (Native American: Pawnee) Sunrise.
SALAH (Arabic) Virtuous. Variations: *Saladdin, Saladin, Saldin, Saleh, Salih.*
SALAMA (Arabic) Secure. Variation: *Saloma.*
SALEHE (African: Swahili) Good.
SALIH (Arabic) Just.
SALIM (Arabic) Tranquillity. Variations: *Saleem, Salem, Salima, Selim.*
SALLU (African: Swahili) Safe.
SALMALIN (Hindu) Taloned.
SALTON (English) Town in the willows.
SALU (Hebrew) Basket.
SALVATORE (Latin) Saviour. When I was a kid, all my friends who were Italian always seemed to have an uncle Sal somewhere in the background. Whether he was going to help fix their bikes or just stop by later on, Uncle Sal seemed to be ubiquitous. All I know, in retrospect, is that Salvatore – which means Saviour – was the best name that these guys could have had. Variations: *Sal, Salvador, Salvator.*
SAMAL (Hebrew) Symbol.
SAMANI (Polynesian) Salmon.
SAMARU (Japanese) Sun.
SAMI (Hebrew) Exalted.
SAMIH (Arabic) Tolerant.
SAMIR (Arabic) Entertainer.
SAMISONI (Polynesian) Sun.
SAMMAN (Arabic) Grocer. Variation: *Sammon.*

SAMOSET (Native American: Algonquin) He who walks a lot. Variation: *Samaset.*
SAMSON (Hebrew) Sun. Variations: *Sampson, Sanson, Sansone.*
SAMUEL (Hebrew) God listens. Though Samuel has tended to be somewhat popular over the last 100 years or so, it seems that it has fallen in and out of favour. Right now, Sam is popular, perhaps owing to the success of playwright Sam Shepard and the history of the TV show *Cheers*, in which Sam Malone tended bar. Sam is a just-another-guy name that should continue to be popular for decades to come. Variations: *Sam, Sammie, Sammy, Samouel, Samuele, Samuello.*

SANBORN (English) Sandy river. Variations: *Sanborne, Sanbourn, Sanburn, Sanburne, Sandborn, Sandbourne.*
SANCHO (Latin) Sacred. Variation: *Sauncho.*
SANDFORD (English) Sandy crossing. Variations: *Sandfurd, Sanford.*
SANDITON (English) Sandy town.
SANG-OOK (Korean) Good.
SANI (Native American: Navajo) Old.
SANJAY (Hindu) Winner.
SANJIV (Hindu) Reinvigorate. Variation: *Sanjeev.*
SANTIAGO (Spanish) Saint.
SANTO (Spanish) Holy. Variation: *Santos.*
SANTOSH (Hindu) Satisfaction.
SARAD (Hindu) Autumn baby.
SARAPH (Hebrew) Burn. Variations: *Saraf, Seraf, Seraph.*
SARGENT (French) Officer. Variations: *Sarge, Sergeant.*
SARIK (Hindu) Bird.

SARNGIN (Hindu) Lotus.

SARPSIS ILPPILP (Native American: Nez Perce) Red moccasins.

SARUGIN (Hindu) Archer.

SASSACUS (Native American: Pequot) Wild man.

SASTARETSI (Native American: Tlonantati) Rat.

SATURNIN (Spanish) Saturn.

SAUL (Hebrew) Asked for. If the parents of Beatle Paul McCartney had given their son the original name of Paul the Apostle, then all those girls back in the 1960s would have been yelling 'Saul! Saul!' Novelist Saul Bellow is probably the most famous celebrity with this name.

SAULA (Polynesian) To request.

SAUTS (Native American: Cheyenne) Bat.

SAVILLE (French) Town of willows. Variations: *Savil, Savile, Savill, Savilla, Savylle.*

SAWNEY (Scottish) Protector of men. Variations: *Sawnie, Sawny.*

SAWYER (English) Woodworker. Variations: *Sayer, Sayers, Sayre, Sayres.*

SAXON (English) Sword. Variations: *Saxe, Saxen.*

SAYYID (Arabic) Leader.

SCANLON (Irish) Little trapper. Variations: *Scanlan, Scanlen.*

SCHUYLER (Dutch) Shield. Variations: *Schuylar, Skuyler, Skylar, Skyler.*

SCOTT (English) One from Scotland. Along with all those Scottie dogs in the 1960s, not to mention the Scottish kilt craze that we had to live through, the name Scott has been popular since the middle of the 20th century. Famous Scotts from the States include F. Scott Fitzgerald and songwriter Francis Scott Key, for whom Fitzgerald was named, pianist Scott Joplin and pop singer Scott Walker. Today, the name still makes the rounds, but it could show signs of moving

up once the phrase 'Beam me up, Scottie', from *Star Trek* disappears from everyday use. Variations: *Scot, Scottie, Scotto, Scotty.*

SCULLY (Irish) Town crier.

SEABERT (English) Shining sea. Variations: *Seabright, Sebert, Seibert.*

SEABROOK (English) River running to the sea. Variation: *Seabrooke.*

SEAFRA (Irish) Peace of God. Variations: *Seafraid, Seartha, Seathra.*

SEAMUS (Irish) He who supplants. Variation of James. Variation: *Shamus.*

SEAN (Irish) God is good. Variation of John. Before the 1920s it was primarily confined to Ireland, but it has been used increasingly widely since the 1960s. There were loads of Seans in my school and they were all cool. Somewhere between then and now, Sean also began to become popular as a girls' name, albeit with different spellings, most frequently Shawn. Today, Sean is still a pretty hip name for babies – perhaps actors Sean Penn, Sean Bean and Sean Connery have something to do with it. The release of the classic western *Shane* in 1953 did much to popularize this version of the name. Variations: *Seann, Shaine, Shane, Shaughn, Shaun, Shawn, Shayn, Shayne.*

SEANAN (Irish) Old and wise. Variations: *Senan, Sinan, Sinon.*

SEARLE (English) Armour.

SEATON (English) Town by the sea. Variations: *Seeton, Seton.*

SEBASTIAN (Latin) One from Sebastia, an ancient Roman city. Shakespeare has two characters called Sebastian, in *Twelfth Night* and *The Tempest*. Like Sean, Sebastian is a really cool name, although it doesn't get one-tenth of the play today that Sean does. This is changing, however; the name does seem to be pop-

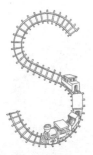

ping up with greater frequency. Variations: *Seb, Sebastien, Sebbie.*

SEDGLEY (English) Sword meadow. Variations: *Sedgeley, Sedgely.*

SEDGWICK (English) Sword place. Variations: *Sedgewick, Sedgewyck, Sedgwyck.*

SEELEY (English) Blessed.

SEEYAKOON ILPPILP (Native American: Nez Perce) Red spy.

SEF (Egyptian) Yesterday.

SEFTON (English) Town in the rushes.

SEFU (African: Swahili) Sword.

SEGEL (English) Treasure. Variations: *Seagel, Segell.*

SEGER (English) Sea fighter. Variations: *Seager, Seeger, Segar.*

SEGUNDO (Spanish) Second.

SEIF (Arabic) Sword of religion.

SEKAN (African: Zimbabwean) Laughter. Variation: *Sekani.*

SEKAR (Hindu) Peak. Variation: *Shekhar.*

SELAH (Hebrew) Song.

SELBY (English) Manor in the village. Variation: *Shelby.*

SELDON (English) Willow valley. Variations: *Selden, Sellden.*

SELEMAEA (Polynesian) God hears.

SELIG (German) Blessed. Variations: *Seligman, Seligmann.*

SELWYN (English) From the forest. Variations: *Selvin, Selwin, Selwinn, Selwynn, Selwynne.*

SEMI (Polynesian) Character.

SEMISTI (Polynesian) Heel. Variation: *Simi.*

SEN (Japanese) Wood sprite.

SENIOR (French) Lord.

SENNETT (French) Venerable. Variation: *Sennet.*

SENWE (African) Stalk.

SEOIRSE (Irish) Farmer. Variation: *Searsa.*

SEOSAMH (Irish) He will add. Variations: *Sedsap, Sedsaph.*

SEPP (German) God will add. Variation of Joseph.

SEPTIMUS (Latin) Seventh.

SEQUOYAH (Native American: Cherokee) Sparrow.

SERAPHIM (Greek) The angels; (Hebrew) Zealous. Variations: *Serafin, Serafino, Seraphimus.*

SERENO (Latin) Calm.

SERGE (Latin) Servant. Variations: *Serg, Sergei, Sergey, Sergi, Sergie, Sergio, Sergius.*

SERVAAS (Scandinavian) Saved.

SESE (Polynesian) Frenchman.

SETANGYA (Native American: Kiowa) Sitting bear.

SETH (Hebrew) To appoint. Notable bearers of the name are found in literature – Seth Bede in George Eliot's novel *Adam Bede* and Seth Starkadder in the satirical novel *Cold Comfort Farm* by Stella Gibbons. Of the popular names today, Seth is unusual because it really has no nicknames or variations. Perhaps the sound of the name is still distinctive enough. Seth was the third son of Adam and Eve and was born after the death of his older siblings, Cain and Abel. It's interesting to note that in the past, the name Seth was frequently given to a newborn son after his parents had already lost a child. Today, Seth has no morbid association. It's just a great name.

SETIMKIA (Native American: Kiowa) Bear who attacks.

SETON (English) Sea town. Variation: *Seaton.*

SET-TAINTE (Native American: Kiowa) White bear. Variation: *Satanta.*

SEVERIN (Latin) Severe. Variation: *Severen.*

SEVERN (English) Boundary.

SEVILEN (Turkish) Beloved.

SEWARD (English) Protector of the sea. Variation: *Sewerd.*

SEWATI (Native American) Bear's claws.

SEWELL (English) Strong at sea. Variations: *Sewald, Sewall.*

SEXTON (English) Church custodian.

SEXTUS (Latin) Sixth. Variation: *Sixtus.*

SEYMOUR (French) From St. Maur, a village in Normandy, France which itself took its name from the little known sixth-century North African St. Maurus. Seymour actually has quite haughty roots and one famous bearer was British actor-manager Sir Seymour Hicks. Variations: *Seamor, Seamore, Seamour, Si, Sy.*

SHACHAR (Hebrew) Sunrise.

SHACHOR (Hebrew) Black. Variation: *Shahor.*

SHADI (Arabic) Singer.

SHADMON (Hebrew) Farm.

SHADRACH (Hebrew) Unknown definition. Variations: *Shad, Shadrack.*

SHAFAN (Hebrew) Rabbit. Variation: *Shafhan.*

SHAFER (Hebrew) Handsome.

SHAFIQ (Arabic) Sympathy. Variations: *Shaff, Shafi.*

SHAHZAD (Hindu) Son of the king.

SHAI (Hebrew) Gift.

SHAIMING (Chinese) Life of sunshine.

SHAKA (African) Unknown definition.

SHAKIL (Hindu) Attractive. Variation: *Shakeel.*

SHAKIR (Arabic) Grateful. Variation: *Shukri.*

SHALEV (Hebrew) Calm.

SHALLUM (Hebrew) Unknown definition. Variations: *Shalem, Shalum.*

SHALMAI (Hebrew) Peace.

Famous Rock and Roll Names

Bruce. Janis. John. Paul. George. Grace. Chuck. Jerry Lee.

As tastes in music change, so do the names of millions of babies each year. But with all of the different kinds of music that have evolved since rock's heyday in the 1950s and 1960s, there's a new trend in baby names that has nothing to do with the singers that are hitting the charts: it's the names of the groups they're singing with.

Ruby. Pearl (as in Jam). Oasis. Soul (as in Collective and Asylum). The first two have been making the rounds of baby name circles for at least a century, but today it's likely that they are named for the rock groups that bear their names. As for the second two, parents who choose either of these more eccentric names for their babies are reflecting a New Age type of consciousness.

Of course, some of the names that will stand out from this period in time are Mariah, Whitney, Britney, Kylie and Alanis for girls. However, boys' names from pop music tend to be relatively rare, since the men who make it big in popular and rock music usually belong to a group, rather than performing as solo singers.

Boys' Names

- David Lee Roth
- Elton John
- Elvis Presley
- Freddie Mercury
- George Harrison
- Jimmy Buffett
- John Lennon
- Kurt Cobain
- Ozzy Osbourne
- Paul McCartney
- Robert Palmer
- Bruce Springsteen

Girls' Names

- Alanis Morrisette
- Alison Moyet
- Annie Lennox
- Bonnie Raitt
- Chrissie Hynde
- Janis Joplin
- Joan Osborne
- Melissa Etheridge
- Natalie Merchant
- Sophie B. Hawkins
- Tina Turner
- Courtney Love

SHALOM (Hebrew) Peace. Variation: *Sholom.*

SHAMIM (Arabic) Fragrant.

SHAMIR (Hebrew) Flint. Variation: *Shamur.*

SHAMMAI (Hebrew) Name. Variation: *Shamai.*

SHANAHAN (Irish) Wise one.

SHANDAR (Hindu) Proud.

SHANDY (English) Noisy. Variations: *Shandey, Shandie.*

SHANI (Hebrew) Red.

SHANK (Irish) God is good. Variations: *Seaghan, Seathan.*

SHANKARA (Hindu) Bringing luck. Variations: *Sankar, Sankara, Shankar.*

SHANLEY (Irish) Small and ancient. Variations: *Shanleigh, Shannleigh, Shannley.*

SHANNON (Irish) Old. Shannon was once solely a name for boys, but sometime in the early 1940s, parents began to choose it for their girls as well. Today, Shannon appears much more frequently among girls than boys, perhaps helped along by the proliferation of girls' names that begin with 'Sh'. Variations: *Shannan, Shannen.*

SHANON (Hebrew) Peaceful. Variation: *Shanan.*

SHANTE (African-American) Newly created. Variations: *Shantay, Shonte.*

SHAPPA (Native American: Sioux) Red thunder.

SHAQUILLE (African-American) Newly created.

SHARAD (Hindu) Autumn.

SHAREF (Arabic) Honest. Variations: *Sharif, Shariff.*

SHARIF (Hindu) Respected. Variations: *Shareef, Shereef, Sherif.*

SHARIL (Arabic) Attractive.

SHARONE (African-American) Flat land. Variation: *Sha Rone.*

SHATEYARONYAH (Native American: Huron) Two clouds.

SHAW (English) Grove of trees.

SHAWL (Hebrew) Request.

SHAWNEL (African-American) Newly created. Variations: *Shawnell, Shawnelle.*

SHEA (English) Requested. Variations: *Shae, Shai, Shaye.*

SHEEHAN (Irish) Calm.

SHEFER (Hebrew) Pleasant.

SHEFFIELD (English) Crooked meadow.

SHELBY (English) Village on the ledge. Shelby seems to be a name with real possibilities, an acceptable alternative to an outdated name like Sheldon. However, as a name that begins with the letters 'Sh', it may continue to be used more for girls than for boys. Variations: *Shelbey, Shelbie.*

SHELDON (English) Steep valley. Variations: *Shelden, Sheldin.*

SHELESH (Hebrew) Third child.

SHELLEY (English) Meadow on a ledge. Variation: *Shelly.*

SHELTON (English) Town on a ledge.

SHEM (Hebrew) Famous.

SHEMAIAH (Hebrew) God has heard. Variations: *Shemaia, Shemaya.*

SHEMARIAH (Hebrew) God protects. Variations: *Shemaria, Shemarya, Shemaryabu, Shmarya, Shmerel.*

SHEN (Chinese) Sacred amulet.

SHENG (Chinese) Victory.

SHENG-LI (Chinese) Very victorious.

SHEPHERD (English) Sheepherder. Variations: *Shep, Shepard, Shephard, Shepp, Sheppard, Shepperd.*

SHEPLEY (English) Sheep meadow. Variations: *Sheplea, Shepleigh, Sheply.*

SHERBORN (English) Clear brook. Variations: *Sherborne, Sherbourn, Sherburn, Sherburne.*

SHERIDAN (Irish) Wild man. Variations: *Sheredan, Sheridon, Sherridan.*

SHERLOCK (English) Bright hair. Variations: *Sherlocke, Shurlock.*

SHERMAN (English) One who cuts cloth. Variations: *Scherman, Schermann, Shermann.*

SHERWIN (English) Bright friend. Variations: *Sherwind, Sherwinn, Sherwyn, Sherwynne.*

SHERWOOD (English) Shining forest. Variations: *Sherwoode, Shurwood.*

SHET (Hebrew) Chosen.

SHEVI (Hebrew) Return. Variations: *Shevuel, Shvuel.*

SHILIN (Chinese) Bright.

SHILLEM (Hebrew) Reward. Variation: *Shilem.*

SHILOH (Hebrew) Unknown definition. Variation: *Shilo.*

SHIMON (Hebrew) Heard. Variation: *Simeon.*

SHIMRI (Hebrew) My protector.

SHIMRON (Hebrew) Observer.

SHIMSHON (Hebrew) Sun.

SHIN (Korean) Trust.

SHING (Chinese) Victory.

SHIN-IL (Korean) Superior trust.

SHIPTON (English) Sheep town.

SHIRO (Japanese) Fourth son.

SHIVA (Hindu) Fortunate. Variations: *Sheo, Shiv, Sib, Siva.*

SHIVAJI (Hindu) fable god.

SHLOMO (Hebrew) Peace.

SHMUEL (Hebrew) God's name. Variations: *Shemuel, Shmelke, Shmiel, Shmulke.*

SHOBHAN (Hindu) Magnificent.

SHOLTO (Scottish) Sower of seeds.

SHOMER (Hebrew) Guardian.

SHONI (Hebrew) Change.

SHONKAH SABE (Native American: Osage) Black dog.

SHOVAI (Hebrew) Gem.

SHOVAL (Hebrew) Road.

SHUZO (Japanese) Third son.

SHYAM (Hindu) Dark beauty. Variation: *Sham.*

SIADHAL (Irish) Sloth. Variation: *Siaghal.*

SIAKI (Polynesian) God is gracious. Variations: *Sione, Soane, Sone.*

SIAOSI (Polynesian) Farmer.

SIARL (Welsh) Man.

SIDNEY (English) One from Sidney, a town in France. Sidney was once quite the aristocratic name; however, a slow and gradual adoption of the name by girls (with a 'y' in place of the 'i') has made this name a rarity for young boys today. Variations: *Sid, Siddie, Sidon, Sidonio, Syd, Sydney.*

SIDWELL (English) Wide stream.

SIENCYN (Welsh) God is gracious.

SIGBJORN (Scandinavian) Victory bear. Variations: *Sigge, Sikke.*

SIGFRID (German) Victory and peace. Variations: *Siegfried, Sigfredo, Sigfrido, Sigfroi, Sigifredo, Sigvard.*

SIGMUND (German) Victory shield. Variations: *Siegmund, Sigmond.*

SIGURD (Scandinavian) Guardian of victory. Variation: *Sjurd.*

SIGWALD (German) Victorious leader. Variation: *Siegwald.*

SIKWAII (Native American: Cherokee) Sparrow.

SILVA (Latin) Forest. Variations: *Silas, Silvain, Silvan, Silvano, Silvanus, Silvio, Sylas, Sylvain, Sylvan, Sylvanus.*

SIMA (Hebrew) Treasure.

SIMBA (African: Swahili) Lion.

SIMCHA (Hebrew) Joy.

SIMIDH (Scottish) Supplanter.

SIMON (Hebrew) God hears. Simon is gaining ground today among parents who see an almost French distinction in the name. Variations: *Simeon, Simion, Simm, Simms, Simone, Symms, Symon.*

SIMPSON (English) Son of Simon. Variation: *Simson.*

SINCLAIR (French) Town in France. Variations: *Sinclare, Synclair.*

SINJON (English) From St. John. Variation: *Sinjun*.

SINTE GLESKA (Native American: Sioux) Spotted tail. Variation: *Sinte Galeska*.

SINTE MAZA (Native American: Sioux) Iron tail.

SIOR (Welsh) Farmer. Variations: *Siors, Siorys*.

SIPHO (South African) Gift.

SIR (English) Sire.

SIRAJ (Arabic) Light.

SIUA (Polynesian) To fish.

SIVA (Hindu) Hindu god of destruction.

SIVAN (Hebrew) Ninth month of the Jewish year.

SIWILI (Native American) Fox tail.

SKELLY (Irish) Storyteller. Variations: *Scully, Skelley*.

SKENANDOA (Native American: Iroquois) Deer.

SKERRY (Scandinavian: Norwegian) Island of stones.

SKIP (Scandinavian) Boss of a ship. Variations: *Skipp, Skipper, Skippie, Skippy*.

SKIRIKI (Native American: Pawnee) Wolf.

SLADE (English) Valley. Variations: *Slaide, Slayde*.

SLANE (Czech) Salty.

SLAVIN (Irish) Mountain man. Variations: *Slaven, Slawin, Sleven*.

SLAVOMIR (Czech) Great and famous.

SLAWOMIERZ (Polish) Great glory.

SLEM-HAK-KAH (Native American: Kalispel) Bear claw.

SLOAN (Irish) Soldier. Variation: *Sloane*.

SMEDLEY (English) Flat meadow. Variations: *Smedleigh, Smedly*.

SMITH (English) Blacksmith. Variations: *Smitty, Smyth, Smythe*.

SNOWDEN (English) Snowy mountain. Variation: *Snowdon*.

SO (Vietnamese) First-born.

SOBESLAV (Czech) To overtake with glory. Variations: *Sobes, Sobik*.

SOBIESLAW (Polish) One who upsets glory.

SOCRATES (Greek) Named for the Greek philosopher. Variations: *Socratis, Sokrates*.

SOFIAN (Arabic) Devoted.

SOHAN (Hindu) Charming.

SOHIL (Hindu) Beautiful.

SOLOMON (Hebrew) Peaceable. One of the most obviously Old Testament names around, Solomon was the son of David and Beersheba whose wise rule over Israel brought about a lengthy peace. Solomon seems to be be making headway among parents who are looking for a Biblical name that is also somewhat hip. Variations: *Salamen, Salamon, Salamun, Salaun, Salman, Salmon, Salom, Salomo, Salomon, Salomone, Selim, Shelomoh, Shlomo, Sol, Solaman, Sollie, Solly, Soloman, Solomo, Solomonas, Solomone*.

SOMERLED (Scottish) Sailor.

SOMERSET (English) Summer estate. Variations: *Sommerset, Summerset*.

SOMERTON (English) Summer town. Variations: *Somervile, Somerville*.

SOMHAIRLE (Irish) Summer sailor. Variation: *Sorley*.

SON (Vietnamese) Mountain.

SONGAN (Native American) Strong.

SONNY (English) Son. Variation: *Sonnie*.

SOREN (Scandinavian) Apart.

SORLEY (Scottish) Viking.

SORRELL (French) Reddish brown. Variations: *Sorrel, Sorrelle*.

SOSAIA (Polynesian) God helps. Variation: *Siosaia*.

SOTERIOS (Greek) Saviour.

SOUTHWELL (English) Southern well.

SOVANN (Cambodian) Gold.

SPALDING (English) Divided field. Variation: *Spaulding*.

SPANGLER (English) Unknown definition.

SPEAR (English) Man with a spear. Variations: *Speare, Spears, Speer, Speers, Spiers*.

SPEMICALAWBA (Native American: Shawnee) Lofty horn. Variation: *Spamagelabe.*

SPENCER (English) Seller of goods. It was originally reserved for the stewards who dispensed supplies in English manor houses. The name is on the upswing in popularity, and not only because actor Spencer Tracy continues to permeate the consciousness through his films with Katharine Hepburn, which are frequently rerun on television. But the simple fact of the matter is that this name is just really cool. Look for it to become more popular well into the 21st century. Variations: *Spence, Spense, Spenser.*

SPIRIDON (Greek) Spirit. Variations: *Spiridion, Spiro, Spiros, Spyridon, Spyros.*

SPOORS (English) Spur maker.

SQUIRE (English) Medieval landlord.

STACY (Greek) Fertile. Variation: *Stacey.*

STAFFORD (English) Landing with a ford. Variations: *Stafforde, Staford.*

STAMOS (Greek) Crown.

STANBOROUGH (English) Unknown definition.

STANBURY (English) Fort made of stone. Variations: *Stanberry, Stanbery.*

STANCIE (English) Unknown definition.

STANCLIFF (English) Stony cliff. Variation: *Stancliffe.*

STANCOMBE (English) Unknown definition.

STANDISH (English) Stony park.

STANFIELD (English) Stony field. Variation: *Stansfield.*

STANFORD (English) Stony ford. Variations: *Stamford, Stan, Standford.*

STANHOPE (English) Stony hollow.

STANISLAUS (Polish) Glorious camp. With countless Polish relatives surrounding me throughout my childhood, I was very familiar with the name Stanislaus. I always thought it was just the Polish version of Stanley; however, I recently discovered that this is not the case. The most common nickname for Stanislaus was Stash. Variations: *Stach, Stanislao, Stanislas, Stanislau, Stanislus, Stanislav, Stanislaw, Stas, Stash, Stashko, Stashko, Stasio.*

STANLEY (English) Stony meadow. Back in its day – which was around the middle of the 19th century – Stanley was quite a noble name. The most famous Stanley we know is the comic actor Stan Laurel, the better half of Laurel and Hardy. Variations: *Stan, Stanlea, Stanlee, Stanleigh, Stanly.*

STANMORE (English) Stony lake.

STANNARD (English) Hard as a stone.

STANTON (English) Stony town. Variations: *Stanten, Staunton.*

STANWAY (English) Stony road. Variations: *Stanaway, Stannaway, Stannway.*

STANWICK (English) Resident of the stony town. Variations: *Stanwicke, Stanwyck.*

STANWOOD (English) Stony woods.

STARR (English) Star.

STAVROS (Greek) Crowned.

STEADMAN (English) One who lives on a farm. Variations: *Steadmann, Stedman.*

STEELE (English) One who resists. Variation: *Steel.*

STEIN (German) Stone. Variation: *Steen.*

STEINAR (Scandinavian) Stone warrior. Variations: *Steen, Stein, Steiner, Sten.*

STEPHEN (Greek) Crowned. Stephen holds the distinction of being the name of the first Christian on record; and its history has served as a built-in boost in any country where Christianity is practised. The name was borne by many saints and ten popes as well as England's King Stephen. The different variations of the name each provide clearly distinct feels. For instance, Steve McQueen had a somewhat swaggering

personality, while Stephen Sondheim, Stephen King, and Steven Spielberg convey a more artistic image. The less formal version 'Stevie' is claimed by a well-known musician: Stevie Wonder. Nowadays, Stephen with a 'ph' is used less often than Steven with a 'v'. Though the name is not as popular as it once was, it is still used with some regularity, and it will be with us for quite some time. Variations: *Stefan, Stefano, Stefanos, Stefans, Steffan, Steffel, Steffen, Stefos, Stepa, Stepan, Stepanek, Stepek, Stephan, Stephane, Stephanos, Stephanus, Stephens, Stephenson, Stepka, Stepousek, Stevan, Steve, Steven, Stevenson, Stevie.*

STERLING (English) First-class. Variation: *Stirling.*

STERNE (English) Unyielding. Variations: *Stearn, Stearne, Stearns, Stern.*

STEWART (Scottish) Steward. Only emerged as a first name in the early 19th century. It became quite fash-ionable in the 1950s but became less common since the 1970s. One famous bearer is British film actor Stewart Granger. Variations: *Stew, Steward, Stu, Stuart.*

STIG (Scandinavian) Wanderer. Variations: *Styge, Stygge.*

STIGGUR (Gypsy) Gate.

STILLMAN (English) Silent man.

STOCKLEY (English) Meadow of tree stumps. Variations: *Stocklea, Stocklee, Stockleigh.*

STOCKTON (English) Town of tree stumps.

STOCKWELL (English) Spring with tree stumps.

STODDARD (English) Protector of horses.

STORM (English) Storm. A name suggesting a passionate, lively nature. It does not appear to have been used before the early 20th century.

STRAHAN (Irish) Minstrel. Variation: *Strachan.*

STRATFORD (English) River crossing near a street.

Strange but True Names

First, you laugh. The next thought you have is, what could these parents have been thinking?

We've all known people who have names that are just, well, not the prettiest or most handsome names around. However, these names – which include Helga, Chumley, and other names from decades past – usually don't sound mellifluous to us now as the result of years and years of association and how each generation regards the most common names of their time.

No, these names are just plain strange – and funny. You'll see!

- Bottled Beer
- Windsor Castle
- Groaner Digger
- Dr. Zoltan Ovary
- Praise-God Barebones
- Siblings: Tonsilitis, Meningitis, Appendicitis and Peritonitis Jackson
- More Siblings: One, Two, Three, Four, Five and Six Dupuis
- Yet More Siblings: Finis, Addenda, Appendix, Supplement and Errata (last name unknown)
- Zachary Zzzra (last in the phone book)
- Reverend Christian Church
- Lavender Sidebottom
- Jordan River
- Stone Wall
- Mineral Waters

STROM (German) River.
STRONG (English) Powerful.
STRUTHERS (Irish) Brook.
STURE (Scandinavian) Contrary.
STYLES (English) Stile, or steps that go over a wall.
SUBHASH (Hindu) Speaks well.
SUCK-CHIN (Korean) Stable foundation.
SUDAS (Hindu) Good helper.
SUDHIR (Hindu) Wise.
SUDI (African: Swahili) Fortune.
SUFFIELD (English) Southern field.
SUGDEN (German) Valley of pigs.
SUHAYL (Arabic) Star. Variation: *Suhail*.
SUIBHNE (Irish) Pleasant. Variation: *Sivney*.
SUJAY (Hindu) Successful victory.
SUJIT (Hindu) Winner.
SULAYMAN (Arabic) Peaceful. Variations: *Shelomon, Siliman, Sulaiman, Suleiman, Suleyman*.
SULKTALTHSCOSUM (Native American: Salish) Half of the sun. Variation: *Sulktashkosha*.
SULLIVAN (Irish) Black-eyed. With its last name origins and Irish roots, the stage is set for Sullivan to become more popularly used. Variations: *Sullavan, Sullevan, Sulliven*.
SULLY (English) Southern meadow. Variations: *Sulleigh, Sulley*.
SULTAN (African: Swahili) Leader.
SULWYN (Welsh) Bright sun.
SUMAN (Hindu) Smart.
SUMANTRA (Hindu) Good advice.
SUNDARA (Hindu) Beautiful. Variations: *Sundar, Sundarama, Sunder*.
SUNDEEP (Punjabi) Enlightened being.
SUNIL (Hindu) Dark blue.
SURAJ (Hindu) Sun.

SUSHOBAN (Hindu) Very attractive.
SUSRUTA (Hindu) Good reputation. Variations: *Sushrut, Sushruta*.
SUTCLIFF (English) Southern cliff. Variation: *Sutcliffe*.
SUTHERLAND (Scandinavian) Southern land. Variation: *Southerland*.
SUTTON (English) Southern town.
SVATOPULK (Czech) Bright people.
SVATOSLAV (Czech) Glorious and holy.
SVEINN (Scandinavian) Strong youth. Variations: *Svein, Sven, Svend, Svends*.
SWAIN (Scandinavian) Competent.
SWALEY (English) Winding stream. Variations: *Swailey, Swale, Swales*.
SWATANEY (Native American: Iroquois) Teacher. Variation: *Swateny*.
SWEENEY (Irish) Small hero. Variation: *Sweeny*.
SWIETOMIERZ (Polish) Holy and famous.
SWIETOPELK (Polish) Holy people.
SWIETOSLAW (Polish) Holy glory.
SWINBOURNE (English) Brook used by swine. Variations: *Swinborn, Swinborne, Swinburn, Swinbyrn, Swynborne*.
SWINDEL (English) Swine valley. Variations: *Swyndel, Swyndell, Swyndelle*.
SWINFORD (English) Swine ford. Variation: *Swynford*.
SWINTON (English) Swine town.
SYLVESTER (Latin) Forested. From Sylvester Stallone to Sylvester the Cat all the way to Sylvester the disco singer from the 1970s, this name is a real mixed bag of images and associations. Variations: *Silvester, Silvestre, Silvestro, Sly*.
SYON (Hindu) Happy.
SZCZESNY (Polish) Lucky.

TAB (German) Brilliant. Variation: *Tabb*.

TABBAI (Hebrew) Good.

TABBEBO (Native American: Paiute) Man of the sun.

TABIB (Turkish) Doctor. Variation: *Tabeeb*.

TABOR (Hungarian) Camp. Variations: *Taber, Taibor, Tayber, Taybor*.

TAD (Welsh) Father. Variation: *Tadd*.

TADHG (Irish) Poet. Variations: *Taidhgin, Teague, Teige*.

TADI (Native American: Omaha) Wind.

TADZI (Native American: Carrier Indian) Loon.

TAGGART (Irish) Son of a priest.

TAGHEE (Native American: Bannock) Chief. Variations: *Taighe, Taihee, Tyee, Tyhee*.

TAHA (Arabic) The Arabic letters 'T' and 'H'; (Polynesian) One.

TAHATAN (Native American: Sioux) Hawk.

TAHE GAHE (Native American: Osage) Buck antlers.

TAHETON (Native American: Sioux) Crow.

TAHI (Polynesian) Ocean.

TAHIR (Arabic) Pure, unsullied. Variation: *Taheer*.

TAHOMA (Native American: Navajo) Shoreline. Variation: *Tohoma*.

TAI (Vietnamese) Skill.

TAIMAH (Native American: Fox) Thunder. Variations: *Taima, Taiomah, Tama, Tamah*.

TAIWO (African: Nigerian) First-born twin.

TAIZO (Japanese) Third son.

TAJ (Hindu) Crown.

TAKESHI (Japanese) Bamboo.

TAKLISHIM (Native American: Apache) Grey.

TAKODA (Native American: Sioux) Friends.

TAL (Hebrew) Rain. Variation: *Talor*.

TALBOT (English) Last name. Variations: *Talbert, Talbott, Tallbot, Tallbott*.

TALE (African: Botswana) Green.

TALFRYN (Welsh) High hill.

TALIB (Arabic) Searcher.

TALIESIN (Welsh) Radiant brow. Variation: *Taltesin*.

TALLI (Native American: Lenapi) Lenapi leader.

TALMAI (Hebrew) Furrow. Variation: *Talmi.*

TALMAN (Hebrew) To injure. Variations: *Tallie, Tally, Talmon.*

TALOF HARJO (Native American: Creek) Crazy bear.

TALOR (Hebrew) Morning dew.

TAM (Vietnamese) Eight.

TAMELA PASHME (Native American: Sioux) Dull knife.

TAMIR (Arabic) One with many dates.

TAMAN (Serbo-Croatian) Black.

TAMMANY (Native American: Delaware) The affable. Variation: *Tamanend.*

TAN (Vietnamese) New.

TANAFA (Polynesian) Drumbeat.

TANAKI (Polynesian) Keep score.

TANAY (Hindu) Son.

TANDIE (African-American) Masculine.

TANG THUY (Vietnamese) Deep pool.

TANGALOA (Polynesian) Big stomach.

TANH (Vietnamese) Attitude.

TANI (Japanese) Valley.

TANK (Polynesian) God of the sky.

TANNER (English) One who tans leather. There are a slew of last names beginning with 'T' that are currently very popular for use as a first names for boys. Tanner is one of a group that includes Tucker, Taylor and Travis. Tanner is beginning to show strength, so I wouldn't be surprised if this name ends up on the top fifty or hundred names for the decade. Variations: *Tan, Tanier, Tann, Tanney, Tannie, Tanny.*

TANTON (English) Town on a silent river.

TANO (African: Ghanian) River. Variation: *Tanno.*

TARHE (Native American: Wyandot) Tree.

TARIK (Hindu) Door knock. Variations: *Taril, Tarin, Tariq.*

TARLETON (English) Thor's town.

TARO (Japanese) First male.

TARRANT (Welsh) Thunder. Variation: *Tarrent.*

TARUN (Hindu) Young.

TAS (Gypsy) Bird's nest.

TASHUNKA (Native American: Sioux) Horse. Variation: *Tasunke.*

TASHUNKA WITCO (Native American: Sioux) Crazy horse.

TASI NAGI (Native American: Sioux) Yellow robe. Variation: *Tashinagi.*

TATANKA IYOTANKA (Native American: Sioux) Sitting bull.

TATANKA PSTCA (Native American: Sioux) Jumping bull.

TATANKAMIMI (Native American: Sioux) Walking bull.

TATE (English) Happy. Variations: *Tait, Taitt, Tayte.*

TATONGA (Native American: Sioux) Male deer.

TAU (African: Botswana) Lion.

TAVA (Polynesian) Tree with fruit.

TAVARES (Spanish) Son of a hermit.

TAVAS (Hebrew) Peacock.

TAVI (Hebrew) Good.

TAVISH (Irish) Twin. Variations: *Tavis, Tevis.*

TAVOR (Hebrew) Unlucky. Variation: *Tabor.*

TAWA (Native American: Hopi) The sun.

TAWAGAHE (Native American: Osage) One who builds a town.

TAWANIMA (Native American: Hopi) Movement of the sun. Variation: *Tewanima.*

TAWAQUAPTEWA (Native American: Hopi) Sun on the horizon. Variation: *Tewaquoptiwa.*

TAWFIQ (Arabic) Good luck. Variation: *Tawfi.*

TAWL (Arabic) Tall. Variation: *Taweel.*

TAWNO (Gypsy) Small.

TAYIB (Arabic) Good.

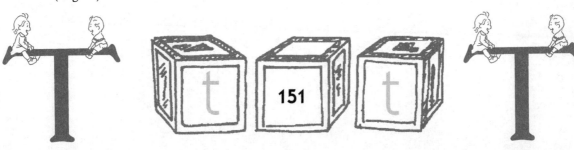

TAYLOR (English) Tailor. Taylor is really gaining ground for both boys and girls, but there are signs that it will soon become the sole property of girls. Boys will have to switch to Tyler or another popular last name as first name that begins with 'T'. Variations: *Tailer, Tailor, Tayler, Taylour.*

TEARLACH (Scottish) Man.

TECHOMIR (Czech) Great consolation.

TECHOSLAV (Czech) Glorious consolation.

TECUMSEH (Native American: Shawnee) Traveller.

TEDMUND (English) Watcher over land. Variation: *Tedmond.*

TEJOMAY (Hindu) Glorious. Variation: *Tej.*

TEKONSHA (Native American: Algonquin) Little caribou.

TELAMON (Greek) Ancient mythological figure.

TELEK (Polish) Ironworker.

TELEM (Hebrew) Furrow.

TELESPHOROS (Greek) To bring the end of an event.

TELFORD (French) One who works with iron. Variations: *Telfer, Telfor, Telfour.*

TEM (Gypsy) Country.

TEMAN (Hebrew) On the right.

TEMPEST (French) Storm.

TEMPLE (English) Temple.

TEMPLETON (English) Town near the temple. Variations: *Temple, Templeten.*

TENDOY (Native American: Bannock) To climb. Variation: *Tendoi.*

TENEANGOPTE (Native American: Kiowa) Kicking bird.

TENNANT (English) Tenant. Variations: *Tenant, Tennent.*

TENNESEE (Native American: Cherokee) The state.

TENNYSON (English) Son of Dennis. Variations: *Tenney, Tennie, Tenny.*

TENSKWATAWA (Native American: Shawnee) Door ajar.

TEO (Polynesian) Gift from God.

TERACH (Hebrew) Goat. Variations: *Tera, Terah.*

TERENCE (Latin) Roman clan name. Twenty and thirty years ago, boys called Terry had Terence as their real names. Today, Terence has become somewhat of a relic since parents have been brave enough to name their sons Terry from the start. Terry is yet another instance of a name that started out being exclusively male, crossed over to become popular for both boys and girls, and then in the end, began to be associated almost exclusively with girls. Variations: *Tarrance, Terencio, Terrance, Terrence, Terrey, Terri, Terry.*

TERRILL (German) Follower of Thor. Variations: *Terrall, Terrel, Terrell, Terryl, Terryll, Tirrell, Tyrrell.*

TERYL (African-American) Mix of Terry and Daryl. Variation: *Terrell.*

TESHER (Hebrew) Donation.

TET (Vietnamese) Festival.

TEVA (Hebrew) Nature.

TEVIN (African-American) Variation of Kevin.

TEVITA (Polynesian) Cherished.

TEX (American) Nickname for Texas.

THABITI (African: Kenyan) A man.

THADDEUS (Aramaic) Brave. Variations: *Taddeo, Tadeo, Tadio, Thad, Thaddaus.*

THAI (Vietnamese) Many.

THANDIWE (African: Zulu) Beloved.

THANE (English) Landlord. Variations: *Thain, Thaine, Thayn, Thayne.*

THANG (Vietnamese) Conquer.

THANH (Vietnamese) End.

THANOS (Greek) Royal. Variation: *Thanasis.*

THAONAWYUTHE (Native American: Seneca) One who interrupts. Variation: *Thaowayuthe.*

THATCHER (English) Roof thatcher. Variations: *Thacher, Thatch, Thaxter.*

THAW (English) Melt.

THAYENDANEGEA (Native American: Iroquois) Gambler.

THEMBA (South African) Hope.

THEOBALD (German) Brave people. Variations: *Thebaud, Thebault, Thibault, Thibaut, Tibold, Tiebold.*

THEODORE (Greek) Gift from God. Variations: *Teador, Ted, Tedd, Teddey, Teddie, Teddy, Tedor, Teodor, Teodoro, Theo, Theodor.*

THEODORIC (German) Leader of the people. Variation: *Thierry.*

THEOPHILUS (Greek) Loved by God. Variations: *Teofil, Theophile.*

THERON (Greek) Hunter.

THESEUS (Greek) Ancient mythological figure.

THIASSI (Scandinavian) Ancient mythological figure. Variations: *Thiazi, Thjazi.*

THO (Vietnamese) Long life.

THOMAS (Aramaic) Twin. St. Thomas was the impetus for this name as it started to become popular around the time of the Middle Ages. Today, Thomas is popular all over the world, and is one of the names that parents are looking to in order to instill a sense of history and tradition in their own sons. Variations: *Tam, Tameas, Thom, Thoma, Thompson, Thomson, Thumas, Thumo, Tom, Tomas, Tomaso, Tomasso, Tomaz, Tomcio, Tomek, Tomelis, Tomi, Tomie, Tomislaw, Tomm, Tommy, Tomsen, Tomson, Toomas, Tuomas, Tuomo.*

THONG (Vietnamese) Smart.

THOR (Scandinavian: Norwegian) Thunder. No matter which version of Thor you choose for your son, you are choosing one of the most popular names in

Animal and Plant Names from Around the World

Glancing through the names in this book, it seems that almost every culture has its favourite nature names it likes to bestow on its newborn girls and boys.

In America, for example, Fawn has been popular for girls and Leo – the lion – has often been used for boys. In France, Linette – a type of little bird – is a popular girls' name, and Numair, Arabic for panther, enjoys popularity for boys among France's growing Muslim population.

Insects are not commonly used to name either girls or boys except in many Native American tribes – the insects represented in the names usually appear in the process of doing something, either crawling up a leaf or being eaten by a bird. Fruits, vegetables, and other plants, however, are frequent sources of names for boys and girls around the world: Rimon is pomegranate for Jews and Ringo is an apple for Japanese people; both are common names for boys. Bakula, Hindi for a type of flower, and Algoma, meaning valley of the flowers for Native Americans, are names for girls.

As you leaf through the thousands of names in this book, you'll see that there are many names you can choose from that originate from a plant or animal in a particular culture.

Boys' Names

- Ash
- Birch
- Clay
- Forest
- Hawk
- River
- Sage
- Thorn

Girls' Names

- Amber
- Cherry
- Daisy
- Fern
- Ginger
- Holly
- Lily
- Olive
- Rose
- Terra
- Violet
- Willow

Denmark. It's a powerful name and should continue to become more popular. Variations: *Tor, Torr.*

THORALD (Scandinavian: Norwegian) One who follows Thor. Variations: *Thorold, Torald.*

THORBERT (Scandinavian: Norwegian) Thor's brightness. Variation: *Torbert.*

THORBURN (Scandinavian: Norwegian) Thor's bear.

THORER (Scandinavian) Thor's warrior. Variation: *Thorvald.*

THORLEY (English) Thor's meadow. Variations: *Thorlea, Thorlee, Thorleigh, Thorly, Torley.*

THORMOND (English) Defended by Thor. Variations: *Thurmond, Thurmund.*

THORNDIKE (English) Thorny riverbank. Variations: *Thorndyck, Thorndyke.*

THORNE (English) Thorn. Variation: *Thorn.*

THORNLEY (English) Thorny meadow. Variations: *Thornlea, Thornleigh, Thornly.*

THORNTON (English) Thorny town.

THORPE (English) Village. Variation: *Thorp.*

THU (Vietnamese) Autumn.

THUC (Vietnamese) Alert.

THUONG (Vietnamese) Chase.

THURLOW (English) Thor's hill.

THURSTON (Scandinavian) Thor's stone. Variations: *Thorstan, Thorstein, Thorsteinn, Thorsten, Thurstain, Thurstan, Thursten, Torstein, Torsten, Torston.*

THUY (Vietnamese) Tender.

TIARNACH (Irish) Godly. Variation: *Tighearnach.*

TIBOR (Slavic) Sacred place. Variations: *Tiebout, Tybald, Tybalt, Tybault.*

TIEN (Vietnamese) First.

TIERNAN (Irish) Little lord. Variations: *Tierney, Tighearnach, Tighearnan.*

TIKI (Polynesian) The first man.

TILDEN (English) Fertile valley.

TILFORD (English) Fertile ford.

TILL (German) Leader of the people.

TILON (Hebrew) Hill.

TILTON (English) Fertile town. Estate.

TIMIN (Arabic) Sea serpent.

TIMOTHY (Greek) Honouring God. Any name that rhymes with Jimmy – like Timmy does – is a great name for a kid. Variations: *Tim, Timmothy, Timmy, Timo, Timofeo, Timon, Timoteo, Timothe, Timotheo, Timotheus, Timothey, Tymmothy, Tymothy.*

TIMUR (Hebrew) Tall.

TIN (Vietnamese) Think.

TIPU (Hindu) Tiger.

TIRU (Hindu) Devoted.

TIRUVALLUVAR (Hindu) Devout village.

TITO (Spanish) To honour.

TITUS (Latin) Unknown definition. Variations: *Tito, Titos.*

TIVON (Hebrew) Lover of nature.

TOA (Polynesian) Brave.

TOAFO (Polynesian) Forest.

TOAL (Irish) Strong people. Variations: *Tuathal, Tully.*

TOBIAS (Hebrew) God is good. Variations: *Tobe, Tobey, Tobia, Tobiah, Tobie, Tobin, Toby.*

TOBBAR (Gypsy) Road.

TOBIKUMA (Japanese) Cloud.

TODD (English) Fox. Variation: *Tod.*

TOHON (Native American) Cougar.

TOH YAH (Native American: Navajo) Walking by a stream.

TOIRDEALBHACH (Irish) Like Thor, the Norse god of thunder. Variations: *Tirloch, Turlough.*

TOKALA (Native American: Sioux) Fox.

TOKUTARO (Japanese) Virtuous.

TOMER (Hebrew) Tall.

TOMI (Japanese) Wealthy.

TOMLIN (English) Little twin. Variation: *Tomlinson*.

TOMOCHICHI (Native American: Creek) To fly up. Variation: *Tomocheechee*.

TONG (Vietnamese) Aromatic.

TONY (Latin) Nickname for Anthony that has evolved into its own freestanding name. Variations: *Toney*, *Tonie*.

TOOHULHULSOTE (Native American: Nez Perce) Noise. Variation: *Toohoolhoolzote*.

TOOPWEETS (Native American: Ute) Strong.

TOPWE (African) Vegetable.

TOR (African: Nigerian) Ruler.

TORAO (Japanese) Tiger.

TORD (Scandinavian) Peace of Thor.

TORGER (Scandinavian) Thor's spear. Variations: *Terje*, *Torgeir*.

TORIL (Hindu) Attitude.

TORIN (Irish) Chief.

TORIO (Japanese) Bird's tail.

TORKEL (Scandinavian) Thor's cauldron. Variations: *Thorkel, Torkil, Torkild, Torkjell, Torquil*.

TORMOD (Scottish) Man from the North.

TOROLF (Scandinavian) Thor's wolf. Variations: *Thorolf, Tolv, Torolv, Torulf*.

TORRANCE (Irish) Little hills. Variations: *Torin, Torrence, Torrey, Torrin, Torry*.

TORU (Japanese) Ocean.

TOSHIHIRO (Japanese) Wise.

TOSHIO (Japanese) Year boy. Variation: *Toshi*.

TOSHIRO (Japanese) Skillful.

TOV (Hebrew) Good. Variations: *Tovi, Toviel, Toviya, Tuvia, Tuviah, Tuviya*.

TOVE (Scandinavian) Thor's rule. Variation: *Tuve*.

TOWNLEY (English) Town meadow. Variations: *Townlea, Townlee, Townleigh, Townlie, Townly*.

TOWNSEND (English) Town's end.

TRACY (French) Area in France. Variations: *Trace, Tracey, Treacy*.

TRAHAEARN (Welsh) Strong as iron. Variations: *Trahern, Traherne*.

TRAI (Vietnamese) Pearl.

TRAVIS (French) Toll-taker. No one knows for sure why this name has suddenly become popular in the last ten or fifteen years, except for the fact that it is a last name that begins with the letter 'T', which accounts for many of the newly popular boys' names. By the 1970s it ranked among the top fifty names in Australia. The success of the British band Travis may help its profile in Britain. Variations: *Traver, Travers, Travus, Travys*.

TRAYTON (English) Town near trees.

TREMAIN (Celtic) Stone house. Variations: *Tremaine, Tremayne*.

TRENT (Latin) Rushing waters. Variations: *Trenten, Trentin, Trenton*.

TREVOR (Welsh) Large homestead. Since Trevor seems to be cut from the same cloth as Travis, you'd think it would be nearly as popular. This is not the case, however, so feel free to use it and think of it as unique. Variations: *Trefor, Trev, Trevar, Trever, Trevis*.

TREY (English) Three.

TRISTAM (Celtic) Famous folklore character. It made its appearance in England in the 12th century and was borne by Sir Tristram of Lyoness, one of the most noble of King Arthur's legendary knights of the Round Table. The tragic story of Sir Tristram and his fatal passion for Princess Isolda was the basis of Wagner's opera *Tristan und Isolde*. The name has also occured in literature as the central character in Laurence Sterne's novel *Tristram Shandy*. Variations: *Tris, Tristan*.

TROND (Scandinavian) From Trondelag, an area in central Norway.

TROWBRIDGE (English) Bridge by a tree.

TROY (Irish) Soldier. Variations: *Troi, Troye.*

TRUMAN (English) Loyal one. Variations: *Trueman, Trumaine, Trumann.*

TRUMBLE (English) Powerful. Variations: *Trumball, Trumbell, Trumbull.*

TSALANI (African: Malawian) Goodbye.

TSATOKE (Native American: Kiowa) Horse who hunts. Variation: *Tsa-Ta-Ke.*

TSELA (Native American: Navajo) Stars lying down.

TSEN TAINTE (Native American: Kiowa) White horse.

TSIN (Native American: Cherokee) Canoe.

TSOAI (Native American: Kiowa) Rock tree.

TSOTOHAH (Native American: Kiowa) Red cliff.

TU (Vietnamese) Four.

TUAN (Vietnamese) Unimportant.

TUCKER (English) One who works with cloth.

TUDOR (Welsh) Royal dynasty.

TUKULI (Native American: Miwok) Caterpillar crawling down a tree in summer.

TULLY (Irish) Peaceful. Variations: *Tull, Tulley, Tullie.*

TULSI (Hindu) Basil.

TUMAINI (African: Kenyan) Hope.

TUNG (Vietnamese) Peace.

TUNU (Native American: Miwok) Deer eating wild onions.

TUONG (Vietnamese) Everyone.

TUPI (Native American: Miwok) To pull a salmon onto the river bank.

TURNER (English) Woodworker.

TUWA (Hebrew) God's goodness.

TUYEN (Vietnamese) Angel.

TWAIN (English) Split in two. Variations: *Twaine, Twayn.*

TWYFORD (English) Place where rivers converge.

TY (American) Unknown definition. Variation: *Tye.*

TYCHO (Scandinavian) On the mark. Variations: *Tyge, Tyko.*

TYDEUS (Greek) Ancient mythological figure.

TYEE (Native American) Chief.

TYKE (Native American) Captain.

TYLER (English) Tile maker. Tyler was an extremely popular name in the 1990s for both boys and girls, though it is more widely used for boys. If you already have a child in nursery school, there's a good chance that one or more of the boys in your child's class is named Tyler. Parents like the name because it is both formal and casual. Variations: *Ty, Tylar.*

TYMON (Greek) Praise the Lord.

TYMOTEUSZ (Polish) To honour God. Variations: *Tomek, Tymek, Tymon.*

TYNAN (Irish) Dark.

TYR (Scandinavian) Shining one.

TYRELL (Latin) Roman clan name. Variations: *Terrell, Tirell, Tyrrell.*

TYRONE (Irish) Land of Owen. Variations: *Tiron, Tirone, Ty, Tyron.*

TYSON (English) Firebrand. Variations: *Tieson, Tison, Tysen.*

TZACH (Hebrew) Clean. Variations: *Tzachai, Tzachar.*

TZADIK (Hebrew) Virtuous. Variations: *Tzadok, Zadik, Zadoc, Zadok, Zaydak.*

TZADKIEL (Hebrew) Virtuous with God. Variation: *Zadkiel.*

TZALMON (Hebrew) Dark. Variation: *Zalmon.*

TZEPHANIAH (Hebrew) God protects. Variations: *Tzefanya, Zefania, Zefaniah, Zephania, Zephaniah.*

TZEVI (Hebrew) Deer. Variations: *Tzeviel, Zevi, Zeviel.*

TZURIEL (Hebrew) God is my rock. Variation: *Zuriel.*

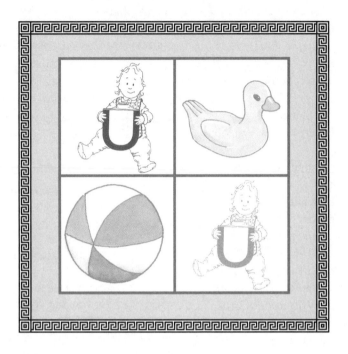

UALTAR (Irish) Ruler of the army. Variations: *Uaitcir, Ualteir.*

UANG (Chinese) Great.

UATA (Polynesian) Army leader. Variation: *Uate.*

UBADAH (Arabic) He who serves God.

UCHECHI (African: Nigerian) God's will.

UDAY (Hindu) To show up. Variation: *Udayan.*

UDELL (English) Yew grove. Variations: *Dell, Eudel, Udall, Udel.*

UDOLF (English) Wealthy wolf. Variations: *Udolfo, Udolph.*

UGO (Italian) Intellect.

UHILA (Polynesian) Lightning.

UHUBITU (Native American) Dirty water.

UILLEOG (Irish) Small protector. Variations: *Uilleac, Uillioc.*

UINSEANN (Irish) One who conquers. Variation: *Uinsionn.*

UJALA (Hindu) Shining. Variation: *Ujaala.*

ULAN (African) First-born of twins.

ULBRECHT (German) Grandeur.

ULEKI (Hawaiian) Hawaiian version of Ulysses. Variation: *Ulesi.*

ULF (Scandinavian) Wolf. Variation: *Ulv.*

ULL (Scandinavian) Glory.

ULMER (English) Famous wolf. Variations: *Ullmar, Ulmar.*

ULRIC (German) Wolf power. Variations: *Ulrich, Ulrick, Ulrike.*

ULRIK (Scandinavian) Noble ruler.

ULYSSES (Latin) Wrathful. Variation of Odysseus. Variations: *Ulises, Ulisse.*

UMAR (Arabic) To bloom.

UMBERTO (Italian) Famous German. Variation of Humbert.

UMED (Hindu) Desire.

UMI (African: Malawian) Life.

UNADUTI (Native American: Cherokee) Wooly head.

UNER (Turkish) Famous.

UNIKA (African: Malawian) To shine.

UNKAS (Native American: Mohegan) Fox. Variations: *Uncas, Wonkas.*

UNWIN (English) Enemy. Variations: *Unwinn, Unwyn.*

UPTON (English) Hill town.

UPWOOD (English) Forest on a hill.

URBAN (Latin) Man from the city. Though rural parents-to-be would probably never consider this name for their baby boys, Urban is slowly catching on as a hip, sophisticated name for parents who are looking for a name that's just a bit different. There were a number of popes who went by the name of Urban, but the name never really made many inroads until very recently. Variations: *Urbain, Urbaine, Urbane, Urbano, Urbanus, Urvan.*

URI (Hebrew) God's light. Variations: *Uria, Uriah, Urias, Urie, Uriel.*

URIAN (Greek) Heaven.

URIEN (Welsh) Privileged birth.

URJASZ (Polish) God is light.

URSAN (Latin) Bear. Variation: *Urson.*

URVIL (Hindu) The sea.

USAMA (Arabic) Lion. Variation: *Usamah.*

USENI (African: Malawian) Tell me.

USI (African: Malawian) Smoke.

USTIN (Russian) Just.

UTATCI (Native American) Bear scratching.

UTHMAN (Arabic) Bird. Variations: *Othman, Usman.*

UTTAM (Hindu) Best.

UZIAH (Hebrew) God is my strength. Variations: *Uzia, Uziya, Uzziah.*

UZIEL (Hebrew) Powerful. Variation: *Uzziel.*

UZOMA (African: Nigerian) Born on a trip.

Last-Names-as-First-Names

Morgan is one last-name-as-first-name that is turning out to be quite a desirable name for girls these days. It's a pleasant, strong name, but it's also androgynous in nature, which some parents feel will bode well for their daughters once they enter the working world.

If family first names Henrietta and Hubert don't do much for you, but you'd like to give your baby a name that reflects some of your family's heritage, you could start by looking at the last names that appear in your family tree. Or you could just look through the phone book to find something you like. Davis or Smith might work for you – boy or girl – but so might Edson, Windsor or Pritchard.

This seems to be a trend that is just beginning to catch on among families who have preferred the tried-and-true names of the past. Some baby name trends are just that: they make a brief fluttering appearance at city and town registries in certain areas of the country, and then they're gone.

I don't think this is the case with last-names-as-first-names. I believe we're just getting started.

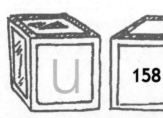

VACHEL (French) Small cow. Variation: *Vachell.*

VADIN (Hindu) Educated orator.

VAIL (English) City in ado. Variations: *Vaile, Vale, Vayle.*

VAINO (Scandinavian: Finnish) Wagon-builder.

VALA (Polynesian) Loincloth.

VALDEMAR (German) Famous leader.

VALENTINE (Latin) Strong. St. Valentine was a third-century martyr whose feast day is celebrated on 14 February. This name is inextricably linked with romance. Variations: *Val, Valentin, Valentino, Valentyn.*

VALERIAN (Latin) Healthy. Variations: *Valerie, Valerien, Valerio, Valery, Valeryan.*

VALI (Scandinavian) Ancient mythological figure.

VALIN (Hindu) Mighty soldier. Valin is a variation of the name Balin. In the Hindu religion, however, Valin is the monkey king. Variations: *Valen, Valyn.*

VALMIKI (Hindu) Ant hill.

VALU (Polynesian) Eight.

VAN (Vietnamese) Appearance. Famous Vans include US actor Van Heflin and Northern Irish singer song-writer Van Morrison.

VANCE (English) Swampland. Variations: *Van, Vancelo, Vann.*

VANDA (Lithuanian) Ruling people. Variation: *Vandele.*

VANDAN (Hindu) Salvation.

VANDYKE (Dutch) From the dyke. Variation: *Van Dyck.*

VANNEVAR (English) Unknown definition.

VANSLOW (English) Unknown definition. Variations: *Vansalo, Vanselow, Vanslaw.*

VANYA (Russian) God is good. Variation of John. Variations: *Vanek, Vanka.*

VARDEN (French) Green mountains. Variations: *Vardon, Verden, Verdon, Verdun.*

VARDHAMMA (Hindu) Growth. Variation: *Vardhaman.*

VAREN (Hindu) Superior.

VARESH (Hindu) God is superior.

VARICK (German) Defending ruler. Variation: *Varrick*.

VARIL (Hindu) Water.

VARTAN (Armenian) Rose.

VARUN (Hindu) God of water. Variations: *Varin, Varoon*.

VASANT (Hindu) Spring.

VASIL (Czech) Kingly. Form of Basil. Variations: *Vasile, Vasilek, Vasili, Vasilios, Vasilis, Vasilos, Vasily, Vassily*.

VASIN (Hindu) Leader.

VASU (Hindu) Prosperous.

VATSYAYANA (Hindu) The author of the *Kama Sutra*.

VAUGHN (Welsh) Small. Perhaps the most famous man with the name Vaughn was the British composer Ralph Vaughan Williams. Even though the name is of Welsh origin, in the middle of the 20th century, the name was very popular. It's a great name, and not used nearly enough today. Variation: *Vaughan*.

VEA (Polynesian) Chief. Variations: *Veamalohi, Veatama*.

VEASNA (Cambodian) Lucky.

VELESLAV (Czech) Great glory. Variations: *Vela, Velek, Velousek*.

VELTRY (African-American) Unknown definition.

VENCEL (Hungarian) Wreath.

VENCESLAV (Czech) Glorious government.

VENEDICT (Russian) Blessed. Variation of Benedict. Variations: *Venedikt, Venka, Venya*.

VERDUN (French) City in France. Variations: *Verden, Verdon*.

VERE (French) Area in France.

VERED (Hebrew) Rose.

VERLIE (French) Town in France. Variation: *Verley*.

VERLIN (American) Spring. Variations: *Verle, Verlon*.

VERNON (French) Alder tree. Variations: *Vern, Verne*.

VERRILL (French) Loyal. Variations: *Verill, Verrall, Verrell, Verroll, Veryl*.

VICTOR (Latin) Conqueror. Owing to its definition, Victor was one of the most popular names during the time of the Romans. It fell out of favour throughout most of the Middle Ages, until it became popular again in the early part of the 20th century. Two famous Victors were Victor Borge and Victor Mature. Variations: *Vic, Vick, Victoir, Victorien, Victorino, Victorio, Viktor, Vitenka, Vitor, Vittore, Vittorio, Vittorios*.

VIDA (English) Beloved.

VIDAR (Scandinavian) Ancient mythological figure.

VIDKUN (Scandinavian) Vast experience.

VIDOR (Hungarian) Happy.

VIET (Vietnamese) Destroy.

VIHS (Hindu) Increase.

VIJAY (Hindu) Victory. Variations: *Bijay, Vijen, Vijun*.

VIJAYENDRA (Hindu) Victorious god of the sky. Variation: *Vijendra*.

VILA (Czech) From William, Will + helmet. Variations: *Vilek, Vilem, Vilhelm, Vili, Viliam, Vilko, Ville, Vilmos*.

VILIAMI (Polynesian) Protector.

VILJO (Scandinavian: Finnish) Guardian.

VILMOS (German) Steady soldier.

VILOK (Hindu) To see.

VIMAL (Hindu) Pure.

VINAY (Hindu) Courteous.

VINCENT (Latin) I once went out with a man named Vincent who had changed his name to Vincent. I'm not sure why he chose the name, unless he took it at face value and wanted to conquer something. Vincent has always been a popular name throughout the ages. However, today, some people equate Vincent solely with the nicknames Vinnie and Vince. Famous Vincents have included Vincent Price and Vincent van Gogh, whose tragic death was recalled in Don Maclean's song 'Vincent'. Although the name today seems a bit dated, I think it's an attractive name that parents-to-be should consider more often. A famous bearer of the variant Vinnie is British footballer turned actor Vinnie Jones. Variations: *Vikent, Vikenti, Vikesha, Vin, Vince, Vincente, Vincenz, Vincenzio, Vincenzo, Vinci, Vinco, Vinn, Vinnie, Vinny.*

VINE (English) One who works in a vineyard.

VINOD (Hindu) Fun.

VINSON (English) Son of Vincent.

VIRGIL (Latin) Roman clan name. The name Virgil seems to have been taken up at an early date in tribute to a revered French monk or an Irish bishop of the same name rather than to the great first-century Roman poet with whom the name is associated today. English settlers subsequently took the name with them to the USA and other parts of the English-speaking world and it has been in use into modern times. Famous Virgils have been US composer Virgil Thomson and the fictional Virgil Tibbs in John Ball's detective novel *In The Heat of the Night*. The name may be ready to make something of a comeback. Variations: *Vergil, Virgilio.*

VITALIS (Latin) Life.

VITO (Latin) Alive. Variations: *Vital, Vitale, Vitalis.*

VITUS (French) Forest. Variation: *Vitya.*

VIVEK (Hindu) Wisdom. Variations: *Vivekanand, Vivekananda.*

VIVIAN (Latin) Full of life.

VLADLEN (Russian) Vladimir + Lenin.

VLADIMIR (Slavic) Famous prince. The popularity of this name was boosted by St. Vladamir, the Russian prince who was largely responsible for bringing Christianity to his country. Variations: *Vlad, Vladamir, Vladimeer, Vladko, Vladlen.*

VLADISLAV (Czech) Glorious ruler. Variation: *Ladislav.*

VLAS (Russian) One who stammers.

VOJTECH (Czech) Comforting soldier. Variations: *Vojta, Vojtek, Vojtresek.*

VOLKER (German) Protector of the people.

VOLNEY (German) Spirit of the people.

VOLYA (Russian) Ruler of the people. Variation of Walter. Variations: *Vova, Vovka.*

VON (Scandinavian) Hope.

VOSHON (African-American) God's grace.

VUI (Vietnamese) Cheerful.

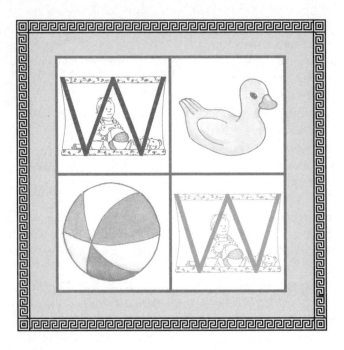

WABAN (Native American) Easterly wind.

WABANAQUOT (Native American: Chippewa) White cloud.

WABAUNSEE (Native American: Potawatomi) Sunrise. Variation: *Wahbon-seh*.

WABONISHI (Native American: Potawatomi) Winter survival.

WACHIRU (African: Kenyan) Son of a law maker.

WADE (English) To cross a river. Wade is one of those short, compact names that seem to command respect without inviting teasing. Margaret Mitchell used the name in her novel *Gone With the Wind*.

WADLEY (English) Meadow near a river crossing. Variations: *Wadleigh, Wadly*.

WADSWORTH (English) Village near a river crossing. Variation: *Waddsworth*.

WAGNER (German) Wagon maker. Variation: *Waggoner*.

WAHCHUMYUS (Native American: Nez Perce) Rainbow.

WAHIB (Arabic) To give.

WAHNAHTAH (Native American: Sioux) Pursuer. Variation: *Wahnaataa*.

WAHOTKONK (Native American: Kiowa) Black eagle.

WAHSHEHAH (Native American: Osage) Fat.

WAHTSAKE (Native American: Osage) Eagle.

WAIL (Arabic) One who returns to Allah.

WAITE (English) Watchman. Variations: *Waits, Wayte*.

WAJIH (Arabic) Extraordinary. Variation: *Wagih*.

WAKEFIELD (English) Damp field. Variation: *Wake*.

WAKELEY (English) Damp meadow. Variations: *Wakelea, Wakeleigh, Wakely*.

WAKEMAN (English) Watchman.

WAKIZA (Native American) Bold warrior.

WAKOYANTANKE (Native American: Sioux) Loud thunder.

WAKUNTCHAPINKA (Native American: Winnebago) Great thunder.

WALAKA (Hawaiian) Ruler of the people. Hawaiian version of Walter. Variation: *Walata*.

WALCOTT (English) Cottage by the wall. Variations: *Wallcot, Wallcott, Wolcott.*

WALDEMAR (German) Famous ruler.

WALDEN (English) Forested valley. Walden is an attractive choice for parents today, because it falls into the category of nature names as well as last name as first name. Some parents will choose it out of deference to Henry David Thoreau, while others will select it because of its fine upstanding manner and tone. Variation: *Waldon*.

WALDO (German) Strong.

WALDRON (German) Strong raven.

WALELIANO (Hawaiian) Strong.

WALENA (Hawaiian) Hawaiian version of Warren.

WALENEKINO (Hawaiian) Hawaiian version of Valentine. Variations: *Walakino, Walekino.*

WALERIAN (Polish) Strong. Variation: *Waleran*.

WALFORD (English) River crossing.

WALFRED (German) Peaceful ruler.

WALID (Arabic) Newborn. Variation: *Waleed*.

WALKARA (Native American: Ute) Yellow. Variation: *Wakara*.

WALKER (English) One who walks on cloth. Last name.

WALLACE (Scottish) One from Wales. Variations: *Wallach, Wallie, Wallis, Wally, Walsh, Welch, Welsh.*

WALLER (English) Wall maker.

WALTER (German) Ruler of the people. Though to some ears Walter may sound a bit outdated, it seems it may be rapidly gaining ground among parents-to-be. It is a name that is at once dignified and affable, although obviously the name isn't used as frequently as it was in the 1930s and 1940s. It was introduced into England in its modern form by the Normans in the 11th century and it reached its peak of popularity in the late 19th century. Famous Walters include Sir Walter Raleigh, Scottish writer Sir Walter Scott, British poet Walter de la Mare, Walt Disney, and poet Walt Whitman. Today, African-American families are choosing the name Walter more frequently than their white counterparts. Variations: *Walt, Walther, Waltr, Watkin.*

WALTON (English) Walled town.

WALWORTH (English) Walled farm.

WALWYN (English) Welsh friend. Variations: *Walwin, Walwinn, Walwynn, Walwynne.*

WAMBLEESKA (Native American: Sioux) White eagle.

WAMBUA (African: Kenyan) Born during the rainy season.

WANEKIA (Native American: Paiute) Creator of life.

WANETA (Native American: Sioux) He who charges another.

WANIG SUCHKA (Native American: Winnebago) Red bird.

WANJOHI (African: Kenyan) Brewer.

WANONCE (Native American: Sioux) Place of attack.

WAPASHA (Native American: Sioux) Red leaf. Variations: *Wabasha, Wapusha.*

WAPI (Native American) Lucky.

WARBURTON (English) Old fortress.

WARD (English) Observer. Variations: *Warde, Warden, Worden.*

WARDELL (English) Watchman's hill.

WARDLEY (English) Watchman's meadow. Variations: *Wardlea, Wardleigh.*

WARE (English) Observant.

WARFIELD (English) Field by the weir (a device placed in a river to catch fish).

WARFORD (English) River crossing by the weir.

WARLEY (English) Meadow by the weir.

WARREN (German) Protector friend. Actor Warren Beatty has injected the name with a reputation of sex appeal and worldliness. Another famous Warren was the British statesman Warren Hastings. Variations: *Warrin, Warriner.*

WARWICK (English) House near a dam. Variations: *Warick, Warrick.*

WASECHUNTASHVNKA (Native American: Sioux) Son of Sitting Bear.

WASHAKIE (Native American: Shoshone) Gourd.

WASHBURN (English) Flooded river.

WASHINGTON (English) Town of smart men.

WASIM (Arabic) Attractive.

WASONAUNEQUA (Native American: Chippewa) Yellow hair.

WASSAJA (Native American: Yavapai) Indication. Variation: *Wasagah.*

WATHOHUCK (Native American: Sauk) Shining road.

WATSON (English) Son of Walter.

WATTAN (Native American: Arapaho) Black. Variation: *Waatina.*

WAUNAKEE (Native American: Algonquin) Peaceful.

WAVERLY (English) Meadow of aspen trees. Variations: *Waverlee, Waverleigh, Waverley.*

WAYA (Native American: Cherokee) Wolf.

WAYLON (English) Roadside land. Variations: *Way, Waylan, Wayland, Waylen, Waylin.*

WAYNE (English) Wagon maker. Version of Wainwright. It became a popular choice in the 1940s, promoted by John Wayne, who took his stage name from Anthony Wayne a general in the American War of Independence. It peaked in popularity in the English-speaking world in the 1970s, but has since suffered a decline. Variations: *Wain, Wainwright, Wayn, Waynwright.*

WEBLEY (English) Weaver's meadow. Variations: *Webbley, Webbly, Webly.*

WEBSTER (English) Weaver. Variations: *Web, Webb, Weber.*

WEI-QUO (Chinese) Leader of a nation.

WEKESA (African: Kenyan) Born during the harvest.

WELBORNE (English) Spring-fed river. Variations: *Welborn, Welbourne, Welburn, Wellborn, Wellbourn, Wellburn.*

WELBY (English) Waterside farm. Variations: *Welbey, Welbie, Wellbey, Wellby.*

WELDON (English) Well near a hill. Variations: *Welden, Welldon.*

WELFORD (English) Well near a river crossing. Variation: *Wellford.*

WELLINGTON (English) Temple in a clearing. There's Beef Wellington and the Duke of Wellington – not to be confused with Duke Ellington.

WELLS (English) Source of water.

WELTON (English) Well for a town.

WEMILAT (Native American) He has everything.

WEMILO (Native American) Everyone talks to him.

WEN (Armenian) Born in winter.

WENCESLAUS (Slavic) Glorious garland. Variation: *Wenceslas.*

WENDELL (German) Wanderer. Variations: *Wendel, Wendle.*

WENDICE (African-American) Unknown definition.

WENTWORTH (English) White man's town.

WENUTU (Native American) Sky clearing.

WERNER (German) Defending army. Variations: *Warner, Wernher.*

WESH (Gypsy) Forest.

WESLEY (English) Western meadow. Wesley first gained prominence as a religious last name, as two brothers, John and Charles Wesley, were the founders of the

Methodist church in England. Parents who belonged to the church soon began to use the brothers' last name for their newborn sons' first names as a tribute to them. Today, Wesley is not among the most popular of names, but it could definitely be a sleeper. Variations: *Wes, Wesly, Wessley, Westleigh, Westley.*

WESTBROOK (English) Western stream. Variations: *Wesbrook, West, Westbrooke.*

WESTBY (English) Western farm.

WESTCOTT (English) Western cottage. Variations: *Wescot, Wescott, Westcot.*

WESTON (English) Western town. Variations: *Westen, Westin.*

WETHERBY (English) Farm of male sheep, known as wether. Variations: *Weatherbey, Weatherbie, Weatherby, Wetherbey, Wetherbie.*

WETHERELL (English) Sheep corner. Variations: *Weatherell, Weatherill, Wetherill, Wethrill.*

WETHERLY (English) Sheep meadow. Variations: *Weatherley, Weatherly, Wetherleigh, Wetherley.*

WHALLEY (English) Forest by a hill. Variation: *Whallie.*

WHARTON (English) Town on a river bank. Though Wharton is more commonly used as a last name, it is beginning to show signs of acknowledgment as a first name. Variation: *Warton.*

WHEATLEY (English) Wheat field. Variations: *Wheatlea, Wheatleigh, Wheatlie, Wheatly.*

WHEATON (English) Town of wheat.

WHEELER (English) Wheel maker.

WHISTLER (English) Occupational name: whistler or piper.

WHITBY (English) Farm with white walls. Variations: *Whitbey, Whitbie.*

WHITCOMB (English) White valley. Variation: *Whitcombe.*

WHITELAW (English) White hill. Variation: *Whitlaw.*

WHITFIELD (English) White field.

What About a Middle Name?

The first name is the most important name, or so most people think. The middle, or second name, is where they can be really creative.

True, some people believe that the middle name should flow naturally from the first, as in the name Mary Ann, but there is a select group of people who believe that when it comes to a child's middle name, anything goes.

Of course, in these days of hyphenated last names, the first half of the combined last name could rightly be considered to be the middle name. But many of these kids get a middle name as well.

This practice, as well as the Catholic tradition of providing a child with a number of names depending upon his or her age in the church, has opened the floodgates to the trend of children who have not one but several middle names. I once heard about a child who has not one, not two middle names, but a total of ten middle names. Why?

Because Eric Michael David Stephen Joshua Kevin Carl Quentin Jesse Alexander William Peters had six siblings when he came into the world, and each one wanted to give him a name. Plus, the parents say they like round numbers, so that meant that Eric got a few more than anyone had bargained for.

Time will tell exactly how many of these names people will have the patience to use on a daily basis. Certainly not most parents, who only call a child by its full name when the son or daughter has done something bad. If a child has ten middle names, by the time an angry parent has finished reciting the child's full name, the parent will have forgotten what to be angry about.

WHITFORD (English) White ford.

WHITLEY (English) White meadow.

WHITLOCK (English) White lock of hair. When I was growing up, I was friends with a girl who had the last name of Whitlock, and I thought it was a great name. I'd never thought of the possibility of using it as a first name for a son, but I think it would work out fine, especially if your baby has whitish-blond hair.

WHITMAN (English) White man.

WHITMORE (English) White moor. Variations: *Whitmoor, Whittemore, Witmore, Wittemore.*

WHITNEY (English) White island.

WHITTAKER (English) White field. Variations: *Whitacker, Whitaker.*

WICAHPI ISNALA (Native American: Sioux) Lone star.

WICHADO (Native American) Compliant.

WICKHAM (English) Village paddock.

WIELISLAW (Polish) Glory is great. Variations: *Wiesiek, Wiesiulek, Wiestaw.*

WIKOLI (Hawaiian) Hawaiian version of Victor. Variation: *Vitori.*

WILANU (Native American) Mixing water with flour.

WILBUR (German) Brilliant. This name is rarely encountered outside the USA today, where it may have been imported by Dutch settlers. Famous Wilburs include US flying pioneer Wilbur Wright and Zambian-born US novelist Wilbur Smith. Variations: *Wilber, Wilbert, Wilburt, Willbur.*

WILDON (English) Wild valley.

WILEY (English) Water meadow. Variations: *Willey, Wylie.*

WILFORD (English) River crossing by willow trees.

WILFRED (English) Purposeful peace. Variations: *Wilfredo, Wilfrid, Wilfried, Wilfryd.*

WILKINSON (English) Son of little Will. Variations: *Wilkes, Wilkie, Wilkins, Willkins, Willkinson.*

WILLIAM (German) Constant protector. William is one of the most popular names throughout English-speaking countries. There are a slew of famous Williams, including Prince William, who will become William V when he ascends to the throne, William Shakespeare, William Blake, William Wordsworth, Billy Crystal, Billy Idol, Willem Dafoe, Will Smith, William Faulkner, William Holden, Billy Wilder, Billy Connolly, Bill Clinton, Willy Russell, Willy Carson and Will Hay; four American presidents, several kings, and plenty of knights. William is as popular today as it was in the 1040s. Currently, African-American parents appear to be choosing this name for their sons more frequently than white parents are.

Although there are a myriad of variations of the name, the traditional William is most common as both a given name and the everyday name that parents use to refer to their sons.

Variations: *Bill, Billie, Billy, Guillaume, Guillaums, Guillermo, Vas, Vasilak, Vasilious, Vaska, Vassos, Vila, Vildo, Vilek, Vilem, Vilhelm, Vili, Viliam, Vilkl, Ville, Vilmos, Vilous, Will, Willem, Willi, Williamson, Willie, Willil, Willis, Willy, Wilson, Wilhelm.*

WILLIAMSON (English) Son of William. Variations: *Willey, Willi, Willie, Willis, Wylie.*

WILLOUGHBY (English) Willow tree farm. Variations: *Willoughbey, Willoughbie.*

WILMER (German) Resolute fame. Variations: *Willimar, Willmer, Wylmer.*

WILNY (Native American) Screaming eagle.

WILSON (English) Son of Will. Variation: *Willson.*

WILTON (English) Town with a well. Variations: *Wilt, Wylton.*

WILU (Native American) Chicken hawk warbling.

WINDHAM (English) Friend of the town. Variations: *Win, Winn, Wyndham, Wynne.*

WINDSOR (English) From Windsor. Variation: *Wyndsor.*

WINFIELD (English) Friend's field. Variations: *Winnfield, Wynfield, Wynnfield.*

WINFRED (English) Peaceful friend.

WINGATE (English) Winding gate.

WINGI (Native American) Willing.

WINIKENEKE (Hawaiian) Hawaiian version of Vincent. Variation: *Vinikeneke.*

WINNEMUCCA (Native American: Paiute) Chief.

WINSLOW (English) Friend's hill.

WINSTON (English) Friend's town. This name has never been very popular in the UK, perhaps because of the overwhelming association with Winston Churchill. It is quite popular in other parts of the world with long-established links to Britain like the Caribbean. John Lennon's middle name was Winston, and the central character in George Orwell's novel about the future *1984* was called Winston Smith. Variations: *Winsten, Winstone, Winstonn, Winton, Wynstan, Wynston.*

WINTHROP (English) Friend's village.

WINWARD (English) My brother's forest.

WIT (Polish) Life.

WLADYSLAW (Polish) Glorious ruler. Variation: *Wtodzistaw.*

WLODZIMIERZ (Polish) Famous ruler.

WOJTEK (Polish) Soldier of consolation. Variation: *Wojteczek.*

WOLCOTT (English) Wolf's cottage.

WOLFE (English) Wolf. Variations: *Wolf, Woolf.*

WOLFGANG (German) Wolf fight. The most famous bearer of this name was Wolfgang Amadeus Mozart. Wolf and Wolfie are great nicknames for the name as long as you tell your son not to bite.

WONAHLLAYHUNKA (Native American: Winnebago) Chief.

WON-SHIK (Korean) Leader.

WOODFIELD (English) Field in the forest.

WOODFORD (English) River crossing in the forest. Variation: *Woodforde.*

WOODROW (English) Row in the woods. Variations: *Wood, Woody.*

WOODVILLE (English) Forest town.

WOODWARD (English) Protector of the forest. Variation: *Woodard.*

WORTH (English) Enclosed farm.

WORTHY (English) Enclosure. Variations: *Worthey, Worthington.*

WRIGHT (English) Carpenter.

WUHAUTYAH (Native American: Nez Perce) Blowing wind.

WUIRTON (Native American) Thrive.

WULITON (Native American) To succeed.

WUNAND (Native American) God is good.

WUSAMEQUIN (Native American: Algonquin) Yellow feather. Variation: *Ousamequin.*

WUYI (Native American) Flying turkey vulture.

WYANDANCH (Native American: Montauk) Wise orator. Variation: *Wiantance.*

WYATT (French) Little fighter. If you name your son Wyatt, the immediate reaction from both adults and children will be to think of a cowboy, as in Wyatt Earp. Variations: *Wiatt, Wyat.*

WYBERT (English) Brilliant at war.

WYCLIFF (English) White cliff. Variation: *Wycliffe.*

WYNDHAM (English) Town near the path. Variation: *Windham.*

WYNN (English) Friend. Variations: *Win, Winn, Wynne.*

WYNONO (Native American) First-born son.

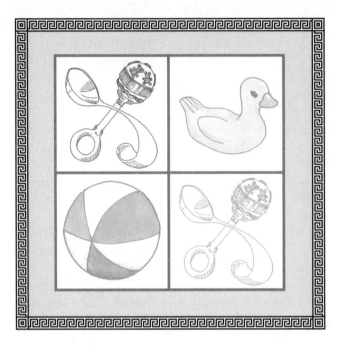

XANTHUS (Greek) Blond. Variation: *Xanthos.*

XAVIER (English) New house. In a game of word association, the name Xavier will bring one of two reactions to most people's minds. It will either be the Cuban musician Xavier Cugat or, if they grew up in Catholic school, the ubiquitous Saint Francis Xavier. Although first names with an 'x' in them are pretty popular these days, most parents like the letter to be in the middle of the name somewhere and not announcing its presence right up front. I think that Xavier is still best used as a middle name. Variations: *Saverio, Xaver.*

XAYVION (African-American) The new house. Variations: *Savion, Sayveon, Sayvion, Xavion, Xayveon, Zayvion.*

XENOPHON (Greek) Alien voice.

XENOS (Greek) Guest. Variations: *Xeno, Zenos.*

XERXES (Persian) Ruler.

XIAOPING (Chinese) Small bottle.

XIMEN (Spanish) Obedient. Variations: *Ximenes, Ximon, Ximun.*

XING-FU (Chinese) Happiness.

XI-WANG (Chinese) Desire.

XYLON (Greek) One who lives in the forest.

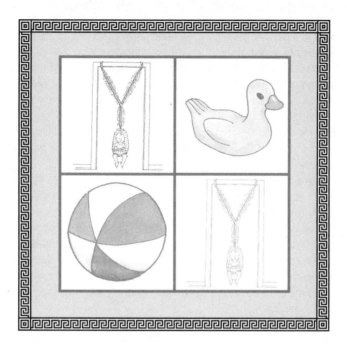

YAAKOV (Hebrew) Supplanter or heel. Variation: *Yankov.*

YAAR (Hebrew) Forest.

YADID (Hebrew) Beloved.

YADIN (Hebrew) God will judge. Variation: *Yadon.*

YAFEU (African: Ghanian) Bold.

YAHOLO (Native American: Creek) One who hollers.

YAHYA (Arabic) God is good. Variation: *Yihya.*

YAIR (Hebrew) God will teach. Variation: *Jair.*

YAKAR (Hebrew) Dear. Variation: *Yakir.*

YAKECEN (Native American) Song from the sky.

YAKEZ (Native American) Heaven.

YAKIM (Hebrew) God develops. Variation: *Jakim.*

YALE (English) Up on the hill. The name is sometimes found in the USA where it is associated with Yale University which was founded by Elihu Yale in 1701.

YAMAL (Hindu) One of a twin.

YAMIN (Hebrew) Right hand. Variation: *Jamin.*

YANA (Hebrew) He answers. Variations: *Janai, Jannai, Yan, Yannai.*

YANCY (Native American) Englishman. Variations: *Yance, Yancey, Yantsey.*

YANKA (Russian) God is good.

YANNIS (Greek) God is good. Variation of John. Variations: *Yannakis, Yanni, Yiannis.*

YANOACH (Hebrew) Rest.

YAPHET (Hebrew) Attractive. Variations: *Japhet, Japheth, Yapheth.*

YAQUB (Arabic) To grab by the heel. Variation: *Yaqoob.*

YARB (Gypsy) Herb.

YARDAN (Arabic) King.

YARDLEY (English) Enclosed meadow. Variations: *Yardlea, Yardlee, Yardleigh, Yardly.*

YARIN (Hebrew) To understand.

The Hispanic Use of the Diminutive

If you're like most people, you'd be hard-pressed to talk to a baby using the same words and tone that you'd use with your boss. You probably make up babyish words, or put a spin on certain words that you think will make the baby understand you better. You know: instead of saying, 'Oh, look at your cute little foot!' you may spout about the itty-bitty foot, in a voice to match.

Hispanic people simply add the suffix -ito (for boys) or -ita (for girls) to the end of a word. And it works whether you add it to the baby's name or a part of his or her body.

For instance, Carlos becomes Carlito and Pippa turns into Pippita. Likewise, that cute little hand can go from mano to manito simply because it belongs to a baby.

The use of a diminutive isn't relegated to the Spanish language, of course. Maybe our own itsy-bitsy and other made-up words and names serve as the English version of the Hispanic diminutive. One thing's for sure, however. No matter what language it's used in, mothers will still be using the diminutive form on their grown children, much to their children's embarrassment.

YASAHIRO (Japanese) Peaceful.

YASAR (Arabic) Wealth. Variations: *Yaser, Yasir, Yasser, Yassir.*

YASH (Hindu) Famous.

YASHASKAR (Hindu) One who brings fame.

YASIN (Arabic) The Arabic letters 'y' and 's'.

YASUO (Japanese) Calm.

YATES (English) Gates. Variation: *Yeats.*

YAZID (African: Swahili) To increase.

YE (Chinese) Universe.

YECHEZKEL (Hebrew) God strengthens. Variations: *Chaskel, Chatzkel, Keskel.*

YEHOCHANAN (Hebrew) God is good. Variations: *Yochanan, Yohannan.*

YEHONATAN (Hebrew) God provides.

YEHOSHUA (Hebrew) God is salvation. Variation: *Yeshua.*

YEHOYAKIM (Hebrew) God will establish. Variations: *Jehoiakim, Yehoiakim, Yoyakim.*

YEHUDI (Hebrew) Praise. The virtuoso violinist Yehudi Menuhin has made many people familiar with this name. Variations: *Yechudi, Yechudil, Yehuda, Yehudah.*

YELUTCI (Native American) Quiet bear.

YEMON (Japanese) Guardian.

YEN (Vietnamese) Calm.

YEOMAN (English) Servant.

YERED (Hebrew) To come down. Variation: *Jered.*

YERIEL (Hebrew) Founded by God. Variation: *Jeriel.*

YERIK (Russian) God is exalted. Variation of Jeremiah. Variation: *Yeremey.*

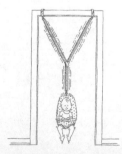

YESHAYAHU (Hebrew) God saves. Variation: *Yeshaya.*

YEVGENYI (Russian) Well born.

YIRMEYAHU (Hebrew) God will restore.

YISHACHAR (Hebrew) Reward. Variations: *Issachar, Sachar, Yisaschar.*

YISRAEL (Hebrew) Israel.

YITRO (Hebrew) Plenty. Variation: *Yitran.*

YITZCHAK (Hebrew) Laughter. A Hebrew version of Issac. Polish-born Israeli Prime Minister Yitzhak Shamir has made us aware of the name. Variations: *Itzhak, Yitzhak.*

YMIR (Scandinavian) Ancient mythological figure.

YO (Chinese) Bright.

YONATAN (Hebrew) Gift from God.

YONG (Chinese) Brave.

YONG-SUN (Korean) Courage.

YOOMTIS KUNNIN (Native American: Nez Perce) Grizzly bear blanket.

YORATH (English) Worthy god. Variations: *Iolo, Iorwerth.*

YORK (English) Yew tree. Variations: *Yorick, Yorke, Yorrick.*

YOSEF (Hebrew) God increases. Variations: *Yoseff, Yosif, Yousef, Yusef, Yusif, Yusuf, Yuzef.*

YOSHA (Hebrew) Wisdom.

YOSHI (Japanese) Quiet.

YOTIMO (Native American) Bee flying to its hive.

YOTTOKO (Native American) Mud from the river.

YOUKIOMA (Native American: Hopi) Flawless. Variations: *Youkeoma, Yukeoma, Yukioma.*

YOUNG-JA (Korean) Forever stable.

YOUNG-JAE (Korean) Forever prosperous.

YOUNG-NAM (Korean) Forever south.

YOUNG-SOO (Korean) Forever rich.

YUAN (Chinese) Round.

YUCEL (Turkish) Noble.

YUKIKO (Japanese) Snow. Variations: *Yuki, Yukio.*

YUL (Chinese) Past the horizon.

YULE (English) Christmas.

YUMA (Native American) Son of the chief.

YUNIS (Arabic) Dove. Variations: *Younis, Yunus.*

YURCHIK (Russian) Farmer. Variation of George. Variations: *Yura, Yuri, Yurik, Yurko, Yurli, Yury.*

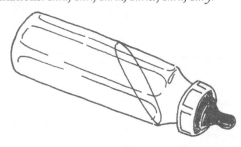

YURI (Russian) Equivalent of the name George. Well-known Yuris include Russian President Yuri Andropov and cosmonaut Yuri Gagarin. Variantion: *Yury, Juri*

YUSHUA (Arabic) God's help.

YUSTYN (Russian) Just.

YUSUF (Arabic) God will increase. A varient of Joseph. Variations: *Youssef, Yousuf, Yusef, Yusif, Yussef.*

YUTU (Native American) Coyote hunting.

YUVAL (Hebrew) Brook. Variation: *Jubal.*

YVES (French) Yew wood. Designer Yves St. Laurent brings glamour and fashion to this high-class French name, though its definition points to lowlier pursuits. The name came to Britain with the Normans in the 11th century. Another famous Yves is French actor Yves Montand. Yvonne, the feminine version of Yves, has always been more popular than the male form of the name. Variation: *Yvon.*

ZACCHEUS (Hebrew) Pure.

ZACHARIAH (Hebrew) The Lord has remembered. Zachariah and its many variations is one of the more popular names around today, probably because it has that Biblical connotation as well as the trendy lightning-rod letter 'Z'. It features in the Bible as the name of John the Baptist's father and of around thirty other people. Little Zacharys are all over the place these days, and all the little boys with the name who are digging in the sandbox at the playground have done a lot to demystify this name. There was also a US president called Zachary Taylor. Variations: *Zacaria, Zacarias, Zach, Zacharia, Zacharias, Zacharie, Zachary, Zachery, Zack, Zackariah, Zackerias, Zackery, Zak, Zakarias, Zakarie, Zako, Zeke.*

ZAFAR (Arabic) To win. Variation: *Zafir.*

ZAHAVI (Hebrew) Gold.

ZAHID (Arabic) Strict.

ZAHIR (Hebrew) Bright. Variations: *Zaheer, Zahur.*

ZAHUR (Arabic) Flower.

ZAIDE (Hebrew) Older.

ZAIM (Arabic) General.

ZAKAI (Hebrew) Pure. Variations: *Zaki, Zakkai.*

ZAKARIYYA (Arabic) God knows.

ZAKI (Arabic) Smart.

ZAKUR (Hebrew) Masculine. Variation: *Zaccur.*

ZALE (Greek) Strength from the sea. Variation: *Zayle.*

ZALMAN (Hebrew) Peaceful.

ZAMIEL (German) God has heard. Variation of Samuel.

ZAMIR (Hebrew) Song.

ZAN (Hebrew) Well-fed.

ZANE (English) God is good. Variation of John. Zane is a great name with the potential to become even bigger than Zachary. The recent popularity of this name can be traced to the writer Zane Grey, who chose it as a suitable substitute for his real name, Pearl. In fact, he took the name from one of his great-grandfathers, Ebenezer Zane, who founded the town of Zanesville in Ohio. Variations: *Zain, Zayne.*

ZAREB (African) Guardian.

ZARED (Hebrew) Trap.

ZAREK (Polish) May God protect the king.

ZAVAD (Hebrew) Present. Variation: *Zabad.*

ZAVDIEL (Hebrew) Gift from God. Variations: *Zabdiel, Zebedee.*

ZAYD (Arabic) To increase. Variations: *Zaid, Zayed, Ziyad.*

ZAYN (Arabic) Beauty.

ZBIGNIEW (Polish) To get rid of anger. Variation: *Zbyszko.*

ZBYHNEV (Czech) Rid of anger. Variations: *Zbyna, Zbynek, Zbysek.*

ZDENEK (Czech) God of wine. Variations: *Zdenecek, Zdenko, Zdenousek, Zdicek.*

ZDESLAV (Czech) Glory is here. Variations: *Zdik, Zdisek, Zdislav.*

ZDZISLAW (Polish) Glory is here. Variations: *Zdzich, Zdziech, Zdziesz, Zdzieszko, Zdzis, Zdzisiek.*

ZEBADIAH (Hebrew) Gift from God. Variations: *Zeb, Zebediah.*

ZEBULON (Hebrew) To exalt. Variations: *Zebulen, Zebulun.*

ZEDEKIAH (Hebrew) God is just. Variations: *Tzedekia, Tzidkiya, Zed, Zedechiah, Zedekia, Zedekias.*

ZEEMAN (Dutch) Seaman.

ZE'EV (Hebrew) Wolf.

ZEHARIAH (Hebrew) Light of God. Variations: *Zeharia, Zeharya.*

ZEHEB (Turkish) Gold.

ZEKE (Hebrew) The strength of God. Zeke got its start as a nickname for Ezekiel, and gradually came into its own as an independent name. For parents who like this name, it may be best to use the original as a given name, so your son can have some variety.

ZEKI (Turkish) Smart.

ZELIG (Hebrew) Holy.

ZELIMIR (Slavic) Desires peace.

ZEMARIAH (Hebrew) Song. Variations: *Zemaria, Zemarya.*

ZENAS (Greek) Generous. Variations: *Zeno, Zenon.*

ZENDA (Czech) Well born.

ZEPHANIAH (Hebrew) Protection. Variations: *Zeph, Zephan.*

ZEPHYRUS (Greek) West wind.

ZERACH (Hebrew) Light. Variations: *Zerachia, Zerachya, Zerah.*

ZEREM (Hebrew) Stream.

ZERIKA (Hebrew) Rainshower.

ZERO (Arabic) Worthless. Can you imagine any parents willingly giving their son this name? In Arabic, it could be the equivalent to the Chinese tradition of giving a child a name that will fend off evil spirits, but I think that even zero is taking things a bit too literally.

ZESIRO (African: Ugandan) First-born of twins.

ZETHUS (Greek) Son of Zeus who built the great stone wall around the town of Thebes, which was named for his wife.

ZEUS (Greek) Living. King of the gods. Variations: *Zeno, Zenon, Zinon.*

ZEVACH (Hebrew) Sacrifice. Variation: *Zevachia, Zevachtah, Zevachya, Zevah.*

ZEVADIAH (Hebrew) God bestows. Variations: *Zevadia, Zevadya.*

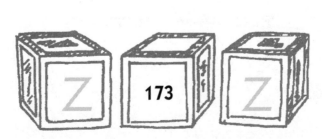

Names of Saints

People who can be the most atheistic souls around unwittingly can choose a name for their baby that got its start when it was named after a saint. Yes, such names as Michael went largely unnoticed until the Catholic church turned a mere mortal into Saint Michael. After that, the name grew in popularity.

Though saint names are now commonly given in some countries without regard to the exact connotation, in other countries, people give their babies the name of a saint specifically because it is associated with the church.

For example, in Italy, saints are frequently turned to for inspiration when choosing a name. However, each region of the country also has its own patron saints, and they are pretty much unknown in other parts of the country, which means that a saint-based name that is popular in Naples, for example, is rare in the area around Venice.

And though it may be hard to believe in this day and age, an obscure law from 1813 in France dictates baby-naming practices to French parents even today. Though it does go largely ignored, in essence, it says that any child born in France must bear the name of either a saint from the Catholic church or a figure from the country's ancient history.

Of course, you can pick the patron saint first instead of choosing the name, especially if it is appropriate to your life. For instance, if you or your spouse are involved in music and you'd like to give your baby a name that relates to your profession, you might look to the patron saints for musicians: Cecilia or Gregory. Interestingly, there is a patron saint of television, and that's Clare of Assisi. Other professional saints include Barbara for architects, Sebastian for athletes, and Matthew for the tax collector. And you don't necessarily have to be Catholic to enjoy picking the name of a patron saint – you just need a good sense of humour. And you thought that your in-laws wanted to have too much influence in helping you name your baby!

Here's a list of selected saints:

Boys' Names

- Antony: Patron saint of domestic animals and butchers.
- Bernard: Patron saint of candle makers.
- Christopher: Patron saint of motorists.
- Francis: Patron saint of the deaf.
- George: Patron saint of boy scouts.
- Jerome: Patron saint of librarians.
- Jude: Patron saint of lost causes.
- Martin: Patron saint of hairdressers.
- Matthew: Patron saint of bankers, bookkeepers, and accountants.
- Nicholas: Patron saint of brides.
- Sebastian: Patron saint of archers and soldiers.
- Stephen: Patron saint of bricklayers.
- Vitus: Patron saint of comedians and dancers.

Girls' Names

- Agnes: Patron saint of girls.
- Anastasia: Patron saint of weavers.
- Anne: Patron saint of housewives and women in labour.
- Apollonia: Patron saint of dentists.
- Brigid: Patron saint of scholars.
- Catherine: Patron saint of art.
- Cecilia: Patron saint of singers and musicians.
- Martha: Patron saint of cooks.
- Monica: Patron saint of married women and mothers.
- Paula: Patron saint of widows.

ZEVID (Hebrew) Present.

ZEVULUN (Hebrew) House. Variations: *Zebulon, Zebulun, Zevul.*

ZHONG (Chinese) Second brother.

ZHU (Chinese) Wish.

ZHUANG (Chinese) Strong

ZIA (Hebrew) Unknown definition.

ZIKOMO (African: Malawian) Thank you.

ZIMRAAN (Arabic) Celebrated.

ZIMRAN (Hebrew) Sacred.

ZIMRI (Hebrew) Valuable.

ZINAN (Japanese) Second son.

ZINDEL (Hebrew) Protector of mankind. Variation of Alexander. A lot of kids might think that the name Zindel is actually pretty cool, due to the fact that a popular children's author is named Paul Zindel. An advantage of this name is that if your kid decides that later on he doesn't care for it, he can go to its original root, Alexander, and select another one of that name's many variations. Variation: *Zindil.*

ZION (Hebrew) Guarded land.

ZIPKIYAH (Native American: Kiowa) Big bow. Variations: *Zipkoeete, Zipkoheta.*

ZITKADUTA (Native American: Sioux) Red bird.

ZITOMER (Czech) To live in fame. Variations: *Zitek, Zitousek.*

ZIV (Hebrew) To shine. Variations: *Zivan, Zivi.*

ZIVAN (Czech) Alive. Variations: *Zivanek, Zivek, Zivko.*

ZIVEN (Slavic) Lively. Variations: *Ziv, Zivon.*

ZIYA (Arabic) Light. Variation: *Zia.*

ZIYAD (Arabic) To increase.

ZLATAN (Czech) Golden. Variations: *Zlatek, Zlaticek, Zlatik, Zlatko, Zlatousek.*

ZOLTIN (Hungarian) Life. Variation: *Zoltan.*

ZOMEIR (Hebrew) One who prunes trees. Variation: *Zomer.*

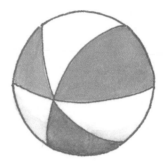

ZORYA (Slavic) Star.

ZOTOM (Native American: Kiowa) One who bites.

ZOWIE (Greek) Life.

ZUBERI (African: Swahili) Strong.

ZUHAYR (Arabic) Young flowers. Variation: *Zuhair.*

ZURIEL (Hebrew) The Lord is my rock.

ZWI (Scandinavian) Gazelle.

ZYA TIMENNA (Native American: Nez Perce) Heartless.

ZYGMUNT (Polish) Victorious protection.

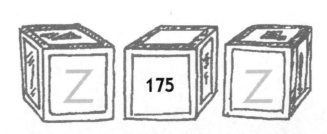

IT'S A GIRL!

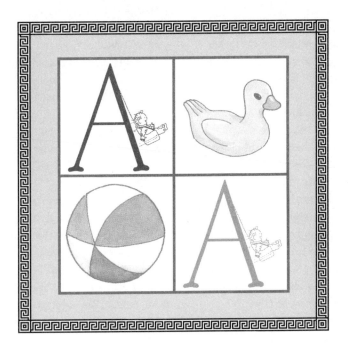

AALIYAH (African-American) To rise.

AANANDINI (Hindu) Happy. Variation: *Ananda.*

ABA (African: Ghanian) Born on Thursday.

ABABUO (African: Ghanian) A child that keeps coming back.

ABAGBE (African: Nigerian) Much-desired child.

ABAM (African: Ghanian) Second child born after twins.

ABAYOMI (African: Nigerian) Happiness.

ABEBI (African: Nigerian) We asked for her, and she came to us. Variations: *Abeje, Abeni.*

ABEDABUN (Native American: Chippewa) Sunrise.

ABEGAILA (Hawaiian) Father's joy. Hawaiian version of Abigail. Variations: *Abigaila, Apikaila.*

ABEKE (African: Nigerian) We asked for her to pet her.

ABELIA (Hebrew) A sigh. Feminine version of Abel. Variations: *Abella, Abelle.*

ABELLONA (Scandinavian: Danish) Feminine version of Apollo. Variations: *Abbelina, Abbeline, Abelone, Apolline, Apollinia, Appoline, Appolinia.*

ABENA (African: Ghanian) Born on a Thursday. Variations: *Aba, Abana, Abina.*

ABEO (African: Nigerian) She brings joy.

ABEQUA (Native American: Chippewa) Homebody. Variation: *Abeque.*

ABEY (Native American: Omaha) Leaf.

ABEYTU (Native American: Omaha) Green leaf.

ABEYTZI (Native American: Omaha) Yellow leaf. Variation: *Abetzi.*

ABHA (Hindu) Light. Variations: *Aabha, Aabhaa, Abhaa.*

ABIA (Arabic) Great.

ABIAH (Hebrew) God is my father. Variations: *Abiela, Abiella, Avia, Aviah, Aviela, Aviella, Aviya.*

179

ABICHAYIL (Hebrew) Strong father. Variations: *Avichayil, Avihayil.*

ABIDA (Arabic) To worship.

ABIDEMI (African: Nigerian) Born during the father's absence.

ABIGAIL (Hebrew) Father's joy. Abigail is one of those wonderful girls' names that conjures up images of a bygone age. It has been in and out of fashion, but is currently enjoying a renaissance. It appears in the Bible both as the beautiful and intelligent wife of Nabal of Carmel who went on to marry King David, and as that of King David's sister. The biblical Abigail described herself as King David's handmaid, and with another literary Abigail featuring as a lady's maid in a 1616 play *The Scornful Lady*, it became slang for any such servant, which caused it to decline in popularity. The name enjoyed a revival in the 1970s and it should continue to be well used in the years to come. Variations: *Abagael, Abagail, Abagale, Abbey, Abbi, Abbie, Abbigael, Abbigail, Abbigale, Abby, Abbye, Abbygael, Abbygail, Abbygale, Abigale, Abigayle, Avigail.*

ABIKANILE (African: Malawian) Listen.

ABIMBOLA (African: Nigerian) Wealthy.

ABIONA (African: Nigerian) Born during a trip.

ABIR (Arabic) Aroma.

ABIRA (Hebrew) Strong. Variation: *Abi.*

ABISHA (Hebrew) God is my father. Variations: *Abijah, Abishah.*

ABITAL (Hebrew) My father comes from dew. Variation: *Avital.*

ABLA (Arabic) Full. Variation: *Ablah.*

ABMABA (African: Ghanian) Born on a Tuesday.

ABRA (Hebrew) Mother of many children. Feminine counterpart of Abraham.

ACACIA (Greek) The acacia tree.

ACADIA (Native American: Micmac) Village.

ACAIJA (Greek) Joy.

ACANTHA (Greek) Thorn.

ACCALIA (Latin) Roman mythological figure.

ACELINE (French) Of noble birth. Variation: *Asceline.*

ACENITH (African) Goddess of love.

ACHALA (Hindu) Steady. Variation: *Achalaa.*

ACHAVA (Hebrew) Friendship.

ACHSAH (Hebrew) Anklet. Variation: *Achsa.*

ACIMA (Hebrew) God judges. Variations: *Achima, Achimah, Acimah.*

ACTON (English) A town in England.

ADA (German) Though it can be a derivative of Adelaide, in German the name Ada means a woman who comes from aristocracy. Variations: *Adamine, Adaminna, Addie, Mina, Minna.*

ADAH (Hebrew) Decoration. Variations: *Ada, Adaya, Adda, Addie, Adi, Adia, Adiah, Adie, Adiel, Adiella, Adiya.*

ADALHEIDIS (Scandinavian) Noble one. Variations: *Aalt, Aaltje, Adalheid, Adelheid, Aleida, Alida.*

ADALIA (Hebrew) God as protector.

ADALINA (Hawaiian) Hawaiian version of Adeline. Variations: *Adela, Akela, Akelina.*

ADAMINA (Hebrew) Feminine version of Adam. God made Adam out of red-coloured earth, and the name can also mean red earth.

ADAMMA (African: Nigerian) A pretty child.

ADANNA (African: Nigerian) Father's daughter.

ADARA (Hebrew) Noble. Variations: *Adena, Adene, Adina, Adra.*

ADEBOLA (African: Nigerian) Her honour.

ADEDAGBO (African: Nigerian) Happiness.

ADELAIDE (English) This once-unfashionable name dates back centuries to William IV's popular German-born wife Queen Adelaide. It is making a comeback as

people turn to more solid, traditional, albeit just-a-bit different names for their babies. Also like Abigail, Adelaide has a bevy of variations: *Adal, Adala, Adalaid, Adalaide, Adalee, Adali, Adalie, Adalley, Addal, Addala, Adelaida, Adele, Adelia, Adelice, Adelicia, Adeline, Adelis, Adelita, Adeliya, Adell, Adella, Adelle, Aline, Della, Delle, Edeline, Eline.*

ADELEKE (African: Nigerian) The crown brings happiness.

ADELIZA (English) Created by combining Adelaide and Liza.

ADELPHA (Greek) Caring sister.

ADEOLA (African: Nigerian) Crown. Variations: *Adola, Dola.*

ADERES (Hebrew) Cape. Variations: *Aderet, Aderetz.*

ADESIMBO (African: Nigerian) Noble birth.

ADESINA (African: Nigerian) This girl is the first of many more children to come.

ADHIKA (Hindu) Increase.

ADHITA (Hindu) Student.

ADIA (African: Swahili) Gift from God.

ADIBA (Arabic) Cultured, refined. Variation: *Adibah.*

ADILA (Arabic) Just. Variation: *Adilah.*

ADINA (Hebrew) Gentle, delicate. Variations: *Adeana, Adin, Adine.*

ADITI (Hindu) Free. Aditi is the mythological mother of Hindu gods; Hindus frequently pray to her to bless the myriad cattle who roam free over the countryside as well as to ask for forgiveness.

ADIVA (Arabic) Gentle.

ADMETE (Greek) Ancient mythological figure.

ADOEETE (Native American: Kiowa) Big tree.

ADOLPHA (German) Noble wolf. Feminine version of Adolph.

ADONCIA (Spanish) Sweet.

ADONIA (Greek) Beauty. It is also a festival held after the annual harvest. Feminine name for the Greek god Adonis.

ADORA (Latin) Much adored. Variations: *Adoree, Adoria, Adorlee, Dora, Dori, Dorie, Dorrie.*

ADOWA (African: Ghanian) Born on Tuesday.

ADRASTEA (Greek) The nymph who cared for Zeus when he was a baby.

ADRIA (English) Black, dark. Feminine version of Adrian. Variations: *Adrea, Adreea, Adria, Adriah.*

ADRIANE (German) Black earth. I always liked the name Adriane, and wondered why parents didn't choose it for their daughters more often. Adriane should appeal to parents who are looking for a pretty name that stands out. Variations: *Adriana, Adriane, Adrianna, Adriannah, Adrianne, Adrien, Adriena, Adrienah, Adrienne.*

ADSILA (Native American: Cherokee) Blossom.

ADUKE (African: Nigerian) Beloved.

ADYA (Hindu) Sunday.

ADZAAN-TSINAJINNIE (Native American: Navajo) Tribal name.

ADZO (African: Ghanian) Born on Monday. Variations: *Adjoa, Adwoa.*

AE-CHA (Korean) Loving daughter.

AEGINA (Greek) Ancient mythological figure.

AEGLE (Greek) Ancient mythological figure.

AENEA (Greek) Worthy.

AEOLA (Greek) Goddess of the winds.

AETHRA (Greek) Ancient mythological figure.

AFAF (Arabic) Virtuous. Variations: *Afifa, Afifah.*

AFAFA (African: Ghanian) First child from second husband.

AFEI (Polynesian) Wrap around.

AFIYA (African: Swahili) Health.

AFPRICA (Irish) Pleasant. Variations: *Afric, Africa, Aifric.*

AFRA (English) The colour of the earth; young deer. Variations: *Affera, Affra, Aphra.*

AFRAIMA (Hebrew) Fertile.

AFRICA (African-American) The continent. Variation: *Afrika.*

AFRYEA (African: Ghanian) Born during happy times.

AFUA (African: Ghanian) Born on Friday.

AFUVALE (Polynesian) Mulberry tree.

AGALIA (Greek) Happy.

AGAPI (Greek) Love. Variations: *Agape, Agappe.*

AGATHA (Greek) Good. Agatha is the patron saint of firefighters and nurses and was the name of one of William the Conqueror's daughter. Except for fans of mystery writer Agatha Christie, most new parents will crinkle up their noses at the suggestion of using this name for their young daughters. Of course, this situation could change, but someone has to be first. Variations: *Aga, Agace, Agacia, Agafia, Agasha, Agata, Agate, Agathe, Agathi, Agatta, Ageneti, Aggi, Aggie, Aggy, Akeneki.*

AGAVE (Greek) Noble.

AGLAIA (Greek) Ancient mythological figure.

AGNES (Greek) Virginal, chaste. Actress Agnes Moorehead, from the TV series *Bewitched*, is probably the most famous Agnes of the last thirty years. Though Agnes is rarely chosen by parents-to-be today, a century ago it was one of the most popular names, especially in Scotland. Variations: *Agnella, Agnesa, Agnesca, Agnese, Agnesina, Agneska, Agness, Agnessa, Agneta, Agneti, Agnetta, Agnola, Agnolah, Agnolla, Agnolle, Nesa, Ness, Nessa, Nessi, Nessia, Nessie, Nessy, Nesta, Senga, Ynes, Ynesita, Ynez.*

AGRIPPA (Latin) If you give your daughter this name, you should be sure that she was born feet-first, because that's just what this name means. Variations: *Agrafina, Agrippina, Agrippine.*

AHALYA (Hindu) Beautiful.

AHAUANO (Polynesian) People.

AHAVA (Hebrew) Beloved. Variations: *Ahavah, Ahavat, Ahouva, Ahuda, Ahuva.*

AHAWHYPERSIE (Native American: Crow) Unknown definition.

AHAWI (Native American: Cherokee) Deer.

AHIA (Polynesian) Enticement.

AHILYA (Hindu) Compassionate.

AHLAM (Arabic) To dream.

AH KUM (Chinese) Good as gold.

AH LAM (Chinese) Like an orchid.

AHOLELEI (Polynesian) Good day.

AHOLO (Polynesian) Plenty.

AHONUI (Hawaiian) Patience.

AHOPOMEE (Polynesian) Dance at night.

AHULANI (Hawaiian) Heavenly altar.

AH-YOKA (Native American: Cherokee) She brings happiness.

AI (Japanese) Love.

AIBBLIN (Irish) Bright, shining girl. Variations: *Aibhlin, Ailbhe.*

AIDA (Arabic) Reward; also an opera by the Italian composer Guiseppe Verdi.

AIDAN (Irish) Fire. Aidan is an androgynous name, though it's more common for boys than girls. If girls continue to appropriate this name, however, look for Aidan almost exclusively as a girls' name within twenty years. Variations: *Aidana, Aydana, Edana*.

AIDEEN (Irish) Unknown definition. Variations: *Adene, Etain*.

AIKO (Japanese) Little one.

AILA (Scandinavian: Finnish) Bright light. Variations: *Aile, Ailee, Ailey, Aili, Ailie, Ailis, Ailse*.

AILAINA (Scottish) Rock. Variations: *Alaine, Alanis*.

AILBHE (Irish) White. Variation: *Oilbhe*.

AILINE (Polynesian) Peace. Variation: *Elina*.

AILSA (Scottish) Place name; there is an island in Scotland called Ailsa Craig.

AIMILIONA (Irish) Hardworking.

AIN (Arabic) Treasure.

AINA (African: Nigerian) Difficult birth.

AINAKEA (Hawaiian) Fair earth.

AINALAN (Hawaiian) Heavenly earth.

AINANANI (Hawaiian) Beautiful earth.

AINE (Irish) Joyous. Name of a fertility goddess and a fairy queen in Irish folklore.

AINO (Scandinavian: Finnish) Ancient mythological figure.

AINSLEY (Scottish) A meadow. Variations: *Ainslee, Ainsleigh, Ainslie, Ansley, Aynslee, Aynsley*.

AIRLEA (Greek) Airy, fragile. Variation: *Airlia*.

AISHA (Arabic) Life. This has become a popular name in the last two decades for African-American girls and for those who follow the Arabic religion, since Aisha was Mohammed's favourite wife. Perhaps the first time that many of us heard of this name was through Stevie Wonder's song 'Isn't She Lovely', which he wrote to honour of his daughter Aisha's birth.

Variations: *Aishah, Aisia, Aisiah, Asha, Ashah, Ashia, Ashiah, Asia, Asiah, Ayeesa, Ayeesah, Ayeesha, Ayeeshah, Ayeisa*.

AISLING (Irish) Dream. Variations: *Aislinn, Ashling, Isleen*.

AITHNE (Irish) Small fire. Another feminine version of Aidan. Variations: *Aine, Aithnea, Eithne, Ethnah, Ethnea, Ethnee*.

AIYANA (Native American) To bloom forever.

AIYETORO (African: Nigerian) Peace on earth.

AJA (Hindu) Goat; aroma. Steely Dan's great jazz album *Aja* has served as the inspiration for many baby girls around the world, not its true Hindu definition. I know one couple who gave their daughter this name because it was the record that was playing while she was conceived.

AJALAA (Hindu) The earth.

AJEYA (Hindu) Victorious.

AJUA (African: Ghanian) Born on Monday.

AJUJI (African) Child of the trash heap.

AKA (Hawaiian) Hawaiian version of Ada.

AKAHANA (Japanese) Red flower. Variation: *Akina*.

AKAHELE (Hawaiian) Careful.

AKAKA (Hawaiian) Good. Hawaiian version of Agatha.

AKAKO (Japanese) Red.

AKALA (Hawaiian) Raspberries.

AKAMAI (Hawaiian) Wise.

AKANESI (Polynesian) Pure.

AKANKE (African: Nigerian) To want her is to love her. Variation: *Akanki*.

AKASUKI (Japanese) One who loves red.

AKAULA (Hawaiian) Sunset.

AKEAKAMAI (Hawaiian) To desire knowledge.

AKELA (Hawaiian) Noble.

AKHILA (Hindu) Total.

AKI (Japanese) Born in the autumn.

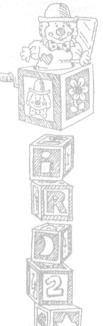

Asian Names – Cultural Traditions

In an ancient country like China, it's to be expected that the practice of naming babies reflects how people tend to honour their heritage, specific facets of the culture, or even ancient superstitions.

For instance, Chinese parents often decide to give a boy a run-of-the-mill name so that the evil spirits will pass him by – because his name is so boring. Girls, on the other hand, tend to be named after plants or creatures in nature. In the Chinese culture, as in others, boys are more highly prized than girls, especially since the country's one-child-per-family rule. Unfortunately, it's possible that parents may feel that girls with pretty names may attract those evil spirits, which would allow parents to try for another child, hopefully a boy.

In Japan, parents bestow certain names on their children for more benevolent reasons. But like Chinese parents, Japanese mothers and fathers tend to give their daughters more descriptive names than their sons. Boys in Japan are frequently named for their position in the birth order in their family, or after their parents' desire that their sons live a long life: Chi, which means thousand in Japanese, is one such name.

Japanese girls are frequently given names that reflect the Japanese culture's attitude towards women: Kazu, which translates to meek and loyal, is a favourite. Girls also receive names inspired by nature but that also reflect the moral attitudes of the society: Miyuki, or pure snow, is one such example.

AKIBA (African) Unknown definition.

AKILAH (Arabic) Smart.

AKILINA (Greek) Eagle. Variations: *Acquilina, Aquilina*.

AKISATAN (African: Nigerian) Clothing for burial.

AKIVA (Hebrew) Shelter. Variations: *Kiba, Kibah, Kiva, Kivah*.

AKOSUA (African: Ghanian) Born on Sunday.

AKUA (African: Ghanian) Born on Wednesday.

AKWETE (African: Ghanian) First-born of twins.

AKWOKWO (African: Ghanian) Younger of twins.

ALA (Hawaiian) Fragrant.

ALABA (African: Nigerian) Second child born after twins.

ALAIA (Arabic) Virtuous.

ALAINE (Gaelic) Rock. Feminine version of Alan. Variations: *Alaina, Alane, Alanna, Alannah, Alayna,*

Alayne, Alena, Alene, Alenne, Aleyna, Aleynah, Aleyne, Allaine, Allayne, Alleen, Alleine, Allena, Allene, Alleynah, Alleyne, Allina, Allinah, Allyna, Allynn, Allynne, Alynne, Alana.

ALAKE (African: Nigerian) One to be fussed over.

ALALA (Greek) In Greek mythology, Alala is the sister of Ares, the god of war.

ALAME (Polynesian) Flower wreath.

ALAMEA (Hawaiian) Ripe, verdant. Variation: *Ahlumea.*

ALAMEDA (Native American) Cottonwood tree.

ALANA (Hawaiian) To float. Variations: *Alaina, Alani, Alanna, Alayne, Alene, Alenne, Allane.*

ALANI (Hawaiian) Orange.

ALAQUA (Native American) Sweet gum tree.

ALARICE (Greek) Noble. Variation: *Alarica.*

ALASTRINA (Irish) Guardian. Variation: *Alastriona.*

ALAUDA (French) Lark.

ALAULA (Hawaiian) Dawn.

ALBA (English) A town on a white hill. Variations: *Albane, Albina, Albine, Albinia, Albinka, Alva.*

ALBERGA (Latin) Noble; inn. Variation: *Alberge.*

ALBERTA (English) Noble. Albert, its masculine counterpart, was once a common name, but Alberta never seemed to catch on.

ALBINA (Italian) White. Variations: *Alba, Albertine, Albertyna, Albinia, Albinka, Alverta, Alvinia, Alwine, Elberta, Elbertina, Elbertine, Elbi, Elbie, Elby.*

ALBREDA (German) Counsellor for elves.

ALCESTIS (Greek) The heroine of a play by Euripides.

ALCINA (Greek) A sorceress. Variations: *Alcine, Alcinia, Alsina, Alsinia, Alsyna, Alzina.*

ALDA (Italian) Old. Variations: *Aldabella, Aldea, Aldina, Aldine, Aleda, Alida.*

ALDARA (Greek) A winged gift. Variation: *Aldora.*

ALDIS (English) Experienced in war. Variations: *Ailith, Aldith.*

ALDONZA (Spanish) Sweet.

ALDREDA (English) Elder counsellor.

ALEA (Arabic) Honourable. Variation: *Aleah.*

ALEEKA (African: Nigerian) Pretty girl.

ALEELA (African) Girl who cries.

ALEEN (Dutch) Bright light. Variations: *Aleena, Aleene, Aleezah, Aleine, Alena, Alene, Alisa, Alitza, Aliza, Alizah.*

ALEGRIA (Spanish) Joy. Variations: *Alegra, Allegria.*

ALEI (Hebrew) Leaf.

ALEKA (Hawaiian) noble.

ALEMA (Hawaiian) Soul.

ALEPEKA (Hawaiian) Bright and noble. Variation: *Alebeta.*

ALESA (Hawaiian) Noble one. Variations: *Aleka, Alika.*

ALESHANEE (Coos) Constantly playing.

ALETA (Spanish) Little winged one.

ALETHEA (Greek) Truth. Variations: *Alathea, Alathia, Aleethia, Aleta, Aletea, Aletha, Alethia, Aletta, Alette, Alithea, Alithia.*

ALEXANDRA (Greek) One who defends. Feminine version of Alexander. Alexandra and its many variations have always seemed to have an elitist, upper-crust aura to them. In the 1980s, the visibility of Alexandra et al was undoubtedly encouraged by Joan Collins's character Alexa on the TV show *Dynasty* as well as Billy Joel and Christy Brinkley's choice for their daughter, Alexa. The name has also been long associated with the royalty, including Queen Victoria, whose real name was Alexandrina, Edward VII's Danis-born wife Queen Alexandra, and Queen Elizabeth II's cousin Princess Alexandra. Variations: *Alejandrina, Aleka, Aleksasha, Aleksey, Aleksi, Alesia, Aleska, Alessandra, Alessa, Alessi, Alex, Alexa, Alexanderia, Alexanderina, Alexena, Alexene, Alexi, Alexia, Alexie, Alexina, Alexiou, Alexis.*

ALEY (English) Hayfield.

ALFONSINE (German) Noble. Feminine version of Alphonse. Variations: *Alfonsia, Alonza, Alphonsine*.

ALFREDA (English) Counsellor of elves. Feminine version of Alfred. Variations: *Alfre, Alfredah, Alfredda, Alfreeda, Alfrieda, Alfryda, Allfredda, Allfrie, Allfrieda, Allfry, Allfryda, Elfre, Elfrea, Elfredah, Elfredda, Elfreeda, Elfrida, Elfrieda, Elfryda, Elfrydah, Elva, Elvah, Freda, Freddi, Freddie, Freddy, Fredi, Fredy, Freeda, Freedah, Frieda, Friedah, Fryda, Frydah*.

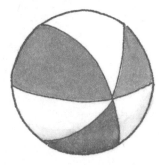

ALGOMA (Native American) Flower valley.

ALHENA (Arabic) Ring.

ALI (Arabic) Highest. Variations: *Alia, Alie, Allie, Ally*.

ALICE (English) Noble. Originally a variation of the name Adelaide, Alice came into its own as a popular name in the 1940s and 1950s. Variations: *Alis, Alles, Allice, Allyce, Alyce*.

ALICIA (English, Hispanic, Swedish) Truthful. Alicia and its variations are very popular today among parents who want lush, beautiful names for their daughters. Actress Jodie Foster's real name is actually Alicia. Alicia and its variants are regularly in the top twenty lists of names for girls, and will undoubtedly continue to become more and more popular. Variations: *Alesha, Alesia, Alisha, Alissa, Alycia, Alysha, Alyshia, Alysia, Ilysha*.

ALIDA (Hispanic) Wing. Variations: *Alaida, Alda, Aldina, Aldine, Aldyne, Aleda, Aleta, Aletta, Alette, Alidah, Alidia, Alita, Allda, Alleda, Allida, Allidah, Allidia, Allidiah, Allyda, Allydah, Alyda, Alydah*.

ALIKE (African: Nigerian) Nobility. Variation: *Alih*.

ALILE (African: Malawian) She cries. Variation: *Alila*.

ALIMA (Arabic) Strong. Variation: *Ahlima*.

ALINA (Russian) Nobility; light. Variations: *Aleen, Aleena, Alenah, Aline, Alline, Allyna, Alyna, Alynah, Alyne, Leena, Leenah, Lena, Lenah, Lina, Lyna, Lynah*.

ALISA (Hebrew) Happiness. Although there isn't really much difference between Alicia and Alisa just from the look of it, the origins of these two names are notably different. Christian parents tend to prefer Alicia, while Jewish parents clearly favour Alisa, because its origins are in the Hebrew language. When I was growing up, the most popular form of the name Elizabeth was my own name, Lisa, and Alisa was rare. However, as you can see by the number of girls' names that begin with 'Al', Lisa has been phased out in favour of the more modern-sounding Alisa. Variations: *Alisah, Alisanne, Alissa, Alissah, Aliza, Allisa, Allisah, Allissa, Allissah, Allyea, Allysah, Alyssa, Alyssah*.

ALISI (Polynesian) Noble.

ALISON (German) Diminutive version of Alice. Today, the name Alison has a most interesting distinction. It is said to be the second-most popular name that mothers who have completed four years of college and beyond choose for their daughters. Alison is a feminine name that doesn't go overboard. Famous Alisons include British children's writer Alison Uttley, British actress Alison Steadman and British singer Alison Moyet. Variations: *Alisann, Alisanne, Alisoun, Alisun, Allcen, Allcenne, Allicen, Allicenne, Allie, Allisann, Allisanne, Allison, Allisoun, Ally, Allysann, Allysanne, Allyson, Alyeann, Alysanne, Alyson*.

ALITA (Spanish) Nobility.

ALITZAH (Hebrew) Happy. Variation: *Aleeza.*

ALIYA (Arabic) Exalted. Variations: *Aliye, Allyah, Alya.*

ALIZA (Hebrew) Joyful. Variations: *Alitza, Alitzah, Aliz, Alizka.*

ALKA (Hindu) Young.

ALKAS (Native American) A scared girl.

ALLTRINNA (African-American) Unknown definition.

ALLYA (Hebrew) To arise.

ALLYRIANE (French) A lyre.

ALMA (Latin) Nurturing one. Variations: *Allma, Almah.*

ALMEDA (Latin) Determined; destined for success. Variations: *Allmeda, Allmedah, Allmeta, Almedah, Almeta, Almetah, Almida, Almidah, Almita.*

ALMENA (English) Constant protector. Feminine version of William. Variations: *Almeena, Almena, Almina, Elmena, Elmina.*

ALMERA (Arabic) Refined woman. Variations: *Allmeera, Allmera, Almeria, Almira, Almyra, Elmerya, Elmyrah, Meera, Merei, Mira, Mirah, Myra, Myrah.*

ALMODINE (Latin) Stone.

ALMOND (English) Nut.

ALNABA (Native American) Two wars fought simultaneously.

ALOHA (Hawaiian) Greeting, welcome.

ALOHALANI (Hawaiian) Spiritual love.

ALOHI (Hawaiian) Bright.

ALOHILANI (Hawaiian) Shining sky.

ALOHINANI (Hawaiian) Shining beauty.

ALONA (Hebrew) Oak tree. Variations: *Allona, Allonia, Alonia, Eilona.*

ALONSA (Spanish) Ready to fight. Variation: *Alonza.*

ALPHA (Greek) Alpha is the first letter of the Greek alphabet. It also represents the beginning of things, specifically as they pertain to religion and family. Variation: *Alfa.*

ALTA (Latin) High. Variation: *Allta.*

ALTAIR (Arabic) Bird.

ALTHAEA (Greek) Healer.

ALTHEA (Greek) With the potential to heal. Althea is a breathy, feminine name. It became famous as the pseudonym by which English poet Richard Lovelace addressed his beloved in his celebrated poem 'To Althea, from Prison'. Another example was the great tennis player of the 1950s, Althea Gibson. Variations: *Altha, Althaia, Altheta, Althia.*

ALTHEDA (Greek) Blossom.

ALTSOBA (Native American: Navajo) At war.

ALUDRA (Greek) Virgin.

ALUMIT (Hebrew) Secret. Variations: *Aluma, Alumice.*

ALUNA (African: Kenyan) Come here.

ALURA (English) Religious counsellor. Variations: *Allura, Alurea.*

ALVA (Spanish) White, pure. Alva is a pretty name. It is not very common but can be found as the middle name of the inventor Thomas Alva Edison. Variations: *Alvah, Alvy, Elva, Elvy.*

ALVINA (English) Counsellor of elves. Variations: *Alvedine, Alveena, Alveene, Alveenia, Alverdine, Alvine, Alvineea, Alvinia, Alwinna, Alwyna, Alwyne, Elveena, Elvena, Elvene, Elvenia, Elvina, Elvine, Elvinia.*

ALVITA (Latin) Energetic.

ALYA (Arabic) To rise up.

ALZBETA (Czech) Consecrated.

ALZENA (Arabic) Woman. Variations: *Alzeena, Alzina.*

ALZUBRA (Arabic) A star in the constellation Leo.

AM (Vietnamese) The moon.

AMA (African: Ghanian) Born on Saturday. Variation: *Amma.*

AMABEL (Latin) Lovable. Variations: *Ama, Amabelle.*

AMADEA (Latin) Feminine version of Amadeus, which means a lover of god. Variations: *Amadee, Amedee.*

187

AMADI (African: Nigerian) Celebration.

AMADIKA (African: Zimbabwean) Beloved.

AMADORE (Italian) Gift of love. Variation: *Amadora.*

AMAL (Arabic) Hope. Variations: *Amahl, Amahla, Amala.*

AMALA (Hindu) Pure. Variation: *Amalaa.*

AMALTHEA (Greek) Ancient mythological mountain goat.

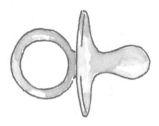

AMANA (Hebrew) Loyal. Variations: *Amania, Amaniah, Amanya.*

AMANDA (Latin) Loved. Amanda is a very popular name these days, having reached a peak in the 1960s. People like it possibly because it has a bit of a patrician air to it, but also because one of its variations – Mandy – is such a casual, approachable name. The name Amanda has appeared in literary vehicles since it featured in two 17th-century plays, *Love's Last Shift* and *The Relapse.* More recently, Noel Coward wrote about Amanda Prynne in his work *Private Lives.* Playwright Tennessee Williams followed Coward's example in his play *The Glass Menagerie.* Famous actresses with the name include Amanda Donahoe and Amanda Holden. Variations: *Amandi, Amandie, Amandine, Amandy, Amata, Manda, Mandaline, Mandee, Mandi, Mandie, Mandy.*

AMANI (Arabic) To want. Variation: *Amany.*

AMARA (Greek) Lovely, immortal girl. Variations: *Amarande, Amaranta, Amarante, Amarantha, Amarinda, Amarra, Amarrinda, Mara, Marra.*

AMARIS (Hebrew) Covenant of God. Variations: *Amaria, Amariah.*

AMARJAA (Hindu) Everlasting.

AMARYLLIS (Greek) Flower.

AMATA (Spanish) Loved.

AMAUI (Hawaiian) A bird.

AMAYA (Japanese) Night rain.

AMAYETA (Native American) Berries.

AMBARISH (Hindu) Saint.

AMBER (English) Semi-precious stone. Jewel names were taken up towards the end of the 19th century, but the book and later the film *Forever Amber* was probably responsible for bringing the name Amber to the attention of people back in the 1960s. Though the Amber in the book title was used to refer to the colour of a man's eyes, people are more familiar with the term today as it refers to a hardened nugget of fossil resin that has trapped a tiny bug or the leaf of a plant inside. Back in the 1960s, when the name was first used for girls, Amber was associated with hippie children. Variations: *Ambar, Amberetta, Amberly, Ambur.*

AMBIKA (Hindu) God of fertility.

AMBROSINE (Greek) Immortal. Variations: *Ambrosia, Ambrosina, Ambrosinetta, Ambrosinette, Ambroslya, Ambrozetta, Ambrozia, Ambrozine.*

AMEE (Hindu) Nectar of life.

AMELIA (English) Hardworking. The avatrix Amelia Earhart was perhaps the most famous example of this name; however, Amelia also has a traditional kind of sound to it. Variations: *Amalea, Amalie, Amelcia, Ameldy, Amelie, Amelina, Amelinda, Amelita, Amella.*

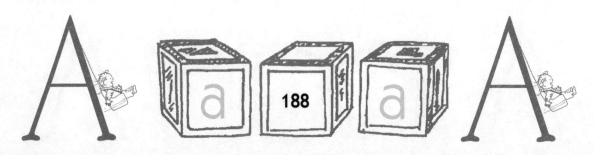

AMENTI (Egyptian) Goddess of the west. Variations: *Ament, Iment.*

AMERICA (English) Guess.

AMETHYST (English) Violet quartzstone.

AMICA (Italian) Close friend. Variation: *Amice.*

AMIDAH (Hebrew) Moral. Variation: *Amida.*

AMIELA (Hebrew) God's people. Variation: *Ammiela.*

AMINA (Arabic) Honest. Variations: *Ameena, Aminah, Amine, Amineh, Amna.*

AMINTA (Latin) Guardian. Variation: *Amynta.*

AMIRA (Arabic) Leader. Variations: *Ameera, Ameerah, Amirah, Meerah, Mira.*

AMISSA (Hebrew) Friend. Variations: *Amisa, Amita.*

AMITA (Hindu) Infinite. Variation: *Amiti.*

AMITOLA (Native American) Rainbow.

AMITY (Latin) Friendship. Variation: *Amitie.*

AMKIMA (Native American: Kiowa) Unknown definition.

AMMA (Hindu) Mother goddess; (Scandinavian) Grandmother.

AMOKE (African: Nigerian) To know her is to love her.

AMOLI (Hindu) Valuable.

AMOR (Spanish) Love. Variation: *Amorette.*

AMY (English) Loved. Author Louisa May Alcott was the first to use the name Amy in a popular work of fiction. Perhaps because of this association, I always think of Amy as a name for a little girl, and not for a grown woman. But it is such a popular name today that thousands of parents are proving me wrong. In the 1970s, Amy was a popular name, but it fell out of favour in the 1980s. Today, it's back with a vengeance. Variations: *Aimee, Aimie, Amada, Amata, Ami, Amice, Amie, Amil.*

AMYMONE (Greek) Ancient mythological figure.

AN (Vietnamese) Peace.

ANA (Polynesian) Cave.

ANABA (Native American: Navajo) Comes back from war.

ANADARIA (Hawaiian) Woman. Variation: *Anakalia.*

ANAHITA (Persian) The goddess of rivers and water.

ANAIS (Hebrew) Gracious.

ANAKA (African-American) Sweet face. Variations: *Anaca, Anika, Anikee.*

ANAKONIA (Hawaiian) Valuable. Variation: *Anatonia.*

ANALA (Hindu) Fire. Variation: *Analaa.*

ANAMOSA (Native American: Sauk) White fawn.

ANANDA (Hindu) A disciple of Buddha.

ANANDITA (Hindu) Happy.

ANASTASIA (Greek) Resurrection. Anastasia is a wonderfully romantic name that is a natural should you want your daughter to study ballet, visit Russia, or tend an organic garden in the country. Variations: *Anastace, Anastacia, Anastacie, Anastase, Anastasie, Anastasija, Anastasiya, Anastassia, Anastatia, Anastazia, Anastice, Anastyce.*

ANATOLA (Greek) Easterly.

ANCELOTE (French) Sevant. Feminine version of Lancelot.

ANCI (Hungarian) Grace of God.

ANDELA (Czech) Angel. Variations: *Andel, Andelka.*

ANDREA (Scottish) Womanly. Feminine version of Andrew. Andrea has regularly appeared in the top fifty names for girls list since the 1950s; however,

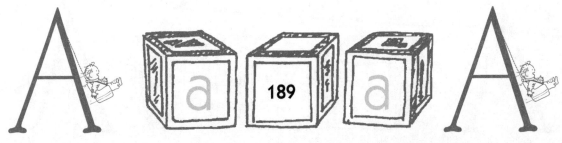

today, the name is more commonly used in one of its more exotic variations, especially the name Andie, after the American film actress Andie MacDowell. In the 1970s, Andrea seemed to be a utilitarian kind of name, but apparently that has changed and it has taken on a more sophisticated air. Other famous bearers of the name include British writer Andrea Newman and American tennis player Andrea Jaegar. Variations: *Andera, Andra, Andreana, Andree, Andreea, Andrene, Andrette, Andria, Andriana, Andrianna, Andrienne, Andrietta, Andrina, Andrine.*

ANDROMEDA (Greek) One who ponders.

ANDULA (Czech) Grace of God. Variation: *Andulka*

ANEKA (Hawaiian) Grace. Variation: *Aneta.*

ANELA (Hawaiian) Angel.

ANEMONE (Greek) Flower of the wind. Variations: *Annamone, Annemone.*

ANESH (Czech) Virginal, pure. Variations: *Anesa, Anezka, Neska.*

ANEVAY (Native American) Superior.

ANGANAA (Hindu) Beautiful.

ANGEE (Hindu) Adequate arms and legs.

ANGELA (Greek) Messenger of God, angel. Actresses Angela Lansbury, Angie Dickenson and Anjelica Huston have given us three different variations of the name. Variations: *Aingeal, Ange, Angel, Angele, Angelene, Angelia, Angelica, Angelika, Angelina, Angeline, Angelique, Angelita, Angie, Angiola, Anjelica, Anngilla.*

ANGHARAD (Welch) Beloved.

ANGPATU (Native American: Sioux) Daytime. Variation: *Anpaytoo.*

ANI (Hawaiian) Beautiful.

ANIANI (Hawaiian) Clear.

ANILA (Hindu) Children of the wind.

ANIMA (Hindu) Small.

ANINA (Hebrew) Answer to a prayer.

ANISAH (Arabic) Friendly. Variations: *Anisa, Anise, Anisha, Anissa, Annissa.*

ANITARA (Hawaiian) Hawaiian version of Anitra. Variation: *Anikala.*

ANIWETA (African: Nigerian) A Nigerian spirit.

ANJU (Hindu) Glory.

ANN (English) Grace. Ann, along with its many variations, was one of the most commonly used names – as either a first or middle name – until the craze for unusual names first hit in the late 1960s. My middle name is Anne, and I always thought it was pretty boring. It's interesting, however, that the two major spellings – Ann and Anne – have gone back and forth in popularity. For instance, from 1900 to 1950, Ann was the most popular form. However, in 1950, after Princess Anne was named, that version became more popular than Ann, ten times over. Variations: *Ana, Anita, Anitra, Anitte, Anna, Annah, Anne, Annie, Annita, Annitra, Annitta, Hannah, Hannelore.*

ANNABELLE (English) Lovable. Variations: *Anabel, Anabele, Anabell, Anabelle, Annabel, Annabell.*

ANNAMARIE (English) Ann + Marie. It was once very popular to take the 'Plain Jane' name Ann and combine it with other girls' names to create something that was just a bit more beautiful than either of the words by themselves. Especially when the version of Ann is Anna, the resulting names are particularly romantic and roll off the tongue. Variations of the 'Ann +' combo include: *Annalie, Annalisa, Annamae, Annamaria, Annamarie, Annamay, Anneliese, Annelise, Annelle, Annemae, Annemarie, Annetta, Annette.*

ANNORA (English) With honour. Variations: *Anora, Anorah, Nora, Norah, Onora.*

ANNUNCIATA (Latin) The Annunciation. Variations: *Annunziate, Anonciada, Anunciacion, Anunciata, Anunziata.*

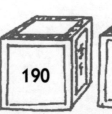

ANOI (Hawaiian) Desire.

ANONA (Latin) Pineapple. Variation: *Anonna*.

ANSONIA (Greek) Son of god.

ANTHEA (Greek) Flower. Anthea is a close cousin of Althea. It enjoyed a peak of popularity in the 1950s but since has become much less common. Hera, the Roman queen of Olympus, was often referred to as Anthea. Famous television personalities with the name include Anthea Turner and Anthea Redfern from *The Generation Game* in the 1970s. Variations: *Anthe, Annthea, Antia*.

ANTIGONE (Greek) The daughter of Oedipus and Jocasta.

ANTOINETTE (French) Priceless. Feminine version of Anthony. Antoinette and its variants are very beautiful names; however, the notorious Frenchwoman Marie Antoinette and her tyrannical views toward her people have probably tarnished this name for a long time to come. Variations: *Antonella, Antonetta, Antonette, Antonia, Antonie, Antonieta, Antonietta, Antonina, Antonine, Tonelle, Tonette, Toney, Toni, Tonia, Tonie, Tony*.

Narrowing Down Your Choices

Okay, so you've started to spend some serious time flipping through the pages of this book and have marked some of the names that sound particularly attractive to you.

Some parents will glance at a name and know instantly that it's the perfect name for their baby.

However, if you're like most parents-to-be, you're not in that category. Some sound great, while others are definite possibilities. Others feel that there are so many choices that it's close to impossible to decide.

So what do you do? How do you begin to choose among the hundreds of names for ones that could be possible names for your baby?

The first thing to do is to write down the names that sound good to you with your last name. Your partner should do the same thing, but separately. It's a good idea to see what the other person thinks; if, by chance, you share some of the same names on your lists, that may be a sign that you should choose that name.

When you've drawn up a list, the next thing you should do is to say the full name out loud to see how it sounds. After all, your child will hear that name directed at him or her tens of thousands of times over the next several decades or more. You have to make sure that first and last names at least sound like they're part of the same name.

You may have a middle name in mind. Though it's less important than the first name you select, it's still a good idea to hear how everything fits together. So after you have some solid candidates for your first name picked out, go ahead and see how some possible middle names fit into the mix.

To further narrow down your choices, you could ask some friends or relatives what they think; but to tell the truth, picking a name is such a personal matter that I think the more people you involve in your search for your baby's perfect name, the more confused you're going to be. So take time on your own to get to your short list. If, at that point, you still don't have a favourite, you just might need a dart board to finalize things.

ANUENUE (Hawaiian) Rainbow.

ANUHEA (Hawaiian) Fragrant.

ANUKA (Hindu) Envious.

ANULI (African: Nigerian) Joyous.

ANUPA (Hindu) Unique. Variation: *Anupaa*.

ANUPRIYAA (Hindu) Exceptional.

ANURA (Hindu) Information.

ANUSHEELA (Hindu) Fan.

ANWEN (Welsh) Fair, beautiful. Variation: *Anwyn*.

ANYA (Latvian) Grace of God. Variation: *Anyuta*.

ANZU (Japanese) Apricot.

AOI (Japanese) Hollyhock.

AOIBHEANN (Irish) Beautiful. Variations: *Aibfinnia, Aoibh, Aoibhinn, Eavan*.

AOIFE (Irish) Pretty. Variation: *Aoiffe*.

AOLANI (Hawaiian) A cloud in heaven.

AONANI (Hawaiian) Beautiful light.

APANGELA (African) One who will not finish a trip.

APARA (African: Nigerian) One who comes and goes. Traditionally used to prevent the girl's death in childhood.

APERILA (Hawaiian) April. Variation: *Apelila*.

APHRA (Hebrew) Dust. Variations: *Affery, Afra, Afrat, Afrit, Aphrat, Aphrit*.

APHRODITE (Greek) The goddess of love and beauty.

APIKATILA (Hawaiian) Father rejoices. Variation: *Api*.

APONA (Hawaiian) Encompassing.

APONI (Native American) Butterfly.

APRIL (English) Named for the month. Many parents choose the name April for their daughters who are born during the month, but to me that seems just a little too obvious. Variations: *Abrial, Abril, Aprilete, Aprilette, Aprili, Aprille, Apryl, Averil, Avril*.

APSARA (Hindu) Heavenly woman.

AQUENE (Native American) Peace.

ARA (Arabic) Rain. Variations: *Ari, Aria, Arria*.

ARABELLA (English) In prayer. Variations: *Arabel, Arabela, Arbell, Arbella, Bel, Bella, Belle, Orabella, Orbella*.

ARACHNE (Greek) Spider.

ARADHANA (Hindu) Devotion.

ARAMINTA (English) Literary name created in the eighteenth century.

ARCADIA (Greek) Pastoral. Variation: *Arcadie*.

ARCELIA (Spanish) Treasure chest.

ARDAH (Hebrew) Bronze. Variations: *Arda, Ardath, Ardona, Ardonah*.

ARDELLE (Latin) Enthusiastic. Variations: *Arda, Ardelia, Ardelis, Ardella, Arden, Ardia, Ardra*.

ARDEN (Latin) Excited.

ARELLA (Hebrew) Angel. Variation: *Arela*.

ARETA (Greek) Virtuous. Variations: *Arete, Aretha, Arethi, Arethusa, Aretina, Aretta, Arette*.

ARETHUSA (Greek) Woodland nymph.

ARGENTA (Latin) Silver.

ARIA (Italian) Melody.

ARIADNE (Greek) Very holy one. Variations: *Araidna, Arene, Argana*.

ARIANA (Welsh) Silver. Variations: *Ariane, Arianie, Arianna, Arianne*.

ARIEL (Hebrew) Lioness of God. The name Ariel burst onto the scene in the early 1990s with the Disney film *The Little Mermaid*. Ariel was previously known as a water sprite as well as a male sprite in Shakespeare's *The Tempest*. Ariel also appears as the title of one of Sylvia Plath's works, and these various sources provide a wide array of inspiration. Variations: *Aeriel, Aeriela, Ari, Ariela, Ariella, Arielle, Ariellel*.

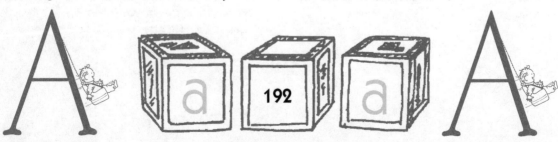

ARISTA (Greek) Harvest.

ARIZA (Hebrew) Made from cedar wood.

ARLENE (English) Pledge. Back in the 1940s and 1950s, Arlene was one of the more popular names for girls, perhaps owing to actresses Arlene Francis and Arlene Dahl. Today, because of this earlier association, the name will strike most parents as dated. Variations: *Arleen, Arlie, Arliene, Arlina, Arline, Arlise, Arlys.*

ARLETTE (French) Feminine version of Charles. Variations: *Arlet, Arletta.*

ARMINA (English) Woman in war. Variations: *Armida, Armine.*

ARNA (Hebrew) Cedar tree; (Scandinavian) Eagle. Variations: *Arni, Arnice, Arnit.*

ARNINA (Hebrew) Mountain. Variations: *Arnice, Arnie, Arnit.*

ARPANA (Hindu) Devoted one.

ARTEMIS (Greek) Goddess of hunting. Variation: *Artemesia.*

ARTHA (Hindu) Great wealth.

ARTHURINA (Gaelic) Rock; nobility. Variations: *Artheia, Arthelia, Arthene, Arthuretta, Arthurine, Artina, Artis, Artri.*

ARUB (Arabic) Affectionate wife.

ARUNA (Hindu) Reddish brown in colour. Variations: *Arunika, Arunima.*

ARVINDAA (Hindu) Lotus.

ARWA (Arabic) Young goat.

ASA (Japanese) Morning. Variation: *Asako.*

ASABI (African: Nigerian) An infant of noble background.

ASELA (Spanish) Ash tree.

ASENAHANA (Polynesian) Red berry.

ASENATA (Hawaiian) Thorny bush. Variation: *Akenaka.*

ASENATH (Hebrew) Bush of thorns.

ASENCION (Spanish) To ascend.

ASHA (Hindu) Desire. Variation: *Ashia.*

ASHANTI (African-American) Ashanti is a name used to commemorate a part of western Africa from which American slaves were captured. Variations: *Ashaunta, Ashuntae.*

ASHIRA (Hebrew) Wealthy.

ASHLEY (English) Ash tree. Ashley started out as a boys' name, with Ashley Wilkes from *Gone With the Wind* popularizing the name. But from that point on, Ashley seemed destined to be a girls' name, possibly because of the sensitivity of the Margaret Mitchell character. Today, giving a boy the name Ashley would almost certainly set him up for a daily dose of ridicule, since Ashley is one of the most popular girls' name around at the moment. Variations: *Ashely, Ashla, Ashlan, Ashlea, Ashlee, Ashleigh, Ashlie, Ashly, Ashton.*

ASHNI (Hindu) Lightning.

ASHURA (African: Swahili) Born during the Islamic month of Ashur.

ASIA (English) Named after the continent.

ASIMA (Arabic) Protector.

ASISA (Hebrew) Ripe.

ASISYA (Hebrew) Juice of God. Variation: *Asisia.*

ASIZA (African-American) Spirit of the forest.

ASLAUG (Scandinavian) Consecrated to God. Variation: *Aslog.*

ASMA (Arabic) Renown.

ASMEE (Hindu) Confident.

ASOKA (Hindu) Flower.

ASPASIA (Greek) Welcome. Variations: *Aspa, Aspia.*

ASPEN (English) Tree. Aspen is a city in the western United States, which is all that some place names need to become popular as names for boys and girls.

ASPHODEL (Greek) Lily.

ASSHEWEQUA (Native American: Sauk) Singing bird.

ASTERA (Hebrew) Star. Variations: *Asta, Asteria, Asteriya, Astra.*

ASTERIA (Greek) Ancient mythological figure.

ASTRAEA (Greek) Starry skies. Variation: *Astrea.*

ASTRID (Scandinavian) Godlike beauty and strength. Astrid is a great alternative to another Norwegian name for girls that is used in this country, Ingrid. Astrid, however, has a softer feel to it and more parents should consider it. Variations: *Astrud, Astryd.*

ASYA (Hebrew) Response. Variation: *Assia.*

ATALANTA (Greek) Greek mythological figure.

ATARA (Hebrew) Crown.

ATHALIA (Hebrew) Praise the Lord. Variations: *Atalia, Ataliah, Atalie, Atalya, Athalee, Athalie, Athalina.*

ATHENA (Greek) Goddess of wisdom. Variation: *Athene.*

ATIDA (Hebrew) Future.

ATIFA (Arabic) Sympathetic. Variation: *Atifah.*

ATIRA (Hebrew) Prayer.

ATIYA (Arabic) Present.

ATRINA (Hawaiian) Peaceful.

AUBREY (English) Counsellor of elves.

AUD (Scandinavian: Norwegian) Unpopulated.

AUDHILD (Scandinavian) Prosperous in battle. Variations: *Aud, Audny.*

AUDREY (English) Nobility and strength. The name became well known as the name of a seventh-century saint but it was not until the early years of the 20th century that it was used in the modern form. Of course, the late actress Audrey Hepburn was responsible for making this name a popular choice through the end of the 1950s. Today, it's not as popular, but it's one of those great old-fashioned names that is due for a comeback. Variations: *Audey, Audi, Audie, Audra, Audre, Audree, Audreen, Audri, Audria, Audrie, Audry, Audrye, Audy.*

AUGUSTA (Latin) Majestic. Feminine version of August and Augustus. It enjoyed a peak in popularity towards the end of the 19th century but has since become rare. Variations: *Agusta, Augustia, Augustina, Augustine, Augustyna, Augustyne, Austina, Austine, Austyna, Austyne.*

AUINA (Hawaiian) Slope. Variation: *Auwina.*

AUKAKA (Hawaiian) Wise. Variations: *Augata, Auguseta.*

AULII (Hawaiian) Delicate.

AUNGATTAY (Native American: Kiowa) Standing in the track.

AURA (Greek) Slight breeze. Variations: *Aure, Aurea, Auria.*

AURELIA (English) Gold. Variations: *Arela, Arella, Aurene, Aureola, Aureole, Auriel, Aurielle.*

AURORA (Latin) Roman goddess of dawn. Variation: *Aurore.*

AUTONOE (Greek) Ancient mythological figure.

AUTUMN (American) Named for the season.

AVA (English) Birdlike. Thought to have evolved as a variant of Eve, it had early exposure through the ninth-century St. Ava of Hainault but appears to have fallen into disuse before the end of the medieval period. Like Audrey, the name Ava is permanently connected with one actress: Ava Gardner. Variations: *Aualee, Avah, Avelyn, Avia, Aviana, Aviance, Avilina, Avis, Aviva.*

AVALON (Gaelic) Island of apples.

AVANI (Hindu) Earth.

AVELINE (Irish) Unknown definition.

AVENA (Latin) Oat pasture.

AVERILL (English) April. Variations: *Avaril, Averil, Averilla, Averyl.*

AVERY (English) Elf advisor. There is an increased usage of this name among girl babies. Avery fits the

baby-naming trends of the times perfectly, since it is unisex as well as a last name.

AVI (Hebrew) My father. Variations: *Avey, Avie, Avy*.

AVIS (Latin) Old Roman family name. Variation: *Avice*.

AVIVAH (Hebrew) Spring. Variations: *Abiba, Abibah, Abibi, Abibit, Avivi, Avivit*.

AVTALIA (Hebrew) Lamb. Variation: *Avtalya*.

AWANATU (Native American: Niwok) Turtle. Variations: *Awanata, Awanta*.

AWENDELA (Native American) Sunrise.

AWINITA (Native American: Cherokee) Fawn. Variation: *Awenita*.

AYA (Hebrew) Bird

AYAH (African: Swahili) Bright.

AYAKO (Japanese) Damask.

AYALAH (Hebrew) Gazelle. Variation: *Ayala*.

AYAMEKO (Japanese) Iris. Variation: *Ayame*.

AYANNA (African-American) Created as a variation of Anna. Variations: *Ayana, Ayania*.

AYASHA (Arabic) Wife.

AYDA (Arabic) Help.

AYELET (Hebrew) Deer.

AYESHA (Persian) Small girl.

AYITA (Native American) The worker.

AYLA (Hebrew) Oak tree. Variation: *Ayala*.

AYOBAMI (African: Nigerian) I am blessed.

AYOBUNMI (African: Nigerian) Joy is mine.

AYODELE (African: Nigerian) Joy in our home.

AYOFEMI (African: Nigerian) Joy likes me.

AYOKA (African: Nigerian) Joyful.

AYONDELA (African) Bending tree.

AYOLUWA (African: Nigerian) The joy of our people.

AYOOLA (African: Nigerian) Joy in wealth.

AYUMI (Japanese) Walk.

AZA (Arabic) Comfort.

AZABA (Hebrew) Biblical name. Variation: *Azabah*

AZALEA (Latin) Flower. Variation: *Azalia*.

AZAMI (Japanese) Flower.

AZARIA (Hebrew) Helped by God. Variations: *Azariah, Azelia*.

AZHAR (Arabic) Flower.

AZIZA (Hebrew) Strong.

AZIZE (Turkish) Dear.

AZRA (Hindu) Virgin.

AZRIELA (Hebrew) God is my strength.

AZUA (African: Swahili) Beloved.

AZURA (French) Blue. Variations: *Azor, Azora, Azure, Azzura, Azzurra*.

AZZA (Arabic) Gazelle.

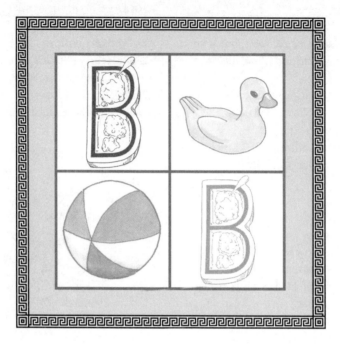

BAAKO (African: Ghanian) First-born.

BABA (African: Ghanian) Born on Thursday.

BACHIKO (Japanese) Happy child.

BADERINWA (African: Nigerian) Worthy of respect.

BADRIYYAH (Arabic) Full moon. Variation: *Budur*.

BAHAAR (Hindu) Spring.

BAHATI (African: Swahili) Lucky.

BAHIJA (Arabic) Happy. Variation: *Bahiga*.

BAHIRA (Arabic) Electric.

BAILEY (English) Bailiff. Bailey has become a popular name for both boys and girls in the last decade and this name should become more widely used for girls. Variations: *Bailee, Baylee, Bayley, Baylie*.

BAKA (Hindu) Crane. Variation: *Baca*.

BAKARA (Hebrew) To visit.

BAKUL (Hindu) Flower. Variation: *Bakula*.

BAKURA (Hebrew) Ripe. Variation: *Bikura*.

BALALA (African) You must eat much to grow.

BALANIKI (Hawaiian) White.

BALBINA (Italian) Stutterer. Variation: *Balbine*.

BAMBI (Italian) Child. Variations: *Bambie, Bambina, Bamby*.

BANAN (Arabic) Fingertips.

BANHT (Hindu) Fire.

BANITA (Hindu) Woman.

BANJOKO (African: Nigerian) One who stays.

BANO (Hindu) Bride.

BAO (Chinese) Precious.

BAO-YO (Chinese) Precious jade.

BAPTISTA (Latin) One who baptizes. Variations: *Baptiste, Batista, Battista, Bautista*.

BARA (Hebrew) To choose. Variations: *Bari, Barra*.

BARBARA (Greek) Foreign. It is thought that the Greek word was originally intended to imitate the stammering foreigners who were unable to speak Greek fluently. It was once one of the most popular names for girls and reached a peak in the early 1950s. However, its usage has dropped off dramatically as parents today associate the name with their parents' generation. Popular Barbaras have included Barbara Stanwyck and Barbra Streisand. As part of its legacy, however, it has left behind lots of variations on a theme: *Babb, Babbett, Babbette, Babe, Babett, Babette, Babita, Babs, Barb, Barbary, Barbe, Barbette, Barbey, Barbi, Barbie, Barbra, Barby, Basha, Basia, Vaoka, Varenka, Varina, Varinka, Varka, Varvara, Varya, Vava.*

BARIAH (Arabic) To succeed.

BARIKA (Arabic) Bloom.

BARKAIT (Hebrew) Morning star. Variation: *Barkat.*

BARRAN (Irish) Little top.

BARRIE (English) Pointed object. Feminine version of Barry.

BASHIYRA (Arabic) Joy.

BASIA (Hebrew) Daughter of God. Variations: *Basha, Basya.*

BASILIA (Greek) Royal. Feminine version of Basil. Variations: *Basila, Basilea, Basilie.*

BASIMA (Arabic) To smile. Variations: *Basimah, Basma.*

BAT (Hebrew) Daughter. Variation: *Bet.*

BATHIA (Hebrew) Daughter of God. Variations: *Basha, Baspa, Batia, Batya, Bitya, Peshe, Pessel.*

BATHILDA (German) Female soldier. Variations: *Bathild, Bathilde, Berthilda, Berthilde.*

BATHSHEBA (Hebrew) Biblical name, wife of Uriah and then David. Variations: *Bathseva, Batsheba, Batsheva, Batshua, Sheba.*

BATINI (African: Swahili) Intimate thoughts.

BATZRA (Hebrew) Fort.

BAYO (African: Nigerian) Happiness.

BEATA (Latin) Blessed. Variation: *Beate.*

The Real Names of Celebrities

Hollywood has really shaped the way we perceive celebrity names. I remember the laughs that burst out when Judy Garland was revealed to be Frances

Gumm and Michael Caine turned out to be Maurice Micklewhite.

Here are some other before-and-after names of some well-known celebrities:

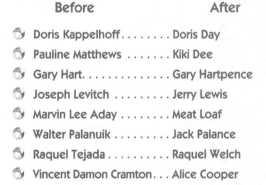

Before	After
Allen Konigsberg	Woody Allen
Bernice Frankel	Beatrice Arthur
Charles Buchinsky	Charles Bronson
Frederick Austerlitz	Fred Astaire
Betty Joan Perski	Lauren Bacall
Edna Rae Gillooly	Ellen Burstyn
Anthony Dominick	Tony Bennett
Cherilyn La Pierre	Cher

Before	After
Doris Kappelhoff	Doris Day
Pauline Matthews	Kiki Dee
Gary Hart	Gary Hartpence
Joseph Levitch	Jerry Lewis
Marvin Lee Aday	Meat Loaf
Walter Palanuik	Jack Palance
Raquel Tejada	Raquel Welch
Vincent Damon Cramton	Alice Cooper

BEATHA (Irish) Life. Variation: *Betha*.

BEATRICE (Latin) She brings joy. I remember being very young the first time I saw this name in print. Beat the rice? I thought. What does that mean? And who would name their child Beat Rice? Beatrice was popularized through Dante's work *The Divine Comedy* and in the Shakespeare play *Much Ado About Nothing*, but the Beatrice that most American kids know is Beatrix Potter, who wrote the stories about Peter Rabbit. Since I've grown up, I've changed my tune about this name – some of the following variations are actually lovely names for a girl or woman. Variations: *Bea, Beatrisa, Beatrise, Beatrix, Beatriz, Beattie, Bebe, Bee, Beitris, Beitriss*.

BEBHINN (Irish) Sweet woman.

BECHIRA (Hebrew) Select.

BEDRISKA (Czech) Peaceful ruler.

BEEJA (Hindu) Beginning. Variation: *Beej*.

BEHIRA (Hebrew) Bright light.

BEL (Hindu) Apple wood.

BELEN (Spanish) Bethlehem.

BELIA (Spanish) Oath of God. Variations: *Belica, Belicia*.

BELINDA (English) Dragon. Variation: *Belynda*.

BELITA (Spanish) Little beauty.

BELLE (French) Beautiful. Variations: *Bela, Bell, Bella, Belva, Belloma*.

BEMEDIKTA (Scandinavian) Blessed. Feminine version of Benedict. Variation: *Benedikte*.

BENA (Hebrew) Wise.

BENE (African) Born during market week.

BENEDETTA (Italian) Blessed. Feminine version of Benedict. Variations: *Benedicta, Benedicte, Benedikta, Benetta, Benita, Benni, Benoite*.

BENITA (Latin) God has blessed. Variations: *Bena, Benitri, Bennie, Binnie*.

BENTLEY (English) Meadow of grass. Variations: *Bentlea, Bentlee, Bentleigh, Bently*.

BERA (German) Bear.

BERACHAH (Hebrew) Benediction. Variations: *Beracha, Berucha, Beruchiya, Beruchya*.

BERDINE (Greek) Bright maiden.

BERECYNTIA (Phrygian) Goddess of the earth.

BERIT (Scandinavian) Brilliant.

BERNADETTE (French) Brave as a bear. Feminine version of Bernard. I think that Bernadette is a pretty name and should be used more often than it is. Actress Bernadette Peters is perhaps the most famous Bernadette around. Variations: *Berna, Bernadene, Bernadett, Bernadina, Bernadine, Bernarda, Bernardina, Bernardine, Bernetta, Bernette, Berni, Bernie, Bernita, Berny*.

BERNEEN (Irish) Strong as a bear.

BERNICE (Greek) She brings victory. Variations: *Bema, Beranice, Berenice, Bernelle, Bernetta, Bernette, Bernicia, Bernie, Bernyce*.

BERNITA (African-American) Variation of Bernard.

BERRY (American) Berry. Variation: *Berri, Berrie*.

BERTHA (German) Bright. This name hit its peak in both the United States and Great Britain in the 1870s. Certainly the name Big Bertha, given to Germany's cannons during World War I, and the fact that it was the name of Mr Rochester's mad wife in *Jane Eyre* helped to determine all the negative connotations of this name. Even my grandmother hated it back in the 1930s. Variations: *Berta, Berthe, Berti, Bertie, Bertilda, Bertilde, Bertina, Bertine, Bertuska, Bird, Birdie, Birdy, Birtha*.

BERTILLE (German) Heroine.

BERURA (Hebrew) Pure.

BERURIA (Hebrew) Chosen by God.

BERYL (Greek) Green gemstone. Variations: *Beril, Berrill, Berry, Beryla, Beryle.*

BETA (Czech) Grace of God. Variations: *Betka, Betuska.*

BETHANY (English) House of poverty; a Biblical village near Jerusalem. As we all seem a bit Tiffanyed out, Bethany has been starting to appear a little bit more often as a close enough substitute. Variations: *Bethanee, Bethani, Bethanie, BethAnn, Bethann, Bethanne, Bethannie, Bethanny.*

BETHEL (Hebrew) Temple.

BETHESDA (Hebrew) Biblical place.

BETHIA (Hebrew) Daughter of Jehovah. Variations: *Betia, Bithia.*

BETI (Gypsy) Small.

BETUEL (Hebrew) Daughter of God. Variation: *Bethuel.*

BETULAH (Hebrew) Young woman. Variations: *Bethula, Bethulah, Betula.*

BEULAH (Hebrew) Married. Variations: *Bealah, Beula.*

BEVERLY (English) Beaver stream. Beverly is a perfect example of a name that was previously exclusive to men. Once it started to be given to girls, though, parents dropped it for their sons like a hot potato. Beverly was a more popular girls' name during the first half of the 20th century than it is today. Variations: *Bev, Beverelle, Beverle, Beverlee, Beverley, Beverlie, Beverlye.*

BEVIN (Gaelic) Singer.

BHAMINI (Hindu) Beautiful lady.

BHANUMATI (Hindu) Sunlight.

BHARATI (Hindu) Cared for.

BHAVIKA (Hindu) Devoted.

BHUMA (Hindu) Earth. Variation: *Bhumika.*

BIAN (Vietnamese) Secretive.

BIANCA (Italian) White. Variations: *Beanka, Biancha, Bionca, Bionka, Blanca, Blancha.*

BIBI (Arabic) Lady. Variations: *Bibiana, Bibianna, Bibianne, Bibyana.*

BIBIANE (Latin) Lively.

BICH (Vietnamese) Jewellery.

BIDELIA (Irish) Strong. Variations: *Bedilia, Biddy, Bidina.*

BIENVENIDA (Spanish) Welcome.

BILLIE (English) Constant protector. Feminine version of William. Billie Holiday, Billie Jean King, and even Michael Jackson's 'Billie Jean' have all made this casual name an appealing choice for a daughter. Though it might cause some confusion in the classroom with a boy named Billy present, he'll grow up and out of the name while a girl so named will tend to hang onto Billie forever. Variations: *Billa, Billee, Billey, Billi, Billy.*

BINA (Hebrew) Knowledge. Variations: *Bena, Binah, Byna.*

BINALI (Hindu) Musical instrument.

BINTI (African) Daughter.

BINYAMINA (Hebrew) Right hand.

BIRA (Hebrew) Fortress. Variations: *Biria, Biriya.*

BIRCIT (Scandinavian: Norwegian) Power. Variation: *Birgit.*

BIRDIE (English) Variations: *Bird, Birdey, Byrd, Byrdie.*

BITHIA (Hebrew) Daughter of God.

BITHRON (Hebrew) Daughter of song.

BITKI (Turkish) A type of plant.

BITTAN (Scandinavian: Swedish) Strength.

BLAINE (Gaelic) Thin.

BLAIR (English) A flat piece of land. In the 1950s, Blair was a commonly used name for a certain class of boys training to fill their father's grey flannel suits. In the 1970s and 1980s, Blair turned into a girls' name, although it still connotes the same social class. Variations: *Blaire, Blayre.*

BLAKE (English) Light or dark.

BLANCHE (English) White. Variations: *Blanca, Blanch, Blancha, Blanka, Blanshe, Blenda.*

BLANCHEFLEUR (French) White flower.

BLANDA (Latin) Seductive. Variations: *Blandina, Blandine.*

BLASIA (Latin) Stutterer. Variation: *Blaise.*

BLATH (Irish) Flower. Variations: *Blaithm, Blathnaid, Blathnait.*

BLESSING (English) To sanctify.

BLIMA (Hebrew) Blossom. Variations: *Blimah, Blime.*

BLODWEN (Welsh) White flower. Variations: *Blodwyn, Blodyn.*

BLOM (African) Flower.

BLONDELLE (French) Blonde one. Variations: *Blondell, Blondie, Blondy.*

BLOSSOM (English) Flower. Among the flowers and related words that were adopted as first names among English speakers towards the end of the 19th century. Even though flower names are popular, Blossom still seems far too close to similar-vintage hippie names to really catch on.

BLUEBELL (English) Flower. Variation: *Bluebelle.*

BLUM (Hebrew) Flower. Variation: *Bluma.*

BLY (Native American) High.

BLYTHE (English) Happy. Variations: *Blithe, Blyth.*

BO (Chinese) Precious.

BOBBIE (English) Bright fame. Feminine version of Robert. Variations: *Bobbee, Bobbette, Bobbi, Bobby, Bobbye, Bobina.*

BODIL (Scandinavian) Battle. Variations: *Bothild, Botilda.*

BOGDANA (Polish) Gift from God. Variations: *Boana, Bocdana, Bogna, Bohdana, Bohdana, Bohna.*

BOGUMILA (Polish) Grace of God.

BOGUSLAWA (Polish) Glory of God.

BOINAIV (Native American: Shoshone) Grass maiden.

BOLADE (African: Nigerian) Honour is here.

BOLANILE (African: Nigerian) Wealth in our house.

BOLESLAWA (Polish) Strong glory.

BONA (Hebrew) Builder.

BONFILIA (Italian) Good daughter.

BONG-CHA (Korean) Best daughter.

BONITA (Spanish) Pretty. Variations: *Bo, Boni, Bonie, Nita.*

BONNIE (English) Good. To me, Bonnie always seemed like a nickname for something, but I could never find out what. Bonnie has been somewhat popular, gaining visibility through the movies *Gone with the Wind* and *Bonnie and Clyde*, and singer Bonnie Raitt. Variations: *Boni, Bonie, Bonne, Bonnebell, Bonnee, Bonni, Bonnibel, Bonnibell, Bonnibelle, Bonny.*

BORGHILD (Scandinavian) Fortified for battle.

BORGNY (Scandinavian) Newly fortified.

BOSKE (Hungarian) Lily.

BOUPHA (Cambodian) Flower.

BOZIDARA (Czech) Divine gift. Variations: *Boza, Bozena, Bozka.*

BRACHA (Hebrew) Blessing. Variation: *Brocha.*

BRADLEY (English) Wide meadow. Variations: *Bradlee, Bradleigh, Bradlie, Bradly.*

BRANCA (Portuguese) White.

BRANDY (English) A liquor. Variations: *Brandais, Brande, Brandea, Brandee, Brandi, Brandice, Brandie, Brandye, Branndea.*

BREANA (Celtic) Strong. Feminine version of Brian. Variations: *Breann, Breanna, Breanne, Briana, Briane, Briann, Brianna, Brianne, Briona, Bryanna, Bryanne.*

BRECK (Gaelic) Freckled.

BREE (English) Person from England. Variations: *Brea, Bria, Brielle.*

BRENDA (English) On fire. Feminine version of Brendan. Became widespread during the 19th century and enjoyed a peak of popularity in the middle of the

20th century. Famous Brendas include US singer Brenda Lee and British actress Brenda Fricker. Variations: *Bren, Brendalynn, Brenn, Brennda, Brenndah.*

BRENNA (English) Raven; black hair.

BRETISLAVA (Czech) Glorious noise. Variations: *Breeka, Breticka.*

BRETT (Latin) From Britain. Variation: *Brette.*

BRICE (English) Quick. Variation: *Bryce.*

BRIDE (Irish) Irish goddess of poetry and song.

BRIDGET (Irish) Strength. Bridget sounds like a good Catholic-girl kind of name. Actress Meredith Baxter Birney played a Bridget in the 1970s TV show *Bridget Loves Bernie*. Variations: *Birgit, Birgitt, Birgitte, Breeda, Brid, Bride, Bridgett, Bridgette, Bridgitte, Brigantia, Brighid, Brigid, Brigid, Brigida, Brigit, Brigitt, Brigitta, Brigitte, Brygida, Brygitka.*

BRIE (French) Region in France.

BRIER (French) Heather. Variation: *Briar.*

BRINA (Slavic) Defender. Variations: *Breena, Brena, Brinna, Bryn, Bryna, Brynn, Brynna, Brynne.*

BRISA (Spanish) Greek mythological figure. Variations: *Breezy, Brisha, Brisia, Brissa, Briza, Bryssa.*

BRISEIS (Greek) Mythological queen of Lyrnessus, whom Achilles won in a war.

BRIT (Celtic) Freckled.

BRITES (Portuguese) Strength.

BRITTANY (English) Feminine version of Britain. This is one of the most popular names for girls since the mid-1980s. Nowadays it appears that girls' names with three syllables that end in the letter 'y' and have at least one 'n' in them are destined for the top ten list. Brittany falls into this category and its cause may be greatly helped by the fame of a certain singer – Miss Spears. Variations: *Brinnee, Britany, Britney, Britni, Brittan, Brittaney, Brittani, Brittania, Brittanie, Brittannia, Britteny, Brittni, Brittnie, Brittny.*

BRONA (Czech) She who wins.

BRONISLAVA (Czech) Glorious armour. Variations: *Brana, Branislava, Branka, Brona, Bronicka, Bronka.*

BRONISLAWA (Polish) Glorious protection. Variation: *Bronya.*

BRONWYN (Welsh) Pure of breast. Variation: *Bronwen.*

BROOKE (English) One who lives by a brook. Actress and child model Brooke Shields started the trend of baby girls named Brooke back in the 1970s. Variation: *Brook.*

BRUCIE (French) Thick brush. Feminine version of Bruce. Variations: *Brucina, Brucine.*

BRUNA (Italian) Having brown skin or brown hair. Feminine version of Bruno.

BRUNELLE (French) Little brown-haired girl. Variations: *Brunella, Brunetta, Brunette.*

BRUNHILDA (German) Armour-clad maiden who rides into battle. This name conjures up images of matronly women. It is the name of the legendary warrior in Richard Wagner's opera cycle *The Ring of the Nibelung*. Variations: *Brunhild, Brunhilde, Brunnhilda, Brunnhilde, Brynhild, Brynhilda.*

BRYN (Welsh) Mountain. Variations: *Brinn, Brynn, Brynne.*

BRYONY (English) Vine. Variations: *Briony, Bronie, Bryonie.*

BUA (Vietnamese) Good-luck charm

BUENA (Spanish) Very good.

BUNMI (African: Nigerian) My gift.

BUNNY (English) Good; also rabbit. Nickname for Bonnie. Variations: *Bunni, Bunnie.*

BUSEJE (African: Malawian) Ask me.

BUTHAYNA (Arabic) Pasture. Variations: *Busayna, Buthaynah.*

BYHALIA (Native American: Choctaw) White oak trees.

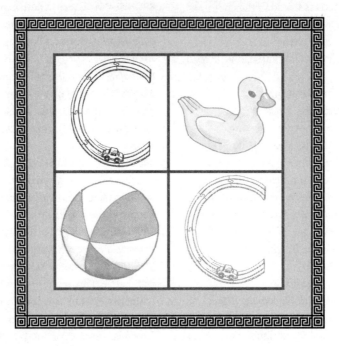

CACHAY (African-American) Prestigious. Possibly derives from French word 'cachet'. Variations: *Cashay, Kachay, Kashay.*

CADENCE (Latin) Rhythmic. Variations: *Cadena, Cadenza, Kadena, Kadence, Kadenza.*

CADY (English) Unknown definition. Variations: *Cade, Cadee, Cadey, Cadie, Kade.*

CAI (Vietnamese) Girl.

CAILIDA (Spanish) Adoring.

CAILIDORA (Greek) Gift of beauty.

CAILIN (Scottish) Triumphant people. Variations: *Caelan, Caileen, Cailyn, Calunn, Cauleen, Caulin.*

CAIMILE (African) Taken from an African proverb where life goes on.

CAINWEN (Welsh) Blessed fair one. Variations: *Ceinwen, Kayne, Keyne.*

CAITLIN (Irish) Pure. Caitlin, created by the combination of Katherine and Lynn, has become a very popular name in the 1990s. Caitlin first became widely known to the majority of us in the early 1980s, and it probably zoomed onto the top ten lists because it was derived from a popular, familiar name that was spelled in a fashion that seemed very exotic. Variations: *Caitilin, Caitlan, Caitlion, Caitlon, Caitlyn, Caitlynne, Catlin, Kaitlin, Kaitlyn, Kaitlynn, Kaitlynne, Katelin, Katelynn.*

CAKUSOLA (African) Love.

CALA (Arabic) Fortress.

CALANDRA (Greek) Lark. Variations: *Cal, Calandria, Calendre, Calinda, Callee, Callie.*

CALANTHA (Greek) Flower. Variations: *Cal, Calanthe, Callee, Calley, Calli, Callie, Cally.*

202

CALATEA (Greek) Ancient mythological figure. Variation: *Calatee*.

CALEDONIA (Latin) Area in Scotland.

CALIDA (Greek) Most beautiful; (Spanish) Affectionate, warm. Variation: *Callida*.

CALLA (Greek) Lily.

CALLIDORA (Greek) Beauty.

CALLIGENIA (Greek) Ancient mythological figure.

CALLIOPE (Greek) Pretty muse. Variations: *Kalliope, Kallyope*.

CALLISTA (Greek) Beautiful. Best known as a result of the success of US actress Callista Flockhart of *Ally McBeal* fame. Variations: *Cala, Calesta, Cali, Calissa, Calista, Calisto, Callie, Cally, Callysta, Calysta, Kala, Kallie*.

CALLULA (Latin) Little beauty.

CALTHA (Latin) Yellow flower. Variation: *Kaltha*.

CALUMINA (Scottish) Dove. Variation: *Calaminag*.

CALVINA (Latin) Without hair. Feminine version of Calvin. Variation: *Calvine*.

CALYPSO (Greek) Girl in hiding. Greek nymph.

CAM (Vietnamese) Citrus.

CAMELIA (English) Flower. Variations: *Camellia, Camilla, Kamelia*.

CAMEO (Italian) A piece of profile jewellery. Variation: *Cammeo*.

CAMILLE (French) Assistant in the church. The name Camille used to have an aura of despair about it based on the tragic figure played by Greta Garbo in the film of the same name. Enough time has passed, however, to make the name an attractive choice again for a daughter. Variations: *Cam, Cama, Camala, Cami, Camila, Camile, Camilia, Camilla, Cammi, Cammie, Cammy, Cammylle, Camyla, Kamila, Kamilka*.

CANDACE (English) Royal title used by Ethiopian queens; white. Candace has become more popular in the last ten years as several TV actresses with the name have starred in hit shows, including Candice Bergen. Variations: *Candee, Candice, Candie, Candis, Candiss, Candy, Candyce, Kandace, Kandi, Kandice, Kandy, Kandyce*.

CANDIDA (Latin) White. Variation: *Candide*.

CANDRA (Latin) Radiant.

CANEADEA (Native American: Iroquois) The horizon.

CANTARA (Arabic) Small bridge.

CAOILFHIONN (Irish) Thin and fair. Variation: *Coelfinnia*.

CAPRICE (Italian) On a whim. Variations: *Capriana, Capricia, Caprie, Kapri, Kaprice, Kapricia, Kaprisha*.

CAPUCINE (French) Cowl, collar. With the popularity of coffee bars serving eighty-eight different types of cappuccino and other coffee drinks, not to mention the roaring popularity of a certain TV series set in a coffee bar, this somewhat obscure name may just become more popular as the years go by. Variations: *Cappucine, Capucina*.

CARA (Italian) Dear. Variations: *Caralea, Caralee, Caralisa, Carella, Cari, Carita, Carra, Kara, Karah, Karry*.

CARESSE (French) Touch. Variations: *Caress, Caressa*.

CAREY (Welsh) Near a castle. Carey is also frequently used as a boys' name. Variations: *Caree, Carree*.

CARI (Turkish) Gentle stream.

CARINA (Italian) Darling; (Scandinavian) Keel of a ship. Variations: *Carena, Cariana, Carin, Carinna, Karina*.

CARINTHIA (German) A region in Germany.

CARISSA (Greek) Refined. Variations: *Carisa, Carisse*.

CARITA (Italian) Charity. Variation: *Caritta*.

CARLA (Italian) Woman. Feminine version of Carl. The name Carla was taken up by English speakers on both sides of the Atlantic in the 1940s and achieved a peak in popularity in the 1980s. Famous bearers of the name include British TV screenwriter Carla Lane and

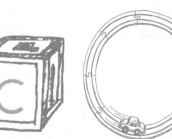

US pop singer Carly Simon. Variations: *Carli, Carlie, Carly, Carlye.*

CARMA (Hebrew) Orchard. Variations: *Carmania, Carmaniya, Carmel, Carmela, Carmeli, Carmen, Carmia, Carmiela, Carmit, Carmiya, Karmel, Karmela, Karmeli, Karmia, Karmit, Karmiya.*

CARNI (Hebrew) Horn. Variations: *Carna, Carney,*

Carnia, Carnie, Carniela, Carniella, Carniya, Carny, Karni, Karnia, Karniela, Karniella, Karniya.

CAROL (German) Woman. Carol was the girl-next-door, goody-two-shoes name when I was growing up. Judging from the lack of toddlers running around with this name today, I'd say that most parents feel the same way. Variations: *Carel, Carey, Cari, Carleen,*

Popular Celebrity Names

Celebrities have always been trend-setters, and Hollywood stars are no exception. Many people are so inspired by the beauty, glamour, machismo, or comedic talent of certain entertainers that they hope their children could draw those qualities from taking on their name alone.

Other times, these entertainers might be bringing to light a name that was never heard before. The following list of actors and actresses have turned their names into household words – literally – by inspiring new parents:

Boys' Names

- Andy Garcia
- Anthony Hopkins
- Antonio Banderas
- Billy Zane
- Brad Pitt
- Bud Abbott
- Christopher Reeve
- Clint Eastwood
- Danny DeVito
- Dean Cain
- Dennis Quaid
- Denzel Washington
- Eddie Murphy
- Gabriel Byrne
- Harry Hamlin
- Harvey Keitel
- Jack Nicholson
- James Dean
- Jimmy Stewart
- Johnny Depp
- Keanu Reeves
- Kevin Costner
- Kyle McLachlan
- Lenny Bruce
- Lou Diamond Phillips
- Macaulay Culkin
- Matt Dillon
- Mel Gibson
- Ralph Maccio
- Robert Downey, Jr.
- Sammy Davis, Jr.
- Stephen Seagal
- Wesley Snipes
- William Baldwin

Girls' Names

- Alicia Silverstone
- Andie MacDowell
- Angela Bassett
- Bette Davis
- Candice Bergen
- Claire Danes
- Cybill Shepherd
- Demi Moore
- Emma Thompson
- Geena Davis
- Gilda Radner
- Glenn Close
- Goldie Hawn
- Halle Berry
- Holly Hunter
- Ingrid Bergman
- Jennifer Jason Leigh
- Joan Crawford
- Julia Roberts
- Katharine Hepburn
- Kathleen Turner
- Maria Conchita Alonso
- Marisa Tomei
- Meg Ryan
- Meryl Streep
- Michelle Pfeiffer
- Nicole Kidman
- Sandra Bullock
- Sharon Stone
- Sigourney Weaver
- Sissy Spacek
- Susan Sarandon
- Vanessa Redgrave
- Winona Ryder

Carlene, Carley, Carlin, Carlina, Carline, Carlita, Carlota, Carlotta, Carlyn, Carlynn, Caro, Carola, Carole, Carolee, Caroll, Carri, Carrie, Carroll, Carry, Caru, Cary, Caryl, Caryle, Caryll, Carylle, Kari, Karie, Karri, Karrie, Karry, Karrye.

CAROLINE (German) Woman. Feminine version of Carl, as well as Charles in diminutive form. Caroline always sounded more regal than just plain Carol, which may explain why Caroline is used more commonly today. Though Caroline could have received the same fate as Carol, several highly visible Carolines have served to redeem the name. First there was Caroline Kennedy; then came Princess Caroline of Monaco. And some parents are adding yet another regal spin on the name with one of the following Variations: *Carolenia, Carolin, Carolina, Carolyn, Carolynn, Carolynne, Karolin, Karolina, Karoline, Karolyn, Karolyna, Karolyne, Karolynn, Karolynne.*

CARON (Welsh) Love. An unusual way to spell the more common Karen. Variations: *Carren, Carrin, Carron, Carrone, Caryn, Carynn.*

CARSON (Scottish) Last name.

CARYS (Welsh) Loved.

CASEY (Irish) Observant. Also common as a boys' name. Out of all the boys' names that become popular as girls' names, Casey may actually be one of the few that remain popular in both camps. Casey is a great name to take a girl from babyhood all the way through life. It's also a classic name, and even though it's just recently become popular, it isn't likely to suffer from the same trendiness as Tiffany and Brittany. Variations: *Cacia, Casee, Casie, Cassie, Caycey, Caysey, Kacey, Kacia, Kasee, Kasie, Kaycey, Kaysey.*

CASILDA (Latin) House.

CASSANDRA (Greek) Protector. Ancient mythological figure. Cassandra is one of those names that almost everyone likes, unless they associate it with a girl whom they hated in school. It's a lush name that first really started to take off in America among African-American parents back in the 1960s, but now it seems to be gaining ground in all kinds of families. Variations: *Casandera, Casandra, Cass, Cassandre, Cassaundra, Casson, Cassondra, Kasandera, Kasandra, Kass, Kassandra, Kassandre, Kassaundra, Kassie, Kasson, Kassondra.*

CASSIA (Greek) Cinnamon.

CASSIDY (Gaelic) Clever. Variations: *Cassidey, Cassidi, Cassidie, Kasady, Kassidey, Kassidi, Kassidie, Kassidy.*

CASTALIA (Greek) Mythological nymph.

CATAVA (African) Sleep.

CATHERINE (English) Pure. Cathy-with-a-C has always been a bit more formal than Kathy-with-a-K. Catherine and all of its derivatives evoke violin lessons, afternoon tea, and gentlemen callers. The 'K' form of Katherine spells tomboys, pigtails, and sleepovers. Famous Catherines include Katharine Hepburn, Catherine Zeta-Jones, Catherine Cookson, St. Catherine of Alexandria, and the Catherine in the novel *Wuthering Heights*. The diminutive *Cat* seems to be gaining in popularity with the likes of TV presenter Cat Deeley. Variations: *Catalina, Catarina, Catarine, Cateline, Catharin, Catharine, Catharyna, Catharyne, Cathe, Cathee, Cathelin, Cathelina, Cathelle, Catherin, Catherina, Cathi, Cathie, Cathy, Catrin, Catrina, Catrine, Catryna, Caty.*

CECILIA (Latin) Blind. Feminine version of Cecil. Paul Simon's song 'Cecilia' probably did more to put this name on the map than the Catholic saint of the same name who is the patron saint of music. Today, variations of Cecilia, especially Cecily, seem to be more popular than the original. Variations: *C'Ceal, Cacilia, Cecely, Ceci, Cecia, Cecile, Cecilie, Cecille, Cecilyn,*

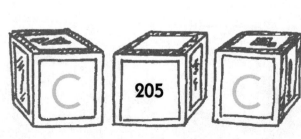

Cecyle, Cecylia, Ceil, Cele, Celenia, Celia, Celie, Celina, Celinda, Celine, Celinna, Celle, Cesia, Cespa, Cicely, Cicilia, Cycyl, Sessaley, Seelia, Seelie, Seely, Seslia, Sesseelya, Sessile, Sessilly, Sheelagh, Sheelah, Sheila, Sheilagh, Sheilah, Shela, Shelah, Shelia, Shiela, Sile, Sileas, Siseel, Sisely, Siselya, Sisilya, Sissela, Sissie, Sissy.

CEDRICA (Welsh) Gift.

CEINWEN (Welsh) Beautiful jewellery.

CEITEAG (Scottish) Pure.

CELANDINE (Greek) Yellow flower.

CELESTE (Latin) Heaven. Celeste is a name that both looks great and sounds great but has never totally caught on. Parents who choose this name for their daughters will undoubtedly be complimented on their choice. Variations: *Cela, Celesse, Celesta, Celestia, Celestiel, Celestina, Celestine, Celestyn, Celestyna, Celinka, Celisse, Cesia, Inka, Selinka.*

CELOSIA (Greek) On fire.

CENOBIA (Greek) Strength of Zeus. Variations: *Cenobie, Zenobia, Zenobie.*

CERELLA (English) In springtime. Variation: *Cerelia.*

CERES (Latin) Roman goddess of agriculture.

CERIDWEN (Welsh) Fair poet. Variations: *Ceri, Ceridwyn.*

CERISE (French) Cherry. Variations: *Cherice, Cherise, Cherrise, Sarise, Sharise, Sherice, Sherise, Sheriz.*

CERYS (Welsh) Love. Variations: *Ceri, Ceries, Cerri, Cerrie.*

CESARINA (Latin) Hairy. Feminine version of Cesar. Variations: *Cesarea, Cesarie, Cesarin.*

CHAANACH (Hebrew) Gracious. Variations: *Chana, Chanah, Chani, Hana, Hende, Hendel, Hene, Heneh, Henna.*

CHAFSIYA (Hebrew) Free. Variations: *Chaishia, Haishia.*

CHAHNA (Hindu) Love.

CHAITALI (Hindu) Active.

CHALESE (African-American) Unknown definition.

CHALINA (Spanish) A rose.

CHAMANIA (Hebrew) Sunflower. Variations: *Chamaniya, Hamania, Hamaniya.*

CHAMELI (Hindu) Jasmine.

CHAN (Cambodian) Tree.

CHANDA (African-American) Unknown definition. Variation: *Chandah.*

CHANDAA (Hindu) Moon. Variations: *Chandra, Chandrakanta.*

CHANDANI (Hindu) Moonlight. Variations: *Chandni, Chandree, Chandrika, Chandrima, Chandrimaa, Chandrjaa.*

CHANDELLE (African-American) Variations: *Chan, Chandell, Shan, Shandell, Shandelle.*

CHANDI (Hindu) Mad.

CHANEL (French) This relatively new name was inspired by the French designer Coco Chanel. Variations: *Chanell, Chanelle, Channell, Channelle, Shanell, Shanelle, Shannelle.*

CHANIA (Hebrew) Camp. Variations: *Chaniya, Hania, Haniya.*

CHANINA (Hebrew) Grace. Variation: *Hanina.*

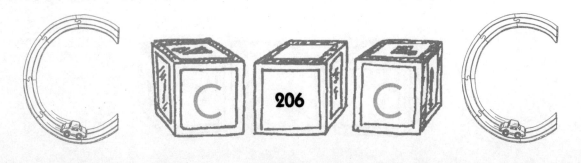

CHANIT (Hebrew) Spear. Variations: *Chanita, Hanit, Hanita.*

CHANNA (Hindu) Chickpea.

CHANNARY (Cambodian) Moon-faced girl.

CHANTAL (French) Rocky area. Variations: *Chantale, Chantalle, Chante, Chantele, Chantelle, Shanta, Shantae, Shantal, Shantalle, Shantay, Shante, Shanteigh, Shantel, Shantell, Shantella, Shantelle, Shontal, Shontalle, Shontelle.*

CHANTERELLE (French) Cup. Variation: *Chantrelle.*

CHANTOU (Cambodian) Flower.

CHANTREA (Cambodian) Moonlight.

CHANYA (Hebrew) God's grace. Variation: *Hanya.*

CHAONAINE (African: Malawian) It has seen me.

CHAOXING (Chinese) Morning star.

CHAPA (Native American: Sioux) Beaver.

CHAPAWEE (Native American: Sioux) Busy like a beaver.

CHARA (Spanish) Rose. Variation: *Charo.*

CHARDE (Arabic) One who leaves.

CHARIS (Greek) Grace. Variations: *Charissa, Charisse.*

CHARITA (Spanish) Princess.

CHARITY (Latin) Dear. In the 18th century, Charity was one of the temperance names along with Prudence and Patience. In recent years, it's fallen more into the category of a 1960s hippie name, at least to my ears. Though it seems to be becoming more popular today, it will probably remain relatively rare. Variations: *Charita, Charitee, Charitey, Sharitee.*

CHARLA (English) Man. Feminine version of Charles. Variations: *Charlaine, Charlayne, Charlena, Charlene, Charli, Charlie, Charline, Cherlene, Cherline, Sharlayne, Sharleen, Sharlene.*

CHARLOTTE (French) Small beauty. Variant of Charles.

CHARMAINE (French) Song. Variations: *Charmain, Charmane, Charmayne.*

CHARMIAN (Greek) Joy.

CHARO (Spanish) Rose.

CHARRON (African-American) Flat land. Variations: *Char Ron, Charryn, Cheiron.*

CHARU (Hindu) Attractive.

CHARUMAT (Hindu) Wise mind.

CHASHMONA (Hebrew) Princess. Variation: *Chashmonit.*

CHASIA (Hebrew) Protected by God. Variations: *Chasya, Hasia, Hasya.*

CHASIDA (Hebrew) Ethical. Variations: *Chasidah, Hasida.*

CHASINA (Hebrew) Strong. Variation: *Hasina.*

CHASTITY (Latin) Purity. Variations: *Chasta, Chastina, Chastine.*

CHAU (Vietnamese) Pearl.

CHAUSIKU (African: Swahili) Born at night.

CHAVA (Hebrew) Life. Variations: *Chabah, Chapka, Chaya, Hava, Haya.*

CHAVI (English, Gypsy) Daughter. Variation: *Chavali.*

CHAVIVA (Hebrew) Beloved.

CHAVON (Hebrew) God is good. Variation: *Chavonne.*

CHAZMIN (African-American) Flower. Variation of Jasmine.

CHAZONA (Hebrew) One who forecasts.

CHE-CHO-TER (Native American: Seminole) Sunrise.

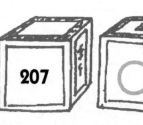

CHEDRA (Hebrew) Happiness. Variation: *Hedra*.

CHEFTZIBA (Hebrew) I am delighted by her. Variations: *Cheftzibah, Cheftziya, Hefibah, Hefzi, Hefzia, Hefziba, Hephziba, Hephzibah, Hepzi, Hepzia, Hepziba, Hepzibah*.

CHEIFA (Hebrew) Haven. Variations: *Chaifa, Haifa, Heifa*.

CHELSEA (English) Ship port. Currently a popular name: it incorporates the certain sophisticated aura plus it's the name of a particular place – a region of London and of New York. Former President Clinton's daughter has given a huge boost to the visibility of this name today, and its popularity should continue to grow long after Clinton has left office. Variations: *Chelsa, Chelsee, Chelsey, Chelsi, Chelsie, Chelsy*.

CHEMDA (Hebrew) Charm. Variation: *Hemda*.

CHEMDIAH (Hebrew) God is my hope. Variations: *Chemdia, Chemdiya, Hemdia, Hemdiah*.

CHENIA (Hebrew) Grace of God. Variations: *Chen, Chenya, Hen, Henia, Henya*.

CHENOA (Native American) White dove. Variation: *Shonoa*.

CHER (French) Dear. This name has made occasional appearances among English speakers since the 1940s and was boosted in the 1960s due to success of the singing duo Sonny and Cher and the subsequent solo fame of Cher, whose real name is Cherilyn. Variations: *Chere, Cherey, Cheri, Cherice, Cherie, Cherise, Sheralynne, Shereen, Shereena, Sherena, Sherene, Sheri, Sherianne, Sherilin, Sherina, Sherralin, Sherrilyn, Sherry, Sherrylene, Sherryline, Sherrylyn, Sherylin, Sherylyn*.

CHERMONA (Hebrew) Holy mountain. Variation: *Hermona*.

CHERRY (French) Cherry; usually pronounced with a 'sh-' sound. Variations: *Chere, Cheree, Cherey, Cherida, Cherise, Cherita, Cherreu, Cherri, Cherrie*.

CHERYL (English) It is thought to have originated from the combination of Cherry and Beryl. It may be ready for a new lease of life, with singer Sheryl Crow being one famous person bearing the name. Variations: *Cherill, Cherrill, Cherryl, Cheryle, Cheryll, Sherryll, Sheryl*.

CHESNA (Slavic) Peaceful.

CHEYENNE (Native American: Algonquin) Specific tribe. Cheyenne is a western place name that is bound to become more popular. Because it is more limiting than, say, Dakota (in that Cheyenne is merely a city while Dakota represents an entire region), it will probably remain somewhat on the fringes. Plus, the suicide of the most famous woman by this name – Marlon Brandon's daughter – might cause parents to shy away from it. Variations: *Cheyanna, Cheyanne, Chiana, Chianna*.

CHHAYA (Hindu) Shadow.

CHIARA (Italian) Clear.

CHIBA (Hebrew) Love. Variation: *Hiba*.

CHICA (Spanish) Girl.

CHIDORI (Japanese) A bird.

CHIKA (Japanese) Intelligence. Variation: *Chikako*.

CHIKU (African: Swahili) Talker.

CHILALI (Native American) Snowbird.

CHIMALIS (Native American) Bluebird.

CHIMENE (French) Gracious.

CHINA (English) Country. Variations: *Chyna, Chynna*.

CHIN-SUNG (Korean) Decency.

CHINUE (African: Nigerian) Blessings of God.

CHIPO (African: Zimbabwean) Gift.

CHIQUITA (Spanish) Little girl.

CHIRIGA (African) Daughter of poor parents.

CHISLAINE (French) Pledge. Variation: *Ghislaine*.

CHITA (Italian) Pearl.

CHITSA (Native American) Fair girl.

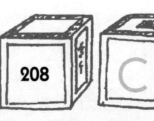

How Abbreviations Can Change the Meaning of a Name

Sometimes, when you choose to abbreviate parts of a name, you can end up with a meaning that turns out to be something totally unexpected. Especially when you fill out a form with those same abbreviations. Witness the following story:

It seems there was an eager new army recruit who was faced with the ordeal of filling out a large stack of papers for a number of different departments that essentially all needed the same kind of information: name, rank, and serial number. He figured he would save a little time and also tell the Army what he liked to be called: R. B. On his forms, he wrote: R. (only) B. (only) Jones.

Remember, this is the army we're talking about. So from that point on, R. B. Jones was known as Ronly Bonly. It was impossible to tell the military brass that they had made a mistake, so poor R. B. decided to give in, and for the rest of his days in the army he learned to respond to Ronly Bonly Jones.

CHIYO (Japanese) A thousand generations. Variation: *Chiyoko*.

CHIZU (Japanese) A thousand storks. Variation: *Chizuko*.

CHLOE (Greek) Young blade of grass. When I was growing up, Chloe was the name of a girl who fashioned herself after the dancer Isadora Duncan: long wavy hair, dressed in Indian print dresses by her parents, and constantly scolded by the teacher for daydreaming in class. Out on the playground, she'd usually go off by herself. Today, Chloe is becoming a very popular name. Over the years, its major appearances have included many novels in the 17th century and, in the Bible, I Corinthians. In the 1970s, Chloe began to appear with increasing frequency in Britain, and the name travelled over to America in the early part of the 1990s. Variations: *Clo, Cloe*.

CHLORIS (Greek) The goddess of vegetation.

CHO (Japanese) Dawn. Variations: *Choko, Choyo*.

CHOFA (Spanish) Wise. Variation: *Chofi*.

CHOLENA (Native American) Bird.

CHOON-HEE (Korean) Daughter of spring.

CHRISTINE (English) Anointed one. Feminine version of Christian. Though Christine was the norm a couple of decades ago, today its variations reign. With their multiple syllables and varying endings, the variations hold much appeal for parents who are looking for a girls' name that is traditional yet still unusual. Famous Christine variations include actress Kirstie Alley, model Christie Brinkley, and the actress Kirsten Dunst from the *Spiderman* films. Variations: *Chris, Chrissy, Christa, Christen, Christi, Christiana, Christiane, Christiann, Christianna, Christie, Christina, Christy, Teena, Teina, Tena, Tina, Tinah*.

CHU-HUA (Chinese) Chrysanthemum.

CHUKI (African: Swahili) Born during a time of hatred.

CHULA (Hebrew) Musician.

CHULDA (Hebrew) Weasel. Variations: *Hulda, Huldah*.

CHUMA (African) Bead; (Hebrew) Heat. Variations: *Chumi, Huma, Humi*.

CHUMANA (Native American) Rattlesnake girl.

CHUMANI (Native American: Sioux) Dew.

CHUMINA (Spanish) God.

CHUN (Chinese) Spring.

CHUNG-AE (Korean) Virtuous love.

CHUNG-CHA (Korean) Virtuous daughter.

CHYNNA (English) China, the country. Variation: *China*.

CIANNAIT (Irish) Ancient. Variation: *Ciannata*.

CIARA (Irish) Black. Variations: *Ceara, Ciarra, Ciera, Cierra*.

CINDERELLA (French) Little cinder girl from the fairy tale.

CIORSTAIDH (Scottish) One who follows Christ. Variations: *Ciorstag, Curstag, Curstaidh*.

CIPRIANA (Greek) From Cyprus. Variations: *Cipriane, Ciprianna, Cypriana, Cyprienne*.

CLARA (English) Bright. Clara seems to be a name from the old days that has the potential for becoming widely used today. Famous Claras include British singer Dame Clara Butt and US actress Clara Bow. If you think it's still a bit old-fashioned, better to choose one of the many variations, except for Clarissa, because then your daughter's friends will always be asking her to explain it all. Variations: *Clair, Claire, Clairette, Clairine, Clare, Claresta, Clareta, Clarette, Clarice, Clarie, Clarinda, Clarine, Claris, Clarisa, Clarissa, Clarisse, Clarita, Claryce, Clerissa, Clerisse, Cleryce, Clerysse, Klara, Klari, Klarice, Klarissa, Klaryce, Klaryssa*.

CLAUDIA (French) Lame. Feminine version of Claude. Variations: *Claudelle, Claudette, Claudina, Claudine*.

CLELIA (Latin) Glorious.

CLEMATIA (Greek) Vine.

CLEMATIS (Greek) Flower.

CLEMENTINE (English) Gentle. Best known as the name of the wife of Sir Winston Churchill. Variations: *Clementia, Clementina, Clemenza*.

CLEOPATRA (Greek) Technically, Cleopatra translates to mean her father's fame, but we think of her as the historical queen of Egypt and the partner of Mark Antony. Variations: *Clea, Cleo*.

CLEVA (English) One who lives on a hill.

CLIANTHA (Greek) Flower. Variations: *Cleantha, Cleanthe, Clianthe*.

CLIO (Greek) One of the nine Greek muses. Clio is the muse of history.

CLIODHNA (Irish) Unknown definition. Variations: *Clidna, Cliona*.

CLODAGH (Irish) A river.

CLORIS (Latin) White, pure. Variation: *Chloris*.

CLOTILDA (German) Famous in battle. Variations: *Clothilda, Clothilde, Clotilde*.

CLOVER (English) Flower.

CLYMENE (Greek) Famous.

CLYTIE (Greek) Splendid. Variations: *Clyte, Clytia*.

COAHOMA (Native American: Choctaw) Red panther.

COCHAVA (Hebrew) Star.

COCHETA (Native American) Foreign.

COLANDA (African-American) Variation of Yolanda.

COLBY (English) Dark farm.

COLETTE (French) Triumphant people. The French novelist who helped to bring this name into the public eye was actually using her last name for her pen name. Its origin is a variation of the name Nicolette. Variations: *Coletta, Collet, Collete, Collett*.

COLLEEN (Gaelic) Girl. Variations: *Coleen, Colene, Coline, Colline*.

COLUMBINE (Latin) Dove. Variations: *Colombe, Columba, Columbia, Columbina*.

COMFORT (English) To comfort.

CONCEPCION (Latin) Conception. Variations: *Concetta, Concettina*.

CONCHOBARRE (Irish) Unknown definition.

CONCORDIA (Greek) The goddess of harmony.

CONNOR (Irish) High desire. Though Connor is very popular for boys, any name that's this striking and this popular will make it over to the girls' side, and we can see that this is already happening. In twenty years,

today's small boys named Connor will probably rue the fact that it has changed into a girls' name – when their own kids tease them for having a girls' name.

CONSTANCE (English) Steady. Variations: *Connie, Constancia, Constancy, Constanta, Constantia, Constantina, Constanza.*

CONSUELA (Spanish) Consolation. Variation: *Consuelo.*

CORAL (English) Coral. Variations: *Coryl, Koral.*

CORAZON (Spanish) Heart. Variation: *Corazana.*

CORBY (English) Town in Britain.

CORDELIA (English) Heart. Variations: *Cordella, Cordelle.*

COREY (Irish) The hollow. Variations: *Cori, Corie, Corri, Corrie, Corry.*

CORINNE (French) The hollow. Variations: *Carine, Carinna, Carinne, Carynna, Corina, Corine, Corinna, Correna, Corrianne, Corrienne, Corrine, Corrinn, Korina, Korinne, Korrina.*

CORINTHIA (Greek) Woman from Corinth.

CORLISS (English) Generous. Variation: *Corlyss.*

CORNELIA (English) Horn. Feminine version of Cornelius. Variations: *Cornela, Cornelie, Cornella, Neelia, Neely, Neelya, Nela, Nelia, Nila.*

CORONA (Spanish) Crown. Variation: *Coronetta.*

CORVINA (Latin) A raven.

COSIMA (Greek) Order. Feminine version of Cosmo. Variation: *Cosma.*

COURTNEY (English) Dweller in the court, or farm. Before it became such a cool name, the image that most of us had of the name was of a privileged, upper-class girl who dutifully went from piano to ballet lessons over the course of one very crowded afternoon. Now, it seems all that has changed. In the 1990s, the name enjoyed a resurgence of popularity with the rise to fame of rock singer Courtney Love, and then the name experienced another wave with the success of the US television series *Friends.* The celebrity status of Courteney Cox has made sure that the name will not be going out of fashion any day soon. Variations: *Cortney, Courtenay, Courteney, Courtnie.*

COZETTE (African-American) Cozy.

CREIRWY (Welsh) Jewel.

CRESCENT (French) Shape. Variations: *Crescentia, Cressant, Cressent, Cressentia.*

CRESSIDA (Greek) Gold. Best known as one half of Shakespeare and Chaucer's *Trolius and Cressida.*

CRISPINA (Latin) Curly hair. Feminine version of Crispin.

CRYSTAL (Greek) Ice, gem. Up until the 1980s, when the name was widely popularized by Linda Evans's character, Krystle, on the TV show *Dynasty,* Crystal already was popular among African-Americans. And back in the 19th century, in England, it actually had its start as a name for boys. Another famous Crystal is US country music singer Crystal Gayle. Variations: *Christal, Cristalle, Cristel, Crystol, Kristal, Kristle, Kristol, Krystal, Krystalle, Krystel, Krystle.*

CYANEA (Greek) Blue.

CYBELE (Greek) The goddess of the earth.

CYMA (Greek) Blossoming. Variation: *Syma.*

CYNARA (Greek) Unknown definition. Variation: *Zinara.*

CYNTHIA (Greek) Goddess of the moon. Variations: *Cindi, Cindie, Cindy, Cinthia, Cintia, Cyndi, Cynth, Cynthie, Cyntia, Kynthia.*

CYRA (Persian) Sun.

CYRENE (Greek) Ancient mythological figure.

CYRILLA (Latin) Godly. Feminine version of Cyril.

CYTHEREA (Greek) The goddess of love and beauty. Variation: *Cytheria.*

CZARINA (Latin) Empress.

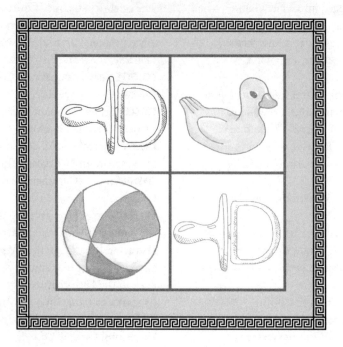

DABORA (Czech) To fight far away. Variations: *Dalena, Dalenka.*

DABUDA (Native American: Washo) Big hips.

DACEY (Irish) From the south. Variations: *Dacee, Daci, Dacia, Dacie, Dacy, Daicee, Daicy.*

DADA (African: Nigerian) Curly hair.

DAFFODIL (French) Flower. Variations: *Daffi, Daffie, Daffy.*

DAGANA (Hebrew) Grain. Variations: *Dagan, Dagania, Deganya.*

DAGMAR (German) Glory. Variations: *Daga, Daggi, Dagi, Dagmara.*

DAGNA (Scandinavian) New day. Variations: *Dagne, Dagney, Dagny.*

DAHLIA (English) Flower. Variations: *Dahla, Dalia, Daliah.*

DAI (Japanese) Grand.

DAISY (English) Flower. Variations: *Dacey, Dacia, Dacy, Daisey, Daisha, Daisi, Daisie, Daizy, Daysi, Deyci.*

DAIYA (Polish) Present.

DAKOTA (English) State name; also used for boys. Dakota is currently very popular, but that could mean that pretty soon it may well be on the wane again. If you don't want to be seen as one who automatically goes along with the crowd, pick a place with a less popular name.

DALAL (Arabic) To flirt. Variation: *Dhelal.*

DALE (English) Valley. Variations: *Dael, Daelyn, Dahl, Dalena, Dalene, Dalenna Dayle, Dalina, Dallana, Daly.*

DALILA (African: Swahili) Gentle. Variations: *Dalia, Dalice.*

DALILI (African: Swahili) Omen.

DALIT (Hebrew) Running water.

DALLAS (English) Town in Scotland. Dallas is also showing up as a boys' name. Variation: *Dallis*.

DALMACE (Latin) An area in Italy. Variations: *Dalma, Dalmassa, Dalmatia*.

DALYA (Hebrew) Branch. Variations: *Dalia, Daliya*.

DAMALIS (Greek) Calf. Variations: *Dainala, Damalas, Damali, Damalla*.

DAMARIS (Latin) Calf. Variations: *Damara, Damaress, Dameris, Dameryss, Damiris*.

DAMAYANT (Hindu) Flirt.

DAMHNAIT (Irish) Poet. Variations: *Deonet, Devnet, Downet, Downett, Dympha*.

DAMIA (Greek) To tame.

DAMITA (Spanish) Princess.

DANA (English) From Denmark. Dana is quickly becoming popular among both boys and girls, but it is more common as a girls' name. Though I've known both a good number of both boys and girls with the name Dana, it appeared for a while that neither took precedence – until now. In some ways, the popularity of the name and the sex it belongs to seems to depend on which Hollywood celebrities with the name are in the majority. A male Dana I know now, in his 20s, tells me that he's currently feeling the pinch of the changeover. Variations: *Daina, Danay, Danaye, Dane, Danee, Danet, Danna, Dayna, Denae*.

DANAE (Greek) Ancient mythological figure.

DANEAN (African-American) Unknown definition. Variations: *DaNeen, DNean*.

DANIAH (Hebrew) God's judgment. Variations: *Dania, Daniya, Danya*.

DANICA (Slavic) Morning star. Variations: *Danika Dannika, Dannica*.

DANIELLE (English) God is my judge. Feminine version of Daniel. Even if Danielle ever became as prevalent a name as Tiffany and other popular modern names, I don't think it would feel as overused. It was popular when I was in school and it's popular now. Of course, the author Danielle Steele has caused many parents to perceive this as a beautiful name for a girl, but I think it would have risen in popularity with or without the prolific author's help. Other famous bearers of the name include TV presenter Dani Behr and Australian singer Dannii Minogue. Variations: *Danee, Danela, Danele, DaNell, Danella, Danette, Daney, Dani, Dania, Danica, Danice, Danie, Daniela, Daniella, Danika, Danila, Danita, Danyelle*.

DANU (Welsh) The mother of the gods.

DANUTA (Polish) Given by God.

DAO-MING (Chinese) The right path.

DAPHNE (Greek) Ancient mythological nymph who was transformed into a laurel tree when pursued by Apollo. Daphne first became popular in America back in the 19th century, when it was commonly given to women who were slaves. It was well used up until the 1930s, when it was among the many flower names taken up in the English-speaking world. Although parents today of all ethnic backgrounds are choosing the name for their daughters in small numbers, Daphne remains most popular among African-American women. One famous Daphne is Daphne Du Maurier, the British novelist. Variations: *Dafne, Daphney, Daphny*.

DARA (Hebrew) Wisdom. Variations: *Dahra, Dareen, Darice, Darissa, Darra, Darrah*.

DARAH (African-American) Princess. Variation of Sarah.

DARALIS (English) Cherished. Variation: *Daralice*.

DARBY (English) A place where deer graze. Darby can also be a boys' name.

DARCI (Irish) Dark one. Variations: *D'Arcy, Darcee, Darcey, Darcie, Darcy, Darsi, Darsie*.

DARDA (Hebrew) Pearl of wisdom.

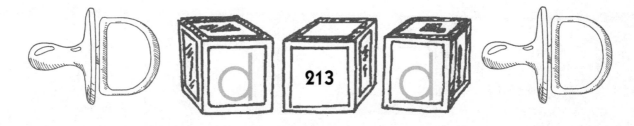

DARIA (Greek) Luxurious. Variations: *Darian, Darianna, Dariele, Darielle, Darienne, Darrelle.*
DARLENE (English) Darling. Variations: *Darla, Darleane, Darleen, Darleena, Darlena, Darlina, Darline.*
DARLONNA (African-American) Darlene + Donna.
DARNELL (English) Disguise. Variations: *Darnae, Darnelle, Darnetta, Darnisha.*
DARPITAA (Hindu) Proud.
DARRELLYN (English) Combination of Darrell and Lynn. Variation: *Daryllyn.*

DARSHA (Hindu) Sighted. Variations: *Darshika, Darshina, Darshini, Darshna.*
DARSHELLE (African-American) Unknown definition.
DARU (Hindu) Cedar tree.
DARYL (English) Last name; area in France. Darryl is traditionally a boy's name; however, the popularity of the actress Daryl Hannah has probably helped to increase its appearance in little girls born in the last ten years. Variations: *Darel, Darrel, Darrell, Darrelle, Darryl, Darrylene, Darrylin, Darryline, Darrylyn, Darylin, Daryline, Darylyne.*
DARYN (Greek) Present, gift. Variations: *Daryan, Darynne.*
DASHA (Greek) God's exhibition.
DATIAH (Hebrew) God's law. Variations: *Datia, Datiya, Datya.*
DAVIDA (Scottish) Cherished friend. Feminine version of David. Variations: *Daveen, Davene, Davia, Daviana, Daviane, Davianna, Davidine, Davina, Davine, Davinia, Davita, Davonna, Davy, Davynn.*

DAWN (English) Sunrise, the dawn. Dawn was a really popular name in the late 1960s and early 1970s because, while it had the feel of many of the hippie names that were popular back then, it still had a long upstanding tradition. This fact made it more acceptable among parents who knew their daughters had to get along in the real world someday. Variations: *Dawna, Dawne, Dawnelle, Dawnetta, Dawnette, Dawnielle, Dawnika, Dawnn.*
DAY (English) Day.
DAYAA (Hindu) Sympathy. Variation: *Dayanita.*
DAYANA (Arabic) Divine.
DAYO (African: Nigerian) Joy is here.
DEA (Latin) Goddess.
DEANA (English) Valley. Feminine version of Dean. Variations: *Deane, Deanna, Deena, Dene, Denna.*
DEANDRA (African-American) Newly created name. Variations: *Deanda, Deandrea, Deandria, Deeandra, Dianda, Diandra, Diandre.*
DEANNA (English) Ocean lover. Variations: *Deane, Deann, Deanne, Deeana, Deeann, Deeanna, Deena, Deona, Deondra, Deonna, Deonne.*
DEBORAH (Hebrew) Bee. When I was in primary school in the 1970s, I remember that there were maybe three or four Debbies spread among one year. Today, the name doesn't seem as popular. Variations: *Deb, Debbi, Debbie, Debby, Debi, Debora, Deborrah, Debra, Debrah, Devora, Devorah, Devra.*
DECEMBRA (Persian) Ten times.
DECIMA (Latin) Tenth. Feminine version of the obscure male name Decimus.
DECLA (Irish) Of the family. Feminine version of Declan.
DEDE (African) First-born daughter.
DEEDEE (Hebrew) Cherished.
DEGULA (Hebrew) Famous.

DEIANIRA (Greek) Ancient mythological figure.

DEIDRE (Irish) Fear, anger. One Deidre I knew in school always complained that no one ever knew how to spell her name: did it have two 'r's, or just one? Was it 'Dei' or 'Die'? Surely, her parents couldn't have known the aggravation she experienced because of her name. Variations: *Dedra, Deidra, Deirdra, Deirdre, Deirdrie, Diedre, Dierdre.*

DEIRBHILE (Irish) Poet's daughter. Variations: *Dervila, Dervla.*

DEKA (African: Somali) Pleasant.

DELANEY (Irish) Child of a competitor. Variations: *Delaina, Delaine, Delayna, Delayne.*

DELIA (Greek) Visible. Name derived from the island Delos, which in Greek mythology was the home of Artemis and Apollo. The best-known bearer of the name is British cookery writer and broadcaster Delia Smith. Variations: *Del, Delise, Delya, Delys, Delyse.*

DELICIA (African-American) Delight. Variations: *Daleesha, Dalicia, Dalisia, Deleesha, Delesha, Delesia, Delice, Delisa, Delise, Delisha, Delisia, Delys, Delyse.*

DELILAH (Hebrew) Delicate. Delilah is perhaps best known as Samson's mistress in the Biblical book of Judges, and as the title and subject of one of the singer Tom Jones's songs. But Delilah is a feminine, lilting name that should be used more often for girls born today. Variations: *Dalila, Delila.*

DELIA (Polish) Daughter of the sea.

DELLA (English) Della literally translates to 'of the', but it's also a form of Adelaide.

DELLE (Hebrew) Jar.

DELMELZA (English) Fort.

DELORA (Spanish) From the ocean.

DELPHA (Greek) Derived from Philadelphia, brotherly love. Variations: *Delphe, Delphia.*

DELPHINE (French) A dolphin. Variations: *Delfina, Delphi, Delphina.*

DELTA (Greek) Delta is the fourth letter of the Greek alphabet, but it could also be a favourite name in southern regions where geographic deltas are prevalent. Actress and singer Delta Goodrem gave this name a boost in the recent years.

DELU (African) Delu is typically given to the first girl born after the first three children were boys.

DELWYN (Welsh) Pretty and blessed.

DELYTH (Welsh) Pretty myth.

DEMETRIA (Greek) From Demeter, the Greek goddess of agriculture. Though many of you have probably not heard the name Demetria before, you are likely to be familiar with the short version of this name through an actress who uses it: actress Demi Moore. I am not aware that the name Demetria – or Demi – is becoming increasingly popular among baby girls born today, but it may just be a matter of time. Variations: *Demeter, Demetra, Demetris, Demi, Demitra, Demitras, Dimetria.*

DENA (Native American) Valley. Variations: *Denav, Dene, Deneen, Denia, Denica.*

DENAE (Hebrew) Innocent.

DENELL (African-American) Dee + Nell. Variation: *Denelle.*

DENISE (French) Lame god. Feminine version of Dennis. The name Denise has been around since the days of the Roman Empire, and it was used with some regularity through the early 17th century. Then it became virtually extinct until the 1950s, when it grew to be very visible. Many parents today, however, may feel that the name is too evocative of the 1950s and 1960s, when it appeared in the top fifteen girls' names. Variations: *Denese, Deni, Denice, Deniece, Denisha, Denize, Dennise, Denyce, Denys, Denys.*

DEOIRIDH (Scottish) Gazelle.

DEOLINDA (Portuguese) Beautiful God.

DEONAID (Scottish) God is gracious.

DERENDA (American) Newly created name. Unknown definition. Variation: *Derinda*.

DERICA (English) Dear. Variations: *Dereka, Derrica*.

DERORA (Hebrew) Independence. Variations: *Derorice, Derorit*.

DERRY (Irish) Red-haired. Variations: *Deri, Derrie*.

DERYN (Welsh) Bird. Variations: *Derren, Derrin, Derrine, Derron, Deryn*.

DESDEMONA (Greek) Misery; also a Shakespearean character. Variation: *Desdemonia*.

DESIREE (French) Longing. Though some people see this name as being a bit too adult to tag on a little girl, I think it is a pretty, feminine name. Its roots stem from Puritanical times, when Desire was the basic name. Today, Desiree seems to be used most often in African-American families, although it is being given to girls of all ethnic backgrounds. Variations: *Desarae, Desira, Desyre, Dezarae, Dezirae, Diseraye, Diziree, Dsaree*.

Famous Characters in Films and Literature

Some people give their babies names from current films and books because they think they are trendy. Others believe, for some reason, that if they give their baby the name of a person that is close to their hearts, whether it's the character in a book they read as a child or a favourite film they viewed as an adult, perhaps their baby will embody some positive trait of that beloved character.

Certainly the kids named Scarlett and Rhett who came out of the 1940s were named as a result of people just going crazy over *Gone with the Wind*.

Today, we are exposed to new and exotic names not only through the increasing numbers of people from different ethnic groups we are able to come into contact with, but also through soap operas and television reality shows. These male and female names can be on the cutting edge, and many new parents have named their kids after soap opera heroes and villains.

As you leaf through this book, you'll see that some of the more popular names originated not only from famous people, but also from fictional ones: Nicholas Nickleby, Oscar Madison, and Madison (Daryl Hannah's character from the 1980s movie *Splash*). There may be a whole new generation of Harrys coming up after the success of the *Harry Potter* books. Sometimes Hollywood scriptwriters and reclusive book authors provide a wealth of new names for parents-to-be to ponder.

Boys

Dirk Pitt		character in Tom Clancy novels
Forrest Gump		*Forrest Gump*
Heathcliff Linton		*Wuthering Heights*
Jim Stark		*Rebel Without a Cause*
Luke Skywalker		*Star Wars*
Tom Sawyer		*The Adventures of Huckleberry Finn*
William Wallace		*Braveheart*

Girls

Becky Thatcher		*Tom Sawyer*
Dorothy Gale		*The Wizard of Oz*
Elizabeth Bennett		*Pride and Prejudice*
Jo March		*Little Women*
Lois Lane		*Superman*
Molly Bloom		*Ulysses*
Scarlett O'Hara		*Gone with the Wind*

DESMA (Greek) Pledge.

DESNA (American) Newly created name; unknown definition. Variations: *Desne, Desney.*

DESSA (Greek) Nomad.

DESTINY (French) Fate. Variations: *Destanee, Destina, Destine, Destinee, Destini, Destinie.*

DEVA (Hindu) Divine.

DEVAHUTI (Hindu) God.

DEVAKI (Hindu) The mother of Krishna.

DEVAL (Hindu) Divine. Variations: *Devanee, Devee, Devi, Devika.*

DEVANY (Gaelic) Dark-haired. Variations: *Davanfe, Devaney, Devenny, Devinee, Devony.*

DEVASHA (Hebrew) Honey. Variation: *Devash.*

DEVENE (Scottish) Beloved. Feminine version of David. Variations: *Devean, Deveen.*

DEVI (Hindu) Goddess of power and destruction.

DEVIN (Irish) Poet. Variations: *Deva, Devinne.*

DEVON (English) Region in southern England. Variations: *Devan, Devana, Devanna, Devona, Devondra, Devonna, Devonne, Devyn, Devynn.*

DEVORGILLA (Scottish) Truth. Variations: *Dearbhforgail, Diorbhail, Diorbhorguil.*

DEWANDA (African-American) Combination of De + Wanda.

DEXTRA (English) One who dyes clothing; right-handed. Feminine version of Dexter.

DEZBA (Native American: Navajo) War.

DHANADAA (Hindu) One who gives wealth.

DHARA (Hindu) Earth. Variations: *Dharinee, Dharitri, Dharti.*

DHAVALA (Hindu) White.

DIAMOND (English) Jewel. Also occasionally used as a boys' name. Variations: *Diamanda, Diamante, Diamonique, Diamontina.*

DIANA (Latin) Divine. Roman goddess of the moon and of hunting. Despite its pagan associations, it was taken up after the Reformation. Diana has always been a popular name, but it has been made more widespread in the last twenty years by such high-profile Dianas as Diana Ross, Diane Keaton, and of course, Princess Diana. Other famous Dianas include British actresses Diana Dors and Diana Rigg. Variations: *Dee, Diahann, Dian, Diane, Dianna, Dianne, Didi, Dyan, Dyana.*

DIANTHA (Greek) Divine flower. Variations: *Diandre, Dianthe, Dianthia.*

DICKLA (Hebrew) Palm tree. Variations: *Dikla, Diklice, Diklit.*

DIDO (Greek) Ancient mythological figure. This name may be set for a revival with the success of British singer Dido at the end of the 1990s and into the 21st century.

DIDRIKA (German) Leader of the people. Feminine version of Dietrich.

DIELLE (French) God. Variation: *Diella.*

DIET (Vietnamese) Conquer.

DIEU-KIEM (Vietnamese) Look for love.

DIGNA (Latin) Valuable. Variation: *Dinya.*

DIJA (African-American) Premature baby.

DILWEN (Welsh) Genuine and blessed.

DILYS (Welsh) Faithful. Variations: *Dylis, Dyllis, Dylys.*

DIMA (Arabic) Rain.

DINAH (Hebrew) God will judge. Variations: *Deena, Denora, Dina, Dinorah, Diondra, Dyna, Dynah.*

DINIA (Hebrew) Wisdom of God. Variation: *Dinya.*

DINKA (African) Family.

DIONNE (Greek) Dione is a Greek mythological figure. Dionne is also the feminine version of Dennis, which in turn is formed from the name of another Greek god, Dionysus, the god of wine. Singer Dionne Warwick was the most popular Dionne around – and

probably the only one – but using her name for a girl today will make it seem like 1973 all over again. Variations: *Deonne, Dion, Diona, Dione, Dionia, Dionna, Dionysia.*

DISA (Scandinavian: Norwegian) Sprite.

DITA (Czech) Wealth; also derivative of Edith, which means property in war. Variation: *Ditka.*

DIVINE (English) Beloved friend. Feminine version of David. Divine and its derivatives have never been terribly popular. Variations: *Divina, Divinia.*

DIVONAH (Hebrew) South. Variations: *Dimona, Dimonah, Divona.*

DIVYA (Hindu) Brilliant.

DIXIE (French) Tenth; also a last name. Variations: *Dix, Dixee.*

DIZA (Hebrew) Joy. Variations: *Ditza, Ditzah.*

DO (African: Ghanian) First child after twins.

DOBA (Native American) No war.

DOBRILA (Czech) Good.

DOBROMILA (Czech) Good grace.

DOBROMIRA (Czech) Good and famous.

DOBROSLAVA (Czech) Good and kind.

DODIE (Hebrew) Beloved. Nickname for Dorothy. Borne by the British writer Dodie Smith. Variations: *Dodee, Dodey, Dodi, Dody.*

DOFI (African: Ghanian) Second child after twins.

DOLI (Native American: Navajo) Bluebird.

DOLLY (English) Doll. Nickname for Dorothy. Dolly Levi from Thorton Wilder's play *The Matchmaker*, which became the musical *Hello Dolly*, and country and western singer Dolly Parton are both examples of famous Dollys. Variations: *Doll, Dollee, Dolley, Dollie.*

DOLORES (Spanish) Sorrow. Variations: *Delores, Doloras, Doloris, Doloritas.*

DOLPHIN (English) Mammal.

DOMINA (Latin) Woman. Variation: *Domini.*

DOMINIQUE (Latin) Lord. Feminine version of Dominick. The boys' name Dominick has been around since the 13th century; no one knows exactly when the feminine form of the name came into being. Currently it is gaining ground in popularity, and its peak seems to be a few years down the road. Variations: *Dominica, Dominika.*

DONA (English) Mighty. Feminine version of Donald. Variations: *Donella, Donelle, Donetta.*

DONATA (Latin) Given.

DONDI (African-American) Unknown definition.

DONELLE (Irish) Ruler of the world. Variation: *Donla.*

DONNA (Italian) Woman of the home. The name Donna was at its peak of popularity in the 1950s and 1960s. The thing to do then was to combine Donna with other names, like Marie and Sue. Perhaps the Osmond parents had similar ideas in mind when they named Donny and Marie. Variations: *Dahna, Donielle, Donisha, Donetta, Donnalee, Donnalyn, DonnaMarie, Donni, Donnie, Donya.*

DONNAG (Scottish) World ruler. Variations: *Doileag, Dolag, Dollag.*

DONOMA (Native American: Omaha) Sun.

DOORIYA (Irish) Ocean.

DORA (Greek) Present. Nickname for Theodora. Variations: *Doralia, Doralyn, Doralynn, Doreen, Dorelia, Dorelle, Dorena, Dorenne, Dorette, Dori, Dorie, Dorinda, Dorita, Doru.*

DORCAS (Greek, Hawaiian) Gazelle. Variation: *Doreka*

DORE (French) Ornate. Dore is pronounced with the 'e' as an 'a', and with the accent on the second syllable. Variations: *Doree, Doretta, Dorette.*

DOREEN (Irish) Gloomy. Variations: *Doireann, Dorene, Dorine, Dorinnia, Doryne.*

DORIAN (Greek) A region in Greece. Also used as a boy's name. Variations: *Doriana, Dorianne, Dorrian.*

DORIS (Greek) A region in Greece. Though Doris was the name of a Greek goddess, the name only became known when writer Charles Dickens placed it on the map as an unusual alternative to Dorothy, which was popular at the time. And who can forget the actress and singer Doris Day, with whom the name will always be linked. Variations: *Dorice, Dorisa, Dorlisa, Dorolice, Dorosia, Dorrie, Dorrys, Dorys, Doryse.*

DORIT (Hebrew) Generation.

DOROTHY (Greek) Gift from God. Famous bearers of the name include British crime novelist Dorothy L. Sayers, US writer Dorothy Parker and Judy Garland's character in the classic film, *The Wizard of Oz.* Variations: *Dollie, Dolly, Dorethea, Doro, Dorotea, Dorotha, Dorothea, Dorothee, Dorothia, Dorrit, Dortha, Dorthea, Dot, Dottie, Dotty.*

DORY (French) Yellow-haired girl. Variations: *Dori, Dorri, Dorrie, Dorry.*

DOTO (African: Tanzanian) Second of twins.

DOUCE (French) Sweet.

DOVEVA (Hebrew) Limber. Variations: *Dovevet, Dovit.*

DOWANHOWEE (Native American: Sioux) Singing.

DRAHOMIRA (Czech) Dearly beloved.

DRAUPADI (Hindu) Famous.

DREW (Greek) Manly; wise. Diminutive of Andrew. Variation: *Dru.*

DRINA (Greek) Protector. Variations: *Dreena, Drena.*

DRISANA (Hindu) Daughter of the sun.

DRUSILLA (Latin) In the Bible, Drusilla is the name of Herod's daughter. Variations: *Drewsila, Drucella, Drucie, Drucilla, Drucy, Druscilla.*

DUA (Arabic) To pray.

DUANA (Irish) Dark-skinned. Feminine version of Duane. Variations: *Duna, Dwana.*

DUDEE (Gypsy) A star.

DUENA (Spanish) Chaperone.

DUHA (Arabic) Unseen.

DULAREE (Hindu) Beloved daughter.

DULCIE (Latin) Sweet. Variations: *Delcina, Delcine, Delsine, Dulce, Dulcea, Dulci, Dulcia, Dulciana, Dulcibella, Dulcibelle, Dulcina, Dulcine, Dulcinea.*

DUMIA (Hebrew) Quiet. Variation: *Dumiya.*

DURGA (Hindu) Unreachable.

DURVA (Hindu) Grass.

DUSANA (Czech) Spirit. Variations: *Dusa, Dusanka, Dusicka, Duska.*

DUSCHA (Russian) Soul.

DUSTINE (English) Dusty place. Feminine version of Dustin. Variations: *Dustee, Dusty.*

DWYNWEN (Welsh) White wave.

DYANI (Native American) Deer.

DYLANA (Welsh) Born of the sea. Feminine version of Dylan.

DYMPNA (Irish) Dympna is the patron saint of mentally ill people. I don't know, but I wouldn't give my daughter – or my cat – this name. Variation: *Dymphna.*

DYVETTE (African-American) Arrow's bow. Variation of Yvette.

DZIKO (South African) The world.

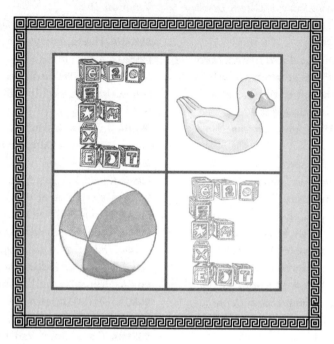

EADOIN (Irish) She has lots of friends.

EALASAID (Scottish) God is my oath.

EALGA (Irish) Noble.

EAMHAIR (Scottish) Unknown definition. Variation: *Eimhear*.

EANNA (Babylonian) Home of the god of gods, Anu.

EARLENE (English) Leader. Feminine version of Earl. Variations: *Earla, Earleen, Earley, Earlie, Earlinda, Earline, Erlene, Erlina, Erline*.

EARTHA (English) Earth. Variations: *Erta, Ertha, Hertha*.

EASTER (English) Named for the holiday.

EBBA (Scandinavian) Strong as a boar. Variations: *Eba, Ebbe*.

EBERTA (German) Bright.

EBONY (African-American) Black wood. Ebony is one of the ten most popular names that African-American parents are giving their daughters these days. Given the trend in the community to give children names that reflect the pride they have in their African-American backgrounds, Ebony is a good choice for parents who don't care for the trend of putting 'La-' in front of a more common name for their daughters. Variations: *Ebbony, Eboney, Eboni, Ebonie*.

EBUN (African: Nigerian) Gift.

ECA (African: Nigerian) Bird.

ECHO (Greek) Ancient mythological nymph.

EDA (English) Happy. Variations: *Edda, Edde, Ede*.

EDDA (Scandinavian) Ancient mythological figure.

EDDI (English) Protector of property. Feminine version of Edward. Variations: *Eddie, Eddy, Eddye*.

EDELINE (German) Noble.

EDEN (Hebrew) Pleasure. Variations: *Eaden, Eadin, Edena, Edenia Edana, Edin*.

EDIAH (Hebrew) Decoration for God. Variations: *Edia, Ediya, Edya, Edyah.*

EDINA (English) One from Edinburgh, capital of Scotland. Variations: *Edeena, Edena, Edyna.*

EDITH (English) Prosperity in war. Is Edith finally beginning to overcome the frumpy image? It could happen, especially since American novelist Edith Wharton, a chronicler of high society, has become chic again. Other famous Ediths include British children's writer Edith Nisbet, British nurse Edith Cavell, British actress Dame Edith Evans and French singer Edith Paif. Variations: *Edie, Edita, Edithe Edy, Edyth, Edytha, Edythe, Eydie, Eydith.*

EDLYN (English) Small noble girl.

EDMEE (Scottish) To love. Variation: *Edme.*

EDMONDA (English) Rich protector. Feminine version of Edmund.

EDNA (Hebrew) Pleasure. Variation: *Ednah.*

EDREA (English) Rich. Variations: *Edra, Eidra, Eydra.*

EDRICE (English) Strong property owner. Feminine version of Edric. Variations: *Edris, Edryce, Edrys, Eidris.*

EDWARDINE (English) Rich protector. Feminine version of Edward. Variations: *Edwarda, Edwardeen, Edwardene, Edwardyne.*

EDWIGE (French) Joyful war. For some parents who are tempted to use Edna as a name for their daughters but think it's still entirely out of the loop, Edwige may be a good alternative. However with the success of J. K. Rowling's *Harry Potter*, books there is probably not a child around who does not know that the variant Hedwig is the name of Harry's pet owl. Variations: *Edvig, Edwig, Hedwig, Hedwige, Yadwigo.*

EDWINA (English) Rich friend. Feminine version of Edwin. Variations: *Edween, Edweena, Edwena, Edwiena, Edwuna, Edwyna.*

EEPA (Hawaiian) Supernatural.

EFAH (Hebrew) Gloom. Variations: *Efa, Eifa, Eifah, Ephah.*

EFFIE (Greek) Singing talk. Variations: *Eff, Effy, Ephie, Eppie, Euphemia, Euphemie, Euphie.*

EFIA (African: Ghanian) Born on Friday.

EFRATA (Hebrew) Fertile. Variations: *Efrat, Ephrat, Ephrata.*

EGA (African: Nigerian) Bird.

EGIDIA (Scottish) Young goat.

EGLAH (Hebrew) Cow. Variation: *Egla.*

EGLANTINE (French) Sweetbriar. Variations: *Eglantilne, Eglantyne.*

EGYPE (English) The country Egypt.

EHANI (Hindu) Desire. Variation: *Ehina.*

EHAWEE (Native American: Sioux) She laughs.

EIBHLIN (Irish) Shining, bright; derivative of Helen.

EIDDWEN (Welsh) Fond and blessed.

EIFIONA (Welsh) Area in Wales.

EILAH (Hebrew) Oak tree. Variations: *Aila, Ailah, Ala, Alah, Ayla, Eila, Eilona, Ela, Elah, Elona, Eyla.*

EILEEN (Irish) Shining, bright. Familiar version of Helen. When I was a kid, Eileen was almost a given among the families of Irish heritage. Today, however,

221

it rarely appears as a first name, and is more common as a middle name. It was probably most popular in the 1920s. Variations: *Aileen, Ailene, Alene, Aline, Ayleen, Eilean, Eilleen, Ilene.*

EILEITHYIA (Greek) The goddess of childbirth. Variation: *Ilithyia.*

EILUNED (Welsh) Idol.

EILWEN (Welsh) Fair.

EIMHEAR (Irish) Swift. Variation: *Emer.*

EINMYRIA (Scandinavian) Ancient mythological figure.

EIR (Scandinavian: Norwegian) Mercy.

EIRA (Scandinavian) Goddess of medicine; (Welsh) Snow. Variation: *Eyra.*

EIRALYS (Welsh) Snowdrop. Variation: *Eirlys.*

EIRIAN (Welsh) Silver.

EIRPNE (Greek) Peace.

EIRWEN (Welsh) Fair. Variation: *Eirwyn.*

EISA (Scandinavian) Ancient mythological figure.

EITHNE (Irish) Kernel. Variations: *Eithna, Ena, Enya, Ethenia, Ethna, Ethnah, Ethnea, Ethnee.*

EKELA (Hawaiian) Noble. Variation: *Etela.*

EKUA (African: Ghanian) Born on a Wednesday.

ELA (Hindu) Intelligent woman; (Polish) Noble. Variations: *Elakshi, Elee, Eli, Elina, Elita.*

ELAINE (French) Bright, shining. Derivative of Helen. Elaine was popular as a girls' name in the 1950s, but has recently fallen out of favour. Famous Elaines have include the mother of Sir Galahad and the lover of Sir Lancelot in Arthurian legend, US actress Elaine Stritch, and British singer and actress Elaine Paige. Variations: *Alayna, Alayne, Allaine, Elaina, Elana, Elane, Elanna, Elayn, Elayne, Eleana, Elena, Eleni Alaina, Ellaina, Ellaine, Ellane, Ellayne.*

ELAMA (Hebrew) God's people.

ELAMMA (Hindu) Mother goddess. Variation: *Ellama.*

ELATA (Latin) Held in high esteem.

ELBERTA (English) Noble, shining. Feminine version of Elbert. Variations: *Elbertina, Elbertine, Elbie.*

ELDORA (Spanish) Coated by gold. Variations: *Eldoree, Eldoria, Eldoris.*

ELDREDA (English) Elderly counsellor.

ELEANOR (English) Mercy. Derivative of Helen. Eleanor always struck me as a commonsense type of name, based on Eleanor Roosevelt as well as Elinor Dashwood in Jane Austen's *Sense and Sensibility.* Though it does seems to be picking up steam, Eleanor is not as popular as other traditional girls' names that are being resurrected today. Variations: *Eleanore, Elenore, Eleonora, Eleonore, Elinor, Ellinor.*

ELECTRA (Greek) Shining one. A mythological figure who had her brother kill their mother and her lover in revenge for their father's murder. Variation: *Elektra.*

ELEELE (Hawaiian) Black eyes.

ELELE (Hawaiian) Messenger.

ELEN (Welsh) Nymph. Variations: *Elin, Ellin.*

ELENOLA (Hawaiian) Bright. Variations: *Elenoa, Elenora, Elianora.*

ELERI (Welsh) Unknown definition.

ELEU (Hawaiian) Alive.

ELGA (Slavic) Holy.

ELI (Scandinavian: Norwegian) Light.

ELIANA (Hebrew) God has answered my prayers. Variation: *Eliane.*

ELIDA (American) Newly created name. Variation: *Elinda.*

ELIDI (Greek) Gift from the sun.

ELIEZRA (Hebrew) God is salvation.

ELIKA (Hawaiian) Forever ruler.

ELIKAPEKA (Hawaiian) Pledged to God. Variations: *Eleki, Elesi, Kapeka, Laika.*

ELILI (Polynesian) Periwinkle.

Native American Names – Cultural Traditions

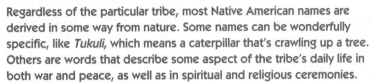

Regardless of the particular tribe, most Native American names are derived in some way from nature. Some names can be wonderfully specific, like *Tukuli*, which means a caterpillar that's crawling up a tree. Others are words that describe some aspect of the tribe's daily life in both war and peace, as well as in spiritual and religious ceremonies.

In many tribes, a naming ceremony takes place to commemorate different rites of passage in a person's life, not just at birth. Therefore, a Native American may have as many as ten different names during his or her lifetime, to honour such events as childhood, marriage, particular life accomplishments, and reaching a certain milestone.

Back in the middle of the nineteenth century, however, the tribes were forced into assimilating into American culture through the efforts of the many zealous missionaries who travelled the country in the name of their religion. Indian names were formally changed to Christian names like John and Mary, as the different tribespeople were forbidden to speak their cultural languages.

Many of the old, more obscure, native languages were lost as the older members of the tribes died out; therefore, many names have been lost forever. Today, however, there is a great push to retrieve some of those ancient languages, as well as those that are on the edge of extinction. Hopefully, this will bring a wealth of new names to baby name books in the future.

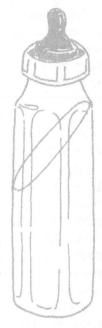

ELINED (Welsh) Idol.

ELIORA (Hebrew) God is light. Variation: *Eleora*.

ELISHA (Hebrew) God is my salvation. Variations: *Eliseva, Elisheba, Elisheva*.

ELITA (Latin) Chosen.

ELIVAH (Hebrew) God is able. Variation: *Eliava*.

ELIZABETH (Hebrew) I pledge to God. As you can see by the numerous variations, if you were to add up all the derivatives of Elizabeth, you'd undoubtedly end up with the most popular girls' name in the world by far. And because of all these wonderful variations, few

girls choose to go by the main root. Variations: *Alzbeta, Babette, Bess, Bessey, Bessi, Bessie, Bessy, Bet, Beta, Beth, Betina, Betine, Betka, Betsey, Betsi, Betsy, Bett, Betta, Bette, Betti, Bettina, Bettine, Betty, Betuska, Boski, Eilis, Elis, Elisa, Elisabet, Elisabeta, Elisabeth, Elisabetta, Elisabette, Elisaka, Elisauet, Elisaveta, Elise, Eliska, Elissa, Elisueta, Eliza, Elizabetta, Elizabette, Elliza, Elsa, Elsbet, Elsbeth, Elsbietka, Elschen, Else, Elsee, Elsi, Elsie, Elspet, Elspeth, Elyse, Elyssa, Elyza, Elzbieta, Elzunia, Isabel, Isabelita, Liazka, Lib, Libbee, Libbey, Libbi, Libbie, Libby, Libbye, Lieschen, Liese, Liesel, Lis, Lisa, Lisbet,*

Lisbete, Lisbeth, Lise, Lisenka, Lisettina, Lisveta, Liz, Liza, Lizabeth, Lizanka, Lizbeth, Lizka, Lizzi, Lizzie, Lizzy, Vetta, Yelisaveta, Yelizaueta, Yelizaveta, Ysabel, Zizi, ZsiZsi.

ELK (Hawaiian) Black.

ELKANA (Hebrew) God has created. Variation: *Elkanah.*

ELKE (German) Noble. Notable bearers of this name include German film actress Elke Sommer and British singer Elkie Brooks. Variation: *Elka.*

ELLA (German) All, total. A famous Ella is US jazz singer Ella Fitzgerald.

ELLEN (English) Variation of Helen that has become a full-fledged name in its own right. A few decades ago, Ellen was the type of name that parents gave to a girl from whom they expected no surprises. Today's Ellens include actresses Ellen Barkin and Ellen DeGeneres. Variations: *Elan, Elen, Elena, Eleni, Elenyl, Ellan, Ellene, Ellie, Ellon, Ellyn, Elyn, Lene, Wily.*

ELLI (Scandinavian) Old age.

ELLICE (Greek) Noble. Feminine version of Elias. Variation: *Elyce.*

ELMA (Greek) Helmet; (Turkish) Apple. Feminine version of Elmo. Largely confined to the USA, it is thought to have evolved from the combination of Elizabeth and Mary.

ELOISE (French) Wise. It is thought this may be a feminie equivalent of Louis, but it has never been widely used. Variations: *Eloisa, Eloisia, Eloiza, Elouise.*

ELORA (Hindu) God gives the laurel to the winner. Variation: *Ellora.*

ELRICA (German) Leader of all.

ELSA (Spanish) Noble. Elsa is a pretty name that has long been popular in Scandinavian as well as Hispanic countries. The name appeared in one of Wagner's operas, *Lohengrin*, and others will remember it as the name of the lioness in Joy Adams' book *Born*

Free, which was turned into a film with Virginia McKenna. Variations: *Else, Elsie, Elsy.*

ELUNED (Welsh) Shape. Variation: *Eiluned.*

ELVA (English) Variation of Olivia.

ELVINA (English) Elf friend. Feminine version of Alvin. Variations: *Elvie, Elvy, Elwina.*

ELVIRA (Spanish) Area in Spain. Variations: *Elva, Elvera, Elvia, Elvirah, Elvire.*

ELYSIA (Latin) From the Elysium Fields, the mythical home of the blessed. Variations: *Eliese, Elise, Elisia, Elyse, Ileesia, Iline, Illsa, Ilyse, Ilysia.*

EMANUELA (Hebrew) God is with us. Feminine version of Emanuel. Variations: *Em, Emanuelle, Emmanuela, Emmanuelle, Emmie, Emmy.*

EME (Hawaiian) Beloved.

EMERA (English) Industrious.

EMERALD (English) A jewel.

EMILY (English) Industrious. Emily is one of those names that automatically implies brains and beauty as well as a nod toward old-fashioned days. It has had a revival since the 1970s. Famous Emilys include British poet Emily Bronte, US poet Emily Dickinson and actress Emily Lloyd. Variations: *Aimil, Amalea, Amalia, Amalie, Amelia, Amelie, Ameline, Amy, Eimile, Em, Ema, Emalee, Emalia, Emelda, Emelene, Emelia, Emelina, Emeline, Emelyn, Emelyne, Emera, Emi, Emie, Emila, Emile,*

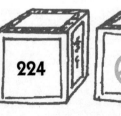

Emilea, Emilia, Emilie, Emilka, Emlynne, Emma, Emmalee, Emmali, Emmaline, Emmalynn, Emele, Emmeline, Emmiline, Emylin, Emylynn, Emlyn.

EMMA (German) Embracing all. A wonderful, Victorian-era name that conjures up images of long, wavy chestnut hair, blue eyes, and cotton petticoats. It has been in use since medieval times and was at its peak in the 19th century, and recently had another revival in the 1980s. Nelson's mistress Lady Emma Hamilton, Emma Woodhouse in Jane Austen's *Emma* and the British actress Emma Thompson all share the name. Variations: *Em, Emmi, Emmie, Emmy.*

EMUNA (Hebrew) Faithful.

ENA (Irish) Bright, shining. Possibly a derivative of Helen.

ENAKAI (Hawaiian) Fiery sea.

ENFYS (Welsh) Rainbow.

ENGRACIA (Spanish) Grace.

ENID (Welsh) Life. This name was most popular in the 1920s, since when it has suffered a marked decline. The prolific British children's writer Enid Blyton is the most famous person with the name. Varations: *Eanid, Enidd, Enud, Enudd.*

ENNIS (Irish) A town in western Ireland. Variation: *Inis.*

ENOLA (Native American) Unknown definition.

ENOMWOYI (African: Nigerian) She is graceful.

ENRICA (Italian) Leader of the house. Feminine version of Henry. Variations: *Enrieta, Enriqueta.*

ENYONYAM (African: Ghanian) It is good for me.

EOGHANIA (Welsh) Youth.

ERELA (Hebrew) Angel.

ERIANTHE (Greek) Lover of flowers.

ERICA (Scandinavian) Leader forever. Feminine version of Eric. Erica is big and has been at least since the early 1970s. In addition to possessing its Scandinavian definition, Erica is also another name for the heather plant. It seems somewhat surprising that this name is still so consistently popular, since it doesn't share the allure that many other traditional names boast today. Well known bearers of the name include US novelist Erica Jong. Variations: *Airica, Airika, Ayrika, Enrica, Enricka, Enrika, Ericka, Erika, Errika, Eyrica.*

ERIKO (Japanese) Child with a collar.

ERIN (Gaelic) Nickname for Ireland; also used occasionally as a boy's name; translates to western island. It has made appearances since the end of the 19th century not only in Ireland but in Australia, the USA and elsewhere increasingly among people who have no Irish connections. Variations: *Erene, Ereni, Eri, Erina, Erinn, Eryn.*

ERINA (Hindu) Speech. Variation: *Erisha.*

ERLINDA (Hebrew) Spirit.

ERMIN (Welsh) Lordly. Variation: *Ermine.*

ERMINE (French) Weasel. Variations: *Ermina, Erminia, Erminie, Ermy.*

ERNA (Scandinavian) Capable.

ERNESTINA (English) Earnest. Variations: *Erna, Ernaline, Ernesta, Ernestine, Ernestyna.*

ERROLYN (English) Area in Britain. Feminine version of Errol.

ERWINA (English) Boar; friend. Feminine version of Erwin.

ERYL (Welsh) Observer.

ESETERA (Hawaiian) Star. Hawaiian version of Esther. Variations: *Ekekela, Eseta.*

ESHANA (Hindu) Desire.

ESHE (African: Swahili) Life.

ESI (African: Ghanian) Born on Sunday.

ESME (French) Esteemed. Variations: *Esma, Esmee.*

ESMERELDA (Spanish) Emerald. Variations: *Emerant, Emeraude, Esma, Esmaralda, Esmarelda, Esmiralda, Esmirelda, Ezmeralda.*

ESPERANZA (Spanish) Hope. Variations: *Esperance, Esperantia.*

ESTELLE (English) Star. Variations: *Essie, Essy, Estee, Estela, Estelita, Estella, Estrelita, Estrella, Estrellita, Stelle.*

ESTHER (Hebrew) Star. Variations: *Essie, Essy, Esta, Ester, Etti, Ettie, Etty.*

ESTRELLA (English) Child of the stars. Variation: *Estrelle.*

ETAIN (Irish) Irish sun goddess.

ETANA (Hebrew) Dedication. Feminine version of Ethan.

ETENIA (Native American) Rich.

ETHEL (English) Noble. Because of its ancient associations it was taken up in the 19th century, when it gained popularity as the name of the main character in William Makepeace Thackerary's *The Newcomes*.

Once upon a time, Ethel was a quite fashionable variation of such names as Ethelinda, Ethelberta and Etheldreda. The singer and dancer Ethel Merman seems to have provided us with this name's last hurrah. Other famous Ethels include British composer Dame Ethel Smyth and US actress Ethel Barrymore. Variations: *Ethelda, Etheline, Ethelyn, Ethelynne, Ethille, Ethlin, Ethyl.*

ETHELINDA (German) Noble serpent. Variations: *Etheleen, Ethelena, Ethelende, Ethelina, Ethelind, Ethylinda.*

ETHETE (Native American: Arapaho) Upright.

ETHNE (Irish) Fire. Variations: *Ethna, Ethnea, Ethnee.*

ETSU (Japanese) Happiness. Variations: *Etsuko, Etsuyo.*

ETTA (English) Diminutive.

ETUMU (Native American) Bear in the sunlight.

ETUMUYE (Native American) Bear climbing a hill.

EUBH (Scottish) Life. Variation: *Eubha.*

EUDORA (Greek) Altruistic gift. Variation: *Eudore.*

Beware of Negative Nicknames

Some nicknames can't be prevented. These spring from deservable physical or emotional characteristics or originate with a member of the family. Nicknames that result from a play on a child's name can be controlled to some extent based on the original name that you choose for your baby.

For example, most nicknames are abbreviated versions of the lengthier given name: Bob, Bobby, or Rob are all nicknames for Robert. While these nicknames are also occasionally given as a child's primary name, many parents prefer the full name as the given name, both so different versions of the name can be used as the child grows into adulthood, and also so the child can have some choice later on as to what works best for him as an adult.

Some nicknames have a babyish feel to them that can be avoided based on the primary name that you choose. But even so, it's impossible to predict the nicknames that your child's peers will pick for him or her. After all, if there's nothing in a name to pick on, kids will make something up – and some parents fall into this category as well. My nickname in school was Lurch, after the butler on the *Addams Family* TV show. Why? Because they thought that I walked like the TV character. Today I laugh about it, but back then, I thought about the nicknames I could hurl back at my tormentors.

So be forewarned: even a name that you think is impossible to turn into a nickname can usually be turned into something else.

EUDOSIA (Greek) Good gift. Variations: *Eudocia, Eudokia, Eudoxia.*

EUGENIA (Greek) Well born. Feminine version of Eugene. It has enjoyed increased visibility since it was the choice of the Duke and Duchess of York for their second daughter, which may well keep this name popular in the coming years. Variations: *Eugena, Eugenie, Eugina.*

EULALIA (Greek) Sweet speaking. Variations: *Eula, Eulalee, Eulalie, Eulaylia, Eulaylie.*

EUN (Korean) Silver.

EUNICE (Greek) Victorious. Variations: *Euniss, Eunys.*

EUN-KYUNG (Korean) Silver.

EUPHEMIA (Greek) Speak well of.

EURYDICE (Greek) Greek mythological figure; wife of Orpheus. Variation: *Euridice.*

EUSTACIA (Greek) Fruitful. Feminine version of Eustace.

EUZEBIA (Polish) Devoted.

EVA (Hebrew) Giver of life. A mixed bunch to choose from: Eva Peron – also known as Evita, Hitler's mistress Eva Braun, and Hungarian-born actress Eva Gabor are all famous Evas. Variations: *Ebba, Evaine, Evathia, Evchen, Eve, Evelina, Eveline, Evi, Evicka, Evike, Evita, Evka, Evonne, Evy, Ewa, Yeuka, Yeva.*

EVADNE (Greek) Good fortune. Variations: *Evadney, Evadnie, Evie.*

EVANGELINE (Greek) Good news. Variations: *Evangelia, Evangelina, Evangeliste.*

EVANIA (Greek) Serene.

EVELYN (French) Hazelnut. Evelyn is a great example of a name that started out as a boys' name – but then parents started to appropriate it for their daughters, rendering the male version all but obsolete. Evelyn became popular in the first couple of decades of the 20th century as a girls' name, and by that point the name had disappeared from general consideration as a boys' name. Novelist Evelyn Waugh is perhaps the sole reminder of this name's true origins. Variations: *Aveline, Eoelene, Eveline, Evelyne, Evelynn, Evelynne, Evlin, Evline, Evlun, Evlynn.*

EVERELDA (English) Boar in battle; also could mean April. Feminine form of Averill.

EVZENIE (Czech) Well born. Variations: *Evza, Evzenka, Evzicka.*

EWALINA (Hawaiian) Hawaiian version of Evelyn. Variation: *Ewa.*

EWANEKELINA (Hawaiian) Good news.

EWELINA (Polish) Life. Variation: *Ewa.*

EYOTA (Native American: Sioux) Great.

EZRELA (Hebrew) God is my strength.

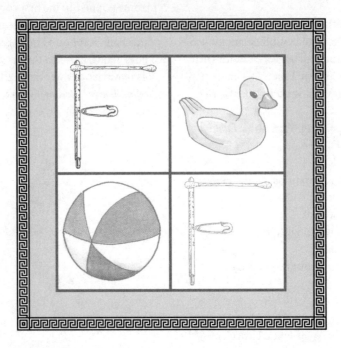

FABAYO (African: Nigerian) Fortunate birth.

FABIA (Latin) One who grows beans. Feminine version of Fabian. Variations: *Fabiana, Fabiane, Fabianna, Fabienne, Fabiola.*

FABRIZIA (Italian) One who works with her hands. Variations: *Fabrice, Fabricia, Fabrienne, Fabritzia.*

FADILA (Arabic) Virtue. Variation: *Fadilah.*

FAHIMA (Arabic) Smart.

FAIDA (Arabic) Abundant. Variation: *Fayda.*

FAITH (English) Faith. Faith was another one of the virtue names that the Puritans liked so much back in the 17th century, and it is one of the few that has survived to this day. Faith, along with Hope, sounds more practical and everyday than either Charity or Prudence. Variations: *Faithe, Faythe.*

FAIVA (Polynesian) Game.

FALAKIKA (Polynesian) Mat.

FALDA (Icelandic) Folded wings.

FALINE (Latin) Catlike.

FALLON (Irish) Related to a leader. Variation: *Falon.*

FALZAH (Arabic) Triumphant.

FANCY (French) Engaged. Nickname for fianceé. Variations: *Fancey, Fancie.*

FANG (Chinese) Fragrant.

FANG HUA (Chinese) Fragrant flower.

FANUA (Polynesian) Land.

FAOILTIARNA (Irish) Lord of the wolves.

FARDOOS (Arabic) Utopia.

FAREWELL (English) Goodbye; beautiful spring.

FARICA (German) Leader of peace.

FARIDA (Arabic) Unique. Variations: *Faridah, Farideh.*

FARIHA (Arabic) Happy. Variation: *Farihah.*

FARRAH (English) Pleasant. Variations: *Fara, Farah, Farra.*

FARREN (English) Last name. Variation: *Faren*.

FATHIYA (Arabic) Victorious.

FATIMA (Arabic) Fatima was the prophet Mohammed's favourite daughter. Fatima has long been used for girls in Muslim families as it implies chastity and other forms of abstention desirable among Muslim women. Devout Muslims in America are now beginning to flock toward this name, following the lead of their relatives in Saudi Arabia, Egypt and India. One possible drawback of the name is its first three letters, which could spawn a slew of teasing in primary school and beyond. Variations: *Fatimah, Fatma, Fatuma*.

FATIN (Arabic) Bewitching. Variations: *Fatina, Fatinah*.

FATUIMOANA (Polynesian) Wreaths.

FAUSTINE (Latin) Lucky. The feminine version of Faust. Variations: *Fausta, Fauste, Faustina*.

FAWN (French) Young deer. Variations: *Faina, Fanya, Fauan, Faun, Faunia, Fawna, Fawne, Fawnia, Fawnya*.

FAY (French) Fairy. Diminutive of Faith. Variations: *Faye, Fayette*.

FAYINA (Ukrainian) Woman from France.

FAYOLA (African: Nigerian) Lucky.

FAYRUZ (Arabic) Turquoise.

FAYZA (Arabic) Winner. Variations: *Faiza, Faizah, Fawzia*.

FEDORA (Greek) Gift from God.

FEIDHELM (Irish) Unknown definition. Variations: *Fedelma, Fidelma*.

FEIGE (Hebrew) Bird. Variations: *Faga, Faiga, Faigel, Feiga, Feigel*.

FELDA (German) From the field.

FELICIA (Latin) Happy; lucky. Feminine version of Felix. As Felicitas it was a fairly common Roman name best known as the third-century saint. Felicia sounds a bit clunky and awkward by itself, but take one of its variations, like Felice or Felicity, and it is transformed into a delicate, feminine name. Felicity, in fact, is becoming more popular for girls these days. A famous Felicity is British actress Felicity Kendall, who first came to fame as Barbara in *The Good Life*. Variations: *Falecia, Falicia, Falicie, Falisha, Falishia, Felice, Feliciana, Felicidad, Felicienne, Felicita, Felicitas, Felicity, Felise, Felita, Feliz, Feliza*.

FELORA (Hawaiian) Flower. Variations: *Felorena, Folora, Polola, Pololena*.

FEMI (African: Nigerian) Love me.

FENG (Chinese) Chinese sweet gum.

FENIA (Scandinavian) Ancient mythological figure. Variation: *Fenja*.

FEODORA (Russian) Gift from God. Feminine version of Theodore.

FERNANDA (German) Peace and courage; brave traveller. Feminine version of Ferdinand.

FERNLEY (English) Valley of ferns. Variations: *Fern, Ferne, Fernlee, Fernleigh, Fernly*.

FETUU (Polynesian) Star.

FIALA (Czech) Violet.

FIAMMETTA (Italian) Sputtering flame. Variation: *Fia*.

FIDDA (Arabic) Silver. Variation: *Fizza*.

FIDELIA (Latin) Faithful. Variations: *Fidela, Fidele, Fidelina, Fidelity, Fidelma, Pikelia*.

FIELIKI (Polynesian) Wanting to be clean.

FIFI (French) Nickname of Josephine. Variations: *Fifine, Fina*.

FIHAKI (Polynesian) Braid of flowers.

FIKRIYA (Arabic) To meditate.

FILIA (Greek) Friendship.

FILIPPINA (Italian) Lover of horses. Feminine version of Philip. Variation: *Filippa*.

FINEEVA (Polynesian) Gabby woman.

FINEONGO (Polynesian) Beautiful woman.

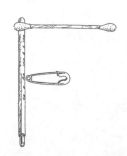

FIONA (Irish) Fair, white. Variations: *Fionna, Fionne.*

FINOLA (Irish) White shoulders. Variations: *Effie, Ella, Fenella, Finella, Fionnaghuala, Fionneuala, Fionnghuala, Fionnuala, Fionnula, Fionola, Fynella, Nuala.*

FIPE (Polynesian) Bright.

FISI (Polynesian) Blossom.

FLAMINIA (Latin) Priest.

FLANNA (Irish) Red hair.

FLANNERY (Irish) Red hair.

FLAVIA (Latin) Yellow hair. Variations: *Flavie, Flaviere, Flavyere, Flayia.*

FLO (Native American) Like an arrow.

FLORA (English) Flower. Flora has potential to become one of the most popular names in the world, since it is one of the more popular names in many countries, including Sweden, Britain, Germany and Russia. A famous Flora is British actress Dame Flora Robson. Variations: *Fiora, Fiore, Fiorentina, Fiorenza, Fiori, Fleur, Fleurette, Fleurine, Flo, Flor, Florance, Florann, Floranne, Flore, Florella, Florelle, Florence, Florencia, Florentia, Florentyna, Florenze, Floretta, Florette, Flori, Floria, Floriana, Florie, Floriese, Florina, Florinda, Florine, Floris, Florrie, Florry, Floss, Flossey, Flossie.*

FLORIDA (Spanish) Flowery.

FLORIMEL (Latin) Flower plus honey.

FLOWER (English) Flower.

FOLA (African: Nigerian) Honourable.

FOLADE (African: Nigerian) She brings honour.

FOLAMI (African: Nigerian) Respect me.

FOLAYAN (African: Nigerian) Walking proudly.

FOLUKE (African: Nigerian) God's care.

FONTANE (French) Fountain.

FORTUNA (Latin) Roman goddess of luck. Variations: *Fortunata, Fortune.*

FRANCES (English) One who is from France. Feminine version of Francis. Frances was a perennial favourite in England through the latter half of the 19th century, but went into a decline in the 20th century. Though it has been considered to be somewhat old fashioned from that time all the way up until the 1980s, Frances is beginning to take off again among parents who are looking for a traditional and classy name for their daughters. Famous Franceses include actress Frances de la Tour and novelist Frances Hodgson Burnett. Variations: *Fan, Fancy, Fania, Fannee, Fanney, Fannie, Fanny, Fanya, Fran, Franca, Francee, Franceline, Francena, Francene, Francesca, Francetta, Francette, Francey, Franchesca, Francie, Francina, Francine, Francisca, Francoise, Frank, Frankie, Franni, Frannie, Franzetta, Franziska, Paquita.*

FRANCOISE (French) Frenchman.

FRANTISKA (Czech) Free woman. Variations: *Frana, Franka.*

FRAYDA (Hebrew) Happy. Variations: *Fradel, Frayde, Freida, Freide.*

FREDA (German) Peaceful. Variations: *Freada, Freddi, Freddie, Freddy, Frederica, Frederique, Freeda, Freida, Frida, Frieda, Fritzi, Fryda.*

FREYA (Scandinavian: Swedish) Noble lady. Variations: *Freja, Freyja, Froja.*

FRIGG (Scandinavian) Beloved. Variation: *Frigga.*

FUJI (Japanese) Wisteria. Variations: *Fujiko, Fujiyo.*

FUJO (African: Swahili) Born to divorced parents.

FUKAYNA (Arabic) Knowledgeable.

FULANDE (Hindu) Flower. Variation: *Fulangi.*

FULLA (Scandinavian) Mythological fertility goddess.

FUSI (Polynesian) Bananas. Variation: *Fusileka.*

FUYU (Japanese) Winter. Variation: *Fuyuko.*

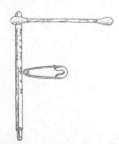

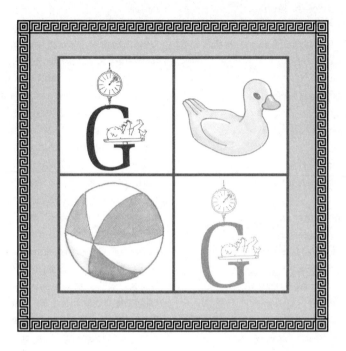

GABRIELLE (Hebrew) Heroine of God. Feminine version of Gabriel. Tennis star Gabriella Sabatini brought new life to this name in many countries around the world. Gabrielle is a wonderfully cultured name that doesn't sound as haughty as some other girls' names that have a sophisticated ring to them. This is probably owing to one of its nicknames, Gaby, which sounds anything but elitist. Gabrielle has already shown signs of cracking the top fifty list of baby names for girls; this trend should continue. Variations: *Gabbi, Gabby, Gabi, Gabriela, Gabriell, Gabriella, Gaby*.

GADA (Hebrew) Lucky.

GAENOR (Welsh) Fair; smooth.

GAETANA (Italian) Area in Italy. Variation: *Gaetane*.

GAFNA (Hebrew) Vine.

GAIA (Greek) Earth. Variations: *Gaioa, Gaya*.

GAIL (Hebrew) My father rejoices. Gail started out as a nickname for Abigail, back in the 1940s when traditional names started to seem a bit stodgy and old-fashioned. Borne by the US actress Gayle Hunnicutt. Variations: *Gael, Gaile, Gale, Gayle*.

GALA (Scandinavian) Singer; celebration. Variation: *Galla*.

GALATEA (Greek) White as milk. Variation: *Galatee*.

GALENA (Greek) Healer.

GALI (Hebrew) Hill, mound. Variations: *Gal, Galice*.

GALIENA (German) High one. Variations: *Galiana, Galianna*.

GALILANI (Native American: Cherokee) Friendly.

GALINA (Russian) Bright one or shining one. Variation of Helen.

GALYA (Hebrew) God has redeemed. Variations: *Galia, Gallia, Gallya*.

GAMBHIRA (Hindu) Noble.

GAMMA (Greek) Third letter of the alphabet.

GANESA (Hindu) Goddess of wisdom.

GANIT (Hebrew) Garden. Variations: *Gana, Ganice.*

GANYA (Hebrew) Garden of God.

GARDENIA (English) Flower.

GARI (German) Spear. Feminine version of Gary.

GARIMA (Hindu) Importance.

GARLAND (French) Wreath. Variations: *Garlanda, Garlande, Garlandera.*

GARNET (English) Jewel. Variations: *Garnetta, Garnette.*

GASHA (Russian) Good. Russian version of Agatha. Variation: *Gashka.*

GAURI (Hindu) White. Variations: *Gori, Gowri.*

GAVRILLA (Hebrew) Heroine.

GAY (French) Joyful. Variations: *Gae, Gai, Gaye.*

GAYORA (Hebrew) Valley of light.

GAZELLE (Latin) Gazelle; graceful. Variation: *Gazella.*

GAZIT (Hebrew) Smooth stone.

GEELA (Hebrew) Joy.

GEFEN (Hebrew) Vine. Variations: *Gafna, Gafnit, Gaphna, Geffen.*

GEFJUN (Scandinavian) She who gives wealth. Variations: *Gefion, Gefjon.*

GELILAH (Hebrew) Rolling hills. Variations: *Gelalia, Gelalya, Gelila, Gelilia, Geliliya.*

GELSEY (English) Last name.

GELYA (Russian) Messenger.

GEMINI (Greek) Twin. Variations: *Gemella, Gemelle, Gemina, Geminine.*

GEMMA (Irish) Jewel; (Italian) Precious stone. Variation: *Gem.*

GEN (Japanese) Spring.

GENEA (Phoenician) The first inhabitants of Phoenicia.

GENESEE (Native American: Iroquois) Wonderful valley.

GENESIS (Hebrew) Beginning. Variations: *Genessa, Genisa, Genisia, Genisis, Jenessa.*

GENEVIEVE (Celtic) White; Celtic woman. Genevieve has tended to be a continental sophisticated name, undoubtedly helped along by actress Genevieve Bujold. It has never been used that frequently, and therefore tends to have a neutral connotation with most people. It received a boost in popularity with the release of the film *Genevieve* in 1953, which was the name of a vintage car. Variations: *Genavieve, Geneva, Geneve, Geneveeve, Genivieve, Gennie, Genny, Genovera, Genoveva, Gina, Janeva, Jenevieve.*

GENNA (Arabic) Small bird.

GENNISHEYO (Native American: Iroquois) Shining wonderful valley. Variation: *Geneseo.*

GEONA (Hebrew) Glorification. Variation: *Geonit.*

GEORGIA (Latin) Farmer. Feminine version of George. Variations: *Georgeann, Georgeanne, Georgeina, Georgena, Georgene, Georgetta, Georgette, Georggann, Georgganne, Georgiana, Georgianne, Georgie, Georgienne, Georgina, Georgine, Giorgia, Giorgina, Giorgyna, Jorgina.*

GERALDINE (French) One who rules with a spear. Feminine version of Gerald. Two actresses with the name are Geraldine James and Geraldine Farrar. Variations: *Ceraldina, Deraldene, Geralda, Geraldeen, Geralyn, Geralynne, Geri, Gerianna, Gerianne, Gerilynn, Geroldine, Gerry, Jeraldeen, Jeraldene, Jeraldine, Jeralee, Jere, Jeri, Jerilene, Jerrie, Jerrileen, Jerroldeen, Jerry.*

GERANIUM (Latin) Flower.

GERD (Scandinavian) Guarded. Gerda is the name of the young heroine in Hans Christian Anderson's fairytale *The Snow Queen.* Variations: *Gard, Gerda.*

GERIANNE (American) Gerry + Anne.

GERMAINE (French) One from Germany. Variations: *Germain, Germana, Germane, Germayn, Germayne.*

GERSEMI (Scandinavian) Gem.

GERTRUDE (German) With the strength of a spear. If you choose to give your daughter the name Gertrude or Germaine, you should be prepared for people to assume that you chose the name to celebrate the two famous feminist writers who lived with them: Gertrude Stein and Germaine Greer. Variations: *Gertie, Gertina, Gertraud, Gertrud, Gertruda, Gerty, Truda, Trude, Trudey, Trudi, Trudie, Trudy, Trudye.*

GERUSHAH (Hebrew) Banishment. Variation: *Gerusha.*

GERVAISE (French) Unknown definition.

GEVA (Hebrew) Hill.

GEVIRAH (Hebrew) Queen. Variation: *Gevira.*

GHADA (Arabic) Graceful. Variations: *Ghadah, Ghayda.*

GHADIR (Arabic) River.

GHALIYA (Arabic) Pleasant odour. Variation: *Ghaliyah.*

GHITA (Greek) Pearl.

GHUFRAN (Arabic) To forgive.

GIA (Italian) Queen.

GIACINTA (Italian) Hyacinth.

GIALIA (Italian) Youthful. Feminine version of Giulio. Variations: *Giala, Gialiana, Gialietta.*

GIANINA (Italian) God is good. Feminine version of John. Variations: *Giancinthia, Gianetta, Gianna, Giannina, Giannine, Jacenda, Jacenta, Jacey, Jacie, Jacinda,*

Names from Nature

Nature is always a great resource for both girls' and boys' names, though girls' names tend to have the upper hand. Of course, some think that parents in the 1960s went overboard by naming their kids Nutmeg, Tofu and Earth, but all in all, Mother Nature is still a good place to turn to for names that are a bit different, but still fitting.

One way to personalize your choice is to name your baby after the birthstone or flower of the month of his or her birthdate. Following are the flowers and gemstones for each month:

January
Birthstone: garnet
Flower: carnation

February
Birthstone: amethyst
Flower: violet

March
Birthstone: aquamarine
Flower: jonquil

April
Birthstone: diamond
Flower: sweet pea

May
Birthstone: emerald
Flower: lily

June
Birthstone: pearl
Flower: lily (of the valley)

July
Birthstone: ruby
Flower: larkspur

August
Birthstone: peridot
Flower: gladiolus

September
Birthstone: sapphire
Flower: aster

October
Birthstone: opal
Flower: calendula

November
Birthstone: topaz
Flower: chrysanthemum

December
Birthstone: turquoise
Flower: narcissus

Jacindia, Jacinna, Jacinta, Jacinth, Jacintha, Jacinthe, Jacinthia, Jacynth, Jacyntha, Jacynthe.

GIBORAH (Hebrew) Strong. Variation: *Gibora.*

GIGI (French) Gigi is an independent name that evolved from Gilberte and Ghislaine. Colette's novel was made into a Hollywood musical of the same-name.

GILADAH (Hebrew) Hill of testimony. Variations: *Galat, Geela, Gila, Gili, Gilia.*

GILANAH (Hebrew) Happy. Variation: *Gilana.*

GILBERTE (French) Shining pledge. Feminine version of Gilbert. Variations: *Gilberta, Gilbertina, Gilbertine, Gill, Gillie, Gilly.*

GILDA (English) Golden.

GILIAH (Hebrew) God's joy. Variations: *Gilia, Giliya, Giliyah.*

GILL (English) Downy.

GILLIAN (English) Youthful. Variations: *Gilian, Gillan, Gillianne, Gillyanne.*

GILSEY (English) Jasmine.

GIN (Japanese) Silver.

GINA (Hebrew) Garden; (Italian) Nickname for names such as Regina and Angelina; (Japanese) Silvery. Gina was one of the more popular exotic names during the 1950s and 1960s, which was probably solely due to the exposure of Italian actress Gina Lollobrigida. Back then, Gina was the epitome of foreign glamour and sophistication. Actress Geena Davis has popularized a new spelling of the name. Variations: *Geena, Gena, Ginat, Ginia.*

GINGER (English) The spice. The most famous Ginger has to be the actress and dancer Ginger Rogers, who partnered Fred Astaire. Diminutive of Virginia.

GINNY (English) Diminutive of Virginia. Variations: *Ginney, Ginnie.*

GIOVANNA (Italian) God is good. Another feminization of John.

GIRISA (Hindu) Lord of the mountain.

GISA (Hebrew) Hewn stone. Variations: *Gissa, Gisse, Giza, Gizza.*

GISELLE (English) Oath; hostage. I've known seven-year-old ballet students who have been green with envy over a classmate named Giselle because it is a picture-perfect name for a ballerina; *Giselle* is a ballet by Gautier. Variations: *Gelsi, Gelsy, Gisela, Gisele, Gisella, Gizela, Gizella.*

GISLAUG (Scandinavian) Consecrated hostage. Variation: *Gislog.*

GITA (Hindu) Song. Variations: *Geeta, Geetika, Gitanjau, Gitika.*

GITANA (Spanish) Gypsy. Variations: *Gitane, Gitanna.*

GITEL (Hebrew) Good. Variations: *Gitela, Gitele, Gittel.*

GITTA (Hungarian) Power. Diminutive of Brigitte. Variation: *Gitte.*

GITUSKA (Czech) Pearl.

GIVOLA (Hebrew) Blossom.

GLADYS (Welsh) Lame. Form of Claudia. About a hundred years ago, Gladys was considered to be the most exotic, sexy name in quite some time. Famous bearers of the name include British actress Dame Gladys Cooper and US soul singer Gladys Knight. Variations: *Gwladus, Gwladys.*

GLEDA (Icelandic) Happy.

GLENDA (Welsh) Holy and good.

GLENN (Irish) Narrow valley. Has been applied to girls since the 1940s. The most well-known female Glenn is actress Glenn Close. Variations: *Glen, Glena.*

GLENNETTE (Scottish) Narrow valley. Feminine version of Glenn.

GLENYS (Welsh) Holy. Variations: *Glenice, Glenis, Glenise, Glennis, Glennys, Glenyse, Glenyss, Glynis.*

GLORIA (Latin) Glory. Seems to have made its first appearance in George Bernard Shaw's play *You Never Can Tell* and became popular around the beginning of

the 20th century. It was at its most frequent in the 1930s, but has since been in decline. There have been lots of famous Glorias over the years: Gloria Steinem, Gloria Swanson, Gloria Gaynor, Gloria Vanderbilt and Gloria Estefan. Variations: *Gloree, Glori, Glorie, Glorria, Glory.*

GLORVINA (Irish) A character in the novel *Wild Irish Girl* by author Lady Morgan.

GLYNIS (Welsh) Small valley. Variations: *Glinnis, Glinys, Glyn, Glynes.*

GOBINET (Irish) Mouth. Variations: *Gobnait, Gobnat, Gobnata, Gobnet, Gubby, Gubnet.*

GODIVA (English) Gift from God.

GOITSEMEDIME (African: Botswana) God knows.

GOLDA (English) Golden. Variations: *Goldarina, Goldarine, Goldia, Goldie, Goldif, Goldina, Goldy.*

GOZALA (Hebrew) Young bird.

GRACE (Latin) Grace. Grace has been around since the Middle Ages, and it has never really gone out of style. It has been especially popular recently, owing to singer Grace Jones and actress Grace Kelly. Variations: *Engracie, Graca, Gracey, Graci, Gracia, Graciana, Gracie, Gracy, Gratia, Grazia, Graziella, Grazielle, Graziosa, Grazyna.*

GRAINNE (Irish) Goddess of grain. Variations: *Grainnia, Grania, Granna.*

GREER (Scottish) Observant. Feminine version of Gregory.

GRESSA (Scandinavian: Norwegian) Grass.

GRETNA (Scottish) Scottish village.

GRISELDA (German) Grey fighting maid. Variations: *Grizelda, Zelda.*

GUADALUPE (Spanish) Valley of wolves.

GUDRUN (Scandinavian) Fight. Variations: *Cudrin, Gudren, Gudrinn, Gudruna, Guro.*

GUIDA (Italian) Guide.

GUILLERMA (Spanish) Will + helmet. Feminine version of William.

GUINEVERE (Welsh) Fair; yielding. Variations: *Gaenor, Gayna, Gaynah, Gayner, Gaynor.*

GULL (Scandinavian) Gold.

GUNHILDA (Scandinavian: Norwegian) Woman warrior. Variations: *Gunda, Gunhilde, Gunilda, Gunilla, Gunnhilda.*

GUNN (Scandinavian) Battle. Variation: *Gun.*

GUNNBORG (Scandinavian) Fortified battle. Variation: *Gunborg.*

GUNNLOD (Scandinavian) Ancient mythological figure.

GUNNVOR (Scandinavian) Cautious in war. Variations: *Gunver, Gunvor.*

GURICE (Hebrew) Lion cub. Variation: *Gurit.*

GUSTAVA (Scandinavian: Swedish) Staff of the gods. Feminine version of Gustav. Variations: *Gusta, Gustha.*

GWENDOLYN (Welsh) Fair brow. Variations: *Guendolen, Guenna, Gwen, Gwenda, Gwendaline, Gwendia, Gwendolen, Gwendolene, Gwendolin, Gwendoline, Gwendolynn, Gwendolynne, Gwenette, Gwennie, Gwenn, Gwenna, Gwenny.*

GWENEAL (Welsh) Blessed angel.

GWENFREWI (Welsh) Blessed peace.

GWENLUAN (Welsh) Blessed flood.

GWERFUL (Welsh) Shy. Variations: *Gweirful, Gwerfyl.*

GWYNETH (Welsh) Happiness. Both Gwyneth and Gwendolyn are popular now because people consider girls' names that begins with 'Gw' to be exotic and sophisticated. But Gwyneth is probably the more popular owing to the actress Gwyneth Paltrow. Variations: *Gwenith, Gwennyth, Gwenyth, Gwynith, Gwynn, Gwynna, Gwynne, Gwynneth.*

GYANDA (Hindu) Learned.

GYPSY (English) Gypsy.

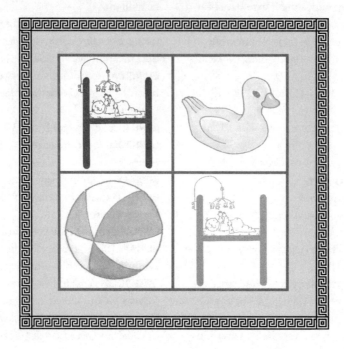

HA (Vietnamese) River.

HABIBA (Arabic) Cherished. Variations: *Habibah, Haviva.*

HACHI (Native American: Seminole) River.

HADASSAH (Hebrew) Myrtle. Variations: *Hada, Hadas, Hadasa, Hadassa, Hodel.*

HADI (Arabic) Calm.

HADIL (Arabic) Cooing pigeon.

HADIYA (African: Swahili) Religious leader. Variation: *Hadiyah.*

HADLEY (English) Meadow of heather. Variations: *Hadlea, Hadlee, Hadleigh.*

HADYA (Arabic) Guide. Variation: *Hadiya.*

HAE-WON (Korean) Grace.

HAFSAH (Arabic) Wife of Mohammed. Variation: *Hafza.*

HAGAR (Hebrew) Forsaken. Variation: *Haggar.*

HAGIA (Hebrew) Joy. Variations: *Hagice, Hagit.*

HAGNE (Greek) Pure.

HAIDEE (Greek) Modest. Variation: *Haydee.*

HAIWEE (Native American: Shoshone) Dove.

HAJAR (Arabic) To abandon. Variation: *Hagir.*

HAKUMELE (Hawaiian) Poet.

HALA (Arabic) Ring of light around the moon. Variation: *Halah.*

HALAPUA (Polynesian) Road near trees.

HALCYON (Greek) Peaceful. If you're a person who believes that we are our names, and you want no surprises in your daughter, Halcyon is a good choice. Then again, there are always those people who will do the opposite of what is expected of them, and unfortunately, when it comes time to fill out the birth certificate, it's impossible to predict which side your daughter will take. Variations: *Halcion, Halcione, Halcyone.*

HALDANA (Scandinavian: Norwegian) One who is half Scandinavian: Danish. Variation: *Haldane.*

HALEAKUA (Hawaiian) God's house.

HALFRIDA (German) Calm heroine.

HALIA (Hawaiian) Remembering a loved one.

HALIAKA (Hawaiian) Leader of the house. Hawaiian version of Harriet. Variations: *Hariaka, Hariata.*

HALIMA (Arabic) Gentle. Variation: *Halimah.*

HALIMEDA (Greek) Of the sea.

HALINA (Russian) Shining one. Russian version of Helen.

HALKU (Hawaiian) Flower.

HALOLANI (Hawaiian) Fly like a bird.

HALONA (Native American) Good luck.

HAMA (Japanese) Beach. Variation: *Hamako.*

HAMIDA (Arabic) To praise. Variations: *Hameedah, Hamidah.*

HANA (Japanese) Flower. Variations: *Hanae, Hanako.*

HANAN (Arabic) Merciful.

HANG (Vietnamese) Full moon.

HANH (Vietnamese) Ethical.

HANI (Hawaiian) Move softly.

HANIA (Hebrew) Resting place. Variation: *Haniya.*

HANIFA (Arabic) Follower of Islam. Variations: *Haneefa, Hanifah.*

HANITA (Hindu) Grace.

HANIYYA (Arabic) Happy. Variation: *Haniyyah.*

HANNAH (Hebrew) Grace. In the Bible, Hannah was mother of the prophet Samuel, but even he couldn't have foreseen how popular his mother's name would remain two millennia later. Hannah was very popular in Britain in the seventeenth through nineteenth centuries when Biblical names were the norm. It appears in the Bible as the name of three women. As it enjoyed a strong revival in the 1970s, today Hannah is still popular, which only means that it will seem dated in a few years time. The reason for this most recent renaissance? Probably Woody Allen's movie *Hannah and her Sisters.* Variations: *Hana, Hanah, Hanna, Hanne, Hannele, Hannelore, Hannie, Honna.*

HANSA (Hindu) Swan. Variations: *Hansika, Hansila.*

HANSINE (Scandinavian) God is good.

HANTAYWEE (Native American: Sioux) Cedar maiden.

HAPPY (English) Glad.

HAQIKAH (Arabic) Truthful.

HARA (Hindu) Tawny.

HARALDA (Scandinavian: Norwegian) Army power. Feminine version of Harold.

HARITA (Hindu) The wind.

HARLEY (English) Rabbit pasture. Variations: *Harleigh, Harlie, Harly.*

HARMONY (Latin) Harmony. Variations: *Harmonee, Harmoni, Harmonia, Harmonie.*

HARPER (English) Harp player. Harper Lee, author of *To Kill a Mockingbird*, first popularized this traditional last-name-as-first-name for girls. Surprisingly, Harper hasn't made much progress on the most popular names list, but it should, since today it pushes all the right buttons.

HARRIET (German) Leader of the house. Feminine version of Harry. Variations: *Harrie, Harrietta, Harriette, Harriot, Harriott, Hatsie, Hatsy, Hattie, Hatty.*

HARSHA (Hindu) Happiness. Variations: *Harshida, Harshika, Harshina.*

HARU (Japanese) Born in spring. Variations: *Harue, Haruko.*

HASANA (African: Nigerian) The first-born of female twins.

HASANATI (Arabic) Good.

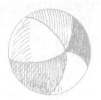

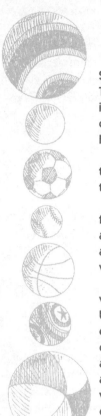

African Names – Cultural Traditions

Sometimes it seems that referring to a name as African doesn't say much. The wide variety of cultures from the African continent as well as the many individual countries means that there are a huge number of names to choose from if you want your son or daughter to exhibit a bit of African heritage in his or her name.

Hundreds of African and African-American names can be found in the name listings in this book. What I found particularly fascinating are the different ways in which parents in Africa choose their babies' names.

In Kenya, some tribes choose several names for the babies born to a family. The first name a baby receives is called a birth name, and is usually picked by a maternal grandmother or grandfather of the baby. About a month and a half later, the baby gets another, more permanent name, which the child's parents or father's parents get to choose.

In Ghana, parents participate in a naming ceremony where the whole tribe takes part. The ceremony occurs a week after the child is born, and the baby's father selects a name, most often taking it from an elderly, dignified relative. In Nigeria, a name is frequently given that is descriptive of the conditions of the birth itself; this name is referred to as an *oraku*. The child also receives a name that is known as an *oriki*, or another name that projects the parents' wishes for the child. You may want to adapt this tradition, making your child's first name the equivalent of an oriki, and the middle name an oraku.

HASIKA (Hindu) Laughter.

HASINA (African: Swahili) Good.

HASNA (Arabic) Strong.

HATEYA (Native American) Push with the foot.

HATHOR (Egyptian) The goddess of love.

HATHSHIRA (Arabic) Seventh daughter.

HATSU (Japanese) First-born.

HAUKEA (Hawaiian) Snow.

HAULANI (Hawaiian) Royalty.

HAUMA (Hindu) Gentle. Variations: *Haleema, Halimah.*

HAUNANI (Hawaiian) Beautiful.

HAUOLI (Hawaiian) Joyful.

HAUSU (Native American) Yawning bear.

HAVEN (English) Refuge.

HAVIVA (Hebrew) Beloved.

HAWA (African: Swahili) Desire.

HAYA (Japanese) Fast.

HAYAT (Arabic) Alive.

HAYFA (Arabic) Dainty.

HAYLEY (English) Meadow of hay. In the 1990s, Hayley was an extremely popular name for girls, but few people know that the name actually originated when child actress Hayley Mills first burst onto the scene. Before her parents took her mother's middle name for their daughter's first name, Hayley – more commonly spelled Haley – was known only as a last name. Variations: *Hailee, Hailey, Haley, Halie, Halley, Halli, Hallie, Hally, Haylee, Hayleigh, Haylie.*

HAZEL (English) The name of a tree. Variations: *Hazal, Hazeline, Hazell, Hazelle, Hazle.*

HEATHER (English) Flower. Its popularity in Britain peaked during the 1950s having first appeared in the 19th century. It is extremely popular in Scotland, where the plant grows readily, but it seems to be on the decline elsewhere.

HEAVEN (English) Paradise.

HEBE (Greek) The goddess of youth.

HEDDA (English) Warfare. Variations: *Heda, Heddi, Heddie, Hetta.*

HEDIAH (Hebrew) Echo of God. Variations: *Hedia, Hedya.*

HEDVIKA (Czech) War of strife.

HEDWIG (German) Struggle. Variations: *Hadvig, Hadwig, Hedvig, Hedviga, Hedvige, Hedwiga, Hedwige.*

HEDY (Greek) Wonderful. Variations: *Hedia, Hedyla.*

HEE-YOUNG (Korean) Pleasurable wealth.

HEIDI (German) Noble. Taken up with some enthusiasm by English speakers in the 1960s after the television adaption of Johanna Spyri's children's story *Heidi*. Variations: *Hedie, Heida, Heide, Heidie, Hydie.*

HELEDD (Welsh) Unknown definition. Variation: *Hyledd.*

HELEN (Greek) Light. Helen has a lengthy track record. Helen was a pivotal figure in Greek mythology as the daughter of Zeus, as well as the real-life mother of emperor Constantine the Great back in the fourth century CE. Over the last few centuries, Helen has gone in and out of fashion, most often alternating with its close relative, Ellen. Though Helen was not too popular in the 1970s and 1980s, it appears to be one of those names that's just waiting to happen. Famous Helens include actresses Helen Mirren, Helen Hayes and singer Helen Shapiro. Variations: *Hela, Hele, Helena, Helene, Hellen, Helli.*

HELGA (Scandinavian: Norwegian) Holy.

HELIA (Greek) The sun.

HELICE (Greek) Spiral.

HELKI (Native American) Touch.

HELMA (German) Helmet. Variations: *Hillma, Hilma.*

HELMINE (German) Constant protector. Feminine version of William.

HELOISE (French) Famous in war. Variation: *Heloisa*

HELSA (Scandinavian: Danish) Glory to God.

HELTU (Native American) Bear that's friendly to people.

HEMALI (Hindu) Golden.

HEMBADOON (African: Nigerian) Victor.

HENRIETTA (German) Leader of the home. Popular at the end of the 19th century. Feminine version of Henry. Variations: *Hattie, Hatty, Hendrika, Henka, Hennie, Henrie, Henrieta, Henriette, Henrika, Hetta, Hettie.*

HEPHZIBAH (Hebrew) My delight is in her. Hephzibah is one of those great old Biblical names that the Puritans loved. It has all the ingredients to become more popular in this country, but I'm afraid that it's just a bit too offbeat for most parents to consider. Variations: *Hephsibah, Hephzabah, Hepzibah.*

HERA (Greek) The mythological queen of the goddesses and wife of Zeus.

HE-RAN (Korean) Graceful orchid.

HERLINDIS (Scandinavian) Gentle army.

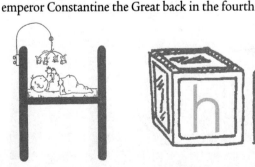

HERMIA (Greek) The mythological messenger for the Greek gods. Feminine version of Hermes. Variations: *Herma, Hermaine, Hermina, Hermione.*

HERMOSA (Spanish) Beautiful.

HESPER (Greek) Evening star. Variations: *Hespera, Hesperia.*

HESTER (Greek) Star. Variation of Esther. Though Esther may be on the verge of a comeback, don't look for Hester to hit the top ten list anytime soon. Hester is the name of the lead character in Nathaniel Hawthorne's novel *The Scarlet Letter*, which is bad enough, and the film probably succeeded at finishing off whatever urge to use this name any parent would have had. Variations: *Hesther, Hestia.*

HETA (Native American) Rabbit hunt.

HEULWEN (Welsh) Sunshine.

HIALEAH (Native American: Seminole) Beautiful pasture.

HIAWASSEE (Native American: Cherokee) Meadow.

HIBA (Arabic) Present.

HIBERNIA (Latin) Latin name for Ireland.

HIBISCUS (Latin) Flower.

HIDE (Japanese) Excellent. Variation: *Hideyo.*

HIILANI (Hawaiian) Carried by heaven.

HIKMAT (Arabic) Wise.

HIKULEO (Polynesian) Echo.

HILARY (Greek) Glad. For at least the next few decades, this name will be indelibly connected with former President Clinton's wife. Variations: *Hilaria, Hilarie, Hillary, Hillery, Hilliary.*

HILAUA (Hawaiian) Loud.

HILDA (German) Battle woman. Variations: *Hilde, Hildie, Hildy, Hylda.*

HILDEGARDE (German) Stronghold in war. Variations: *Hildagard, Hildagarde.*

HILDEMAR (German) Famous in war.

HILDRETH (German) War counsellor. Variation: *Hildred.*

HILLEVI (Scandinavian) Safe in battle.

HILMA (German) Nickname for Wilhelmina.

HIMANI (Hindu) Snow-covered. Variation: *Heemani.*

HIND (Arabic) Unknown definition.

HINDA (Hebrew) Female deer. Variations: *Hindel, Hindelle, Hynda.*

HINOOKMAHIWIKILINAKA (Native American: Winnebago) Floating clouds.

HIPAKEIKI (Hawaiian) Lamb.

HIPPOLYTA (Greek) Horses. The mythological queen of the Amazons.

HIRAL (Hindu) Brilliant.

HIROKO (Japanese) Benevolent.

HISA (Japanese) Everlasting. Many of the more popular names for Japanese girls and boys are meant to impart the hope for longevity to the person with the name. Hisa is one of these names. Superstitions are frequently involved in picking a name for your baby, and this ancient Japanese custom could very well catch on in this country. Hisa is a beautiful name, regardless of its meaning, which may encourage non-Japanese parents to choose it. Variations: *Hisae, Hisako, Hisayo.*

HISANO (Japanese) Meadow.

HITI (Eskimo) Hyena.

HIVA (Polynesian) Song.

HIWAHIWAKEIKI (Hawaiian) This child is loved.

HJORDIS (Scandinavian) Goddess of the sword.

HLIN (Scandinavian) Ancient mythological figure.

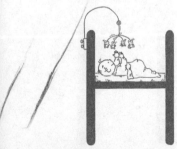

Some Popular Names from the 1980s

Who knows why people in the 1980s did the things they did? The trends that occur in each decade are somehow affected by the events of the previous one, and in the 1980s, the names that parents chose seemed to have the sound of money to them. Or maybe we were just watching too many of those nighttime soap operas that starred people with too much money and too much time on their hands to boot.

But a common belief about what goes in and out of style is determined by what was popular three decades earlier. So look at the top names of the 1950s, especially the boys' names. You'll see that the top fifty names from the 1980s are almost a carbon copy of the names from that decade.

Boys' Names

Michael	Scott
Christopher	Paul
Matthew	Kevin
David	Anthony
Jason	Richard
Daniel	Sean
Robert	Charles
Eric	Aaron
Brian	Bradley
Joseph	Timothy
Ryan	Benjamin
James	Patrick
Steven	Jeremy
John	Derek
Jeffrey	Gregory
Adam	Kenneth
Justin	Philip
Andrew	Alexander
Mark	Donald
Nicholas	Edward
William	Kyle
Jonathan	Nathan
Brandon	Jesse
Thomas	Ronald
Joshua	Carl

Girls' Names

Jennifer	Kimberly
Sarah	Michelle
Nicole	Laura
Jessica	Danielle
Katherine	Jacqueline
Stephanie	Mary
Elizabeth	Heather
Amanda	Tiffany
Melissa	Christine
Lindsay	Shannon
Rebecca	Erica
Lisa	Katie
Rachel	Renee
Lauren	Maria
Andrea	Susan
Christina	Monica
Emily	Natalie
Kristen	Courtney
Megan	Amber
Angela	Diana
Crystal	April
Kelly	Dana
Julie	Dawn
Erin	Samantha
Amy	Victoria

241

HOA (Vietnamese) Flower.

HOAKA (Hawaiian) Bright.

HOALOHALANI (Hawaiian) Spiritual friend.

HOALOHANANI (Hawaiian) Beautiful friend.

HOKUALOHI (Hawaiian) Shining star.

HOKUAO (Hawaiian) Morning star.

HOKUAONANI (Hawaiian) Beautiful star.

HOKULANI (Hawaiian) Divine star. Variation: *Hoku.*

HOLA (Spanish) Hello; greeting.

HOLDA (German) Hidden. Variations: *Holde, Holle, Hulda.*

HOLLIS (English) Near the holly. Variation: *Holice.*

HOLLY (English) Plant. Holly has been popular since the 19th century and reached a peak at the end of the 20th century. First, it's a seasonal name that many parents choose for their daughters who are born close to Christmastime. Second, it's a plant name, and this category of names seems particularly poised to grow in usage in the years to come. And as a bonus, Holly Hunter is a talented, prolific actress, which never hurts when it comes to the popularity of a name. Variations: *Hollee, Holley, Holli, Hollie, Hollyann.*

HOLOMAKANI (Hawaiian) Wind. Variations: *Kani, Makani.*

HONEKAKALA (Hawaiian) Honeysuckle.

HONEY (English) Sweetener; term of affection.

HONG (Vietnamese) Pink.

HONORA (English) Honourable woman. Variations: *Honner, Honnor, Honnour, Honor, Honorah, Honorata, Honore, Honoria, Honorine, Honour.*

HONOVI (Native American: Hopi) Powerful buck.

HOOLANA (Hawaiian) Happy.

HOPE (English) Hope.

HORATIA (English) A Roman clan name. Feminine version of Horatio. Variation: *Horacia.*

HORTENSE (Latin) Roman clan name; hydrangea flower. Variations: *Horsensia, Hortencia, Hortensia, Ortensia.*

HOSANNA (Greek) Cry of prayer. Variation: *Hosannie.*

HOSHI (Japanese) Star. Variations: *Hoshie, Hoshiko, Hoshiyo, Hosiko.*

HO-SOOK (Korean) Pure lake.

HRISOULA (Greek) Golden.

HUA (Chinese) Flower.

HUATA (Native American) A basket of seeds.

HUAU (Hawaiian) Bright.

HUBERTA (German) Intelligent. Feminine version of Hubert. Variation: *Huette.*

HUDA (Arabic) Direction. Variation: *Hoda.*

HUE (Vietnamese) Old-fashioned.

HUI-FANG (Chinese) Fragrant.

HULDAH (Hebrew) Weasel or mole. Variations: *Hulda, Huldi, Huldie, Huldy.*

HULUAVA (Polynesian) Lighthouse.

HUMITA (Native American: Hopi) Shelled corn.

HUNTER (English) Hunter.

HUONG (Vietnamese) Blossom.

HURRIYYAH (Arabic) Angel.

HUSNI (Arabic) Beauty. Variations: *Husniya, Husniyah.*

HUSNIYA (Arabic) Excellence. Variation: *Husniyah.*

HUSO (African) A bride's sadness.

HUYANA (Native American: Miwok) Falling rain.

HUYNH (Vietnamese) Yellow.

HWA-YOUNG (Korean) Beautiful flower.

HYACINTH (Greek) Flower.

HYE (Korean) Graceful.

HYO-SONN (Korean) Tender.

HYPATIA (Greek) Highest.

HYUN-AE (Korean) Smart and loving.

HYUN-OK (Korean) Wise pearl.

IANEKE (Hawaiian) God is good. Variations: *Ianete, Iani.*

IANTHE (Greek) Flower. Variation: *Iantha.*

IBTIHAJ (Arabic) Happiness.

IBTISAM (Arabic) To smile. Variations: *Ebtissam, Essam, Ibtissam , Issam.*

ICHCHANI (Hindu) Queen of twelfth century.

IDA (English) Youth. Ida was a big name fifty to one hundred years ago, which brought forth the Gilbert and Sullivan opera *Princess Ida*, the song 'Ida, Sweet as Apple Cider', and the actress Ida Lupino. Although other names from that period are popular today, Ida has not made much of a comeback. Variations: *Idalene, Idalia, Idalina, Idaline, Idalya, Idalyne, Ide, Idell, Idella, Idelle, Idetta, Idette, Idia.*

IDAA (Hindu) Earth. Variation: *Ila.*

IDE (Irish) Thirst. Variation: *Ita.*

IDONY (Scandinavian) Goddess of spring. Variations: *Idonea, Idun, Itiunnr.*

IDOWU (African: Nigerian) First child born after twins.

IDRA (Hebrew) Fig tree.

IDRIYA (Hebrew) Duck. Variation: *Idria.*

IDUNA (Scandinavian: Norwegian) Beloved. Variation: *Idonia.*

IENIPA (Hawaiian) Fair lady.

IFAMA (African: Nigerian) All is well.

IFE (African: Nigerian) Love.

IFETAYO (African: Nigerian) Love is joyful.

IGNACIA (Latin) On fire. Feminine version of Ignatius. Variations: *Ignatia, Ignazia, Iniga.*

IHAB (Arabic) To give.

IHSAN (Arabic) Benevolent. Variations: *Ihsana, Ihsanah.*

IKABELA (Hawaiian) Pledged to God. Variation: *Ikapela.*

IKIA (Hebrew) God helps me.

IKU (Japanese) Nurturing. Variation: *Ikuko.*

IKUSEGHAN (African: Nigerian) Peace is better than war. Variation: *Ikusegham.*

ILANA (Hebrew) Tree. Variations: *Elana, Elanit, Ilanit.*

ILESHA (Hindu) God of the earth.

ILIA (English) One who comes from the town of Troy, also known as Ilium.

ILIMA (Hawaiian) Flower.

ILKA (Slavic) Admirer.

ILMA (English) Variation of William.

ILONA (Hungarian) Pretty.

ILSE (German) Pledge of God. Variation of Elizabeth. Variations: *Ilsa, Ilsie.*

IMA (Japanese) Now. Variations: *Imae, Imako.*

IMALA (Native American) Discipline.

IMAN (Arabic) Faith.

IMANA (African: Rwandan) God of all.

IMARA (African: Swahili) Firm.

IMELDA (Italian) Embracing the fight. Perhaps best-known as the name of Filipino politician Imelda Marcos. Variation: *Imalda.*

IMIN (Arabic) Conviction.

IMMACULADA (Spanish) Innocent. Variation: *Immaculata.*

IMMOKALEE (Native American: Cherokee) Falling water.

IMOGEN (Latin) Last-born; innocent. This name came into favour towards the end of the 19th century and enjoyed a peak of popularity late in the 20th century. A famous Imogen is British actress Imogen Stubbs. Variations: *Imogene, Imogenia, Imogine.*

IMPERIA (Latin) Imperial.

IN (Korean) Mankind.

INA (Greek) Pure. Variation: *Ena.*

INAM (Arabic) Charitable. Variation: *Enam.*

INANNA (Babylonian) The goddess of war.

INAS (Arabic) Friendly. Variations: *Inaya, Inayah.*

INDIA (English) The country. The name of a character in Margaret Mitchell's *Gone with the Wind*.

INDIGO (Latin) Dark blue.

INDIRA (Hindu) Beauty.

INDRA (Hindu) Supreme god; god of the sky.

INDRE (French) River.

INDRANEE (Hindu) Wife of Indra, the god of the sky. Variation: *Indrayani.*

INDU (Hindu) Moon.

INES (Spanish) Pure. Variation of Agnes. Variations: *Inesita, Inessa, Inetta, Inez, Ynes, Ynesita, Ynez.*

INGA (Scandinavian) In Norse mythology, god of fertility and peace. Variations: *Ingaar, Inge, Ingo, Ingvio.*

INGEBORG (Scandinavian) Protector of Ing, Norwegian god of peace. Variations: *Ingaberg, Ingaborg, Ingeberg, Inger, Ingmar.*

INGEGERD (Scandinavian) Ing's fortress. Variations: *Ingegard, Ingjerd.*

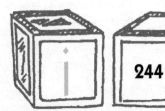
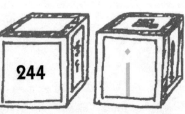

INGRID (Scandinavian) Beautiful. Of all the feminine names from Scandinavia that begin with 'Ing', Ingrid is the most widely used, owing to the renown of actress Ingrid Bergman. There was a flurry of activity surrounding the name back in the 1950s and 1960s, but it faded until just recently and is now beginning to show signs of strength again.

INOA (Hawaiian) Chant.

INOCENCIA (Spanish) Innocence. Variations: *Inocenta, Inocentia.*

INOLA (Native American: Cherokee) Black fox.

INSHTATHEUMBA (Native American: Omaha) Bright eyes.

IOLA (Welsh) Worthy god. Variation: *Iole.*

IOLANA (Hawaiian) Violet.

IOLANTHE (English) Violet.

IONA (Greek) Scottish island.

IONE (Greek) Violet. Variations: *Ionia, Ionie.*

IOSEPINE (Hawaiian) God adds. Variations: *Iokepina, Iokepine, Kepina.*

IPHIGENIA (Greek) Sacrifice. Variation: *Iphigenie.*

IRENE (Greek) Peace. Irene has a long and rich history. One Irene became a saint in the fourth century CE. Even before that, Irene was one of the more popular names during the Roman Empire. Its popularity continued right until the middle of the 20th century, when it suddenly seemed to run out of steam. Today, the many variations of the name are more common than the original root. Variations: *Arina, Arinka, Eirena, Eirene, Eirini, Erena, Erene, Ereni, Errena, Irayna, Ireen, Iren, Irena, Irenea, Irenee, Irenka, Irina, Irine, Irini, Irisha, Irka, Irusya, Iryna, Orina, Orya, Oryna, Reena, Reenie, Rina, Yarina, Yaryna.*

IRIS (Greek) Flower. Greek goddess of the rainbow. Variations: *Irisa, Irisha.*

IRMA (German) Complete.

IRVETTE (English) Friend of the sea. Feminine version of Irving.

ISABEL (Spanish) Pledge of God. Isabel is the Spanish equivalent and Isabella is the Italian version of Elizabeth. Though Isabel seems like it might be too old-fashioned to be popular, the truth is that it is one of the more popular names around and still growing. Actress Isabella Rossillini has helped to bring exposure to this name. Variations: *Isa, Isabeau, Isabelita, Isabella, Isabelle, Isobel, Issi, Issie, Issy, Izabel, Izabele, Izabella, Izabelle, Izebela, Ysabel.*

ISADORA (Latin) Gift from Isis. Best known as the name on US dancer Isadora Duncan. Feminine version of Isidore. Variation: *Isidora.*

ISAMU (Japanese) Active.

ISATAS (Native American) Snow. Variation: *Istas.*

ISAURA (Greek) Ancient country in Asia. Variation: *Isaure.*

ISEULT (Irish) Ruler of the ice. Variations: *Hisolda, Isolda, Isolde, Ysenit, Ysolte.*

ISHA (Hebrew) Woman; (Hindu) Protector.

ISHANA (Hindu) Desire. Variation: *Ishani.*

ISHI (Japanese) Stone. Variations: *Ishie, Ishiko, Ishiyo, Shiko, Shiuo.*

ISIS (Egyptian) Goddess of ancient Egypt.

ISLA (Scottish) Based on the name of a Scottish island – Islay.

ISMAELA (Hebrew) God listens. Variations: *Isma, Mael, Maella.*

ISMAT (Arabic) To protect.

ISMENE (Greek) The daughter of Oedipus and Jocasta.

ISOKA (African: Nigerian) Gift from God. Variations: *Isoke, Soka.*

ISRA (Arabic) Night trip.

ISTVAN (Greek) Crowned with laurels.

ITALIA (Latin) From Italy. Variation: *Talia.*

 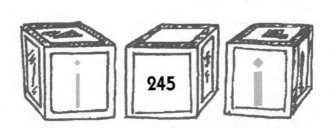 

ITIAH (Hebrew) God is here. Variations: *Itia, Itiel, Itil, Itiya*.

ITIDAL (Arabic) Middle of the road.

ITINSA (Native American: Tlingit) Waterfall.

ITO (Japanese) Fibre.

Hispanic Names – Cultural Traditions

In Spanish countries in Europe and in Central and South America, the Roman Catholic church has played a vital part in helping to determine what generations of boys and girls are called.

Maria is the name most often given to Hispanic girls, while Cristobal and Manuel are common for boys, as is the name Jesus. The given first name, however, is often only one that appears in a long line of names, since Hispanic families frequently give the surname of both the father and mother to a baby, and sometimes even tack on a grandparent's or other elderly relative's last name and/or maiden name. Then there's always a baptism name, a name conferred on a child by his or her godparents, and a confirmation name added later on. It's also not unusual for a child to be christened with the name of a religious holiday, like Natividad for girls. A little tiny baby with eight or more names, as it turns out, is not an uncommon occurrence.

ITUHA (Native American) Oak tree.

IUANA (Native American) Wind blowing over a bubbling stream.

IUDITA (Hawaiian) God is praised. Variation: *Iukika*.

IUGINIA (Hawaiian) Well-bred. Variations: *Iugina, Iukina, Iukinia*.

IULAUA (Hawaiian) Good talker. Variation: *Ulalia*.

IULIA (Hawaiian) A Roman clan name that also means young. Hawaiian version of Julia. Variations: *Iuliana, Kulia, Kuliana*.

IUNIA (Hawaiian) Good victory. Variation: *Eunika*.

IUSITINA (Hawaiian) Righteous. Variation: *Iukikina*.

IVANA (Slavic) God is good. Feminine version of Ivan. Variations: *Iva, Ivania, Ivanka, Ivanna, Ivannia*.

IVEREM (African: Nigerian) Good luck.

IVORY (Latin) Ivory. Ivory is as popular among African-American parents as its counterpart, Ebony, though I think it might be too much to name twins Ebony and Ivory. Parents in many African-American families like the name Ivory because it shows pride in their heritage, whether it alludes to the substance itself or to Africa's Ivory coast. Variations: *Ivoreen, Ivorine*.

IVRIA (Hebrew) In Abraham's land. Variations: *Ivriah, Ivrit*.

IVY (English) Plant. Variations: *Iva, Ivey, Ivie*.

IWA (Japanese) Rock.

IWALANI (Hawaiian) Sea bird.

IWILLA (African-American) I will rise. Newly created name.

IYABO (African: Nigerian) Mother comes back.

IZDIHAR (Arabic) Blossoming.

IZEGBE (African: Nigerian) Long-awaited child. Variation: *Izebe*.

IZUSA (Native American) White stone.

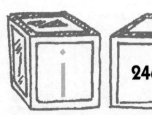

JA (Hawaiian) Fiery.

JAAMINI (Hindu) Night.

JACEY (American) Newly created, possibly from the letters 'J' and 'C'. Variations: *Jace, Jacy.*

JACINTA (Spanish) Hyacinth. Feminine version of Jacinto. Variations: *Glacinda, Glacintha, Jacinda, Jacintha, Jacinthe, Jacinthia, Jacki, Jacky, Jacquetta, Jacqui, Jacquie, Jacynth, Jacyntha, Jacynthe.*

JACQUELINE (French) He who replaces. Feminine version of Jacob. Jacqueline's heritage is undoubtedly French. However, Jackie Kennedy's glamour and poise served to put an American spin on the name. Interestingly enough, although Jackie O is as loved as ever, the name Jacqueline is still not as popular as it was back in the 1920s when it regularly hit the top fifty list. Variations: *Jacaline, Jacalyn, Jackalin, Jackalyn, Jackeline, Jackelyn, Jacketta, Jackette, Jacki, Jackie, Jacklin,* *Jacklyn, Jacky, Jaclyn, Jaclynn, Jacoba, Jacobette, Jacobina, Jacolyn, Jacqualine, Jacqualyn, Jacqualynn, Jacquelean, Jacquelene, Jacquelin, Jacquelyn, Jacquelyne, Jacquelynn, Jacquelynne, Jacqueta, Jacquetta, Jacquiline, Jacquline, Jacqulynn, Jaculine, Jakelyn, Jaqueline, Jaquelyn, Jaquith.*

JADE (Spanish) Jade stone. It became popular in the 1970s when Mick Jagger gave his daughter this name. Variations: *Jada, Jadee, Jadira, Jady, Jaida, Jaide, Jayde, Jaydra.*

JADWIGE (Polish) Safety in war. Variation: *Jadwiga.*

JAE (Latin) Jaybird. Variations: *Jaya, Jaylee, Jayleen, Jaylene, Jaylynn.*

JAE-HWA (Korean) Very beautiful.

JAEL (Hebrew) Mountain goat.

JAFFA (Hebrew) Beautiful. Feminine version of Yaffa. Variations: *Jaffi, Jaffice, Jaffit, Jafit.*

JAHA (African: Swahili) Dignity.

JAIMIE (English) One who replaces. Feminine version of James. Jaimie was first popularized as a great girls' name in the 1970s because it conveys so much energy and fitness, and a bit of tomboyishness – yet a girl with this name wouldn't hesitate to get dressed up to go out to dinner. At least, that's how Lindsey Wagner portrayed the character she played in the TV series *The Bionic Woman*. Variations: *Jaime, Jaimey, Jaimi, Jaimy, Jamee, Jami, Jamie, Jayme*.

JAIRA (Spanish) God teaches.
JALA (Arabic) Clear.
JALAJAA (Hindu) Lotus. Variation: *Jalitaa*.
JALANEELI (Hindu) Moss.
JALEESA (African-American) Jay + Lisa. Variations: *Ja Leesa, Ja Lisa*.
JALILA (Arabic) Great. Variations: *Galila, Galilah, Jalilah, Jallila*.
JALINDA (African-American) Jay + Linda. Variation: *Jalynda*.
JALINI (Hindu) One who lives by the water.
JAMAICA (English) The country.
JAMELIA (Arabic) Handsome. Feminine version of Jamal. Variations: *Jamell, Jamila*.
JAMILA (Arabic) Beautiful. Variations: *Gamila, Gamilah, Jameela, Jamilah, Jamilla, Jamillah, Jamille, Jamillia*.

JAN (Hebrew) God is good. Variations: *Jana, Janina, Janine, Jann, Janna*.
JANAE (Hebrew) God answers. Variations: *Janai, Janais, Janay, Janaya, Janaye, Jannae, Jeanae, Jeanay, Jenae, Jenai, Jenay, Jenaya, Jenee, Jennae, Jennay*.
JANAKI (Hindu) Mother. Variation: *Janika*.
JANAN (Arabic) Spirited.
JANE (English) God's grace. During the 19th century, the name was associated with housemaids and servants. It became more universally popular in the 1920s and again in the 1960s. Famous Janes include Jane Seymour, Jane Austen and Jane Fonda as well as the well-known US singers who bore the variant of Jane – Janis Joplin and Janis Ian. Variations: *Janey, Janica, Janice, Janicia, Janie, Janiece, Janis, Janise, Jannice, Jannis, Jayne, Sheenagh, Sheenah, Sheina, Shena*.
JANESSA (American) Combination of Jan and Vanessa. Variations: *Janesse, Janissa, Jannessa, Jenessa*.
JANET (English) Diminutive of Jane. Janet may have seen some activity in the baby name department owing to the popularity of singer Janet Jackson. However, the name hasn't really been in vogue in this country since the 1960s, when Miss Jackson was born. Other famous Janets include South African actress Janet Suzman, US actress Janet Leigh and British opera singer Dame Janet Baker. Janet became an independent name in its own right around the start of the 1800s, and since then has spawned a number of interesting variations. Variations: *Janeta, Janeth, Janett, Janetta, Janette, Jannet, Janneth, Jannetta, Jenet, Jenett, Jenetta, Jenette, Jennetta, Jennette, Joanet, Sinead, Siobahn, Sioban, Siobhan*.
JANINE (English) God is good. Feminine version of John. Variations: *Janina, Jannine, Jeneen, Jenine*.
JANITA (Scandinavian) God is good. Variations: *Jaantje, Jannike, Jans, Jansje*.

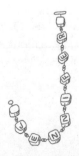

JANY (Hindu) Fire.

JAPERA (African: Zimbabwean) Complete.

JARDENA (Hebrew) To descend. Feminine version of Jordan.

JARITA (Hindu) Mother.

JARKA (Czech) Spring. Variations: *Jaruse, Jaruska.*

JARMILA (Czech) One who loves spring.

JARNSAXA (Scandinavian) Ancient mythological figure. Variation: *Iarnsaxa.*

JAROSLAVA (Czech) Glorious spring.

JASMINE (Persian) Flower. If it wasn't for the great success of the animated Disney movie *Aladdin*, Jasmine would probably have been relegated to a footnote of popular flower names that first hit around the turn of the century. But Princess Jasmine – and, to a lesser extent, model Yasmin Le Bon – have revived this wonderfully feminine name, and it has not yet hit its peak the second time around. Variations: *Jasmeen, Jasmin, Jasmina, Jazmin, Jazmine, Jessamine, Jessamyn, Yasiman, Yasman, Yasmine.*

JASWINDER (Hindu) The god of the sky's thunder.

JATHIBIYYA (Arabic) Attractive. Variations: *Gathbiyya, Gathbiyyah, Gathibiyya, Gathibiyyah, Gazbiyya, Gazbiyyah, Jathbiyya, Jathbiyyah, Jathibiyyah.*

JAVIERA (Spanish) Shining. Variations: *Javeera, Xaviera.*

JAWAHIR (Arabic) Gem. Variation: *Gawahir.*

JAY (Latin) Happy. Variations: *Jai, Jaie, Jaye.*

JAYA (Hindu) Victory. Variations: *Ja Wanti, Janatika, Jayamala, Jayanti, Jayashree, Jayna, Jayt.*

JAYLENE (English) Blue jay. Variations: *Jae, Jaye, Jayline, Jaynell.*

JAYNE (Hindu) Victorious.

JAZLYN (American) Combination of Jazz and Lynn. Variations: *Jasleen, Jaslyn, Jaslynn, Jazlynn, Jazzalyn, Jazzlyn.*

JEAN (Scottish) God is good. Feminine version of John. Variations: *Jeana, Jeanette, Jeanna, Jeanne, Jeannie, Jennette.*

JELENA (Russian) Light.

JEM (English) Supplanter or heel.

JEMIMA (Hebrew) Dove. Variations: *Jamima, Jemimah, Jemmie, Jemmimah, Jemmy, Mima, Mimma.*

JEMINA (Hebrew) Right-handed. Variations: *Jem, Jemi, Jemma, Jemmi, Jemmie, Jemmy, Mina.*

JEMMA (English) Plant bud.

JENA (Hindu) Patience.

JENDAN (African: Zimbabwean) Thankful.

JENDAYA (African: Zimbabwean) To give thanks.

JENELLE (English) Yielding. Version of Guinevere.

JENNA (Arabic) Little bird. Variations: *Jannarae, Jena, Jenesi, Jenn, Jennabel, Jennah, Jennalee, Jennalyn, Jennasee.*

JENNICA (English) God is good. Variation: *Jenica.*

JENNIFER (Welsh) White; smooth; soft. Jennifer is a Cornish version of Guinevere. It is perhaps the best example of the kind of trendy names that exploded in popularity overnight in the mid-1970s all the way up to the early 1990s before almost completely burning out. That was until the arrival on the scene of US actress Jennifer Aniston, star of *Friends* and inspiration for a million haircuts, and singer and actress Jennifer Lopez. Time will tell to see if it has got so popular that many parents might have tended to shy away from using it. Variations: *Genn, Gennifer, Genny, Ginnifer, Jen, Jena, Jenalee, Jenalyn, Jenarae, Jenene, Jenetta Jenita, Jennis, Jeni, Jenice, Jeniece, Jenifer, Jeniffer, Jenilee, Jenilynn, Jenise,*

Jenn, Jennessa, Jenni, Jennie, Jennika, Jennilyn, Jennyann, Jennylee, Jeny, Jinny.

JERALYN (American) Combination of Jerry and Marilyn. Variations: *Jerelyn, Jerilyn, Jerilynn, Jerralyn, Jerrilyn.*

JEREMIA (Hebrew) The Lord is great. Feminine version of Jeremiah.

JERICA (English) Unknown definition. Variations: *Jerika, Jerrica, Jerrika.*

JERSEY (English) Place name.

JERUSHA (Hebrew) Married.

JESSENIA (Arabic) Flower.

JESSICA (Hebrew) He sees. Like Jennifer, Jessica was a regular fixture on the baby name hit parade from the mid-1970s all the way through to the late 1980s. It made its first appearance in the Bible in the Book of Genesis. Shakespeare also used the name in *The Merchant of Venice*, giving the name to the daughter of Shylock. Parents today who like the name but who don't want to be considered trendy are choosing other variations related to Jessica. Variations: *Jesica, Jess, Jessa, Jesse, Jesseca, Jessey, Jessi, Jessie, Jessika.*

JESUSA (Hispanic). Feminine version of Jesus.

JETHRA (Hebrew) Plenty.

JETTE (Scandinavian: Danish) Black. Variation: *Jetta.*

JEWEL (French) Jewel. Variation: *Jewelle*

JEZEBEL (Hebrew) Virginal. Variations: *Jez, Jezzie.*

JIANA (American) Unknown definition.

JILL (English) Young. Shortened version of Juliana. The late actress Jill Ireland was perhaps one of the most famous Jills around along with British writer Jilly Cooper. Jill is a classic name, but it doesn't seem to have enough pizzazz to hit the most-popular charts. Variations: *Gil, Gill, Gyl, Gyll, Jil, Jilli, Jillie, Jilly, Jyl, Jyll.*

JILLIAN (English) Young. Variations: *Gilli, Gillian, Gillie,*

Jilian, Jiliana, Jillana, Jilliana, Jillianne, Jilliyanne, Jillyan, Jillyanna.

JIMENA (Spanish) Heard.

JIN (Japanese) Excellent.

JINA (African: Swahili) Name.

JINAN (Arabic) Paradise.

JINDRISKA (Czech) Ruler at home. Variations: *Jindra, Jindrina, Jindruska.*

ING-WEI (Chinese) Small bird.

JIN-KYONG (Korean) Bright jewel.

JINNAT (Hindu) Heaven.

JINX (Latin) Spell. Variation: *Jynx.*

JIRINA (Czech) Farmer. Variation: *Jiruska.*

JISELLE (American) Allegiance.

JIVANTA (Hindu) To create.

JOAKIMA (Hebrew) God will judge.

JOAN (Hebrew) God is good. Like many of its traditional counterparts, Joan has gone in and out of style over the course of many centuries. Extremely popular during the Middle Ages, it seemed to wane in the 1600s, until the first half of the 20th century, when it became one of the most popular names around. No doubt actresses Joan Crawford, Joan Collins and Joan Fontaine kept the name in the public eye. Variations: *Joani, Joanie, Joannie, Jonee, Joni.*

JOANNE (English) God is good. Variations: *Joana, Joanna, Joannah, Johanna, Johanne.*

JOAQUINA (Spanish) Flower. Variation: *Joaquine.*

JOBY (Hebrew) Persecuted. Feminine version of Job. Variations: *Jobi, Jobie.*

JOCASTA (Italian) Happy.

JOCELYN (English) Unknown definition, possibly a combination of Joyce and Lynn. Variations: *Jocelin, Joceline, Jocelyne, Joci, Jocie, Josaline, Joscelin, Josceline, Joscelyn, Joseline, Joselyn, Joselyne, Josiline, Josline.*

JOCOSA (Latin) Playful.

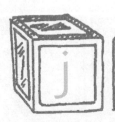
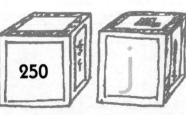

JODELLE (French) Last name. Variations: *Jo Dell, Jodell.*

JODHA (Hindu) Sixteenth century Hindu woman.

JODI (Hebrew) Praised. Variations: *Jodie, Jody.*

JOELLE (French) God is Lord. Feminine version of Joel. Variations: *Joda, Joell, Joella, Joellen, Joellyn, Joely.*

JOKE (Hawaiian) Happy.

JOKLA (African: Swahili) Robe of adornment.

JOLAN (Hungarian) Purple flower.

JOLANTA (Czech) Violet. Variation: *Jolana.*

JOLENE (American) Probably for ever associated with the Dolly Parton song of the same name, Jolene is a combination name, formed by using 'Jo' and 'lene', a popular suffix in the beginnings of the baby boom. As you can see, the variations in spelling tended to get very creative. Jolene is considered by some to be a contemporary version of Josephine. Variations: *Jolean,*

Joleen, Jolian, Jolin, Joline, Jolinn, Jolinne, Jolyn, Jolynn, Jolynne, Jolyon.

JOLIE (French) Pretty. A recent introduction of late 20th-century invention. Variations: *Jolee, Joley, Joli, Joline, Joly.*

JONAVA (African-American) Unknown definition.

JONELLA (English) God is good to all. Variations: *Jonelle, Joni, Jonie, Jony.*

JONINA (Hebrew) Dove. Variations: *Jona, Jonati, Jonit, Yona, Yonit, Yonita.*

JONNA (English) God is good. Variation of John. Variations: *Jahnna, Johnna.*

JONQUIL (English) Flower. Variations: *Jonquila, Jonquille.*

JORA (Hebrew) Autumn rain. Variation: *Jorah.*

JORDAN (English) To descend. The name Jordan has a very curious background: during the Crusades, Christians who returned home brought water from

Family Ties: Juniors, Seniors, III, Etc.

Some people believe that the biggest honour that can be given to another person is to name their newborn baby after him – or her. Though I am aware of several cases in which a daughter was given the same name as her mother, this is a relative rarity; most often, a son is named after a father, with the appropriate Jr. or Roman numeral after the name to indicate the position in the family.

Although this can be a great source of pride for the family, it can always backfire if the child is made to believe that (a) he has to live up to his father's accomplishments, or (b) he comes to equate his identity with his dad's, and never really has a chance to develop his own unique persona.

When naming a child after a parent, it's customary to use Jr. when the son is second in line, though after that, Roman numerals are the norm. After the fourth male in a row with the same name except for a Roman numeral, however, the current child-bearing generation may tire of the repetition – or else putting a 'V' after a kid's name just starts to seem silly. What other explanation can there be? I've never seen this practice carried beyond the fourth generation...except, of course, for Catholic popes, whose numbers have gone into the double digits. Then again, they don't have sons to pass their names on to.

the Jordan river for the express purpose of baptizing their children. As a result, many of those children were named Jordan – the boys at least. The name really didn't start to catch on for girls until the 1980s. Today, alas, Jordan is beginning to show the signs of strain that many androgynous names go through: parents are ceasing to consider the name for their sons. Variations: *Jordana, Jordon, Jordyn*.

JORGINA (Hispanic) Farmer.

JOSEPHINE (Hebrew) God will add. Feminine version of Joseph. Variations: *Jo, Joey, Jojo, Josefa, Josefina, Josefine, Josepha, Josephe, Josephene, Josephina, Josetta, Josette, Josey, Josi, Josie*.

JOVITA (Latin) Gladden.

JOY (English) Happiness. Variations: *Gioia, Joi, Joie, Joya, Joye*.

JOYCE (Latin) Joyous. Joyce actually started out as a boys' name. It was the name of a saint in the seventh century CE. This usage continued occasionally until the late Middle Ages, but Joyce started to be regularly used only during the 19th century. During the Flapper Era, Joyce was the third most common name for girls, which lasted through the 1950s. Variations: *Joice, Joyousa*.

JOYITA (Spanish) Jewel.

JUABAI (Hindu) Mother of the founder of the Maratha confederacy in the 17th century.

JUANA (Spanish) God is good. Feminine form of John. Variations: *Juanetta, Juanita*.

JUDITH (Hebrew) Jewish. Variations: *Jitka, Jucika, Judey, Judi, Judie, Judit, Judita, Judite, Juditha, Judithe, Judy, Judye, Jutka*.

JUH (Hindu) Flower.

JULA (Polish) Downy.

JULIA (English) Young. Roman clan name. Julia is a name that, shall we say, has legs. It's popular all over the world and has been since women in ancient Rome gave the name to their babies in honour of the emperor Julius Caesar. In the 20th century, Julia was popular from the years immediately following World War II throughout the mid-1970s, when it rested for about a decade until actress Julia Roberts burst onto the scene and made it very popular again. Parents seem to prefer Julia over the perkier Julie. Variations: *Iulia, Jula, Julcia, Julee, Juley, Juli, Juliana, Juliane, Julianna, Julianne, Julica, Julie, Julina, Juline, Julinka, Juliska, Julissa, Julka, Yula, Yulinka, Yuliya, Yulka, Yulya*.

JULIET (English) Downy. Much promoted by Shakespeare's tragedy *Romeo and Juliet*, two famous British actresses include Juliet Mills and Juliet Stevenson. Variations: *Julieta, Julietta, Juliette, Julita*.

JUMANA (Arabic) Pearl. Variation: *Jumanah*.

JUMAPIU (African: Kenyan) Born on Sunday.

JUMOKE (African: Nigerian) Loved by all.

JUN (Chinese) Truth of life. Variation: *Junko*.

JUNE (English) The month. Variations: *Junae, Junel, Junella, Junelle, Junette, Juno*.

JUSTINE (French) Just. Feminine version of Justin. Variation: *Justina*.

JUTKA (Hungarian) Praise God.

JYOTI (Hindu) Light of the moon. Variation: *Jyotsana*.

month.

te.

ninine version
ie, *Kacy, Kaycee,*

finition.

Kadia, Kadya.
) Unknown

KAGISO (African: Botswana) Peace.

KAHOKO (Hawaiian) Star.

KAI (Japanese) Forgiveness; (Hawaiian) Sea. A name with a varied background, it is also thought to be Scandinavian of uncertain origin and some think that it is related to the Roman Caius. Although most people haven't heard of Kai as the name for a girl, they may be familiar with it as a name for a boy. Kai has just recently started to appear in some places as a name for girls, most often by African-American parents, but I think that this is a name that is on its way up overall. Variations: *Kaiko, Kaiyo.*

KAILASH (Hindu) Himalayan mountain.

KAIMAUE (Hawaiian) Calm seas.

KAISA (Scandinavian: Swedish) Pure.

KAITCHKMA WINEMA (Native American) Strong woman.

KAITLIN (English) Combination of Kate and Lynn. Variations: *Kaitlinn, Kaitlinne, Kaitlynn, Katelin, Katelyn, Katelynne.*

KAKALA (Polynesian) Flower.

KAKALINA (Hawaiian) Pure. Variations: *Kakarina, Katalina.*

KAKAULANI (Hawaiian) In the sky.

KAKIELEKEA (Hawaiian) White gardenia.

KAKRA (African: Ghanian) Second-born of twins.

KAL (English) Yellow flower.

KALA (Hindu) Black one. Variations: *Kalee, Kali, Kallee.*

KALALA (Hawaiian) Bright. Hawaiian version of Clara. Variation: *Kalara.*

KALAMA (Hawaiian) Flaming torch.

KALAMELA (Hawaiian) Hawaiian version of Carmen.

KALANA (Hawaiian) Flat land.

KALANI (Hawaiian) Heaven.

KALANIT (Hebrew) Flower. Variations: *Kalanice, Kaleena, Kalena, Kalina.*

KALAUDIA (Hawaiian) Lame. Hawaiian version of Claudia. Variations: *Kalaudina, Kalaukia, Kalaukina, Kelaudia, Kelaukia.*

KALAUKA (Hawaiian) Famous. Variation: *Kalarisa.*

KALEI (Hawaiian) Wreath of flowers.

KALERE (African) Short woman.

KALI (Hindu) Energy. Variation: *Kalli*

KALIGENIA (Greek) Beautiful daughter.

KALIKA (Hindu) Flower pod.

KALILA (Arabic) Beloved. As you can see, Kalila has spawned a wide variety of variant spellings. It's used most often in Arabic countries in much the same way that we use Honey or Sweetie. It is a pretty name and not entirely unfamiliar, which makes it a good candidate for increased popularity. Varient Kaleigh has been commonly used in the 1970s and 1980s. Variations: *Kaila, Kailey, Kaleela, Kaleigh, Kalie,*

Kalilla, Kaly, Kayle, Kaylee, Kayleen, Kayleigh, Kaylene, Kayley, Kaylie, Kaylil, Kylila.

KALILEA (Polynesian) Pillow talk.

KALILINOE (Hawaiian) Rain.

KALINA (Polish) Flower. Variations: *Kaleen, Kaleena, Kalena, Kalene.*

KALINDA (Hindu) The sun. Variation: *Kaleenda.*

KALINDI (Hindu) A river. Variation: *Kaleendi.*

KALINI (Hawaiian) Pure. Hawaiian version of Karen.

KALINN (Scandinavian) Stream.

KALINO (Hawaiian) A bright light.

KALIONA (Hawaiian) One lion.

KALISKA (Native American) Coyote pursuing a deer.

KALITA (Hindu) Famous.

KALLI (Greek) Singing lark. Variations: *Cal, Calli, Callie, Colli, Kal, Kallie, Kallu, Kally.*

KALLIRROE (Greek) Beautiful stream. Variations: *Callirhoe, Callirhot, Calliroe, Callirrhoe, Callirroe, Callirrot.*

KALLISTA (Greek) Most beautiful. Variations: *Cala, Calesta, Calista, Callie, Cally, Kala, Kalesta, Kali, Kalie, Kalika, Kalista, Kalli, Kallie, Kally, Kallysta.*

KALLOLEE (Hindu) Happy.

KALOLA (Hawaiian) Woman. Hawaiian version of Carol. Variation: *Karola.*

KALOME (Hawaiian) Peace.

KALONICE (Greek) Beautiful victory.

KALOTE (Hawaiian) Small beauty. Hawaiian version of Charlotte. Variations: *Halaki, Harati, Kaloka, Kaloke, Kalota.*

KALPANA (Hindu) Imagination. It appears in classical Indian texts and was taken up in medieval times in deference to feminine beauty.

KALTHUM (Arabic) Fat-cheeked. Variation: *Kalsum.*

KALUWA (African) Overlooked.

KALUYAN (Cambodian) Supreme.

KALYAN (Hindu) Beautiful.

KALYCA (Greek) Rosebud. Variations: *Kali, Kalica, Kaly.*
KAMA (Hebrew) Ripe.
KAMALA (Hindu) Lotus. One of the alternative names borne by the goddess Lakshmi. Variation: *Kamalika.*
KAMALI (African: Zimbabwean) Guardian angel of infants.
KAMANIKA (Hindu) Beautiful. Variation: *Kamaniya.*
KAMARI (African: Swahili) Like the moon. Variation: *Kamaria.*
KAMATA (Native American) Throwing bones.
KAME (Japanese) Tortoise. Variations: *Kameko, Kameyo.*

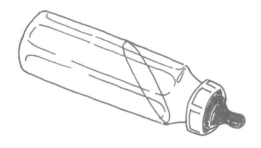

KAMEA (Hawaiian) Sole one.
KAMEKE (African) Blind person.
KAMELI (Hawaiian) Honey.
KAMELIA (Hawaiian) Vineyard. Variation: *Komela.*
KAMI (Polynesian) Love.
KAMILA (Arabic) Perfect. You might think that Kamila is a variation of the name Camille, but it has totally different roots and definition. Of course, some parents have deliberately designed the name so that it is a variation of Camille, but in its original form, Kamila is Arabic through and through. Variations: *Kameela, Kamilah, Kamilla, Kamillah, Kamla.*
KAMINARI (Japanese) Thunder.
KAMOANA (Hawaiian) Ocean.
KANA (Hindu) Tiny. Variation: *Kanika.*
KANANI (Hawaiian) Beautiful.

KANARA (Hebrew) Canary. Variation: *Kanarit.*
KANDA (Native American) Magic.
KANE (Japanese) Talented. Variation: *Kaneko.*
KANEESHA (African-American) Unknown definition. Variation: *Kaneisha.*
KANENE (African) Sty in the eye.
KANERU (Japanese) To do two things at once. Variation: *Kane.*
KANESTIE (Native American: Seneca) Guide.
KANI (Hawaiian) Sound.
KANIH (African: Kenyan) Black cloth.
KANIQUA (African-American) Unknown definition. Variation: *Kanikwa.*
KANJANAA (Hindu) God of love.
KANNITHA (Cambodian) Angel.
KANOA (Hawaiian) Free one.
KANTA (Hindu) Desire. In classical Indian writings, the name is often applied to wives or mistresses.
KANTI (Hindu) Lovely. Variation: *Kantimati.*
KANYA (Hindu) Daughter. Variation: *Kanyaa.*
KAORU (Japanese) Aroma.
KAPIKA (Hawaiian) Gazelle.
KAPONIANANI (Hawaiian) Consecrated beauty.
KAPUA (Hawaiian) Flower.
KAPUAULA (Hawaiian) Red flower.
KAPUKI (African) First-born daughter.
KARA (Latin) Dear. Kara started out life spelled the Italian way with a 'C', but somehow it became more popular with a 'K'. In any case, Kara is both exotic and familiar and parents should start to consider it more. Variations: *Kaira, Karah, Karalee, Karalyn, Karalynn, Kari, Kariana, Karianna, Karianne, Karie, Karielle, Karrah, Karrie, Kary.*
KAREN (Scandinavian) Diminutive of Katerina. An established favourite among Scandinavians for many years, the name was adopted by English speakers in

the USA in the 1920s afer it was imported with Scandinavian settlers. It was subsequently taken up on both sides of the Atlantic and reached a peak in popularity in the 1960s. It is still popular though less frequently used. Famous Karens include Karen Blixen and Karen Carpenter. Variations: *Caren, Carin, Caryn, Karin, Karina, Karon, Kerena.*

KARENZA (Scottish) Love. Variations: *Kerensa, Kerenza.*

KARIDA (Arabic) Virginal.

KARIMA (Arabic) Noble. Variation: *Karimah.*

KARIS (Greek) Grace.

KARISMA (English) Variation of Charisma.

KARISSA (Greek) Dear.

KARLENE (Latvian) Man. Feminine version of Charles. Variations: *Karleen, Karlen, Karlena, Karlina.*

KARMA (Hindu) Fate.

KARMEL (Hebrew) Garden of grapes. Variations: *Cami, Carmel, Carmia, Karmeli, Karmi, Karmia, Karmiel, Karmielle.*

KARMEN (English) Garden. Variation of Carmen. Variations: *Karmina, Karmine, Karmita.*

KARMIL (Hebrew) Red.

KARNEETSA (Native American: Spokan) Unknown definition.

KAROLAINA (Hawaiian) Woman. Variations: *Kalalaina, Kalolaina, Kalolina, Karalaina, Kealalaina.*

KARPURA (Hindu) Princess from the 12th century.

KARUNA (Hindu) Compassion.

KASA (Native American) Dress made of fur. Variations: *Kahsha, Kasha.*

KASI (Hindu) The holy city. Closely linked with the worship of Shiva, it was the ancient name of Varanasi or Benares, a city famous as a place of pilgrimage and inevitably taken up as a name by people who came from there.

KASINDA (African) Child born after twins.

KASMIRA (Slavic) Bringing peace. Feminine version of Casimir.

KASTURBA (Hindu) Musk.

KATANIYA (Hebrew) Small. Variations: *Katania, Ketana.*

KATEKE (African) An overstayed guest.

KATHERINE (Greek) Pure. Katherine and all of its derivatives have been popular since the days of its Greek origin, when it was known as Aikaterina. The diminutive Kate features twice in Shakespere's plays: *Henry V* and the *Taming of the Shrew*, which was later turned into the musical *Kiss Me Kate.* Some famous Katherines have been actress Katharine Hepburn and author Katherine Mansfield. The roll-call of Kates includes British illustrator Kate Greenaway, singer Kate Bush, actress Kate Winslet and model Kate Moss. Though many parents today are favouring the more Gaelic forms of the name – like Katriona and Caitriona – Katherine itself presents a good choice simply based on all the variations you can choose from later. Variations: *Caitriona, Caren, Caron, Caryn, Caye, Kaethe, Kai, Kaila, Kait, Kaitlin, Karen, Karena, Karin, Karina, Karine, Karon, Karyn, Karyna, Karynn, Kata, Kataleen, Katalin, Katalina, Katarina, Kate, Katee, Kateke, Katerina, Katerinka, Katey, Katharin, Katharina, Katharine, Katharyn, Kathereen, Katherin, Katherina, Kathey, Kathi, Kathie, Kathleen, Kathlyn, Kathlynn, Kathren, Kathrine, Kathryn, Kathryne, Kathy, Kati, Katia, Katica, Katie, Katina, Katrina, Katrine, Katriona, Katryna, Kattrina, Katushka, Katy, Karrin, Katya, Kay, Kisan, Kit, Kitti, Kittie, Kitty, Kotinka, Kotryna, Yekaterina.*

KATRIEL (Hebrew) Crowned by God.

KATSU (Japanese) Triumphant. Variation: *Katsuko.*

KATURA (African: Zimbabwean) Relief.

KATYAYANI (Hindu) Goddess.

KAU-AU-OINTY (Native American: Kiowa) Goose cry.

256

KAUILA (Hawaiian) Acclaimed woman.

KAULA (Hawaiian) Clairvoyant.

KAULANA (Hawaiian) Famous one.

KAULUWEHI (Hawaiian) One garden.

KAUSALYA (Hindu) Mother of Rama. Variations: *Kaushali, Kaushalya*.

KAVERI (Hindu) River.

KAVINDRA (Hindu) Poet.

KAWAIMOMONA (Hawaiian) Sweet water.

KAWENA (Hawaiian) Fire.

KAWENAULA (Hawaiian) Red sunset.

KAYA (Native American: Hopi) Older sister.

KAYLA (English) Pure. Variation of Katherine. Kayla may have started to become popular about the same time that the name Caleb started to appear more frequently for boys. Although in definition they are not closely related, they both share a lyrical but compact sound. Once Kayla hit, it hit big and spread like wildfire. Today, Kayla is solidly entrenched as a favourite girls' name, even though it was nowhere to be seen even ten years ago. Variations: *Kaela, Kaelee, Kaelene, Kaeli, Kaeleigh, Kaelie, Kaelin, Kaelyn, Kaila, Kailan, Kailee, Kaileen, Kailene, Kailey, Kailin, Kailynne, Kalan, Kalee, Kaleigh, Kalen, Kaley, Kalie, Kalin, Kalyn, Kayana, Kayanna, Kaye, Kaylan, Kaylea, Kayleen, Kayleigh, Kaylene, Kayley, Kayli, Kaylle*.

KAYA (Native American) Wise child.

KAZU (Japanese) Obedient. Variation: *Kazuko*.

KEAHDINEKEAH (Native American: Kiowa) Tossing.

KEALA (Hawaiian) Road.

KEALANI (Hawaiian) White heaven.

KEALOHA (Hawaiian) Cherished friend.

KEALOHI (Hawaiian) Shining friend.

KEARA (Irish) Dark. Variations: *Keira, Kiara, Kiera, Kierra*.

KEEAOLA (Hawaiian) Breath of life.

KEEHABAH (Native American: Navajo) Unknown definition.

KEENA (English) Unknown definition.

KEESHA (African-American) Newly created. Variations: *Keisha, Keshia, Kiesha*.

KEEZHEEKONI (Native American: Chippewa) Fire.

KEHACHIWINGA (Native American: Winnebago) Wolf den.

KEHINDE (African: Nigerian) Second-born of twins.

KEI (Japanese) Awe. Variation: *Keiko*.

KEIKI (Hawaiian) Child.

KEIKIKALANI (Hawaiian) Divine child.

KEITA (English) Forest. Feminine version of Keith.

KEKE (Hawaiian) Chaste. Variation: *Kete*.

KEKEPANIA (Hawaiian) Crown. Variation: *Setepania*.

KEKILIA (Hawaiian) Poor eyesight. Variations: *Kekila, Kikilia, Sesilia, Sisilia*.

KEKONA (Hawaiian) Second child.

KELA (Hawaiian) Valley. Variation: *Dela*.

KELALANI (Hawaiian) Limitless sky.

KELDA (Scandinavian) Fountain or spring. Variation: *Kilde*.

KELDAY (English) Unknown definition.

KELEKA (Hawaiian) To harvest. Variation: *Kelekia*.

KELEKEA (Hawaiian) Gardenia flower.

KELETINA (Hawaiian) Heavenly. Variation: *Kelekina*.

KELILA (Hebrew) Crown. Variations: *Kaile, Kaille, Kalia, Kayla, Kayle, Kyle, Kylia*.

KELINA (Hawaiian) Moon goddess.

KELLY (Irish) Female soldier. Kelly has had multiple personalities over the last hundred years: first it was a last name, then many parents with Irish roots chose it for their boys, and today it is almost exclusively a girls' name. Kelly was at its most popular in the 1970s, and parents who have selected the name for their daughter since then have, more often than not,

Native American Names – Current Trends

As cultural awareness of Native American customs has grown in the last decade or so, more non-Indians are looking toward using Native American names for their own children. I've heard that a Native American child's name is based on what his or her parents see at the moment of conception, which may explain the girls' name *Awenita*, which means a fawn, or the boys' name *Ouray*, which translates to 'arrow'. However, when you learn that the boys' name *Hulwema* means a grizzly bear that has been killed with a shotgun, you can't help but wonder what the ambiance was like.

Though their parents may have Anglicized names like Elizabeth and Henry, the Native American babies that are being born today are, more likely than not, being given names that reflect their heritage. Often they are given two names: a traditional name that clearly reflects their heritage, along with a more modern, 'American' name. The majority of parents give the more modern name as the first name, with the native name serving as the middle name. However, some have reversed this, and there are a sizable number of parents – both native and non-native Americans – who are opting for only the Indian name.

Boys' Names

- Alahmoot: Elm branch.
- Chaska: First son.
- Diwali: Bowl.
- Eskaminzim: Big mouth.
- Galegina: Male deer.
- Hohots: Bear.
- Irateba: Beautiful bird.
- Kahatunka: Crow.
- Len: Flute.
- Mankato: Blue earth.
- Nashoba: Wolf.
- Ohanzee: Shadow.
- Pezi: Grass.
- Sani: Old.
- Tawa: Sun.
- Wahotkonk: Black eagle.
- Zotom: One who bites.

Girls' Names

- Acadia: Village.
- Chapa: Beaver.
- Doli: Bluebird.
- Eyota: Great.
- Genesee: Pretty valley.
- Inola: Black fox.
- Kaya: Older sister.
- Litonya: Hummingbird.
- Mahwah: Beautiful.
- Natane: Daughter.
- Opa: Owl.
- Pana: Partridge.
- Sahkyo: Mink.
- Taima: Fox.
- Una: Remember.
- Weayaya: Sunset.
- Zitkala: Bird.

selected one of the name's expressive variations. Variations: *Kealey, Kealy, Keeley, Keelie, Keellie, Keely, Keighley, Keiley, Keilly, Keily, Kellee, Kelley, Kellia, Kellie, Kellina, Kellisa.*

KELSEY (English) Island. Although actor Kelsey Grammer has made us aware that Kelsey can also be a male name – and actually the name started out as being for boys only – Kelsey captivated many parents-to-be during the mid-to-late 1980s, when Mr Grammer was still a part-time patron on *Cheers.* Variations: *Kelcey, Kelci, Kelcie, Kelcy, Kellsie, Kelsa, Kelsea, Kelsee, Kelseigh, Kelsi, Kelsie, Kelsy.*

KELULA (Yiddish) Girlfriend.

KENDA (Native American) Magic. Variations: *Kenada, Kenadi, Kendi, Kendie, Kendy, Kennda, Kenndi, Kenndie, Kenndy.*

KENDALL (English) Valley of the river tent. Last name. Variations: *Kendal, Kendel, Kendell.*

KENDRA (English) Origin unknown; possibly a combination of Kenneth and Sandra. Kendra is particularly popular among African-American parents today, although no one can trace where the name first appeared or what it means. Kendra first surfaced in the United States in the 1940s, and it didn't reach Britain until the later part of the 1960s. Variations: *Kena, Kenadrea, Kendria, Kenna, Kindra, Kinna, Kyndra.*

KENISHA (African-American) Beautiful woman. Variations: *Keneisha, Keneshia, Kennesha.*

KENTON (English) Place name.

KENYA (Hebrew) African country.

KENZIE (Scottish) Light one.

KEOHI (Hawaiian) One woman.

KEOKIANA (Hawaiian) Farmer. Variations: *Geogiana, Geogina, Keokina.*

KEOLA (Hawaiian) One life.

KEOLAKUPAIANAHA (Hawaiian) Good life.

KEPILA (Hawaiian) Fortune-teller. Variations: *Kipila, Sebila, Sibila.*

KERANI (Hindu) Sacred bells. Variations: *Kera, Kerie, Kery.*

KEREM (Hebrew) Orchard.

KEREN (Hebrew) Animal horn. Variations: *Kerrin, Keryn.*

KERENSA (Cornish) Love. Variations: *Karensa, Karenza.*

KERRY (Irish) County in Ireland. Like its counterpart, Kelly, Kerry was once a very popular name. However, it seems as though its variations and creative spellings have got the better of it, rendering the original form almost obsolete. Like Kelly, Kerry started out as a boys' name. Variations: *Kera, Keree, Keri, Keriana, Keriann, Kerianna, Kerianne, Kerra, Kerrey, Kerri, Kerrianne, Kerrie.*

KESAVA (Hindu) Lots of hair.

KESHET (Hebrew) Rainbow.

KESI (African: Swahili) Daughter with a difficult father.

KESIA (African-American) Favourite. Variation: *Keshia.*

KESSEM (Hebrew) Magic.

KESSIE (African: Ghanian) Fat.

KETI (Polynesian) Pure.

KETIFA (Hebrew) To pick. Variation: *Ketipha.*

KETINA (Hebrew) Girl.

KETURAH (Hebrew) Perfume. Variation: *Ketura.*

KETZIA (Hebrew) Tree bark. Variations: *Kazia, Kesiah, Ketzi, Ketziah, Kezi, Kezia, Keziah, Kissie, Kizzie, Kizzy.*

KEVINA (Irish) Handsome. Feminine version of Kevin. Variations: *Keva, Kevia, Kevyn.*

KEWANEE (Native American: Potawatomi) Prairie hen. Variation: *Kewaunee.*

KHADIJA (Arabic) Premature baby. Variations: *Khadiga, Khadua.*

KHADQAH (Arabic) Honourable.

KHALIDA (Arabic) Forever. Variations: *Kaleeda, Khalidah.*

KHALILA (Arabic) Good friend. Variation: *Khalilah.*

KHAPKHAPONIMI (Cayuse) Bark.

KIANNAH (American) Variation of Hannah. Variations: *Kia, Kiana, Kianah, Kianna.*

KIARA (American) Unknown definition. Variations: *Keira, Kiarra, Kiera, Kierra.*

KIBIBI (African: Swahili) Little girl.

KICHI (Japanese) Lucky. Variation: *Kicki.*

KIELE (Hawaiian) Gardenia flower. Variations: *Kieley, Kieli.*

KIEU (Vietnamese) Graceful.

KIFIMBO (African: Swahili) A twig.

KIKI (Spanish) Nickname for Enriqueta.

KIKILIA (Hawaiian) Blind.

KIKU (Japanese) Chrysanthemum. Variations: *Kikue, Kikuko.*

KILEY (Gaelic) Handsome. Variation: *Kilee.*

KILIA (Hawaiian) Heaven.

KILIWIA (Hawaiian) Forest. Variation: *Silivia.*

KIMAMA (Native American: Shoshone) Butterfly.

KIMAYA (Hindu) Godlike.

KIMBERLY (English) King's meadow. Kimberly was a well-used name at the start of the 20th century for boys, since it was a town in South Africa and many men were fighting a war there. To commemorate the battles, parents named their sons after the town. By the 1940s, Kimberly had already begun to take root as a girls' name, and it turned into one of the most popular names in the 1960s and 1970s. Today, however, it appears less frequently. Variations: *Kim, Kimba, Kimba Lee, Kimball, Kimber, Kimberlea, Kimberlee, Kimberlei, Kimberleigh, Kimberley, Kimberli, Kimberlie, Kimberlyn, Kimbley, Kimmi, Kimmie, Kymberlee.*

KIMI (Japanese) Superb. Variations: *Kimie, Kimiko, Kimiyo.*

KIMIMELA (Native American: Sioux) Butterfly.

KIN (Japanese) Gold.

KINA (Hawaiian) To judge.

KINETA (Greek) Dynamic.

KINI (Hawaiian) God is good. Variations: *Kinikia, Kinitia, Sinitia.*

KINNERET (Hebrew) Harp.

KINSEY (English) Family member.

KINSHASA (African-American) The capital of Congo.

KINTA (Native American: Choctaw) Beaver.

KINU (Japanese) Silk. Variations: *Kinuko, Kinuyo.*

KIOKO (Japanese) Happy.

KIRA (Bulgarian) Throne. Variations: *Kiran, Kirana, Kiri, Kirra.*

KIRAN (Hindu) Light. Variation: *Kirina.*

KIRBY (English) Farm near a church.

KIRI (Hindu) Amaranth. Variation: *Kirsi.*

KIRIAH (Hebrew) Village. Variations: *Kiria, Kirya.*

KIRIMA (Intuit) Hill.

KIRITINA (Hawaiian) Christ. Variations: *Kilikina, Kirikina.*

KIRSI (Hindu) Amaranth flower.

KIRSTEN (Scandinavian) Anointed. Feminine version of Christian. Kirsten and its variations have always seemed to be underused, compared to their relatives Kristen and Christine. However, because it's been underused, Kirsten is becoming more popular than its counterparts today. Also, the visibility of the actress Kirstie Alley doesn't hurt. Variations: *Keerstin, Kersten, Kersti, Kerstie, Kerstin, Kiersten, Kierstin, Kirsta, Kirsti, Kirstie, Kirstin, Kirstine, Kirsty, Kirstyn, Kirstynn, Kyrstin.*

KISA (Russian) Kitten. Variations: *Keesa, Kysa.*

KISHA (African-American) Newly created.

KISHANDA (African-American) Newly created.

KISHI (Japanese) Beach. Variation: *Kishiko.*

KISHORI (Hindu) Young girl.

KISKA (Russian) Pure.

KISMET (American) Destiny.

KISSA (African: Ugandan) Born after twins.

KITA (Japanese) North.

KITRA (Hebrew) Wreath.

KIWA (Japanese) Born on the border. Variations: *Kiwako, Kiwayo.*

KIWIDINOK (Native American: Chippewa) Woman of the wind.

KIYO (Japanese) Happy families. Variation: *Kiyoko.*

KIYOSHI (Japanese) Shining.

KIZZY (Hebrew) Cinnamon. Variations: *Kissie, Kissy, Kizzie.*

KNASGOWA (Native American: Cherokee) Heron.

KNESHIA (African-American) Unknown definition.

KO (Japanese) Daughter's obligation.

KOANA (Hawaiian) God is good. Variation: *Ioana.*

KODELIA (Hawaiian) Daughter of the sea. Variation: *Kokelia.*

KOFFI (African) Born on Friday.

KOHANA (Japanese) Little flower.

KOHINOOR (Arabic) Light.

KOKO (Japanese) Stork.

KOKUMO (African: Nigerian) This child will not die.

KOLAB (Cambodian) Rose.

KOLEKA (Hawaiian) Gift from God. Variation: *Kolekea.*

KOLENELIA (Hawaiian) Horn. Hawaiian version of Cornelia. Variation: *Korenelia.*

KOLENYA (Native American) To cough.

KOLIKA (Hawaiian) Hawaiian version of Doris.

KOLINA (Hawaiian) Maiden; (Scandinavian: Swedish) Pure.

KOLOE (Hawaiian) Blooming.

KOLOLIA (Hawaiian) Glory. Variation: *Goloria.*

KOMA (Japanese) Pony. Variation: *Komako.*

KOMAL (Hindu) Dainty. Variation: *Komala.*

KOME (Japanese) Rice. Variation: *Komeko.*

KONA (Hindu) Bony.

KONANE (Hawaiian) Lunar glow.

KONEKO (Japanese) Kitten.

KONIA (Hawaiian) Talent.

KOOSKOOSKIA (Native American: Nez Perce) Water.

KOPEA (Hawaiian) Wise. Variations: *Kopaea, Sopia.*

KORA (Greek) Girl. Variations: *Cora, Corabel, Corabella, Corabelle, Corabellita, Corake, Coralyn, Corella, Corena, Coretta, Corey, Cori, Corie, Corilla, Corinna, Corinne, Corissa, Corlene, Corri, Corrie, Corrin, Corrissa, Corry, Cory, Coryn, Coryna, Corynn, Korabell, Koree, Koreen, Korella, Korenda, Korette, Korey, Korie, Korilla, Korissa, Korri, Korrie, Korrina, Korry, Kory, Korynna, Koryssa.*

KORINA (English) Maiden. Korina has been around since the middle of the 19th century, but seems to have always been slightly on the sidelines. This should make it a good choice for parents today who are looking for something just a bit different. Variations: *Korinna, Korinne, Korrina.*

KOSOKO (African: Nigerian) Born to die.

KOSTYA (Russian) Faithful.

KOTO (Japanese) Harp.

KRISTEN (English) Anointed. Feminine version of Christian. Kristen is stuck in the middle: not as common as Christine but not as unusual as Kirsten. The other names have been around for centuries, however, while Kristen has actually only been around in any measure since the 1960s. I personally like the name when there is at least one 'y' in it – for instance, Kristyn – but any parent choosing this name today should feel comfortable knowing that it's highly probable that their daughter will be the only Kristen

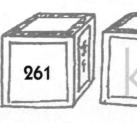

in her class. Variations: *Krista, Kristan, Kristin, Kristina, Kristine, Kristyn, Kristyna, Krysta, Krystyna.*

KUAI HUA (Chinese) Flower blossom.
KUALII (Hawaiian) Queen.
KUAULI (Hawaiian) Fertile.
KUDIO (African) Born on Monday.
KUKANA (Hawaiian) Hawaiian version of Susannah.
KUKIKO (Japanese) Snow girl.
KUKUA (African: Ghanian) Born on Wednesday.
KULANI (Hawaiian) Reaching heaven.
KULUKULUTEA (Polynesian) Dove.
KULWA (African: Tanzanian) First-born of twins.
KULYA (Native American) Burnt pine nuts.
KUMA (Japanese) Bear.
KUMARI (Hindu) Daughter.
KUMI (Japanese) Braid. Variations: *Kumiko, Kumiyo.*
KUMUDA (Hindu) Lotus.
KUNANI (Hawaiian) Beautiful.
KUNI (Japanese) Rural baby. Variation: *Kuniko.*
KUNIGONDE (Scandinavian) Brave in battle. Variation: *Cunegonde.*
KUNTHEA (Cambodian) Aromatic.
KUNTO (African: Ghanian) Third-born child.
KURI (Japanese) Chestnut.
KUSA (Hindu) Grass.
KUSHALI (Hindu) Smart girl.

KUSUM (Hindu) Flower.
KUTATTOA (Native American) Bear pawing through garbage.
KUTCUYAK (Native American) Hairy bear.
KUURAGA (African: Malawian) Crying.
KVETA (Czech) Flower. Variations: *Kvetka, Kvetuse, Kvetuska.*
KWABINA (African) Born on Tuesday.
KWANESHA (African-American) Unknown definition.
KWANITA (Native American: Zuni) God is good.
KWASHI (African) Born on Sunday.
KWAU (African) Born on Thursday.
KYALAMBOKA (African: Tanzanian) God save me.
KYLA (Hebrew) Crown.
KYLE (Scottish) Narrow land. Of course, by now, you can see the signs: this highly popular 1990s name for boys has already started to develop a following among girls.
KYLIE (Australian Aboriginal) Boomerang. This name has become more widely accepted throughout the English speaking world snce the late 1970s. Its popularity can be attributed to the huge success of the Australian soap opera *Neighbours* and a young actress called Kylie Minogue who starred in it. When she left the show she launched what was to become a huge singing career and is now an international pop superstar. Variations: *Kye, Kyla, Kylene.*
KYOKO (Japanese) Mirror.
KYRA (Greek) Lady. Variations: *Keera, Keira, Kira, Kyrene, Kyria.*
KYRIE (Irish) Dark.
KYUNG-SOON (Korean) Gentle respect.

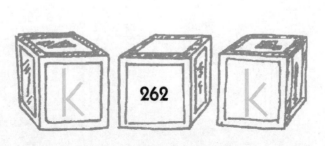

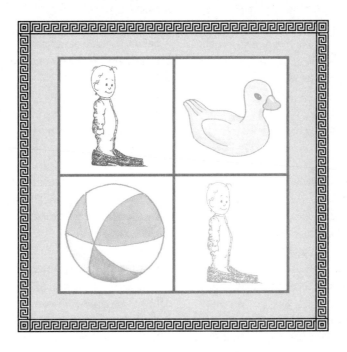

LA CHELLE (African-American) Unknown definition. Variation: *Lachelle.*

LA DAWN (African-American) Unknown definition. Variations: *Ladawn, Ladawna.*

LA DEAN (African-American) Unknown definition.

LA DELLE (African-American) Unknown definition. Variations: *La Dell, Ladelle.*

LA NEESHA (African-American) Unknown definition. Variations: *La Neisha, La Neishah, Laneesha, Laneeshah, Laneisha, Laneishah, Lanisha.*

LA VON (African-American) Unknown definition.

LABANA (African-American) Rocky. Variation: *Labahna.*

LABHAOISE (Irish) Famous in war.

LABRENDA (African-American) Newly created.

LACARA (African-American) Newly created.

LACEY (French) Last name. The original source of the name was a Norman place name Lassy in Calvados. However, some name experts consider Lacey to be a version of Larissa. Lacey was a common French name in the 19th century. Variations: *Laci, Lacie, Lacy.*

LACHANA (African-American) Newly created.

LACHINA (African-American) Newly created.

LACHONDA (African-American) Newly created.

LACHRESA (African-American) Newly created.

LACOLE (African-American) Newly created.

LACRECIA (African-American) Newly created.

LACYNDORA (African-American) Newly created.

LADAISHA (African-American) Newly created.

LADIVA (African-American) Newly created.

LADONNA (African-American) Newly created. The uninitiated might think that Ladonna is just a cheap imitation of the famous singer's name Madonna, but in fact it is one of the more common 'La' names that African-Americans have created for their daughters out of more common names. This trend began in the early 1980s, and has been wildly popular ever since. Variations: *Ladon, Ladonne, Ladonya.*

LADY (English) Noble title.

LAEL (Hebrew) From God.

LAFONDRA (African-American) Newly created.

LAHELA (Hawaiian) Lamb.

LAINA (English) Road.

LAINE (English) Bright one. Variation of Helen. Variations: *Lainey, Lane, Layne.*

LAJESSICA (African-American) Newly created.

LAJLI (Hindu) Humble. Variation: *Lajita.*

LAJNI (Hindu) Shy.

LAJOIA (African-American) Newly created.

LAJULIETTE (African-American) Newly created.

LAKA (Hawaiian) Docile.

LAKALYA (African-American) Newly created.

LAKEA (African-American) Newly created. Variation: *Lakia.*

LAKEDIA (African-American) Newly created.

LAKEISHA (African-American) Newly created. Lakeisha is one of the most popular African-American 'La' names. Compared to the other 'La' names, there are numerous ways to spell this name. Lakeisha also can be traced to Ayesha, which many Muslim families chose for their daughters before the 'La' trend began. Variations: *Lakecia, Lakeesha, Lakesha, Lakeshia, Laketia, Lakeysha, Lakeyshia, Lakicia, Lakiesha, Lakisha, Lakitia, Laquiesha, Laquiesha, Laquisha, Lekeesha, Lekeisha, Lekisha.*

LAKEN (African-American) Newly created.

LAKENDRA (African-American) Newly created.

LAKENDRIA (African-American) Newly created.

LAKENYA (African-American) Newly created.

LAKILA (African-American) Newly created.

LAKITA (African-American) Newly created.

LAKIYA (African-American) Newly created.

LAKRESHA (African-American) Newly created. Variation: *Lakrisha.*

LAKSHA (Hindu) White rose.

LAKSHANA (Hindu) Sign. Variations: *Lakshmi, Laxmi.*

LAKYA (Hindu) Born on Thursday.

LALA (Czech) Tulip.

LALAGE (Greek) Talkative. Variations: *Lallie, Lally.*

LALIKA (Hindu) Beautiful woman.

LALISA (African-American) Newly created.

LALITA (Hindu) Mischievous.

LAMEEKA (African-American) Newly created.

LAMIS (Arabic) Soft.

LAMONICA (African-American) Newly created.

LAMYA (Arabic) Dark lips. Variation: *Lama.*

LAN (Vietnamese) Flower. Variation: *Lang.*

LANA (English) Rock. Variation of Alanna. Sometimes used as an abbreviation of Svetlana. It seems to have made its first appearance in the 1920s. Lana Turner, of course, was probably the most famous Lana that many of us have known. By the way, her original name was Julia, just about the most popular name going today. Variations: *Lanae, Lanice, Lanna, Lanne*tte.

LANAKILA (Hawaiian) Triumph.

LANATA (African-American) Newly created.

LANEETRA (African-American) Newly created.

LANETTA (African-American) Newly created. Variation: *Lanette.*

LANGIKULA (Polynesian) Sunset.

LANI (Hawaiian) Sky.

LANIECE (African-American) Newly created.

LANORA (African-American) Newly created.

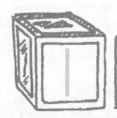

LANTHA (Greek) Purple flower. Variations: *Lanthe, Lanthia, Lanthina.*
LAPAULA (African-American) Newly created.
LAQUALIA (African-American) Newly created.
LAQUANDA (African-American) Newly created.
LAQUARIUS (African-American) Newly created.
LAQUEENA (African-American) Newly created.
LAQUELA (African-American) Newly created.
LAQUILLA (African-American) Newly created.

LAQUINDA (African-American) Newly created.
LAQUITA (African-American) Newly created. Variation: *Laqueta.*
LARA (English) Famous. The song 'Lara's Theme', from the romantic film *Dr. Zhivago*, was probably the sole determining factor in a seeming surplus of baby girls named Lara after 1965. The trend didn't last that long, however; parents today are leaning more toward Larissa, which is the Russian version of the name.

Hindu Names – Cultural Traditions

Hinduism cannot be thought of as a religion where its participants think about God for an hour once a week in a church. Instead, people who follow the Hindu religion believe that God is everywhere they look. They take the same path when naming their children. Frequently, Hindu baby names reflect the main tenet of religion – that of polytheism, or many gods – and so a good majority of Hindus are named after gods. For each god, moreover, there can be hundreds of different names to choose from.

The names Sita for a girl and Vishnu for a boy are quite common. Nature names are also prevalent, again, due to the Hindu belief that God is everywhere you look: a tree, a bird, a rock. In essence, according to Hindu tradition, each time you say that name, you are actually saying the name of God.

Like many Chinese parents, some Hindu parents may also choose an ugly or boring name for their child because they think that the evil spirits won't be as tempted to snatch the child away into death. This practice, however, is not separate from the practice of giving a name that represents a god; indeed, Hindus can also view God in children who are given a name that means worm or pestilence.

Boys' Names

Adri	Krishna
Amar	Nandin
Anand	Pramod
Balin	Rohin
Dalal	Sarad
Hardeep	Siva
Hasin	Vadin
Kala	Valin
Kapildev	Vasin
Kesin	Vinod

Girls' Names

Aditi	Lalita
Anala	Maya
Bakul	Natesa
Chandi	Rani
Deva	Rudra
Ganesa	Sagara
Jaspreet	Sita
Kalinda	Tulsi
Karma	Veda
Karuna	

Variations: *Laralaine, Laramae, Lari, Larina, Larinda, Larita.*

LAREINA (Spanish) The queen. Variations: *LaRayne, Lareine, Larena, Larraine.*

LARESHA (African-American) Newly created.

LARINDA (African-American) Newly created.

LARINE (African-American) Newly created.

LARISSA (Greek) Happy. Though Lara and Larissa seem to be related, they are actually derived from different roots. Larissa first began to appear in the 1960s, as did Lara, but today it is Larissa that is still around. Variations: *Laresa, Laressa, Larisa, Laryssa.*

LARITA (African-American) Newly created.

LARK (English) Bird.

LARSHELL (African-American) Newly created.

LASHANDA (African-American) Newly created.

LASHANNA (African-American) Newly created. Variation: *Lashana.*

LASHANNON (African-American) Newly created.

LASHANTA (African-American) Newly created.

LASHARON (African-American) Newly created.

LASHAUN (African-American) Newly created. Variations: *Lashauna, Lashaunda, Lashaunia, Lashaunta, Lashawna, Lashawnda.*

LASHEA (African-American) Newly created.

LASHEBA (African-American) Newly created.

LASHEELE (African-American) Newly created.

LASHELL (African-American) Newly created. Lashell provides a pretty variation on the traditional Michelle. Variation: *Lashelle.*

LASHENIA (African-American) Newly created.

LASHERRI (African-American) Newly created.

LASHONA (African-American) Newly created. Variations: *Lashonda, Lashunda, Lashundra.*

LASONDA (African-American) Newly created.

LASONIA (African-American) Newly created. Variation: *Lasonya.*

LASSIE (English) Young girl.

LASTARR (African-American) Newly created.

LATA (Hindu) Vine.

LATAISHA (African-American) Newly created. Variations: *Lateisha, Latesha.*

LATANIA (African-American) Newly created. Variations: *Latanya, Latonia, Latonya.*

LATARISHA (African-American) Newly created.

LATARRA (African-American) Newly created. Variation: *Latara.*

LATASHA (African-American) Newly created. I like Latasha because it sounds so close to Natasha, the name that many of us automatically associate with a female Russian spy. A lot of other people out there must like it too, since Latasha has shown up in the top fifty names for African-American girls since the mid-1980s. Variation: *Latashia.*

LATAVIA (Arabic) Pleasant.

LATAVIS (African-American) Newly created.

LATENNA (African-American) Newly created.

LATIFA (Arabic) Tender, gentle. Variations: *Lateefa, Lateefah, Latifah.*

LATIVIA (African-American) Newly created.

LATONA (Latin) In Roman mythology, the mother of Diana and Apollo. Variations: *Latonia, Leto.*

LATORA (African-American) Newly created. Variation: *Latoria.*

LATOSHA (African-American) Newly created. Variation: *Latoshia.*

LATOYA (African-American) Newly created. The visibility of Michael Jackson's sister LaToya Jackson has made her first name one of the more popular 'La' names around. As her reputation and that of her family ebbs and flows, it will be interesting to see how

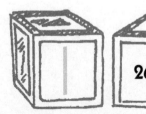

that affects the popularity of Latoya as a baby name. Variations: *Latoia, Latoyia, Latoyla*.

LATRECIA (African-American) Newly created.

LATRICE (African-American) Newly created. Variations: *Latricia, Latrisha*.

LATRINA (African-American) Newly created.

LAUDOMIA (Italian) Praise the house.

LAUFEIA (Scandinavian).Leafy island. Variation: *Laufey*.

LAURA (Latin) Laurel. Laura was a common name in my primary school, but some of us thought it was a bit nerdy. Many parents today, however, don't agree with me, since Laura has appeared in the top twenty-five list of girls' names since the mid-1970s. Laura can trace its roots back to the 14th century in Italy, when it was spelled Lora. The Italian poet Petrarch addressed his love poetry to Laura. The name has been equally popular both in Britain and in the United States. Famous Lauras include British fashion designer Laura Ashley and US actress Laura Dern. Variations: *Larette, Laural, Laure, Laureana, Laurel, Lauren, Laurena, Lauret, Laureta, Lauretta, Laurette, Laurie, Laurin, Lauryn, Lora, Loren, Lorena, Loret, Loreta, Loretta, Lorette, Lori, Lorin, Lorita, Lorrie, Lorrin, Lorry, Loryn*.

LAVANNA (African-American) Newly created.

LAVEDA (Latin) Washed clean. Variations: *Lavella, Lavelle*.

LAVERNE (French) Springlike. Variations: *Lavern, Laverna, Lavyrn, Lavyrne*.

LAVETTA (African-American) Newly created.

LAVINIA (Latin) Roman woman. According to legend Lavinia was the wife of Aeneas and thus the mother of the Roman people. It was considered an aristocratic name and was popular during the Renaissance. Variations: *Lavena, Lavenia, Lavina, Laviner, Lavinie, Levina, Levinia, Livinia, Lovina*.

LAVITA (African-American) Life. Variation: *Laveeda*.

LAVONNE (African-American) Newly created. Variation: *Lavon*.

LAWAHIZ (Arabic) To glance.

LAWANDA (African-American) Newly created.

LAWANNA (African-American) Newly created.

LAWANZA (African-American) Newly created.

LE (Vietnamese) A pear. Vietnam.

LEAH (Hebrew) Weary. Slowly but surely, Leah is starting to appear more frequently among baby girls born today, especially among Jewish families. Leah, in the Book of Genesis, was first used as a given name in 16th-century Puritan England. Variations: *Lea, Leia, Leigha, Lia, Liah*.

LEALA (French) Loyal. Variations: *Lealia, Lealie, Leola*.

LEALIKI (Polynesian) Waves.

LEANDA (English) Lion man. Variations: *Leandra, Leodora, Leoine, Leoline, Leona, Leonanie, Leonelle, Leonette, Leonice, Leonissa*.

LEANNA (Gaelic) Flowering vine. Variations: *Leana, Leane, Leann, Leanne, Lee Ann, Lee Anne, Leeann, Leeanne, Leianna, Leigh Ann, Leighann, Leighanne, Liana, Liane, Lianne*.

LEANORE (English) Bright one. Variation of Helen. Variations: *Leanor, Leanora, Lenor, Lenora, Lenorah, Lenore, Leonara, Leonora, Leonore*.

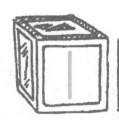

LECIA (Latin) Short for Alicia or Felicia. Variations: *Lecy, Lisha, Lishia.*

LEDAH (Hebrew) Birth. Variations: *Leda, Leida, Leta, Leyda, Lida, Lidah, Lyda.*

LEEBA (Hebrew) Heart.

LEENA (Hindu) Devoted.

LEFNA (Estonian) Light.

LEHUA (Hawaiian) Sacred.

LEI (Chinese) Openhearted, upright, honest.

LEIGH (English) Meadow. In its simpler spelling, Lee, this name has always been more popular for boys than for girls, but Leigh is beginning to gain a following. I've always liked the name Leigh, but it always seemed that with its exotic spelling it should have an unusual pronunciation as well. Variation: *Lee.*

LEIKO (Japanese) Proud.

LEILA (Arabic) Night. Variations: *Laila, Layla, Leela, Leelah, Leilah, Leilia, Lela, Lelah, Lelia, Leyla, Lila, Lilah.*

LEILANI (Hawaiian) Heavenly.

LEILI (Hebrew) Night. Variations: *Laili, Lailie, Laylie, Leilie.*

LEINANI (Hawaiian) Beautiful wreath.

LEISI (Polynesian) Lace.

LEMUELA (Hebrew) Devoted to God. Feminine version of Lemuel.

LENA (English) Bright one. One famous bearer of the name is US singer Lena Horne. Variation of Helen. Variations: *Lenah, Lene, Leni, Lenia, Lina, Linah, Line.*

LEN-AG-SEE (Native American: Shawnee) Wife of Chief Blackhoof. Variation: *Lenexa.*

LENICE (African-American) Newly created. Variations: *La Neece, LaNiece, Laniece.*

LENIS (Latin) Smooth, silky.

LENKA (Czech) Light.

LENNA (German) The strength of a lion. Variations: *Lenda, Lennah.*

LEODA (German) Of the people. Variation: *Leota.*

LEOLANI (Hawaiian) Tall.

LEONA (Latin) Lion. Feminine version of Leon. I've always liked the name Leona. It first surfaced in the 19th century and began to appear more frequently after World War II. Variations: *Leonia, Leonie, Leonine, Leonissa, Leontyne.*

LEONANI (Hawaiian) Beautiful voice.

LEONARDA (German) Roar of the lion. Variations: *Lenda, Leonarde.*

LEONIE (French) Lioness. Variations: *Leona, Leonda, Leondra, Leondrea, Leonela.*

LEOPOLDINE (German) Brave people. Feminine version of Leopold. Variations: *Leopolda, Leopoldina.*

LEORA (Greek) Light. Variations: *Leorah, Leorit, Lior, Liora, Liorah, Liorit.*

LEOTIE (Native American) Prairie flower.

LEPEKA (Hawaiian) To bind.

LERATO (African: Botswana) Love.

LESIELI (Polynesian) Lamb.

LESLIE (Scottish) Low meadow. Leslie has had a rich and colourful history, adapted from its original use as a last name in one of Robert Burns's poems. Burns spelled it as Lesley, but when parents began to use the name for their boys, they used the spelling of Leslie. The name remained popular among both sexes and in both spellings up until the 1940s. Today, Leslie is primarily a girls' name, although neither spelling predominates. Variations: *Leslea, Leslee, Lesley, Lesli, Lesly, Lezlee, Lezley, Lezli, Lezlie.*

LETA (Latin) Happy. Variation: *Lida.*

LETHA (Greek) Amnesia.

LETITIA (Latin) Happiness. Variations: *Leticia, Letisha, Letizia, Lettitia, Letycia.*

LEVANA (Hebrew) White. Variations: *Leva, Levania, Levanit, Levanna, Livana, Livna, Livnat, Livona.*

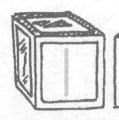
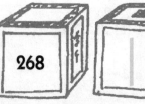

LEVIA (Hebrew) Attached. Feminine version of Levi.

LEVIAH (Hebrew) God's lioness. Variation: *Levia*.

LEVINA (Latin) Lightning.

LEVONA (Hebrew) Frankincense. Variation: *Levonat*.

LEWANA (Hebrew) The moon. Variations: *Lewanna, Liva*.

LEXA (Czech) Protector of man. Feminine version of Alexander. Lexa and its variations are starting to appear more widely today, probably owing to the existence of an 'x' within the name. Though most parents are using this name as a pet name for the more formal Alexandra, a few are choosing it as their daughter's given name. Variations: *Lexi, Lexia, Lexie, Lexina, Lexine*.

LEYA (Spanish) The law.

LI (Chinese) Pretty.

LI HUA (Chinese) Pear blossom.

LIA (Hebrew) Tired.

LIAN (Chinese) Graceful willow.

LIANA (French) Twist like a vine. Variations: *Li, Lia, Lian, Liane, Liann, Lianna, Lianne*.

LIBE (Hebrew) Love. Variations: *Liba, Libbe, Libbeh, Libi, Libke, Libkeh, Lipke, Lipkeh*.

LIBENA (Czech) Love. Variations: *Liba, Libenka, Libuse, Libuska, Luba*.

LIBERTY (English) Freedom.

LIBYA (African-American) Country in North Africa.

LICHA (Spanish) Nobility.

LIDA (Slavic) Loved by all. Variations: *Lidah, Lyda*.

LIDWINA (Scandinavian) Friend of the people.

LIEN (Chinese) Lotus. Variation: *Lien Hua*.

LIESL (German) Nickname for Elizabeth. Variations: *Leizl, Liesa, Liese, Liesel, Liezel, Lisel, Lisl, Lisle*.

LIFTHRASIR (Scandinavian) She desires life.

LILA (Hindu) Dance of God.

LILAC (English) Flower.

LILIA (Hawaiian) Lily flower.

LILAVATI (Hindu) Free will.

LILIA (Hawaiian) Lilies.

LILIHA (Hawaiian) Loathing.

LILITH (Arabic) Night demon. It's a good bet that few people would have heard of Lilith without the character Dr. Lilith Sternin, the psychiatrist played by actress Bebe Neuwirth on the TV show *Cheers*. Lilith is actually the name of the wife that Adam had before Eve. According to legend, Lilith didn't like having a man calling the shots, so she departed, turning herself into a demon instead. Variation: *Lillis*.

LILLIAN (English) Lily + Ann. Variations: *Lileana, Lilian, Liliana, Lilias, Lilika, Lillia, Lillianne, Lillyan, Lillyanna, Lilyan*.

LILUYE (Native American) Chicken hawk.

LILY (Latin) Flower. Variations: *Lili, Lilia, Lilie, Lilli, Lillie, Lillye, Lilye*.

LIMBER (African: Nigerian) Happiness.

LIN LIN (Chinese) Cheerful.

LINA (Arabic) Palm tree.

LINDA (Spanish) Pretty one. In the 1960s and 1970s, it seemed that there were always a couple of girls with this name in every classroom. This was to be expected, since back in the 1950s, Linda was the name that replaced Mary as number one. Today, Linda is almost nowhere to be seen. And when it is used today, the most frequent spelling is Lynda. Variations: *Lin, Linday, Linde, Lindee, Lindi, Lindie, Lindy, Linn, Lyn, Lynada, Lynadie, Lynda, Lynde, Lyndy, Lynn, Lynnda*.

LINDEN (English) Tree.

LINDSAY (English) Island of linden trees. Perhaps Lindsay was the reason that Linda hasn't remained more popular, even though except for sharing a few letters, the names have nothing in common. Lindsay was mostly a boys' name until the 'bionic woman' –

Some Popular Names from the 1990s

What do people think of when they look back to the 1990s? Turmoil on the job? Home? Family? Strange weather?

The jury is still out as to why parents are choosing these most popular names during this decade, but take a look at the name lists for the previous five decades: you'll find names on this list that appear on every previous one. Perhaps parents were looking back to simpler times and choosing names from the years that were perceived as easier to live in. Boys' names chosen in the 1990s were also heavy in Biblical influence – Daniel, Matthew, John – while girls' names had a wealthy sound to them: Ashley, Amanda, Brittany.

No matter the reasons, the only thing you can be sure of is that parents will continue to select names for their kids that reflect the times they're living in – or the years they're nostalgic about. Because some things never change!

Boys' Names

Michael	Kevin
Christopher	Adam
Matthew	Tyler
Joshua	Jacob
Andrew	Jeffrey
Daniel	Jason
Justin	Timothy
David	Benjamin
Ryan	Corey
John	Aaron
Steven	Mark
Robert	Alexander
James	Richard
Nicholas	Cody
Joseph	Jeremy
Brian	Nathan
Jonathan	Travis
Kyle	Derek
Sean	Jared
William	Patrick
Brandon	Scott
Eric	Charles
Zachary	Dustin
Thomas	Jordan
Anthony	Jesse

Girls' Names

Ashley	Rebecca
Jessica	Michelle
Amanda	Kelly
Sarah	Chelsea
Brittany	Courtney
Megan	Crystal
Jennifer	Amy
Nicole	Laura
Stephanie	Kimberly
Katherine	Allison
Caitlin	Erica
Lauren	Alicia
Rachel	Jamie
Samantha	Katie
Heather	Erin
Elizabeth	Mary
Danielle	Alyssa
Christina	Kelsey
Emily	Andrea
Amber	Alexandra
Melissa	Christine
Tiffany	Angela
Lindsey	Jacqueline
Kristen	Casey
Kayla	Shannon

played by Lindsay Wagner – helped to bring this name to the forefront. Lindsay and its variant spellings appeared on the top ten baby name lists in the 1980s, but as with all very popular names, ten or fifteen years can make a huge difference in how the name is perceived. Variations: *Lindsaye, Lindsey, Lindsi, Lindsie, Lindsy, Linsay, Linsey, Linzey, Lyndsay, Lyndsey, Lynsay, Lynsey.*

LINETTE (Welsh) Idol. Variations: *Lanette, Linet, Linetta, Linnet, Linnetta, Linnette, Lynetta, Lynette, Lynnet, Lynnette.*

LING (Chinese) Delicate.

LINIT (Hebrew) Relax.

LINNEA (Scandinavian) Lime tree.

LIONA (Hawaiian) Roaring lion.

LIRIT (Hebrew) Lyrical.

LISA (English) Pledged by oath to God. Version of Elizabeth. Though I don't particularly think of my own parents as being faithful to the trends of their day, the fact that they named me Lisa is testament to how attuned they really were. In terms of popularity, Lisa was number four on the baby name hit parade in 1970, and number twelve in 1980, but today parents are clearly preferring to use one of the other deriva-tives of Elizabeth such as Liza or Libby. My parents may have been swayed by Nat King Cole's number-one song, 'Mona Lisa'. Variations: *Leesa, Leeza, Leisa, Liesa, Liese, Lisanne, Lise, Liseta, Lisetta, Lisette, Lissa, Lissette, Liza, Lizana, Lizanne, Lizette.*

LISANDRA (Greek) Liberator. Variations: *Lissandra, Lizandra, Lizann, Lizanne, Lysandra.*

LISELI (Native American) Unknown definition.

LISSILMA (Native American) Be there.

LITONYA (Native American: Miwok) Hummingbird.

LIVANGA (African) Think before you act.

LIVIYA (Hebrew) Lioness. Variation: *Leviya.*

LIVONA (Hebrew) Spice. Variations: *Livia, Liviya.*

LOFN (Scandinavian) Ancient mythological goddess.

LOIS (English) Famous soldier. Feminine version of Louis.

LOIYETU (Native American) Blooming flower .

LOKALIA (Hawaiian) Garland of roses.

LOKAPELA (Hawaiian) Beautiful rose.

LOKE (Hawaiian) Rose. Variations: *Loka, Lokelani.*

LOKEMELE (Hawaiian) Rose from the sea.

LOKOMAIKAI (Hawaiian) Generous.

LOKOMAIKAINANI (Hawaiian) Beautiful and generous.

LOLA (English) Sorrow. Nickname for Dolores. Long established across the Spanish-speaking world, the British pop group The Kinks released a hugely successful single entitled 'Lola' in 1970. Variations: *Loleta, Loletta, Lolita.*

LOLLY (English) Laurel. Nickname for Laura.

LOLOTEA (Native American) Gift from God.

LOMASI (Native American) Pretty flower.

LONI (English) Ready for battle. Feminine version of Alphonso. Variations: *Lona, Lonee, Lonie, Lonna, Lonnie.*

LOPEKA (Hawaiian) Bright fame.

LORELEI (German) Area in Germany. Variations: *Loralee, Loralie, Loralyn, Lorilee, Lura, Lurette, Lurleen, Lurlene, Lurline.*

LORNA (Scottish) Area in Scotland. Thought to have been invented by the British novelist R. D. Blakemore for his heroine *Lorna Doone.* Variation: *Lorrna.*

LORRAINE (French) Area in France. Thought to be a variant of Laura, it may have become familiar in the 16th century through Mary, Queen of Scots' mother Mary of Lorraine. It enjoyed a peak of popularity in the 1950s and 1960s, but has since been in decline. In Ireland, it was one of the most popular names for girls in the 1970s. Variations: *Laraine, Lauraine, Laurraine, Lorain, Loraine, Lorayne, Lorine, Lorrayne.*

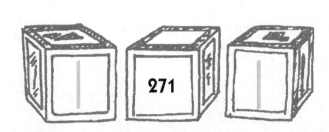

LOSA (Polynesian) Rosa. Variations: *Losana, Lose.*

LOSAKI (Polynesian) To meet.

LOTA (Hindu) Cup.

LOTTA (Scandinavian: Swedish) Woman. Variations: *Lotie, Lotte, Lottey, Lotti, Lottie, Lotty.*

LOTUS (Greek) A fruit.

LOUISE (English) Famous soldier. Feminine version of Louis. Famous Louises include the author of *Little Women*, Louisa May Alcott and US actress Louise Brooks. The name may have also been given a boost by the popular movie *Thelma and Louise*. Variations: *Aloise, Aloysia, Louisine, Louiza, Luisa, Luise.*

LOURDES (French) Area in France. The name Madonna chose for her daughter.

LOVE (English) Love. Variations: *Lovey, Lovi, Lovie.*

LUAN (Vietnamese) Talk over.

LUANA (German) Combination of Louise and Anne. Variations: *Luann, Luanne.*

LUBORNIRA (Czech) Great love. Variations: *Luba, Lubena, Lubina, Lubinka, Lubka, Luboska.*

LUCA (Italian) Feminine version of Lucas.

LUCERNE (Latin) Lamp. Variation: *Lucerna.*

LUCINDA (Latin) Beautiful light.

LUCITA (Spanish) Light.

LUCKY (English) Fortunate. Variations: *Luckie, Luckye.*

LUCRETIA (Latin) Roman clan name. Variations: *Lucrece, Lucrecia, Lucreecia, Lucrezia.*

LUCY (English) Light. Feminine version of Lucius. Lucy is a great old name that has finally made the comeback that it deserves. Lucia, the root for all Lucy-related names, is in turn the feminine version of an ancient Roman family name. Today, it seems that parents are choosing Lucy more often; I think it is destined to become one of the hipper names of the last few years. A famous Lucy includes Lucille Ball, star of the *I Love Lucy* shows. Variations: *Lucetta, Lucette, Lucia, Luciana, Lucie, Lucienne, Lucilla, Lucille, Lucina, Lucinda, Lucita.*

LUDMILA (Czech) Loving people. Variations: *Lidka, Lidmila, Lidunka, Liduse, Liduska, Ludmilla, Luduna, Lyudmila.*

LUDOVICA (Scandinavian) Famous in war.

LUIGHSEACH (Irish) Unknown definition.

LUJAYN (Arabic) Silver.

LULANI (Hawaiian) Heaven's peak.

LULU (African: Swahili) Pearl. Best-known as the stage name of pop singer Lulu, whose real name is Marie Lawrie.

LUMUSI (African: Ghanian) Born face-downward.

LUNA (Latin) Roman moon goddess. Variations: *Lunetta, Lunette, Lunneta.*

LUPE (Hawaiian) Ruby.

LUPETU (Native American) Bear climbing over a man.

LURLEEN (German) Place name. Variations: *Lura, Lurette, Lurlene, Lurline.*

LURA (English) Unknown definition.

LUSELA (Native American) Bear foot.

LUTE (Polynesian) Friend.

LUYU (Native American) Beak.

LUZ (Spanish) Light. Variations: *Luzi, Luzie.*

LYDIA (Greek) Woman from Lydia, a region in ancient Greece. Variations: *Lidi, Lidia, Lidie, Lidka, Likochka, Lydiah, Lydie.*

LYNN (English) Pretty. Diminutive of Linda. Lynn was one of the more widely used names in the 1940s both as a first and a middle name. It reached a peak in the 1950s and 1960s. Famous Lynns include British actress Lynn Redgrave and Canadian ballet dancer Lynn Seymour. Variations: *Lin, Lina, Linell, Linelle, Linn, Linne, Lyn, Lyndall, Lyndel, Lyndell, Lyndelle, Lynelie, Lynell, Lynna, Lynne, Lynnelle.*

LYRIS (Greek) Lyre; a small harp. Variation: *Lyra.*

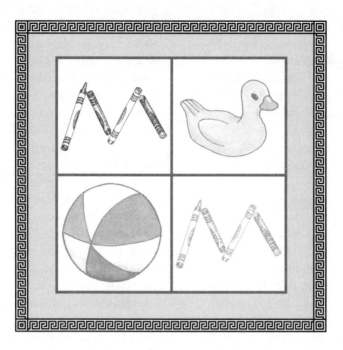

MAATA (Polynesian) Lady.

MAAYAN (Hebrew) Mountain. Variation: *Mayana*.

MAB (Irish, Gaelic) Joy. Queen Mab is a legendary Irish fairy queen.

MABEL (English) Lovable. One well-known Mabel is children's writer Mabel Lucy Atwell. Mabel is starting to appear on birth certificates today as often as it did a hundred years ago, when it was a popular name in this country. Variations: *Mabelle, Mable, Maybel, Maybell, Maybelle*.

MACHI (Japanese) Ten thousand. Variation: *Machiko*.

MACIA (Polish) Defiant.

MACKENZIE (Irish) Daughter of a wise leader.

MACY (English) Last name.

MADELINE (French) Mary Magdalen. Most parents today are familiar with the *Madeleine* books by the author Ludwig Bemelmans. The character that Cybill Shepherd played in the TV show *Moonlighting* in the 1980s named Maddy may be responsible for the small upward blip we see today connected with the name. Variations: *Mada, Madalaina, Maddalena, Maddi, Maddie, Madelaine, Madelayne, Madeleine, Madelena, Madelene, Madelina, Madge, Magda*.

MADHAVI (Hindu) Spring.

MADHU (Hindu) Honey. Variation: *Madhur*.

MADHULEKHA (Hindu) Sweet daughter.

MADIA (Arabic) To praise. Variations: *Madiha, Madihah*.

MADISON (English) Last name.

MADONNA (Latin) My lady. This name has received worldwide exposure since the 1980s and 1990s with the success of superstar Madonna Louise Veronice Ciccone.

MADRA (Spanish) Mother.

MAEIKO (Japanese) Honest child.

MAEMI (Japanese) Honest smile.

MAEVE (Irish) Delicate. The name of the legendary queen of Connacht and is still largely confined to Ireland. Maeve Binchy is a famous Irish writer.

MAGARA (African: Zimbabwean) To sit.

MAGASKAWEE (Native American: Sioux) Swan girl.

MAGDALENA (Spanish) Woman from Magdala, area in the Middle East. Variations: *Magdala, Magdalen, Magdalene.*

MAGENA (Native American) New moon.

MAGNILDA (German) Successful in battle.

MAGNOLIA (Latin) Flower name.

MAHA (Arabic) Big eyes. The name evokes the large expressive eyes of cattle, often considered to be a metaphor for feminine beauty in the Arab world.

MAHALA (Hebrew) Tenderness. The name features in the Bible as the wife of Esau and also the wife of Rehoboam. It seems to have made its first appearance in the 17th century and is most commonly found in the USA. The late singer Mahalia Jackson popularized this name. Perhaps this would be a good name for a daughter born into a musical family, but for some, the connection may just be too obvious. Variations: *Mahalah, Mahalia, Mahaliah, Mahalla, Mahelia, Mehalia.*

MAHANGA (Polynesian) Twins.

MAHASITN (Arabic) Good.

MAHASKA (Iowa) White cloud.

MAHEESA (English) The Hindu god Siva. Variations: *Mahesa, Mahisa.*

MAHI (Hindu) Earth. Variation: *Mahika.*

MAHIMA (Hindu) Eminence.

MAHINA (Hawaiian) Moon.

MAHIRA (Hebrew) Quick. Variation: *Mahera.*

MAHWAH (Native American: Algonquin) Beautiful.

MAI LY (Vietnamese) Plum blossom.

MAI (Vietnamese) A flower.

MAIA (Greek) Mother. Greek nymph.

MAIBA (African: Zimbabwean) Serious.

MAIDA (English) Maiden. Variations: *Maidie, Mayda.*

MAIKAI (Hawaiian) Good.

MAILI (Polynesian) Breeze.

MAIMI (Hindu) Gold.

MAIRA (Hawaiian) Myrrh. Variation: *Maila.*

MAISIE (Scottish) Pearl. Diminutive of Margaret. Variations: *Maisey, Maisy, Maizie.*

MAITERYI (Hindu) Philosopher's wife.

MAIZA (Arabic) Discerning.

MAJ (Scandinavian) Pearl. Variations: *Mai, Maia, Maja.*

MAJESTA (Latin) Majesty.

MAJIDAH (Arabic) Magnificent. Variation: *Maiida.*

MAKA (Native American: Sioux) Earth.

MAKAALOHI (Hawaiian) Shining eyes.

MAKADISA (African) Selfish.

MAKALEKA (Hawaiian) Pearl. Variations: *Makalika, Makelesi.*

MAKANA (Hawaiian) Gift.

MAKANI (Hawaiian) The wind.

MAKANAAKUA (Hawaiian) Gift from God. Variation: *Makana.*

MAKANAMAIKAI (Hawaiian) Good gift. Variation: *Makana.*

MAKAWEE (Native American: Sioux) Abundant. Variation: *Macawi.*

MAKEDA (Hebrew) Bowl.

MALA (Hawaiian) Garden.

MALAK (Arabic) Angel.

MALALANI (Hawaiian) Holy garden.

MALAMA (Polynesian) Shine.

MALAMHIN (Scottish) Smooth brow.

MALANA (Hawaiian) Cheerful.

MALATI (Hindu) Jasmine.

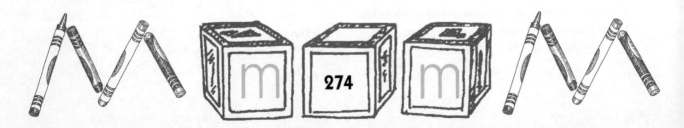

MALI (Hindu) Farmer.

MALIA (Hawaiian) Defiance. Variation: *Mali.*

MALIAKA (Hawaiian) Hawaiian version of Marietta. Diminutive of Mary. Variations: *Mariata, Meliaka.*

MALIE (Polynesian) Lucky.

MALILA (Native American) Salmon swimming upstream.

MALINA (Hawaiian) Peaceful.

MALKAH (Hebrew) Queen. Variations: *Malcah, Malka, Malkia, Malkiah, Malkie, Malkit, Malkiya.*

MALKIN (German) Battle maiden.

MALKOSHA (Hebrew) Recent rain.

MALKUYU (Native American) Dried flowers.

MALLORY (French) Unfortunate. Derived from a Norman French nickname. It is usually a last name,

but has been used mostly in America in the 1980s. Variations: *Malloreigh, Mallorey, Mallorie, Malorey, Malori, Malorie, Malory.*

MALOMO (African: Nigerian) Evil spirits.

MALU (Hawaiian) Peace. Variations: *Maloo, Malou.*

MALUHI (Hawaiian) Peaceful.

MALULANI (Hawaiian) Guarded by angels.

MALVA (Greek) Delicate. Variations: *Malvina, Melva, Melvena, Melvina.*

MAMA (African: Ghanian) Born on Saturday.

MAMAKIAEH (Native American: Cheyenne) Curly hair.

MAMO (Hawaiian) Yellow bird.

MAMTA (Hindu) Tenderness.

MANA (Hawaiian) Supernatural power.

MANAALII (Hawaiian) Powerful queen.

Famous Writers and Artists

Some parents read Shakespeare aloud during pregnancy, in the hopes that some of that culture just may rub off on their kids later on. Others play Mozart almost non-stop from the results of the pregnancy test to the delivery room, hoping that their babies will grow into musical prodigies.

Others cut to the chase and name their babies after famous writers or artists in order to increase the chances that they may turn into budding Picassos or Hemingways. Is it wishful thinking?

Now, I know that not all parents name babies after a famous writer or artist because they would like their progeny to follow in the namesake's footsteps; some say they just like the name. Remember that the young star of a number of successful films may turn people from thinking of your Leonardo as a 'da Vinci' to a 'DiCaprio'. And his peers, who may have previously looked down on the child's name, may suddenly think that it's cool.

Boys' Names

- Claude Monet
- David Hockney
- Edgar Allan Poe
- Gabriel Garcia Marquez
- Geoffrey Chaucer
- Gustave Klimt
- Herman Melville
- Maurice Sendak
- Nathaniel Hawthorne
- Pablo Picasso
- Salvador Dali
- Walt Whitman

Girls' Names

- Agatha Christie
- Alice Walker
- Charlotte Bronte
- Elizabeth Barrett Browning
- Frida Kahlo
- Georgia O'Keeffe
- Gloria Steinem
- Jane Austen
- Laura Ingalls Wilder
- Maya Angelou
- Nora Ephron
- Sidonie Gabrielle Colette

MANABA (Native American) Returned to war.

MANAL (Arabic) Accomplished.

MANALANI (Hawaiian) Heavenly power.

MANAOIO (Hawaiian) Faith.

MANAOLANA (Hawaiian) Confidence.

MANAOLANAKEIKI (Hawaiian) Faithful child.

MANAR (Arabic) Beacon.

MANAWALEA (Hawaiian) Generous.

MANDARA (Hindu) Tree.

MANETTE (French) Defiant.

MANGENA (Hebrew) Song. Variation: *Mangina*.

MANI (Chinese) Buddhist prayer.

MANIDISA (African: Ghanian) Sweet. Variation: *Mandisa*.

MANIKARNIKA (Hindu) Jewel maker.

MANJIKA (Hindu) Sweet sounds.

MANJULIKA (Hindu) Sweet.

MANSI (Native American) Picked flower. Variations: *Mancey, Manci, Mancie, Mancy, Mansey, Mansie, Mansy*.

MANUELA (Spanish) God is among us. Feminine version of Emanuel. Variation: *Manuelita*.

MANWANGOPATH (Miami) Light breeze.

MANYA (Russian) Nickname for Mary.

MAPIYA (Native American: Sioux) Heaven.

MAPUANA (Hawaiian) Sweet-smelling.

MARA (Hebrew) Bitter. Variation: *Marah*.

MARAALIKA (Hindu) Swan.

MARABEL (English) Beautiful Mary. Variations: *Marabelle, Marable, Marbella*.

MARAEA (Hawaiian) Sea woman. Variations: *Malaea, Malia, Mele, Mere*.

MARATA (Hawaiian) Woman. Variations: *Malaka, Maleka, Mareka*.

MARATINA (Hawaiian) Warlike. Variation: *Malakina*.

MARCIA (Latin) Warlike. Feminine version of Mark. There were three early Christian saints with this name, which became current in the late 19th century. However, as everything old becomes new again, eventually, Marcia just may start to catch on among parents. Variations: *Marce, Marcee, Marcela, Marcelia, Marcella, Marcelle, Marcena, Marcene, Marcey, Marci, Marcie, Marcina, Marcy, Marsha*.

MARDI (French) Tuesday.

MARELDA (German) Famous battle maid. Variation: *Marilda*.

MARELLA (English) Combination of Mary and Elle. Variation: *Marelle*.

MARETTA (English) Defiant. Variation: *Marette*.

MARGANIT (Hebrew) Flower.

MARGARET (English) Pearl. Margaret has very deep roots, reaching back to the third century when it was the name of a popular saint. Later on, in the 11th century, it was so popular that it was known as the national Scottish female name. It was also very popular in England and the United States: Margaret was a consistent member of the top ten girls' names list for the better part of the first half of the 20th century. Today, many parents are beginning to take a second look. Variations: *Greeta, Greetje, Grere, Gret, Greta, Gretal, Gretchen, Gretel, Grethal, Grethel, Gretje, Gretl, Gretta, Groer, Maggi, Maggie, Maggy, Mair, Maire, Mairi, Mairona, Margara, Margareta, Margarethe, Margarett, Margaretta, Margarette, Margarita, Margarite, Marge, Margeret, Margerey, Margery, Margrett, Marguerette, Marguerite, Marj, Marjorie, Meagan, Meaghan, Meaghen, Meg, Megan, Megen, Meggi, Meggie, Meggy, Meghan, Meghann, Peg, Pegeen, Pegg, Peggey, Peggi, Peggie, Peggy, Reet, Reeta, Reita, Rheeta, Riet, Rieta, Ritta*.

MARGAUX (French) The name of a champagne. Variations: *Margo, Margot.*

MARGEA (Hebrew) Peace.

MARGI (Hindu) Direction.

MARI (Japanese) Ball. Variation: *Mariko.*

MARIA (Latin) Variation of Mary. Variations: *Marea, Mariah, Marie, Marya.*

MARIAN (French) Combination of Mary and Ann. Variations: *Mariana, Mariane, Mariann, Marianna, Marianne, Marion, Marrian, Marrion, Mary Ann, Maryann, Maryanna, Maryon, Maryonn.*

MARICARA (Romanian) Bitter. Variation of Miriam. Variations: *Marice, Marieca, Marise.*

MARIE (French) Variation of Mary. It's funny what the difference a letter will make to determine the popularity of a given name. Marie is a perfect example. While some parents wouldn't consider Mary or Maria, it seems that Marie has found a middle ground. French in origin, it was taken up in the 19th century and reached a peak of popularity in the 1960s and 1970s. Well known Maries include French physicist Marie Curie and music hall performer Marie Lloyd.

MARIETTA (French) Diminutive of Mary. Variation: *Mariette.*

MARIGOLD (English) Flower.

MARILYN (English) Combination of Mary and Lynn. Taken up on wide scale in the 1950s after the international success of American film actress Marilyn Monroe, whose real name was Norma Jean Baker. Variations: *Maralin, Maralynn, Marelyn, Marilee, Marilin, Marilynne, Marralynn, Marrilin, Marrilyn, Marylin, Marylyn.*

MARINA (Latin) From the sea. Variations: *Marena, Marinda, Marine, Marinna, Marna.*

MARINI (African: Swahili) Healthy.

MARIS (Latin) Star of the sea. Though many people consider the up-and-coming Maris and its variations to be derivatives of Mary, it actually comes from the Latin marine term *stella maris*, which means 'star of the sea'. Maris first started to appear in the United States, and some of the variations – Marissa, for example – began to pop up in the 1950s, but it was only in the 1990s that the name has taken a real foothold. Actress Marisa Tomei has been responsible for providing most of the exposure. Variations: *Marieca, Marisa, Marise, Marish, Marisha, Marissa, Marisse, Meris, Merisa, Merissa.*

MARISOL (Spanish) Bitter sun.

MARJANI (African: Swahili) Coral.

MARJOLAINE (French) Marjoram.

MARKETA (Czech) Pearl.

MARLENE (English) Combination of Maria and Magdalene. Variations: *Marla, Marlaina, Marlaine, Marlana, Marlane, Marlayne, Marlea, Marlee, Marleen, Marleina, Marlena, Marley, Marlie, Marlina, Marlinda, Marline, Marlyn.*

MARLO (English) Last name. Variation: *Marlow.*

MARMARA (Greek) Sparkling. Variation: *Marmee.*

MARNI (Hebrew) To rejoice. Variations: *Marna, Marne, Marney, Marnia, Marnie, Marnina, Merina.*

MARONA (Hebrew) Flock of sheep.

MAROULA (Greek) Defiant.

MARTHA (English) Lady. When I was a child, Martha was the name that your grandmother had, not the girl who sat next to you in class. Today, Martha is one of those previously unpopular names that seems to have attained a high degree of chic. Variations: *Macia, Marit, Marite, Marlet, Mart, Marta, Martell, Marth, Marthe, Marthena, Marti, Martie, Martina, Martita, Martus, Martuska, Marty, Martyne, Martynne, Masia, Matti, Mattie.*

MARTINA (Latin) Warlike. Feminine version of Martin. Variation: *Martine*.

MARVEL (French) A marvel. Variations: *Marva, Marvela, Marvele, Marvella, Marvelle*.

MARWA (Arabic) Rock.

MARY (Hebrew) Bitterness. The Virgin Mary. Back in the Middle Ages, you could be tried for blasphemy if you chose the name Mary for your daughter; back then, it was considered to be too sacred to use for a mere mortal. Of course, once attitudes changed, Mary quickly grew to become one of the most popular names among English-speaking countries. After the 1950s, Mary rapidly began to decline in popularity, to the point where today it is a fairly uncommon name. Famous Marys of the past include Mary Pickford, Mary Poppins and Mary Tyler Moore. Today, without a famous face spreading the good news about Mary, I wouldn't expect it to reach its previous heights of popularity. Variations: *Maree, Marella, Marelle, Mari, Marial, Marieke, Mariel, Mariela, Mariele, Mariella, Marielle, Marika, Marike, Maryk, Maura, Moira, Moll, Mollee, Molley, Molli, Mollie, Molly, Mora, Moria, Moyra*.

MARYAMT (Arabic) Sadness.

MASA (Japanese) Direct.

MASAGO (Japanese) Sand.

MASELA (Hawaiian) Warlike. Hawaiian version of Marcella. Variation: *Makela*.

MASHAVU (African: Swahili) Chubby cheeks.

MASIKA (African: Swahili) Born during the rainy season.

MASKINI (African: Swahili) Poor.

MATANA (Hebrew) Present.

MATANMI (African: Nigerian) Do not lie to me.

MATAOAKA (Native American: Pamunkey) She plays. Variations: *Matoax, Matowaka*.

MATELITA (Polynesian) Powerful warrior.

MATILDA (Old German) Maiden in battle. Matilda is a wonderful, lyrical name that many parents are finding to be a perfect match for their newborn daughters. It's expressive enough on its own, but the many different variations are also very distinctive. Variations: *Maddi, Maddie, Maddy, Mat, Matelda, Mathilda, Mathilde, Matilde, Mattie, Matty, Matusha, Matylda, Maud, Maude, Tila, Tilda, Tildie, Tildy, Tilley, Tilli, Tillie, Tilly, Tylda*.

MATRIXA (Hindu) Mother. Variation: *Matrika*.

MATSU (Japanese) Pine. Variations: *Matsuko, Matsuyo*.

MATTEA (Hebrew) Gift from God. Feminine version of Matthew. Variations: *Mathea, Mathia, Matthea, Matthia, Mattia*.

MAUDISA (South African) Sweet

MAULI (Hindu) Hair.

MAULIDI (African: Swahili) Born during the Islamic month of Maulidi.

MAUREEN (Irish) Variation of Mary. Maureen was a quintessentially Irish name that appeared to be equally popular in Ireland, Britain, and the United States, at least up until 1960, when it began to become used less frequently. Famous Maureens include Maureen O'Sullivan and Maureen O'Hara, both movie stars who seemed to go into retirement about the same time that the name began to fade. Variations: *Maurene, Maurine, Moreen, Morreen, Moureen*.

MAUSI (Native American) Picking flowers.

MAUVE (French) The mallow plant. Variation: *Malva*.

MAVIS (French) Thrush. Variation: *Mayvis*.

MAWIYAH (Arabic) Life.

MAWUSI (African: Ghanian) In God's hands.

MAXINE (English) Greatest in excellence. Feminine version of Maximilian. Variations: *Maxeen, Maxene, Maxi, Maxie, Maxima, Maximina, Maxina*.

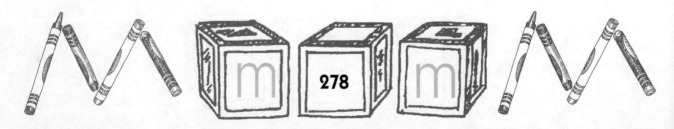

MAY (English) Calendar month. Back in the 1920s, it was all the rage to use months of the year as names for girls, although this exclusive group seemed to focus on springtime: April, May and June. Also Mae – a variant popularized by actress Mae West, whose statuesque figure resulted in her name being taken up for the inflatable life jackets worn by RAF flying crews. It seems to be catching on among parents today. Variations: *Mae, Mai, Mayleen, Maylene.*

MAYA (Hindu) God's power. Variation: *Mya.*

MAYSA (Arabic) Walk proudly. Variation: *Maisah.*

MAZAL (Hebrew) Fate.

MAZHIRA (Hebrew) Gleaming.

MEAD (English) Meadow. Variation: *Meade.*

MEADHBH (Irish) Great joy.

MEARA (Irish) Jolly.

MECA (Spanish) Gentle.

MECHOLA (Hebrew) To dance. Variation: *Mahola.*

MECISLAVA (Czech) Glorious sword. Variations: *Mecina, Mecka.*

MEDA (Native American) Prophet.

MEDEA (Greek) Leader. Ancient mythological figure.

MEDINA (Arabic) City in Saudi Arabia.

MEDORA (English) Gift from mother.

MEE-KYONG (Korean) Shining beauty.

MEENA (Hindu) Fish. Variations: *Meenal, Minal, Minali, Minisha.*

MEE-YON (Korean) Beautiful lotus blossom.

MEGA (Spanish) Gentle.

MEHAL (Hindu) Rain.

MEHIRA (Hebrew) Quick.

MEHITABEL (Hebrew) Benefited by God. In the old Don Marquis stories, Mehitabel was the streetwise cat friend of Archy, the cockroach, who took it upon himself to tell their stories by hopping across typewriter keys. Though some people may associate Mehitabel with other ancient names of less repute, like Medusa, Mehitabel is a wonderfully unusual name. Variation: *Mehetabel.*

MEHJIBIN (Hindu) Face like a temple.

MEHLI (Hindu) Rain.

MEI (Hawaiian) Hawaiian version of May. Variation: *Mahina.*

MEI-HWA (Chinese) Beautiful flower.

MEIKO (Japanese) Bud

MEI-LIEN (Chinese) Beautiful lotus.

MEIRA (Hebrew) Light. Variations: *Meiri, Meirit, Meora, Meorah.*

MEIRONA (Hebrew) Lamb. Variation: *Merona.*

MEI-XING (Chinese) Beautiful star.

MEI-ZHEN (Chinese) Beautiful pearl.

MEL (Portuguese) Honey.

MELA (Hindu) Religious congregation.

MELANIE (Greek) Dark-skinned. Variations: *Mel, Mela, Melaine, Melana, Melane, Melani, Melaniya, Melanka, Melany, Melanya, Melashka, Melasya, Melenia, Melka, Mellanie, Mellie, Melloney, Mellony, Melly, Meloni, Melonie, Melony, Milena, Milya.*

MELANTHA (Greek) Dark flower.

MELBA (English) Variation of Melbourne; city in Australia. Variations: *Mellba, Mellva, Melva.*

MELCIA (Polish) Ambitious.

MELIA (Spanish) Yellow.

MELIAME (Polynesian) Bitter.

MELINDA (Latin) Honey. Variations: *Malina, Malinda, Malinde, Mallie, Mally, Mel, Meleana, Melina, Melinde, Meline, Mellinda, Melynda, Mindi, Mindie, Mindy.*

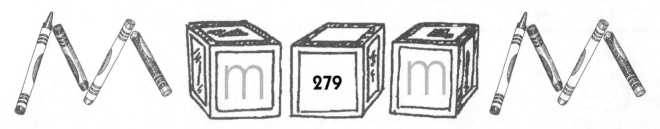

MELIORA (Latin) Better.

MELISANDE (French) Powerful. Variations: *Melasandre, Mellisande.*

MELISSA (Greek) Bee. Today Melissa hovers around the bottom half of the top twenty-five list. The name is destined to move up the ranks slightly, owing to the success and popularity of singer Melissa Etheridge. Melissa is an ancient name that was first popular during the early Roman Empire as it was the name of the woman who nursed the mighty god Juno when he was a baby. Variations: *Melisa, Melisande, Melisandra, Melisandre, Melissande, Melissandre, Melisse, Mellisa, Mellissa.*

MELITA (Greek) Honey. Variations: *Malita, Meleta, Melitta.*

MELODY (Greek) Song. Variations: *Melodee, Melodey, Melodia, Melodice, Melodie.*

MELORA (Latin) Improve.

MELOSA (Spanish) Sweet.

MELVINA (Celtic) Chief. Variations: *Malvina, Melva, Melvena.*

MEMA (Spanish) Hardworking.

MEMBTA (Native American) To taste crushed seeds.

MENA (Dutch) Strength. Variation: *Menna.*

MENASHA (Native American: Algonquin) Island.

MENIA (Scandinavian) Ancient mythological figure. Variation: *Menja.*

MENORA (Hebrew) Candelabra. Variation: *Menorah.*

MEONAH (Hebrew) Home. Variation: *Meona.*

MEOQUANEE (Native American: Chippewa) Red dress.

MERAB (Hebrew) Fertile.

MERAV (Hebrew) To increase. Variations: *Meirav, Merab.*

MERCEDES (Spanish) Mercy. Though it might be assumed that any girl named Mercedes today would be directly inspired by the luxury car, the fact is that the car received its name from the Spanish version of one of the popular ways to refer to the Virgin Mary, Our Lady of the Mercies. However, if you already have a son named Ben, don't choose this name. Variations: *Merced, Mercede.*

MERCIA (English) Ancient British kingdom.

MERCY (English) Mercy. Variations: *Mercey, Merci, Mercia, Mercie, Mersey.*

Scandinavian Mythological Figures

Turn to the boys' names and look at Thor. There you will see at least ten different variations of the old Norse name that serves as the old Norse god of thunder known as Thor.

Thor was the god who watched over humans and their foibles, and rescued them when necessary. In art and in literature, Thor appears as a Zeus-like being with lots of muscles and a hairy body, who rides in a small chariot pulled by goats. According to legend, Thor was so big and the sound of his goats' hooves so loud, that the sound when he was being pulled across the skies of heaven was like thunder and the weapons he hurled down to earth were bolts of lightning.

Because of Thor's position as ruler over all the other Norse gods, a number of Scandinavian names for boys use Thor as a root: Thorvald, Thormond and Thorbert. And Thor also serves as the root for the word *Thursday*.

You don't have to be of Scandinavian origin to name your baby boy after Thor, but if you do choose this route, don't scold your baby the first time he throws all of his toys out of his playpen; he's only living up to his namesake.

MEREDITH (Welsh) Great leader. Variations: *Meredithe, Merideth, Meridith, Merridith.*

MEREUNA (Hawaiian) Hawaiian version of Marilyn. Variation: *Melelina.*

MERI (Scandinavian: Finnish) Ocean. Variation: *Meriata.*

MERIEL (Gaelic) Brilliant seas. Variations: *Merial, Meriol, Merrill.*

MERIMA (Hebrew) To lift up. Variation: *Meroma.*

MERIWA (Intuit) Thorn.

MERLE (French) Blackbird. Variations: *Merl, Merla, Merlin, Merlina, Merline, Merlyn.*

MERRY (English) Happy. Variations: *Meri, Merri, Merrie, Merrilee, Merrily.*

MERYL (English) Bright as the sea. Actress Meryl Streep is an obvious reason why this name has become popular for girls since the early 1980s. Nevertheless, parents today are more likely to choose one of the variations that sounds androgynous and resembles a last name. Of course, these two trends are responsible for many of the new girls' names out there. Variations: *Merill, Merrall, Merrel, Merrell, Merrill, Meryle, Meryll.*

MESHA (Hindu) Ram.

MESI (African: Malawian) Water.

MESSINA (Latin) Middle.

MEUSA (Hawaiian) Bee. Variations: *Meli, Melika.*

MINA (Native American: Sioux) First daughter.

MIA (Italian) Mine.

MI-CHA (Korean) Lovely girl.

MICHAELA (Hebrew) Who is like the Lord? Feminine version of Michael. Variations: *Makaela, Micaela, Mical, Michael, Michaella, Michal, Michala, Mickaula, Micki, Mickie, Micky, Mikella, Mikelle, Mychaela.*

MICHELLE (French) Who is like the Lord? More common feminine version of Michael. Michelle has been one of the few names that has been in the top ten list since the 1960s. The song 'Michelle' by The Beatles can take credit for some of this popularity, as well as Michelle Pfeiffer, who grabbed the torch in the mid-1980s. Used quite frequently in African-American families today, it is beginning to see a challenge by a close relative, Michaela, and its variations that sound more androgynous to the ear. Variations: *Michele, Nichelle.*

MICHIKO (Japanese) The righteous way. Variation: *Michi.*

MICINA (Native American) New moon.

MIDORI (Japanese) Green.

MIEKO (Japanese) Wealthy.

MIEU (Vietnamese) Salt.

MIGINA (Native American) New moon.

MIGISI (Native American: Chippewa) Eagle.

MIGNON (French) Cute. Variations: *Mignonette, Minnionette, Minnonette.*

MI-HI (Korean) Lovely joy.

MIKA (Japanese) New moon.

MIKALA (Hawaiian) Who is like the Lord? Hawaiian version of Michelle.

MIKAZUKI (Japanese) New moon.

MIKI (Japanese) Family tree. Variations: *Mikie, Mikiko, Mikiyo, Mikki, Mikky.*

MIKILANA (Hawaiian) Flower. Variation: *Misilana.*

MIKKA (Japanese) Third day.

MILA (Slavic) Loved by the people.

MILADA (Czech) My love. Variation: *Mila*

MILAGROS (Spanish) Miracles. Variations: *Mila, Milagritos, Miligrosa.*

MILCAH (Hebrew) Adviser. Variations: *Milca, Milka, Milkah.*

MILDRED (English) Tender strength. Variation: *Mildrid.*

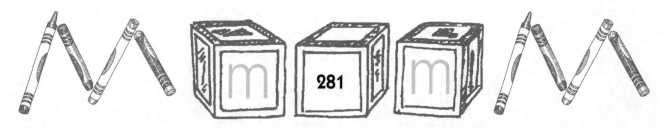

281

MILENA (Czech) Grace. Variations: *Milada, Miladena, Miladka, Milana, Milanka, Milenka, Milka, Miluse, Miluska, Mlada, Mladena, Mladka, Mladuska.*

MILI (Hebrew) Virtuous.

MILIANI (Hawaiian) Tender caress. Variations: *Milana, Miliana.*

MILICA (English) Hard-working.

MILILANI (Hawaiian) Give praise.

MILIMILI (Hawaiian) Cherished.

MILISENA (Hawaiian) Strong at work. Variation: *Milikena.*

MILLICENT (German) Born to power. In the 1950s and 1960s, Millie – short for Millicent – seemed to be the ubiquitous name of every next-door neighbour on television. Today, however, Millicent seems feminine and unusual but not strange: it's ripe for adoption into the top names list. Variations: *Melicent, Meliscent, Mellicent, Milley, Milli.*

MILOSLAVA (Czech) Lover of glory.

MILOSLAWA (Polish) Love of glory.

MIMITEH (Native American: Blackfoot) New moon.

MIN (Chinese) Sensitive.

MINA (Czech) Child of the earth. Variations: *Meena, Minette, Minna, Minnette, Minnie.*

MINAKO (Japanese) Three seven child.

MINAL (Native American) Fruit.

MINAMI (Japanese) South. Variation: *Miniami.*

MINDA (Hindu) Wisdom.

MINE (Japanese) Apex. Variation: *Mineko*

MINEKO (Japanese) Peak.

MINERVA (Latin) The Roman goddess of wisdom.

MINETTA (English) Feminine nickname of William; Will + helmet. Variations: *Minette, Minna.*

MING (Chinese) Tomorrow.

MINNEOKADAWIN (Native American: Sioux) Flows into water.

MINNIE (English) Feminine diminutive of William. Variations: *Minni, Minny.*

MINOWA (Native American) Moving voice.

MIO (Japanese) Triple cord.

MI-OK (Korean) Lovely pearl.

MIRA (Hindu) Rich. Variations: *Meera, Miraata.*

MIRABEL (Latin) Wonderful. An increasing number of parents are looking toward Mirabel and its variations as a suitable first name for their daughters. Though it seems that every girls' name that ends in 'bel' is rising on the popularity scale, Mirabel is probably the most melodious. Variations: *Mirabell, Mirabella, Mirabelle.*

MIRANDA (Latin) Admirable. Variations: *Maranda, Meranda, Mira, Myranda, Randa, Randee, Randene, Randey, Randi, Randie, Randy.*

MIRELLA (Hebrew) God speaks. Variations: *Mireille, Mirelle, Mireya, Myrelle.*

MIRENA (Hawaiian) Beloved. Variation: *Milena.*

MIRI (Gypsy) Mine.

MIRIAM (Hebrew) Bitter. Variations: *Maijii, Maikki, Mair, Maire, Mairi, Mairona, Mame, Mamie, Mamy, Manon, Masha, Mashenka, Mashka, Miliana, Mima, Mimi, Mimma, Mimmie, Miri, Miriama, Mirian, Mirriam, Mirrian, Miryam, Myriam.*

MIROSLAVA (Czech) Great and famous. Variations: *Mirka, Miruska.*

MIROSLAWA (Polish) Great glory. Variation: *Mirka.*

MISAE (Native American: Osage) White sun.

MISAO (Japanese) Loyal.

MISOKA (Japanese) Last day of the month.

MISSY (English) Diminutive of Melissa.

MISTY (English) Mist. Became familiar in the 1970s inspired by the film *Play Misty for Me.*

MITENA (Native American: Omaha) Born under a new moon.

MITSU (Japanese) Light. Variation: *Mitsuko.*

MITUNA (Native American) Enclose a piece of salmon with leaves.
MITZI (German) Variation of Mary. Variations: *Mitsu, Mitzee, Mitzie, Mitzy.*
MIULANA (Hawaiian) Magnolia tree.
MIWA (Japanese) Clairvoyant. Variation: *Miwako.*
MIYA (Japanese) Temple.
MIYO (Japanese) Beautiful generations. Variation: *Miyoko.*

MIYUKI (Japanese) Snow.
MIZELA (English) Unknown definition. Variations: *Marzalie, Masella, Mazala, Mazella, Mazila, Mesella, Messella, Mezillah, Mizella, Mizelle, Mizelli.*
MIZUKO (Japanese) Water child.
MLISS (Cambodian) Flower.
MLO (Japanese) Strong.
MO LAN (Chinese) Magnolia blossom.
MOANA (Hawaiian) Ocean.
MOANANANI (Hawaiian) Beautiful sea.
MOANI (Hawaiian) Light breeze.
MODESTY (Latin) Modesty. Variations: *Modesta, Modestia, Modestina, Modestine.*
MOEMU (Native American) Two bears.
MOHALA (Hawaiian) Flower petals.
MOHANA (Hindu) Engaging. Variations: *Mohini, Mohonie.*
MOMONE (Native American: Montauk) Heather.
MONA (Irish) Noble.
MONDAY (English) Day of the week.
MONEKA (Native American: Sioux) Earth. Variation: *Moneca.*

MONICA (Latin) Adviser or nun. I've always thought that the name Monica has a lot of energy to it; this trait is perhaps best embodied by the tennis champion Monica Seles. Another reason for its popularity is due to its appearance as one of the characters in the TV series *Friends.* On the other hand, one of its variations, Monique, always sounds sultry; it's one of the best French names that you could give your daughter. Today, Monique is most popular among African-American families, who have placed it in the top fifty list of names for their daughters. Variations: *Monika, Monique.*
MONIFA (African: Nigerian) I am lucky.
MONISHA (African-American) Unknown definition.
MONTANA (Spanish) Mountain.
MOR (Scottish) Great.
MORA (Spanish) Blueberry.
MORAN (Hebrew) Teacher. Variation: *Moranit.*
MORASHA (Hebrew) Gift.
MORAY (Scottish) Great.
MORELA (Polish) Apricot.
MORENA (Portuguese) Brunette. Variations: *Moreen, Morella.*
MORGAN (Welsh) Great and bright. Though in the past, Morgan has been more widely known as both a last name and a name for boys, actress Morgan Fairchild provided great exposure for this name. Originally, the step-sister of King Arthur, the sorceress, Morgan Le Fay, helped to create some feminine allure to the name. Variations: *Morgana, Morganne, Morgen.*
MORI (Japanese) Forest. Variations: *Moriko, Moriyo.*
MORIAH (Hebrew) The Lord is my teacher. Variations: *Moria, Morice, Moriel, Morit.*
MORIE (Japanese) Branch.
MORNA (Scottish) Tender.

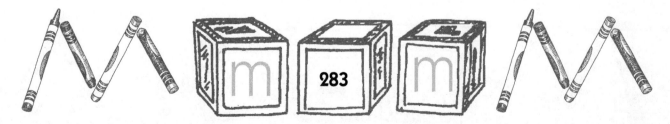

MOROWA (African: Ghanian) Queen.

MORWENNA (Welsh) Maiden.

MOSELLE (Hebrew) Drawn from the water. Feminine version of Moses. Variation: *Mozelle*.

MOSI (African: Swahili) First-born.

MOSWEN (African: Botswana) White.

MOTO (Japanese) Source. Variation: *Motoko*.

MOUNA (Arabic) Desire. Variations: *Mounia, Muna*.

MOWEAQUA (Native American: Potawatomi) Wolf woman.

MOYNE (Irish) Flat land. Variation: *Moyna*.

MU LAN (Chinese) Magnolia blossom.

MU TAN (Chinese) Peony blossom.

MUADHNAIT (Irish) Little noble one. Variations: *Moina, Monat, Moyna*.

MUDIWA (African: Zimbabwean) Beloved.

MUGAIN (Irish) Slave.

MUHAYYA (Arabic) Welcome.

MUIKA (Japanese) Sixth day of the week.

MUIREANN (Irish) Long hair. Variations: *Muirinn, Murainn, Murinnia*.

MUIRNE (Irish) Cherished.

MULLYA (Native American) Acorns falling off a tree. Variation: *Mulya*.

MUMINAH (Arabic) Believer.

MUNA (Arabic) Desire.

MUN-HEE (Korean) Educated.

MUNIRAH (Arabic) Teacher.

MURA (Japanese) Village.

MURASAKI (Japanese) Purple.

MURDAG (Scottish) Sea warrior. Variations: *Murdann, Murdina*.

MURIEL (Irish) Bright as the sea. Began to be used with increasing frequency in the 19th century and was particularly popular in Scotland. It was most used in the 1920s and 1930s but has since been in decline. Scottish-born writer Muriel Spark bears the name. Its popularity may have received a boost owing to the success of the Australian movie *Muriel's Wedding*. Variations: *Muirgheal, Murial, Muriell, Murielle*.

MUSETTA (French) Little bagpipe. Variation: *Musette*.

MUSIDORA (Greek) Gift from the Muses.

MUSLIMAH (Arabic) One who is religious.

MUTETELI (African: Rwandan) Dainty.

MUTSIAWOTAN AHKI (Native American: Blackfoot) Armoured woman.

MWANAHAMISI (African: Swahili) Born on Thursday.

MWANAJUMA (African: Swahili) Born on Friday.

MWANAWA (African: Tanzanian) First-born.

MY (Vietnamese) Pretty.

MY KHANH (Vietnamese) Pretty stone.

MYFANVVY (Welsh) Child of the water. Variations: *Myff, Myvanwy*.

MYLA (American) Merciful. Variations: *Milena, Myleen, Mylene*.

MYLSHA (Arabic) Woman.

MYRA (Latin) Scented oil. Feminine version of Myron. Variations: *Murah, Myria, Myriah*.

MYRDDIN (Welsh) Fortress by the sea.

MYRNA (Irish) Beloved. Variations: *Merna, Mirna, Muirna*.

MYRTLE (English) Plant. Variations: *Myrta, Myrtilla*.

MYSTIQUE (French) Mysterious. Variations: *Mistique, Misty, Mystica*.

MYUNG-HEE (Korean) Smart daughter.

MYUNG-OK Brilliant pearl.

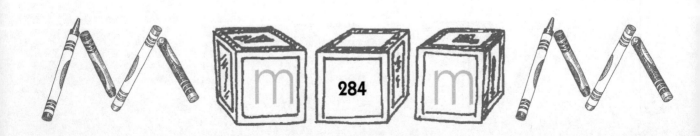

NAAMAH (Hebrew) Sweet. Variations: *Naama, Naamana, Naami, Naamia, Naamiah, Naamiya.*

NAARAH (Hebrew) Girl. Variation: *Naara.*

NAAVAH (Hebrew) Delightful.

NABIHA (Arabic) Smart. Variation: *Nabihah.*

NABILA (Arabic) Highborn. Variations: *Nabeela, Nabilah, Nabilia.*

NABULUNGI (African: Ugandan) Beautiful.

NADA (Arabic) Dew at sunrise. Variation: *Nadya.*

NADETTE (German) Brave bear.

NADEZDA (Czech) Unknown definition. Variation: *Nadeia.*

NADIA (Russian) Hope. This name was virtually unknown in the English-speaking world until the early 20th century. Variations: *Nada, Nadeen, Nadene, Nadina, Nadine, Nadiya, Nadja, Nadya, Natka.*

NADIDA (Arabic) Equal. Variation: *Nadidah.*

NADIRA (Arabic) Rare. Variations: *Nadirah, Nadra.*

NADYAN (Hebrew) Pond. Variation: *Nadian.*

NADZIEJA (Polish) Hope. Variations: *Nadzia, Nata, Natia, Natka.*

NAEEMAH (Arabic) Generous.

NAFSHIYA (Hebrew) Friendship.

NAGIDA (Hebrew) Wealthy. Variations: *Nagia, Nagiah, Nagiya, Najiah, Najiya, Najiyah, Negida.*

NAGISA (Japanese) Beach.

NAHARA (Hebrew) Light. Variations: *Nehara, Nehora.*

NAHIDA (Hindu) Daughter with swollen breasts. Variation: *Nahid.*

NAHLA (Arabic) Drink.

NAIA (Hawaiian) Dolphin.

NAIDA (Greek) Water nymph. Variations: *Naiad, Nayad, Nyad.*

NAILAH (Arabic) One who succeeds. Variation: *Naila.*

NAIMA (Arabic) Content. Variations: *Naeemah, Naimah.*

NAJAT (Arabic) Safe. Variation: *Nagat.*

NAJIBA (Arabic) Well born. Variations: *Nagiba, Nagibah, Najibah.*

NAJLA (Arabic) Pretty eyes. Variations: *Nagla, Najila, Najlaa, Najlah.*

NAJWA (Arabic) Confide. Variation: *Nagwa.*

NALIN (Native American: Apache) Young woman.

NALUKEA (Hawaiian) White wave.

NAMI (Japanese) Wave. Variation: *Namiko.*

NAMISHA (Hindu) Truthful.

NAMONO (African: Ugandan) Second-born of twins.

NAMPEYO (Native American: Hopi) Girl with a snake. Variations: *Nampayo, Nampayu.*

NANA (Hawaiian) Spring month.

NANABAH (Native American: Navajo) Wife of a tribal chairman.

NANALA (Hawaiian) Sunflower.

NANCY (Hebrew) Grace. This name is thought to have evolved as a familiar form of Ann. It emerged as an independent name in its own right during the 18th century. It was particularly popular in the USA and Canada in the middle years of the 20th century. The famous Nancys that most of us know include former First Lady Nancy Reagan, a character in Charles Dickens novel *Oliver Twist*, fictional detective Nancy Drew, US-born politician Nancy Astor, who became Britian's first female member of parliament, and author Nancy Mitford. Variations: *Nan, Nana, Nance, Nancee, Nancey, Nanci, Nancie, Nancsi, Nanette, Nann, Nanna, Nanncey, Nanncy, Nanni, Nannie, Nanny, Nanscey, Nansee, Nansey.*

NANDANA (Hindu) Happiness. Variations: *Nandini, Nandita.*

NANEK (Hawaiian) Merciful. Variations: *Naneka, Naneki, Naneta.*

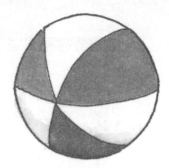

NANI (Hawaiian) Beautiful.

NANIAHIAH (Hawaiian) Beautiful evening.

NANISE (Polynesian) Gracious.

NANVAH (Hebrew) Lovely.

NANYAMKA (African: Ghanian) Lamb.

NANYE-HI (Native American: Cherokee) Wanderer.

NAO (Japanese) Truthful.

NAOMI (Hebrew) Pleasant. Naomi seems poised for newfound popularity for several reasons. It's a pretty name, it has strong Biblical overtones that appeal to many parents today as it appears in the old Testament as the name of Ruth's mother-in-law. It has enjoyed renewed popularity, especially in Australia since the 1970s. It has also been spread by the fame of model Naomi Campbell. Given this combination, Naomi should continue to flourish at least for the next few years. Variations: *Naoma, Naomia, Naomie, Neoma, Noami, Noemi, Noemie.*

NARA (Japanese) Oak tree.

NARCISSA (Greek) Daffodil. Variations: *Narcisa, Narcisse, Narkissa.*

NARDA (Latin) Scented lotion.

NARELLE (Australian) Unknown definition.

NARESHA (Hindu) Leader.

NARI (Japanese) Thunderclap. Variation: *Nariko.*

NARILLA (English, Gypsy) Unknown definition. Variation: *Narrila*.

NASCHA (Native American: Navajo) Owl.

NASEEM (Hindu) Morning breeze.

NASHOTA (Native American) Twin.

NASNAN (Native American) Surrounded with music.

NASPA (Hebrew) The Lord's miracle. Variations: *Nasia, Nasya*.

NASRIN (Arabic) Rose. Variation: *Nasreen*.

NASYA (Hebrew) Miracle of God. Variation: *Nasia*.

NATA (Native American) Creator.

NATALIE (Latin) Birthday. A traditional favourite in Russia, the name is often given to girls born on or near Christmas Day. It was borne by a fourth-century saint whose feast day is celebrated on 1 December. It was introduced to Britain in the 19th century and enjoyed a peak of popularity in the 1970s. Of course, its being associated with the actress Natalie Portman won't exactly hurt the name. Variations: *Natala, Natalee, Natalene, Natalia, Natalina, Nataline, Natalka, Natalya, Natelie, Nathalia, Nathalie*.

NATANE (Native American: Arapaho) Daughter.

NATANIAH (Hebrew) Gift of God. Feminine version of Nathan. Variations: *Natania, Nataniela, Nataniella, Natanielle, Natanya, Nathania, Nathaniella, Nathanielle, Netana, Netanela, Netania, Netaniah, Netaniela, Netaniella, Netanya, Nethania, Nethaniah, Netina*.

NATASHA (Greek) Rebirth. Natasha is a name that has many exotic connotations associated with it. It is the name of one of the characters in Leo Tolstoy's epic *War and Peace*. In the 1970s and 1980s, actress Natassja Kinski kept the name alive, and today it's Natasha Richardson who is the pre-eminent example. But leaving all that aside, Natasha is just a beautiful name for a girl and later a woman. There was one famous Natasha who settled for a more American form of her name: the late Natalie Wood. Variations: *Nastasia, Nastassia, Nastassja, Nastassya, Nastasya, Natashia, Tashi, Tashia, Tasis, Tassa, Tassie*.

NATESA (Hindu) Lord of the dance.

NATHITFA (Arabic) Pure. Variations: *Nathifa, Nathifah, Natifa, Natifah*.

NATIVIDAD (Spanish) Christmas.

NATKA (Russian) Promise.

NATSU (Japanese) Summer. Variations: *Natsuko, Natsuyo*.

NAUASIA (Native American: Sauk) The daughter of Black Hawk and Asshewequa.

NAVIT (Hebrew) Beautiful. Variations: *Naavah, Nava, Navice*.

NAWAL (Arabic) Present.

NAYANA (Hindu) Beautiful eyes.

NAYO (African: Nigerian) She is our joy.

NAZIHAH (Arabic) Trustworthy.

NAZIRA (Arabic) Equal. Variation: *Nazirah*.

NEALA (Irish) Champion. Feminine version of Neil. Variations: *Nealie, Nealy, Neeli, Neelie, Neely, Neila, Neile, Neilla, Neille*.

NECEDAH (Native American: Winnebago) Yellow.

NECHAMA (Hebrew) Comfort. Variations: *Nachmi, Necha, Neche, Nehama*.

NECHE (Native American) Friend.

NECHONA (Hebrew) Appropriate.

NECI (Latin) On fire.

NEDA (Czech) Born on Sunday. Variations: *Nedda, Neddie, Nedi*.

NEDAVIAH (Hebrew) God is charitable. Variations: *Nedavia, Nedavya, Nediva*.

NEEMA (African: Swahili) Born during good times.

NEENAH (Native American: Winnebago) Running water.

NEH (Native American) Goose.

NEHA (Hindu) Loving. Variations: *Nehali, Nehi.*
NEHANDA (African: Zimbabwean) Strong.
NEIMA (Hebrew) Powerful.
NEITH (Egyptian) The goddess of the home. Variation: *Neit.*
NEKA (Native American) Wild goose.
NEKOMA (Native American: Chippewa) Grandmother.
NELKA (Polish) Stone or fortress. Variation: *Nela.*
NELL (English) Light. Jodie Foster's film entitled *Nell*, in which she played the main character, brought this name with a Victorian flair into our consciousness again. Back around the start of the 20th century, when the name was first popular, the variation Nellie was more common than its root. Other famous bearers of the name include Nell Gwyn, the much-loved actress who became mistress to Charles II, Little Nell in Charles Dickens' *The Old Curiosity Shop*, and the Australian opera singer Dame Nellie Melba. Today, both should grow in popularity as both a first and middle name. Variations: *Nella, Nelley, Nelli, Nellie, Nelly.*
NEMERA (Hebrew) Leopard.
NENET (Egyptian) Goddess.
NEOLA (Greek) Young girl. Variation: *Neolah.*
NEPA (Arabic) Walking backwards.
NERA (Hebrew) Light. Variations: *Neria, Neriah, Neriya.*
NERIDA (Greek) Sea nymph. Variations: *Nerice, Nerina, Nerine, Nerisse, Neryssa, Rissa.*
NERISSA (Greek) Sea snail. The name of Portia's sharp-witted maid servant in Shakespeare's *A Merchant of Venice*. Variations: *Nerisa, Nerise.*
NERTHUS (Scandinavian) Ancient mythological goddess.
NERYS (Welsh) Lord. A relatively newly invented name, it is seldom encountered outside Wales. Well-known actress Nerys Hughes bears the name.

NESIAH (Hebrew) Miracle of God. Variations: *Nesia, Nessia, Nesya, Nisia, Nisiah, Nisva.*
NEST (Welsh) Pure. Variation: *Nesta.*
NETIA (Hebrew) Plant.
NETIS (Native American) One who can be trusted.
NETTIE (English) Derived as a nickname for girls' names that end in '-ette' or '-etta'. Variations: *Neta, Netta, Nettia, Netty.*
NEVA (Spanish) Snow.
NEVADA (English) The state. Like Montana, Nevada is quickly becoming one of the more popular girls' names that are taken from a place name.
NEVIAH (Hebrew) Forecaster. Variation: *Nevia.*
NEZA (Slavic) Lamb. Variation: *Neysa.*
NGABILE (African: Tanzanian) It belongs to me.
NGOZI (African: Nigerian) Blessing.
NGU (Vietnamese) Sleep.
NGUYET (Vietnamese) Moon.
NIABI (Native American) Young deer.
NIAMH (Irish) Bright
NIBAL (Arabic) Arrow.
NICOLA (English) People of victory. Feminine version of Nicholas. French version is Nicole. It has been commonly used since the 12th century and enjoyed a peak in popularity in the UK in the 1970s. It has been borne by many famous actresses in its various forms, including Nicole Kidman. The French version of the name received a boost in the 1990s when it featured in a long running series of car adverts on television. Variations: *Nichol, Nicole, Nichole, Nicholle, Nicki, Nickola, Nickole, Nicola, Nicoleen, Nicolene, Nicoletta, Nicolette, Nicolina, Nicoline, Nicolla, Nicolle, Nikki, Nikola, Nikoletta, Nikolette.*
NIDA (Native American) The bones of extinct creatures.
NIHAL (Arabic) One who drinks.

Trendy Celebrity Names

If you look at some of the lists of top names for years gone by, you'll see that many were influenced by the film stars of the day. In the 1940s, for example, Betty (Grable) and Barbara (Stanwyck) were both in the top ten, as were Richard (Harris) and Jose (Ferrer).

There are hazards to this method, of course. In the film *Clueless*, the main character played by Alicia Silverstone was named Cher, after, well, *Cher*. If a name is particularly trendy or unusual, it's hard to believe that it will ever make it into the mainstream. Like the nature names that parents in the 1970s gave their children – Spring and Oak are just two of these organic and wholesome names – any unusual name that suddenly becomes popular and that hasn't been around before is a perfect candidate for appearing dated whenever someone asks your grown child her name twenty years later.

Certainly, Bo, Dack and Krystle were innocently chosen by parents influenced by TV and films in the late 1970s and early 1980s, but where are they now? Of the three, only Krystle – spelled in its more common variation, Crystal – has survived, though it is still pretty obscure.

So you may have fallen head over heels in love with a particular film or actor, and you think the ultimate compliment would be to name your own flesh-and-blood after him. My advice? Don't, unless you really like the name Whoopi and promise yourself that your child can change it later to something he or she really likes.

NIKE (Greek) Goddess of victory. One of the most established brand names in the world Variation: *Nika*.

NIKEESHA (African-American) Variations: *Niceesha, Nickeesha, Nickisha, Nicquisha, Niquisha, Nykesha*.

NILI (Hebrew) An acronym for 'The glory of Israel will not repent'.

NILSINE (Scandinavian) Victory of the people.

NIMA (Hindu) Tree. Variations: *Neema, Neemah, Nema*.

NIMESHA (Hindu) Fast. Variations: *Naimishi, Nimmi*.

NINA (Spanish) Girl. Nina is an ancient name that has been around for several millennia. In Babylonian mythology, Nina was the goddess of the seas, and in the Incan culture, Nina ruled over fire. It seems as if Nina is a name that could always be just a bit more popular, and given the slight stirrings the name has had since the mid-1970s, it may well start to become more visible. Famous Ninas include US jazz singer Nina Simone and British novelist Nina Bawden.

Variations: *Neena, Ninelle, Ninet, Nineta, Ninete, Ninetta, Ninette, Ninita, Ninnette, Ninotchka, Nynette.*

NINOVAN (Native American: Cheyenne) Home.
NIOBE (Greek) Fern. Ancient mythological figure.
NIPA (East Indian) River.
NIRANJANA (Hindu) Full moon.
NIREL (Hebrew) Cultivated pasture.
NIRVELI (East Indian) Water.
NISHA (Hindu) Night. Variation: *Nishi.*
NISHI (Japanese) West. Variations: *Nishie, Nishiko, Nishiyo.*
NISSA (Hebrew) Examine. Variation: *Nisa.*
NITA (Hindu) Friendly. Variations: *Neeta, Nitali.*
NITARA (Hindu) Settled.
NITSA (Greek) Shining girl.
NITUNA (Native American) Daughter.
NIVA (Hebrew) Talk. Variation: *Neva.*
NIXIE (German) Water nymph.
NIZANA (Hebrew) Bud. Variations: *Nitza, Nitzana, Zana.*
NJEMILE (African: Malawian) Honourable.
NKOSAZANA (South African) Princess.
NLMAH (Arabic) Blessing. Variation: *Nimat.*
NNEKA (African: Nigerian) Important mother.

NOBANTU (South African) Popular.
NOEL (French) Christmas. Names that reflect the seasons in some way are starting to become very popular, and Noel is no exception. Traditionally, parents named their baby boys and girls born on Christmas day with a variation of Noel, but today's parents have taken the liberty of giving the name to children who are born throughout the month of December. The variation Nowell appears to have come about because this is how the holiday is spelled in many Christmas carols. Variations: *Noela, Noelani, Noele, Noeleen, Noelene, Noeline, Noell, Noella, Noelle, Noelline, Noleen, Nowell.*
NOELAN (Hawaiian) Divine mist.
NOGA (Hebrew) Morning light.
NOICHA (Native American) Sun. Variation: *Nolcha.*
NOIRIN (Irish) Honourable light.
NOKSU (Native American) A hawk's nest.
NOLA (English) White shoulder. Variations: *Nolah, Nolana.*
NOLETA (Latin) Reluctant. Variation: *Nolita.*
NOMALANGA (South African) Sunny.
NOMBEKO (South African) Respect.
NOMBESE (African: Nigerian) Good child.
NOMBLE (South African) Beauty.
NOMUSA (African: Zimbabwean) Merciful.
NONA (Latin) Ninth. Variations: *Nonah, Noni, Nonie, Nonna, Nonnah.*
NONOOKTOWA (Native American) Unusual child.
NONYAMEKO (South African) Patience.
NOOR (Hindu) Light. Variation: *Noora.*
NORA (Greek) Light. US singer Norah Jones may have given this name a boost in recent years and taken away some of the associations with wrinkled-stocking-wearing Nora Batty from *The Last of the Summer Wine*. Variation: *Norah.*

NORAZAH (Malaysian) Light. Variation: *Norhaneza.*

NORBERTA (German) Famous northerner. Feminine version of Norbert.

NOREEN (English) Diminutive of Nora, light. Variations: *Noreena, Norene, Norina, Norine.*

NORELL (Scandinavian) From the north. Variations: *Narelle, Norelle.*

NORI (Japanese) Principle. Variation: *Noriko.*

NORLAILI (Malaysian) Light

NORMA (Latin) Pattern. Though Norma was once fashionable enough to belong to several film actresses including Norma Shearer, off the screen the name always seemed to belong to mothers and grandmothers and never little girls. Though a similar-sounding name – Martha – caught on in the 1990s in some circles, Norma doesn't seem as if it will have the same clout. Variation: *Normah.*

NORNA (Scandinavian) Fate.

NORRIS (English) Last name.

NOTAKU (Native American) Growling bear.

NOULA (Greek) Grace. Variation: *Noulah.*

NOURA (Arabic) Light. Variation: *Nourah.*

NOURBESE (African: Nigerian) Special child.

NOVA (Latin) New. Variation: *Novah.*

NOVELLA (Spanish) New little thing.

NOVIA (Spanish) Girlfriend.

NTMATUALLAH (Arabic) God's blessing.

NU (Vietnamese) Girl.

NUDAR (Arabic) Golden.

NUHA (Arabic) Smart.

NUKULUVE (Polynesian) Where doves live.

NUMA (Arabic) Beautiful.

NUNA (Native American) Land.

NUNIA (Polynesian) Leader.

NUR (Arabic) Illuminate. Variations: *Nura, Nuri, Nurya.*

NURIA (Hebrew) Fire of the Lord. Variations: *Nuriah, Nuriel.*

NURIT (Hebrew) Small flower. Variations: *Nurice, Nurita.*

NURU (African: Swahili) Daylight.

NUSI (Hungarian) Grace of God.

NUTAN (Hindu) New.

NYDIA (English, Latin) Nest. Variations: *Nidia, Nidiah, Nydiah.*

NYLA (Native American: Creek) Winner. Variation: *Nila.*

NYREE (Maori) Unknown definition.

NYURA (Russian) Grace.

NYX (Greek) Night.

291

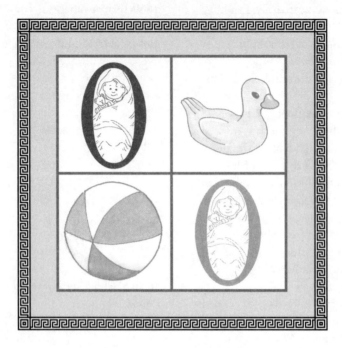

OBA (African: Nigerian) Goddess of the river.

OBEDIENCE (English) Loyalty.

OBELIA (Greek) Needle.

OBIOMA (African: Nigerian) Kind.

OCEAN (English) Ocean. Variations: *Oceana, Oceania*.

OCIN (Native American) Rose.

OCTAVIA (Latin) Eighth. Octavia is a wonderfully intriguing name. The name brings up images of reruns of the old TV series *I, Claudius*, which exhibited some of the more decadent characteristics of the Roman Empire. Nearly everyone will admit to liking the name, but you'll have to be brave to give it to your own daughter. Variations: *Octavie, Ottavia*.

ODDRUN (Scandinavian) Point. Variations: *Oda, Odd, Oddr*.

ODDVEIG (Scandinavian) Woman with a spear.

ODE (African: Nigerian) Born while travelling.

ODEDA (Hebrew) Powerful.

ODELE (German) Wealthy. Variations: *Oda, Odeela, Odela, Odelia, Odelinda, Odell, Odella, Odelle, Odelyn, Odila, Odile, Odilia*.

ODELETTE (French) Little song. Variations: *Odelet, Odette*.

ODELIA (Hebrew) Praise God. Variation: *Odeleya*.

ODERA (Hebrew) Plough.

ODESSA (Greek) Long journey.

ODETTE (French) Wealthy. Variation: *Odetta*.

ODHARNAIT (Irish) Green. Variations: *Orna, Ornat*.

ODINA (Native American: Algonquin) Mountain.

ODIYA (Hebrew) Song of God.

OFA (Polynesian) Love.

OGIN (Native American) Rose.

OHELA (Hebrew) Tent.

OHEO (Native American: Iroquois) Beautiful.

OKALANI (Hawaiian) Of the heavens.

OHNICIO (Irish) Honour.

OJASVEE (Hindu) Shining. Variation: *Ojasvita*.

OJININTKA (Native American: Sioux) Rose.

OKI (Japanese) Middle of the ocean.

OKIIANI (Hawaiian) From heaven.

OKTAWJA (Polish) Eighth.

OLA (Polish) Protector of men; (Scandinavian) Ancestor's relic. Variations: *Olesia, Olesya*.

OLABISI (African: Nigerian) To increase.

OLABUNMI (African) Award.

OLANIYI (African: Nigerian) Wealth.

OLATHE (Native American: Shawnee) Beautiful.

OLAUG (Scandinavian) Devoted to ancestors.

OLDRISKA (Czech) Prosperous ruler. Variations: *Olda, Oldra, Oldrina, Olina, Oluse*.

OLEDA (English) Noble. Variations: *Oleta, Olethea*.

OLENA (Russian) Brilliant light. Variation: *Olenya*.

OLESIA (Polish) Protector of humanity.

OLGA (Russian) Holy. Variant of the name Helga. The two Olgas who are perhaps best known are a saint from the tenth century and the petite gymnast Olga Korbut, who helped bring a new grace to the name during the 1976 Summer Olympics. Olga is still one of the more popular names in Russia today, but it is also widely used across Europe. Variations: *Elga, Ola, Olenka, Olesya, Olia, Olina, Olka, Olli, Olly, Olunka, Oluska, Olva, Olya, Olyusha*.

OLIANA (Hawaiian) Flowering evergreen.

OLINA (Hawaiian) Happy. Variations: *Oleen, Oline*.

OLINDA (Latin) Perfumed.

OLISA (African) God.

OLIVIA (Latin) Olive tree. Olivia, currently very popular and hovering near the top ten list, has a long and illustrious history in the arts and on TV. The name was not in regular use until the 1970s, since when it has enjoyed a strong resurgence in popularity. It is associated with actress Olivia De Havilland and Australian singer Olivia Newton-John. Olivia made its first appearance in literature in Shakespeare's play *Twelfth Night*, but today its popularity seems to stem from its wide usage on TV: Olivia was not only the name of the sainted mother on the 1970s show *The Waltons*, but has also appeared as a character in no fewer than three soap operas. Parents like the name because it has eloquence and sophistication, and yet a homely feel to it. Variations: *Lioa, Lioia, Liovie, Liv, Olia, Oliva, Olive, Olivet, Olivette, Olivine, Ollie, Olva*.

OLUBAYO (African: Nigerian) Great joy.

OLUFEMI (African: Nigerian) God loves me.

OLUFUNMILAYO (African: Nigerian) God gives me joy.

OLUREMI (African: Nigerian) God consoles me.

OLVYEN (Welsh) White footprint.

OLWEN (Welsh) White footprint. Variations: *Olwenn, Olwin, Olwyn, Olwyne*.

OLYMPIA (Greek) Mount Olympus, home of the Greek gods. Variations: *Olimpia, Olympya, Pia*.

OMA (Arabic) Leader.

OMANA (Hindu) Lady.

OMEGA (Greek) Last letter of the Greek alphabet.

OMEMEE (Native American) Pigeon.

OMINOTAGO (Native American: Chippewa) Wonderful voice.

OMOLARA (African: Nigerian) Born at the right time.

OMOROSE (African: Nigerian) Beautiful child.

OMUSA (Native American) Fail to hit a deer with a bow and arrow.

OMUSUPE (African: Nigerian) She is precious.

ONA (Lithuanian) Grace.

ONAIWAH (Native American) Alert. Variation: *Onawa*.

ONATAH (Native American) God of corn.

ONDINE (Latin) Little wave. Variations: *Ondina, Ondine, Ondyne, Undina, Undine*.

ONDREA (Czech) Fierce woman. Variation: *Ondra*.

ONEIDA (Native American) Anticipation. Variations: *Onida, Onyda*.

ONELLA (Greek) Light.

ONI (African: Nigerian) Desired.

ONIDA (Native American) The one we search for.

ONIATARIO (Native American: Iroquois) Beautiful lake. Variation: *Ontario*.

ONORA (Latin) Honour. Variations: *Onoria, Onorine*.

OONA (Irish) Unity. Variations: *Oonagh, Oonah*.

OPA (Native American: Choctaw) Owl.

OPAL (English) Gem. Some of the old-fashioned jewel names, like Opal, were pretty common around the 1900s. Opal was traditionally given to girls born in October, the opal being the birthstone of that month. Today, while Ruby and Jade are quickly becoming hot names, Opal doesn't seem to be keeping up. Variations: *Opalina, Opaline*.

OPHELIA (Greek) Help. Variation: *Ofelia*.

OPHIRA (Hebrew) Gold. Variation: *Ofira*.

ORA (Latin) Prayer. Variation: *Orra*.

ORAH (Hebrew) Light. Variations: *Ora, Orali, Orit, Orlee, Orli, Orlice, Orly*.

ORALIE (French) Golden. The 'Ora' part of Oralie is actually the feminine version of 'oro', which in Spanish means gold. While gold technically isn't a jewel, many of the girls' names that contain this root first began to be popular, appropriately enough, in the 1980s, when names that sounded rich and sophisticated were all the rage. One variation of this name, Oriel, represents the angel of fate; and the popularity of a similar-sounding name, Ariel, (which parents began to flock to after the success of the Disney movie *The Little Mermaid*) seem to have set the stage for a more widespread acceptance of these unusual but beautiful names. Variations: *Oralee, Oralia, Orelie, Oriel, Orielle, Orlena, Orlene*.

ORANGE (English) Orange. Variation: *Orangetta*.

ORELA (Latin) Revelation.

ORENDA (Native American) Magic spell.

ORFHLAITH (Irish) Golden lady. Variations: *Orflath, Oria, Oriana, Oriane, Orianna, Orla, Orlagh, Orlaith, Orlann, Orlene*.

ORIANA (Latin) Sunrise. Variations: *Oraine, Oralia, Orane, Orania, Orelda, Orelle, Oriane*.

ORINO (Japanese) Weaver's loom. Variation: *Ori*.

ORIOLE (English) Bird. Variations: *Auriel, Orella, Oriel, Oriola*.

ORITHNA (Greek) Mythological daughter of the king of Athens.

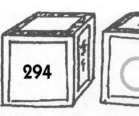

Famous Composers

Even though classical music has a reputation for being somewhat stodgy and old-fashioned, it offers a rich variety of names that any parent today could choose from.

Even though Ludwig, Wolfgang and Felix get most of the attention, the truth is that there are many other composers from whom you could choose a suitable name for your child: Samuel Barber, Aaron Copland, Charles Ives, Amy Beach and Virgil Thomson are just a few. In fact, to emphasize the musical connection even more, you may want to use a composer's full name for your child's first and middle names.

There are hundreds of first and middle names you can select from composers from other countries. Following is a sampling of them:

- Antonin Dvorak
- Benjamin Britten
- Camille Saint-Saens
- Clara Schumann
- Claudio Monteverdi
- Domenico Scarlatti
- Enrique Granados
- François Couperin
- Franz Schubert
- Jean Sibelius
- Jules Massenet
- Karl Czerny
- Orlando Gibbons
- Ralph Vaughan Williams
- Sergei Rachmaninoff
- Thomas Tallis

ORLAIN (African-American) Unknown definition.

ORLENDA (Russian) Female eagle. Variation: *Orlinda*.

ORNICE (Hebrew) Pine tree. Variations: *Orna, Ornit*.

ORPAH (Hebrew) A fawn. Variations: *Ofra, Ofrat, Ofrit, Ophra, Ophrah, Ophrat, Ophrit, Oprah, Orpa, Orpha, Orphy*.

ORQUIDEA (Spanish) Orchid.

ORSA (Latin) Female bear. Variations: *Orsala, Orsaline, Orsel, Orselina, Orseline, Orsola*.

ORTHIA (Greek) Straight.

ORYA (Russian) Peace. Variation: *Oryna*.

OSEN (Japanese) Thousand. One of the more popular Japanese superstitions is that numbers that are rounded off are luckier than odd numbers that are left intact. Osen is one of the many names that grew out of this superstition.

OSEYE (African: Nigerian) Happy one.

OSYKA (Native American: Choctaw) Eagle.

OSYTH (English) Unknown definition.

OTILIE (Czech) Wealthy.

OTTHILD (German) Successful in battle. Variations: *Ottila, Ottilia, Ottilie, Otylia*.

OTYLIA (Polish) Wealth.

OTZARA (Hebrew) Wealth. Variation: *Ozara*.

OUIDA (English) Famous soldier.

OURANIA (Greek) Heavenly one.

OVYENA (Welsh) Unknown definition.

OWENA (Welsh) Well born. Feminine version of Owen.

OYA (Native American: Miwok) To give a name to something.

OZERA (Hebrew) Help.

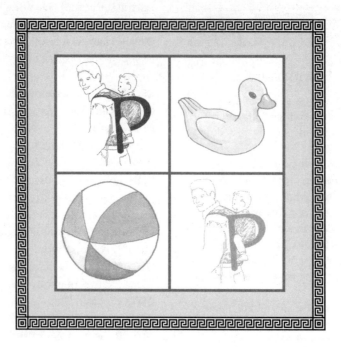

PAAVANA (Hindu) Pure.

PAAVANI (Hindu) The Ganges river.

PACA (Spanish) Frenchman.

PADGETT (Greek) Wisdom. Variations: *Padget, Paget, Pagett, Pagette.*

PADMA (Hindu) The lotus. Variations: *Padmasundara, Padmavati, Padmini.*

PAGE (French) Intern. Page is a girls' name that isn't used too frequently, but when it is, it seems to command a sense of respect and power. Medieval pages were young men who served in the households of the noble families of England and were always male. It is curious therefore that nowadays it is reserved exclusively for girls. The name Page will probably continue to be used sparingly, but when it does appear, it will always pack a punch. Variation: *Paige.*

PAKA (African: Swahili) Kitten.

PALA (Native American) Water.

PALAKIKA (Hawaiian) Hawaiian version of Frances. Variation: *Farakika.*

PALILA (Hawaiian) Bird.

PALLAS (Greek) Another name for Athena, goddess of the arts; goddess of wisdom.

PALMA (Spanish) Palm.

PALMER (English) Palm tree. Last name. Variations: *llmirah, Palima, Pallimirah, Pallma, Pallmara, Pallmyra, Palma, Palmira, Palmyra.*

PALOMA (Spanish) Dove. Variations: *Palloma, Palometa, Palomita, Peloma.*

PAMELA (Greek) Honey. Despite the fame of former *Baywatch* vixen Pamela Anderson, the name actually has quite a number of strong literary connections. Pamela's first known usage was by author Sir Philip Sidney in his work entitled *Arcadia*, which dates from the very end of the 16th century. Next, it appeared in a popular novel entitled *Pamela* by another author, Samuel Richardson, in the middle of the 18th century. Latter-day authors who were actually christened with the name include Pamela Moore and Pamela Hansford Johnson. Other famous women with the diminutive form include poet Pam Ayres and tennis player Pam Shriver. Pamela fell into the top ten list from the 1950s through the 1970s, but then tended to fall off in popularity. Pamela Anderson could very well bring the name back into popular usage once again. Variations: *Pam, Pamala, Pamalia, Pamalla, Pamelia, Pamelina, Pamella, Pamilia, Pamilla, Pammela, Pammi, Pammie, Pammy.*

PANA (Native American) Partridge.

PANDITA (Hindu) Scholar.

PANDORA (Greek) All-gifted. According to Greek legend, Pandora was the name of the very first mortal woman. She had a mysterious box she couldn't stop herself from opening, thus unleashing all of man's troubles and woes. All that was left inside was hope. Variations: *Panda, Pandorra, Panndora.*

PANGIOTA (Greek) All holy.

PANNA (Hindu) Emerald.

PANOLA (Native American: Choctaw) Cotton.

PANPHILA (Greek) She loves all. Variations: *Panfila, Panfyla, Panphyla.*

PANSY (English) Flower. Variations: *Pansey, Pansie.*

PANTHEA (Greek) All the gods.

PANYA (African: Swahili) Mouse.

PANYIN (African: Ghanian) First-born of twins.

PAPINA (Native American: Miwok) Vine on an oak tree.

PARIS (English) The city. In keeping with the current trend toward naming girls after cities, states and regions, Paris is right up there as a name for a baby girl, although I do know of parents who have chosen

this name for their daughter because it was where they believe she was conceived. Variations: *Parisa, Parris, Parrish.*

PARTHENIA (Greek) Virginal. Variations: *Parthania, Parthena, Parthenie, Parthina, Parthine, Pathania, Pathena, Pathenia, Pathina.*

PARTHENOPE (Greek) Ancient mythological figure.

PARVANI (Hindu) Celebration. Variation: *Parvina.*

PARVATI (Hindu) The goddess Devi.

PARVIN (Hindu) Star. Variation: *Parveen.*

PASCALE (French) Child of Easter. Feminine version of Pascal. Variations: *Pascalette, Pascaline, Pascalle, Paschale.*

PASHA (Greek) Of the ocean. Variation: *Palasha.*

PASUA (African: Swahili) Born by Caesarean section.

PATEREKIA (Hawaiian) Aristocrat. Variation: *Pakelekia.*

PATI (Native American: Miwok) Twisting willows.

PATIA (Spanish) Leaf.

PATIENCE (English) Patience. Variations: *Paciencia, Patient.*

PATRICIA (English) Noble. Feminine version of Patrick. Though Patricia has a long, esteemed history dating from the sixth century, when it began to be used within the Catholic church, a surge in Patricia's popularity can clearly be distinguished from the time that one of Queen Victoria's granddaughters was given the name. From there, it basically exploded in both Great Britain and the United States. This fervour lasted until well into the 1970s. As with many other formal names, even though Patricia may be the given name, it's more likely that you'll use one of Patricia's nicknames. And when parents are choosing the name today, they are leaning toward one of the more exotic variations listed here. Famous Patricias include actress Patricia Neal. Variations: *Pat, Patreece, Patreice, Patria, Patric, Patrica, Patrice, Patricka, Patrizia, Patsy, Patti, Pattie, Patty, Tricia, Trish, Trisha.*

PAULA (Latin) Small. Feminine version of Paul. Variations: *Paola, Paolina, Paule, Pauleen, Paulene, Pauletta, Paulette, Paulie, Paulina, Pauline, Paulita, Pauly, Paulyn, Pavla, Pavlina, Pavlinka, Pawlina, Pola, Polcia, Pollie, Polly.*

PAUSHA (Hindu) Month in the Hindu year.

PAVANA (Hindu) Wind. Variation: *Pavani.*

PAX (Latin) Peace.

PAZ (Hebrew) Gold. Variations: *Paza, Pazia, Paziah, Pazice, Pazit, Paziya, Pazya.*

PEAKALIKA (Hawaiian) She brings happiness. Variation: *Beatarisa, Biatirisa.*

PEARL (Latin) Pearl. Variations: *Pearla, Pearle, Pearleen, Pearlena, Pearlette, Pearley, Pearline, Pearly, Perl, Perla, Perle, Perlette, Perley, Perlie, Perly.*

PEDZI (African) Last child.

PEKE (Hawaiian) Bright.

PELA (Hawaiian) Pretty. Variation: *Bela.*

PELAGIA (Greek) The ocean; (Polish) Sea-dweller. Variations: *Pelage, Pelageia, Pelagie, Pelegia, Pelgia, Pellagia.*

PELEKA (Hawaiian) Bright. Variations: *Beke, Bereta.*

PELEKILA (Hawaiian) Primitive. Variations: *Peresekila, Peresila, Perisila.*

PELENAKINO (Hawaiian) Strong as a bear. Variations: *Berenadeta, Berenadino.*

PELIAH (Hebrew) God's miracle. Variation: *Pelia.*

PELIKA (Hawaiian) Peaceful. Hawaiian version of Freda. Variation: *Ferida.*

PELIPA (Native American) Lover of horses.

PELULIO (Hawaiian) Emerald. Variation: *Berulo.*

PEMBA (African) Meteorological power.

PENDA (African: Swahili) Beloved.

PENELOPE (Greek) Bobbin weaver. Penny is a great worldly name that dates back to the ancient Greek myth in which Penelope remained faithful to Ulysses.

The name was taken up in the 16th century and has remained popular ever since, reaching a peak in the 1950s and 1960s. Famous Penelopes include Penelope Cruz and Penelope Keith. Variations: *Lopa, Pela, Pelcia, Pen, Penelopa, Penina, Penine, Penna, Pennelope, Penni, Penny, Pinelopi, Piptisa, Popi.*

PENI (Native American) His mind.

PENINAH (Hebrew) Coral. Variations: *Peni, Penie, Penina, Penini, Peninit.*

PENINIYA (Hebrew) Hen. Variation: *Peninia.*

PEONY (English) Flower.

Watch Those Initials

So you've finally picked the name you want for your new baby. It sounds great with your last name, you've selected a middle name that works well, too, but there's one more thing you should consider:

What do the initials spell out?

Frequently, parents-to-be agonize so much over choosing a name for their baby that once they've settled on a great name, they breathe a huge sigh of relief and forget about it until the birth certificate needs to be signed. Unfortunately, this little oversight of forgetting about what the initials spell out could cause years of agony when your child's name is Tara Imogen Thompson. Think of your grown daughter refusing to wear anything with a monogram or your adult son covering up the monogram on his suitcase before he ever gets to the airport.

So watch those initials. Make sure they don't spell anything offensive or it could call attention to the combination. If you've overlooked this, you may have to start from scratch, but I think it's worth it.

PEPITA (Spanish) God will add. Diminutive feminine form of Joseph. Variations: *Pepa, Peta.*

PERACH (Hebrew) Blossom. Variations: *Perah, Pericha, Pircha, Pirchia, Pirchit, Pirchiya, Pirha.*

PERDITA (Latin) Lost.

PERFECTA (Spanish) Perfect.

PERRY (French) Pear tree; (Greek) Nymph of mountains. Perry started out as a boys' name that was actually a nickname for Peregrine. Parents began to consider the name for their daughters around the middle of the 20th century, but it seems to be so rarely used by either sex that it has remained a gender-neutral name even after all these years. I think that more parents should consider this name, which meets several of the current baby-naming trends. Variations: *Peri, Perrey, Perri, Perrie.*

PERSEPHONE (Greek) The goddess of spring and rebirth.

PERSIS (Latin) From Persia. Variation: *Perssis.*

PETA (Greek) Rock. Feminine version of Peter. Variations: *Petra, Petrice, Petrina, Petrona.*

PETRONELLA (Latin) Roman clan name. Variations: *Pernel, Pernelle, Peronel, Peronelle, Petrina, Petronelle, Petronia, Petronilla, Pier, Pierette.*

PETRONILLA (Scandinavian) Stone. Variations: *Pella, Pernilla, Pernille, Petrine.*

PETULA (Latin) Sassy. Variation: *Petulah.*

PETUNIA (English) Flower.

PHEAKKLEY (Cambodian) Loyal.

PHEDRA (Greek) Bright. Variations: *Faydra, Fedra, Phadra, Phaedra, Phedre.*

PHEODORA (Greek) Gift from God. Feminine version of Theodore.

PHILADELPHIA (Greek) City, brotherly love. Variations: *Philli, Phillie.*

PHILANA (Greek) Lover of people.

PHILANTHA (Greek) Lover of flowers.

PHILBERTA (English) Bright.

PHILIPPA (Greek) Lover of horses. Feminine version of Philip. I know a woman named Philipa. We call her Phil, and I've always wanted to ask her what it was like to live with the name while she was growing up. After all, back in the 1960s, it wasn't cool for a girl to have a boys' name. In her case, however, it's worked out: she's a veterinarian who spends a good part of her day taking care of horses. Is this a case of someone who grew into her name? Variations: *Philipa, Philippine, Phillipina, Pippa, Pippy.*

PHILOMENA (Greek) Beloved. Variations: *Filomena, Philomene, Philomina.*

PHOEBE (Greek) Brilliant. Phoebe was the daughter of Uranus and Gaia. Variations: *Pheabe, Phebe, Pheby, Phobe.*

PHYLLIS (Greek) Green tree branch. Variations: *Philis, Phillis, Philliss, Phillys, Phylis, Phyllida, Phylliss.*

PIA (Latin) Pious.

PIEDAD (Spanish) Devotion.

PILAR (Spanish) Pillar.

PILI (African: Swahili) Second-born.

PILIKIKA (Hawaiian) Strong. Variation: *Birigita.*

PILILANI (Hawaiian) Close to heaven.

PILISI (Greek) branch.

PILUKI (Hawaiian) Leaf.

PINEKI (Hawaiian) Peanut.

PINGA (Hindu) Bronze.

PINGJARJE (Native American: Apache) Small deer.

PINQUANA (Native American: Shoshone) Fragrant.

PIPER (English) Bagpipe player.

PIRENE (Greek) The daughter of the river god, Achelous.

PITA (African) Fourth daughter.

PIXIE (English) Tiny.

PLACIDA (Spanish) Calm. Variation: *Plasida.*

PLEASANCE (English) Pleasure. Variations: *Pleasant, Pleasants, Pleasence*.

POCAHONTAS (Native American: Algonquin) Capricious.

POLETE (Hawaiian) Small. Variations: *Poleke, Polina*.

POLLY (English) Variation of Molly, which in turn is a diminutive form of Mary, which means bitter. In the minds of most people, Polly will forever be connected with the name for a parrot or the irrepressible optimist in the novel by author Eleanor H. Porter, *Pollyanna*. Variations: *Pauleigh, Pollee, Polley, Polli, Pollie, Pollyann, Pollyanna, Pollyanne*.

POLLYAM (Hindu) Goddess of the plague.

POLYXENA (Greek) Very hospitable.

POMAIKAI (Hawaiian) Fortunate.

POMONA (Latin) Apple.

PONI (African) Second daughter.

POPPY (Latin) Flower. A very popular name in Edwardian England which reached a peak in the 1920s despite the associations with the flower and the men who died in the First World War. Variation: *Popi*.

PORTIA (Latin) Roman clan name. Variations: *Porcha, Porscha, Porsche, Porschia, Porsha*.

POSALA (Native American: Miwok) Flower.

PRAGYATA (Hindu) Wisdom.

PRARTHANA (Hindu) Prayer.

PRATIBHA (Hindu) Tolerance.

PRECIOUS (English) Precious. Variations: *Precia, Preciosa*.

PREMA (Hindu) Love.

PREMLATA (Hindu) Vine.

PRIBISLAVA (Czech) To help glorify. Variations: *Pribena, Pribka, Pribuska*.

PRIMA (Latin) First. Variations: *Primalia, Primetta, Primina, Priminia, Primula*.

PRIMAVERA (Italian) Spring.

PRIMROSE (English) First rose.

PRINCESS (English) Royal title. Variations: *Prin, Princesa, Princessa*.

PRISCILLA (English) Old. Once upon a time, Priscilla seemed to have the same kind of reputation as Polly. It was a popular Puritan name and came back into fashion in the 19th century too. Today, however, the widow of Elvis Presley, Priscilla Presley, has given new visibility to this name and singlehandedly altered its reputation from prim and proper to smart and alluring. Variations: *Precilla, Prescilla, Pricilla, Pris, Priscila, Priss, Prissie, Prissilla, Prissy, Prysilla*.

PRISMA (Greek) Cut glass. Variation: *Prusma*.

PRIYA (Hindu) Beloved. Variations: *Priyal, Priyam, Priyanka, Priyasha, Priyata, Priyati*.

PROSERPINE (Roman) Mythological queen of the underworld.

PROTIMA (Hindu) Prominent Indian dancer.

PRUDENCE (Latin) Wariness. Established as one of the 'virtue' names by the Puritans in the 17th century. Variations: *Pru, Prudencia, Prudie, Prudu, Prudy, Prue*.

PRUNELLA (Latin) Small plum. Best known as the name of actress Prunella Scales who co-starred with John Cleese in *Fawlty Towers*.

PSYCHE (Greek) The soul.

PTAYSANWEE (Native American: Sioux) White buffalo.

PUA (Polynesian) Flowering tree.

PUAKAI (Hawaiian) Ocean flower. Variation: *Pua*.

PUAKEA (Hawaiian) White flower.

PUALANI (Hawaiian) Flower. Variation: *Puni*.

PUANANI (Hawaiian) Beautiful flower.

PULUPAKI (Polynesian) Flower wreath.

PURITY (English) Pure.

PURNIMA (Hindu) Full moon.

PYRRHA (Greek) Red.

QUAHAH (Native American: Pueblo) White coral beads.

QUARTILLA (Latin) Fourth.

QUBILAH (Arabic) Agreement.

QUEEN (English) Queen. Variations: *Queena, Queenation, Queeneste, Queenette, Queenie, Queeny.*

QUERIDA (Spanish) Beloved.

QUESTA (French) Hunter.

QUETA (Spanish) Home ruler.

QUIANA (American) Grace. Variation: *Quianna.*

QUINCI (English) The fifth son's estate. Variations: *Quincie, Quincy.*

QUINN (Gaelic) Advisor. Variation: *Quincy.*

QUINTINA (English) Fifth. Quintina and all of its melodious variations are often used when a daughter's birth falls under very specific categories: frequently, a girl named Quintina will either be the fifth child in a family or born on the fifth day of a certain month. Some parents even choose the name when their daughter is born in the month of May, the fifth month of the year. Personally, I'd  reserve it for a daughter who is born in the fifth month, on the fifth day, at 5:55 in the morning. Variations: *Quin, Quinella, Quinetta, Quinette, Quintana, Quintessa, Quintona, Quintonice.*

QUITERIE (French) Peaceful.

RAANANA (Hebrew) Fresh. Variation: *Ranana.*
RABAB (Arabic) Pale cloud.
RABIAH (Arabic) Breeze. Variations: *Rabi, Rabia.*
RACHAV (Hebrew) Large. Variation: *Rahab.*
RACHEL (Hebrew) Lamb. Rachel is essentially one of the oldest names in the Bible, appearing as Rahel, the name of Jacob's second wife. It has proven to be a popular name ever since the Puritans' times in the 1600s. During the Middle Ages, however, Christians wouldn't touch the name since they considered it to be a strictly 'Jewish' name. After the Puritans broke through with its more common use, it remained popular among parents who wished their daughters to eventually emulate the mother of Joseph in the Bible, and as time went on, parents from all walks began to see the beauty in the name. In the 1990s, Rachel consistently appeared in the top twenty names list.

Variations *Rachael, Racheal, Rachele, Rachell, Rachelle, Rae, Raelene, Raquel, Raquela, Raquella, Raquelle.*
RADHA (Hindu) Prosperity; success.
RADHIYA (African: Swahili) Agreeable.
RADINKA (Czech) Active.
RADMILLA (Slavic) Industrious for the people. Variation: *Radmila.*
RADOMIRA (Czech) Glad and famous.
RADOSLAVA (Czech) Glorious and happy.
RADOSLAWA (Polish) Glad for glory. Variation: *Rada.*
RAE (Hebrew) Lamb. Variations: *Raeann, Raelene, Ray, Raye, Rayette.*
RAFA (Arabic) Well-being. Variation: *Rafah.*
RAFAELA (Spanish) God heals. Feminine version of Raphael. Variations: *Rafa, Rafaelia, Rafaella, Rafella, Rafelle, Raffaela, Raffaele, Raphaella, Raphaelle, Refaela, Rephaela.*

RAFYA (Hebrew) God heals. Variations: *Rafia, Raphia.*

RAGHIDA (Arabic) Happy.

RAGNBORG (Scandinavian) Counsel. Variations: *Ragna, Ramborg.*

RAGNILD (German) Power. Variations: *Ragnhild, Ragnhilda, Ragnhilde, Ragnilda, Ranillda, Renilda, Renilde.*

RAI (Japanese) Next. Variation: *Raiko.*

RAIDAH (Arabic) Guide.

RAINBOW (English) Rainbow.

RAINELL (English) Newly created, combination of 'rain' and 'elle'. Variation: *Rainelle.*

RAISA (Hebrew) Rose. Borne by an early Christian martyr put to death in 308. Variations: *Raise, Raisel, Raissa, Raisse, Raizel, Rayzil, Razil.*

RAJA (Arabic) Anticipation. Variations: *Raga, Ragya, Rajya.*

RAJALAKSHMI (Hindu) Goddess of fortune. Variation: *Raji.*

RAJANI (Hindu) Night. Variations: *Rajana, Rajni.*

RAJATA (Hindu) King. Variation: *Raji.*

RAJNANDINI (Hindu) Princess.

RAKU (Japanese) Pleasure.

RALPHINA (English) Wolf-counsellor. Feminine version of Ralph. Variation: *Ralphine.*

RAMAA (Hindu) Lovely. Variations: *Ramana, Ramani.*

RAMIA (African) Fortune-teller.

RAMLA (African: Swahili) Predicts the future.

RAMONA (Hindu) Wise protector. Feminine version of Raymond. Many parents casting around for a suitable name for their daughters will remember Ramona primarily as the impish character in the children's books by author Beverly Cleary.

RAN (Scandinavian) Goddess of the sea.

RANA (Spanish) Frog. Variations: *Raniyah, Ranna, Ranya.*

RANDA (Arabic) Tree.

RANI (Hindu) Queen. Variations: *Rania, Ranique, Ranita.*

RANIELLE (African-American) God is my judge. Variation of Danielle.

RANITA (Hebrew) Song of joy. Variations: *Ranice, Ranit, Ranite, Ranitra, Ranitta.*

RANJANA (Hindu) Beloved.

RANT-CHE-WAI-ME (Iowa) Female pigeon.

RANVEIG (Scandinavian) Housewife. Variation: *Ronnaug.*

RANYA (Hindu) To gaze.

RASHA (Arabic) Gazelle.

RASHEDA (Turkish) Righteous. Feminine version of Rashid. Variations: *Rasheeda, Rasheedah, Rasheida, Rashidah.*

RASIA (Greek) Rose. Variations: *Rasine, Rasya.*

RATHNAIT (Irish) Grace. Variations: *Ranait, Rath.*

RATI (Hindu) Goddess of love. Derived from the Sanskrit for rest or repose.

RATRI (Hindu) Night.

RAVEN (English) The bird. Variation: *Ravenne.*

RAWNIE (Gypsy) Lady.

RAVVA (Hindu) The sun.

RAWIYA (Arabic) Tell a story. Variations: *Rawiyah, Rawya.*

RAYA (Hebrew) Friend.

RAYNA (Hebrew) Song of the Lord. Variations: *Raina, Rana, Rane, Rania, Renana, Renanit, Renatia, Renatya, Renina, Rinatia, Rinatya.*

RAYYA (Arabic) Quenched thirst.

RAZI (Hebrew) Secret. Variations: *Razilee, Razili.*

RAZIAH (Hebrew) Secret of God. Variations: *Razia, Raziela, Razilee, Razili, Raziya.*

RAZIYA (African: Swahili) Agreeable.

REA (English) Manly. Variations: *Rhia, Ria.*

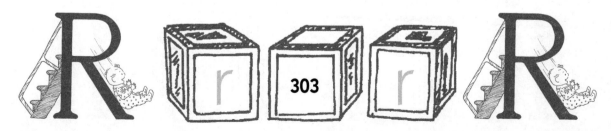

303

REBECCA (Hebrew) Joined together. The first Rebecca known to us was the Biblical wife of Isaac and the mother of Jacob. Other famous Rebeccas since then have been Rebecca of Sunnybrook Farm from Kate Douglas's novel, as well as another literary figure, novelist Rebecca West. Novelist Daphne Du Maurier also wrote a novel called *Rebecca*, later turned into a movie by Alfred Hitchcock. Name-watchers point to Du Maurier's book as the main influence that put Rebecca on the map back in the 1940s. Variations: *Becca, Becky, Reba, Rebbecca, Rebbie, Rebeca, Rebeccah, Rebecka, Rebeckah, Rebeka, Rebekah, Rebekka, Rebekke, Rebeque, Rebi, Reby, Reyba, Rheba.*

REGAN (Irish) Son of the small ruler. Variation: *Reagan.*

REGINA (Latin) Queen. Variations: *Raenah, Raina, Raine, Rainy, Rana, Rane, Rayna, Regena, Reggi, Reggie, Reggy, Regi, Regie, Regiena, Regine, Reginia, Reginna, Reinette, Reyna.*

REHEMA (African: Swahili) Compassion.

REI (Japanese) Appreciation.

REICHANA (Hebrew) Aromatic. Variations: *Rechana, Rehana.*

REIKO (Japanese) Very pleasant child. Variation: *Rei.*

REKHA (Hindu) Line.

REMAZIAH (Hebrew) Sign from God. Variations: *Remazia, Remazya.*

REMEDIOS (Spanish) Help.

REMY (French) Champagne. Variations: *Remi, Remie.*

REN (Japanese) Lotus.

RENA (Hebrew) Melody. Variation: *Reena*

RENÉE (French) Reborn. French names with accent marks appeared to be pretty popular during the 1970s and Renée fit right in. The Latin version of Renée is Renata, and it was commonly used by people in the Roman Empire for their daughters. Somewhere between back then and the 1600s, Renata turned into Renée; Renata rarely appears anymore. Variations: *Renata, Renay, Rene, Renelle, Reney, Reni, Renia, Renie, Renni, Rennie, Renny.*

RENITA (Latin) Defiant. Variation: *Reneeta*

RESEDA (Latin) Flower.

REUBENA (English) Behold a son. Feminine version of Reuben. Variations: *Reubina, Rubena, Rubenia, Rubina, Rubine, Rubyna.*

REUMA (Hebrew) Lofty. Variation: *Raomi.*

REVA (Hindu) Sacred river.

REVAYA (Hebrew) Satisfied. Variation: *Revaia.*

REXANA (Latin) King and grace. Combination of Rex and Anna. Variations: *Rexanna, Rexanne.*

REZA (Czech) Harvest. Variation of Teresa. Variations: *Rezi, Rezka.*

RHEA (Greek) Earth. Variations: *Rhia, Ria.*

RHETA (Greek) Eloquent.

RHIANNON (Welsh) Goddess. Variations: *Rheanna, Rheanne, Rhiana, Rhiann, Rhianna, Rhiannan, Rhianon, Rhuan, Riana, Riane, Rianna, Rianne, Riannon, Riannon, Rianon, Riona.*

RHIANVYEN (Welsh) Fair maiden.

RHODA (Greek) Rose. Of course, the most famous Rhoda that those of us who remember the 1970s know is Rhoda Morgenstern, Valerie Harper's successful TV role. Rhoda's roots are actually Biblical – the name first appeared in the New Testament Book of Acts – and it was commonly used during the late 1800s. Variations: *Rhodante, Rhodanthe, Rhodia, Rhodie, Rhody, Roda.*

RHONDA (Welsh) Grand. Variations: *Rhonnda, Ronda.*

RHONWEN (Welsh) Slender, fair. Variations: *Ronwen, Roweena, Roweina, Rowena, Rowina.*

RHU (Hindu) Pure.

RIA (Spanish) Mouth of a river.

304

RIANE (Irish) Feminine version of Ryan.

RICARDA (Italian) Powerful ruler. Feminine version of Richard. Variations: *Rica, Ricca, Richarda, Richel, Richela, Richele, Richella, Richelle, Richenda, Richenza, Ricki, Rickie, Ricky, Riki, Rikki, Rikky.*

RIDA (Arabic) Content. Variations: *Radeya, Radeyah.*

RIGBORG (Scandinavian) Strong fortification.

RIGMOR (Scandinavian) Powerful courage.

RIHANA (Arabic) Sweet basil.

RIKU (Japanese) Land. Variation: *Rikuyo.*

RILLA (German) Stream. Variations: *Rilletta, Rillette.*

RIMA (Arabic) Antelope.

RIMONA (Hebrew) Pomegranate.

RIN (Japanese) Park.

RINA (English) Newly created.

RINDA (Scandinavian) Ancient mythological figure. Variation: *Rind.*

RIOGHNACH (Irish) Queen. Variation: *Riona.*

RISA (Latin) Laughter. Variations: *Rise, Risha, Riza.*

RISHONA (Hebrew) Initial.

RISSA (English) Nickname for Nerissa, a sea nymph.

RITA (English) Pearl. Diminutive of Margaret. Rita reached its height during the 1940s with the popularity of the actress Rita Hayworth, and it is that association that makes the name seem unfortunately dated today. Other famous Ritas around since Hayworth's heyday have largely been fictional characters: one was lovely Rita, meter maid, from The Beatles' song, and the other is Rita, the patron saint of couples who are having trouble in their marriage. No wonder the name isn't more widely used! Variations: *Reeta, Reta, Rheta, Rhetta.*

RITIKA (Hindu) Active.

RITZPAH (Hebrew) Coal. Variations: *Ritzpa, Rizpah.*

RIVA (Hebrew) Joined. Variations: *Reva, Rivah.*

RIVKA (Hebrew) Noose. Variations: *Rifka, Rifke, Riki, Rivai, Rivca, Rivcka, Rivi, Rivvy.*

ROBERTA (English) Bright fame. Feminine version of Robert. Introduced in the 1870s, it was especially popular in Scotland and the USA, and made popular in 1933 by Jerome Kern's musical *Roberta*. Another famous bearer of the name is US singer Roberta Flack. Variations: *Bobbet, Bobbett, Bobbi, Bobbie, Bobby, Robbi, Robbie, Robby, Robena, Robertena, Robertha, Robertina, Robin, Robina, Robine, Robinette, Robinia, Robyn, Robyna, Rogan, Roynne.*

ROCHELLE (French) Little rock. Variations: *Rochele, Rochell, Rochella, Roshele, Roshelle.*

RODA (Polish) Rose.

RODERICA (German) Famous ruler. Feminine version of Roderick. Variations: *Rica, Roderiqua, Roderique.*

ROHANA (Hindu) Sandalwood. Variation: *Rohanna.*

ROKUKO (Japanese) Sixth-born.

ROLANDA (German) Famous land. Feminine version of Roland. Variations: *Rolande, Rollande, Rolonda, Rolonde.*

ROMA (Italian) Rome.

ROMAINE (French) One from Rome. Variation: *Romayne.*

ROMANA (Polish) Citizen of Rome.

ROMOLA (Latin) Woman from Rome. Variations: *Romella, Romelle, Romi, Romolla, Romula, Romy.*

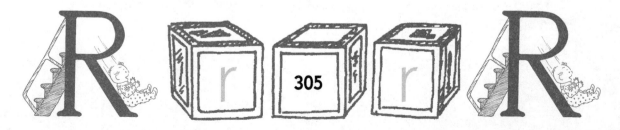

RONA (Scandinavian: Norwegian) Rough isle. Variations: *Rhona, Roana, Ronella, Ronelle, Ronna.*

RONI (Hebrew) Joy is mine. Variations: *Ronia, Ronice, Ronit, Ronli.*

RONIYA (Hebrew) Joy of God. Variations: *Ronela, Ronella, Ronia.*

RONNELL (African-American) Feminine version of Ron. Variations: *Ronell, Ronelle, Ronnel.*

RONNI (English) Strong counsel. Feminine version of Ronald. Variations: *Ronnette, Ronney, Ronnica, Ronny.*

ROSALBA (Latin) White rose.

ROSALIND (Spanish) Pretty rose. Variations: *Rosalina, Rosalinda, Rosalinde, Rosaline, Rosalyn, Rosalynd, Rosalyne, Rosalynn, Roselind, Roselynn, Roslyn.*

ROSAMOND (German) Famous protector. Variation: *Rosamund.*

ROSANNA (English) Combination of Rose and Anna. Variations: *Rosana, Rosannah, Rosanne, Roseana, Roseanna, Roseanna, Roseannah, Rosehannah, Rozanna, Rozanne.*

Greek Mythological Figures

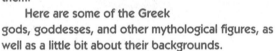

If you have no clue about Greek mythology, the last thing you may want to do is to name your baby after an obscure Greek god that seems to have no relevance to the world today.

But actually, if you take a look at the following list, you'll see that it's not such a bad idea, if you broaden your outlook and allow yourself to find out more. Greek gods and goddesses have been the recipients of some of the most mellifluous names around and have some great stories associated with them.

Here are some of the Greek gods, goddesses, and other mythological figures, as well as a little bit about their backgrounds.

Male Gods

- Adonis: God of beauty.
- Apollo: God of war.
- Ares: God of war.
- Atlas: Held the world on his shoulders.
- Cronos: God of harvests; father of Zeus.
- Eros: God of love.
- Helios: God of the sun.
- Hephaestus: God of fire.
- Hermes: Messenger for the gods.
- Orion: God of the hunt.
- Pan: God of shepherds.
- Pontus: God of the sea.
- Thanatos: God of death.
- Triton: God of the sea.
- Zeus: King of the gods.

Female Gods

- Aphrodite: Goddess of love and beauty.
- Artemis: Goddess of nature.
- Athena: Goddess of wisdom.
- Demeter: Goddess of the earth.
- Eris: Goddess of debate.
- Hera: Queen of the goddesses.
- Hestia: Goddess of the home.
- Iris: Goddess of the rainbow.
- Nike: Goddess of victory.
- Persephone: Goddess of spring and rebirth.
- Rhea: Mother of Zeus.
- Selena: Goddess of the moon.

ROSCHAN (Hindu) Dawn. Variations: *Rochana, Rochani, Roschana, Roshan, Roshana, Roshanara, Roshni.*

ROSCISLAWA (Polish) Glory in conquest.

ROSE (Latin) Flower. A name that has always been popular owing to the fact that is a symbol of the Virgin Mary. It reached a peak in popularity in the late 19th and early 20th century and benefitted from the comeback of flower names in the 1990s, when Rose seemed to be the runaway leader. It has Victorian overtones, it's elegant, and it's also becoming extremely popular as a middle name. Rose should continue to bloom through the rest of this decade and beyond. Variations: *Rosabel, Rosabell, Rosabella, Rosabelle, Rosalee, Rosaley, Rosalia, Rosalie, Rosalin, Rosella, Roselle, Rosetta, Rosette, Rosey, Rosi, Rosie, Rosita, Rosy, Ruza, Ruzena, Ruzenka, Ruzsa.*

ROSELANI (Hawaiian) Heavenly rose.

ROSEMARY (Latin) Dew of the sea. Variations: *Rosemaree, Rosemarey, Rosemaria, Rosemarie.*

ROSSALYN (Scottish) Cape. Feminine version of Ross. Variations: *Rosslyn, Rosslynn.*

ROSTISLAVA (Czech) One who seizes glory. Variations: *Rosta, Rostina, Rostinka, Rostuska.*

ROULA (Greek) Defiant. Variation: *Rula.*

ROXANNE (Persian) Dawn. Variations: *Roxana, Roxane, Roxann, Roxanna, Roxianne, Roxie, Roxy.*

ROYALE (French) Royal. Variations: *Royalene, Royall, Royalle.*

RUANA (Hindu) Indian violin.

RUBY (English) Jewel. Ruby was part of the first wave of jewel names that began to hit at the end of the 19th century. It slowly fell out of fashion during the 20th century. However today, Ruby is slowly beginning to become more popular again. I like it the best among jewel names. Famous Rubys include Ruby Wax and US singer and dancer Ruby Keeler. Variations: *Rube, Rubey, Rubie, Rubye.*

RUCHI (Hindu) Love.

RUCHIKA (Hindu) Attractive.

RUDELLE (German) Famous. Variation: *Rudella.*

RUDRA (Hindu) Plant.

RUFARO (African: Zimbabwean) Happiness.

RUFINA (Latin) Red-haired. Feminine version of Rufus.

RUKAN (Arabic) Confident.

RUKIYA (African: Swahili) To arise.

RUKMINI (Hindu) Golden.

RUNA (Scandinavian) Secret lore. Variation: *Rula.*

RUPAL (Hindu) Beautiful. Variations: *Rupala, Rupali, Rupinder.*

RUQAYYA (Arabic) Arise. Variations: *Ruqayah, Ruqayyah.*

RURI (Japanese) Emerald.

RUSALKA (Czech) Wood nymph.

RUT (Czech) Devoted companion.

RUTA (Hawaiian) Friend.

RU-TAN-YE-WEE-MA (Iowa) Strutting pigeon.

RUTH (Hebrew) Companion. The name of King David's great-grandmother in the Bible. Variations: *Ruthe, Ruthella, Ruthelle, Ruthetta, Ruthi, Ruthie, Ruthina, Ruthine, Ruthy.*

RUWAYDAH (Arabic) Graceful walk.

RYBA (Czech) Fish.

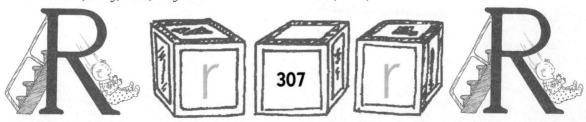

SAADA (African: Swahili) Help.

SABAH (Arabic) Morning. Variation: *Sabah.*

SABETHA (Native American: Ute) Unknown definition.

SABINA (Latin) Roman clan name. Variations: *Savina, Sebina.*

SABRA (Hebrew) Rest. Variations: *Sabrah, Sabre, Sabreen, Sabreena, Sabrena, Sabrinna, Sebra.*

SABRIYYA (Arabic) Patience. Variations: *Sabira, Sabirah, Sabriyyah.*

SACAJAWEA (Native American: Shoshone) Unknown definition. Variation: *Sacagawea.*

SACHI (Japanese) Bliss. Variation: *Sachiko.*

SADA (Japanese) Virginal.

SADHANA (Hindu) Devotion.

SADHBH (Irish) Goodness. Variations: *Sabha, Sabia, Sadbha, Sadhbha, Saidhbhe, Saidhbhin, Sive.*

SADIRA (Persian) Lotus tree.

SADZI (Native American) Sun heart.

SAFA (Arabic) Pure. Variations: *Safiyya, Safiyyah.*

SAFFRON (English) Flower. Variations: *Saffren, Saffronia, Saphron.*

SAFI (Hindu) Friend.

SAFIYYA (African: Swahili) Best friend. Variations: *Safiya, Safiyeh, Safiyyah.*

SAGA (Scandinavian) Ancient mythological figure.

SAGARA (Hindu) Ocean.

SAGE (Latin) Wise. Variations: *Saige, Sayge.*

SAHAR (Arabic) Sunrise.

SAHKYO (Native American: Navajo) Mink.

SAHPOOLY (Native American: Kiowa) Owl.

SAIDAH (Arabic) Happy.

SAINT (English) Holy.

SAKAE (Japanese) Wealth.

SAKARI (Hindu) Sweet one.

SAKI (Japanese) Cape.

SAKTI (Hindu) Energy.

SAKUNA (Hindu) Bird.

SAKURA (Japanese) Cherry.

SALA (Hindu) Sacred tree.

SALALI (Native American: Cherokee) Squirrel.

SALAMA (African: Swahili) Security.

SALE (Hawaiian) Princess. Variations: *Kala, Kalai, Kale, Kela, Sarai, Sera.*

SALENA (Hindu) The moon.

SALHA (Arabic) Ethical.

SALIDA (Hebrew) Happy. Variations: *Selda, Selde.*

SALIHAH (Arabic) Virtuous.

SALIMA (Arabic) Safe. Variations: *Salama, Salimah, Salma.*

SALMA (Hindu) Safe. Variation: *Salima.*

SALOME (Hebrew) Peace. Variations: *Saloma, Salomey, Salomi, Salomia.*

SALOTE (Polynesian) Woman.

SALUS (Latin) The goddess of health.

SALVADORA (Spanish) Saviour.

SALVIA (Latin) Healthy. Variations: *Sallvia, Salvina.*

SALWA (Arabic) Comfort.

SAMALA (Hebrew) Requested of God. Variations: *Samale, Sammala.*

SAMANTHA (English) His name is God. Samantha is widely considered to be the feminine version of Samuel, and though it's been around from the 1600s, when it was used mostly by black Americans, it wasn't until the TV series *Bewitched* first appeared in the 1960s that this name really took off. Samantha was still one of the most popular girls' name in the mid-1990s. Cole Porter also wrote a song called 'I Love You Samantha', which featured in the film *High Society* and also brought prominence to the name. Besides Samantha Stevens, another famous Samantha is Samantha Fox, the former model and singer. Variations: *Sam, Samella, Samentha, Sammantha, Sammee, Sammey, Sammi, Sammie, Sammy, Semanntha, Semantha, Simantha, Symantha.*

SAMAR (Arabic) Night talk.

SAMARA (Hebrew) Protected by God. Variations: *Samaria, Sammara.*

SAMEH (Arabic) One who forgives.

SAMHAOIR (Irish) Unknown definition.

SAMIA (Arabic) Understanding. Variations: *Samihah, Samira, Samirah.*

SAMINA (Hindu) Happy. Variations: *Sameena, Sameenah.*

SAMIRA (Hebrew) Evening talk.

SAMUELA (Hebrew) God has heard. Feminine version of Samuel. Variations: *Samelle, Samuella, Samuelle.*

SAMYA (Arabic) To rise up. Variations: *Samiya, Samiyah.*

SANA (Arabic) To shine. Variations: *Saniyya, Saniyyah.*

SANANDA (Hindu) Joy.

SANCIA (Latin) Holy. Variations: *Sancha, Sanchia, Santsia, Sanzia.*

SANDEEP (Punjabi) Enlightened.

SANDRA (English) Protector of men. Made an early appearance in the 19th century in George Meredith's novel *Sandra Belloni*. In common use in the 1930s and reached a peak of popularity in the 1950s. Feminine version of Alexander. Variations: *Sandee, Sandi, Sandie, Sandrea, Sandria, Sandrina, Sandrine, Sandy, Saundra, Sondra, Zana, Zandra, Zanna.*

SANDYHA (Hindu) Twilight.

SANJANA (Hindu) Gentle.

SANSANA (Hebrew) Leaf of the palm.

SANTANA (Spanish) Saint.

SANTAVANA (Hindu) Hope.

SANURA (African: Swahili) Like a kitten.

SANUYE (Native American: Miwok) Red cloud.

SANYA (Hindu) Born on a Saturday.

SANYOGITA (Hindu) Twelfth-century queen.

SAPATA (Native American) Dancing bear.

SAPPHIRE (Hebrew) Jewel. Variations: *Safira, Saphira, Sapir, Sapira, Sapirit, Sapphira, Sephira.*

SARAB (Arabic) Fantasy.

SARAH (Hebrew) Princess. Sarah was once primarily notable for its popularity as a name for Jewish girls, but in the 1990s Sarah hovered among the most popular names for all daughters. In the Bible, Sarah was the wife of Abraham, and the name has been well-used and well-liked in both Great Baritain and the United States since Puritan times. Famous Sarahs today include Sarah Jessica Parker and Sara Gilbert. Though some fear Sarah will become overused if its popularity continues, others believe that it's destined to be a timeless classic. Variations: *Sadee, Sadie, Sadye, Saidee, Saleena, Salena, Salina, Sallee, Salley, Sallianne, Sallie, Sally, Sallyann, Sara, Sarai, Saretta, Sarette, Sari, Sarita, Saritia, Sarra.*

SARALA (Hindu) Straight.

SARASWATI (Hindu) Lake.

SARAUNLYA (African: Nigerian) Queen.

SARIL (Turkish) Running water.

SARITA (Hindu) River.

SAROJA (Hindu) Born by a lake. Variation: *Saroj.*

SAROJINI (Hindu) Lotuses.

SARONNA (African-American) Unknown definition.

SASHA (Russian) Protector of men. Feminine diminutive version of Alexander. Variations: *Sasa, Sascha.*

SASKIA (Dutch) Unknown definition.

SASONA (Hebrew) Joy.

SASSACUS (Pequot) Unknown definition.

SATIN (French) Satin.

SATINKA (Native American) Magic dancer.

SATO (Japanese) Sugar.

SATORIA (African-American) Unknown definition.

SATYARUPA (Hindu) Truth. Variation: *Satarupa.*

SAUDA (African: Swahili) Dark-skinned.

SAURA (Hindu) Sun worshipper.

SAVANNA (Spanish) Treeless. Place name. Savanna is hot. It seems that in every other film, as well as many books, the name of the female protagonist who must jump through hoops and face seemingly insurmountable challenges all in 300 pages or 90 minutes, is named Savanna. Melinda Dillon played Savannah in the movie *The Prince of Tides*, and Whitney Houston played Savannah in the movie *Waiting to Exhale*. Variations: *Savana, Savanah, Savannah, Savonna, Sevanna.*

SAVITRI (Hindu) Sun god.

SAWA (Japanese) Swamp.

SAWNI (Native American: Seminole) Echo. Variation: *Suwanee.*

SAWSAN (Arabic) Lily.

SAYO (Japanese) Evening birth.

SCARLETT (English) Red. Popularized by Margaret Mitchell's heroine Scarlett O'Hara in *Gone with the Wind*. Variations: *Scarlet, Scarlette.*

SCENANKI (Native American: Creek) Unknown definition.

SEASON (Latin) Season.

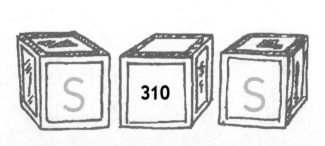

SEBASTIANE (Latin) One from an ancient Roman city. Feminine version of Sebastian. Variations: *Sebastiana, Sebastienne*.

SECUNDA (Latin) Second.

SEDA (Armenian) Forest echo.

SEDNA (Intuit) Goddess of food.

SEEMA (Hebrew) Treasure. Variations: *Seemah, Sima, Simah*.

SEIKO (Japanese) Accomplishment.

SEINI (Polynesian) God is gracious.

SEKELAGA (African: Tanzanian) Rejoice.

SEKI (Japanese) Stone.

SELA (Polynesian) Princess.

SELENA (Greek) Goddess of the moon. I think that many of the girls' names that begin with 'S' and have lots of vowels in them are very pretty and Selena is no exception. Though Selena's first use was as a Greek goddess, the name began to become popular in the 1800s promoted by the British Calvanist leader Selina Hastings, Countess of Huntingdon. Variations: *Celena, Celina, Celinda, Celine, Celyna, Salena, Salina, Salinah, Sela, Selene, Selina, Selinda, Seline, Sena*.

SELIMA (Hebrew) Peace. Variation: *Selimah*.

SEMA (Greek) Omen.

SEMEICHA (Hebrew) Happy. Variation: *Semecha*.

SEMELE (Latin) The mother of Bacchus by Jupiter.

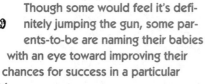

Best Names for Particular Careers

Though some would feel it's definitely jumping the gun, some parents-to-be are naming their babies with an eye toward improving their chances for success in a particular field.

Of course, there are no guarantees, and things will probably change regarding how particular names are perceived twenty or more years from now; but for the most part, here is some advice that may increase your child's chances in reaching the pinnacle of a particular field:

If you'd like your child to be successful in an academic career as a scholar or professor, you should pick a suitably studious or plain name: Susan, Harold, Edward (not Ed), and Ruth all work well.

If you envision a child who is active in the arts, names that are a bit eccentric and volatile but expressive are your best bet: Look at Rula and Zoe for girls and Julian and Damian for boys.

The corporate world is also easy to work out, since, for the most part – at least for now – names that are simple and provide no surprises are best when it comes to fitting within the social structure that is the modern-day office: James and William, Carol and Debbie.

And if you would like your offspring to succeed in a back-to-nature field like gardening or running a health food store, Sophie, Raina, Timothy and Cass are all good choices.

Of course, you run the risk of stereotyping your child, who may or may not agree with your idea of the ideal career. You might end up with a child with a name in a field that is somewhat incongruous, or else a child who will change his or her name in later years owing to a conviction that you erred completely.

Here's a hint, though. A recent corporate research study surveyed students and asked them which women they would choose to hire based on only the names that appeared on their CVs. The truth: women with names that were viewed as unsexy were chosen more often than women with sexy names. Among the so-called 'winners' were Ethel, Florence, Doris and Edna. The 'losers' were Melanie, Jacqueline, Jennifer and Alicia.

SEMIRAMIS (Hebrew) Highest heaven. Variation: *Semira.*

SENALDA (Spanish) Sign.

SENGA (Scottish) Thin.

SEONA (Scottish) God is gracious. Variations: *Seonag, Shona.*

SEOSAIMHTHIN (Irish) To increase.

SEPTEMBER (English) Month.

SEPTIMA (Latin) Seventh.

SERACH (Hebrew) Plenty.

SERAPHINA (Hebrew) Angel. Variations: *Sarafina, Serafina, Serafine, Seraphine, Serofina.*

SERENA (Latin) Serene. If you'd like your daughter to be cute and a little bit mischievous, then Serena is a good name for her. It is sometimes considered to be an aristocratic name and has been selected by the Royal Family in recent times as the name Serena Stanhope, Viscountess Linley. It may also become more popular with the success of the tennis-playing Williams sisters, the younger one being called Serena. Variations: *Sareen, Sarena, Sarene, Sarina, Sarine, Sereena, Serenah, Serenna, Serina.*

SERILDA (German) Female soldier. Variations: *Sarilda, Serhilda, Serhilde, Serrilda.*

SESHETA (Egyptian) The goddess of the stars. Variation: *Seshat.*

SETSU (Japanese) Faithful. Variation: *Setsuko.*

SEVILLA (Spanish) Mythical Roman priestess. Variation: *Seville.*

SHAANANA (Hebrew) Peaceful.

SHACHARIYA (Hebrew) Sunrise. Variations: *Schacharia, Shacharit, Shacharita, Shaharit, Shaharita.*

SHADA (Native American) Pelican.

SHADYA (Arabic) Singer. Variations: *Shadiya, Shadiyah.*

SHAFAYE (African-American) Newly created.

SHAFIQA (Arabic) Sympathetic. Variations: *Shafia, Shafiqah.*

SHAHAR (Arabic) Moonlight.

SHAHINA (Hindu) Gentle.

SHAHIRA (Arabic) Famous. Variation: *Shahirah.*

SHAHNAZ (Hindu) Proud king.

SHAHRAZAD (Arabic) One who lives in the city. Variations: *Shahrizad, Sheherazad, Sheherazade.*

SHAILA (Hindu) Small mountain.

SHAINA (Hebrew) Beautiful. Variations: *Shaine, Shanie, Shayna, Shayne.*

SHAITA (African-American) Newly created.

SHAJUAN (African-American) Newly created.

SHAJUANA (African-American) Newly created.

SHAKA (African-American) Newly created. Variation: *Chaka.*

SHAKEENA (African-American) Newly created. Variation: *Shakina.*

SHAKELA (African-American) Newly created.

SHAKIA (African-American) Newly created. Variation: *Shakeya.*

SHAKILAH (African-American) Newly created.

SHAKIRA (African-American) Newly created. Variations: *Shakera, Shaketa, Shakirah, Shakirra.*

SHAKITA (African-American) Newly created. Variation: *Shaquita.*

SHAKONDA (African-American) Unknown definition.

SHAKTI (Hindu) Divine woman.

SHAKUNTALA (Hindu) Bird.

SHALANDA (African-American) Newly created. Variation: *Shalinda.*

SHALANE (African-American) Newly created.

SHALAUN (African-American) Newly created.

SHALAY (African-American) Newly created. Variation: *Shalaya.*

SHALEELA (African-American) Newly created. Variations: *Shaleelah, Shalila.*

SHALENA (African-American) Newly created.

SHALETA (African-American) Newly created. Variation: *Shaletta.*

SHALIKA (African-American) Newly created.

SHALISA (African-American) Newly created.

SHALONDA (African-American) Newly created. Putting the prefix 'Sha-' before the suffix of a popular name – like 'Londa' – or placing it before an independent name – like 'Linda' – is another popular way that African-Americans are creating new names for their daughters. Though the 'La-' prefix seems to be more popular, 'Sha-' presents an original, though not entirely unfamiliar, way to create a new name.

SHALONDE (African-American) Newly created.

SHALVAH (Hebrew) Peace. Variation: *Shalviya.*

SHALYN (African-American) Newly created.

SHAMEENA (Hindu) Beautiful.

SHAMICA (African-American) Newly created. Variations: *Shameeka, Shameka, Shamika, Shamikah.*

SHAMIRA (Hebrew) Protector.

SHAMITA (African-American) Newly created.

SHAMMARA (Arabic) Prepare for battle.

SHANA (English) Diminutive of Shannon. Variations: *Shanae, Shanay.*

SHANASA (Hindu) Wish.

SHANDA (African-American) Newly created.

SHANDRA (African-American) Variation of Sandra.

SHANEA (African-American) Newly created.

SHANEEN (African-American) Newly created.

SHANEIKA (African-American) Newly created. Variations: *Shaneka, Shanekia, Shanequa.*

SHANELLE (African-American) Newly created.

SHANETHA (African-American) Newly created.

SHANETHIS (African-American) Newly created.

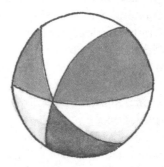

SHANETTA (African-American) Newly created.

SHANETTE (African-American) Newly created.

SHANI (African: Swahili) Marvellous.

SHANICE (African-American) Newly created. Variations: *Shaneice, Shanese, Shaniece, Shanise, Shannice.*

SHANIDA (African-American) Newly created.

SHANIKA (African-American) Newly created. Variations: *Shaneeka, Shaneeke, Shanicka, Shanikah, Shaniqua, Shanique, Shenika.*

SHANINGO (Native American: Algonquin) Beautiful one. Variation: *Shenango.*

SHANISHA (African-American) Newly created.

SHANITA (African-American) Newly created.

SHANITHA (African-American) Newly created.

SHANITRA (African-American) Newly created.

SHANIYA (African-American) Newly created.

SHANNON (Irish) Ancient. Though Shannon is thoroughly Irish in its origin, it has primarily only been used as a last name in that country. It is often assumed that it comes from the name of the Irish river. It seems to have made its debut as a first name in the 1950s and is today much more common in Canada and USA than elsewhere. Variations: *Shanan, Shann, Shanna, Shannah, Shannan, Shannen, Shannie, Shanon.*

SHANTAINA (African-American) Newly created. Variations: *Shantainah, Shantayna, Shantaynah.*

SHANTEKA (African-American) Newly created.

SHANTIA (African-American) Newly created.

SHANTILLI (African-American) Newly created.

SHANTINA (African-American) Newly created.

SHANTRICE (African-American) Newly created.

SHAPIRA (Hebrew) Good.

SHAPPA (Native American) Red thunder.

SHARADA (Hindu) Mature. Variation: *Sharda.*

SHARAI (Hebrew) Princess. Variation of Sarah. Variations: *Shara, Sharayah.*

SHARAMA (African-American) Unknown definition. Variations: *Sharamah, Shirama.*

SHARANEE (Hindu) Guardian. Variations: *Sharanya, Sharna.*

SHARDA (English) Runaway. Variations: *Sade, Shardae, Sharday, Sharde.*

SHARIFA (Arabic) Noble. Variations: *Sharifah, Sharufa, Sherifa, Sherifah*

SHARLENE (German) Woman. Feminine version of Charles. Relatively recently taken up, dating only to the middle of the 20th century. It was popular in the 1980s as Sharlene was the name of Kylie Minogue's character in *Neighbours*. Variations: *Sharleen, Sharleyne, Sharlina, Sharline, Sharlyne.*

SHARLON (African-American) Variation of Sharon.

Advantages and Disadvantages of Unusual Names

No matter what name you choose for your baby, whether it's one of the more popular names around or one nobody has ever heard of, there are going to be both pros and cons to the name. And the more unusual the name is, the more regularly you and your child will be made aware of it as you encounter mispronunciations and questions about its spelling or what it means.

This is the first major disadvantage to having an unusual name. The second is that your child will be made to feel a bit different from everyone else in his or her class. Some kids, of course, will take pride in their uniqueness from an early age, but most don't. The flip side is that if you give your baby a name that is pretty common, then he or she will probably complain that everyone else has it. So, in a way, no matter what you choose, you should know in advance that you can't win.

In the end, I recommend selecting a name that is different, but yet not *too* different. This can be a difficult balance to achieve, but after you try out several names that you feel fall into this category, your instinct tends to take over – you'll know it when a name works for you and your baby.

SHARMAINE (English) Roman clan name. Variations: *Sharma, Sharmain, Sharman, Sharmane, Sharmayne, Sharmian, Sharmine, Sharmyn.*

SHARON (Hebrew) A plain. The name features in the Bible as the name of a valley in Palestine famed for its natural beauty. Sharon is a pretty name that feels just a bit dated, since it regularly appeared on lists of the top twenty most popular girls' names in the 1940s, 1950s and 1960s. Variations: *Sharan, Sharen, Sharin, Sharona, Sharonda, Sharone, Sharran, Sharren, Sharron, Sharronda, Sharronne, Sharyn, Sheren, Sheron, Sherryn.*

SHASTA (Native American) Name of a mountain.

SHATARA (Arabic) Hard-working.

SHATHA (Arabic) Perfume.

SHAUNA (English) God is good. Feminine variation of John. Variations: *Shaunda, Shaune, Shauneen, Shaunna, Shawna, Shawnda, Shawnna.*

SHAUNDA (African-American) Newly created. Variations: *Shawnda, Shawndah, Shonda, Shondah.*

SHAVONDA (African-American) Unknown definition.

SHAVONNE (Hebrew) God is good. Feminine variation of John. Variations: *Shavon, Shavone, Shevon, Shevonne, Shivonne, Shyvon, Shyvonne.*

SHAWANNAH (African-American) Unknown definition.

SHAWN (Hebrew) God is good. Another feminine variation of John. Variations: *Sean, Shawnee, Shawni.*

SHAYLEEN (African-American) Unknown definition.

SHEA (Hebrew) Request. Variations: *Shay, Shayla, Shaylee.*

SHEAUGA (Native American: Iroquois) Raccoon.

SHEBA (Hebrew) Pledged daughter. Short for Bathsheba.

SHEELA (Hindu) Gentle. Variation: *Sheeli.*

SHEINA (Hebrew) Beautiful. Variations: *Shaina, Shaindel, Shaine, Shana, Shayna, Shayndel, Sheindel, Shona, Shoni, Shonie.*

SHEKEDA (Hebrew) Almond tree. Variations: *Shekedia, Shekediya.*

SHELAVYA (Hebrew) To gather. Variation: *Shelavia.*

SHELBY (English) Estate on a ledge. Shelby is most commonly thought of as a name for boys and as a last name, but it was one of the hottest names in the mid-1990s for baby girls. Julia Roberts played a woman named Shelby in the movie *Steel Magnolias,* and the rest is history. Variations: *Shelbee, Shelbey, Shellby.*

SHELIYA (Hebrew) My God. Variations: *Sheli, Shelia, Shelli.*

SHELLEY (English) Meadow on a ledge. In the mid-19th century it emerged as a first name under the influence of poet Percy Bysshe Shelley. It enjoyed a peak in popularity in the1970s and 1980s, then went into decline. Well-known actresses Shelley Winters and Shelley Long share this name. Variations: *Shellee, Shelli, Shellie, Shelly.*

SHENANDOAH (Native American: Algonquin) Beautiful girl from the stars.

SHERA (Hebrew) Light.

SHERICE (American) A plain. Variations: *Sharice, Shericia.*

SHERIDA (English) Feminine version of Sheridan. Last name. Variation: *Sheridawn.*

SHERIKA (Arabic) Easterner.

SHEVA (Hebrew) Pledge.

SHIFA (Hebrew) Plenty.

SHIFRAH (Hebrew) Pretty. Variations: *Schifra, Shifra.*

SHIKA (Japanese) Deer.

SHILO (Hebrew) Biblical site in Israel.

SHILRA (Hebrew) Lovely. Variations: *Schilra, Shilrah.*

SHIMONA (Hebrew) To listen. Variations: *Simeona, Simona.*

SHIMRIAH (Hebrew) God protects. Variations: *Shimra, Shimria, Shimrit, Shimriya.*

SHINA (Japanese) Loyal. Variation: *Shinako.*

SHINO (Japanese) Bamboo.

SHIRAH (Hebrew) Song. Variations: *Shira, Shiri, Shirit.*

SHIRIN (Hindu) Sweet. Variation: *Shirina.*

SHIRLEY (English) Bright meadow. Though Shirley was a common name for boys from Puritan times all the way through to the mid-1800s, two female Shirleys – almost a century apart – helped to turn the tide. The first was a novel by Charlotte Bronte entitled *Shirley,* and the second was Shirley Temple. Though theirs is an uncommon name today, a number of famous Shirleys from decades past helped the name to remain popular throughout the 1960s: Shirley Jones, Shirley Bassey, Shirley MacLaine, and Shirley Horne. Variations: *Shirlean, Shirleen, Shirlene, Shirlynn, Shurly.*

SHIRLI (Hebrew) My song. Variation: *Shirlee.*

SHIZU (Japanese) Quiet. Variations: *Shizue, Shizuko, Shizuyo.*

SHOBHANA (Hindu) Beautiful. Variations: *Shobha, Shobbini.*

SHOMERA (Hebrew) Protect. Variations: *Shomria, Shomriah, Shomrit, Shomriya, Shomrona.*

SHONA (Irish) God is good. Feminine variation of John. Variations: *Shonah, Shone.*

SHONAK (Native American: Pima) Creek.

SHOSHANA (Hebrew) Lily. Variations: *Shosha, Shoshanah, Shoshanna.*

SHRILEKHA (Hindu) Good writing.

SHU (Chinese) Tender.

SHUALA (Hebrew) Fox.

SHUKRIYA (Arabic) Thanks. Variation: *Shukriyyah.*

SHUKURA (African: Swahili) Grateful. Variation: *Shukuma.*

SHULAMIT (Hebrew) Peaceful. Variations: *Shelomit, Shlamit, Shula, Shulamith, Sula, Sulamith.*

SHUMANA (Native American) Rattlesnake girl. Variation: *Shuma.*

SHUWANI (African-American) Newly created.

SHYAMA (Hindu) Dark beauty.

SHYLA (Hindu) The goddess Parvati.

SIANY (Irish) Healthy. Variations: *Slaine, Slainie, Slania.*

SIBETA (Native American: Miwok) Fishing under a rock.

SIBONGILE (African: Zimbabwean) Appreciation.

SIBYL (Greek) Seer, oracle. When some people hear the name Sibyl today, they may think of the woman with multiple personality disorder. More than a century earlier, however, a novel written by Benjamin Disraeli entitled *Sybil* helped to popularize the name. Actress Cybill Shepherd has also helped to add some glamour to the name in recent years. Variations: *Sibbell, Sibel, Sibell, Sibella, Sibelle, Sibilla, Sibyll, Sibylla, Sybel, Sybella, Sybelle, Sybil, Sybill, Sybilla, Sybille, Sybyl.*

SIDONIE (French) From Sidon, a town in the ancient Middle East. The French author Colette's full name was Sidonie Gabrielle Colette. Variations: *Sidaine, Sidonia, Sidony, Sydonia, Syndonia.*

SIDRA (Latin) Stars.

SIERRA (English) Mountain. Variation: *Siera.*

SIF (Scandinavian) Relationship. Variation: *Siv.*

SIGELE (African: Malawian) Left.

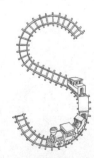

SIGFREDA (German) Peaceful victory. Feminine version of Sigfried. Variations: *Sigfreida, Sigfrida, Sigfrieda, Sigfryda.*

SIGNE (Scandinavian: Norwegian) Beautiful. Variations: *Signa, Signild, Signilda, Signilde.*

SIGNY (Scandinavian) New victory. Variations: *Signe, Signi.*

SIGOURNEY (English) Unknown definition.

SIGRID (Scandinavian: Norwegian) Beautiful victory. Variation: *Siri.*

SIGRUN (Scandinavian) Secret victory.

SIGYN (Scandinavian) Victory.

SIHAM (Arabic) Arrow.

SIHU (Native American) Flower.

SIKO (African) Crying.

SILENCE (English) Quiet.

SILJA (Scandinavian) Blind.

SILPE (Native American: Flathead) Unknown definition.

SILVA (Latin) Forest. Variations: *Silvaine, Silvana, Silvania, Silvanna, Silvia, Silviana.*

SIMCHA (Hebrew) Joy.

SIMI (Native American: Chumash) Wind valley.

SIMONE (French) God listens. Feminine version of Simon. Simone may initially resemble Renée, since it was a French name that was popular in the 1970s, but I think Simone has a much more timeless quality, perhaps owing to the actress Simone Signoret and the author Simone de Beauvoir. Look for the name to become more popular in the coming years. Variations: *Simona, Simonetta, Simonette, Simonia, Simonina, Symona, Symone.*

SINA (Irish) God is good. Variations: *Sinah.*

SINOPA (Native American: Blackfoot) Fox.

SIPETA (Native American) Fishing.

SIRENA (Greek) One who gets caught up. Variations: *Sireena, Sirene, Syrena.*

SISIKA (Native American) Swallow.

SISILIA (Polynesian) Blind.

SISSY (English) Blind. Nickname for Cecilia. Variations: *Sissee, Sissey, Sissi, Sissie.*

SITA (Hindu) The goddess of agriculture. Variations: *Seeta, Seetha, Siti.*

SITI (African: Swahili) Lady.

SIVANA (Hebrew) Ninth month of the Jewish calendar.

SIXTEN (Scandinavian) Victory stone.

SJOFN (Scandinavian) Love.

SKYLER (Dutch) Shelter. Variations: *Schuyler, Skye.*

SMASHI (Hindu) Moonbeam. Variations: *Shashibala, Shashini.*

SNANA (Native American: Sioux) Ringing sounds.

SNOWDROP (English) Flower.

SOBESLAVA (Czech) To overtake glory. Variations: *Sobena, Sobeska.*

SOCORRO (Spanish) Help.

SOFRONIA (Greek) Wise.

SOLANA (Spanish) Sunshine. Variations: *Solenne, Solina, Soline, Souline, Soulle, Zelena, Zelene, Zelia, Zelie, Zelina, Zeline.*

SOLANGE (French) Dignified. Name of a ninth-century saint. Variation: *Solance.*

SOLEDAD (Spanish) Solitude. Variation: *Sola.*

SOLVEIG (Scandinavian) House of strength. Variations: *Solvag, Solve, Solvig.*

SOMA (Hindu) Moon.

SONA (Hindu) Gold. Variations: *Sonal, Sonala, Sonali, Sonika, Sonita.*

SONIA (English) Wisdom. Variation of Sophia. Variations: *Sonja, Sonya.*

SOOK (Korean) Purity.

SOOK-JOO (Korean) Pure gem.

SOON-BOK (Korean) Tender.

Roman Mythological Figures

Like their Greek counterparts, Roman gods and other mythological figures have long influenced how we see each other and how we view the ancient world that has shaped so much of our present-day thought. Roman mythological figures have provided us with names that are ubiquitous. They are names not only for people but also for the planets (Mars and Venus).

Following are some of the more common baby names that parents can choose for their little gods and goddesses:

Male Names

- Bacchus: God of wine.
- Cupid: God of love.
- Faunus: God of shepherds; Roman counterpart of Pan.
- Hercules: Jove's son.
- Janus: God of doorways.
- Jove: King of the gods; Roman counterpart of Zeus.
- Jupiter: God of all.
- Mars: God of war.
- Mercury: Messenger for the gods.
- Neptune: God of the sea.
- Remus: Brother of Romulus.
- Romulus: Founder of Rome.
- Saturn: God of harvests; father of Jove.
- Sol: God of the sun.
- Ulysses: King of Ithaca.
- Vulcan: God of fire.

Female Names

- Aurora: Goddess of sunrise.
- Ceres: Goddess of farming.
- Diana: Goddess of the moon and the hunt.
- Flora: Goddess of flowers.
- Fortuna: Goddess of fate and fortune.
- Juno: Queen of the goddesses.
- Latona: Mother of Diana and Apollo by Zeus.
- Luna: Goddess of the moon.
- Minerva: Goddess of wisdom.
- Pomona: Goddess of fruit trees.
- Terra: Goddess of the earth.
- Vesta: Goddess of the home.
- Victoria: Goddess of victory.

SOPHEARY (Cambodian) Lovely.

SOPHIA (Greek) Wisdom. Sophia and its close relation Sophie both zoomed onto the top ten list in the United States and Great Britain in the 1990s. The names have had a great deal of exposure from celebrities, starting with the seemingly ageless Sophia Loren, continuing with the novel and film *Sophie's Choice*, and, in the 1990s, model Sophie Dahl. Sophie holds a slight edge over Sophia in popularity. Variations: *Sofi, Sofia, Soficita, Sofka, Sofya, Sophey, Sophie, Sophy, Zofe, Zofia, Zofie, Zofka, Zosha, Zosia.*

SOPHRONIA (Greek) Sensible, prudent. Variations: *Soffrona, Sofronia.*

SOPORTEVY (Cambodian) Angelic.

SORA (Native American) Songbird.

SORAYA (Persian) Unknown definition.

SORCHA (Irish) Clear.

SOREKA (Hebrew) Vine.

SORREL (English) Herb. Variation: *Sorrell, Sorrelle.*

SOSO (Native American) Squirrel eating a nut.

SPERANZA (Italian) Hope.

SPRING (English) Spring.

SRI (Hindu) Wealth. Variations: *Shree, Shri.*

STACY (Greek) Resurrection. Diminutive of Anastasia. Variations: *Stace, Stacee, Stacey, Staci, Stacia, Stacie, Stasee, Stasia.*

STANISLAVA (Czech) Glorious government. Variations: *Stana, Stanuska, Stinicka.*

STAR (English) Star. Variations: *Starla, Starlene, Starr.*

STARLING (English) Bird.

STELLA (Latin) Star.

STEPANA (Czech) Crown.

STEPHANIE (English) Crown. Feminine version of Stephen. Stephanie is turning into one of those perennially popular names. It has a timeless quality that parents like and sounds like a name that will fit the shy, retiring girl as well as the active and more outgoing daughter. Famous Stephanies include Princess Stephanie, singer/actress Stephanie Mills, and Stefanie Powers. When Stephanie first began to become popular back in the 1970s, few people would have foreseen that the name would still be hot decades later, as it regularly appears on the list of the top twenty-five names for girls. Variations: *Stefania, Stefanie, Steffi, Stepania, Stepanie, Stephana, Stephanine, Stephannie, Stephena, Stephene, Stepheney, Stephenie, Stephine, Stephne, Stephney, Stevana, Stevena, Stevey, Stevi, Stevie.*

STOCKARD (English) Last name.

STORM (English) Storm. Variations: *Stormi, Stormie, Stormy.*

SUBIRA (African: Swahili) Patience.

SUDARSHANA (Hindu) Good eyesight.

SUGI (Japanese) Cedar tree.

SUHAD (Arabic) Insomnia. Variations: *Suhair, Suhar, Suhayr.*

SUHAILA (Hindu) Star. Variation: *Suhayila.*

SUHAILAH (Arabic) Gentle.

SUJATA (Hindu) Noble.

SUKEY (English) Lily. Diminutive of Susan. Variations: *Suke, Sukee, Suki, Sukie, Suky.*

SUKOJI (African) First daughter born after a son.

SULA (Icelandic) Large bird.

SULAKHNA (Hindu) The name of the wife of the founder of the Sikh religion.

SULETU (Native American: Miwok) Flight.

SULWEN (Welsh) Bright sun. Variation: *Sulwyn.*

SUMA (African: Tanzanian) Ask.

SUMATI (Hindu) Unity. In ancient times used mainly as a boys' name, but today it is almost exclusively female.

SUMI (Japanese) Clear.

319

SUMIKO (Japanese) Charcoal.

SUMMER (English) The season. Variations: *Somer, Sommer.*

SUNAYANA (Hindu) Beautiful eyes. Variation: *Sunayani.*

SUNDARI (Hindu) Beautiful. Variation: *Sundara.*

SUN-HI (Korean) Loyalty.

SUNI (Native American) Zuni Indian.

SUNITA (Hindu) Well-behaved.

SUNKI (Native American) Successful hunter.

SUNNIVA (Scandinavian) Gift of the sun. Variations: *Synnova, Synnove.*

SUNSHINE (English) Sun. Variations: *Sunnie, Sunni, Sunita, Sunny.*

SURAGANA (Hindu) Divine.

SURATA (Hindu) Joy.

SURI (Hindu) Knife.

SURINA (Hindu) Goddess.

SURYA (Hindu) Sun god.

SUSAN (Hebrew) Lily. Susan today tends to appear more frequently as a middle name than as a first name, but some of its exotic variations are beginning to be used more often. Variations: *Susann, Susanna, Susannah, Susanne, Susetta, Susette, Susi, Susie, Susy, Suzan, Suzane, Suzanna, Suzannah, Suzanne, Suzetta, Suzette, Suzi, Suzie, Suzy, Zsa Zsa, Zusa, Zuza.*

SUSHANTI (Hindu) Silence.

SUSHOBHANA (Hindu) Beautiful.

SUTKI (Native American) A broken clay pot.

SUZU (Japanese) Bell.

SUZUKI (Japanese) Little bell tree. Variations: *Suzue, Suzuko.*

SUZUME (Japanese) Sparrow.

SVANHILD (Scandinavian) Battle swan.

SVANNT (Scandinavian) Slender.

SVEA (Scandinavian) Kingdom.

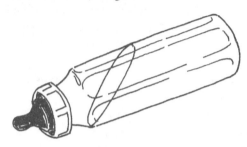

SVETLANA (Czech) Star. Variations: *Svetla, Svetlanka, Svetluse, Svetluvska.*

SWARUP (Hindu) Nehru's mother.

SWOOSIE (American) Newly created. Definition unknown. Variations: *Swoozie, Swoozy.*

SYDNEY (French) Feminine version of Sidney. Saint Denis. Variations: *Sydnie, Sydny.*

SYLVIA (Latin) From the forest. According to legend Rhea Silvia was the mother of Romulus and Remus, the founders of Rome. Variations: *Silvana, Silvia, Silvianne, Silvie, Sylva, Sylvana, Sylvanna, Sylvee, Sylvie.*

SYONA (Hindu) Happy.

SYREETA (Arabic) Companion.

TABIA (African: Swahili) Talented.

TABINA (Arabic) Follower of Mohammed.

TABITHA (English) Gazelle. About the only character in the hit TV series *Bewitched* whose name hasn't caught on among baby-naming parents is the irrepressible Darren. As with Samantha, the show was singlehandedly responsible for promoting the name Tabitha into popular culture. It continues to be used quite frequently, even today, all these years later. Variations: *Tabatha, Tabbitha, Tabby, Tabetha, Tabotha, Tabytha.*

TACEY (English) Quiet. Variations: *Tace, Tacita.*

TACI (Native American) Tub.

TADEWI (Native American: Omaha) Wind. Variation: *Tadi.*

TADITA (Native American) Runner. Variation: *Tadeta.*

TAFFY (Welsh) Beloved.

TAGHRID (Arabic) Singing bird.

TAHCAWIN (Native American: Sioux) Doe.

TAHIRA (Arabic) Pure. Variation: *Tahirah.*

TAHIYYA (Arabic) Welcome. Variation: *Tahiyyah.*

TAHNEE (English) Little one.

TAIMA (Native American: Fox) Thunder. Variations: *Taimah, Taiomah.*

TAIN (Native American: Omaha) New moon. Variation: *Tainee.*

TAIPA (Native American) Quail.

TAIWO (African: Nigerian) First-born of twins.

TAKA (Japanese) Honourable.

TAKALA (Native American: Hopi) Cornstalk. Variation: *Takalah.*

TAKARA (Japanese) Treasure.

TAKAYREN (Native American: Tlingit) Commotion.

TAKEKO (Japanese) Bamboo child.

TAKENYA (Native American: Miwok) Falcon in flight.

TAKI (Japanese) Waterfall.

TAKIA (Arabic) Worshipper.

TAKUHI (Armenian) Queen. Variation: *Takoohi*.

TALA (Native American) Wolf.

TALAL (Hebrew) Dew. Variation: *Talila*.

TALASI (Native American) Cornflower.

TALE (African: Botswana). Green.

TALIA (Hebrew) Dew. Talia is a sweet and unique name that its fans feel is terribly underexposed. Some people are familiar with the name through the actress Talia Shire, who appeared in many of the *Rocky* films. However, its history is a bit loftier: in the Old Testament, Talia was the name of one of the angels who escorted the Sun from Dawn to Dusk. Variations: *Talie, Talley, Tallie, Tally, Talora, Talya, Thalie, Thalya*.

TALIBA (Arabic) Seeker of knowledge. Variation: *Talibah*.

TALISA (African-American) Variation of Lisa. Variation: *Telisa*.

TALISE (Native American: Creek) Beautiful water.

TALITHA (English) Girl. Variations: *Taleetha, Taletha, Talicia, Talisha, Talita*.

TALLIS (English) Forest.

TALLULAH (Native American: Choctaw) Leaping water. The most famous bearer of the name has been actress Tallulah Bankhead. Variations: *Tallula, Talula, Talulah, Talulla*.

TALMA (Hebrew) Hill.

TALUTAH (Native American: Sioux) Red.

TALYA (Hebrew) Lamb. Variation: *Talia*.

TAM (Vietnamese) Heart.

TAMA (Japanese) Jewel.

TAMAH (Hebrew) Marvel. Variation: *Tama*.

TAMAKI (Japanese) Bracelet. Variations: *Tamako, Tamayo*.

TAMANNA (Hindu) Want.

TAMARA (Hebrew) Palm tree. Variations: *Tama, Tamah, Tamar, Tamarah, Tamarra, Tamera, Tami, Tamma, Tammara, Tammee, Tammera, Tammey, Tammie, Tammy, Tamor, Tamour, Tamra, Thamar, Thamara, Thamarra*.

TAMAS (Hindu) Night. Variations: *Tamasa, Tamasi, Tamasvini*.

TAMASINE (English) Twin. Feminine version of Thomas. Variations: *Tamasin, Tamsin, Tamsyn, Tamzen, Tamzin*.

TAMI (Japanese) People. Variations: *Tamie, Tamiko*.

TAMIKA (Japanese) Child of the people. Variations: *Tamike, Tamiko, Tamiya, Tamiyo*.

TAMOHARA (Hindu) The sun.

TAMRIKA (African-American) Newly created. Variation: *Tamreeka*.

TANAKA (Japanese) Swamp dweller.

TANAY (African-American) Newly created. Variation: *Tanee*.

TANAYA (Hindu) Daughter. Variation: *Tanuja*.

TANE (Japanese) Seed.

TANI (Japanese) Valley.

TANISHA (African-American) Newly created. Variations: *Taneesha, Taneisha, Tanesha, Taneshea, Tanicha, Taniesha, Tanitia, Tannicia, Tannisha, Tenecia, Teneesha, Teneisha, Tenesha, Teniesha, Tenisha, Tinecia, Tiniesha, Tynisha*.

TANITH (Irish) Estate. Variations: *Tanita, Tanitha*.

TANNISHTHA (Hindu) Devoted.

TANSY (Greek) Immortality.

TANVI (Hindu) Young woman.

TAO (Vietnamese) Apple.

TAPASYA (Hindu) Bitter.

TAQIYYA (Arabic) Devotion. Variations: *Takiyah, Takiyya, Takiyyah, Taqiyyah*.

TARA (Irish) Hill. Of course, the most famous Tara around was the name of the estate in *Gone With the Wind* inherited by Scarlett O'Hara. The name of her home seems to have served as the catalyst for the increasing presence of this name in the United States and in England. British audiences in the 1960s were equally likely to know the name from the character in the television series *The Avengers*. Today the likes of Tara Palmer-Tompkinson and actress Tara Fitzgerald may be responsible for another surge in popularity. Also a common name for males and females in India. Variations: *Tarah, Taran, Tareena, Tarena, Tarin, Tarina, Tarra, Tarrah, Tarren, Tarryn, Taryn, Taryna, Teryn.*

TARAL (Hindu) Rippling.

TARANI (Hindu) Light. Variation: *Tarini.*

TAREE (Japanese) Tree branch.

TARIKA (Hindu) Star.

TARJA (African-American) Unknown definition.

TARLAM (Hindu) Flowing,

TARUB (Arabic) Cheerful.

TARUNIKA (Hindu) Girl.

TASHA (Russian) Christmas. Diminutive of Natasha. Variations: *Tashina, Tashka, Tasia.*

TASHANEE (African-American) Unknown definition.

TASHINA (African-American) Unknown definition. Variations: *Tasheena, Tasheenah, Tashinah.*

TASIDA (Native American) Rides a horse.

TASINA SAPEWIN (Native American: Oglala Sioux) Black blanket.

TASMINE (English) Twin. Feminine version of Thomas. Variation: *Tasmin.*

TATE (Scandinavian) Bubbly. Variation: *Tatum.*

TATIANA (Russian) Ancient Slavic king. Feminine version of Tatius. Variations: *Latonya, Tahnya, Tana, Tania, Tanis, Tanka, Tannia, Tannis, Tarnia, Tarny, Tata, Tatianna, Tatyana, Tatyanna, Tonia, Tonya, Tonyah.*

TATSU (Japanese) Dragon.

TAULAKI (Polynesian) Waiting.

TAWIA (African) Born after twins.

TAWNIE (English) Child. Variation: *Tawny.*

TAYANITA (Native American: Cherokee) Beaver.

TAYLOR (English) Tailor. Variations: *Tailor, Talor, Tayler.*

TAZU (Japanese) Stork.

TCU MANA (Native American: Hopi) Snake girl.

TEAGAN (English) Pretty. Variations: *Tegan, Teige.*

TEAMHAIR (Irish) Hill.

TEGVYEN (Welsh) Lovely maiden.

TEKAHIONWAKE (Native American: Mohawk) Double wampum.

TELERI (Welsh) Unknown definition.

TELEZA (African: Malawian) Slippery.

TEMIRA (Hebrew) Tall. Variations: *Temora, Timora.*

TEMPERANCE (Latin) Moderation.

TEMPEST (French) Storm.

TENNILLE (French) Last name. Variation: *Tenille.*

TENUVAH (Hebrew) Fruit and vegetables. Variation: *Tenuva.*

TERENA (English) Roman clan name. Feminine version of Terence. Variations: *Tereena, Terenia, Terina, Terrena, Terrina, Teryna.*

TERESA (Greek) Harvest. Teresa and all of its variations are wonderfully feminine names that are as timely

today as they were back in the 1960s, when they first started to become popular. Two Catholic saints made this name part of the lexicon: St. Teresa of Avila from the 16th century and St. Therese from 19th-century France, who was commonly referred to as a little flower. And of course, there is also Mother Theresa. Variations: *Terasa, Teree, Terese, Teresia, Teresina,* *Teresita, Teressa, Teri, Terie, Terise, Terrasa, Terresa, Terresia, Terri, Terrie, Terrise, Terry, Terrya, Tersa, Terza, Tess, Tessa, Tessie, Tessy, Theresa, Therese, Theressa, Thereza, Thersa, Thersea.*

TERLAH (Hebrew) Fresh. Variations: *Tari, Taria, Teria.*
TERRA (Latin) The earth. Variations: *Tera, Terah, Terrah.*
TERTIA (Latin) Third. Variation: *Tersia.*

Muslim Names

The Koran is the holy book of the Islamic faith, which was founded by the prophet Mohammed in 610 CE. As a result, many Muslim boys are given the name Mohammed. Some believe that it is the most popular name in the world, with close to one thousand variations.

Other names from the Koran for boys are frequently derived from the ninety-nine beneficial qualities of God that are written in the Muslim holy book: Hakeem and Nasser, which respectively translate to wise and victorious, are two such names.

For girls, virtuous names also rule, though they aren't directly derived from the Koran. Fatima is 'daughter of the prophet', and Ayasha means wife.

Muslim names for both boys and girls tend to have a positive meaning to them; the Asian tradition of giving babies ugly or plain names so that the evil spirits will pass them by is close to non-existent among Muslims. Instead, there are Tahira (pure) and Malak (angel) for girls, and Nadir (precious) and Baha (magnificent) for boys. In fact, it's difficult to find a Muslim name that does not have a positive spin to it.

Whether a boys' or girls' name, Muslim names are – like Native American names – derived from nature and everyday objects, as well as admirable character qualities.

Boys' Names

Abdul	Kamal
Alim	Khalid
Amir	Mahmud
Cemal	Mohammad
Dekel	Numair
Fadil	Rahman
Habib	Salih
Halim	Sharif
Hussein	Tahir
Jamal	Yasir
Kadir	Zaim

Girls' Names

Alima	Lilith
Amina	Malak
Ayasha	Medina
Basimah	Noura
Fatima	Qiturah
Genna	Sana
Iman	Tahira
Jamila	Takia
Kalila	Zakia
Latavia	

TESHUAH (Hebrew) Reprieve. Variations: *Teshua, Teshura*.

TESSA (Polish) Beloved by God. Variations: *Tess, Tessia, Tessie*.

TETSU (Japanese) Iron.

TEVY (Cambodian) Angel.

THADDEA (Greek) Brave. Feminine version of Thaddeus. Variations: *Thada, Thadda*.

THALASSA (Greek) Ocean.

THALEIA (Greek) To bloom. Variation: *Thalia*.

THANA (Arabic) Thanksgiving.

THANDIWE (South African) Affectionate.

THANH (Vietnamese) Brilliant.

THAO (Vietnamese) Respect.

THE (Vietnamese) Pledged.

THEA (Greek) Goddess.

THEIA (Greek) Divine one. Variation: *Thia*.

THEKIA (Greek) Famous God.

THEKLA (Greek) Divine fame. Variations: *Tecla, Tekla, Thecla*.

THELMA (Greek) Will. Variation: *Telma*.

THEMA (African: Ghanian) Queen.

THEMBA (African: Zulu) Trusted.

THEODORA (Greek) Gift of God. Feminine version of Theodore. Theodora has been one of those unexpectedly popular names that appear from nowhere basically overnight. It's a weighty name that also shows its fun side through its abbreviated version, Theo. Theodora has only begun to catch on, so look for more girls with this name over the next ten to fifteen years. Variations: *Teddy, Teodora, Theadora, Theda, Theodosia*.

THEONE (Greek) Godly. Variations: *Theona, Theoni, Theonie*.

THEOPHANIA (Greek) God's appearance. Variation: *Theophanie*.

THEOPHILA (Greek) Beloved by God. Variation: *Theofila*.

THETA (Greek) Greek letter. Variation: *Thetis*.

THETIS (Greek) The mother of Achilles.

THI (Vietnamese) Poem.

THIRZA (Hebrew) Pleasant. Variations: *Thyrza, Tirza, Tirzah*.

THOCMETONY (Native American: Paiute) Flower. Variation: *Tocmetone*.

THOMASINA (English) Twin. Feminine version of Thomas. Variations: *Thomasa, Thomasena, Thomasine, Toma, Tomasina, Tomasine, Tommi*.

THORA (Scandinavian) Thor's battle. Variations: *Thordia, Thordis, Thyra, Tyra*.

THU (Vietnamese) Autumn. Variation: *Tu*.

THURAYYA (Arabic) Star. Variations: *Surayya, Surayyah, Thuraia, Thuraypa, Thurayyah*.

THUY (Vietnamese) Gentle.

TIA (Spanish) Aunt. Variations: *Tiana, Tianna*.

TIARA (Spanish) Crown. Variation: *Tiera*.

TIBERIA (Latin) Tiber River. Variations: *Tibbie, Tibby*.

TIERNAN (English) Lord. Variation: *Tierney*.

TIFARA (Hebrew) Festive. Variations: *Tiferet, Tifhara*.

TIFFANY (Greek) God's appearance. Modern version of Theophania. As the 1980s went, so did certain baby names, and Tiffany was one of these. In the anything-goes decade of luxury, Tiffany was one of the most popular girls' names around. Even earlier, the name was especially popular with African-American parents in the 1970s. Tiffany first got its start back in ancient Greece, when it was commonly given to girls who were born on 6 January, also known as the Epiphany. But in the modern era, as with many other names that seem to come out of nowhere, this one was in a film: Audrey Hepburn in *Breakfast at Tiffany's* put this name on the map in the 1960s. Today, the name is

starting to fall out of fashion. Variations: *Tifani, Tiff, Tiffaney, Tiffani, Tiffanie, Tiffiney, Tiffini, Tiffney, Tiffy*.

TIGRIS (Irish) Tiger.

TIMOTHEA (Greek) Honouring God. Feminine version of Timothy. Variations: *Timaula, Timi, Timie, Timmi, Timmie*.

TIPONYA (Native American) Owl eating an egg.

TIPPAH (Native American: Chickasaw) Unknown definition.

TIRA (Hebrew) Camp.

TIRION (Welsh) Gentle.

TIRTHA (Hindu) Ford.

TIRZA (Hebrew) Kindness. Variations: *Thirza, Tirza, Tirzah*.

TISA (African: Swahili) Ninth child.

TISH (English) Happiness. Variation of Letitia. Variation: *Tisha*

TISHRA (African-American) Newly created. Variation: *Tishrah*.

TITANIA (Greek) Giant. Variation: *Tita*.

TITILAYO (African: Nigerian) Eternal happiness.

TIVONA (Hebrew) Nature lover.

TIWA (Native American) Onion.

TIWOLU (Native American) Chicken hawk sitting on eggs.

TOBY (Hebrew) God is good. Feminine version of Tobias. Toby seems like a great name for a little girl, and I also have the feeling that it's great for a female corporate executive. Variations: *Tobe, Tobee, Tobey, Tobi, Tobie*.

TOHUIA (Polynesian) Flower.

TOIREASA (Irish) Strength. Variations: *Treise*.

TOKI (Japanese) Chance.

TOKIWA (Japanese) Steady.

TOLIKNA (Native American) Coyote ears.

TOLOISI (Native American) Hawk killing a snake.

TOMAZJA (Polish) Twin.

TOMIKO (Japanese) Content child.

TOMO (Japanese) Intelligence.

TOOKA (Japanese) Ten days. Variation: *Tookayo*.

TOPAZ (Latin) Jewel. Has made occasional appearances as a first name since the 19th century.

TOPSY (English) The topsail. Variations: *Toppsy, Topsey, Topsie*.

TORA (Japanese) Tiger; (Scandinavian) Thunder.

TORBORG (Scandinavian) Thor's hall. Variations: *Thorborg, Torbjorg*.

TORDIS (Scandinavian) Thor's goddess.

TORI (Japanese) Bird.

TORUNN (Scandinavian) Loved by Thor.

TOSHALA (Hindu) Satisfied. Variation: *Tripta*.

TOSHIO (Japanese) Year-old child. Variations: *Toshi, Toshie, Toshiko, Toshikyo*.

TOSKI (Native American) Bug.

TOTSI (Native American) Moccasins.

TOVA (Scandinavian) Beautiful Thor. Variations: *Tove, Turid*.

TOVAH (Hebrew) Pleasant. Variations: *Toba, Tobit, Tova, Tovat, Tovit*.

TRACY (English) Summer. Variation of Teresa. Tracy was one of the more popular gender-neutral names back in the 1960s when it was in the middle of its transition from boys' name to girls' name. Today, other gender-neutral names are more popular, but a number of famous Tracys helped renew interest in this name, including Tracy Chapman, Tracy Ullman and Tracy Austin. Variations: *Trace, Tracee, Tracey, Traci, Tracie, Trasey, Treacy, Treesy.*

TRANG (Vietnamese) Smart.

TRAVA (Czech) Grass.

TRAVIATA (Italian) Woman who wanders.

TREVA (English) Homestead at sea. Feminine version of Trevor. Variation: *Trevina.*

TRICIA (English) Noble. Feminine version of Patrick. Variations: *Treasha, Trichia, Trish, Trisha.*

TRILBY (English) Literary name that dates from the Victorian era. Variations: *Trilbie, Trillby.*

TRINH (Vietnamese) Virgin.

TRINITY (Latin) Triad. Variations: *Trini, Trinita.*

TRISTA (Latin) Sad. Variations: *Trgsta, Tristan, Tristen, Tristin, Tristina, Tristyn.*

TRIXIE (English) She brings happiness. Variation of Beatrice. Variations: *Trix, Trixi, Trixy.*

TRUC (Vietnamese) Desire.

TRYPHENA (Greek) Delicacy. Variations: *Triphena, Tryphana, Tryphene, Tryphenia, Tryphina.*

TSIFIRA (Hebrew) Crown.

TSISTUNAGISKA (Native American: Cherokee) Rose.

TSOMAH (Native American: Kiowa) Yellow hair.

TSUHGI (Japanese) Second daughter.

TSULA (Native American: Cherokee) Fox.

TSURUKO (Japanese) Crane.

TUA (Polynesian) Outdoors.

TUALAU (Polynesian) Talking outdoors.

TUESDAY (English) Tuesday.

TUHINA (Hindu) Snow.

TUKI (Japanese) Moon. Variations: *Tukiko, Tukiyo.*

TULA (Native American: Choctaw) Apex; (Hindu) The astrological sign Libra.

TULINAGWE (African: Tanzanian) God is with us.

TULSI (Hindu) Basil.

TUSA (Native American: Zuni) Prairie dog.

TUSAJIGWE (African: Tanzanian) We are blessed.

TUWA (Native American: Hopi) Earth.

TUYEN (Vietnamese) Angel.

TUYET (Vietnamese) Snow.

TWYLA (African-American) Newly created. Variations: *Twila, Twylla.*

TYANA (African-American) Newly created.

TYESHA (African-American) Newly created. Variation: *Tyisha.*

TYLER (English) Last name.

TYRA (Scandinavian) Thor's battle.

TZADIKA (Hebrew) Loyal. Variation: *Zadika.*

TZAFRA (Hebrew) Morning. Variation: *Tzefira, Zafra, Zefira.*

TZAHALA (Hebrew) Happy. Variation: *Zahala.*

TZEIRA (Hebrew) Young.

TZEMICHA (Hebrew) In bloom. Variation: *Zemicha.*

TZEVIYA (Hebrew) Gazelle. Variations: *Civia, Tzevia, Tzivia, Tzivya, Zibiah, Zivia.*

TZIGANE (Hungarian) Gypsy. Variations: *Tsigana, Tsigane.*

TZILA (Hebrew) Darkness. Variations: *Tzili, Zila, Zili.*

TZINA (Hebrew) Shelter. Variation: *Zina.*

TZIPIYA (Hebrew) Hope. Variations: *Tzipia, Zipia.*

TZIYONA (Hebrew) Hill. Variations: *Zeona, Ziona.*

TZOFI (Hebrew) Scout. Variations: *Tzofia, Tzofit, Tzofiya, Zofi, Zofia, Zofit.*

TZURIYA (Hebrew) God is powerful. Variations: *Tzuria, Zuria.*

UCHENNA (African: Nigerian) God's will.

UDELE (English) Wealthy. Variations: *Uda, Udella, Udelle.*

UDIYA (Hebrew) Fire of God. Variations: *Udia, Uriela, Uriella.*

UINISE (Polynesian) Fair victory.

UJILA (Hindu) Bright light. Variations: *Ujala, Ujjala, Ujvala.*

ULA (Irish) Jewel from the ocean.

ULIMA (Arabic) Wise. Variation: *Ullima.*

ULRICA (German) Wolf power.

ULRIKA (Scandinavian) Noble ruler. Variation: *Ulla.*

ULTIMA (Latin) The end. Variation: *Ultimah.*

ULU (African: Nigerian) Second-born girl.

ULUAKI (Polynesian) First.

ULVA (German) Wolf.

UMA (Hindu) Flax.

UMALI (Hindu) Generous.

UMAYMA (Arabic) Little mother.

UME (Japanese) Plum blossom. Variations: *Umeki, Umeko.*

UMEEKA (Hindu) The goddess Parvati.

UMIKO (Japanese) Child of the sea.

UM-KALTHUM (Arabic) Mother of a plump-cheeked baby. Variation: *Um-Kalsum.*

UMM (Arabic) Mother.

UMNIYA (Arabic) Desire.

UNA (Irish) Lamb; (Latin) One.

UNITY (English) Oneness. Variation: *Unita.*

UNN (Scandinavian) Love.

UPALA (Hindu) Beach.

URANIA (Greek) Heavenly. Once upon a time in the 19th-century, there were a number of parents who thought it ought to be all the rage to name their daughters after Greek goddesses and muses. Urania, the muse of astronomy, was one of those names. A handful of parents might be tempted to use it today. Variations: *Urainia, Uraniya, Uranya.*

URANJA (Polish) The muse of astronomy.

URBANA (Latin) Of the city. Variation: *Urbanna.*

URBI (African: Nigerian) Princess.

URIT (Hebrew) Brightness.

URSULA (Latin) Little bear. Variations: *Ursala, Ursella, Ursule, Ursulina, Ursuline.*

USHA (Hindu) Dawn. Variation: *Ushas.*

USHI (Chinese) Ox.

USHMIL (Hindu) Warm. Variation: *Ushmila.*

USHRIYA (Hebrew) God's blessing. Variation: *Ushria.*

UT (Vietnamese) East.

UTA (Japanese) Song. Variation: *Utako.*

UWIMANA (African: Rwandan) Daughter of God.

Famous Country Music Names

Tammy, Johnny, Jerry, Dolly. Why does it seem that if you want to make it big in country music, the last syllable of your first name has to end in '-y'? I'm exaggerating, but along with big hair, sequins, and a ten-gallon hat, in country music, you need a name that leaves no mistake about which kind of music you favour.

Certainly after Garth Brooks started selling millions of records, along with Wynonna (Judd, not to be confused with Winona Ryder, the actress), some parents began to give their babies country-music names to reflect the passion that they feel for this genre of music. Of course, there are country music purists out there who believe that any country music singer who became popular after Hank Williams, Jr., left the scene is not worthy of their ears. This would by necessity limit the number of baby name choices, but fortunately, for the most part, the people who fall into this category are grandparents, and not parents.

As country music continues to change, I'll bet so will the names that fans choose for their babies.

Boys' Names

- Charlie McCoy
- Chet Atkins
- Clay McMichen
- Garth Brooks
- George Jones
- Hank Williams, Jr.
- Kenny Rogers
- Lee Clayton
- Travis Tritt
- Waylon Jennings

Girls' Names

- Barbara Mandrell
- Crystal Gayle
- Dolly Parton
- Loretta Lynn
- Naomi Judd
- Patsy Cline
- Patty Lovelace
- Reba McEntire
- Shania Twain
- Tammy Wynette
- Wynonna Judd

VACHYA (Hindu) To speak.

VAILEA (Polynesian) Water that talks.

VALA (German) Chosen.

VALDA (Norse) Ruler. Variations: *Valida, Velda, Vellda.*

VALENTIA (Latin) Healthy. Variations: *Valence, Valencia, Valene, Valentina, Valentine, Valenzia.*

VALERIE (Latin) Strong. A popular name during the Roman Empire, Valerie tends to be underused today. Famous Valeries include Valerie Singleton, and British film actress Valerie Hobson. Although some parents may feel that the name sounds like a relic from the 1960s, others will feel slightly nostalgic about the name and choose it for their own daughters. Variations: *Val, Valaree, Valarey, Valaria, Valarie, Vale, Valeree, Valeria, Valeriana, Valery, Vallarie, Valleree, Vallerie, Valli, Vallie, Vally.*

VALESKA (Polish) Glorious ruler.

VALONIA (Latin) Shallow valley.

VALORA (Latin) Brave. Variations: *Valoria, Valorie, Valory, Valorya.*

VANA (Polynesian) Sea urchin.

VANAJA (Hindu) Daughter from the woods.

VANALIKA (Hindu) Sunflower.

VANDA (Czech) Variation of Wanda. Tribal name. Variation: *Vandah.*

VANDANI (Hindu) Honour. Variation: *Vandana.*

VANECIA (English) Venice; Italian city. Variations: *Vanetia, Vanicia, Venecia, Venetia, Venezia, Venice, Venise, Venize.*

VANESSA (Greek) Butterflies. Variations: *Vanesa, Vanesse, Vania, Vanna, Vannessa, Venesa, Venessa.*

VANETTA (English) Newly created.

VANI (Hindu) Voice.

VANIKA (Hindu) Small forest.

VANJA (Scandinavian) God is good.

VANNA (Cambodian) Golden.

VANORA (Welsh) White wave. Variation: *Vannora*.

VARANA (Hindu) River.

VARDA (Hebrew) Rose. Variations: *Vardia, Vardice, Vardina, Vardis, Vardit*.

VARSHA (Hindu) Rain shower. Variation: *Varisha*.

VASHTI (Persian) Beautiful.

VASUNDHARA (Hindu) Earth.

VATUSIA (African) The dead leave us behind.

VEATA (Cambodian) Wind.

VEDA (Hindu) Knowledge, wisdom. Variation: *Veeda*.

VEDETTE (Italian) Sentry. Variation: *Vedetta*.

VEERA (Hindu) Strong.

VEGA (Arabic) Falling; (Scandinavian) Star.

VELESLAVA (Czech) Great glory. Variations: *Vela, Velina, Velinka, Velka, Veluska*.

VELIKA (Slavic) Great. Variation: *Velia*.

VELINDA (African-American) Variation of Melinda. Variation: *Valinda*.

VELMA (English) Newly created. Variation: *Vellma*.

VENETTA (English) Newly created. Variations: *Veneta, Venette*.

VENUS (Latin) Roman goddess of love. Variations: *Venise, Vennice, Venusa, Venusina*.

VERA (Slavic) Faith. Vera was at its height in both the United States and Britain during the flapper days of the 1920s. Variations: *Veera, Veira, Verasha, Viera*.

VERBENA (Latin) Holy plants. Variations: *Verbeena, Verbina*.

VERDAD (Spanish) Truth.

VERENA (Latin) True. Variations: *Vereena, Verene, Verina, Verine, Veruchka, Veruschka, Verushka, Veryna*.

VERITY (Latin) Truth. Variations: *Verita, Veritie*.

VERNA (Latin) Springtime. Variations: *Vernetta, Vernie, Vernita, Virna*.

VERONICA (Latin) True image. Variations: *Veranique, Vernice, Veron, Verona, Verone, Veronice, Veronicka, Veronika, Veronike, Veroniqua, Veronique*.

VESPERA (Latin) Evening star.

VESTA (Latin) Goddess of the home. Variations: *Vessy, Vest*.

VEVINA (Irish) Kind woman.

VIANNA (African-American) Unknown definition.

VICA (Hungarian) Life.

VICTORIA (Latin) Roman goddess of victory. Victoria is a name that has had a number of spurts in popularity since the days of the early Roman Empire, when it was one of the most frequently bestowed names for girls. It lay dormant until Queen Victoria took the throne in Britain in the 1800s, when it began to be used with some regularity until she died. The name was resurrected again in the 1940s and has remained in common usage ever since. Although Victoria's nicknames were more popular in the 1960s and 1970s, today the full name is the most widely used. Variations: *Torey, Tori, Toria, Torie, Torrey, Torri, Torrie, Torrye, Tory, Vicki, Vickie, Vicky, Victoriana, Victorina, Victorine, Victory, Vikki, Vikky, Vitoria, Vittoria*.

VIDA (Hebrew) Beloved. Variations: *Veda, Veeda, Veida, Vidette, Vieda, Vita, Vitia*.

VIDONIA (Portuguese) Vine branch. Variations: *Veedonia, Vidonya*.

VIDYA (Hindu) Instruction.

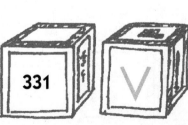

VIGDIS (Scandinavian: Norwegian) War goddess. Variation: *Vigdess.*

VIGILIA (Latin) Alert.

VIKA (Polynesian) Victory. Variation: *Vikaheilala.*

VILLETTE (French) Small town.

VILMA (Russian) Variation of Wilma.

VIMALA (Hindu) Lovely.

VINA (Spanish) Vineyard. Variations: *Veina, Venia.*

VINCENTIA (Latin) To conquer. Feminine version of Vincent. Variations: *Vincenta, Vincentena, Vincentina, Vincentine, Vincetta, Vinia, Vinnie.*

VINH (Vietnamese) Gulf.

VIOLA (Scandinavian) Violet.

VIOLET (Latin) Violet. First adopted in medieval times it has been in decline since the 1920s but in recent years appears to be acquiring cool status again. Variations: *Viola, Violetta, Violette.*

VIRGINIA (Latin) Virgin. The name given by Sir Walter Raleigh to the first English possessions in America in the 16th century in tribute to the Virgin Queen Elizabeth I. Variations: *Vergie, Virgy, Virginie, Vegenia, Virginai, Virgena, Virgene.*

VIRIDIS (Latin) Green. Virdis, Virida, Viridia, Viridiana.

VIRTUE (Latin) Virtue.

VISOLELA (African) Unlimited imagination.

VITA (Latin) Life. Variations: *Veeta, Vitel, Vitella.*

VIVIAN (Latin) Full of life. The name was once solely used by males. Actress Vivien Leigh was responsible for the name's first burst of popularity in the 1940s. Ever since actress Julia Roberts played a hooker named Vivian in the movie *Pretty Woman*, the name has started to appear on birth certificates with a little bit more regularity. Variations: *Viv, Viva, Viveca, Vivecka, Viveka, Vivia, Viviana, Viviane, Vivianna, Vivianne, Vivie, Vivien, Vivienne.*

VLADIMIRA (Czech) Famous ruler. Variation: *Vladmira.*

VLADISLAVA (Czech) Glorious ruler. Variations: *Ladislava, Valeska.*

VONDRA (Czech) A woman's love.

VORSILA (Czech) Little she-bear.

VYOMA (Hindu) Sky. Variation: *Vyomika.*

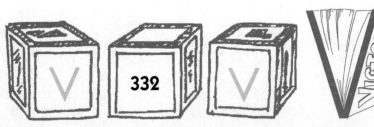

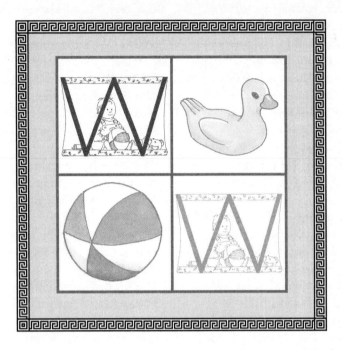

WACHIW (Native American: Sioux) Girl who dances.

WAFA (Arabic) Faithful. Variations: *Wafiyya, Wafiyyah.*

WAHCHINTONKA (Native American: Sioux) Patient.

WAIPSHWA (Native American: Wanapum) One who carries.

WAJA (Arabic) Noble. Variations: *Wagiha, Wagihah, Wajiha, Wajihah.*

WAKANDA (Native American) Magical. Variation: *Wakenda.*

WALANIKA (Hawaiian) True image. Hawaiian version of Veronica. Variations: *Walonika, Welonika.*

WALBURGA (German) Strong protection. Variations: *Walberga, Wallburga.*

WALDA (German) Ruler. Feminine version of Waldo. Variations: *Wallda, Welda, Wellda.*

WALENTYA (Polish) Healthy.

WALIDA (Arabic) Newborn. Variation: *Walidah.*

WALKER (English) Last name. Variation: *Wallker*

WALLIS (English) One from Wales. Feminine version of Wallace. Variations: *Wallie, Walliss, Wally, Wallys.*

WANAAO (Hawaiian) Sunrise.

WANAAONANI (Hawaiian) Beautiful sunrise.

WANAKA (Hawaiian) Hawaiian version of Wanda.

WANDA (German) Wanderer. Variations: *Wandi, Wandie, Wandis, Wonda, Wonnda.*

WANETA (Native American) One who moves forward. Variations: *Wanetta, Wanette, Wannetta, Wannette.*

WANIKA (Hawaiian) God is good.

WAPIN (Native American: Potawatomi) Sunrise.

WARDA (German) Protector. Feminine version of Ward. Variations: *Wardia, Wardine.*

WASEME (African: Swahili) People talking.

WASHI (Japanese) Eagle.

WASHTA (Native American: Sioux) Good.

333

WASULA (Native American: Sioux) Bad hair.

WATSEKA (Native American: Potawatomi) Woman.

WATTAN (Arabic) Homeland.

WAUNA (Native American: Miwok) Calling geese.

WAYLAHSKISE (Native American: Shawnee) Graceful.

WAYNOKA (Native American: Cheyenne) Clean water.

WEAYAYA (Native American: Sioux) Sunset.

WEEKO (Native American: Sioux) Beautiful girl.

WEETAMOO (Native American: Pocasset) Lover. Variations: *Weetamoe, Weetamore, Wetamoo, Wetemoo.*

WEHINAHPAY (Native American: Sioux) Sunrise.

WELENA (Hawaiian) Springtime. Hawaiian version of Verna.

WENDY (English) Wendy was invented by author J. M. Barrie and first appeared as the name of a character in the novel *Peter Pan* in 1904. It maintained its reputation as one of the most popular names on both sides of the Atlantic especially in Scotland and reached its peak of popularity in the 1960s and 1970s. Variations: *Wenda, Wendee, Wendey, Wendi, Wendie, Wendye, Windy.*

WHITLEY (English) White field.

WHITNEY (English) White island. Of course, singer Whitney Houston is the primary reason why this name rapidly travelled from being a corporate fast-track name for boys in the early '80s to one of the more popular names for girls in the '90s, especially in the USA. Although Whitney is still popular, it is beginning to be cast aside in favour of other, more cutting-edge names. Variations: *Whitnee, Whitnie, Whitny, Whittney.*

WHOOPI (French) Unknown definition.

WICAHPI (Native American: Sioux) Star. Variation: *Wicapi.*

WICAHPI ISNALA (Native American: Sioux) Long star. Variation: *Wicapi Isnala.*

WICAHPI WAKAN (Native American: Sioux) Holy star. Variation: *Wicapi Wakan.*

WIDAD (Arabic) Love.

WIHAKAYDA (Native American: Sioux) Youngest daughter.

WIKOLIA (Hawaiian) Victorious.

WILA (Hawaiian) Faith.

WILDA (English) Willow. Variations: *Willda, Wylda.*

WILFREDA (English) Peaceful will. Feminine version of Wilfred.

WILHELMINA (German) Feminine version of William, Will + helmet. Variations: *Wiletta, Wilette, Wilhelmine, Willa, Willamina, Williamina.*

WILLOW (English) Tree.

WILMA (German) Feminine version of William, Will + helmet. Variations: *Wilmette, Wilmina, Wylma.*

WILONA (English) To desire.

WINDA (African: Swahili) Hunt.

WINEMA (Native American: Miwok) Female chief.

WINIFRED (Welsh) Holy peace. Winifred is a pretty name that is both delicate and powerful. The name was at its height in popularity during the 19th and early 20th centuries among English and Scottish parents. Today more people seem to be falling for the sweet quality of the name again. Look for Winifred to become more widely used in the coming years, especially with the letter 'y' replacing one of the vowels in the name. The diminutive Winnie is best known as the name for Pooh Bear. Variations: *Win, Winifrede, Winifride, Winifryde, Winne, Winni, Winnie, Winny, Wyn, Wynn.*

WINNE-COMAC (Native American: Algonquin) Fertile land.

WINOLA (German) Enchanting friend.

WINTER (English) Winter.

WISDOM (English) Wisdom.

WISIA (Polish) Victorious.

WITASHNAH (Native American: Sioux) Chaste.

WIYAKA-WASTEWIN (Native American: Sioux) Pretty feather.

WLADYSLAWA (Polish) Glorious ruler.

WREN (English) Bird.

WYANET (Native American) Beautiful.

WYETTA (African-American) Feminine version of Wyatt.

WYNELLE (African-American) Variation: *Wynette*.

WYNN (Welsh) Fair, white. Variations: *Winne, Wynne*.

WYNONAH (Native American) First-born. Variations: *Wenona, Wenonah, Winona, Winonah, Wynnona*.

WYOME (Native American: Algonquin) Big field

XANDRA (Spanish) Protector.

Superstitions about Names

On the face of things, a name is simply an amalgam of letters arranged in a certain way so that the person who has the name can assume some kind of identity through the name, a symbol of sorts.

That's the scientific side of things. The truth is that generations of parents in every country and in every faith have their beliefs about what they should and shouldn't name their babies owing to superstition. A traditional Ashkenazi Jewish superstition dictated that if you named a baby after a living person, that person would instantly fall ill and die, since the baby needed more of the energy than the adult, and so would only suck the life force out of them. (However, Sephardic Jews believe the opposite!) Many cultures also chose names from nature, like a flower, so that the baby would be sure to blossom and grow.

Today many of us may scoff at these beliefs, but the truth is that individuals hold their own peculiar superstitions about names. For instance, you may choose to not name a baby after an elderly relative because you didn't like the way the older person smelled, while you were growing up, and think that

perhaps your baby will end up with the same aroma. Or you may hate a name that your partner loves – because a friend's mother with the same name died when you were only thirteen and you don't want a similar fate to befall your child. Don't name a baby after a relative who's currently in prison, many people say, no matter how much you love your relative, because your child might end up with the same lifestyle. Some superstitions relate to particular names; you may have been brought up to believe that people named Benjamin cannot be trusted. Or, like one Scottish friend of mine, you might believe that if your firstborn is named Fred, you will have problems with your carburetor (or fuel injection) for the rest of your life. The superstitions that swirl around the names that we do and don't choose for our kids most often involve unreasonable associations we have with the name.

No matter how unreasonable these associations might be, no one can tell you to get rid of your superstitions about names or anything else. And you should know that you're in good company around the world if you choose to abide by them.

XANTHE (Greek) Yellow. Name borne by several minor characters in Greek mythology. Variations: *Xantha, Xanthia.*

XANTHIPPE (Greek) Wife of Socrates.

XAVIERA (English) New house. Feminine version of Xavier. The name Xaviera started out as the name of a saint from the 16th century. Though some parents are beginning to consider Xaviera for their daughters, an increase in usage doesn't seem too likely given the name's indelible connection to Xaviera Hollander, author of the notorious 1960s book, *The Happy Hooker.* Variations: *Xavier, Xavyera.*

XENIA (Greek) Hospitable. Variations: *Xeenia, Xena.*

XIANG (Chinese) Fragrant.

XIAO-NIAO (Chinese) Small bird.

XIAO-XING (Chinese) Morning star.

XIN (Chinese) Elegant, beautiful.

XUAN (Vietnamese) Spring.

XYLIA (Greek) Forest. Variations: *Xyla, Xylina, Xylona.*

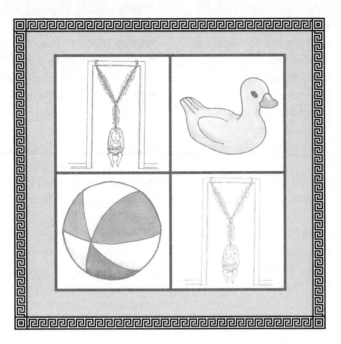

YAA (African: Ghanian) Born on Thursday.

YAARA (Hebrew) Honeycomb. Variations: *Yaari, Yaarit, Yara.*

YACHI (Japanese) Good luck. Variations: *Yachiko, Yachiyo.*

YACHNE (Hebrew) God is good. Variation: *Yachna.*

YAEL (Hebrew) Mountain goat. Variations: *Jael, Yaala, Yaalat, Yaela, Yaella.*

YAFFA (Hebrew) Beautiful.

YAHIVIKA (Native American: Hopi) Spring.

YAKI (Japanese) Snow. Variations: *Yukie, Yukika, Yukiko.*

YAKIRA (Hebrew) Dear. Variations: *Yekara, Yekarah.*

YALIKA (Native American) Spring flowers.

YALUTA (Native American) Women talking.

YAMINA (Arabic) Ethical. Variations: *Yaminah, Yemina.*

YAMINI (Hindu) Night.

YAMKA (Native American) Flower blooming.

YANAHA (Native American: Navajo) She confronts an enemy. Variation: *Yanaba.*

YARDENA (Hebrew) To descend. Variation: *Jardena.*

YARDENIYA (Hebrew) God's garden. Variations: *Jardenia, Yardenia.*

YARINA (Russian) Peace. Variation: *Yaryna.*

YARKONA (Hebrew) Green.

YARMILLA (Slavic) Market seller.

YASHILA (Hindu) Successful.

YASHNA (Hindu) Prayer. Variation: *Yashnah.*

YASHODHANA (Hindu) Prosperous. Variation: *Yashwina.*

YASHODHARA (Hindu) Renowned.

YASMINE (Arabic) Flower. Though Jasmin, the name from which Yasmine is derived, is the more well-known variation of this name, I predict that Yasmine will become more popular in time, simply because many parents will want to put their unique spin on what is becoming a relatively popular name. In fact, Yasmine first became popular in the United States back in the 1920s because of a play entitled *Hassan*, by playwright James Flecker, in which the female protagonist was named Yasmin. Variations: *Yasmeen, Yasmeena, Yasmena, Yasmene, Yasmin, Yasmina.*

YASU (Japanese) Calm. Variations: *Yasuko, Yasuyo.*

YE (African: Ghanian) First-born of twins.

YEHUDIT (Hebrew) God will be praised. Variations: *Yudi, Yudit, Yudita, Yuta, Yutke.*

YEJDE (African: Nigerian) She resembles her mother.

YELENA (Russian) Light. Variation of Helen. Variation: *Yalena.*

YEMINA (Hebrew) Strong. Variation: *Yemena.*

YENENE (Native American) Sorceress.

YENTA (Hebrew) Ruler at home. Variations: *Yente, Yentel, Yentele, Yentil.*

YEPA (Native American) Snow maiden.

YESENIA (Arabic) Flower. Variations: *Yecenia, Yesnia, Yessenia.*

YESHARA (Hebrew) Direct.

YETTA (English) Ruler at home Feminine diminutive version of Henry. Variation: *Yette.*

YEVA (Russian) Life. Variation: *Yevka.*

YIESHA (Arabic) Woman.

YIN (Chinese) Silver.

YOCHEVED (Hebrew) God's glory. Variation: *Yochebed.*

YOI (Japanese) Born in the evening.

YOKI (Native American) Bluebird.

YOKKAKO (Japanese) Four days.

YOKO (Japanese) Child of the ocean.

YOLANDA (Greek) Purple flower. In the United States, Yolanda has long been a name that has been more popular among African-American families than white parents, but that is gradually starting to

Changing Names Later in Life

As you pore through the names in this book, you naturally think about the names that strike you as being the right one for your baby.

But what if your baby begs to differ a couple of decades down the road when he or she grows into an adult? Or what if *you* change your mind later on? More people than you'd imagine decide that they've had enough of their old name and legally change it.

In the case of changing a child's name, there are some parents who adopt a child and decide to give them a name that may have more traditional connections to the baby's adoptive family. People who adopt infants usually don't have to worry about renaming a new baby since the baby tends

to go unnamed until the new parents take over.

Regardless of the reason for a name change, most people alter their name by deed poll. To change a child's name, sometimes just signing a document drawn up by a lawyer that gives both the new and old names is enough. In the UK you cannot change the details on a birth certificate except in limited circumstances.

Thousands of people decide to change their names every year in this country and for many different reasons. Because of the intrinsically personal nature of a name, in most cases, these people are very reluctant to disclose what their previous names were.

change. Yolanda first appeared as the name of a saint in 13th-century Spain, and later belonged to Hungarian royalty. Though some parents might feel the name is dated and too unusual to use today, it's clear that others disagree. Variations: *Eolanda, Eolande, Iolanda, Iolande, Yalanda, Yalinda, Yalonda, Yola, Yoland, Yolande, Yolane, Yolette, Yoli, Yolonda, Yulanda.*

YOLOTA (Native American) Farewell to spring.

YOLUTA (Native American) Seed.

YON (Burmese) Rabbit.

YONINA (Hebrew) Dove. Variations: *Yona, Yonah, Yoninah, Yonit, Yonita.*

YONKELA (African-American) Unknown definition.

YORI (Japanese) Honest.

YOSHA (Hindu) Woman.

YOSHE (Japanese) Lovely.

YOSHIKO (Japanese) Quiet. Variations: *Yoshi, Yoshie, Yoshiyo.*

YOSHINO (Japanese) Fertile land.

YOUNG-IL (Korean) Excellence.

YOUNG-SOON (Korean) Tender flower.

YOVELA (Hebrew) Rejoicing.

YU (Chinese) Jade.

YUKI (Japanese) Snow. Variations: *Yukie, Yukiko.*

YULA (Russian) Young. Variation of Julia. Variations: *Yulenka, Yuliya, Yulya.*

YURIKO (Japanese) Lily child.

YUSRA (Arabic) Rich. Variations: *Yusrivva, Yusrivvah.*

YUTKIYE (Native American) Chicken hawk hunting.

YUTTCISO (Native American) Lice on a hawk.

YVETTE (French) Arrow's bow.

YVONNE (French) Yew wood. Yvonne is a name that conjures up images of black-and-white dramas from the 1940s, when Yvonne was often chosen as the name of the unsuspecting tragic female heroine. It as been popular since the1900s, reaching a peak in frequency in the 1950s and1960s. Famous bearers of the name include French actresses Yvonne Arnaud and Yvonne Printemps and the US pop singer Yvonne Elliman. Variations: *Yvetta, Yvette, Yvone.*

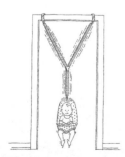

ZADA (Arabic) Fortunate. Variations: *Zaida, Zayda.*

ZAFINA (Arabic) Triumphant.

ZAFIRA (Arabic) Success. Variation: *Zafirah.*

ZAHARA (Hebrew) Shine. Variations: *Zahari, Zaharit.*

ZAHAVA (Hebrew) Golden. Variation: *Zahavah.*

ZAHIRA (Arabic) Bright. Variations: *Zaheera, Zahirah.*

ZAHRA (Arabic) Blossom. Variations: *Zahara, Zahirah, Zahrah, Zara, Zuhra.*

ZAHREH (Persian) Happiness.

ZAINAB (Hindu) Plant.

ZAIRA (Italian) Princess. Variations: *Zarah, Zaria, Zayeera.*

ZAKAH (Hebrew) Pure. Variations: *Zaka, Zakia, Zakiah.*

ZAKIYA (African: Swahili) Pure. Variation: *Zakiyah.*

ZAKIYYA (Hindu) Pure. Variations: *Zakia, Zakiah, Zakiyyah.*

ZALIKA (African: Swahili) Well born.

ZALTANA (Native American) Tall mountain.

ZAN (Chinese) Support; favour; praise.

ZANETA (Polish) God is gracious.

ZARA (Hebrew) Dawn. In the 1990s, names that have a 'z', 'x' or 'q' in them were popular, but parents still prefer names that aren't totally unfamiliar. Zara fits the bill nicely, as it is close to both Tara and Sarah. It is also the name of the daughter of Princess Anne. Variations: *Zarah, Zaria.*

ZARIFA (Arabic) Graceful.

ZARINA (Hindu) Golden.

ZARITA (Spanish) Princess. Variation of Sarah.

ZAWADI (African: Swahili) Present.

ZAYIT (Hebrew) Olive.

ZAYNAB (Arabic) Plant. Variation: *Zainab.*

ZAZA (Hebrew) Action. Variation: *Zazu.*

ZBYHNEVA (Czech) To get rid of anger. Variations: *Zbyha, Zbysa.*

ZDENKA (Czech) Variations: *Zdena, Zdenicka, Zdenina, Zdeninka, Zdenuska.*

ZDESLAVA (Czech) Glory is here. Variations: *Zdevsa, ZdeVska, Zdisa, Zdiska, Zdislava.*

ZEA (Latin) Grain. Variation: *Zia.*

ZEBORAH (African-American) Variation of Deborah.

ZEFFA (Portuguese) Rose.

ZEFIRYN (Polish) Goddess of the west wind.

ZEHARA (Hebrew) Light. Variation: *Zehorit.*

ZEHAVA (Hebrew) Gold. Variations: *Zahava, Zehovit, Zehuva, Zehuvit.*

ZEHIRA (Hebrew) Careful.

ZEL (Persian) Cymbal.

ZELENKA (Czech) Fresh.

ZELFA (African-American) Unknown definition.

ZELLA (German) Hostile one.

ZELMA (German) Divine helmet.

ZEMIRA (Hebrew) Song.

ZEMORAH (Hebrew) Tree branch. Variation: *Zemora.*

ZENAIDA (Greek) Wild dove.

ZENANA (Hebrew) Woman. Variations: *Zena, Zenia.*

ZENDA (Hebrew) Holy.

ZENOBIA (Greek) Strength of Zeus. Zenobia is a powerful name that served a queen in the third century CE in the early Roman Empire. Novelists Nathaniel Hawthorne and Edith Wharton both used the name in their stories.

ZEPHYR (Greek) Wind from the west. Variations: *Zefir, Zephira, Zephyra.*

ZEPPELINA (English) Definition unknown.

ZERA (Hebrew) Seeds.

ZERALDINA (Polish) Spear ruler.

ZERDALI (Turkish) Wild apricot.

ZERLINDA (Hebrew) Beautiful dawn. Variation: *Zerlina.*

ZERREN (English) Flower.

ZESIRO (African: Ugandan) First of twins.

ZETTA (Hebrew) Olive. Variations: *Zeta, Zetana.*

ZEVIDA (Hebrew) Present. Variation: *Zevuda.*

ZEYNEP (Turkish) Ornament.

ZHANE (African-American) Unknown definition.

ZHEN (Chinese) Pure.

ZHO (Chinese) Character.

ZHONG (Chinese) Honest.

ZHUO (Chinese) Smart.

ZIGANA (Hungarian) Gypsy.

ZIHNA (Native American) Spinning.

ZILLA (Hebrew) Shadow. Variations: *Zilah, Zillah, Zylla.*

ZILPAH (Hebrew) Dignity. Many of the girls' names that begin with 'Z' are Biblical in origin, and Zilpah is no exception, first appearing in the Book of Genesis as the name of Jacob's mistress. If you wander around old cemeteries, you'll find the name Zilpah on many of the headstones. Variations: *Zillpha, Zilpha, Zulpha, Zylpha.*

ZIMRIAH (Hebrew) Songs. Variations: *Zimria, Zimriya.*

ZINA (English) Hospitable. Variation: *Zena.*

ZINNIA (English) Flower. Variations: *Zinia, Zinnya, Zinya.*

ZIPPORA (Hebrew) Little bird. Biblical wife of Moses. Variations: *Cipora, Tzipeh, Tzipora, Tzippe, Zipeh, Zipora, Ziporah, Zipporah.*

ZIRACUNY (Native American: Kiowa) Water fiend.

ZIRAH (Hebrew) Coliseum. Variation: *Zira.*

ZITA (Greek) Seeker. Probably best known in Catherine Zeta Jones' name. Variation: *Zitella.*

ZITKALA (Native American: Sioux) Bird.

ZITKALASA (Native American: Sioux) Red bird.

ZITOMIRA (Czech) To live famously. Variations: *Zitka, Zituse.*

ZIVA (Hebrew) Brilliant. Variations: *Zeeva, Ziv.*

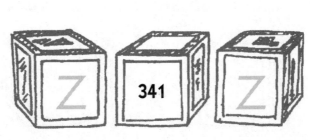

ZIVANKA (Czech) Alive. Variations: *Zivka, Zivuse, Zivuska.*

ZLATA (Czech) Golden. Variations: *Zlatina, Zlatinka, Zlatka, Zlatuna, Zlatunka, Zlatuse, Zlatuska.*

ZLHNA (Native American: Hopi) Spinning.

ZOCHA (Polish) Wisdom.

ZOE (Greek) Life. Zoe is perhaps the most popular 'Z' name for girls, and it seemed to pick up steam in the 1990s. The first Zoe surfaced in the third century CE; she was later martyred as a saint. Today parents can choose to add an umlaut above the 'e' or to leave it as is. Parents will continue to look to Zoe for a daughter they expect to have considerable artistic talent. Famous bearers of the name include British actress Zoe Wanamaker and TV and radio presenter Zoe Ball. Variations: *Zoey, Zoie.*

ZOHERET (Hebrew) She shines.

ZOLA (Italian) Piece of earth. Popularized as the surname of French novelist Emile Zola, it became well known as the name of South African bare-foot runner Zola Budd.

ZONA (Latin) Belt.

ZONIA (English) Unknown definition.

ZONTA (Native American: Sioux) Honest.

ZORA (Slavic) Dawn. Variations: *Zara, Zorah, Zorra, Zorrah.*

ZORINA (Slavic) Golden. Variation: *Zorana.*

ZUBA (English) Unknown definition.

ZUBAIDA (Arabic) Marigold. Variations: *Zubaidah, Zubeda.*

ZUDORA (Hindu) Labourer.

ZULEIKA (Arabic) Brilliant.

ZULEMA (Hebrew) Peace. Variation: *Zulima.*

ZURI (African: Swahili) Beautiful.

ZUWENA (African: Swahili) Good. Variation: *Zwena.*

ZUZANA (Czech) Rose.

ZUZELA (Native American: Sioux) A wife of Sitting Bull.

ZYTKA (Polish) Rose.

Famous Scientists, Doctors and Inventors

Like politicians, there are a lot of famous scientists, doctors and inventors who share the same names: John, William, George, James. Of course, this is an indication of the tenor of the times in which they were born, but this class of famous people also has more than its fair share of people named Antoine, Gabriel, Giuseppe and Nathan. Among women in the field, a few inspirations are Florence (Nightingale), Marie (Curie) and Grace (Hopper, who invented the COBOL computer language).

If you'd like your child to make strides in the field of science, don't feel that you have to give him or her a geeky name; Alessandro would work just fine.

Many people once regarded politicians as the most upstanding citizens around. Today, scientists and engineers have clearly replaced politicians in the category most people admire.